# Lifelines
## Famous Contemporaries
## from 600 B.C. to the Present

# Lifelines

## Famous Contemporaries
## from 600 B.C. to the Present

Frank W. Weis

**Facts On File Publications**
460 Park Avenue South
New York, N.Y. 10016

# Lifelines
**Famous Contemporaries**
**from 600 B.C. to the Present**

**Library of Congress Cataloging in Publication Data:**
Weis, Frank W.
   Lifelines: famous contemporaries from 600 B.C. to the present

   Includes index.
   1. Biography.   2. Chronology, Historical.   I. Title.
CT104.W45   920′.02   80-23132
ISBN 0-87196-760-X   AACR1

Printed in the United States of America
10 9 8 7 6 5 4 3 2 1

# How to Use This Book

The aim of this book is to provide a chronological overview of the history of the world from 600 B.C. to the present, concentrating particularly on the men and women who contributed importantly to shaping their times—and our own. To that end, the book is divided into sections covering each 25-year period from 600 B.C. through 1975. Each section opens with a brief description of historical events and trends of the time; this description is followed by brief biographies of the most important figures who were active during that period.

The book is arranged in two-page spreads; on the left there is a column listing the names of people who were living at the opening of each period, but who were no longer as active as they had been earlier; their ages as the period began are supplied. On the right readers will find a list of the historical figures who would attain importance in a later period, but who had not yet reached the peak of their activity when the period closed; their ages at the end of the period are supplied. See, as an example, pages 6-7: During the period 550-525 B.C., Pythagoras and Belshazzar, among others, were at their prime. As the period opened, in 550 B.C., Thales, Lao-tzu and Croesus were living but past their periods of primary activity. In 525 B.C., when the period came to an end, Buddha, Darius I and Confucius were living but had not yet come to the forefront.

An index is provided to permit immediate access to every historical figure listed in the book. In addition, portraits of many of the figures whose biographies appear here are supplied.

It is the hope of the author and the publisher that LIFELINES will be of value to readers both as a biographical directory and as a chronology of the events—and, even more, the people—who helped to shape our world.

# Lifelines

**Famous Contemporaries
from 600 B.C. to the Present**

# 600–575 B.C.

Six hundred B.C. is a landmark date. While the worn-out autocracies of Western Asia were falling, one by one, Hellenic civilization was rising in Europe. When Jeremiah and Ezekiel warned of the imminent doom of Jerusalem, they might as well have included the conquerors with the conquered, for after thirty centuries twilight was at last falling on the Asiatic gods and mocking their claims of immortality. The Assyrian empire had ceased to exist with the capture of Nineveh in 612 B.C.; Babylonia was soon to follow, although Babylon was still the greatest city in the world; and Egypt's days of power and glory lived only as fading memories. In 722 B.C. Israel had fallen, and in 597, twelve years after King Josiah died on the field of Megiddo, the last king of Judah ascended the throne of David.

## 600 B.C.

**Jeremiah,** age 50?; one of the major Old Testament prophets, who preached in Jerusalem from 628 to 586 B.C. He fortold the destruction of the temple in Jerusalem and the enslavement of the Jews as the vengeance of the Lord for their wickedness and idolatry. When Jerusalem fell to the Babylonian king Nebuchadnezzar II, he was allowed to remain and went with other Jews to Egypt.

**Draco,** age ?; Greek statesman who gave Athens its first written code of laws in 621 B.C. He is sometimes called the founder of Athenian civilization, for his laws brought feuds, vendettas and private retaliation for injuries under control. They also eliminated from the community those unable or unwilling to live amicably and honestly with their neighbors. For most crimes, including the smallest theft, the penalty was death.

**Solon,** age c. 38; Athenian statesman and legislator who moderated the harshness of Draco's laws, tempering justice with mercy. He gave Athens a new constitution that reduced the political power of the nobles and laid the foundation for future democracy.

**Nebuchadnezzar II,** age ?; king of Babylonia from 605 to 562 B.C. The son of Nabopolassar, who founded the Chaldean empire, Nebuchadnezzar is remembered for his destruction of the city and temple of Jerusalem in 586 B.C. after a 16-month siege. His armies then marched five to 10 thousand Jews, mostly from the upper classes, across the desert to Babylon, where they remained in captivity for nearly half a century, until 538.

**Zedekiah,** age ?; last king of Judah, from 597 to 586 B.C. A descendant of David, he was placed on the throne as a puppet by Nebuchadnezzar in 597. Zedekiah later grew bold, however, and revolted in 588. In 586 B.C., after the city was captured and destroyed, he was blinded and led in chains to Babylon.

Greeks breathed a purer and freer air, that the spirit of freedom arose and flourished as a result of the difficulty of the Greek terrain. It may be so, for its mountains and long, irregular seacoast—broken with deep indentations—restricted overland travel and produced small valley communities, enclosed and isolated by mountain ranges. Necessity produced self-sufficiency, and from self-sufficiency in turn came the courage to be free. The Asiatic "sciences" of divination and astrology never grew well in the stony Greek soil. We find Thales observing the heavens—not as the temple astrologers did, to discover the will of Enlil, Enki or Nanna—but in a scientific spirit, to understand planetary movements. For astrology the Greeks substituted astronomy, and a new age was born.

About the same time in Persia, Zoroaster, or Zarathustra, was also breaking ground as the founder of a new kind of religion—for religion was soon to become a matter of individual choice, no longer determined by place of birth or dependent upon official human intermediaries.

# 575 B.C.

**Zoroaster, or Zarathustra,** age 28?; religious prophet born in Persia. As a young man Zoroaster received revelations from Ahura-Mazda (the Lord of Wisdom) and founded Zoroastrianism, which displaced Persian polytheism. Some see Zoroastrianism as the source of the Jewish (and Christian) concepts of Satan, the archangels and the Last Judgment.

**Ezekiel,** age ?; major Hebrew prophet. Ezekiel, a priest in Jerusalem, was exiled to Babylon in 597 after the first capture of Jerusalem by the Babylonians. From 597 to 586 he continued to prophesy in Babylon, as Jeremiah was doing in Jerusalem, but after his prophecies came true in 586, he became the comforter of the Jews in captivity and foretold the coming of a messiah and the restoration of the Jewish kingdom.

**Thales,** age 24?; Greek philosopher and scientist born in Miletus, in Asia Minor. He was perhaps the first to search for rational explanations of natural phenomena, making the leap from superstition to science. It is commonly said that he held water to be the origin of all things, but the essence of his accomplishment is that he did not attribute events to the whims of the gods, but looked for the explanation of nature within nature itself. He predicted the solar eclipse of 585 B.C.

**Aesop,** age 20?; Greek writer of animal fables. Supposedly a slave on the island of Samos, Aesop was originally from Phrygia, in Asia Minor. The fables, rewritten in Greek verse by Babrius in the second century A.D. and in Latin verse by Phaedrus in the first century A.D., appeared in the 10th century in a prose collection by an author named Romulus. Velasquez painted Aesop's portrait as he imagined him to have looked.

**Sappho,** age 20?; Greek lyric poet born on the island of Lesbos. The ancients greatly admired her and compared her to Homer, but only fragments of her work remain. From the celebration in her poems of the love of women comes the term *lesbian,* after her native island.

Anaximander
 (c.611-546 B.C.), age c.36
Nabonidus
 (   -538? B.C.), age ?
Lao-tzu
 (604?-531? B.C.), age 29?
Croesus
 (   -546 B.C.), age ?
Cyrus the Great
 (600?-529 B.C.), age 25?
Peisistratus
 (605/600-527 B.C.),
 age c.25
Anaximenes
 (c.585-528 or 524 B.C.),
 age c.10
Pythagoras
 (582/580-500 B.C.), age c.7

# 575–550 B.C.

It was once believed that a stirring of the mind passed over the world's population in the sixth century B.C., a mysterious stimulus from an unknown source; no other explanation could be found for the simultaneous appearance, in widely scattered parts of the world, of religious innovators. From every country they came forth—prophets and seers, holy men and saviors—preaching, teaching and pointing the way to salvation. Zoroaster in Persia, Lao-tzu in China and Ezekiel in Babylon were among the first. Then came Pythagoras in southern Italy, followed by Buddha and Mahavira in India and Confucius in China. Within a comparatively short span of time, most of the great religions of the world—the so-called higher religions—were born.

## 575 B.C.

Solon
  (c.638-c.559 B.C.), age c.63
Nebuchadnezzar II
  (     -562 B.C.), age ?
Zoroaster
  (630/628-551/541 B.C.),
   age 53?
Thales
  (624?-546 B.C.), age 49?
Aesop
  (620?-560? B.C.), age 45?
Sappho
  (620/615-c.565 B.C.), age 45?

**Anaximander,** age c. 36; Greek philosopher and astronomer. Born in Miletus, Anaximander was a disciple and friend of Thales. He continued the search for rational explanations of natural phenomena and correctly calculated the angle of the earth's tilt (about 23 degrees) from the apparent path of the sun.

**Nabonidus,** age ?; last king of the Chaldean Empire of Babylonia (from 556 to 538 B.C.). An officer unrelated to the royal family, he was made king by a rebellion of officers six years after the death of Nebuchadnezzar. He is said to have incurred the enmity of the priests by his neglect of the worship of Marduk; the priests' treachery may have enabled the Persians to enter the city without opposition. In 538 B.C. Babylonia became part of the Persian empire.

**Lao-tzu,** age 29?; Chinese philosopher. Lao-tzu was reputedly the founder of Taoism and, possibly, the author of the *Tao-te-ching*. His philosophy of quietism urged renunciation of all desire and the attainment, through mystical contemplation, of harmony with the underlying principle of the universe. Frequently misunderstood in later times, Taoism eventually degenerated into magic and superstition.

The decline of theocratic states, the weakening of ancient traditions and customs, the havoc caused by marching armies, the destruction of temples, the dispersal of the priests, the abrogation of the sacrifices: these were common occurrences of the time. The late Assyrian empire was notorious for uprooting peoples, for transporting whole populations from one end of the empire to the other, as when they deported the Jews from Samaria and brought in people from the Euphrates valley, creating a jumble of races, creeds and traditions. The new religions addressed themselves to the plight of the individual, and though the comforts they offered were to seem uninviting to many in a later age, their discovery of unsuspected resources within the human mind was no small contribution to progress and enlightenment.

The religious efflorescence of the sixth century B.C. would seem to indicate that it was an unhappy age, a period of transition and decline when old ties had been severed and new ones, that might restore life, had not yet formed.

# 550 B.C.

**Croesus,** age ?; last king of Lydia (from 560 to 546 B.C.); noted for his great wealth and the splendor of his capital at Sardis. He enlarged his kingdom to embrace most of Asia Minor, including the Ionian cities on the coast. After his defeat by Cyrus the Great in 546 B.C., Lydia was incorporated into the Persian empire. The fate of Croesus is not known.

**Cyrus the Great,** age 25?; king of Persia from 550 to 529 B.C. and founder of the Persian empire. Succeeding his father as king of Anshan, a Persian district subject to the Medes, he revolted, defeated the Median king and proclaimed himself king of the Medes and Persians. Although Egypt, Babylonia and Lydia allied against him, he defeated Lydia in 546 and captured Babylon in 538, making Persia the most powerful state in the world.

**Peisistratus,** age c. 25; Greek general and statesman; tyrant of Athens 560–527 B.C. He opposed the aristocratic party and favored the distribution of land to the poor. Peisistratus encouraged literature and art and increased the splendor of religious festivals, thereby setting the stage for the birth of Greek drama.

Anaximenes
(c.585-528 or 524 B.C.),
age c.35
Pythagoras
(582/580-500 B.C.), age c.32
Belshazzar
(6th cent. B.C.), age ?
Anacreon
(572/570-488 B.C.), age c.22
Cleisthenes
(c.570-after 500 B.C.),
age c.20
Xenophanes
(c.570-c.480 B.C.), age c.20
Tarquinus Superbus
(6th cent. B.C.), age ?
Buddha
(c.563-483 B.C.), age c.13
Mahavira
(6th cent. B.C.), age ?
Darius I
(558?-486 B.C.), age 8?
Simonides
(c.556-468 B.C.), age c.6
Cambyses II
(c.555-522 B.C.), age c.5
Confucius
(551-479 B.C.), age 1

# 550–525 B.C.

Three great kings ruled Western Asia in 550 B.C.: Croesus, Nabonidus and Cyrus the Great. Before Croesus created a small empire by conquering adjacent territory, Lydia was a small, prosperous kingdom in western Asia Minor, the principal commercial link between the Ionian cities and the interior. It was rich in minerals, including gold, and the first country to use metal coins. After its army was taken by surprise by Cyrus the Persian and Croesus was taken prisoner, it lost its independence; thenceforth it would be merely a province of other states. This was also true of the Greek cities on the coast of Asia Minor. They had been settled before 1000 B.C., according to tradition, by Ionians fleeing from the mainland to escape a wave of migrating Dorian Greeks. The cities had grown prosperous from trade and maintained their independence until they were subjugated

## 550 B.C.

Thales
(624?-546 B.C.), age 74?
Anaximander
(c.611-547 B.C.), age c.61
Nabonidus
(     -538? B.C.), age ?
Lao-tzu
(604?-531? B.C.), age 54?
Croesus
(     -546 B.C.), age ?
Cyrus the Great
(600?-529 B.C.), age 50?
Peisistratus
(605/600-527 B.C.), age c.50

**Anaximenes,** age c. 35; Greek philosopher of Miletus, pupil of Anaximander. He continued the scientific quest, perhaps with less success than his predecessors. He maintained that the earth was flat and rested on air.

**Pythagoras,** age c. 32; Greek philosopher and mathematician born on the island of Samos. He settled at Croton, in southern Italy, and taught his disciples a philosophy that blended mathematics with the doctrine of metempsychosis and other Orphic elements. He held earthly life to be a preparation for a better world.

**Belshazzar,** age ?; Babylonian prince, son of King Nabonidus (incorrectly identified in the Bible as the son of Nebuchadnezzar). According to the Old Testament story (Daniel 5), handwriting appeared on the wall during Belshazzar's feast, prophesying doom, and that very night the Persians captured the city.

by Croesus; after his defeat they belonged to Persia, a circumstance that would prove hazardous to the Persian Empire.

Nabonidus ruled Babylonia for nearly 20 years and was an able and conscientious monarch. The great capital city continued to bask in the Indian summer of its neo-Babylonian age, but the vast sums spent by Nebuchadnezzar II on new temples and various public improvements had unsettled the economy. Inflation was a problem. Between 560 and 550 B.C. prices rose 50 percent. Furthermore, the priests of Marduk resented the king's attempt to introduce the worship of Nanna, the ancient god of Erech, into Babylon. Consequently, when the Persian army diverted the Euphrates River from its course and entered the city along the river bed, the alarm that should have been sounded was not sounded, and the long, long life of the great kingdom of Babylonia ended. Subjection by Greeks, Romans, Arabs and Turks lay ahead. Cyrus released the Jews, and some returned immediately to Jerusalem.

# 525 B.C.

**Anacreon,** age c. 22; Greek lyric poet born in Teos, in Asia Minor. He lived for many years at the court of Polycrates, tyrant of Samos, and at the court of Hipparchus, tyrant of Athens. Anacreon was noted for his short lyrics celebrating love and wine.

**Cleisthenes,** age c. 20; Greek statesman, called the founder of Athenian democracy. He allied himself with the popular assembly, broke the political power of the four major aristocratic clans and established a democratic constitution.

**Xenophanes,** age c. 20; Greek philosopher, poet, and religious reformer, born in Colophon, in Asia Minor. Xenophanes was a wandering poet and singer until he settled in Elea, in southern Italy, where he founded the Eleatic school of philosophy. He rejected and ridiculed anthropomorphic gods, and was the author of the famous saying that if oxen could paint and sculpt, they would depict the gods as oxen.

Tarquinius Superbus
(6th cent.), age?
Buddha
(c.563-483), age c.38
Mahavira
(6th cent.), age ?
Darius I
(558?-486), age 33?
Simonides
(c.556-468), age c.31
Cambyses II
(c.555-522), age c.30
Confucius
(551-479), age 26
Lucius Junius Brutus
(6th cent.), age ?
Publius Valerius
(6th cent.), age ?
Heraclitus
(540 or 535-475), age 15?
Miltiades
(550 or 540-489), age 15?
Leonidas I
( -480), age ?
Pausanias
( -470), age ?
Aristides
(530?-468), age 5?
Themistocles
(527/524-460), age c.2

# 525–500 B.C.

The quarter century from 525 to 500 B.C. was an unusual epoch in world history, remembered as significant from China to Rome. The two great moral teachers of Asia, Buddha and Confucius, were in the middle of their careers—Buddha was 38 when the period began and 63 when it ended; Confucius was 26 when it began and 51 when it ended. In Western Asia, Persia had swallowed up the weaker states, including Egypt and Asia Minor. Darius the Great, king of kings, ruled an empire more extensive than any previously known.

In Athens, Cleisthenes was laying the foundation of democratic government and giving Athens a new constitution; farther west, Rome, not to be outdone, established a republic. Modern historians are reluctant to accept the traditional accounts of early Roman history as factual, for they are much too dramatic, or melodramatic, and too romantic. Sober scholars are little inclined to believe that a republic was established because of the rape and suicide of a young woman. Equally dramatic circumstances, it is said, attended the first codification of Roman law. The story begins as a

## 525 B.C.

Anaximenes
(c.585-528 or 524), age c.60
Pythagoras
(582/580-500), age c.57
Anacreon
(572/570-488), age c.47
Cleisthenes
(c.570-after 500), age c.45
Xenophanes
(c.570-c.480), age c.45

**Tarquinius Superbus** (Tarquin the Proud), age ?; seventh and last king of Rome (from 534–510 B.C.), probably of Etruscan origin. An unpopular despot, he was expelled, according to Roman tradition, after the rape of Lucretia by his son, Tarquinius Sextus. Led by Lucius Junius Brutus, the Romans then established a republic (in 509 B.C.).

**Buddha** (Siddhartha Gautama), age c. 38; Indian philosopher, founder of Buddhism; son of a king in what is now Nepal. Renouncing the world at the age of 29 and leaving his wife and small child, he exchanged conventional comforts for a wandering life in search of enlightenment. After six years he declared that the realization of the blessed spiritual state of Nirvana is possible only through self-abnegation and the extinction of all desire.

**Mahavira** (great hero), or Vardhamana, age ?; Indian religious teacher; founder of Jainism. A contemporary of Buddha, he organized a brotherhood of monks, urged solicitude for all forms of life and practiced rigid asceticism as a means of escaping the cycle of rebirth.

**Darius I** (Darius the Great), age 33?; king of Persia from 521–486 B.C., son-in-law of Cyrus the Great. He is remembered for the extensive and excellent road system built under his leadership, for the rock carvings and inscriptions at Behistun, for the new capital of Persepolis and for the defeat of his army by the Greeks at the celebrated Battle of Marathon in 490 B.C. He died while preparing another expedition.

**Simonides,** age c. 31; Greek lyric poet born on the island of Ceos, famous for his poems in honor of the heroes of Marathon and Thermopylae. At the end of a long life spent mostly at the courts of wealthy

young girl, 15 or 16, daughter of a centurion, is on the way to the Forum, where she attends a literary school. She is accompanied by her governess, a proper middle-aged woman. Suddenly a man calls to her to stop, and firmly lays hold of her arm, exclaiming loudly that she is his property, a slave stolen from his house when very young. The girl is speechless, the nurse shrieks, and a crowd gathers.

Most historians will agree, however, that a republic was established about 509 B.C., whatever the reasons. Some might even agree that Rome's future could have been foreseen in those early days. From the beginning they were a warlike people, and it was an uncommon year when the city remained at peace. Every male citizen was a soldier and every patrician a military strategist. It was taken for granted that the elected consuls should know how to plan a campaign and should personally lead the army in battle. Rome at its height never lacked seasoned leaders or valiant soldiers. It is not surprising that Rome's neighbors said it was not a city, but an armed camp. These were the people who carried the banner reading SPQR (for *senatus populusque Romanus,* the senate and the people of Rome) alongside the wolf standard—the symbols of the Republic—to every continent of the Old World.

# 500 B.C.

patrons, he engaged in poetic rivalry with Pindar at the court of Hiero I, tyrant of Syracuse. Poetry, it appears, had no exalted origin. Its early practitioners were men skilled with words who employed their skill in flattering their patrons, attributing to them fine qualities and graces in exchange for room at their tables.

**Cambyses II,** age c. 30; king of Persia from 529–522 B.C., son and successor of Cyrus the Great. Reported to have been not quite sane and given to drunken rages, he is known chiefly for his conquest of Egypt. He defeated the pharaoh Psamtik III in 525 B.C. and added Egypt to the Persian empire. He died, possibly committing suicide, on the way home.

**Confucius** (K'ung Fu-tzu), age 26; Chinese sage and moral teacher. He neither founded a religion nor constructed a philosophical system, but, motivated by the insecurity and disorder of his time, he formulated principles of right conduct and practical wisdom, emphasizing good family relationships as the basis of social stability. A collection of his sayings, the *Analects,* was made by his disciples.

**Lucius Junius Brutus,** age ?; Roman statesman, reputedly one of the founders of the Republic in 509 B.C. and one of the first two consuls. According to tradition, as related by Livy and Shakespeare, he took the lead in expelling Tarquin.

**Publius Valerius** (Publicola), age ?; Roman statesman, colleague of Junius Brutus in founding the Republic. He served as consul four times.

Heraclitus
(540 or 535-475), age 40?
Miltiades
(550 or 540-489), age 40?
Leonidas I
(    -480), age ?
Pausanias
(    -470), age ?
Aristides
(530?-468), age 30?
Themistocles
(527/524-460), age c.27
Aeschylus
(525-456), age 25
Xerxes I
(519?-465), age 19?
Pindar
(522/518-443/438), age 18?
Parmenides
(c.514-    ), age c.14
Cimon
(510/507-449), age c.10

9

"As many days as there are in the whole journey, so many are the men and horses that stand along the road, each horse and man in the interval of a day's journey, and these are stayed neither by snow nor rain, nor heat nor darkness from accomplishing their appointed courses with all speed."

The words are Herodotus', in praise of the postal service of the Persians, whose riders sped in relays over the excellent roads carrying official documents. The Persian Empire surpassed its predecessors not only in the extent of its territory, but also in efficient and, for that time, humane and tolerant rule. It was fortunate in having at the outset three vigorous and capable monarchs: Cyrus the Great, from 550-529 B.C.; Darius the Great, from 521-486 B.C., and Xerxes I, also called the Great, from 486-465 B.C.

When Cyrus conquered Lydia in 546 B.C., he acquired

## 500 B.C.

Pythagoras
(582/580-500), age c.82
Anacreon
(572/570-488), age c.72
Cleisthenes
(c.570-after 500), age c.70
Xenophanes
(c.570-c.480), age c.70
Buddha
(c.563-483), age c.63
Darius I
(558?-486), age 58?
Simonides
(c.556-468), age c.56
Confucius
(551-479), age 51

HERACLITUS
Greek philosopher
540 or 535-475 B.C.

**Heraclitus,** age 40?; Greek philosopher born in Ephesus, in Asia Minor, of an aristocratic family. He is famous for introducing the idea of flux as a basic reality. Familiar sayings originated by Heraclitus include: "Nothing is; everything is becoming," "Everything flows; nothing remains constant," and "You cannot step into the same river twice."

**Miltiades,** age 40?; Athenian general, commander in the celebrated victory at Marathon in 490 B.C. He was acclaimed as a national hero, but his moment of glory ended quickly. The following year he died in prison. He was charged with deceiving the people in employing a fleet of 70 ships to avenge a private grudge.

**Leonidas I,** age ?; (?–480 B.C.), king of Sparta from 491/90–480 B.C., renowned for his heroic stand in the mountain pass of Thermopylae against the overwhelming forces of Xerxes I. A Greek traitor eventually showed the Persians another way through the mountains, and they attacked from the rear; Leonidas, 300 Spartans, and 1,000 other Greeks died in the pass.

**Pausanias,** age ?; (?–470 B.C.), Spartan general, nephew of Leonidas and commander of the combined Greek forces at Plataea (near Thebes) in 479. Accused twice of treasonable negotiations with Xerxes I, he was twice acquitted, but when later accused of conspiring with the

the Ionian Greek cities on the coast of Asia Minor—Miletus, Ephesus, Colophon and a number of others. In 499 B.C. these cities, under the leadership of Aristagoras, tyrant of Miletus, revolted and proclaimed their independence. The revolt was suppressed as soon as the Persians could give it their attention. Miletus was captured and razed in 492 B.C. and its inhabitants deported. The mainland cities of Athens and Eretria had assisted the revolt, an act which Darius could not forgive. His resentment and his desire to punish these cities resulted in the Persian-Greek wars. The familiar Greek accounts proudly recall the heroism at Thermopylae in 480 B.C. and the brilliant victories at Marathon in 490 B.C., at Salamis, a sea battle, in 480 B.C. and at Plataea in 479 B.C., where the Greek phalanx and spear proved superior to the Persian bow. However, despite the evidence of Greek valor, both Athens and Eretria were captured and burned to the ground. On the advice of Themistocles, the Athenians had abandoned their city. Opinions differ as to whether the Persians departed because they admitted defeat or because they were satisfied with their vengeance.

# 475 B.C.

Athenian Themistocles to overthrow the government, he took sanctuary in the temple of Athena, where, after the Spartans had barricaded the exits, he starved to death.

**Aristides,** age 30?; Athenian statesman and general, called Aristides the Just. He commanded a contingent at Marathon and in 479 B.C., aided by Pausanias and the Spartans, won a great victory at Plataea, which ended the Persian threat.

**Themistocles,** age c. 27; Athenian statesman and general, foremost champion of naval power. After his victory at Salamis in 480 B.C., his fortunes declined, and when in 468 B.C. he was accused of treachery, he took refuge with his old enemies the Persians. Artaxerxes kindly made him ruler of Magnesia (in southeastern Thessaly), where he remained the rest of his life, imprinting Magnesian coins with his own image.

**Aeschylus,** age 25; Greek dramatist, born in Eleusis, called the creator of tragedy. He fought in the Persian wars at Marathon, Salamis and Plataea. He also wrote 80 or 90 plays, winning first prize in the annual competition 13 times. Only seven plays have survived in complete form, including *Prometheus Bound, Seven against Thebes,* and *Agamemnon.*

**Xerxes I,** age 19?; king of Persia from 486–465 B.C., son and successor of Darius the Great. After three years of preparation, fitting out a great fleet and mobilizing two million men, he set sail for Athens, landed unopposed and burned the deserted city. After his defeats at Salamis and Plataea he returned to Persia. Dissolute living occupied his later years until he was murdered by the captain of the palace guard.

**Pindar,** age 18?; Greek lyric poet born near Thebes, famous for his choral lyrics sung to the accompaniment of music. A professional poet, he wrote odes and hymns for hire, employing his undisputed poetic gifts to magnify with lofty moral sentiments the special occasions of his clients.

Parmenides
  (c.514-    ), age c.39
Cimon
  (510/507-449), age c.35
Anaxagoras
  (500-428), age 25
Phidias
  (500/498-432), age c.25
Sophocles
  (c.496-406), age c.21
Pericles
  (495-429), age 20
Empedocles
  (495 or 490-435/430),
   age 15?
Zeno
  (495/490-430), age c.15
Artaxerxes I
  (    -425), age ?
Herodotus
  (485/484-425), age c.9
Euripides
  (485/480-406), age c.5
Protagoras
  (485/480-411/410), age c.5

# 475–450 B.C.

The history of the second quarter of the fifth century B.C. is the story of the ascendancy of Athens. After the Persians had withdrawn from mainland Greece, they still held some of the islands off the coast of Asia Minor. In order to dislodge them, it was proposed that the Greek city-states form an alliance, each contributing men and ships according to its resources. It was also proposed that this League of Delos, or Delian League, should be made a permanent confederation in order to repel future aggression. The principal organizers were the Athenians Aristides and Cimon; headquarters were established on the island of Delos in 478 B.C., and each of the more than 200 members was assigned its quota.

Within a few years all the islands had been liberated, and with no immediate danger on the horizon, many of the smaller states stopped supplying men and ships and made their contributions in money. In 454 B.C. the treasury was removed from Delos to Athens, and by 449 B.C. all but three states were making cash payments. When attempts to se-

## 475 B.C.

Simonides
   (c.556-468), age c.81
Heraclitus
   (540 or 535-475), age 65?
Pausanias
   (      -470), age ?
Aristides
   (530?-468), age 55?
Themistocles
   (527/524-460), age c.52
Aeschylus
   (525-456), age 50
Xerxes I
   (519?-465), age 44?
Pindar
   (522/518-443/438), age 43?

**Parmenides,** age c. 39; Greek philosopher of the Eleatic school, born in southern Italy, a pupil of Xenophanes. In his beliefs Parmenides was a precursor of Platonic idealism. He is said to have visited Athens late in life, where the young Socrates heard him speak. He maintained that nothing changes and nothing passes away, because the visible world of transient objects is itself an illusion.

**Cimon,** age c. 35; Athenian general and statesman, son of Miltiades. He aided Aristides in forming the Delian League and commanded the fleet in several engagements with the Persians, but is better known as a leader of the conservative, aristocratic party and an enemy of democracy.

**Anaxagoras,** age 25; Greek philosopher of the Ionian school, born in Asia Minor. The first philosopher to establish a school in Athens, he taught there for 30 years, from 462–432 B.C.; Pericles and Euripides were among his pupils and friends. A naturalist, he was exiled on charges of impiety brought by enemies of Pericles.

cede from the League were restrained by force, the members began to suspect they were no longer partners in a free alliance, but vassals of Athens. When the Athenians began to spend the League's treasury on public improvements for their city, it looked even more ominous. The money was important to Athens, for without it, the Parthenon would not have been built; neither would any of the other buildings erected by Pericles in his endeavor to make Athens the most beautiful city in Greece. Athens would not have attracted artists, poets and philosophers from many lands. Perhaps there would not have been an audience large enough to induce Socrates to speak publicly.

When Pericles came to power in 460 B.C. Athens entered its famed Golden Age; when Thucydides, the son-in-law of Cimon, accused him of robbing the treasury of the Delian League, his reply was that since Athens had undertaken to guarantee the defense of all Greece, the city might use the money as it saw fit. If the Delian League had indeed been an alliance of free states, then the reply of Pericles would have been nonsense. But the truth is that Athens, in the Age of Pericles, had become an imperial power.

# 450 B.C.

**Phidias,** age c. 25; Greek sculptor, called the greatest of antiquity. He designed the sculptures of the Parthenon and executed a 60-foot statue of Zeus at Olympia. A member of the Periclean circle and superintendent of public works projects, he was accused of impiety and exiled, although some say he died in prison.

**Sophocles,** age c. 21; Greek tragic dramatist born near Athens of a wealthy family. He wrote about 120 plays and won the annual prize for tragedy 18 or 20 times. His seven extant plays include *Oedipus Rex, Antigone, Electra,* and *Oedipus at Colonus.*

**Pericles,** age 20; Athenian statesman of a distinguished family, eloquent leader of the democratic party. Pericles was the center of a brilliant circle that included Anaxagoras, Sophocles, Phidias, Herodotus, Protagoras and Aspasia. He commissioned architects Ictinus and Callicrates to design the Parthenon (built 447–432 B.C.) and made Athens the most beautiful city in Greece. His death from the plague in 429 during the war with Sparta left the fate of Athenian democracy in the hands of mediocre politicians.

Empedocles
  (495 or 490-435/430), age 40?
Zeno
  (495/490-430), age c.40
Artaxerxes I
  (    -425), age ?
Herodotus
  (485/484-425), age c.34
Euripides
  (485/480-406), age c.30
Protagoras
  (485/480-411/410), age c.30
Nehemiah
  (5th cent.), age ?
Thucydides
  (5th cent.), age ?
Leucippus
  (5th cent.), age ?
Ezra
  (5th cent.), age ?
Socrates
  (470/469-399), age c.20
Nicias
  (c.470-413), age c.20
Cleon
  (    -422), age ?
Critias
  (c.460-403), age c.10
Democritus
  (c.460-370), age c.10
Hippocrates
  (c.460-c.377), age c.10
Thucydides
  (c.460-c.400), age c.10

13

# 450–425 B.C.

The plague was believed to have originated in Ethopia, and spread from there to Egypt and Libya—and to much of the Persian Empire—before it struck Athens in the first year of the Peloponnesian War. The city was overcrowded and lacked adequate lodging for the country people who had flocked in to escape the marauding Spartan soldiers. Among these people the disease raged unchecked. Thucydides paints a sorrowful picture of bodies of dying men lying one upon another and half-dead creatures reeling through the streets and gathering around the fountains to cool the burning fever. In spite of this calamity, the war went on. But after the second summer the Athenians seemed to lose heart. Pericles called an assembly and said that although the enemy had invaded their country, as indeed had been expected, and although the plague had come upon Athens suddenly, nevertheless, "the hand of heaven must be borne with resignation, that of the enemy with fortitude; this was the old

## 450 B.C.

Pindar
   (522/518-443/438), age 68?
Parmenides
   (c.514-    ), age c.64
Cimon
   (510/507-449), age c.60
Anaxagoras
   (500-428), age 50
Phidias
   (500/498-432), age c.50
Sophocles
   (c.496-406), age c.46
Pericles
   (495-429), age 45

**Empedocles,** age 40?; Greek philosopher and rhetorician born in Sicily, teacher of Gorgias, the Sophist. A curious reversionary figure among Greek philosophers, he claimed miraculous and prophetic powers and believed blood to be the thinking organ, able to control the movement of the limbs by its presence in all parts of the body.

**Zeno,** age c. 40; Greek philosopher, native of Elea and disciple of Parmenides, whom he is said to have accompanied to Athens. Plato mentions him briefly. He won fame as an inventor of paradoxes, e.g., that of the race between Achilles and the tortoise, which purported to prove logically that the tortoise could never be overtaken.

**Artaxerxes I,** age ?; king of Persia from 464–425 B.C., son and successor of Xerxes I, whose murderer he killed. He enjoyed peace throughout most of his 40-year reign and remained neutral in the Peloponnesian War. He appears in a favorable light in the Old Testament for his approval of the restoration of Judaism. Both Ezra and Nehemiah (whom he appointed governor of Judea) returned to Jerusalem during his reign.

**Herodotus,** age c. 34; Greek historian born in Asia Minor, called the Father of History. He traveled over most of the known world, taking note of and recording the wonders he encountered, and also wrote a history of the Persian wars. He is the sole source of much of our knowledge of the ancient world.

way at Athens, and do not you prevent it being so still. Remember, too, that if your country has the greatest name in all the world, it is because she never bent before disaster; because she has. . . won for herself a power greater than any hitherto known, the memory of which will descend to the latest posterity. . ."

"Born, however, as you are, citizens of a great state, and brought up, as you have been, with habits equal to your birth, you should be ready to face the greatest disasters and still to keep unimpaired the lustre of your name."

He said much more in the same uplifting vein. Thucydides writes that what was called a democracy was actually government by the leading citizen, a man so gifted that he could persuade the citizens of the rightness of any course and keep them to it. But in 429 B.C., two and a half years after the beginning of the war, he succumbed to the plague himself. Factions sprang up immediately, each wanting to take the lead, and operations in the field were paralyzed by their disagreements over strategy. Although the war dragged on for many years, the Athenians finally let victory slip from their hands.

# 425 B.C.

EURIPIDES
Greek dramatist
485/480-406 B.C.

**Euripides,** age c. 30; Greek dramatist, son of a prosperous family on the island of Salamis, where he spent most of his life, preferring seclusion to the social life of Athens. He wrote about 90 plays and won first prize five times. His plays marked a departure from tradition and were not immediately popular, for he was a skeptic and a realist. Among the 17 or 18 extant plays are *Alcestis, Medea, The Trojan Women, Orestes* and *The Bacchae.*

Nicias
(c.470-413), age c.45
Cleon
( -422), age ?
Critias
(c.460-403), age c.35
Democritus
(c.460-370), age c.35
Hippocrates
(c.460-c.377), age c.35
Thucydides
(c.460-c.400), age c.35
Alcibiades
(450-404), age 25
Aristophanes
(450/448-385/380),
age c.23
Lysander
( -395), age ?
Thrasybulus
( -389), age ?
Antisthenes
(444-after 371), age 19
Isocrates
(436-338), age 11
Aristippus
(c.435-366/356), age c.10
Dionysius the Elder
(c.430-367), age c.5

# 450 B.C.

**Protagoras,** age c. 30; Greek philosopher born in Abdera in Thrace. The first and most famous of the Sophists, Protagoras was a friend of Pericles, and the author of the saying, "Man is the measure of all things." He was also the first to teach grammar systematically, distinguishing parts of speech, tenses and moods. On the way to Sicily, after being exiled for questioning the existence of the gods, he is said to have been shipwrecked and lost.

**Nehemiah,** age ?; Jewish leader, probably a eunuch, who rose to high rank at the court of Artaxerxes I of Persia. An energetic and capable man, he was appointed governor of Judea and authorized to restore Jerusalem. He returned in 440 B.C. and began by rebuilding the city walls from 439–437 B.C. His history is told in the Old Testament Book of Nehemiah.

**Thucydides,** age ?; Athenian statesman, son-in-law of Cimon and his successor as leader of the aristocratic party in opposition to Pericles. He accused Pericles of fraud and misappropriation of funds belonging to the Delian League, which were contributed for mutual defense and not for the beautification of Athens. His ostracism in 443 B.C. left Pericles unchallenged. (He should not be confused with Thucydides, the historian.)

**Leucippus,** age ?; Greek philosopher of Miletus, teacher of Democritus and founder of the atomistic theory. He believed all things, including mind, are constituted of material units of various sizes and shapes.

# 425–400 B.C.

In 415 B.C., after 17 years of the Peloponnesian War, the Athenians undertook the famous Sicilian expedition. Nicias, their general, tried to dissuade them, advising them to conserve their strength and accusing Alcibiades of expecting some private profit from it. But they fitted out a fleet at enormous expense, said to be the most costly and splendid force ever sent out by a single city. It was a gala day when they sailed. Almost the whole population of Athens went down to Piraeus to watch. Thucydides wrote of this spectacle: "The ships being now manned, and everything put on board with which they meant to sail, the trumpets commanded silence, and the prayers customary before putting out to sea were offered, not in each ship by itself, but by all to-

# 425 B.C.

Sophocles
   (c.496-406), age c.71
Artaxerxes I
   (    -425), age ?
Herodotus
   (485/484-425), age c.59

**Nicias,** age c. 45; Athenian general and statesman. A moderate, opposed to the war party of Cleon and Alcibiades, he argued against undertaking the Sicilian expedition, but was made one of its commanders (415–413 B.C.). As the trapped Athenian fleet was being destroyed in the harbor of Syracuse, he attempted to escape overland, was captured and executed.

**SOCRATES**
Athenian philosopher
470/469-399 B.C.

Xenophon
    (431/430-355), age c.5
Plato
    (428/427-348/347), age c.2

**Socrates,** age c. 20; renowned Athenian philosopher whose dialectical skill attracted such famous pupils as Plato, Xenophon, Alcibiades, Antisthenes and Aristippus, and upon whose philosophy, or Plato's account of it, rose the labyrinthian edifice of European idealism. A bold questioner of accepted ideas and conventions, he was condemned to death for impiety in 399 B.C., five years after the fall of Athens.

**Ezra,** age ?; Jewish priest who returned to Jerusalem (perhaps about 428 B.C.) with royal authority to reform and reestablish Jewish religious worship. He took a leading part in shaping the ritual of modern Judaism and wrote the Book of Ezra and Chronicles I and II of the Old Testament.

gether to the voice of a herald; and bowls of wine were mixed through all the armament, and libations made by the soldiers and their officers in gold and silver goblets. In their prayers joined also the crowds on shore, the citizens and all others that wished them well. The hymn sung and the libations finished, they put out to sea, and first sailing out in columns then raced each other as far as Aegina, and so hastened to reach Corcyra, where the rest of the allied forces were also assembling."

Miscalculation, errors of judgment, treachery and chance each played a part in the downfall of Athens, but few events of the war were so disheartening as the loss of this splendid fleet. Nicias and Demosthenes, their ships ignominiously bottled up in the harbor at Syracuse, made a final desperate effort to break through the line of enemy ships. Failing, they abandoned and burned the ships still afloat and attempted to escape overland with the army. They failed in this, too.

# 400 B.C.

**Cleon,** age ?; Athenian politican, leader of the democratic party and the dominant political force in Athens after the death of Pericles. He was of humble birth and poorly educated, but a gifted and persuasive public speaker who urged vigorous prosecution of the war. He was killed in battle in 422 B.C. in Macedonia. Thucydides and Aristophanes portrayed him as vulgar, violent and unprincipled.

Antisthenes
    (444-after 371), age 44
Isocrates
    (436-338), age 36
Aristippus
    (c.435-366/356), age c.35

# 425 B.C.

Euripides
  (485/480-406), age c.55
Protagoras
  (485/480-411/410), age c.55
Socrates
  (470/469-399), age c.45

**Critias,** age c. 35; Athenian political leader and writer, pupil of Socrates and relative of Plato. One of the Thirty Tyrants imposed on Athens by Sparta at the close of the Peloponnesian War, he was a rich aristocrat, cynical and contemptuous of democracy. He appears in Plato's *Protagoras, Timaeus* and *Critias.* Some clever man, he said, invented the gods to enforce obedience to the law through fear of unseen, observant spirits.

**Democritus,** age c. 35; Greek philosopher born in Thrace. He accepted the atomistic theory of matter and attempted a mechanistic explanation of the universe, strongly influencing Epicurus and Lucretius, his philosophical descendants.

HIPPOCRATES
Greek physician
c.460-c.377 B.C.

**Hippocrates,** age c. 35; Greek physician born on the island of Cos, called the father of medicine. He rejected the demonic theory of disease and regarded medicine as a natural science, based on bedside observation of the patient.

# 400 B.C.

# 400–375 B.C.

In 400 B.C., with Athens at its mercy, Sparta was the dominant power in Greece. Spartan social structure was one of the most peculiar ever devised. While the helots, or state slaves, went about like heavily burdened beasts, performing menial and arduous labor, and wearing dogskin caps as a mark of their servitude, young Spartans were taken from their mothers at the age of seven, made wards of the state, removed to barracks where they lived the rest of their lives and trained in strict military discipline. This was the basis of Sparta's reputed invincibility.

After the defeat of Athens, Sparta aspired to rule all of the eastern Mediterranean. Through the intrigues of Lysander, a civil war erupted between Cyrus the Younger and his brother, Artaxerxes II, king of Persia. In the first battle, in 401 B.C., Cyrus was killed. His troops dispersed to their homes, but the band of Greek mercenaries had to make an

**Thucydides,** age c. 35; Greek historian born in Athens. His *History of the Peloponnesian War,* with its accurate and impartial reporting of events, has been called the first modern history. It contains the famous funeral oration delivered by Pericles. (He should not be confused with Thucydides, the son-in-law of Cimon.)

**Alcibiades,** age 25; Athenian general and politician. A friend of Socrates' and nephew of Pericles, he is often blamed for the defeat of Athens. Without his insistence, for purely personal reasons, the fateful expedition to Sicily might not have been undertaken. Going over to the Spartan side after being accused of impiety and sacrilege, he advised them of Athenian weaknesses. From there he went to Persia, and finally to Phryhia, where he was murdered at the instigation of the Thirty Tyrants. His instability and undependability, the Romans said, were typical of Greek character.

**Aristophanes,** age c. 23; Athenian playwright. Of his more than 40 comedies, 11 have survived, including *The Clouds, Lysistrata* and *The Frogs.* He employed his comic talent to attack and ridicule whatever was new and progressive, his principal targets being Socrates, Euripides, the Sophists and the leaders of the democratic party. Throughout the war he wrote plays urging peace with Sparta.

**Lysander,** age ?; brilliant and unscrupulous Spartan statesman, commander of the fleet in the last years of the Peloponnesian War. By destroying nearly every ship of the Athenian fleet, he forced Athens to surrender in 404 B.C. He set up the Thirty Tyrants, but the following year the Spartan ephors reversed his policy and helped restore Athenian democracy. He was killed in battle against the coalition of Thebes and Corinth.

**Thrasybulus,** age ?; Athenian statesman and general, leader of the democratic opposition to the Thirty Tyrants. Exiled in 404 B.C., he enlisted the support of Thebes, marched south and captured Piraeus, the port of Athens, forced the surrender of the Thirty Tyrants and restored democracy with the approval of Sparta.

# 400 B.C.

Dionysius the Elder
(c.430-367), age c.30
Xenophon
(431/430-355), age c.30
Plato
(428/427-348/347), age c.27
Epaminondas
(418?-362), age 18?
Diogenes
(412-323), age 12

arduous march through Armenia to safety (as related by Xenophon in *Anabasis.)* Sparta, undiscouraged, undertook other campaigns and for a while appeared victorious, but Sparta's success aroused jealousy. Thebes and Corinth watched their rival's progress with suspicion, and Athens had so far recovered by 377 B.C. that it was able to form a second maritime league, one this time in which the independence of the members was guaranteed. Before long, Athens, at the head of her league, was fighting Sparta again and driving Spartan ships from the Aegean. This was humiliating, but it was the war Sparta declared on Thebes that brought a speedy end to Spartan dreams of glory. The great Theban general Epaminondas administered a crushing defeat to the Spartans in 371 B.C. The following year he invaded the valley of the Eurotas and dissolved the Peloponnesian League, destroying Sparta's military power forever. Thereafter, Sparta was forced to concentrate on its own internal problems and played only a minor role in Greek politics.

# 375 B.C.

# 400 B.C.

Socrates
  (470/469-399), age c.70
Democritus
  (c.460-370), age c.60
Hippocrates
  (c.460-c.377), age c.60
Thucydides
  (c.460-c.400), age c.60
Aristophanes
  (450/448-385/380), age c.48
Lysander
  (    -395), age ?
Thrasybulus
  (    -389), age ?

**Antisthenes,** age 44; Athenian philosopher, founder of the Cynic school. After the fall of Athens and the death of Socrates, he gave up his old life, dressed as a poor workman and urged a return to the simplicity of nature. Renouncing comforts and luxuries and idle disputation, he created an image of the philosopher as one who, by his wisdom, simplicity of life and fortitude, found true happiness.

**Isocrates,** age 36; Greek rhetorician born of a wealthy family, the most famous teacher of oratory in ancient Greece. Extremely shy and handicapped by a weak voice, he did not make speeches, but wrote dissertations to be read. His flowing prose style and complex sentence structure made him famous and influenced both Demosthenes and Cicero. He was one of Socrates' pupils in his youth.

**Aristippus,** age c. 35; Greek philosopher born in Cyrene, in north Africa. He was the founder of the Cyrenaic school, which stressed the importance of the feelings, teaching that pleasure is the only good and immediate pleasure best of all.

**Dionysius the Elder,** age c. 30; tyrant of Syracuse from 405–367 B.C. A government clerk of humble birth, he rose to power by championing the cause of the poor. With an army of mercenaries, he waged war on the Carthaginians in Sicily and the Greek cities of southern Italy and made Syracuse the strongest Greek city in the West. He maintained a regal court, frequented by poets and philosophers, including Plato.

**Xenophon,** age c. 30; Greek historian born in Athens, a pupil of Socrates'. He wrote *Memorabilia,* his recollections of Socrates, and *Anabasis,* an account of the Persian civil war and the retreat of 10,000 Greek mercenaries to the Black Sea.

# 375 B.C.

# 375–350 B.C.

Sparta's fall left Thebes the strongest power in Greece, but it remained so only while Epaminondas lived. Rivalry among the city-states continued in an unpredictable manner, with alliances continually shifting. Such unstable and confused times, pervaded by war-weariness and disillusionment, were fertile soil for the rise and spread of new philosophies, particularly philosophies which ennobled withdrawal from society as the highest ideal. Antisthenes, a former pupil of Socrates, set up a school in Athens—the Cynic school—of an entirely new kind, which would deal not with words and syllogisms but with life and conduct. He would begin by abolishing all government, all established religion, private property and marriage—all the comforts and amenities to which civilized society accustoms its citizens. The

PLATO
Greek philosopher
428/427-348/347 B.C.

**Plato** (Aristocles), age c. 27; Greek philosopher born in Athens of an aristocratic family, the most distinguished pupil of Socrates and teacher of Aristotle. He founded the Academy in 387 B.C., which in the course of its 900 years' existence turned into the world's first university. Author of the celebrated *Dialogues* (of which 26 are extant), he remains the world's most influential philosopher, even though interest in metaphysical idealism has declined in the 20th century.

Epaminondas
    (418?-362), age 43?
Diogenes
    (412-323), age 37
Speusippus
    (c.400-339), age c.25
Dionysius the Younger
    (c.397-after 344), age c.22
Xenocrates
    (396-314), age 21
Praxiteles
    (c.390-330), age c.15
Demosthenes
    (385/384-322), age c.10
Aristotle
    (384-322), age 9
Antigonus I Cyclops
    (c.382-301), age c.7
Philip II
    (382-336), age 7

true philosopher, he said, lives by the law of nature and is contemptuous of artificial customs and conventions. Individual self-sufficiency was his ideal.

His pupil, Diogenes, taught the same message, but in a spectacular way. A homeless vagrant, he would point to the porticoes of Zeus and the Hall of Processions, saying that the Athenians had thoughtfully provided him with shelter. As the perfect antithesis to Pericles, who, half a century earlier, had spoken for the good citizen who accommodates himself to the demands his society makes of him in exchange for the benefits it confers, Diogenes spoke for the rank outsider, who utterly rejects civilized society and will not be reconciled to it; who scorns its honors no less than its comforts, professing to believe that men of position, generals and statesmen, are not the first among men, but the last.

Clearly something had gone wrong. Society had somehow failed the individual, and the individual was deserting. Greece was in decline, and its future bleak.

# 350 B.C.

Democritus
(c.460-370), age c.85
Antisthenes
(444-after 371), age 69
Isocrates
(436-338), age 61
Aristippus
(c.435-366/356), age c.60
Dionysius the Elder
(c.430-367), age c.55
Xenophon
(431/430-355), age c.55
Plato
(428/427-348/347), age c.52

**Epaminondas,** age 43?; Greek general and statesman born in Thebes, noted for his integrity and simple way of living and for crushing the military power of Sparta at Leuctra in 371 B.C. One of the greatest generals of antiquity, he invented military tactics which were copied by Philip of Maccdonia and Alexander the Great.

The Metropolitan Museum of Art, Rogers Fund, 1922.

DIOGENES
Greek Cynic philosopher
412-323 B.C.

**Diogenes,** age 37; Greek Cynic philosopher born in Sinope on the

# 350–325 B.C.

When Philip II became its ruler in 359 B.C., Macedonia was a backward kingdom, considered barbarous by the Greeks. Its plains were inhabited by industrious farmers and an aristocracy of horse breeders. Within twenty years the new king accomplished what no city-state had been able to do—he united all Greece under one rule. A cunning, unscrupulous, ambitious man, he made his first objective the creation of a powerful army. He adopted and improved the slanting phalanx originated by Epaminondas, whom he had met at Thebes as a youth. At Leuctra the great general had concentrated power on the left slanting wing, which enabled it to break through the Spartan line, swing right and attack from the rear. With an invincible army and a strong fleet, Philip began to intervene in the quarrels of the Greeks. Demosthenes perceived his aim and opposed him violently, but Philip persevered, and after his famous victory at Chaer-

# 350 B.C.

Black Sea, pupil of Antisthenes'. Rejecting all conventions and preferring the role of comic eccentric to that of serious thinker, he became more famous than his teacher and was transformed into the legendary saint of philosophy. Diogenes was venerated for nearly a thousand years, until the final collapse of paganism.

**Speusippus,** age c. 25; Greek philosopher, pupil and nephew of Plato and his successor as head of the Academy. He believed in the interrelatedness of all things and attempted a systematic classification of plants and animals. He believed that pleasure is neither the highest good nor wholly evil; that good is not the source but the goal of being; and that specialization is futile, for if one knows only one thing, he understands nothing. Crippled by paralysis, he committed suicide.

**Dionysius the Younger,** age c. 22; son of Dionysius the Elder, whom he succeeded as tyrant of Syracuse in 367 B.C. Known chiefly for his failure to become a philosopher-king under Plato's tutelage, he was exiled in 356 B.C. and returned in 346 B.C., only to be expelled again in 344 B.C. for his arbitrary rule. He retired to Corinth, where he lived many years as a teacher of rhetoric.

**Xenocrates,** age 21; Greek philosopher born in Chalcedon. Xenocrates was a pupil of Plato's, and accompanied him to Sicily in 361 B.C. He succeeded Speusippus as head of the Academy and is said to have been the first to divide philosophy into the branches of logic, physics and ethics. Because of his virtuous life and reputation for integrity, he was not required to take an oath when appearing in court.

# 350 B.C.

Praxiteles
(c.390-330), age c.40
Demosthenes
(385/384-322), age c.35
Aristotle
(384-322), age 34
Antigonus I Cyclops
(c.382-301), age c.32
Philip II
(382-336), age 32
Darius III
(    -330), age ?
Porus
(    -321?), age ?
Theophrastus
(c.372-c.287), age c.22
Mencius
(371?-288?), age 21?
Chuang-tzu
(c.369-286), age c.19
Ptolemy I
(c.367-283), age c.17
Seleucus I
(c.358-280), age c.8
Alexander the Great
(356-323), age 6

onea in 338 B.C. over the Athenian and Theban armies, he formed the Corinthian League, with the intention of making an assault on Persia. Before it could get under way, he was assassinated in the summer of 336 B.C.

His son Alexander was then 20 and an experienced soldier. In response to the secession of the Greek cities from the Corinthian League, he marched swiftly south, destroyed Thebes and reduced its population to slavery. Nothing was left standing in Thebes but the temples and the house where Pindar had lived. In the spring of 334 B.C. Alexander was ready to realize his ambition of leading all Greece against the Persian Empire. He crossed to Asia Minor with 30,000 infantry and 5,000 cavalry. Only Sparta had not sent troops. After Greek victories at Granicus and Issus, in 333 B.C., Darius III offered to cede the territory west of the Euphrates. Alexander did not bother to reply, but before proceeding with the conquest of Persia, he swung southward to Syria and Phoenicia, where he was delayed seven months by the resistance of Tyre. Towards the end of 332 B.C. he entered Egypt with little opposition and founded the city of Alexandria. He left Egypt in the spring of 331 B.C. and in the fall he

# 325 B.C.

advanced into Mesopotamia, where Darius was waiting on a field chosen to his own advantage—the field of Gaugamela, near Arbela. There, with the slanting phalanx, Alexander annihilated the last Persian army in October 331 B.C. He occupied Babylon, Susa and Persepolis, and in 329 B.C. pushed east into Bactria, where he married a princess, and beyond. He entered India in the summer of 327 B.C., and in

Isocrates
   (436-338), age 86
Plato
   (428/427-348/347), age c.77
Diogenes
   (412-323), age 62
Speusippus
   (c.400-339), age c.50
Dionysius the Younger
   (c.397-after 344), age c.47
Xenocrates
   (396-314), age 46

**Praxiteles,** age c. 40; Athenian sculptor, second in reputation only to Phidias. *Hermes with the Infant Dionysus* (in the museum at Olympia) is thought to be his only surviving original work. The *Apollo Sauroctonus* and the *Aphrodite of Cnidus,* both in the Vatican Museum, are among the best-known Roman copies.

**Demosthenes,** age c. 35; Athenian statesman and orator famous for the *Philippics,* a series of orations warning the Athenians of the imperialistic aims of Philip of Macedonia. After the battle of Chaeronea his cause was lost. In 322 B.C. he ended his life by taking poison.

ARISTOTLE
Greek philosopher
384-322 B.C.

**Aristotle,** age 34; Greek philosopher born in Chalcidice, on the northern coast of the Aegean. A son of the physician to the Macedonian king, he studied 20 years under Plato, tutored Alexander the Great from 342–335 B.C. and returned to Athens to found the Lyceum, where he taught for 12 years. He retired to Chalcis after the death of Alexander to avoid the fate of Socrates. Scientist as well as philosopher, he was esteemed above Plato in the Middle Ages and was accepted as the final authority on all subjects. His best-known works are *Ethics, Politics* and *Poetics.*

**Philip II,** age 32; king of Macedonia from 359–336 B.C., a military genius and founder of the Macedonian Empire. He defeated the combined Athenian and Theban armies at Chaeronea in 338, but was assassinated at a banquet two years later and succeeded by his son, Alexander the Great.

326 B.C. defeated King Porus. At the Indus River his troops refused to go farther. The army then sailed down the Indus to the Indian Ocean and returned to Persia, some by sea and some, with Alexander, by means of an arduous march across the desert. He was back in Susa in the spring of 324 B.C., undisputed master of the Persian Empire, and was planning new campaigns.

**Darius III,** age ?; king of Persia from 336–330 B.C., sixth-generation descendant of Cyrus the Great and last of the Achaemenid dynasty. Fleeing to the East after the destruction of his army at Guagamela (near Arbela) in 331 B.C., he was imprisoned by Bessus, satrap of Bactria, who usurped the crown and murdered him. Alexander, arriving too late to save the king, buried Darius III with royal honors, and in 329 B.C. captured and executed Bessus as a regicide.

**Porus,** age ?; Indian king of the Indus Valley who resisted the invasion of Alexander the Great. His huge army, including 200 war elephants, was defeated in 326 B.C. by a small force of Macedonians, but Alexander restored his kingdom to him in recognition of his bravery.

**Theophrastus** (Tyrtanus), age c. 22; Greek philosopher born on the island of Lesbos. A pupil of Aristotle's and his successor as head of the Lyceum, where he lectured for 35 years, he is best known as the author of *On the History of Plants,* the first comprehensive treatment of botany, and *Characters,* a series of lively sketches of various personality types, imitated by La Bruyere among others.

Antigonus I Cyclops
   (c.382-301), age c.57
Ptolemy I
   (c.367-283), age c.42
Seleucus I
   (c.358-280), age c.33
Alexander the Great
   (356-323), age 31
Roxana
   (    -311), age ?
Chandragupta
   (    -286), age ?
Epicurus
   (342/341-270), age c.17
Menander
   (343/342-291), age c.17
Demetrius I
   (c.337-283), age c.12
Zeno of Citium
   (c.335-c.263), age c.10

MENCIUS
Chinese philosopher
371?-288? B.C.

**Mencius** (Meng-tzu), age 21?; Chinese philosopher who traveled from kingdom to kingdom, urging the rulers to adopt the principles of Confucius. He believed in the natural goodness of men but insisted that it required a favorable environment to be fully manifested. He declared that a ruler whose subjects have been reduced to poverty should be removed. *The Book of Mencius* is a Chinese classic.

**Chuang-tzu,** age c. 19; Chinese mystical philosopher, exponent of the doctrines of Lao-tzu. He maintained that identification with the universal principle of nature (Tao) should be man's goal. His book of essays is profound and humorous and, unlike many ancient books, may be readily understood and appreciated by modern readers.

# 325–300 B.C.

When the wily Egyptian priests hailed him as the son of the god Amon, Alexander did not deny it. In 324 he ordered the Greek cities to establish a cult for the worship of Alexander the god, and he decreed that his personal attendants should fall down and kiss the ground before him in the Oriental manner. Some of his best Macedonian generals, practical soldiers with no patience for such nonsense, were executed for treason. Plots and conspiracies sprang up and rebellion smouldered among his veteran soldiers. Among those accused of conspiracy and executed was Aristotle's nephew, official historian of the Asiatic campaign. It is questionable whether Alexander could have organized his empire. His intention was to establish a theocratic monarchy, but he proceeded slowly and had accomplished very little by June 13, 323 B.C., when he died of malaria in Babylon at the age of 33.

The wars among his successors were long and bitter, but eventually Ptolemy and Seleucus achieved a measure of

## 325 B.C.

Diogenes
(412-323), age 87
Xenocrates
(396-314), age 71
Demosthenes
(385/384-322), age c.60
Aristotle
(384-322), age 59
Porus
(    -321?), age ?
Theophrastus
(c.372-c.287), age c.47
Mencius
(371?-288?), age 46?
Chuang-tzu
(c.369-286), age c.44

**Antigonus I Cyclops,** age c. 57; Macedonian general and king of Macedonia from 306–301 B.C. After the death of Alexander the Great, he became the leading contender for control of the entire empire, but a coalition of envious generals defeated and killed the old man at the battle of Ipsus in 301 B.C. He was succeeded by his son Demetrius I.

**Ptolemy I, Ptolemy Soter** (preserver), age c. 42; Macedonian general in Alexander's army who became satrap of Egypt after Alexander's death. He later assumed the title of king and established a dynasty that ruled for 300 years, whose most famous member was Cleopatra. He made Alexandria his capital and founded the famous library and museum. Almost continuously at war, he abdicated in 285 B.C. in favor of his son.

**Seleucus I Nicator** (conqueror), age c. 33; Macedonian general and king of Hellenistic Syria from 306–280 B.C., founder of the Seleucid dynasty. In the scramble for shares of the empire left by Alexander, he gained for himself most of the former Persian Empire. He founded Greek cities in Asia, including his capital, Antioch, and spread Hellenistic culture throughout the East.

stability in Egypt and Syria that was not possible in Macedonia. There Antipater, one of Philip's generals, had been named regent in 334 B.C. when Alexander departed. But in 323 B.C. the army elected Arrhidaeus king of Macedonia. He was an illegitimate son of Philip's. Perdiccas, another general, was made regent for Roxana and her small son, Alexander IV but Perdiccas was killed in a mutiny of his troops in 321 B.C. in 319 B.C. Antipater was killed in battle, and Polysperchon, another general, was named regent to succeed him; this displeased Cassander, the son of Antipater. In the meantime, Arrhidaeus had been put to death by order of Olympias, widow of Philip and mother of Alexander. The following year, 316 B.C., she was captured by Cassander and put to death, and Cassander assumed the title of king. His authority was challenged by the armies of Antigonus I Cyclops and his son Demetrius, but from 301 B.C., after the battle of Ipsus, until his death in 297 B.C., Cassander was in complete control of Macedonia and Greece. After his death the situation again became fluid. This was the condition of Greece at the opening of the third century B.C. Clearly its role as the political and cultural leader of the world had ended.

# 300 B.C.

**Alexander III,** age 31, king of Macedonia, called Alexander the Great. He succeeded Philip II, his father, in 336 B.C. at the age of 20. He led an army into Asia, defeated the Persians, conquered Tyre, occupied Egypt and built the city of Alexandria. He died of fever in Babylon in 323 B.C.

**Roxana,** age ?; wife of Alexander the Great (they were married in 327 B.C.) and daughter of a Bactrian prince. After Alexander's death, she took her son, Alexander IV, to Macedonia and became entangled in court intrigues. Both were imprisoned and murdered by Cassander, the son of Antipater.

**Chandragupta** (Sandrocottus), age ?; king of Magadha in India, 321?–298 B.C. An ambitious local native leader, he destroyed the Macedonian garrisons left by Alexander, deposed the rightful king (of the Nanda dynasty) and founded the Maurya dynasty, ruling most of Northern India and Afghanistan. He acquired great power and prestige and in fear of assassination, rarely left his ornate palace. In 298 he abdicated, became a Jain monk and wandered to southern India, where 12 years later he fasted to death. He was the grandfather of Asoka.

Epicurus
(342/341-270), age c.42
Menander
(343/342-291), age c.42
Demetrius I
(c.337-283), age c.37
Zeno of Citium
(c.335-c.263), age c.35
Euclid
(fl. c.300), age ?
Manetho
(fl. c.280), age ?
Berossus
(early 3rd cent.), age ?
Bindusara
(    -273), age ?
Pyrrhus
(c.318-272), age c.18
Theocritus
(c.310-250), age c.10
Ptolemy II
(309-246), age 9
Callimachus
(c.305-c.240), age c.5

# 300–275 B.C.

It is generally acknowledged that third century Athens stood on a lower cultural level than Athens of the golden fifth century. Who was there to stand beside Sophocles, Aeschylus, Pindar and Euripides? There were no sculptors the equal of Phidias, no philosophers to compare with Socrates. Or so it is commonly thought. No one can be sure, for Hellenistic literature has almost totally perished. Of the estimated 700,000 papyrus rolls that were once held in the library at Alexandria, a few scraps remain. Such a great loss could indeed conceal from later ages the existence of great writers, historians and philosophers, but, more to the point, it produces a false picture of the age. Actually the third century was better educated and more literate than the fifth. The manufacture of papyrus rolls had been improved, and they were produced in large quantities; educated slaves were employed as copyists. At least 1,100 Hellenistic writ-

## 300 B.C.

Theophrastus
   (c.372-c.287), age c.72
Mencius
   (371?-288?), age 71?
Chuang-tzu
   (c.369-286), age c.69
Ptolemy I
   (c.367-283), age c.67
Seleucus I
   (c.358-280), age c.58
Chandragupta
   (    -286), age ?

**Epicurus,** age c. 42; Greek philosopher born on the island of Samos, founder of the Epicurean school in Athens. He combined the naturalism of Democritus with an ethics that extolled intellectual pleasure, serenity and detachment from the world.

**Menander,** age c. 42; Greek dramatist born in Athens. He wrote over 100 comedies, with love as the theme, which remained popular long after his death. Noted for their style and wit, his plays were imitated and adapted to the Roman stage by Plautus and Terence.

**Demetrius I Poliorcetes** (besieger of cities), age c. 37; king of Macedonia from 294–285 B.C., son of Antigonus I Cyclops. He fought alongside his father in the wars of the Diadochi (successors) and was with him at Ipsus in 301 B.C. His destruction of the Egyptian fleet off Salamis in 306 B.C. was commemorated by the famous statue, *Victory of Samothrace,* found on the island of Samothrace and now in the Louvre.

**Zeno of Citium,** age c. 35; Greek philosopher of Phoenician ancestry born in Cyprus, founder of Stoicism. He established an influential school in Athens about 308 B.C. His emphasis on practical ethics made Stoicism the dominant philosophy of the Roman period, with Cicero, Cato the Younger and Seneca among its adherents.

**Euclid,** age ?; Greek mathematician, founder of a school in Alexandria during the reign of Ptolemy I. He is best known for his treatise on

ers are known by name, though their works have perished. Most of the literary activity was on behalf of a new reading public seeking entertainment. Some historians have professed to see a parallel between the fifth and third centuries of the ancient world and the 19th and 20th centuries of the modern and have suggested that men and women of the 20th century would feel more at home in the third century B.C. than in the fifth.

Comedy flourished in Athens more vigorously than any other literary form during this period. It was a comedy of manners, light and entertaining. About 70 writers of comedy are known, but the greatest name is that of Menander. The 1957 discovery in a Cairo antiquarian's shop of a complete play, the only one known, stimulated interest in his work. Love is his theme; young love is frustrated by society or parents until something unexpected happens or a sudden discovery is made which removes all obstacles. Witty, elegant and extremely popular in the third century, he might well have been equally successful in the early 20th century as a Hollywood screenwriter.

# 275 B.C.

geometry, which for many centuries served as the basis of geometry textbooks.

**Manetho,** age ?; Egyptian priest and historian, author of a history of Egypt from the earliest times to 323 B.C., written to inform the Greek conquerors about his country's past. The fragments that remain have been invaluable to modern scholars.

**Berossus,** age ?; Babylonian priest and historian, contemporary of Manetho; he recorded Babylonian myths, superstitions and science as well as history. Fragments remain, scattered throughout the works of Josephus, Eusebius and other later historians.

**Bindusara,** age ?; king of Magadha in India from 298–273 B.C. He was an able ruler who enlarged the kingdom, but his chief claim to fame is that he was the son of Chandragupta and the father of Asoka, the greatest monarch of ancient India.

**Pyrrhus,** age c. 18; king of Epirus (in northwestern Greece) from 295–272 B.C., remembered for his Pyrrhic victories over the Romans. Responding to a call for assistance from the Greek colony of Tarentum in southern Italy, he sailed with 25,000 men and 20 elephants. He defeated the Romans in a costly battle at Heraclea in 280 B.C. and again at Asculum in 279 B.C. after which he declared, "One more such victory and I am lost."

Theocritus
(c.310-250), age c.35
Ptolemy II
(309-246), age 34
Callimachus
(c.305-c.240), age c.30
Asoka
(     -232), age ?
Valmiki
(3rd cent.), age ?
Archimedes
(287-212), age 12
Ptolemy III
(282-221), age 7
Chrysippus
(c.280-c.207), age c.5

# 275–250 B.C.

As Athens' power and prestige decline, Alexandria's grew. It appeared as if Alexandria would succeed Athens as the world's center of literature and science, though not of philosophy, for Athens still had the Academy and the Lyceum, and the newer Stoic and Epicurean schools were established there. Eminent men of letters and scientists from all parts of the Hellenistic world were attracted to Alexandria, encouraged by the hospitality of the Ptolemies and the reputation of the great library and museum. Callimachus and Theocritus, Euclid and Eratosthenes were among the most famous. The culture of Alexandria was neither Egyptian nor Greek, but a conglomerate of all creeds, traditions and dialects. It could hardly be otherwise, for the Macedonians were in Egypt for a single purpose—to exploit the country. Like the ancient pharaohs, the Ptolemies claimed ownership of all the land and leased it to the natives. It was a land of

## 275 B.C.

Epicurus
  (342/341-270), age c.67
Zeno of Citium
  (c.335-c.263), age c.60
Bindusara
  (     -273), age ?
Pyrrhus
  (c.318-272), age c.43

**Theocritus,** age c. 35; Greek Poet, a native of Sicily. Known as the originator of Arcadian or pastoral poetry, he lived at the court of Hiero II of Syracuse and in Alexandria at the court of Ptolemy II. His work was much imitated in its sensitivity to nature by later poets.

**Ptolemy II,** Ptolemy Philadelphus, age 34; king of Egypt from 285–246 B.C., son of Ptolemy I. Under his rule Egypt became supreme in the eastern Mediterranean and Alexandria rivaled Athens as a center of Hellenistic culture. He built the famous lighthouse at Pharos, one of the Seven Wonders of the Ancient World, destroyed by an earthquake in the 14th century.

**Callimachus,** age c. 30; Greek poet and scholar born in Cyrene, foremost Alexandrian poet of his time, noted for his wit and learning. Appointed chief librarian by Ptolemy II, he made a critical catalog *(Pinakes),* now lost, of the contents of the great library. He is said to

# 250–225 B.C.

By the middle of the third century B.C., Rome had completed the conquest of Italy; however, no single statesman or general, nor even any two or three, could claim the lion's share of the glory. This is one of the peculiarities of Roman history—the absence of outstanding names during the period of its rise to power. The three centuries following the

## 250 B.C.

tenant farmers, and between the sun-baked peasant farmers and the polyglot, cosmopolitan population of Alexandria there was an unbridgeable gulf. It is not surprising that, after the first three Ptolemies, decline set in.

At the other end of the known world the first flowering of Indian art was bursting out in exuberant naturalism, in the benign climate that characterized the reign of Asoka. Grandson of the founder of the Maurya empire, he was also a great conqueror, but about 260 B.C. he renounced wars of conquest, was converted to Buddhism and embraced *ahimsa,* the principle of nonviolence. He made Buddhism the state religion, although he tolerated all religions; he moderated the severity of penal laws and restricted the killing of animals. For the first time in history a great, prosperous empire was administrated on principles of compassion and nonviolence. Asoka is still remembered as the greatest king in Indian history. In the 40 years of his reign, India enjoyed an era of peace, prosperity and just and efficient government.

## 250 B.C.

have written 800 works, but only six hymns, a few epigrams and fragments of *Aetia,* a learned poem on the origins of religious customs, survive.

**Asoka,** age ?; king of Magadha from c. 273–232 B.C. who brought India under one rule for the first time in history. Troubled by the suffering caused by his conquests, he abandoned warfare and about 260 B.C. was converted to Buddhism, then only a small sect, which through his influence developed into a world religion. He sent missionaries as far as Greece and Egypt. India prospered and the arts flourished under his humane government.

**Valmiki,** age ?; Indian poet. He is the author, according to tradition, of the Sanskrit epic, the *Ramayana,* which in its more than 24,000 couplets relates the adventures of the prince Rama and his wife Sita, and is one of the two great Indian epic poems.

Archimedes
(287-212), age 37
Ptolemy III
(282-221), age 32
Chrysippus
(c.280-c.207), age c.30
Eratosthenes
(276/275-196/194),
age c.25
Hamilcar Barca
(270?-228), age 20?
Shih Huang Ti
(259-210), age 9
Titus Maccius Plautus
(254-184), age 4

founding of the Republic about 500 B.C. are curiously lacking in famous men. The first great names that come to attention are those of Plautus, Ennius, Scipio Africanus and Cato the Elder, all alive in 200 B.C., when Rome had already grown powerful. But who transformed Rome from a small agricultural community into the ruler of Italy? It was done by the Senate and the people of Rome, for Rome was a republic, and many able men participated in the achievement. While the great men of Greece and Asia were winning fame for lesser achievements, the Roman consuls were

## 225 B.C.

## 250 B.C.

content to serve their single year, relinquish control to the newly elected consuls and return to the Senate to become one voice among many.

Rome's great enemies, Hamilcar Barca and Hannibal, are world renowned, even figures of historical romances, but the Romans who opposed them are hardly known. Who invaded Africa in the First Punic War? It was Marcus Atilius Regulus. Who destroyed the Carthaginian fleet in 241 B.C. and forced Hamilcar Barca to abandon Sicily and make

Theocritus
   (c.310-250), age c.60
Ptolemy II
   (309-246), age 59
Callimachus
   (c.305-c.240), age c.55
Asoka
   (      -232), age ?

ARCHIMEDES
Greek mathematician and
   physicist
287-212 B.C.

**Archimedes,** age 37; Greek mathematician and physicist born in Sicily. A pioneer in mechanics and hydrostatics, he is remembered for two sayings: "Eureka!" and "Give me a place to stand and I will move the earth." With his mechanical devices, he aided the defense of Syracuse in the Second Punic War and was killed by a Roman soldier.

**Ptolemy III,** called Ptolemy Euergetes (benefactor), age 32; king of Egypt from 246–221 B.C., son of Ptolemy II. During his reign Egypt reached the height of its power and prosperity under the Macedonian dynasty. He generously supported the arts.

# 225–200 B.C.

Hannibal, the Carthaginian, was a man of great ability who devoted his life to one aim—the subjugation of Rome; for he knew, as well as Cato, that only one state—Rome or Carthage—could survive. In the spring of 218 B.C., with 40,000 men, a number of elephants and a troop of Numidian cavalry, he crossed the Pyrenees from Spain and the Rhone River, and went over the high Alps near the little St. Bernard pass, arriving in the Po Valley in September. He defeated the Romans in midwinter at Trebia and again in the spring of 217 B.C. at Lake Trasimenus. The Carthaginians continued south to Apulia, where at Cannae in 216 B.C. the Romans, with a new army, again gave battle. Hannibal executed

## 225 B.C.

peace? It was Gaius Lutatius Catullus. Neither of these names is well known today.

The First Punic War, from 264-241 B.C., was caused, whatever the immediate pretext, by Rome's desire to expand into the western Mediterranean. Carthage controlled the commerce of that area and stood squarely in Rome's way. Following Rome's victory, the sea was open to Roman ships and the larger part of Sicily had become the first Roman province.

**Chrysippus,** age c. 30; Greek Stoic philosopher born in Cilicia (in southeastern Asia Minor), called the second founder of Stoicism. Although Epictetus and Marcus Aurelius are better known, Chrysippus, after Zeno, was the most important Stoic. He systematized the doctrines and gave Stoicism its orthodox form. He espoused the universal brotherhood of men and the principle of inherent natural rights, which became the foundation of Roman law. Only fragments remain of his work.

**Eratosthenes,** age c. 25; Greek scholar, scientist and head of the library at Alexandria, born in Cyrene in North Africa. He measured the obliquity of the ecliptic with great accuracy (cf. Anaximander, P. 4); calculated the circumference of the earth; catalogued over 700 stars; established a system of chronology dating events from the fall of Troy; and wrote the first comprehensive book on geography, which contained a map of the known world. After going blind in his old age, he starved himself to death.

**Hamilcar Barca,** age 20?; Carthaginian general, commander in the First Punic War, and father of Hannibal. The defeat of the Carthaginian fleet in 241 B.C. compelled him to abandon Sicily and make peace with Rome. His brutal suppression of the rebellion of unpaid mercenaries was realistically portrayed by Gustav Flaubert in his novel *Salammbo*.

Shih Huang Ti
  (259-210), age 34
Titus Maccius Plautus
  (254-184), age 29
Hannibal
  (247-183/182), age 22
Liu Pang
  (247-195), age 22
Antiochus III
  (242-187), age 17
Quintus Ennius
  (239-169?), age 14
Scipio Africanus Major
  (237/234-184/183),
  age c.11
Marcus Porcius Cato
  (234-149), age 9

a perfectly planned pincer movement and annihilated the Romans, who are said to have lost 50,000 men. Thereafter Quintus Fabius Maximus, the Roman general, avoided direct encounters, preferring to wear down his enemy by harassment. Hannibal remained in Italy 15 years; his army, firmly entrenched in the mountains of southern Italy, could not be dislodged.

When certain unusual and mysterious occurrences were observed in the area, the priestly interpreters of the Sibylline Books were asked to explain them. After consulting their books, they revealed that the signs indicated that Hannibal would be driven from Italy only through the intervention of the Great Mother of Ida (Cybele); however, she would have to be brought to Rome from her temple in Pessinus near Mount Ida in Asia Minor. Ambassadors were dispatched immediately. The king of Pergamum received them respectfully and presented them with the black stone said to be the abode of the goddess. Thus it was that the worship of Cybele was formally introduced in Rome in 204 B.C. She entered the city in triumph, carried through the streets by the most respected matrons, accompanied by the cheers of the crowds, and solemnly installed in a temple on the Palatine Hill.

Archimedes
  (287-212), age 62
Ptolemy III
  (282-221), age 57
Chrysippus
  (c.280-c.207), age c.55
Eratosthenes
  (276/275-196/194), age c.50

**Shih Huang Ti,** age 34; Chinese emperor from 221–210 B.C., first emperor of the Ch'in Dynasty, from which comes the name China. As Prince Cheng of the feudal state of Ch'in, he unified China by conquering the warring states, and in 221 B.C. assumed the title Shih Huang Ti (the first emperor). He built the Great Wall and burned the books of Confucius and other philosophers to eradicate all traces of the feudal past. He was succeeded by a weak son and his empire soon collapsed.

**Titus Maccius Plautus,** age 29; Roman playwright born in Umbria. He settled in Rome and wrote about 40 comedies, borrowing his plots, characters and settings from Menander. Twenty have survived. Shakespeare's *Comedy of Errors* is taken from Plautus, as is the character of Falstaff in *Henry IV*.

**Liu Pang,** age 22; Chinese emperor from 202–195 B.C., founder of the Han Dynasty (202 B.C.–A.D. 220). A minor village official of peasant origin, he joined the guerrilla warfare that followed the collapse of the Ch'in central government, defeated all rivals and established a more durable dynasty, which controlled the first truly centralized and well-governed Chinese empire.

**Antiochus III** (Antiochus the Great), age 17; king of Syria from 223–187 B.C., great-great-grandson of Seleucus I. The preeminent monarch of his time, he recovered territories lost by his precedessors and partially restored the glory of the Seleucid Empire. In 199 B.C. he recovered Palestine, which had been under Egyptian rule for nearly a

# 200–175 B.C.

Had the Roman senators known more about the worship of Cybele, they might have preferred Hannibal to her. When they understood its nature, they quarantined the religion, fearing the effect of its bizarre rites upon the minds of the people. They forbade Roman citizens to take part in the sacred revels and confined the Asiatic priests to their temple. But, not wishing to offend the goddess after her service to Rome, they granted the priests permission to go about the streets on certain holidays, soliciting gifts to maintain the temple. Dressed like women, long haired and jeweled, the priests marched in processions to the accompaniment of jangling tambourines.

Although they were not yet welcome in Rome, religions from the East had by 200 B.C. already swept over the eastern Mediterranean. After Alexander and his successors had carried Greek culture into Asia in the fourth century B.C.,

The gratitude of the Roman people was unbounded when, soon afterward, Hannibal's army returned to Africa. Some practical-minded people, however, suggested that the landing of Scipio Africanus in Africa might have had more to do with Hannibal's departure than the goddess.

century. Hannibal, in exile from Carthage, advised him on military strategy.

HANNIBAL
Carthaginian general
247-183/182 B.C.

**Hannibal,** age 22; Carthaginian general, son of Hamilcar Barca. Using Spain as a base, he crossed the Alps, advanced into southern Italy and destroyed the Roman army at Cannae in 216 B.C. He maintained his army in Italy for another 13 years, until he was recalled in 203 B.C. to oppose the Roman landing in Africa, where he lost the great Battle of Zama, which ended the Second Punic War in 202 B.C. Exile and suicide by poison was his eventual fate.

Jesus, Son of Sirach
(early 2nd cent.), age ?
Quintus Ennius
(239-169?), age 39
Scipio Africanus Major
(237/234-184/183), age c.36
Marcus Porcius Cato
(234-149), age 34
Antiochus IV
(c.215-163), age c.15
Polybius
(205/203-125/120), age c.5

the tide reversed. In the second century revitalized Oriental faiths flooded the West, spread by Syrian traders and slaves as well as priests. For several centuries the Eastern mystery cults enjoyed the favor of mediterranean peoples, with no other gods to challenge their supremacy. These strange religions (whose name comes not from an implication of mystery in their nature, but from *myste,* meaning an *initiate)* were originally fertility cults, but they had undergone subtle changes and had become in essence forms of a belief in an afterlife. The soul, according to the mystery cults, had been imprisoned in a mortal body; its aim was to transcend this earthly life and return to its heavenly home. These cults, whose initiates were sworn not to reveal any part of the secret rites, propagated for the first time in the history of the West the notion of heavenly immortality. So effectively were the Greeks and Roman gods displaced that when Christianity triumphed, it was not over Zeus, Apollo and Juno, but rather Attis, Adomis, Isis and Osiris, the gods of the mysteries.

# 200 B.C.

Eratosthenes
(276/275-196/194),
age c.75
Titus Maccius Plautus
(254-184), age 54
Hannibal
(247-183/182), age 47
Liu Pang
(247-195), age 47
Antiochus III
(242-187), age 42

**Jesus, Son of Sirach** (Joshua ben Sira), age ?; Jewish scholar of Jerusalem, author of *Ecclesiasticus,* an Apocryphal book of the Old Testament (canonical in the Roman Catholic Bible), containing maxims of worldly wisdom. One familiar line is: "Let us now praise famous men . . . " (44:1).

**Quintus Ennius,** age 39; Roman poet born in Calabria, called the father of Latin poetry. A centurion in Sardinia during the Second Punic War, he was taken to Rome by Cato the Elder. There he became a Roman citizen, taught Greek and translated Greek plays. He wrote tragedies, of which about 400 lines are extant, and the epic poem *Annales* (in 18 books), of which 600 lines remain. His work influenced Virgil, Lucretius and Ovid.

# 175–150 B.C.

The Asiatic backlash against Hellenism was especially violent in Palestine, where the Jews had a long history of resistance to foreign gods. The Ptolemies of Egypt, who controlled Palestine before 200 B.C., practiced noninterference with the religions of their subjects, but in 199 B.C. Antiochus the Great took southern Syria and Palestine from Egypt. The Jews were less comfortable under Syrian rule, but no serious trouble developed until the reign of Antiochus IV Epiphanes, when the bitter contention of two Jewish families for the office of high priest provided an excuse for Syrian intervention. In 169, as Antiochus was invading Egypt, the rivalry broke into open warfare. On his return from Egypt, Antiochus entered Jerusalem and his troops quelled the disturbance. He apparently then resolved that for the sake of stability there should be one culture and one religion for the entire kingdom. Judea, a small and unimportant part of the realm, had to conform.

# 175 B.C.

Quintus Ennius
(239-169?), age 64
Marcus Porcius Cato
(234-149), age 59

**Mattathias,** age ?; Jewish village priest, known as the instigator of the Maccabean revolt. His defiance of Syrian authorities and murder of the king's officer was the spark that set off the rebellion. He and his five sons fled to the mountains and escaped capture.
**Antiochus IV Epiphanes** (illustrious), age c. 40; king of Syria from

**Scipio Africanus Major** (Publius Cornelius Scipio), age c. 36; called Scipio the Elder, most illustrious Roman general before Julius Caesar, famous for his invasion of Africa and defeat of Hannibal at Zama. After his acquittal of charges, brought by Cato, of accepting bribes, he retired to his country house, embittered by Rome's ingratitude. He was the father of Cornelia.

**Marcus Porcius Cato** (Cato the Elder), age 34; Roman statesman and writer, known as an inflexible champion of the moral virtues of the early Republic and famous for ending every Senate speech with "I vote that Carthage should be destroyed." He wrote a treatise on farming, *De Agricultura,* which is the oldest surviving prose work in Latin.

# 175 B.C.

Mattathias
( -166?), age ?
Antiochus IV
(c.215-163), age c.40
Polybius
(205/203-125/120),
age c.30
Judas Maccabeus
( -160), age ?
Cornelia
(2nd cent.), age ?
Terence
(195 or 185-159), age 20?
Hipparchus
(c.190-c.125), age c.15
Scipio Africanus Minor
(185/184-129), age c.10

The city walls were torn down and soldiers garrisoned within the city. A Greek altar was placed upon the Jewish altar in the Temple, which became a temple to Zeus. Many Jews conformed, for there was a large party, mostly of the upper class, who welcomed Greek culture. Others resisted and met death. When a royal officer arrived at Modin, a village 15 miles west of Bethel, he set up an altar and invited the aged priest Mattathias to be the first to offer sacrifice. The old man replied in a loud voice that he would not. When a nervous Jew stepped forward, anxious to placate the officer, the old priest killed him with a single blow and threw him on the altar. Mattathias then killed the Syrian official and the revolt was on.

The miracle of the small country of Judea winning its independence from the mighty Seleucid Empire came about through dissension among the Syrians after the death of Antiochus in 163 B.C. as well as the heroic determination of Judas Maccabeus and his followers. In 142 B.C. the Maccabeans set up an independent state and maintained it until the Romans added Judea to their dominions.

# 150 B.C.

175–163 B.C., son of Antiochus III. He is remembered for his attempt to Hellenize the Jews and outlaw worship of the God of Israel. He desecrated and plundered the temple in Jerusalem and set up altars for the worship of pagan gods. His folly resulted in the expulsion of the Syrians from Judea and the establishment of an independent kingdom.

Hipparchus
(c.190-c.125), age c.40
Scipio Africanus Minor
(185/184-129), age c.35

## 175 B.C.

**Polybius,** age c. 30; Greek historian born in the Peloponnesus. Held in Rome as a political hostage after 160 B.C., he wrote a history of the world from 266 to 146 B.C. and is ranked next to Thucydides among the greatest Greek historians. He accompanied Scipio the Younger to Africa and witnessed the destruction of Carthage.

**Judas Maccabeus** (the hammerer), age ?; third son of Mattathias; leader of the Jewish revolt from 166–160 B.C. He defeated four Syrian armies in two years and led his guerrilla force to Jerusalem, where he cleansed the temple and restored Jewish worship on Dec. 25, 165 B.C.—an event commemorated by the Jewish Feast of Dedication, or Hanukkah. Killed in battle in 160 B.C., he is the subject of Handel's oratorio *Judas Maccabaeus*.

# 150–125 B.C.

The bitter domestic wars in Rome during the second and first centuries B.C. began with the Gracchi—Tiberius Sempronius Gracchus and Gaius Sempronius Gracchus—and their story had, in turn, begun some years earlier.

Roman domestic politics was at that time largely a family affair. Scipio Africanus Major, conqueror of Hannibal, was the father of Cornelia, a Roman matron noted for her devotion to her children (her *jewels*). She married the statesman Tiberius Sempronius Gracchus, who served as consul in 177 B.C. and again in 163 B.C. Of their 12 children, only three lived to adulthood: two sons, Tiberius Sempronius Gracchus and Gaius Sempronius Gracchus, who would become known to history as the Gracchi, and a daughter who married Scipio Africanus Minor. Africanus Minor was not related to Africanus Major, but was the son of Lucius Aemilius Paullus, a Roman general. He was adopted, however, by the eldest son of Africanus Major, which made him the adop-

## 150 B.C.

Marcus Porcius Cato
  (234-149), age 84
Polybius
  (205/203-125/120),
  age c.55
Cornelia
  (2nd cent.), age ?

**Hipparchus,** age c. 40; Greek astronomer born in Asia Minor. He catalogued over 1,000 stars and originated the method of indicating geographical position by latitude and longitude. He was also the originator of the system of astronomy copied by Ptolemy in the second century A.D. and known thereafter as the Ptolemaic System.

**Scipio Aemilianus Africanus Minor,** age c. 35; Roman general and statesman, called Scipio the Younger. In the Third Punic War, he besieged Carthage, destroyed the city and sold the population into

**Cornelia,** age ?; Roman matron noted for her devotion to her children. The daughter of Scipio Africanus Major and mother of the Gracchi, she devoted herself, after the death of her husband, to rearing and educating her children, who brought her undying fame.

**Terence** (Publius Terentius Afer), age 20?; Roman playwright born in Carthage, of African origin. Taken to Rome as a slave while still a child, he was educated and freed and wrote six Latin comedies that were modeled on Greek originals. His comedies were more subtle and refined than Plautus'. His best-known works are *The Woman of Andros* and *The Brothers*. He died on a journey to Greece in search of more plays by Meńander.

Tiberius Sempronius Gracchus
(163-133), age 13
Wu Ti
(157-87), age 7
Gaius Marius
(c.155-86), age c.5
Gaius Sempronius Gracchus
(153-121), age 3

tive cousin of his wife.

Tiberius Sempronius Gracchus, the elder of the Gracci, had fought at Carthage and in Spain, and had observed the fortunes of the middle class decline as wealth poured into the hands of the very rich. He was elected tribune of the people and immediately proposed a redistribution of public lands. Among his bitter opponents was Scipio the Younger, his brother-in-law and adoptive cousin. When Tiberius was murdered, Scipio rejoiced openly; immediately after his bitter public denunciation of Gaius, however, Scipio was himself murdered. The act has been attributed to various people: to his enemies in the democratic faction, to his wife and to Cornelia, his mother-in-law. In any case, after the death of her second son, Gaius, in an election riot in 121 B.C., Cornelia retired to Misenum. When she died, a statue was erected and inscribed "Cornelia, Mother of the Gracchi"; the base of the statue, which bears the inscription, is now held by the Capitoline Museum in Rome.

Not until the early part of the next century was the struggle to redistribute Rome's wealth resumed, with increased bitterness and violence, by Marius and Sulla.

slavery. As leader of the Senatorial party, he violently opposed the reforms urged by the Gracchi. A patron of the arts and member of an aristocratic circle of admirers of Greek culture, he died by assassination.

**Tiberius Sempronius Gracchus,** age 13; Roman statesman, leader of the popular party. He sponsored proposals to restore the class of independent farmers by a redistribution of land and was killed, with 300 of his followers, in a street riot. He enters the record here, at the age of 13, because his career was to be so short.

Wu Ti
(157-87), age 32
Gaius Marius
(c.155-86), age c.30
Gaius Sempronius Gracchus
(153-121), age 28
Ssu-ma Ch'ien
(145?-90/87), age 20?
Alexander Jannaeus
(    -76), age ?
Lucius Cornelius Sulla
(138-78), age 13
Posidonius
(c.135-51), age c.10
Mithradates VI
(c.132-63), age c.7

# 125–100 B.C.

The Han Empire of China was the Eastern counterpart of the Roman Empire. Its armies were as triumphant and its territory as extensive as Rome's, yet there was virtually no contact between them. One reason for this may be that to have traveled safely from the borders of one to the other, one would have had to be accompanied by an army. Lone travelers were easy prey for brigands and wild tribes. Emperor Wu Ti, sometimes called Han Wu Ti, was the fifth and strongest ruler of the Han dynasty. Probably born about 157 B.C., he became emperor at 17 and ruled with vigor and efficiency until he was 70.

The Ch'in (or Tsin) Empire had been the first to unite an extensive area. Founded by Shih Huang Ti (who called himself the First Emperor) in 221 B.C., it proved an ephemeral creation, although "the First Emperor" was a man of exceptional ability. He divided China into 36 provinces, governed by officials directly under his control. He shifted large

## 125 B.C.

Polybius
  (205/203-125/120),
  age c.80
Cornelia
  (2nd cent.), age ?
Hipparchus
  (c.190-c.125), age c.65

**Wu Ti,** age 32; emperor of China from 140–87 B.C., fifth and strongest ruler of the Han Dynasty. He expanded the empire by conquest to include most of the present area of China, north to Korea, south to Tonkin and west far into central Asia. Confucianism was restored as the official ideology, though in a corrupt form, concerned principally with cosmology and magic.

**Caius Marius,** age c. 30; Roman general and statesman, uncle of Julius Caesar (by marriage). Chosen Tribune of the People in 119 B.C. and consul in 107 B.C., the first of seven times, he became leader of the popular party in opposition to Sulla. In the civil war of 88 B.C., he was driven from Rome, but returned with an army, captured the city and proscribed the leaders of the aristocratic party.

segments of the population, as the Assyrians had done in the West, to overcome local resistance to centralized rule. He built the major part of the Great Wall and ordered a general burning of books, exempting only those on medicine, agriculture and divination. Rivalry among his generals after his death destroyed the unity he had created, and China fell into chaos.

A wily politician, Liu Pang, emerged as the strong man. By 202 B.C. he had forged a new unity and established the Han dynasty, which ruled for four centuries. It is called the first truly centralized and soundly administered Chinese empire. In its fifth emperor, Wu Ti, it had a worthy successor of Liu Pang. He further extended the boundaries, repulsed the barbarian Huns, reduced the functions of the nobles to honorary formalities and enlisted the knowledge and skill of the educated classes in the administration. The political framework established by Liu Pang was thus strengthened and consolidated; as a result it would endure as a protective shelter for the development of Chinese civilization, a civilization which, though frequently disrupted by periods of disorder and foreign domination, retained a continuity through the centuries.

# 100 B.C.

**Gaius Sempronius Gracchus,** age 28; Roman statesman, younger brother of Tiberius Gracchus. He renewed agitation for land reform and was killed in an election riot at the age of 32.

**Ssu-Ma Ch'ien,** age 20?; father of Chinese history; court historian to Emperor Wu Ti. His great work, the *Shih Chi,* served as a model for later dynastic histories, and included accounts of all countries and peoples then known. He reformed the calendar and is said to have devised the system of chronology still in use. He chose castration instead of death as punishment for offending the emperor in order to finish his history, which is the only source on Lao-tzu, the philosopher and founder of Taoism.

Alexander Jannaeus
( -76), age ?
Lucius Cornelius Sulla
(138-78), age 38
Posidonius
(c.135-51), age c.35
Mithradates VI
(c.132-63), age c.32
Marcus Terentius Varro
(116-27), age 16
Marcus Licinius Crassus
(115/112-53), age c.15
Lucius Licinius Lucullus
(c.110-56), age c.10
Cataline
(108-62), age 8
Marcus Tullius Cicero
(106-43), age 6
Pompey the Great
(106-48), age 6

# 100–75 B.C.

Internal dissension and civil war dimmed the glory of Rome's brilliant military successes. What is remembered from the first quarter of the first century B.C. is not Roman conquests, but the jealousy and rivalry of Marius and Sulla. Gaius Marius, born in 155 B.C., was in a sense the heir of the Gracchi, but although he was nearly contemporary with them, he did not emerge as a leader of the popular party until the following century, when he was well along in years. Lucius Cornelius Sulla, a younger man, descended from a minor branch of the patrician Cornelia family, had served under Marius in Africa and had effected the capture of Jugurtha, king of Numidia, to conclude the campaign in 106 B.C. Both men were successful generals and consuls several times.

In 88 B.C. Sulla and Cinna were consuls. Sulla was given command of the campaign against Mithradates VI, king of Pontus, but no sooner had he left Rome than one of the

## 100 B.C.

Wu Ti
   (157-87), age 57
Gaius Marius
   (c.155-86), age c.55
Ssu-ma Ch'ien
   (145?-90/87), age 45?

**Posidonius,** age c. 35; Greek Stoic philosopher born in Syria, one of the most learned men of his time; a friend and teacher of Cicero. His celebrated school at Rhodes attracted many Romans and played an important part in the diffusion of Hellenistic culture in the West.

**Mithradates VI Eupator** (the Great), age c. 32; king of Pontus in northeast Asia Minor from 120–63 B.C. Rome's most formidable enemy in the East, he aspired to create a great Hellenistic empire in Asia Minor. In the three Mithradatic Wars (88–66 B.C.), he met and was defeated by Sulla, Lucullus and Pompey. He fled in 65 B.C. to the Crimea and attempted suicide by poison, which failed, it is said, because of his prolonged precautionary use of antitoxins. He is the

tribunes transferred the command to Marius. Sulla immediately turned back, marched into Rome and began the civil war by massacring the partisans of Marius, who had himself already decamped. When Sulla had departed the second time, Cinna, his fellow consul, recalled Marius, who entered Rome with his army and followed Sulla's example by massacring his own political enemies. He then appointed himself consul, but had been in office only a few days when he died at 69.

After Sulla had concluded the campaign in the East, defeated Mithradates and made peace (in 83 B.C.), he returned and began extensive proscriptions. He made himself dictator in 82 B.C., condemned to death or exile great numbers who had supported Marius and confiscated their property. To everyone's surprise, he gave up his office in 79 B.C. and retired to the country to write his memoirs. For a few years Rome was at peace with itself, until rivalry between Caesar and Pompey resumed the sordid melodrama, with Caesar taking the part of Marius and Pompey that of Sulla, as champion of the aristocratic Senate.

# 75 B.C.

subject of Racine's *Mithridate*.

**Alexander Jannaeus,** age ?; king of Judea from 103–76 B.C., great-grandson of Mattathias and the second Hasmonean to assume the title of king. Strife, intrigue and cruelty marked his reign. Some scholars have identified him as the Wicked Priest who persecuted the Teacher of Righteousness in the Dead Sea Scrolls.

**Lucius Cornelius Sulla,** age 38; Roman general and dictator from 82–79 B.C. Leader of the Senatorial party, he gained control of Rome after the death of Marius and proscribed great numbers of his political enemies. In 79 B.C. he relinquished power and retired to his villa, where he died the following year.

Marcus Terentius Varro
  (116-27), age 41
Marcus Licinius Crassus
  (115/112-53), age c.40
Lucius Licinius Lucullus
  (c.110-56), age c.35
Cataline
  (108-62), age 33
Marcus Tullius Cicero
  (106-43), age 31
Pompey the Great
  (106-48), age 31
Spartacus
  (   -71), age ?
Julius Caesar
  (102 or 100-44), age c.25
Lucretius
  (99/96-55), age c.24
Cato the Younger
  (95-46), age 20
Sallust
  (86-34), age 11
Marcus Junius Brutus
  (85?-42), age 10?
Gaius Cassius
  (   -42), age ?
Catullus
  (84-54), age 9
Mark Antony
  (c.83-30), age c.8

# 75–50 B.C.

In the second quarter of the first century B.C. a host of giant figures strides onto the stage, intimating that portentous dramas are about to unfold. Their names are familiar: Cicero, Pompey, Caesar, Spartacus, Cataline, Cato the Younger. Yet in this age dominated by war and politics, scholars, poets and philosophers also flourished. A scholar like Varro could live through these dangerous times, occupied with his books, and reach the age of 89; Catullus could remain obsessed with his passion and the fickleness of his mistress, oblivious of politics; even Cicero, inhabiting two worlds, could find time for philosophy; and, strangest of all, Lucretius could write his philosophical poem in an atmosphere of serenity that belied the very existence of war and proscriptions. It comes as a shock to realize that he was a contemporary of Caesar's, just one year younger.

## 75 B.C.

Posidonius
  (c.135-51), age c.60
Mithradates VI
  (c.132-63), age c.57

**Marcus Terentius Varro,** age 41; Roman scholar, the most erudite and prolific writer of his time, most of whose works have been lost. Only one complete work has survived, *De re rusticana libri III (Three Books on Farming),* an important source on Roman agriculture. A partisan of Pompey, he miraculously escaped proscription during the civil war and lived to extreme old age. Julius Caesar named him to head his proposed public library.

**Marcus Licinius Crassus,** age c. 40; unscrupulous Roman politician; member of the First Triumvirate with Caesar and Pompey. He became one of the richest men in Rome by buying up confiscated or abandoned estates during the proscriptions of Sulla. As governor of Syria in 54 B.C., he robbed the temple of Jerusalem of its treasures. Unsuccessful as a general, he was killed fighting the Parthians.

**Lucius Licinius Lucullus,** age c. 35; Roman general and epicure, famous for his great wealth and his extravagant banquets. He commanded the Roman army in the Third Mithradatic War (74–66 B.C.) with brilliant success, but was recalled and replaced by Pompey for reducing interest rates in the provinces. He retired and lived in luxury as a patron of the arts.

**Catiline** (Lucius Sergius Catilina), age 33; Roman aristocrat, politician and conspirator. After the ruin of his political ambitions, he organized the underworld population of Rome, its criminals and outcasts, in 63 B.C. in a plot to kill the consuls and plunder the city. The patrician mistress of one of the conspirators sold her information to the police, and the scheme was publicly exposed by Cicero in the four famous Catilinarian Orations.

**Marcus Tullius Cicero,** age 31; Roman statesman, orator and writer; consul in 63 B.C. He opposed Caesar's dictatorship but did not join the conspiracy of Brutus and Cassius. He is best remembered for his orations, displaying a mastery of Latin prose style, and his letters, revealing details of Roman private life. Proscribed by the Second Triumvirate, he was killed by followers of Mark Antony.

**Pompey the Great** (Gnaeus Pompeius Magnus), age 31; Roman general and statesman, ally of Sulla against Marius and champion of the

An improbable story about Lucretius has been handed down by St. Jerome: "After a love philtre had turned him mad, and he had written, in the intervals of his insanity, several books which Cicero revised, he killed himself by his own hand in the 44th year of his life." Cicero did publish *De rerum natura,* but it is not likely that he revised it. Lucretius was the poet of naturalism. Although Italian by birth, he expressed a philosophy that was thoroughly Greek, more truly Greek in spirit than that of Socrates or Plato. His philosophy was the materialism of Democritus and Epicurus, in harmony with Greek life and art, and with the moderation and reasonableness of the Hellenic spirit which saw the world not as a shadow of reality, but reality itself. While Caesar and Pompey contended for glory, with the eyes of the world upon them, Lucretius was intent upon the wonder of the world, the spectacle of life and its serene pleasures. At death, he said, the body dissolves into atoms, and nothing of its own nature remains; but more of his nature remains in his poem than is left to us of Caesar and Pompey, despite their triumphs and conquests.

# 50 B.C.

Senatorial party. He captured Jerusalem in 63 B.C. and annexed Syria and Palestine to Rome. After the death of Julia, his wife and Caesar's daughter, in 54 B.C., rivalry between the two men brought on the civil war. Defeated by Caesar at Pharsalus in 48 B.C., he fled to Egypt, where he was killed by order of Ptolemy XII.

**Spartacus,** age ?; Roman gladiator from Thrace who led a revolt of slaves in 73–71 B.C. He took refuge on Mount Vesuvius and was joined by some 90,000 runaway slaves. After defeating several Roman armies, he led his force to Cisalpine Gaul, where he planned to allow them to depart for their own countries. They preferred to remain and plunder Italy and marched south. Spartacus was killed in battle with Crassus, who crucified all the men he captured.

**Gaius Julius Caesar,** age c. 25; Roman general and dictator. Portrayed by Suetonius as an unscrupulous schemer for power and prestige, he was nevertheless one of the great military commanders of history, famous for the conquest of Gaul and invasion of Britain in 55 B.C. As leader of the popular party, he defied the Senate, crossed the Rubicon and marched on Rome, making himself dictator in 49 B.C. His assassination in 44 B.C. ushered in another period of civil war, which ended only with the final triumph of Augustus in 27 B.C. His histories of the Gallic and civil wars are models of straightforward Latin prose.

**Lucretius** (Titus Lucretius Carus), age c. 24; Roman poet and philosopher, author of *De rerum natura (On the Nature of Things),* a long didactic poem based on the philosophy of Epicurus. Stories of his madness and suicide are believed to be unfounded.

**Cato the Younger** (Marcus Porcius Cato), age 20; Roman statesman, soldier and Stoic philosopher, great-grandson of Cato the Elder. A staunch republican, he supported Pompey against Caesar and continued the struggle two years after Pompey's death. His suicide in 46 B.C. cost Brutus and Cassius an ally.

**Gaius Valerius Catullus,** age 9; Roman lyric poet famed for his poems of love and passion, inspired by his love for the beautiful, rich and unprincipled Clodia (Lesbia), wife of Metellus Celer. He died in 54 B.C. at the age of 30.

Sallust
   (86-34), age 36
Marcus Junius Brutus
   (85?-42), age 35?
Gaius Cassius
   (     -42), age ?
Mark Antony
   (c.83-30), age c.33
Vercingetorix
   (     -46), age ?
Herod the Great
   (73?-4 B.C.), age 23?
Gaius Cilnius Maecenas
   (74 or 70- 8 B.C.), age 20?
Virgil
   (70-19), age 20
Cleopatra VII
   (69-30), age 19
Horace
   (65-8 B.C.), age 15
Strabo
   (64/63-A.D. 24), age c.14
Augustus Caesar
   (63-A.D. 14), age 13
Marcus Vipsanius Agrippa
   (63-12 B.C.), age 13
Hillel
   (c.60-A.D.c.10), age c.10
Livy
   (59-A.D.17), age 9
Livia Drusilla
   (56/55-A.D.29), age c.6

# 50–25 B.C.

What kind of a man was Julius Caesar? Certainly his is one of the greatest names of history, among the handful (Napoleon, Washington, Lincoln) that every fourth-grader knows. Equally certain is it that he was not an idealist or reformer, but a thoroughgoing realist. If it is true that he had planned extensive administrative and social innovations which his assassination prevented, it is possible that it was only to have something to do. He was too energetic a man to be held long by the frivolous pleasures some men find sufficient to fill a life. He was eminently sensible and practical, extremely able and intelligent, but also unscrupulous, cruel and ambitious.

Such a man must be resolute in whatever he undertakes, making quick, unerring decisions—never bumbling, never

## 50 B.C.

Marcus Terentius Varro
    (116-27), age 66
Marcus Tullius Cicero
    (106-43), age 56
Pompey the Great
    (106-48), age 56
Gaius Julius Caesar
    (102 or 100-44), age c.50
Cato the Younger
    (95-46), age 45

**Sallust** (Gaius Sallustius Crispus), age 36; Roman historian and politician, a partisan of Julius Caesar. He amassed a great fortune as governor of Numidia, in north Africa, and returned to build luxurious gardens in Rome and a magnificent country house. He wrote a history of the Roman Republic, which is lost, and an account of the conspiracy of Catiline, *Bellum Catilinae,* which is extant.

**Narcus Junius Brutus,** age 35?; Roman politician, son-in-law and nephew of Cato the Younger and one of the richest men in Rome. He is remembered as one of the principal conspirators in the assassination of Julius Caesar on March 15, 44 B.C. Defeated in battle in Macedonia by Mark Antony and Octavian, he committed suicide.

**Gaius Cassius Longinus,** age ?; Roman general and conspirator, originator of the plot against Caesar in which more than 60 men joined. After the first battle of Philippi in 42 B.C., he committed suicide.

**Mark Antony** (Marcus Antonius), age c. 33; Roman soldier and politician. He was a lieutenant of Caesar's in Gaul and his successor as Cleopatra's lover. He joined Octavian to defeat Brutus and Cassius at Philippi and thereafter controlled the eastern half of the empire from Alexandria (or from a barge on the Nile with Cleopatra at his side). His rivalry with Octavian led to his downfall in the great naval battle at Actium in 31 B.C. and his suicide the following year. He is portrayed in two plays by Shakespeare *(Julius Caesar* and *Antony and Cleopatra)* and in one by Dryden *(All for Love).*

**Vercingetorix,** age ?; young Gallic chieftain of the Averni tribe, leader of a general revolt of Gallic tribes against Roman rule in 52 B.C. He defeated Caesar's army at Gergovia, near modern Clermont-Ferrand, but was trapped and captured near present-day Dijon. After being exhibited in Rome at Caesar's triumph, he was put to death. His statue stands in the marketplace at Clermont-Ferrand.

hesitating. Suetonius tells a curious story about this sure-footed practical man, how he lost his way and wandered about all night looking for the road to Rome. Having resolved to march on Rome, he desired to leave his headquarters in Gaul without attracting attention, so that his arrival should come as a surprise. He sent on ahead a small force of 5,000 foot soldiers and 300 cavalry, while he let himself be seen in public throughout the day, watching the gladiators exercise and standing about without any show of urgency. In the evening he dined with guests, but as dusk fell he quietly slipped away. With a few of his staff he got into a hired gig (drawn by a pair of mules) and began the journey to Rome. However, the carriage's lights went out and they lost their way. At daybreak, after wandering all night, they met a fellow who guided them along narrow lanes to the right road. Proceeding with all speed Caesar and his aides joined the soldiers at the Rubicon, which formed the boundary between Gaul and Italy. After some hesitation and weighing of pros and cons, they crossed it. The year was 49 B.C.

# 25 B.C.

**Herod the Great,** age 23?; king of Judea from 37–4 B.C. by favor of the Roman Senate. An Arab (Idumaean, or Edomite), he was the son of Antipater, whom Julius Caesar made ruler of Palestine in 55. He is remembered chiefly for his massacre of the children (Matt. 2) and for the intrigues and quarrels of his family. Of his 10 wives, the second, Mariamne, whom he executed, was the great-granddaughter of Alexander Jannaeus. In his last years he was mentally deranged and afflicted, it is believed, with advanced arteriosclerosis. According to Josephus, parts of his body became gangrenous and produced worms. He was the father of Herod Antipas, later tetrarch of Galilee.

**Gaius Cilnius Maecenas,** age 20?; Roman statesman and wealthy patron of literature, born in Etruria. He was a friend and adviser of Augustus' and the friend and patron of Horace, Virgil and other poets.

**Virgil** (Publius Vergilius Maro), age 20; great Roman poet born near Mantua, son of a farmer made prosperous by marriage. He lived mostly at Neapolis (Naples), where he is entombed. Virgil was a friend of Horace and Maecenas, as well as of Augustus, who took particular interest in the progress of the *Aeneid* and had each section read to him as it was finished. Not physically strong, he became ill and died on a trip to Greece, requesting that the unfinished *Aeneid* be burned. He was regarded in the Middle Ages as a precursor of Christianity because of the messianic predictions in the *Eclogues*.

**Cleopatra VII,** age 19; voluptuous queen of Egypt (51–49 and 48–30 B.C.) and notorious *femme fatale* who nearly gained control of the Roman Empire. The daughter of Ptolemy XI and a descendant of the Macedonian general who founded the dynasty, she lived in Rome as mistress of Julius Caesar from 46–44 B.C. and gave birth to a son, Caesarion, or Ptolemy XIV. She was also the mistress and wife of Mark Antony. Unable to captivate the cool Octavian (Augustus), who planned to exhibit her in Rome as his captive, she committed suicide.

Horace
(65-8 B.C.), age 40
Strabo
(64/63-A.D.14), age c.39
Augustus Caesar
(63-A.D.14), age 38
Marcus Vipsanius Agrippa
(63-12 B.C.), age 38
Hillel
(c.60-A.D.c.10), age c.35
Livy
(59-A.D.17), age 34
Livia Drusilla
(56/55-A.D.29), age c.31
Sextus Propertius
(c.50-c.15 B.C.), age c.25
Ovid
(43-A.D.17), age 18
Tiberius
(42-A.D.37), age 17
Julia
(39-A.D.14), age 14

# 25 B.C. – A.D. 1

The death agonies of the Roman Republic lasted from 49 to 27 B.C. For a long time Rome had not been a republic, but an oligarchy controlled by wealthy senators. Mismanagement and misrule were endemic. Eastern governors regarded their provinces not as charges but as prey, and plundered them unmercifully. Those Eastern cities that looked for a way to satisfy Roman tax collectors by borrowing money suffered the worst disaster, for the Roman bankers and moneylenders (Cicero and Brutus among them), who advanced loans at exorbitant rates of interest, demanded all the property of the city as security and enforced their claims on defaulted loans with the assistance of Roman military forces.

Wealth beyond imagining poured into the hands of the rich, while in the streets an impoverished proletariat of all

## 25 B.C.

Herod the Great
    (73?-4 B.C.), age 48?
Gaius Cilnius Maecenas
    (74 or 70-8 B.C.), age 45?
Virgil
    (70-19 B.C.), age 45

**Horace** (Quintus Horatius Flaccus), age 40; Roman lyric poet born in Apulia, son of a former slave. He fought for Brutus at Philippi and supported himself as a clerk in the government service until he was discovered by Virgil and introduced to Maecenas, who became his patron and gave him a farm in the Sabine hills. He is best known for his odes, celebrating love and wine, friendship, contentment and the joy of living.

**Strabo,** age c. 39; Greek geographer and historian born in Pontus, in Asia Minor. Known for his *Geographica,* a rich source of knowledge of the ancient world, describing Europe, Asia, Egypt and Libya, he also wrote a history of Rome, which is lost.

**Augustus** (Gaius Julius Caesar Octavianus), age 38; called Augustus Caesar. The first Roman emperor, from 27 B.C.–A.D. 14, he was the grandnephew of Julius Caesar, who adopted him as son and heir. An able administrator, he restored internal peace and prosperity, rebuilt temples and revived ancient Roman worship. The Augustan Age was the golden age of Latin literature.

**Marcus Vipsanius Agrippa,** age 38; Roman statesman and general. The trusted adviser, a friend and son-in-law of Augustus, not a few of whose accomplishments would more properly be attributed to Agrippa, he commanded the fleet at Actium in 31 B.C. and was chosen to succeed Augustus, but failed to survive him.

**Hillel,** age c. 35; Jewish scholar born in Babylon. After settling in Palestine, he won recognition as the foremost interpreter of Biblical law and Jewish tradition. President of the Sanhedrin in 30 B.C., and

races and nationalities rioted on any pretext. A man's life was safe neither in the streets of Rome nor in the countryside nearby, where no one went without an armed guard. Money was everyone's paramount concern; poverty had become the greatest disgrace and the greatest crime.

When Augustus assumed the title of *princeps,* he took care to clothe his authority in traditional Republican forms, but his power, backed by the army, was absolute. Nevertheless, the new order he established came as a relief and a blessing. With the terrible period of anarchy behind them, with internal peace and order restored to the empire and reforms introduced into the administration of the provinces, people of all classes counted themselves fortunate to have exchanged Republican chaos for imperial order. All parts of the empire experienced a rebirth of harmony and prosperity, and Rome was at last ready to dominate the Mediterranean world as legitimate monarch rather than pirate, taking its place as the center of the last and greatest Mediterranean empire.

# 1

the first outstanding contributor to the development of the Talmud, he is depicted in legend and story as the ideal Jewish sage.

**Livy** (Titus Livius), age 34; Roman historian born in Padua, author of a monumental history of Rome *(Ab urbe condita libri)* covering the period from the founding of the city to 9 B.C.; it is based partly on legend and tradition and is unsurpassed for its narrative interest. About one quarter of the 142 books are extant, including the first ten.

**Livia Drusilla,** age c. 31; first empress of Rome, third and last wife of Augustus Caesar, and mother, by her first marriage, of Tiberius. Beautiful, intelligent and ambitious, she married Augustus (Octavian) in 30 B.C. after he had forced her husband to divorce her. She secured the succession for her son, Tiberius.

**Sextus Propertius,** age c. 25; Roman poet born near Assisi, son of a wealthy family. A friend of Maecenas, Ovid and Virgil, he is known for his amatory elegies to Cynthia (Hostia, his unfaithful mistress). His masterpiece, an idealization of the noble Roman matron, treats the death of Cornelia.

**Ovid** (Publius Ovidius Naso), age 18; Roman poet born in central Italy of a wealthy landowning family. He won fame with his short erotic elegies and the *Art of Love,* a poetical guide to seduction. He is best known for the *Metamorphoses,* a collection of myths and legends in verse, and the *Fasti,* a poetical calendar of Roman festivals from January to June. Exiled in A.D. 8 by Augustus to a bleak Roman town on the Black Sea, he remained there the rest of his life.

Tiberius
(42-A.D.37), age 42
Julia
(39-A.D.14), age 39
Philo Judaeus
(25/20-A.D.c.50),
age c.20
Herod Antipas
(     -after A.D.40), age ?
Arminius
(18/17-A.D.21), age c.17
Germanicus Caesar
(15 B.C.-A.D.19), age 15
Agrippina the Elder
(14/13 B.C.-A.D.33),
age c.13
Claudius I
(10 B.C.-A.D.54), age 10
Sejanus
(     -A.D.31), age ?
Saint Peter
(     -A.D.67?), age ?
John the Baptist
(8/4 B.C.-A.D.28/30),
age 4/8
Jesus
(8/4 B.C.-A.D.c.29), age 4?
Lucius Annaeus Seneca
(4 B.C.-A.D.65), age 4

# A.D. 1–25

One of the traditions preserved and invigorated by Augustus in his efforts to revive the spirit of old Rome was the Feast of the Saturnalia. He designated three days—December 17, 18 and 19—as legal holidays, although the celebration itself lasted seven days. It was an ancient festival, first observed, according to Livy, just after the battle of Lake Regillus in 496 B.C. Whatever its earlier nature may have been, in later years it became a celebration of brotherhood and good will, and for these few days the slave could regard himself as the equal of his master.

The Saturnalia began on the morning of the 17th with sacrifices in the open air by the Forum in front of the temple

## 1

Strabo
    (64/63 B.C.-A.D. 24),
    age c.64
Augustus Caesar
    (63 B.C.-A.D. 14), age 63
Hillel
    (c.60 B.C.-A.D. c.10),
    age c.60
Livy
    (59 B.C.-A.D. 17), age 59
Livia Drusilla
    (56/55 B.C.-A.D. 29),
    age c.56
Ovid
    (43 B.C.-A.D. 17), age 43

**Tiberius** (Tiberius Claudius Nero Caesar), age 42; Roman emperor from A.D. 14–37, successor to Augustus. Although a brilliant general, he was the victim of bad counsel and the suspicions and intrigues of his family. He lived his last ten years on the island of Capreae (Capri), where the ruins of his 12 villas may still be seen.

**Julia,** age 39; daughter and only child of Augustus Caesar (by his second wife). At 16 she married her second husband, Marcus Vipsanius Agrippa, adviser to Augustus, and had three sons and two daughters (Julia and Agrippina). After Agrippa's death in 12 B.C., she married Tiberius. Notorious for her many adulteries, she was exiled by Augustus in 2 B.C. to the island of Pandataria, near Naples. Her daughter Julia was banished in A.D. 9 for the same reason.

**Philo Judaeus,** age c. 20; Jewish philosopher born in Alexandria of a wealthy family, perhaps the first to attempt to reconcile Hellenism with Judaism, which he accomplished by allegorical interpretation of the Old Testament. He introduced the concept of the Logos, as intermediary between a transcendant God and the created world and influenced Clement of Alexandria and Origen.

to Saturn. An outdoor banquet followed in which slaves sat down first and were served by senators and patricians. The slaves feasted and drank and enjoyed themselves without a word of reproach, and not until they had finished were the tables cleared and set for the patricians. The distinctions between slave and free were abrogated; slaves neglected their ordinary duties, wore the *pilleus,* the badge of freedom, and spoke as they pleased without restraint. The succeeding days were given over to private celebrations, visits to friends and the exchange of gifts. All classes surrendered themselves to the spirit of the occasion, and crowds thronged the public places, filling the air with the traditional greeting, "Io Saturnalia!" This temporary annulment of class distinctions, recalling an age when there had been no differences of social rank, expressed, better than words, a conviction of the unjust and artificial nature of social inequality.

**25**

**Herod Antipas,** age ?; tetrarch (vassal king) of Galilee from 4 B.C.– A.D. 39, son of Herod the Great. His sole claim to fame comes from his historical association with John the Baptist and Jesus Christ (Luke 23:6-12). He divorced his first wife to marry his niece, Herodias; his action provoked the public rebuke of John the Baptist, who was subsequently executed for his rashness (Matt. 14:3-12).

**Arminius,** age c. 17; German chieftain of the Cherusci, who occupied the area of modern Hanover. He is famous for stopping the advance of Roman armies toward the Elbe and forcing them back to the Rhine. In a devastating surprise attack in Teutoberg Forest in A.D. 9, he annihilated three Roman legions. He became a national hero of Germany and the subject of a dramatic trilogy by Klopstock.

**Germanicus Caesar,** age 15; Roman general, son of the younger brother of Tiberius. Much admired as an exemplar of the heroic virtues of old Rome, he was a favorite of all classes. Tiberius, in envy, recalled him from Germany and sent him to the East, where he was poisoned at 33. His wife was Agrippina the Elder; their nine children included Caligula and Agrippina the Younger, mother of Nero.

Pontius Pilate
  (1st cent. A.D.), age ?
Agrippina the Elder
  (14/13 B.C.-A.D.33),
  age c.37
Claudius I
  (10 B.C.-A.D.54), age 34
Sejanus
  (    -A.D.31), age ?
Saint Peter
  (    -A.D.67?), age ?
John the Baptist
  (8/4 B.C.-A.D.28/30),
  age 28/32
Jesus
  (8/4 B.C.-A.D.c.29),
  age 28?
Lucius Annaeus Seneca
  (4 B.C.-A.D.65), age 28
Saint Paul
  (A.D.c.3-65/67), age c.22
Vespasian
  (A.D.9-79), age 16
Caligula
  (12-41), age 13
Salome
  (14?-    ), age 11?
Agrippina the Younger
  (15-59), age 10
Pliny the Elder
  (23-79), age 2

Two distinct and apparently unrelated periods confront the historian of the Roman world of 25 B.C. and that of A.D. 25. The latter age does not seem to have evolved from the former, but to have taken shape independently of it, as if the former had vanished like a punctured bubble. The two ages seem centuries apart in spirit, although a single lifetime might have contained both. Some historians used to rely upon the altered racial composition of the Romans as the explanation, observing that many of the old patrician families had died out and that the sturdy Roman farmers had become all but extinct, displaced by armies of slaves on great plantations. The flood of Asiatics pouring into Italy, bringing their own religions and customs, inundated ancient Roman traditions. Other historians attribute the change to a growing population and to the consequent congestion, noise,

**25**

Livia Drusilla
   (56/55 B.C.-A.D. 29),
   age c.80
Tiberius
   (42 B.C.-A.D. 37), age 66
Philo Judaeus
   (25/20 B.C.-A.D. c.50),
   age c.44
Herod Antipas
   (    -after A.D. 40), age ?

**Pontius Pilate,** age ?; Roman procurator (fiscal agent and governor) of Judea from A.D. 26–36 under the emperor Tiberius. The extent of his responsibility for the execution of Jesus, after the Sanhedrin (Jewish supreme council) had found him guilty of blasphemy, has long been debated. The story is told in Matt. 27; Mark 15; Luke 23; John 18.

**Agrippina the Elder** (Vipsnaia Agrippina), age c. 37; granddaughter of Augustus, daughter of Agrippa and wife of Germanicus Caesar, whom she accompanied on his campaigns in Germany and the East. Although she is often cited as an outstanding example of noble Roman womanhood, she gave birth to Caligula and was the grandmother of Nero. After her husband's death, Tiberius banished her to the island of Pandataria, where she died of starvation.

CLAUDIUS I
Emperor of Rome
10 B.C.-A.D. 54

**Claudius I** (Tiberius Claudius Drusus Nero Germanicus), age 34; fourth emperor of Rome (A.D. 41–54), nephew of Tiberius. Neglected and sickly in his youth, he was, in the opinion of modern historians, an able and efficient ruler, though Tacitus and Suetonius reported otherwise. His second wife (and niece), Agrippina the Younger, persuaded him to disinherit his own son and adopt hers, Nero. Soon after he was served a dish of poisoned mushrooms.

dirt, confusion and poverty.

In 25 B.C. Rome stood on the threshold of the Augustan Age, imbued with a sense of promise and of faith in the future. Virgil, Horace, Livy, Propertius, Ovid and Strabo were alive, as well as their great patrons, Augustus and Maecenas. Fifty years later all were gone, and the promise had vanished. They left no descendants; they had no successors. A different cast of characters occupied the stage: Tiberius, Claudius, Sejanus and Caligula—conspirators and murderers. Would anyone then have undertaken an epic poem on the Roman past, singing the story of Aeneas and Dido? Would anyone have researched the ancient annals and told the whole story of Rome from the founding of the city? It was already too late.

However, other figures had also appeared upon the scene, of a different nature, preparing to play their parts: Paul, John the Baptist, Jesus, Peter and John the Evangelist. They entered quietly and unobtrusively, without attracting the attention of the leading players in Rome, but the future belonged to them, not to the successors of Augustus.

**Sejanus** (Lucius Aelius Sejanus), age ?; Roman politician and conspirator, commander of the Praetorian Guard under Tiberius. A master of intrigue, he plotted to make himself emperor, persuading Tiberius to banish Agrippina and putting others of the family out of the way. He was virtually the master of Rome after Tiberius retired to Capri in A.D. 27, but his duplicity was eventually discovered and he was executed in 31. He is the subject of a play by Ben Jonson.

**St. Peter** (Simon Peter), age ?; principal disciple of Jesus. He was leader of the church in Jerusalem, organizer of a church in Antioch and first bishop of Rome (A.D. 55?–64/67), where he died a martyr. St. Peter's Basilica supposedly stands on the site of his grave.

**John the Baptist,** age 28/32; Jewish prophet, son of the priest Zacharias and second cousin of Jesus. He lived in the desert as an ascetic until about the age of 30, when he began preaching in the Jordan valley, warning of the imminent coming of a messiah. He was imprisoned and executed by Herod Antipas, tetrarch of Galilee.

**Jesus** (Hebrew, *Joshua*), age 28?; called Jesus Christ, the central figure of Christianity, born, according to tradition, in Bethlehem. He lived as a child in Nazareth and about the age of 30 began preaching in the Palestinian countryside, urging baptism and repentance of sins. He was crucified at Jerusalem during the reign of Tiberius. (The Christian scholars, Sextus Julius Africanus, third century, and Dionysius Exiguus, sixth century, who attempted to correlate the dates of classical and Hebrew history, miscalculated by a few years. Modern scholars put the birth of Jesus between 8 and 4 B.C. Using the latter date, we give his age in A.D. 25 as 28, not 29.)

**Lucius Annaeus Seneca,** age 28; Roman statesman, Stoic philosopher and dramatist, born in Spain, tutor and adviser to Nero and for a few years virtual ruler of the empire. He amassed a great fortune and retired in 65 to write moral essays in a highly rhetorical style and nine tragic dramas in verse, which were greatly admired during the Renaissance. He committed suicide by imperial order.

Vespasian
(9-79), age 41
Agrippina the Younger
(15-59), age 35
Pliny the Elder
(23-79), age 27
Saint Clement I
(30?-101?), age 20?
Marcus Cocceius Nerva
(30 or 35-98), age 20?
Gaius Petronius
(   -66), age ?
Gnaeus Julius Agricola
(37-93), age 13
Flavius Josephus
(37-95/100), age 13
Nero
(37-68), age 13
Lucan
(39-65), age 11
Titus
(39/40-81), age c.11
Martial
(c.40-c.104), age c.10
Plutarch
(46-120), age 4

**St. Paul,** age c. 22; Christian missionary and theologian born in Tarsus in Asia Minor, called Apostle to the Gentiles. The principal organizer of the early church and author of many epistles included in the New Testament, he was martyred in Rome during Nero's reign.

**Caligula** (Gaius Caesar), age 13; third emperor of Rome (A.D. 37–41), grandnephew of Tiberius, whom he succeeded. Tyrannical and cruel, one of Rome's most detestable rulers in spite of his excellent parentage, he watched people being tortured and killed as he dined. After he

# 50–75

The problem of succession in the Roman Empire was never solved. On more than one occasion able rulers were followed by incompetents who came to power through a quirk. When Augustus succumbed to the persuasion of his third wife, Livia Drusilla, he opened the way for the Drusus family to gain control of the succession. It was a plebian family, whose first notable member was tribune of the people in 122 B.C. with Gaius Cracchus. There was not a first-rate ruler among them, and there were several monsters.

For failing to establish, by his own example, an orderly method of succession that would insure the selection of the best men, Augustus may be held accountable for much of Rome's subsequent woe. Plotting and scheming became the normal way of life in the palace, and eventually the choice of emperors fell to the army or the Praetorian Guard, who in later years elected and deposed emperors at a dizzying pace. Tiberius, the second emperor and son of Livia Drusilla, ruled 23 years and lived to be 78. He was succeeded by Caligula, 25, his grandnephew, the youngest

Philo Judaeus
   (25/20 B.C.-A.D. c.50),
   age c.69
Claudius I
   (10 B.C.-A.D. 54), age 59
Saint Peter
   (    -A.D.64/67), age ?
Lucius Annaeus Seneca
   (4 B.C.-A.D. 65), age 53
Saint Paul
   (A.D. c.3-65/67), age c.47

**Vespasian** (Titus Flavius Sabinus Vespasianus), age 41; ninth emperor of Rome (69–79), the first Flavian. Proclaimed emperor at the age of 60 by the army, he restored stability after the turbulence caused by the excesses of Nero's reign and the year of three emperors (69). His father was of humble origin, but his mother's brother was a senator. During his reign Britain was conquered (78–79), construction of the Colosseum was begun and Jerusalem was destroyed (70).

**Agrippina the Younger,** age 35; unscrupulous Roman matron, daughter of Germanicus Caesar and Agrippina the Elder, born on the site of modern Cologne (named Colonia Agrippina for her). Her third husband was her uncle, the emperor Claudius. After he had made Nero, her son by her first marriage, his heir, he was poisoned before he could

had ruled for four years officers of the Praetorian Guard put him to death.

**Salome,** age 11?; dancing girl of Judea, stepdaughter of Herod Antipas and granddaughter of Herod the Great. Although not mentioned by name in the New Testament, she is believed to be the girl who danced for Herod and asked for the head of John the Baptist. She would probably have been about 14 or 16 at that time. The story is told in Matt. 14:3-11 and Mark 6:16-28. She is the subject of a play by Oscar Wilde and an opera by Richard Strauss.

son of Germanicus Caesar and Agrippina the Elder, and great-grandson of Livia Drusilla. After officers of the guard had ended his tyranny by putting him to death in A.D. 41, they set a precedent by assuming the right to name his successor. Their choice, Claudius, was the uncle of Caligula and younger brother of Germanicus Caesar, both of whom were grandsons of Livia Drusilla. Claudius took as his second wife his niece, Agrippina the Younger, the sister of Caligula and great-granddaughter of Livia Drusilla. She persuaded Claudius to adopt Nero, her son by a previous marriage. Claudius was emperor 13 years and died at 63. Nero was then 17; he ruled 14 years and was killed at 31. He too was a descendant of Livia Drusilla.

After Nero's death, the Praetorian Guard chose Galba, a respectable patrician, as emperor. Six months later, after his murder, the army proclaimed Otho emperor. Three months later he committed suicide and was succeeded by Vitellius, who ruled from January to December in A.D. 69 and was then defeated and killed by the army of Vespasian, under whom a measure of stability was restored. He was emperor 10 years and was succeeded by his two sons.

The first century of the empire did not end as auspiciously as it had begun. It became transparently clear that the real master of Rome was the army.

change his mind. She dominated Nero until he had her put to death.

**Pliny the Elder** (Gaius Plinius Secundus), age 27; Roman scholar and naturalist born at Como. He served as a cavalry officer in Germany, as an administrator and as commander of the fleet stationed at Misenum from 74 to 79. His *Naturalis historia* is a vast compendium of information on the natural sciences—geography, anthropology and so on. He perished of asphyxiation on the beach at Stabiae when the eruption of Mount Vesuvius buried Pompeii.

**St. Clement I** (Clement of Rome), age 20?; third bishop of Rome (from 88–97) after St. Peter. His *Epistle to the Corinthians*, formerly included in the New Testament, provides the earliest testimony for the martyrdom of Peter and Paul in Rome. Some scholars believe he was the Clement mentioned in Philippians 4:3.

Marcus Cocceius Nerva (30 or 35-98), age 45?

Gnaeus Julius Agricola (37-93), age 38

Flavius Josephus (37-95/100), age 38

Titus (39/40-81), age c.36

Martial (c.40-c.104), age c.35

**50**

**Gaius Petronius,** age ?; Roman satirist, favorite of Nero and master of entertainment at his court. Author of the *Satyricon,* probably the first Western European novel. Accused of conspiracy, he committed suicide by imperial order.

**Nero** (Nero Claudius Caesar Drusus Germanicus), age 13; Roman emperor 54–68. His ambitious mother, Agrippina, made him emperor and dominated him until he had her put to death in A.D. 59. Emotion-

# 75–100

The last quarter of the first century A.D. was an interesting period in many ways. There was renewed interest in literature and history, as Josephus, Martial, Plutarch and Tacitus achieved prominence. Even philosophy, at least in its practical application, enjoyed a revival, as young men attracted to the school of Epictetus imbibed the ethics of Stoicism. The most notable events were the conquest of Britain and the eruption of Mount Vesuvius.

Titus had succeeded his father as emperor when, on the morning of August 24, A.D. 79, a fine ash began to blow into the streets of Pompeii, then a prosperous seaport town. Vesuvius, near the eastern shore of the bay, about ten miles southeast of Naples, rises 4,000 feet above the flat plain and has a circumference of over 30 miles. Its crater is

**75**

Vespasian
  (A.D. 9-79), age 66
Pliny the Elder
  (23-79), age 52

**Marcus Cocceius Nerva,** age 45?; Roman statesman born in Umbria; emperor A.D. 96–98. Elected emperor at an advanced age by the Senate, he ruled only 16 months but is called the first of the five good emperors. He secured the passage of laws providing land for poor citizens and public support of needy children.

ally unbalanced, murderous and unnaturally suspicious, he has been described as a monster of evil. After being declared a public enemy by the Roman Senate, he had himself killed by a slave.

**Lucan** (Marcus Annaeus Lucanus), age 11; Roman poet born in Spain, nephew of Seneca and a member of Nero's court. He wrote the epic poem *Pharsalia,* portraying Pompey and Cato the Younger as Republican heroes in the civil war. Accused of conspiracy against Nero, he committed suicide at the age of 26.

about 2,300 feet in diameter. Bulwer-Lytton's *The Last Days of Pompeii,* a fictional but convincing account, describes how, as the ash continued to fall, alarm grew, although the volcano was generally believed to be extinct. Finally, a great explosion blew off the top of the mountain, and Pompeii and Herculaneum were buried under a rain of ash, cinders and mud.

Pliny the Elder, then commander of the fleet at Misenum, sailed over to investigate, and was asphyxiated on the beach. His nephew, Pliny the Younger, then 17, escaped his uncle's fate and described the eruption in two letters to Tacitus. The cities lay buried and forgotten until 1748, when excavators found houses, streets, murals and mosaics in a marvelous state of preservation.

Titus was a mild and benevolent ruler, but died at 42 after only two years as emperor. His brother Domitian, an unpopular tyrant, ruled 16 years; at the end of the century, however, matters improved when the first of the five good emperors began his rule, in A.D. 96.

**Gnaeus Julius Agricola,** age 38; Roman general and statesman, conqueror of Britain and governor from 78–84. He subdued the tribes of Wales and Yorkshire and extended Roman rule to the Firth of Forth. Sailing north around Scotland, he proved that Britain was an island. He was the father-in-law of Tacitus, who wrote his biography.

# 75

Plutarch
(46-120), age 29
Akiba ben Joseph
(c.50-132/137), age c.25
Domitian
(51-96), age 24
Trajan
(53-117), age 22
Epictetus
(50/60-135), age 20?
Tacitus
(55/57-117/120), age c.20
Juvenal
(c.60-140), age c.15
Pliny the Younger
(62-113), age 13
Suetonius
(c.69-140), age c.6

# 100

Akiba ben Joseph
(c.50-132/137), age c.50
Juvenal
(c.60-140), age c.40

St. Clement I
(30?-101?), age 45?

**Flavius Josephus** (Joseph ben Matthias), age 38; Jewish historian born in Jerusalem of a family of priests. He joined the revolt of the Jews in 66 and was captured, but won the favor of the Roman general Vespasian (later emperor) and his son Titus. Granted Roman citizenship, he lived in Rome under the patronage of three emperors and wrote the history of the Jews in two works, *Antiquities of the Jews* and *The Jewish War*.

PLUTARCH
Greek biographer and
essayist
46-120

**Plutarch,** age 29; Greek biographer and essayist born in Chaeronea in Boeotia. He traveled widely and taught at Rome, but spent most of his life in his native city, where he served as magistrate and priest of Apollo. He is famous for *Parallel Lives,* a collection of short biographies of noted Greeks and Romans, which Shakespeare used as a source for *Julius Caesar*.

# 100–125

For the greater part of its second century the Roman Empire was fortunate in its rulers. From A.D. 96 to 180 it was governed fairly and justly by the five good emperors: Nerva for two years, Trajan for 19, Hadrian for 21, Antoninus Pius for 23 and Marcus Aurelius for 19. It was an era of prosperity and mostly peaceful, although the restlessness of barbarian tribes kept Marcus Aurelius in army camps close to the frontier during much of his reign. All five were exceptional men. Marcus Cocceius Nerva was of senatorial rank, had held high office under Vespasian and Titus and was twice consul. After an honorable and blameless career, he became emperor for the last two years of his life. He chose the best man available as successor when he adopted Trajan, commander of the Roman army on the Rhine. Younger and more vigorous, Trajan was a forthright soldier with a strict sense of justice. Born near Seville, Spain, the son of a general, he entered the army in youth and served in Syria and Spain. He gave the empire one of the best govern-

**100**

**Titus** (Titus Flavius Sabinus Vespasianus), age c. 36; 10th emperor of Rome (79–81), son of Vespasian. He commanded the army that destroyed Jerusalem in 70, when his father was emperor, but was a lenient and popular ruler. During his reign Mount Vesuvius erupted, in 79, and the Colosseum (Amphitheatrum Flavium) was completed, in 80.

**Martial** (Marcus Valerius Martialis), age c. 35; Roman poet born in Spain, best known for his satiric epigrams, the 14 surviving books of which open a window onto contemporary Roman manners and morals. Two emperors were his patrons.

**Domitian** (Titus Flavius Domitianus Augustus), age 24; 11th emperor of Rome (81–96), third Flavian, son of Vespasian and brother of Titus, whom he succeeded. A hated despot who in his later years instituted a reign of terror, he is remembered mainly for recalling Agricola from Britain in 84. He was stabbed to death by a former slave at the instigation of Domitia, his wife, and was succeeded by Nerva.

**Trajan** (Marcus Ulpius Trajanus), age 22; Roman emperor from 98–117, born in Spain, second of the five good emperors. A forceful ruler and indomitable soldier, he extended the boundaries of the empire to their maximum, built roads and bridges and restored cities. He also erected Trajan's column in 114 in his own honor.

**Epictetus,** age 20?; Stoic philosopher born a slave in Asia Minor. A teacher of practical ethics, he founded a school at Nicopolis on the eastern shore of the Adriatic, where his pupil, Flavius Arrianus, wrote down his lectures and conversations which are preserved in the *Discourses* and the *Enchiridion*. He preached the brotherhood of man and the acceptance of one's lot as the will of God.

**Publius Cornelius Tacitus,** age c. 20; Roman historian and statesman born in north Italy, son of a knight and son-in-law of Agricola. He held office under three emperors and is considered Rome's greatest historian, as the author of *Historiae*, covering the years 68-96; *Annales*, on the emperors Tiberius to Nero; and *Germania*, on the Germanic tribes.

Pliny the Younger
(62-113), age 38
Suetonius
(c.69-140), age c.31
Hadrian
(76-138), age 24
Ptolemy
(c.85-c.161), age c.15
Antoninus Pius
(86-161), age 14

ments in its history and adopted as his heir his nephew Hadrian.

Hadrian was born in Spain and became the ward of Trajan after he was orphaned. He accompanied Trajan on his campaigns and received perhaps the best training of any emperor. He was a learned man, an admirer of Greek culture and a connoisseur and patron of art. He is best known for his personal attention to details of administration, as he traveled continually through all parts of the empire. He visited Britain about 120 and ordered the construction of a wall across the narrow waist of Britain, from Solway Firth to the mouth of the Tyne (just south of modern Newcastle) to protect Roman Britain from hostile northern tribes. Built soon after 120 (there is some disagreement about the exact dates), the stone and masonry wall rose 20 feet high and was eight feet thick. At regular intervals along its 74 miles stood stone blockhouses garrisoned with soldiers, and a military road ran along the south side. A few sections still stand, and the government of Britain has undertaken to preserve them as historical monuments.

Hadrian died at 62 and was buried in Rome; his mausoleum is known today as the Castel Sant' Angelo.

125

## 100

St. Clement I
 (30?-101?), age 70?
Flavius Josephus
 (37-95/100), age 63
Martial
 (c.40-c.104), age c.60
Plutarch
 (46-120), age 54
Trajan
 (53-117), age 47
Epictetus
 (50/60-c.135), age 45?
Publius Cornelius Tacitus
 (55/57-117/120), age c.45

## 125

Akiba ben Joseph
 (c.50-132/137), age c.75
Epictetus
 (50/60-c.135), age 70?
Juvenal
 (c.60-140), age c.65
Suetonius
 (c.69-140), age 56
Hadrian
 (76-138), age 49

**Akiba Ben Joseph,** age c. 50; Palestinian rabbi, teacher at the rabbinical school at Jaffa. He is famous for his compilation and systematization of Hebrew oral laws, recognized as the foundation of that section of the Talmud known as the *Mishnah.* A supporter of the ill-fated revolt of Simon Bar Cocheba in 132, he was imprisoned and put to death and is the subject of many legends.

**Juvenal** (Decimus Junius Juvenalis), age c. 40; Roman poet, author of satires savagely attacking immorality, tyranny and the corruption of the age. He deplored the loss of the old Roman virtues and the flood of Asiatics into Rome (the Orontes flowing into the Tiber). He originated many familiar phrases—"bread and circuses," "rara avis" and "a sound mind in a sound body"—and was imitated by Samuel Johnson in the poems *London* and *The Vanity of Human Wishes.*

**Pliny the Younger** (Gaius Plinius Caecilius Secundus), age 38; Roman statesman, nephew of Pliny the Elder. He is famous for his letters

# 125–150

Historians disagree on the causes of the early persecution of Christians. It was not Roman policy to restrict religious worship. A thousand faiths flourished and a thousand gods were worshiped throughout the expansive empire. It seems odd that the Christians should have been singled out. "If we seriously consider," wrote Edward Gibbon, "the purity of the Christian religion, the sanctity of its moral precepts, and the innocence as well as the austere lives of the greater number of those who during the first ages embraced the faith of the Gospel, we should naturally suppose that so benevolent a doctrine would have been received with due reverence even by the unbelieving world; that the learned and the polite, however they might deride the miracles, would have esteemed the virtues of the new sect, and that the magistrates, instead of persecuting, would have protected an order of men who yielded the most passive obedience to the laws. . . ."

**Ptolemy** (Claudius Ptolemaeus), age c. 40; astronomer and geographer of Alexandria. The Ptolemaic system (based on that of Hipparchus) according to which the sun, planets and stars revolve around the earth was universally accepted until the 16th century. The Middle Ages knew his book as the *Almagest,* translated from the Arabic.

**Antoninus Pius** (Titus Aurelius Fulvius Boionius Arrius), age 39; Roman emperor from 138–161, native of Italy. Antoninus Pius was an able, just and moderate ruler in a time of peace and prosperity. One of

(written for publication), the best known being those to the Emperor Trajan on the Christians and to Tacitus describing the death of his uncle on the beach at Stabiae.

**Suetonius** (Gaius Suetonius Tranquillus), age c. 31; Roman biographer and historian. A friend of Pliny the Younger, he was the private secretary to Emperor Hadrian (119–121) and author of *Lives of the Caesars,* history interspersed with scandalous stories.

**Hadrian** (Publius Aelius Hadrianus), age 24; Roman emperor from 117–138, born in Spain, nephew of Trajan. A brilliant, gifted man and an able administrator, he was nonetheless disliked for his imperious manner. Traveling constantly throughout the empire for personal inspections and supervision, he visited Britain and built Hadrian's Wall (120–123). He was a connoisseur of art and one of the five good emperors.

Ptolemy
(c.85-c.161), age c.40
Antoninus Pius
(86-161), age 39
Justin Martyr
(c.100-c.165), age c.25
Lucian
(c.120-after 180), age c.5
Marcus Aurelius
(121-180), age 4
Lucius Apuleius
(123/125-after 170), age c.1

However rational this assumption, the Romans, a people noted for their reasonableness and practical common sense, did not adopt such a policy. The Christians were persecuted not only by tyrants such as Nero and Domitian, but also by Trajan and Marcus Aurelius, honorable and just men whose first concern was for the welfare and prosperity of the empire. Moreover, the persecutions and executions were not carried out capriciously, but officially and legally, in keeping with a policy whose soundness was not questioned. The shifting of perspective over the centuries has made strange and puzzling what was once quite clear. The present age sees the Christians as they saw themselves, as martyrs to their faith unjustly persecuted by cruel tyrants, not as they were universally seen then—as a nefarious band of unbelievers whose impiety offended the Roman gods and imperiled the welfare of the community. They and their secret societies were an affront to the gods. Their offense was atheism; they were not executed because of their religion, but for their lack of it.

# 150

Lucian
(c.120-after 180), age c.30
Marcus Aurelius
(121-180), age 29
Lucius Apuleius
(123/125-after 170), age c.26
Publius Helvius Pertinax
(126-193), age 24
Galen
(129/130-199/200), age c.20
Pausanias
(2nd cent.), age ?
Papinian
(140 or 146-212), age 4?
Lucius Septimius Severus
(146-211), age 4

the five good emperors, he was much admired by his successor, Marcus Aurelius.

**Justin Martyr** (Justin the Martyr or Flavius Justinus), age 25?; Christian apologist born in Samaria. He attempted to reconcile Christian doctrines with pagan culture and held that within all men there is a rational power, the Logos, and that all men who live according to this Logos are Christians even though they are called atheists. His principal work, the *Apology,* was addressed to Antoninus Pius. He was beheaded with six other Christians during the reign of Marcus Aurelius.

# 150–175

In the second century A.D. the Roman Empire reached the zenith of its power and prosperity, and many historians would agree that the 23-year reign (from 138-161) of Antoninus Pius marked its most blessed period. His reign was so peaceful and uneventful as to seem uninteresting; his character was so moderate and reasonable, so little given to excesses of flamboyance, that beside the more notorious emperors he appears colorless. Not much is known about him except that he was a man devoted to the welfare of the empire. He was born in Italy of a family originally from Gaul; he served as consul in 120 and in Asia as proconsul; he was adopted by Hadrian and became emperor at 52. His son-in-law and successor, Marcus Aurelius, said of him that along with mildness of temper he displayed unshakable resolution in pursuing a course once he had decided upon

**150**

Ptolemy
(c.85-c.161), age c.65
Antoninus Pius
(86-161), age 64
Justin Martyr
(100?-c.165), age 50?

**Lucian,** age c. 30; Greek satirist born in Samosata, in Syria. A brilliant writer known for his wit and humor, he was a major figure in the revival of Greek literature in Roman times, writing *Dialogues of the Gods* and *Dialogues of the Dead.*

**Marcus Aurelius** (Marcus Annaeus Verus), age 29; Roman emperor from 161–180 and Stoic philosopher. He lived mostly in army camps, defending the frontiers, and died of the plague on the site of modern Vienna. Author of the *Meditations* and the last of the five good emperors, he said he would have preferred the life of a philosopher to that of an emperor.

**Lucius Apuleius,** age c. 26; Roman writer and orator born in Numidia

# 175–200

Commodus became emperor in 180 at the age of 19. To free himself for his own pleasures, he committed the government into the hands of ministers, who were tyrannical scoundrels like himself. After 13 miserable years the tyranny was ended when three persons Commodus trusted, his favorite concubine, the chamberlain and the captain of

**175**

it, yet remained ready to listen to the advice of others. There was nothing in him harsh, implacable or violent. He examined each matter that came before him unhurriedly and without confusion, as if he had abundant time and nothing else in the world demanded his attention. In him the empire found a worthy ruler, a man of ability and integrity who promoted trade and commerce, encouraged literature and erected many fine buildings. He lived to be 75 and was succeeded by Marcus Aurelius and Lucius Aurelius Verus, both of whom he had adopted, as co-emperors. Verus died eight years later in 169, leaving Marcus Aurelius as sole ruler.

Marcus Aurelius, whose fame is greater than his father-in-law's, was also a good emperor, but said he was not happy and would have preferred the life of a philosopher. His *Meditations,* written for himself rather than for others, reveal a man preoccupied with keeping his balance. He broke the precedent set by his immediate predecessors when he chose as his successor not the best man available, but the worst—his son Commodus.

(modern Algeria) of wealthy parents. He is chiefly known for his popular comic Latin novel, *The Golden Ass,* which strongly influenced later writers, particularly Boccaccio and Cervantes.

**Publius Helvius Pertinax,** age 24; Roman general and statesman chosen emperor at age 67—after a long and honorable career—by the concubine, chamberlain and captain of the guards who had together strangled the tyrant Commodus. His reign and his life ended three months later.

**Galen,** age c. 20; Greek physician born in Pergamum. The foremost medical authority of his time, he settled in Rome in 164. His knowledge remained unsurpassed until the 17th century.

Pausanias
    (2nd cent.), age ?
Papinian
    (140 or 146-212), age 29?
Lucius Septimius Severus
    (146-211), age 29
Clement of Alexandria
    (c.150-215/220), age c.25
Tertullian
    (c.160-230), age c.15
Commodus
    (161-192), age 14
Ulpian
    (170?-228), age 5?

the guards, had him murdered and carried his body secretly out of the palace at night. That same night they went to the house of the prefect of the city, Publius Helvius Pertinax, an aged senator with a long and honorable public career, and offered him the supreme power. With considerable reluctance, he accepted.

In a tumultuous Senate meeting early the next morning, the first day of a new year, the senators rejoiced openly at the news and formally condemned the deceased Commodus as tyrant and public enemy. The new emperor set to work at once to undo part of the evil that had been done. He recalled from exile and released from prison many men who had been falsely accused and restored their honors and fortunes. Upon finding the treasury empty, he cut the emperor's household expenses in half and put up for public sale the gold and silver plate as well as a great number of beautiful slaves of both sexes, and demanded the return of treasure stolen from the state by the favorites of Commodus. He opened up all uncultivated lands in Italy and the

Lucian
   (c.120-after 180), age c.55
Marcus Aurelius
   (121-180), age 54
Publius Helvius Pertinax
   (126-193), age 49
Galen
   (129/130-199/200),
    age c.45

**Pausanias,** age ?; Greek traveler and geographer, author of *Hellados periegesis (Description of Greece),* probably the world's first guidebook for travelers. A great storehouse of knowledge of ancient Greece, it describes architecture and sculptures and gives accounts of local cults, folklore and history. It is best known in James Frazer's translation and commentary in six volumes (1898).

**Papinian** (Aemilius Papinianus), age 29?; Roman jurist, the first of the three great authorities on Roman law. Appointed Praetorian Prefect (chief judicial officer of the empire) by Septimius Severus in 203, he was executed by Caracalla in 212 for disapproving of the murder of Geta, Caracalla's brother.

**Lucius Septimius Severus,** age 29; Roman emperor from 193–211, born in Africa of Carthaginian origin. Proclaimed emperor by the army of Pannonia after the revolt of the Praetorian Guard, he was the first

# 200–225

Rivalry among the generals of the provincial legions, after the death of Pertinax, ended with the triumph of Septimius Severus. As his army approached Rome, he sent word ahead, commanding the Praetorian Guard to wait unarmed outside the city. They did so, and no doubt watched the approach of the heavily armed Pannonian army with some misgiving. Their sentence was mild—perpetual banishment to a distance of 100 miles from the capital.

Severus recruited a new guard, four times as large, comprised of soldiers from the frontier legions who were selected for their strength, courage and loyalty. The status of the Praetorian Prefect was elevated from that of a mere captain of the guards to one ranking next to the emperor. As befitted the chief judicial officer of the empire, the prefect

provinces to those who would work them, with a promise of a ten-year tax exemption. The new year seemed like the dawning of a new era, and it appeared as if Rome had been blessed with a sixth good emperor. But though he wore the purple robes and was nominal master, he could not even save his own life. After three months a band of Praetorians burst into the palace, killed him openly at midday and carried his head back to camp on a lance in full view of the horrified citizens. His economies had been too strict.

**200**

emperor to derive his authority from the army and the first non-Roman emperor. (His wife was the daughter of a Syrian high priest.) He spent his last years in Britain and died at Eboracum (York).

**Clement of Alexandria** (Titus Flavius Clemens), age c. 25; Greek theologian of the early Christian church born in Athens. He taught at Alexandria, with Origen among his pupils, and was the first to attempt to reconcile Platonism with Christian doctrines. He made the catechetical school at Alexandria an important center of learning.

**Lucius Aelius Aurelius Commodus,** age 14; Roman emperor from 180–192, last of the Antonines, son and successor of Marcus Aurelius. He persecuted the most able men of the Senate and divided the rest of his time between his concubines and the professional gladiators with whom he fought in the arena. Poisoned wine and strangulation by a professional wrestler ended his infamous reign, in an assassination plot to which his closest friends conspired.

Tertullian
  (c.160-230), age c.40
Ulpian
  (170?-228), age 30?
Julius Paulus
  (fl. c.200), age ?
Diogenes Laertius
  (early 3rd cent.), age ?
Origen
  (185-254), age 15
Caracalla
  (188-217), age 12

represented the emperor and exercised his authority on frequent occasions. Men of the caliber of Papinian and Ulpian were given the post.

For a long time after the end of the Republic, the ancient traditions had been preserved, following the example of Augustus; it was universally agreed that political power rested ultimately in the will of the people, who had legitimately conferred it, through the action of the Senate, upon the emperor. But Serverus was a forthright soldier and disdained to keep up the pretense. He was a Carthaginian and had married a Syrian woman, both descended from Rome's ancient enemies, and possessed of the indifference of foreigners toward Roman tradition. Through his rash and unstatesmanlike behavior, and his inability to appreciate the advantage of requiring formal legal sanctions to legitimize the emperor's authority, he earned for himself the opprobrious distinction of being the principal author of the decline of the Roman Empire.

**225**

## 200

Galen
 (129/130-199/200), age c.70
Papinian
 (140 or 146-212), age 54?
Lucius Septimius Severus
 (146-211), age 54
Clement of Alexandria
 (c.150-215/220), age c.50

**Tertullian** (Quintus Septimius Florens Tertullianus), age c. 40; Christian theologian born in Carthage, a lawyer before his conversion, and the first important Christian Latin writer. More than 30 of his works defending Christianity have survived. Late in life he joined the ascetic sect of Montanists, which was subsequently declared heretical.

**Ulpian** (Domitius Ulpianus), age 30?; Roman jurist born in Tyre, a younger contemporary of Papinian. He was Praetorian Prefect under Alexander Severus from 222 to 228, when he was murdered by officers objecting to his strict discipline. He was the author of innumerable commentaries, in clear, elegant prose, which supplied one third of Justinian's *Digest*.

**Julius Paulus,** age ?; the third great Roman jurist, successor of Ulpian as Praetorian Prefect. Nearly one sixth of the *Digest* is taken from his

## 225 – 250

To Septimius Severus, the first emperor with no ties to Rome, can be attributed the Syrian invasion of the capital at the close of the second century. In 187 Severus married Julia Domna, daughter of a Syrian high priest. When she came to Rome in 193, a great crowd of relatives hoping for government assignments accompanied her, giving to imperial Rome an exotic, Oriental color. After a reign of 18 years Severus was succeeded by his sons, Caracalla and Geta. Caracalla's disgraceful reign was terminated in 217 by the Praetorian Prefect Macrinus, who made himself emperor after having Caracalla killed, only to be defeated the following year by the Parthians and overthrown. The army then proclaimed a 13-year-old Syrian boy emperor. His name was Varius Avitus Bassianus; he was the grandnephew of Julia Domna (who had committed suicide after the death of her son Caracalla) and high priest of the Syrian sun-god at Emesa. He is better known as Heliogabalus and was one of

## 225

Tertullian
 (c.160-230), age c.65
Ulpian
 (170?-228), age 55?
Julius Paulus
 (3rd cent.), age ?

**Origen** (Origenes Adamantius), age 40; Christian theologian and teacher born in Alexandria, successor at an early age of Clement as head of the catechetical school. He was a prolific writer, a Platonist and Biblical scholar of great influence on the church whose most famous work was *Contra celsum.*

**Ardashir I,** age ?; king of Persia from 226–241 and founder of the Sassanid dynasty, which ruled for four centuries, from 226–641. A vassal prince, he overthrew the last Parthian king, made Ctesiphon on the Tigris his capital and established Mazdaism (orthodox Zoroastrianism) as the official religion. His expansion alarmed the Romans and resulted in his defeat by Emperor Alexander Severus (231–233). He claimed descent from Darius and Xerxes.

writing, which included, most notably, commentaries on civil law and equity law.

**Diogenes Laertius,** age ?; Greek biographer; author of a book on the lives and opinions of the Greek philosophers from Thales to Epicurus, in which much valuable information, otherwise unobtainable, is mixed with entertaining stories and hearsay. Almost nothing is known of his own life.

**Caracalla** (Marcus Aurelius Antoninus), age 12; Roman emperor from 211–217, called Caracalla from the Gallic hooded cloak he wore. A cowardly and treacherous man mostly remembered for his cruelty, he was the son of Septimius Severus and ruled jointly with his younger brother Geta, until he had him murdered in 212. He built the famous Baths of Caracalla and issued an edict granting Roman citizenship to all free inhabitants of the empire.

the oddest emperors in Roman history. He turned the government over to the Syrian women of his family and occupied himself with propagating his bizarre cult throughout the empire and observing its licentious rites. In 222 he was murdered by the Praetorians and succeeded by his cousin, Alexander Severus Bassianus, another Syrian.

His 13-year reign, from 222-235, saw a return to greater stability and conservatism and a restoration to the Senate of some of its former influence. He appointed the great jurist Ulpian, also a Syrian, Praetorian Prefect and relied heavily on him as an adviser. However, the Syrian women remained powerful and influential. His mother, Julia Mamaea, accompanied him on his campaigns and was killed with him when the army of the Rhine mutinied in 235.

While Rome was in turmoil, a revival occurred in the East, as Persia reawakened and grew powerful enough under the Sassanid monarchs to challenge Rome. Founded by Ardashir I, this dynasty outlived the Western Empire. Its great kings, Shapur I and II and Khosru I and II, were long remembered and celebrated in Persian poetry and legend.

**Plotinus,** age c. 20; Roman philosopher born in Egypt of Roman parentage. He studied at Alexandria and established a school in Rome about 244. He is recognized as the founder, or chief exponent, of Neoplatonism, a compound of Platonism and Oriental mysticism, and is the author of the *Enneads*.

**Alexander Severus** (Alexius Bassianus), age c. 17; Roman emperor from 222–235, born in Syria. A relative of the Syrian wife of Septimius Severus and a cousin of Heliogabalus, he was a moderate ruler, with Ulpian as his adviser, and stopped the persecution of Christians. He repelled the Persian advance in the East, but could not maintain army discipline. He and his mother were murdered by his own troops.

225

Origen
(185-254), age 40
Ardashir I
(3rd cent.), age ?
Plotinus
(204/205-270), age c.20
Alexander Severus
(208/209-235), age c.17
Valerian
(    -269?), age ?
Aurelian
(212/215-275), age c.13
Mani
(c.216-276), age c.9

250

Valerian
(    -269?), age ?
Aurelian
(212/215-275), age c.38
Mani
(c.216-276), age c.34
Shapur I
(3rd cent.), age ?
Zenobia
(3rd cent.), age ?
Porphyry
(c.232-304), age c.18
Diocletian
(245-313/316), age 5

# 250–275

In the 49 years between the death of Alexander Severus in 235 and the accession of Diocletian in 284, Rome had 18 emperors, all military despots dependent upon the army for their authority. Their names are little known, and few of them accomplished anything worthwhile in their reigns, which lasted an average of two and a half years. Under their rule the condition of the empire grew steadily more desperate. The ultimate disgrace came with the destruction of a Roman army by Shapur I and the capture of the emperor Valerian, who was kept in captivity the remaining nine years of his life.

The most able of the military emperors was Aurelian, who reasserted the might of Roman arms during his short reign (from 270-275). He recovered much lost territory, but the extremity of Rome's situation may be judged from his deci-

**250**

Origen
(185-254), age 65
Plotinus
(204/205-270), age c.45

**Valerian,** age ?; Roman emperor from 253–260, proclaimed emperor by the army, and the only emperor to be captured and held prisoner by an enemy. Rome's fortunes were sinking, barbarians encroached on every frontier, when in the East, Shapur I destroyed the Roman army and took Valerian prisoner. Valerian's son, Gallienus, whom he had made joint ruler, continued as emperor, while his father remained in captivity until his death. Shapur never ceased boasting of his exploit.

**Aurelian** (Lucius Domitius Aurelianus), age c. 38; Roman emperor from 270–275. A common soldier who rose to high rank, he was proclaimed emperor by the army. He energetically repelled encroaching barbarians; reconquered Egypt; recovered Gaul and Britain; and defeated Zenobia, queen of Palmyra. He was proclaimed Restorer of the Empire by the Senate.

**Mani,** age c. 34; Persian religious prophet, founder of Manichaeism. He held that man's spirit belonged to God and his body to Satan. Women also belonged to Satan and were seducers of men from the

# 275–300

What Aurelian began Diocletian completed; he delivered the *coup de grace* to the spirit of Republican Rome. With enemies stirring on every frontier, he divided the empire and its government into four parts, with four rulers instead of one. There were two senior emperors, designated *Augusti*

**275**

sion to construct a 54-foot wall around the city. Rome's enemies were pressing closely. He was of humble origin, probably born in Pannonia, and little concerned about the preservation of Roman traditions. He brought back from Syria a cult of the sun-god, made it the official religion of the empire and proclaimed himself vicegerent of the Unconquered Sun, Lord of the Roman Empire. Rome still ruled, but it was not the same Rome. The familiar, traditional Rome of Scipio, Cato, Cicero and Caesar—even of Hadrian and Marcus Aurelius—seemed light-years away. In its place had arisen an Oriental despotism. When Ulpian, half a century earlier, had declared that the will of the emperor had the force of law, he immediately justified the exercise of absolute power by adding that it had been legitimately conferred by the Senate and the people. The new order, however, required no such justification and admitted of no compact between ruler and ruled. The boundary had been crossed into the realm of Eastern ideologies, where the sovereignty of the people was unperceived and their rights unrecognized, and where all that was required was prostration before the divinities and obedience to the supreme monarch.

right path. He preached strict celibacy and vegetarianism. Manichaeism was the religion of St. Augustine before his conversion and the basis of several medieval heresies (Albigenses).

**Shapur I,** age ?; king of Persia from 241–272, son and successor or Ardashir I. An able monarch and tolerant ruler, he resumed war with the Romans and at Edessa (in modern Turkey) took the emperor Valerian prisoner in 260. He was the protector of Mani and had Greek and Indian classics translated into Pahlavi.

**Zenobia** (Bathzabbai), age ?; queen of Palmyra, an ancient commercial city in Syria, from 267–272. Widow of King Odenathus and regent for her infant son, she continued her husband's conquests and added eastern Asia Minor and Egypt to her expanding empire. The emperor Aurelian besieged Palmyra and took her captive. Described as uncommonly beautiful, with large dark eyes and teeth of pearly whiteness, she was exhibited at his triumph in Rome (274), but later pardoned and given a villa at Tibur (Tivoli) in Italy.

Porphyry
(c.232-304), age c.43
Diocletian
(245-313/316), age 30
St. Anthony
(250/251-350), age c.25
Arius
(250 or 256 or 280-336),
age 19?
Eusebius of Caesarea
(260/263-339/340), age 15?

and privileged to wear the diadem, and two subordinate colleagues called *Caesars.* Each had his assigned portion of the empire to administer and defend. Maximian, a senior emperor, established his court at Milan, from which location, at the foot of the Alps, the movements of the barbarians could be better kept under observation. Milan acquired the splendor and luxuries of an imperial city: a circus, a theater, baths, a magnificent palace and porticoes lined with statuary.

300

For his capital Diocletian chose Nicomedia in northwestern Asia Minor, which in a few years became the most populous city of the empire, after Rome, Alexandria and Antioch. Diocletian seldom visited Rome, and the Senate, deprived of a voice in the government, was soon reduced to the status of a town council. In removing the imperial court from Rome, Diocletian also abandoned the spirit of Republican informality. In earlier imperial times a certain simplicity of manner and dress had been generally observed. The emperor mingled with the senators as one of them, his only

**275**

Aurelian
    (212/215-275), age c.63
Mani
    (c.216-276), age c.59
Zenobia
    (3rd cent.), age ?

**Porphyry** (Malchus), age c. 43; Neoplatonic philosopher born in Syria. He studied in Rome under Plotinus, whose *Enneads* he edited and published. The most important Neoplatonist after Plotinus, he vigorously defended paganism against Christianity.

**Diocletian** (Gaius Aurelius Valerius Diocletianus), age 30; Roman emperor from 284–305, born in Dalmatia of slave origin. Elected emperor by the army, he transferred the capital from Rome to Nicomedia in Asia Minor, severing the last connection of the Roman Senate with the government. His court resembled that of an Oriental despot, com-

# 300–325

A symptom of the uncertainty of the times, as the fortunes of the Roman Empire continued to decline, was the growing attraction of other-worldly religions and the spread of philosophies that depreciated the temporal world. One such manifestation of a widespread malaise was the Christian monastic movement of the fourth century, which inspired thousands to renounce the world and embrace an arduous life in the Egyptian desert. St. Anthony was the first important Christian hermit. Some few others may have preceded him into the desert (St. Ambrose mentions a Paul of Thebes), but none became widely known. It was through Anthony's fame that the ascetic life won favor and prestige. During his many years of solitary life, Anthony acquired a reputation among the Egyptian peasants as a miracle-worker who could heal the sick and cast out devils. Reports spread of his powers and his piety until, towards the close of his long life, he had become one of the most famous men of his time.

Of those persuaded to follow his example and embrace the religious life, some came from well-to-do families, but the majority were of poor parentage and had little or no education. Many were Egyptian peasants. In the desert they

**300**

distinction of dress being a purple robe among their purple-bordered togas. Spurning such simplicity, Diocletian wore about his head the diadem, a white band set with pearls; he wore robes of silk and gold and shoes studded with gems. Scores of officials, servants and eunuchs surrounded him, preventing easy access to his presence. Nor could anyone converse with him as man to man, but only as subject to master, first prostrating himself on the ground in the Eastern manner. The spirit of Republican Rome could sustain no greater affront than this.

plete with throne and footstool and the elaborate ceremonial of the Persians. He abdicated at 60 and retired to the Dalmation coast, where he built an immense one-story palace covering nine acres, with a 500-foot portico on one side, and found happiness and contentment raising cabbages.

**St. Anthony,** age c. 25; Egyptian hermit, founder of Christian monasticism. At the age of 20 he embraced the ascetic life and is said to have been the first Christian hermit in the Egyptian desert, which soon blossomed with communities of monks attracted by reports of his sanctity and miraculous powers.

Arius
   (250 or 256 or 280-336),
   age 44?
Eusebius of Caesarea
   (260/263-339/340), age 40?
Constantine I
   (274 or 280 or 288-337),
   age 20?
St. Athanasius
   (293/298-373), age c.7

lived on bread and water and dried peas and shut themselves up in their cells for most of the day to meditate and pray. They plaited palm leaves into baskets and mats, which they occasionally took to Alexandria to sell. Quiet and gentle, with no rivalry among themselves except to excel in humility, patience and kindness, many besides Anthony won renown. Their fame shone brightly in the Middle Ages, when the life stories and sayings of Macarius, Arsenius, Poeman and Pastor formed an essential part of the Christian tradition.

Five thousand monks, or close to that number, were reported living on Mount Nitria, 37 miles from Alexandria. The surrounding desert was dotted with their cells as far as Scete, 40 miles from Nitria, in a desolate area where water was hard to find and the only guideposts were the stars. When to all of these are added those living on lonely mountain tops and on islands in the Nile, the 7,000 reported living under the rule of St. Pachomius in numerous separate monastic communities and the 10,000 under Serapion, the accounts of travelers through Egypt and Palestine towards the close of the fourth century seem almost believable. The number of recluses in the desert, they claimed, equaled the population of the towns. The great desert migration that began with St. Anthony continued until about the middle of the fifth century, when it appears to have ceased as abruptly as it had begun.

## 300

Porphyry
  (c.232-304), age c.68
Diocletian
  (245-313/316), age 55
St. Anthony
  (250/251-350), age c.50

**Arius,** age 44?; Greek theologian born in Libya; a priest in Alexandria. His controversial doctrine (Arianism) divided the Christian Church in the fourth century. His conception of the nature of the Trinity was opposed by Athanasius and finally declared heretical by the First Council of Constantinople in 381.

**Eusebius of Caesarea** (Eusebius Pamphili), age 40?; Greek theologian and church historian born in Palestine; bishop of Caesarea Palestinae (in southern Palestine) from 314–340. Author of an important history of the early church, *Historia ecclesiastica,* he is also remembered as the baptizer of Constantine the Great.

**Constantine I,** age 20?; called Constantine the Great (Flavius Valerius Aurelius Constantinus), Roman emperor from 306–337, eldest son of Constantius I. His vision of the cross with the words, *In hoc signo vinces,* led to his conversion to Christianity. He moved the capital of the empire to Byzantium and renamed the city Constantinople.

# 325–350

In the fourth century Christianity, which was well on its way to a complete triumph over the pagan religions, was bitterly divided over a theological dispute. The dispute arose when it became known that Arius, a Christian priest of Alexandria, was teaching a doctrine of doubtful orthodoxy. He maintained that Jesus, as the first created being, was not the equal of the Father, but subordinate to him, in a sense half human and half divine. Arius was condemned and relieved of his duties by his orthodox opponents, who adhered to the doctrine that Jesus Christ is of the same substance as the Father. The complex controversy continued for many years; St. Athanasius, archbishop of Alexandria and the principal opponent of Arianism, was exiled and recalled five times, as the reigning emperor supported or opposed Arianism. Constantius II, son of Constantine the Great, was an Arian and desired to apprehend Athanasius, who took ref-

## 325

St. Anthony
  (250/251-350), age c.75

Arius
  (250 or 256 or 280-336),
  age 69?

**St. Athanasius,** age c. 32; Greek theologian, called the father of orthodoxy, born in Alexandria. Patriarch of Alexandria from 328–373 and principal opponent of Arianism in the dispute over the Trinity, he was exiled five times and found refuge among the desert hermits during his longest exile (356–362). Victorious at last, he was restored as archbishop in 366.

The Metropolitan Museum of Art. Bequest of Mary Clark Thompson, 1926.

CONSTANTINE I (the Great)
Roman emperor
274 or 280 or 288-337

St. Athanasius
  (293/298-373), age c.32
Samudragupta
  (4th cent.), age ?
Shapur II
  (309-379), age 16
Ausonius
  (c.310-393/395), age c.15
Ulfilas
  (c.311-381/383), age c.14
St. Martin of Tours
  (315/316-397/399),
    age c.10
Valentinian I
  (321-375), age 4

uge in the desert.

As Edward Gibbon tells the story, "The deserts of Thebais were now peopled by a race of wild, yet submissive fanatics. . . . The numerous disciples of Anthony and Pachomius received the fugitive primate as their father, admired the patience and humility with which he conformed to their strictest institutions. . . . The archbishop . . . was lost among a uniform and well-disciplined multitude; and on the nearer approach of danger he was swiftly removed, by their officious hands, from one place of concealment to another, till he reached the formidable deserts. . . . The retirement of Athanasius, which ended only with the life of Constantius, was spent, for the most part, in the society of the monks, who faithfully served him as guards, as secretaries, and as messengers."

Years later Athanasius, drawing upon his memories of the desert and of the saint who on his deathbed had left him his sheepskin and his old cloak, wrote a full account of the life of St. Anthony, whose lasting fame is largely due to the scholarly and eloquent archbishop.

**Samudragupta,** age ?; king of India c. 330–c. 380, son and successor of Chandragupta I (founder of the Gupta dynasty). Samudragupta conquered most of northern India and much of the south, and ushered in an era of peace, prosperity and the golden age of Indian art and literature.
**Shapur II** (Shapur the Great), age 16; king of Persia from 309–379, from the day of his birth to his death, in a reign almost as long as that

Ausonius
  (c.310-393/395), age c.40
Ulfilas
  (c.311-381/383), age c.39
St. Martin of Tours
  (315/316-397/399), age c.35

## 325

Eusebius of Caesarea
(260/263-339/340), age 65?
Constantine I
(274 or 280 or 288-337),
age 45?

of Louis XIV in Europe. One of the strongest Sassanid monarchs, he repulsed Central Asian tribes in the East and resumed warfare with the Romans over Armenia. He defeated a great Roman army in 363 near

# 350–375

Although the Roman Empire was not yet officially Christian when Julian the Apostate, nephew of Constantine the Great, became emperor in 361, the progress of the church nevertheless seemed inexorable. Christianity was no longer merely the religion of the underprivileged classes; its members came from all ranks of society. And as Christians no longer looked from day to day for the end of the world and the Last Judgment, they began to be absorbed into the life of the community. They joined the army and served in the government. The last persecutions occurred in the reigns of Diocletian and Galerius, who had been a *Caesar* under Diocletian. In the final years of the reign of Galerius (305-311), it became apparent that the Christians had become too numerous to be checked by violent measures, and it was Galerius who made the first move toward toleration. Shortly

## 350

St. Anthony
(250/251-350), age c.100
St. Athanasius
(293/298-373), age c.57

**Ausonius,** age c. 40; Latin poet and scholar of Gallic origin born in Bordeaux; tutor of Gratian, the son of Valentinian I. He was the prefect of Gaul and consul in 379, after Gratian became emperor. A Christian who appreciated pagan culture, he is known for his *Idyllia*, particularly *Mosella*, a poetic description of the Moselle valley, which is almost romantic in its sensitivity to the beauties of nature.

**Ulfilas** (Wulfila, little wolf), age c. 39; Gothic bishop, missionary to

Ctesiphon, where the emperor Julian the Apostate was killed. His victories over the Romans were commemorated by large rock sculptures.

Valentinian I
  (321-375), age 29
St. Basil
  (c.330-c.379), age c.20
Julian
  (331-363), age 19
Chandragupta II
  (4th cent.), age ?
St. Ambrose
  (339/340-397), age c.10
St. Jerome
  (340 or 345-420), age 5?
St. John Chrysostom
  (345/349-407), age c.5
Theodosius I
  (346/347-395), age c.4

before his death he issued an edict to this effect.

The Edict of Milan of Constantine I followed in 313, in effect establishing the equality of all religions and making a place for the God of the Christians among the other divinities. But such an arrangement was not now acceptable to the church. Subsequent events of Constantine's reign made it clear that nothing short of the total destruction of paganism and a union of church and state would satisfy. All this was accomplished in the course of the fourth century, but when Julian was proclaimed emperor by his troops in 361, it was possible to believe that the tide might yet be reversed. He was a learned young man, a lover of pagan philosophy and culture, and made a valiant effort to revive and restore the pagan deities. Yet even if he had lived, it is doubtful whether he could have done more than temporarily delay the inevitable. His two-year reign ended with his death in the Persian deserts in a war with Shapur II. Eighteen years later Theodosius I began the systematic extermination of paganism.

the Visigoths on the lower Danube River, whom he converted to Arianism. He translated the Bible into Gothic, using a written alphabet that combined Greek letters with Germanic runes. The extant fragments are the earliest known examples of Germanic literature.

**St. Martin of Tours,** age c. 35; French prelate, patron saint of France, born in Pannonia. He left home about 356 and lived as a hermit near Tours in Gaul, where he became famous as a miracle worker. He

Chandragupta II
  (4th cent.), age ?
St. Ambrose
  (339/340-397), age c.35
St. Jerome
  (340 or 345-420), age 30?

Samudragupta
    (4th cent.), age ?
Shapur II
    (309-379), age 41

founded the first monastery in Western Europe in 360, and was bishop of Tours from 371 until his death.

**Valentinian I,** age 29; Roman emperor from 364–375, born in Pannonia of humble parents. He rose to high rank in the army under Julian and Jovian and was elected emperor by the army after Jovian's death. He made his brother Valens emperor of the East. A good emperor, he reduced taxes, promoted education, provided medical care for the poor of Rome and tolerated all religions—although he was an orthodox Christian. He was succeeded by his two sons, Gratian, aged 16, and the infant Valentinian II.

**St. Basil** (Basil the Great), age c. 20; Christian prelate of the Eastern

# 375–400

The last quarter of the fourth century witnessed the triumph of Christianity in the Roman Empire. Henceforth the church would be a power as great or greater than the state, and with an infinitely greater capacity for endurance. Possession, through St. Peter, of the keys of the Kingdom of Heaven was the secret of its power, but its worldly influence derived also from a number of able men who appeared almost simultaneously to provide intelligent and vigorous leadership. Without the energy and vision of St. Ambrose, St. Jerome, St. John Chrysostom, St. Augustine and their imperial convert, Theodosius I, the beginning might have been much less auspicious. The church had better men to lead it than the state, which continued in a condition of widespread debility.

While these events were taking place in the West, a vigorous new dynasty had been established in the Ganges

Samudragupta
    (4th cent.), age ?
Shapur II
    (309-379), age 66
Ausonius
    (c.310-393/395), age c.65
Ulfilas
    (c.311-381/383), age c.64
St. Martin of Tours
    (315/316-397/399), age c.60

**Chandragupta II,** age ?; king of India about 380–413, son and successor of Samudragupta. The kingdom continued to expand and prosper, and according to the Chinese traveler, Fa-Hsien, who spent 10 years in India, it was a country of safe roads, benevolent government, just taxation and religious tolerance. This was the age of the Ajanta cave paintings, of classical Indian sculpture, progress in mathematics, the development of the Vedantic philosophy and the dramas of Kalidasa.
**St. Ambrose** (Ambrosius), age c. 35; bishop of Milan and one of the four original doctors of the Western Church; son of the prefect of southern Gaul. He excommunicated Theodosius I and ordered him to do penance for his military crimes. When the emperor complied, the

Church, bishop of Caesarea. He organized monastic communities in which hard work and charitable services replaced the asceticism and isolation of hermits. St. Basil was the older brother of Gregory of Nyassa and a friend of Gregory of Nazianus—all three were saints, prelates, and Fathers of the Church. In his youth he was a friend of Julian the Apostate's.

**Julian** (Flavius Claudius Julianus), age 19; called Julian the Apostate, Roman emperor from 361–363, nephew of Constantine the Great. In an effort to revive paganism, he reopened pagan temples and planned to establish a hierarchy of bishops and to formulate a catechism. He was killed in battle at the age of 32.

St. John Chrysostom
(345/349-407), age c.30
Theodosius I
(346/347-395), age c.29
St. Augustine
(354-430), age 21
Pelagius
(354/360-420), age 15?
Alaric
(c.370-410), age c.5

valley in India, capable of achieving a high state of civilization. Its founder, Chandragupta I, about whom little is known (and who should not be confused with the earlier Chandragupta who founded the Maurya dynasty in the time of Alexander the Great), reigned only a short time (c.320-330) before being succeeded by his son. Samudragupta's long reign (c.330-375/380) ushered in the golden age of Sanskrit literature, science and art, which continued to flower in the reign of his son, Chandragupta II (375/380-413?). The just government of this monarch achieved prosperity and security for its subjects, and Sanskrit drama attained its finest expression in the plays of Kalidasa. The reign of his successor, Kumadragupta, was equally splendid, but during the reign of the fifth king of the dynasty, Skandagupta (455-480?), the White Huns from central Asia began their incursions. After his death, they came in large numbers and broke up the empire at about the same time the Western Roman Empire was being overrun by barbarians. Although members of the Gupta dynasty continued to rule until well into the next century, they had been reduced to local potentates with limited territories.

# 400

church was established as a powerful, independent force, free of state control. He was a friend of Monica's and instrumental in the conversion of her son, Augustine.

**St. Jerome** (Eusebius Hieronymous), Christian monk and scholar born in Pannonia; in 382 secretary to the pope. He entered a monastery in Bethlehem in 386 and produced the Latin version of the Bible known as the Vulgate. He was made Doctor of the Church in 1298.

**St. John Chrysostom** (golden mouth), age c. 30; Christian prelate born in Antioch of a wealthy family; patriarch of Constantinople from 395–404 and Doctor of the Church. He was an eloquent and popular preacher, but died in exile after being banished by the empress Eudoxia

Pelagius
(354/360-420), age 40?
Alaric
(c.370-410), age c.30
Kalidasa
(c.375-455?), age c.25
Nestorius
(     -c.451), age ?
St. Patrick
(389?-461?), age 11?

Valentinian I
    (321-375), age 54
St. Basil
    (c.330-c.379), age c.45

for attacking the immorality of the Byzantine court. Many of his ser-mons and letters are extant.

**Theodosius I** or Theodosius the Great (Flavius Theodosius), age c. 29; Roman emperor of the East from 379–395 and of the West in 394–395, born in Spain, son of a Roman general. He was the last ruler of the empire before its permanent division. A zealous champion of Christi-

# 400–425

After the death of Theodosius I in 395 at the age of 49 or 50, the disintegration of the empire accelerated, as it was split permanently into East and West. The immediate cause was the incompetence and immaturity of Theodosius' sons, whom he had named as successors. Arcadius in the East was 18 and described as stunted, sleepy-looking and slow of speech. Honorius, emperor of the West, was 11. Both were mere puppets. Already the empire seemed to be in the hands of barbarians; not only was the army predominantly non-Roman—a mixture of Gauls, Franks and other Germans—but the strongest men in the government were also barbarians. Power in the East was held first by the Praetorian Prefect, Rufinus, a Gaul; then by the eunuch Eutropius; and finally by Eudoxia, wife of Arcadius and daughter of a Frankish chief. In the West, the general Stilicho, son of

400

Chandragupta II
    (4th cent.), age ?
St. Jerome
    (340 or 345-420), age 55?
St. John Chrysostom
    (345/349-407), age c.55
St. Augustine
    (354-430), age 46

**Pelagius,** age 40?; British monk and theologian born in Ireland or Scotland. He preached in Rome, challenging Augustine's doctrine of predestination, arguing for freedom of the will and holding out the hope of heaven to all men, not merely to the elect. Accused of heresy in 415, he was acquitted but banished from Rome in 418 by Pope Zosimus.

**Alaric,** age c. 30; Gothic chieftain born near the Black Sea; a merce-nary in the Roman army until 395, when he was elected king of the Visigoths. After plundering the Balkans, he invaded Italy in 401 and

anity, he destroyed pagan temples and terminated the Olympic Games.

**St. Augustine** (Aurelius Augustinus), age 21; Christian theologian and philosopher born in north Africa. Before his conversion by St. Ambrose in 387, he was a teacher of rhetoric in Milan. Bishop of Hippo from 396–430 and the most influential figure of the early church, he is known today as the author of *The City of God* and *Confessions*.

St. Leo I
   (390 or 400-461), age 10?

a Vandal chief, was both Honorius' guardian and his chief minister.

Alaric, a Goth who commanded Visigothic mercenaries in the Roman army, rebelled in 395 and began to pillage the Balkans. When he moved west and invaded Italy in 401, Stilicho marched south to stop his depredations, leaving Gaul undefended. In the meantime, the eruption of the Huns onto the Hungarian plains had set the German tribes in motion. They spilled over the Rhine and the Danube and plundered the northern provinces. Mainz, Trier and other towns went up in flames.

When the incompetent Honorius had Stilicho killed in 408 on suspicion of treason, the West was left without a defender. Alaric seized control of Italy and laid seige to Rome. The walls of Aurelian still stood and could not be breached but he starved the city into submission, and on August 24, 410, entered as conqueror of the city which had stood impregnable for 800 years. Honorius remained holed up in Ravenna, incapable of action. His successors were no better than he, and the empire continued to crumble.

**425**

again in 408. In August 410, he captured Rome after a long siege and sacked the city. He died suddenly the same year and was buried, along with much treasure, under the bed of the Busento River in the south of Italy.

**Kalidasa,** age c. 25; Hindu poet and dramatist, the greatest figure of classical Sanskrit literature. He lived at the courts of Chandragupta II and Kumaragupta (who reigned from 413–455) and wrote dramas, epics and lyric poetry. He is best known for the drama *Sakuntala*, which was highly praised by Goethe.

Nestorius
   (    -c.451), age ?
St. Patrick
   (389?-461?), age 36?
St. Leo I
   (390 or 400-461), age 35?
Genseric
   (400?-477), age 25?
Attila
   (c.406-453), age c.19

# 425–450

When one visualizes historical accounts of the Roman world in the middle of the fifth century, something seems strangely missing. There are saints on every corner, their eyes fixed on heaven, and barbarians on every border, their hearts set on plunder, but there seems to be a scarcity of Romans. Little is heard of those stalwart citizens who sustained the empire for four centuries. The fact is, many had gone to the country. The landowning aristocracy had for some time been leaving the cities, vacating their town palaces to settle on their country estates, where they were isolated from Rome and independent of her. Their villas were capable of obtaining directly from the land all the requirements of the household. In the seasons when there was little work to be done in the fields, other kinds of pro-

**425**

St. Augustine
  (354-430), age 71
Kalidasa
  (c.375-455?), age c.50

**Nestorius,** age ?; Syrian ecclesiastic; patriarch of Constantinople from 428–431 and founder of Nestorian Christianity. He objected to the term "Mother of God," arguing that Mary was mother of the human but not the divine nature of Jesus Christ. Branded a heretic by the Council of Ephesus in 431, he was deposed and exiled. His doctrine spread throughout the East, and the Nestorian Church still exists in some places.

**St. Patrick** (Succat), age 36?; patron saint of Ireland born in southwest Britain of a Celto-Roman family of high rank. Entrusted by the pope with the conversion of the Irish, he organized churches and propagated the faith against the bitter opposition of the druids. When he retired in 457, Ireland was Christian.

**St. Leo I** (Leo the Great), age 35?; Italian ecclesiastic; pope from 440–461. An able administrator, he vigorously combatted heresy and strengthened the authority of the pope over other bishops. He escaped unharmed during the sack of Rome in 455.

# 450–475

The date of 449 for the arrival of Hengist and Horsa in Britain is not verifiable; it is merely a guess. Yet the fact that the Anglo-Saxons should appear at a time when the Western Roman Empire was entering its final stage of disintegration is a striking coincidence. The juxtaposition of events suggests that as one empire was dying, the seeds of another were being planted. In a sense, Britain is a direct

**450**

ductive work were undertaken, such as the manufacture of a variety of articles for domestic use: furniture, clothing, shoes, baskets, pottery and kitchen utensils. Every great villa had its mill for grinding flour, its carpenter shop and its forge, as well as workshops for spinning and weaving. Some households employed embroiderers, goldsmiths, architects, painters and other highly skilled workmen. While this degree of self-sufficiency was not uncommon among great families of earlier periods, the significance of these small closed economies became clearly evident as the central authority decayed. They tended to become little autonomous kingdoms, the villas, protected by men-at-arms, standing like fortresses in the midst of their fields.

These rich families, secure in the tranquility of nature and removed from the tumult of a decaying Rome, could be as indifferent to her fate as the heaven-bent ecclesiastics and saints. In the context of history, their establishment was the connecting link between the classical world and the age of feudalism then taking shape.

**450**

**Genseric** (or Gaiseric), age 25?; barbarian chief, king of the Vandals (a Germanic tribe) from 428–477. In 429 he led his tribe from Spain to Africa, devastated the provinces and established the Vandal kingdom, with Carthage as capital. His pirate fleets ruled the Mediterranean. In 455 he invaded Italy, entered Rome unopposed and plundered the city for 14 days, carrying away the palace furnishings, gold roofs of temples and the gold and silver originally taken from the temple of Jerusalem. He took the empress Eudoxia and her two daughters hostage and enslaved great numbers of Roman citizens. Neither the emperor of the West nor of the East could stop him.

**Attila,** age c. 19; king of the Huns (an Asiatic tribe) from 433–453. He devastated the Balkans (447–450) and extorted annual tribute from the Eastern emperor. His invasion of Gaul was turned back by the combined Roman and Visigothic armies, but he pillaged northern Italy in 452 until his sudden death. He appears in the epic *Nibelungenlied* as the legendary king Etzel.

Hengist
    (5th cent.), age ?
Skandagupta
    (     -480), age ?
Ricimer
    (     -472), age ?
Odoacer
    (433/435-493), age c.17
Childeric I
    (c.436-481), age c.14

descendant of Rome, for in the four centuries of Roman occupation, the institutions, law and Latin language of the conquerors made impressions which lingered for many centuries.

Britain enters the historic record with the landings of Julius Caesar in 55 and 54 B.C. Detailed knowledge of the island begins then, but Caesar's adventure was brief. Only with the partial conquest in A.D. 43 by the emperor Claudius and his general Aulus Plautius, who overran southeastern Kent and the Isle of Wight, did Britain truly enter the historic era. For nearly 40 years, under successive gover-

**475**

nors, the Romans pushed steadily north and west. The tribes of Wales and Yorkshire resisted, until the arrival of Agricola as governor in 78. Between 79 and 84 Agricola completed the conquest of Britain to the Firth of Forth. The northern Picts and Scots were left free, while the south was transformed into a prosperous Roman province called Britannia, separated and protected from the north some years later by Hadrian's Wall. Towns were built wherein the British aristocracy and the wealthy became thoroughly Romanized.

## 450

Kalidasa
(c.375-455?), age c.75
Nestorius
(   -451?), age ?
St. Patrick
(389?-461?), age 61?
St. Leo I
(390 or 400-461), age 60?
Genseric
(400?-477), age 50?
Attila
(c.406-453), age c.44

**Hengist,** age ?; chieftain (with his brother Horsa) of the Jutes, the first Anglo-Saxons in Britain. They landed in Kent about 449 and joined the Britons in repelling an invasion of Picts. He established an independent kingdom in 455.

**Skandagupta,** age ?; king of India from 455–480, fifth and last king of the Gupta dynasty (320–480), during the golden age of Indian literature and science. He was the son and successor of Kumaragupta and the grandson of Chandragupta II. Huns from central Asia destroyed the Gupta Empire after his death (480–490).

# 475–500

Before the Goths split into two groups, they lived on the Baltic coast between the Vistula and Elbe rivers, directly south of Norway and Sweden. They were a Germanic people whose original home, it is believed, was southern Sweden. Their own traditions agreed with this assumption and, moreover, the large island 100 miles south of Stockholm is called Gotland. From the Baltic they migrated south to the region of the lower Danube around the Black Sea. By A.D. 230 they had become a menace to the outer Roman provinces, to the Balkans, the Aegean coasts and the cities of Asia Minor. Athens was sacked in 262. Their depredations continued until the emperor Claudius II (268-270) crushed a Gothic army at Naissus in Upper Moesia (now Bulgaria), after which they divided into two geographically distinct groups.

## 475

The last Roman troops were withdrawn in the first decade of the fifth century, and for 40 or 50 years the Celtic Britons were left to themselves. Britain slipped back into a dark age about which little is known, but the Roman influence remained and was absorbed by the Saxons as they displaced the Celts. So strong and pervasive had been the effects of Latin civilization that even though the Roman Empire collapsed, its heritage was retained and built upon by the next great empire builders.

**475**

**Ricimer,** age ?; Roman general of Germanic (Suevi) origin, the behind-the-scenes ruler of the Western Roman Empire in its last years. After the Vandals had sacked Rome in 455, he destroyed their fleet in the Mediterranean, deposed the Roman emperor Avitus and put Majorian in his place. Thereafter he elected and deposed emperors at will. Four years after his death the empire collapsed.

**Childeric I,** age c. 14; king or tribal chieftain of the Salian Franks c. 457–481, son of Meroveus (for whom the Merovingian dynasty was named) and father of Clovis I. His tomb was discovered in the 17th century near Tournai, Belgium.

Odoacer
   (433/435-493), age c.42
Theodoric the Great
   (c.454-526), age c.21
Romulus Augustulus
   (c.461-    ), age c.14
Clovis I
   (c.466-511), age c.9

The Ostrogoths settled in southern Russia on the shores of the Black Sea; the West Goths, or Visigoths, settled between the Danube and Dneister rivers in what is now Rumania, the region where Alaric was born. In the fourth century the Visigoths were granted permission by the emperor to cross the Danube and settle in Moesia, where many became farmers and many more joined the Roman army. After the death of the emperor Theodosius in 395, however, they returned to their barbarous ways and under Alaric's leadership moved west into Italy. From there, after Alaric's death, they crossed the Pyrenees into Spain, where they established a Visigothic kingdom that included most of Spain and southern Gaul.

The Ostrogoths, driven from the Black Sea about 370 by the Huns, moved west and with the permission of Rome settled in Pannonia (now northern Yugoslavia). Theodoric became their king in 474 and in 493 he established the Ostrogothic Kingdom of Italy. Eventually the Goths were absorbed by other Germanic peoples and were lost in the mingling of European races.

**500**

Genseric
   (400?-477), age 75?
Skandagupta
   (     -480), age ?
Childeric I
   (c.436-481), age c.39

**Odoacer,** age c. 42; chieftain of a Teutonic tribe called the Heruli, mercenaries in the Roman army. In 476 he led an insurrection, killed the Roman general Orestes, deposed the boy emperor and proclaimed himself king of Italy, bringing to a close a thousand years of Roman history. He ruled from 476 to 493.

**Theodoric the Great,** age c. 21; king of the Ostrogoths, born in Pannonia. Sent by the emperor of the East in 488 to expel Odoacer from Italy, he defeated him in battle and gave a banquet where Odoacer

# 500–525

In the early third century, as the Goths were migrating south from the shore of the Baltic Sea, there was a general movement of undetermined cause among other Germanic tribes. Saxons, Franks, Alemans and Burgundians moved nearer the borders of the Roman Empire. By the middle of the third century, the Franks were settled in two groups along the Rhine River: the Salian Franks in the north, along the lower Rhine, on low, marshy land, and the Riparian Franks along the middle course of the river. No one knows where they had come from. They were a brutal, violent people whose favorite weapon was the *francisca,* a light, single-edged throwing axe.

About the middle of the fourth century the Franks and the Alemans crossed the Rhine and overran northeastern Gaul.

500

Theodoric the Great
   (c.454-526), age c.46

**Clovis I,** age c. 34; king of the Franks from 481–511. Succeeding his father, Childeric I, as king of the Salian Franks, in 486 he overthrew the last Roman governor of Gaul, united all Frankish peoples in one kingdom and established his court at Paris in 507. He was baptized by the archbishop of Rheims in 496.

**Aryabhata,** age c. 24; Hindu mathematician and astronomer of the later Gupta era. He knew that the earth rotated on its axis and understood the cause of eclipses. He wrote books on algebra and trigonometry and influenced the development of Arabic science.

**Anicius Manlius Severinus Boethius,** age c. 20; Roman philosopher and convert to Christianity born in Rome; a high official in the gov-

was treacherously murdered. He founded the Ostrogothic Kingdom of Italy and ruled from Ravenna from 493–526, respecting Roman institutions and promoting agriculture and commerce. He appears in the *Nibelungenlied* as Dietrich von Bern.

**Romulus Augustulus,** age c. 14; Roman emperor 475–476, last emperor of the West. A puppet ruler supported by his father Orestes, the Roman general, he was deposed by Odoacer in 476 and allowed to retire to Campania, where he disappeared from history. The abrogation of his title and office marked the end of the Western Empire.

# 500

Clovis I
   (c.466-511), age c.34
Aryabhata
   (c.476-550), age c.24
Boethius
   (c.480-524), age c.20
St. Benedict
   (c.480-543/547), age c.20
Bodhidharma
   (    -c.530), age ?
Justinian I
   (483-565), age 17
Arthur
   (    -537), age ?

Julian, then a *Caesar* under the emperor Constantius II, succeeded in driving them back, defeating 35,000 Alemans in a great battle in the summer of 357. The Salian Franks were permitted to settle within the borders of the empire in 358, where they became peaceful subjects of Rome. A half century later (c.400) the last Roman troops withdrew from the Rhine and the Salian Franks moved deeper into Gaul. They remained on good terms with the Romans and many took service at the Roman court. It is more than likely that Childeric, the father of Clovis, was in the service of Rome.

Rome fell in 476, and Clovis, a cunning, treacherous chieftain, succeeded his father in 481. He united all the Franks, and in 486 defeated and killed Syagrius, the last Roman governor of Gaul. He proceeded to subjugate Alemans, Burgundians and other Germans, forging a powerful Frankish kingdom. His baptism in 496 assured him the Church's support against the Arian Theodoric in Italy and cleared the way for the Frankish kingdom to develop into Charlemagne's empire and, finally, into the Holy Roman Empire.

# 525

ernment of Theodoric. His translations and commentaries on Aristotle provided the Middle Ages with its best source on Aristotelian thought. Accused of high treason and imprisoned, he wrote *The Consolation of Philosophy* in 523 while awaiting execution.

**St. Benedict of Nursia,** age c. 20; Italian monk, founder of the Benedictine order, the first monastic organization in the West. He lived in a cavern for three years and won fame for his sanctity, and then founded a number of monasteries, including Monte Cassino (529).

**Bodhidharma,** age ?; Buddhist monk from southern India, missionary to China in the late fifth or early sixth century. He introduced a form of Buddhism that emphasized the importance of meditation over doctrines and scriptures, which became known as Zen (dhyana) Buddhism.

Justinian I
   (483-565), age 42
Arthur
   (    -537), age ?
Khosru I
   (    -579), age ?
Belisarius
   (505-565), age 20
Justin II
   (    -578), age ?
Alboin
   (    -572), age ?
St. Columba
   (521-597), age 4

# 525–550

In the first half of the sixth century the advance of the West Saxons into Wales and Cornwall was halted by a great Celtic warrior king whose heroic deeds have been so overlaid wth the accretions of later ages that many historians deny his existence. The first mention of this heroic figure occurs in the sixth-century chronicle of Gildas, who refers to the great battle of Mount Badon (c. 520) without naming the victorious king. A mighty unnamed warrior is again mentioned in the Welsh poem *Gododdin* (c. 600). Nennius, a Welsh chronicler of the eighth century, is somewhat more explicit and records the deeds of a Celtic warrior who fought and defeated the Saxons in 12 battles. Another chronicle, the *Annales Cambriae,* of a later, uncertain date, gives 537 as the year of his death. Geoffrey of Monmouth's *Historia* (c. 1135) treats him as a historical personage and

**525**

Theodoric the Great
(c.454-526), age c.71
Aryabhata
(c.476-550), age c.49
St. Benedict of Nursia
(c.480-543/547), age c.45
Bodhidharma
(      -c.530), age ?

**Justinian I,** age 42; Justinian the Great (Flavius Petrus Sabbatius Justinianus), Roman emperor from 527–565, born in Illyria. He brought the empire briefly back to life by recovering lost territories in northern Africa and all the Mediterranean lands except Gaul and Spain. He appointed a commission to compile and systematize Roman laws; they produced the *Corpus juris civilis,* which became the basis of Western European law.

**Arthur,** age ?; king of the Celtic Britons, son of Uther Pendragon. Opposing the advance of West Saxons into Wales in the sixth century (516–537), he won a great victory at Mount Badon in 520 and was killed in battle at Camlan in 537. He is often regarded as purely

# 550–575

**550**

Justinian I, often called the greatest of the Eastern Roman emperors, reigned from 527-565. Khosru I, the greatest Sassanid king of Persia, reigned from 531-579. Both were powerful, ambitious rulers. Justinian is famous for recovering lands of the Western empire lost to the barbarians, including Africa, Italy and parts of Spain. Gaul was beyond his grasp, but

adds more details. When the spirit of romantic chivalry is introduced into the story by Wace's *Roman de Brut* (c. 1155), the transformation of the Celtic warrior into a medieval knight is well underway.

Beneath the stories of the noble knights of the Round Table—of the magic sword Excalibur; the wizard Merlin; evil Modred; the sorceress Morgan le Fay; the illicit romance of Sir Lancelot of the Lake; the quest of his son, Sir Galahad, for the Holy Grail; the death of the king and his magical transport to Avalon—beneath all the romantic inventions of later ages, which have appareled a sixth-century warrior in the shining armor of a medieval knight, may still be seen the lineaments of a historical figure. The legendary accretions do not affect the credible historical fact that the Saxons were resisted by a doughty warrior, and defeated, as long as he lived. To such an impressive figure would naturally accrue a wealth of romance and legend, but it is more than likely that there was such a mighty Celtic king, though he may not have had a Round Table and may have borne an unpronounceable Welsh name instead of Arthur.

legendary, but two early chroniclers, Gildas and Nennius, vouched for his existence and recorded more than 12 battles in which he took part.

**Khosru I** (Chosroes), age ?; king of Persia from 531–579, one of the greatest of the Sassanid dynasty. He extended the boundaries of Persia to the Indus River, to the Black Sea and far into central Asia. In the process he waged a series of wars with Justinian I, compelling him to pay tribute. Khosru is the subject of many legends portraying him as a just but firm ruler.

**Belisarius,** age 20; Byzantine general born in Illyria whose conquests under Justinian restored the empire. He conquered the Vandal kingdom and brought King Gelimer captive to Constaninople. He also conquered Italy, occupying Rome in 536.

Justin II
( -578), age ?
Alboin
( -572), age ?
St. Columba
(521-597), age 29
Antara
(525?-615?), age 25?
Brunhilde
( -613), age ?
St. Gregory I
(c.540-604), age c.10
St. Columban
(c.543-615), age c.7

the Mediterranean became once more a Roman lake. Modern historians have argued that it was all wasted effort, a futile expenditure of men and resources. Constantinople was too far from Europe to rule over it effectively, a fact made evident when Justinian's successors soon lost what he had gained.

In 526 Antioch, the second largest and richest city of the Eastern empire, was struck by a terrible earthquake which is said to have killed 250,000 people, but in 540 it experienced a worse disaster. Khosru captured the city and utterly destroyed it, leaving not a house standing. He massacred the inhabitants or enslaved them. Many years passed before it was rebuilt. More concerned with his western adventure, Justinian bought a five-year peace treaty with gold and twice renewed it.

Justinian's two most lasting achievements are his codification of Roman law and the construction of Hagia Sophia or Santa Sophia, the Church of the Divine Wisdom, an awe-inspiring masterpiece of Byzantine architecture. Built in 532-37, Hagia Sophia is famous for its great central dome, which,

## 550

Aryabhata
   (c.476-550), age c.74
Justinian I
   (483-565), age 67
Khosru I
   (     -579), age ?
Belisarius
   (505-565), age 45

**Justin II,** age ?; Roman emperor of the East from 565–578, nephew and successor of Justinian I. After the death of the great emperor, troubles mounted. The Lombards crossed the Alps into Italy and founded the Lombard kingdom. Subject to fits of insanity, Justin turned the government over to his general Tiberius, who succeeded him in 578.

**Alboin,** age ?; first Lombard king of Italy (569–572?). As chief of the Germanic tribe of Lombards, who had moved from the lower Elbe River into Pannonia and Austria, he led them across the Alps, capturing Milan in 569. After a three-year siege Alboin took Pavia, which he made his capital. His violent and murderous married life with Rosamond, daughter of a Germanic chief he had killed in battle, was the subject of dramas by Swinburne and Alfieri.

# 575–600

An almost forgotten age is the golden age of Irish Christian scholarship of the sixth and succeeding centuries, when Ireland was a bright spot of learning in the darkness of northern Europe. It is a phenomenon not readily explained, unless it may be attributed to the isolation of the land and its remoteness from the paths of migrating barbarians. For centuries the native Celtic population had been left undisturbed. The Romans, during their 400-year occupation of Britain, apparently never crossed the Irish Sea to attempt another conquest. The Anglo-Saxons from the Continent, who in-

## 575

while actually supported by a system of lesser domes and arches, gives the impression of being entirely unsupported. The dome is 102 feet in diameter and 164 feet high, while the vast interior of the church is 102 feet wide and 265 feet in length. Forty arched windows surrounding the base of the dome light up the interior, with its multicolored marble walls and gold mosaics. When Constantinople fell in 1453, the church was converted into a mosque and four minarets were built at the corners. It is no longer a mosque but a museum of Byzantine art and stands in all its glory in Istanbul, where it has stood for close to 1,500 years.

**575**

**St. Columba** (Colum), age 29; Irish missionary to Scotland, called the Apostle of Caledonia. The son of an Ulster chief (of the O'Donnells of Donegal), he sailed to Scotland in 563 with 12 disciples to convert the Picts. He traveled throughout the Highlands founding monasteries. When he died in 597 northern Scotland was Christian.

**Antara,** age 25?; Arabian warrior and poet, hero of countless legends and romances. Born a Christian slave, he grew up to become a Bedouin chief; courageous, handsome, and proud—the ideal desert sheik of romantic novels and motion pictures. His single extant poem is one of the seven incomparable poems of the collection known as the *Muallaqat.*

Brunhilde
( -613), age ?
St. Gregory I
(c.540-604), age c.35
St. Columban
(c.543-615), age c.32
Ethelbert
(552?-616), age 23?
St. Isidore of Seville
(560?-636), age 15?
St. Augustine
( -604), age ?
Khosru II
( -628), age ?
Li Yuan
(565-635), age 10
Mohammed
(c.570-632), age c.5
Abu Bakr
(573-634), age 2

vaded Britain and largely displaced the Celts, left the Irish Celts to themselves.

The first recorded outsiders to land on Irish shores were missionaries from Rome, sent by Pope Celestine I in the fifth century. St. Palladius and St. Patrick built churches and monasteries, planting the seeds of learning that flowered the following century. As the reputation of Irish scholarship spread to the Continent, a flood of students came to the monasteries to further their education. Among the most famous Irish monks were St. Columba (521-597), St. Columban (543-615) and St. Gall (550-645), all scholars and missionaries. Many arts were cultivated, including the illumination of manuscripts. This splendid age was brought to a close by Norse raids, which began about 800 and continued for two centuries,

**600**

leaving the country in chaos.

Near the town of Ceanannus Mor (formerly Kells) in northeastern Ireland, on the Blackwater River northwest of Dublin, stand the ruins of an ancient monastery founded in the

Khosru I
    (    -579), age ?
Justin II
    (    -578), age ?
St. Columba
    (521-597), age 54
Antara
    (525?-615?), age 50?

**Brunhilde,** age ?; Frankish queen; wife of Sigebert I, king of the East Franks; daughter of the Visigothic king of Spain; and central figure of the Merovingian nightmare. Murder, revenge and war filled the 40 years following the murder of her sister Galeswintha, wife of the king of the West Franks, in 567. Sigebert I and Chilperic I were grandsons of Clovis I, brothers and deadly enemies. The bloody history ended when Brunhilde, nearly 80, was dragged to her death behind wild horses.

**St. Gregory I** (Gregory the Great), age c. 35; Italian ecclesiastic born in Rome of a wealthy family; prefect of Rome at 30 and pope from 590–604. Despite chronic ill health, he upheld and strengthened the church in a barbarous age. He encouraged monasticism and insisted on clerical celibacy and exemption from trial in civil courts. In 597 he

# 600–625

With startling suddenness the focus of history shifts to a region of the East long dormant. The conspicuous scarcity of prominent names in the West during the barbarian centuries contrasts sharply with the wealth of Eastern names. A prophet was born who promised eternal bliss in paradise, and the whole desert sprang to life. The tribes of Arabia were united by the new religion of Islam and emboldened to spill out from their arid wastes and seize the wealth of the cultivated lands. Some historians have suggested that the pressure of overpopulation, coupled with a drought of exceptional severity in the Arabian interior, added economic motivations to religious ones in the holy war against the infidels.

In regard to Islam and the historical personages associated with its rise, there has been much confusion over the

600

sixth century by St. Columba. It was here that the Book of Kells, an illuminated manuscript of the Latin Gospels, was found. It is believed to date from the eighth century and is now in the library of Trinity College, Dublin. This is the last relic of the vanished golden age of Irish scholarship.

sent St. Augustine to Britain as a missionary. The Gregorian chant was named for him.

**St. Columban,** age c. 32; Irish monk born in Leinster during the golden age of Irish monastic scholarship; missionary to the continent of Europe in its darkest age. With 12 monks, including St. Gall, he sailed to France in 585, hoping to eradicate the impiety and immorality at the Frankish courts. Discovering upon arrival the hopelessness of his mission, he contented himself with founding monasteries, including the famous Bobbio Abbey in Lombardy where he died.

**Ethelbert,** age 23?; king of Kent from 560–616, the first Christian Anglo-Saxon king of England. His wife, daughter of a Frankish king, was already a Christian when St. Augustine arrived in 597 to baptize the king. His capital at Canterbury became a center of Christianity.

St. Isidore of Seville
  (560?-636), age 40?
St. Augustine
  (    -604), age ?
Khosru II
  (    -628), age ?
Li Yuan
  (565-635), age 35
Mohammed
  (c.570-632), age c.30
Abu Bakr
  (573-634), age 27
Heraclius
  (c.575-641), age c.25
Othman
  (575?-656), age 25?
Omar
  (581?-644), age 19?
Harsha
  (c.590-647), age c.10
T'ai Tsung
  (597-649), age 3

spelling of names. The prophet's name in Arabic is Muhammad, his followers are Muslims, and two of his successors (caliphs) were 'Umar and 'Uthman. However, from very early times he has been known in the West as Mohammed. The use of this form is so general that it seems pedantic to insist on Muhammad. Likewise, the names of Omar and Othman are the familiar forms and seem more natural than 'Umar and 'Uthman, just as Omar Khayyam has always been Omar rather than 'Umar. However, Mohammedanism as a common form for Islam and Moslem for Muslim are patently wrong and inappropriate. The recourse to so-called familiar forms results in a hodge-podge. Moreover, purists who demand consistency at all costs—insisting of Muhammad, 'Umar and 'Uthman—invariably make an error with the Turkish sultans, whom they designate as Muhammad I, II and III. This is irrational by their own rules, for the Turkish form is, properly, Mahomet.

But if consistency is really unattainable, then the use of Mohammed, Muslim, Omar, Othman, and Muhammad I, II and III may be acceptable.

Antara
  (525?-615?), age 75?
Brunhilde
  (      -613), age ?
St. Gregory I
  (c.540-604), age c.60
St. Columban
  (c.543-615), age c.57
Ethelbert
  (552?-616), age 48?

**St. Isidore of Seville,** age 40?; Spanish prelate and scholar; archbishop of Seville from 600–636. Reputed to be the most learned man in Europe, he compiled a great encyclopedia which was held in high esteem for many centuries.

**St. Augustine,** age ?; Christian monk born in Rome, first archbishop of Canterbury, called Apostle to the English. Sent with 40 monks to England by Pope Gregory I, he landed in 597 and baptized Ethelbert, king of Kent. He founded the monastery of Christ Church in Canterbury.

**Khosru II** (Chosroes), age ?; king of Persia from 590–628, grandson of Khosru I. When a usurper seized the throne of the Eastern Roman Empire, he invaded Syria and Palestine, occupied Egypt and captured Chalcedon on the Bosporus opposite Byzantium. He also expanded eastward and controlled the caravan routes across Asia. The last important Sassanid king, he was deposed and killed by his son, Kavadh II. Thirteen years later the dynasty was overthrown by the Muslims.

**Li Yuan,** age 35; first emperor (618–627) of the T'ang dynasty of China (618–907), one of the most brilliant periods of Chinese history. Although he is usually called the founder of the dynasty, some historians give credit to the military exploits of his son, Li Shihmin (later Emperor T'ai Tsung) for the overthrow of the Sui dynasty.

**Mohammed** (Muhammad), age c. 30; Arabian prophet born in Mecca; founder of Islam. An orphan, a shepherd boy and camel driver, at 24 he married Khadija, a wealthy widow, and became a prosperous mer-

# 625–650

The period of the T'ang dynasty in China, from 618-907, was a highly civilized, literate and cultured period—the golden age of Chinese literature. While Western Europe was mired in barbarism, China was boasting such famous names as Li Po, Tu Fu, Po Chu-i, Wang Wei and Han Yu, writers and poets whose equal would not be seen in Europe for six or eight centuries. The T'ang dynasty was established by Li Yuan, a general formerly in the service of the short-lived Sui dynasty (589-618), and his son Li Shihmin. They continued the work of unification begun by the Sui dynasty and took advantage of the administrative system and excellent networks of roads already in existence. Within a comparatively short time, the T'ang emperors controlled an area that in-

St. Isidore of Seville
  (560?-636), age 65?
Khosru II
  (      -628), age ?

**Omar** ('Umar), age 44?; second Muslim caliph (634–644), chosen by Abu Bakr on his deathbed as successor. He was the driving force behind the irresistible expansion of Islam. As his armies pushed into Egypt, Syria and Persia, he laid the foundation of a centralized administration and established a system of taxation. He also introduced the

chant. About the age of 40, prompted by visions, he began preaching a new religion, but opposition forced him to take flight *(Hegira)* in 622. He was more successful in Medina, establishing a theocratic state that included all of Arabia and provided the stimulus for the great territorial and cultural expansion of the Arab peoples. His sayings and revelations were collected in the Koran after his death.

**Abu Bakr,** age 27; friend, father-in-law and successor (caliph) of Mohammed. The first convert, outside Mohammed's family, and a fervent believer, he accompanied the prophet on the *Hegira*. As the first caliph (632–634), he began the extension of Islam beyond Arabia and fought both Persia and the Byzantine Empire. He was succeeded by Omar.

**Heraclius,** age c. 25; Byzantine emperor from 610–641, son of a Roman general who aided him in deposing the tyrant Phocas. An able ruler in a difficult time, he saw Syria, Palestine and Egypt fall to Khosru II, then recovered them briefly, only to lose them again to the Muslims. The permanent loss of the Eastern provinces reduced the empire by half. In his later years he devoted himself to theology.

**Othman** ('Uthman), age 25?; third Muslim caliph (644–656), son-in-law of Mohammed and successor of Omar. Although an aged man, he made conquests in Bactria, Armenia and north Africa, but dissension arose over his favoritism toward his family, the wealthy Umayyads. He issued a standardized, official text of the Koran and ordered other versions destroyed. Revolts broke out among the troops, and a mob stormed his house in Medina and killed him. He was succeeded by Ali.

# 625

Omar
(581?-644), age 44?
Harsha
(c.590-647), age c.35
T'ai Tsung
(597-649), age 28
Ali
(600?-661), age 25?
Muawiya
(c.602-680), age c.23
Fatima
(606-632), age 19
Aisha
(611-678), age 14
Hasan
(c.624-669), age c.1

cluded parts of Korea, Manchuria, Mongolia, Tibet and Turkestan—unquestionably the most extensive empire in the world. Reforms were undertaken to protect the rights of peasants against the rich landlords, and a remarkable cultural efflorescence followed the territorial expansion. In addition to its famous names in literature, the T'ang period is noted for its sculpture and painting. It was the classical age of Chinese art.

The greatest emperors of the T'ang dynasty were Kao Tsung, who reigned from 649-683 and was the grandson of Li Yuan, and Hsuan Tsung, who reigned from 712-756. Both maintained brilliant courts that attracted philosophers, poets and artists and spread the cultural influence of China to Japan, southeast Asia and other adjacent areas. Throughout most of the period the empire was at peace, and though it experienced occasional periods of weakness and instability under inferior rulers, it recovered its stability and endured until 907.

# 650

practice of dating events from the *Hegira* (622). He was assassinated by a Persian slave at Medina.

**Harsha,** age c. 35; king of India from 606-647, the last native Indian ruler of importance until the 20th century. He revived the Gupta empire by uniting northern India in a strong kingdom with its capital at

Muawiya
(c.602-680), age c.48
Aisha
(611-678), age 39

Kanauj on the Ganges. He patronized art and literature and was a poet and dramatist himself, author of *The Pearl Necklace*. After his conversion to Buddhism, he built monasteries and hospitals and forbade the killing of animals. Shortly after his death the empire dissolved into petty warring states, and the killing of animals as well as people was resumed.

**T'ai Tsung** (Li Shihmin), age 28; Chinese emperor from 627–649, of the T'ang dynasty, son and successor of Li Yuan. His expansion and strengthening of the empire laid the foundation for the cultural flowering of the later T'ang period. At the end of his reign he controlled an area that extended into Korea, Manchuria, Mongolia and Tibet. Relations were established with Harsha's court at Kanauj by the Buddhist

Li Yuan
    (565-636), age 60
Mohammed
    (c.570-632), age c.55
Abu Bakr
    (573-634), age 52
Heraclius
    (c.575-641), age c.50
Othman
    (575?-656), age 50?

# 650–675

The division of Islam into Sunnites and Shi'ites is not based on doctrinal differences, but on political quarrels that originated in the seventh century. The term Sunnite or Sunni is derived from the Arabic *sunnah,* meaning way, path or rule; the Sunnites are orthodox, traditional Muslims, who comprise 85 percent of all Muslims. The term Shi'ite is derived from the Arabic *Shi'ah,* meaning a follower of Ali. Shi'ites comprise 10 percent of all Muslims and are found principally in Iran and Iraq, but also in Yemen, Syria, Lebanon, northern India and Pakistan.

When the Prophet Mohammed died in 632, he was succeeded as religious and political leader by his chief disciple and close friend, Abu-Bakr, a man of 57 and the father of Aisha, the Prophet's youngest wife. He was caliph (successor) for only two years, and when he died in 634 he was

650

Othman
    (575?-656), age 75?
Ali
    (600?-661), age 50?

**Muawiya,** age c.48; fifth Muslim caliph (661–680), successor of Hasan and founder of the Umayyad dynasty. A member of a wealthy merchant family of Mecca and a relative of Othman, he had been secretary to Mohammed and a general under Abu Bakr. He restored stability to the Muslim empire, moved the capital to Damascus and made the office of caliph hereditary.

**Aisha,** age 39; favorite wife of the prophet Mohammed (after the death in 620 of Khadija), daughter of Abu Bakr. She is said to have married soon after the *Hegira,* at which time she would have been about 11 and Mohammed 52. Known as the Mother of the Believers, she opposed Ali and fomented a revolt during his caliphate.

**Hasan,** age c.26; fifth Muslim caliph (661), grandson of Mohammed, son of Ali and Fatima. On the death of Ali he was proclaimed caliph,

monk Hsuan Tsang.

**Ali** ('Ali ibn-abi-talib), age 25?; fourth Muslim caliph (656–661), successor of Othman; cousin of Mohammed and husband of his daughter Fatima. Although he was an early convert and faithful follower, his right to the succession was contested. The ensuing dispute led to the schism between Shi'ites and Sunnites. He was assassinated by three zealots.

**Fatima,** age 19; daughter of Mohammed by his first wife, the wealthy Khadija. She married Ali, the prophet's cousin, and had two sons, Hasan and Husain. She died young, in the same year as her father, and is revered by all Muslims. The Fatimid dynasty of north Africa claimed descent from her.

succeeded by Omar (634-644), Othman (644-656) and Ali (656-661). Ali, the fourth caliph, was Mohammed's son-in-law, having married his daughter Fatima.

At this point the schism began. The Shi'ites maintain that the Prophet meant for Ali and his family to be his successors and had prepared him for the role by imparting to him certain knowledge and wisdom requisite for the leader of Islam. When Ali was assassinated in 661, his sons, Hasan and Husain, claimed the right of succession, but were forcibly restrained by Muawiya, the fifth caliph (661-680); Muawiya founded the Umayyad dynasty, which ruled Islam until 750. A conspiracy in which the Shi'ites participated was organized in 750 against the Umayyads. All members of the Umayyad family were massacred—except one, who escaped and founded an independent caliphate at Cordoba. In the Middle East the caliphate passed to the Abbasid family, who were Shi'ites. They moved the capital to Baghdad and ruled Islam until 1258. Among their caliphs were the famous Harun al-Rashid and al-Mamun.

but soon abdicated when Muawiya challenged him and threatened war. He retired to Medina and was killed, it is said, in a harem intrigue. The Shi'ites believe he was poisoned by the Umayyads and revere him as a martyr.

**Kao Tsung,** age 22; emperor of China from 649–683, of the T'ang dynasty, son and successor of T'ai Tsung (Li Shihmin). He annexed all of Korea, as the empire continued to expand and prosper. At his death the concubine Wu Hou usurped the throne.

**Husain,** age c.21; pretender to the caliphate, grandson of Mohammed, son of Ali and Fatima and brother of Hasan. Upon Muawiya's death in 680, he claimed succession to the caliphate, but was intercepted and killed by the troops of Yazid, son of Muawiya, on Oct. 10, 680, a holy day celebrated by Shi'ites.

# 650

Hasan
 (c.624-669), age c.26
Kao Tsung
 (628-683), age 22
Husain
 (c.629-680), age c.21
Caedmon
 (7th cent.), age ?
Abd al-Malik
 (c.646-705), age c.4

# 675

Caedmon
 (7th cent.), age ?
Abd al-Malik
 (c.646-705), age c.29
Wu Hou
 ( -704), age ?
Bhavabhuti
 (fl. 700), age ?
Tarik
 ( -720), age ?
St. Bede
 (673-735), age 2

# 675–700

During the period when the brilliance of the T'ang court was dimmed by falling into the hands of a usurping courtesan, and Western Europe had not emerged from its darkness, the Muslim caliphate continued to expand and prosper. The 75th anniversary of the founding of Islam as a religion and a political state fell in the reign of Abd al-Malik (685-705). The territorial expansion of the Muslims had been extraordinary, but there was no comparable development of religious doctrines. There are no names in the early history of Islam to be compared with the famous Christian theologians, who were to forge orthodox doctrine in the heat of intense

**675**

Muawiya
(c.602-680), age c.73
Aisha
(611-678), age 64
Kao Tsung
(628-683), age 47
Husain
(c.629-680), age c.46

**Caedmon,** age ?; earliest known Anglo-Saxon Christian poet. According to St. Bede, he was an uneducated cowherd who wrote poetic versions of various Old and New Testament stories. Scholars disagree about the authorship of certain extant poems thought to be his.

**Abd Al-Malik,** age c.29; fifth Umayyad caliph (685–705), chosen after Muawiya's grandson died without heirs. His father had been secretary and adviser to Othman. With the aid of his general, al-Hajjaj,

# 700–725

At the opening of the eighth century the two major powers in the world were China and Islam. The two lesser powers were the Byzantine Empire and the Frankish Empire in Europe. Islam could expand no farther in the east, for the T'ang Empire could defend its borders, and if aroused might expand them at the expense of Islam. The Byzantine Em-

**700**

controversies. In sharp contrast to Christianity, Islam was created whole, for all truth was said to be contained in the Koran.

Islam is a derivative religion; its sources are Judaism and Christianity, and many of the stories in the Koran are versions of those in the Old Testament. It is essentially a formal religion, enjoining the faithful to believe in God, angels, the scripture, the prophets (one of whom is Alexander the Great), the day of judgment and predestination. It requires the believer to stop whatever he is doing five times a day, face Mecca and recite certain predetermined prayers or scriptures. It is a religion of resignation and passivity, declaring that whatever happens is the will of God, and thrives in a latitude where the hot season is barely endurable. Its tenets enable the faithful to cope with the intense heat and survive, and leave the rest to Allah.

**700**

he crushed rival factions and unified the empire. He introduced Arabic coins and made Arabic the official language.

**Wu Hou,** age ?; empress of China from 683–704, a former concubine of Kao Tsung. Although sometimes called the emperor's widow, she is believed to have been an ambitious imperial concubine who seized the throne from the rightful heir. She remained in power for 20 years, a period filled with court intrigues and scandals.

Bhavabhuti
  (fl. 700), age ?
Tarik
  (    -720), age ?
St. Bede
  (673-735), age 27
St. John of Damascus
  (c.675-c.750), age c.25
Walid I
  (c.675-715), age c.25
Leo III (Byzantine emperor)
  (c.680-741), age c.20
Hsuan Tsung
  (685-762), age 15
Charles Martel
  (688/689-741), age c.12
Abd ar-Rahman
  (    -732), age ?
Wang Wei
  (699-759), age 1

pire, in Asia Minor and the Balkans, barred the way to Europe, preventing the Muslims from pouring across the Bosporus. The Arabs ferociously stormed the barrier, but Byzantium, though shaken, sustained the attack. Since Justinian, the empire had been in decline and had lost much territory. The Lombards, a Germanic tribe who had settled on the lower Elbe River, invaded Italy (568-70) under their chieftain Alboin and wrested central Italy from the empire— although Rome, Sardinia, Corsica and the coasts of Italy and Sicily remained under imperial control. Muslim conquests

**725**

had taken Syria, Palestine, Egypt and north Africa, but not Constantinople. Muawiya's six-year siege (672-678) failed, as did the siege of 717-18. Leo III stood firm. His Greek fire, an incendiary compound that reputedly ignited when it became wet, destroyed the Arab fleet; it was a terrible new weapon that gave the advantage to his side. This was the last Arab attempt to take the capital.

Somewhat earlier, however, they had found another way to Europe. In the far West there was a weak spot. It was

## 700

Abd al-Malik
  (c.646-705), age c.54
Wu Hou
  (    -704), age ?

**Bhavabhuti,** age ?; Indian dramatist, second only to Kalidasa; best known as the author of a tragic drama, *Malati Madhava,* called the Hindu *Romeo and Juliet.* He lived at Kanauj at the court of a successor of Harsha.

**Tarik,** (Tariq ibn-Ziyad), age ?; Berber chieftain who led the Muslim invasion of Spain in 711. He landed near Gibraltar (which is named for him) with 7,000 men and overthrew the Visigothic kingdom.

**St. Bede or Baeda** (the Venerable Bede), age 27; English historian and theologian born in Northumbria. Ordained a priest in 703, he lived at the monastery of Jarrow and taught Greek, Latin, Hebrew and theology. He was the author of the *Ecclesiastical History of England* (in Latin), completed in 731.

**St. John of Damascus,** age c.25; Syrian Christian theologian born in Damascus, son of an official of the caliph. Although recognized as a leading theologian of the early Greek Church, the author of books defining orthodoxy, throughout his life he was a subject of the Muslim

# 725-750

The Muslim occupation of Spain disturbed European princes, few of whom expected the Muslims to be content with one corner of Europe, and indeed their raids across the Pyrenees into Gaul steadily increased in number and depth of penetration. By 725 they had taken Arles and Toulouse and forced the duke of Aquitaine to retreat to the north. The Moors seemed on the point of adding Gaul to the realm of Islam.

Fortunately for Europe, the Frankish Empire had only recently been taken over by new and vigorous rulers. Toward the end of the preceding century the Merovingians had seen their kingdom break into many pieces; small principalities were created by adventurous princes and dukes who proclaimed their independence and refused service to the king. If the Moors had arrived at that time, they might

## 725

during the caliphate of Walid I (705-715) that the Berber general, Tarik, led an army of 7,000 across the Strait of Gibraltar into Spain. At the Rio Barate he met the Visigothic army led by King Roderick, and Tarik's victory on July 19, 711, marked the end of the Visigothic kingdom of Spain. Tarik continued his advance and occupied Cordoba and Toledo. The Muslim governor of north Africa, Musa ibn-Nusair, followed with 10,000 troops and by 713 had occupied all of Spain. The Arab army was then on the doorstep of Europe, poised to thrust into Gaul.

caliph, living after about 700 in a monastery near Jerusalem. He was one of the church fathers.

**Walid I,** age c.25; Muslim caliph from 705–715, son of Abd al-Malik. His reign marked the zenith of Umayyad power. The Muslim realm under his rule extended from the borders of the T'ang Empire in the east, across Asia and north Africa to southern France. Among his generals were al-Hajjaj and Tarik, who led an army into Spain in 711. He was the builder of the great cathedral mosque at Damascus.

**Leo III** (the Syrian), age c.20; Byzantine emperor from 717–741, famous for checking the advance of the Muslims and starting the Christian offensive that finally halted their expansion. Employing Greek fire (an incendiary mixture containing naptha) and assisted by a violent storm, he sank or dispersed a fleet of 1,800 Arab ships blockading Constantinople (717–718). He is also known for his struggle to eradicate the popular superstitious worship of images (icons), which he banned in 726.

Hsuan Tsung
(685-762), age 40
Charles Martel
(688/689-741), age c.37
Abd ar-Rahman
(      -732), age ?
Wang Wei
(699-759), age 26
Li Po
(701-762), age 24
Tu Fu
(712-770), age 13
al-Mansur
(c.712-775), age c.13
Pepin the Short
(714-768), age 11

have picked off the small duchies like apples from a tree. But the Franks had since been reunited, not by Merovingians, but by upstart mayors of the palace, the majordomos or stewards who managed the estates of the king. Ebroin was the first mayor of the palace to establish himself as sole ruler of the Franks, although he allowed the king to remain as a figurehead. Ebroin died in 681, and Pepin of Herstal was the next to establish himself as ruler of the Franks (687–714). His illegitimate son, Charles Martel, succeeded him and ruled from 715–741. Martel built up a powerful cavalry force which greatly assisted him in repulsing the Arabs, whose raids had begun to reach Bordeaux and Autun. Abd ar-Rahman, the governor of Spain, led a raid across the Pyrenees in 732 and advanced as far as Tours. On his return journey he had reached Poitiers when he was surprised by the army of Charles Martel and left dead on the field. Gaul was saved on that October day, for the Arabs could no longer carry out widespread raids with impunity. They remained north of the Pyrenees until 759, when they lost their last foothold in Gaul.

St. Bede
  (673-735), age 52
St. John of Damascus
  (c.675-c.750), age c.50
Leo III (Byzantine emperor)
  (c.680-741), age c.45

**Hsuan Tsung** (Ming Huang), age 40; emperor of China from 712–756, of the T'ang dynasty. During his reign territorial expansion, prosperity and civilization achieved unprecedented heights. He presided over a brilliant court in a great age of poetry, painting and sculpture (including the famous T'ang horses). Troubles mounted in the last years of his reign, and he abdicated in 756.

**Charles Martel,** age c.37; ruler of the Franks (mayor of the palace) from 715–741, grandfather of Charlemagne. He ended the Muslim threat with his victory over Abd ar-Rahman near Poitiers in 732.

**Abd ar-Rahman,** age ?; Arab governor of Spain from 721-732. By 731 Muslim raids into France had reached Bordeaux, and parts of Aquitaine were under their control. Abd ar-Rahman led an army across the Pyrenees in 732 and unexpectedly met Charles Martel near Tours. In the ensuing battle he was defeated and killed. (He should not be

# 750–775

As the power and wealth of the Islamic empire continued to increase, jealousy, intrigue and unrest threatened its stability. Impregnable to external attack, it succumbed to vendettas from within. Midway through the eighth century the Shi'ite Abbasids seized power and destroyed the Sunnite Umayyad dynasty. After Walid I, during whose caliphate (705-715) the Umayyads were at the height of their power, there were eight additional Umayyad caliphs, none of whom enjoyed a lengthy reign except Hisham, who ruled from 724-743. The last of the line was Marwan II, whose rule lasted from 744-750. Administrative inefficiency, revolts among the subject peoples and conspiracies plagued the last Umayyads. One of the conspirators was Abu al-Abbas, who claimed descent from a merchant of Mecca named Abbas who had been the uncle of both Mohammed and Ali. Abu al-Abbas gathered together and band of malcontents: disgruntled soldiers, over-

St. John of Damascus
  (c.675-c.750), age c.75
Hsuan Tsung
  (685-762), age 65
Wang Wei
  (699-759), age 51
Li Po
  (701-762), age 49

**Tu Fu,** age 38; Chinese poet born in Shensi province, friend of Li Po and considered by some a better poet. Unable to pass the civil service examination, he lived a wandering life and wrote with bitterness of his misfortunes, of the corruption at court and the suffering of the poor.

**al-Mansur,** age c.38; second Abbasid caliph (754–775), brother and successor of the first, Abu al-Abbas, who reigned only four years. He made the new dynasty (which ruled for five centuries) strong and

confused with Emir Abd ar-Rahman I.)

**Wang Wei,** age 26; Chinese poet, painter and physician at the court of Hsuan Tsung. Called the founder of southern Chinese landscape painting, he is known for his delicate landscapes in black ink. In both poetry and painting he depicted the quiet beauty of nature. He retired to a Buddhist monastery in his later years.

**Li Po,** age 24; Chinese lyric poet born in what is now Szechwan province, called the greatest poet of China. A romanticist, a lover of the beauties of nature and of women and the pleasures of wine, he lived for some years at the court of Hsuan Tsung, but was banished and resumed a wandering life. His surviving poems are believed to be only one tenth of the total. On a moonlit night, according to tradition, he fell from a boat while drunk and drowned in the Yellow River.

## 750

Tu Fu
   (712-770), age 38
al-Mansur
   (c.712-775), age c.38
Pepin the Short
   (714-768), age 36
Abd ar-Rahman I
   (731-788), age 19
Alcuin
   (735-804), age 15
Charlemagne
   (742-814), age 8

taxed landowners and Shi'ites still fighting century-old wars. When the revolt flared, the aged Marwan II was overcome and killed; simultaneously, a general massacre of the Umayyad family was carried out, from which only one member, Abd ar-Rahman I, escaped.

The establishment of the Abbasid caliphate, which was Persian and Shi'ite, meant that Islam was no longer to be dominated by Arabs. When Abu al-Abbas died in 754, he was succeeded by his brother, al-Mansur, an able ruler (754–775) who gave the new regime a firm foundation and moved the capital in 762 from Damascus to the new city of Baghdad on the Tigris River. Islam turned from the simplicity and frugality of the nomadic Arabs toward an Oriental extravagance and luxury. Additionally, the transfer of power to the Abbasids meant the displacement of the nomadic conquerors by the settled peoples they had subjugated and converted. The Abbasid caliphs ruled until 1258, but their greatest period was the eighth and ninth centuries, when the famous Harun al-Rashid and al-Mamun maintained courts of legendary splendor.

## 775

stable, and in 762 he built the city of Baghdad and made it his capital. In the luxury and splendor of their courts, the caliphs soon rivaled the ancient Persian kings. A great patron of learning, he encouraged the translation of Western classics into Arabic.

**Pepin the Short** (Pepin le Bref), age 36; king of the Franks from 751–768, son of Charles Martel and father of Charlemagne. As mayor of the palace from 741–751, he deposed Childeric III, last of the

Cynewulf
   (8th or 9th cent.), age ?
Alcuin
   (735-804), age 40
Charlemagne
   (742-814), age 33
St. Leo III (Pope)
   (c.750-816), age c.25

Merovingians, and established the Carolingian dynasty.

**Abd ar-Rahman I,** age 19; emir of Cordoba from 756–788. A grandson of Hisham (Umayyad caliph 724–743) and the only survivor of the

# 775–800

The resistance of the Byzantine emperior, Leo III, and the Muslim defeat in the West by Charles Martel marked the end of Islamic expansion and the beginning of a Christian counteroffensive. Both Charles Martel and his son and successor, Pepin the Short, were more truly the heirs of Clovis than the weak Merovingians of the seventh century. Charlemagne succeeded his father, Pepin the Short, in 768, when he was not yet 30. A tall, stout, blue-eyed man with an iron constitution and a thin, piping voice, he had eight wives, several concubines and 14 children. He outlived all but one of his sons. Hunting and war were his main occupations. The image of a benign, fatherly figure perpetuated by the Church does not accord with his deeds, which were those

al-Mansur
  (c.712-775), age c.63
Abd ar-Rahman I
  (731-788), age 44

CHARLEMAGNE
Frankish emperor
742-814

**Charlemagne** (Charles the Great), age 33; king of the Franks from 768–814. He expanded and unified the kingdom and was crowned Carolus Augustus, Emperor of the Romans, on Christmas Day, 800, by Pope Leo III. He was a patron of literature, science and art and a defender of Christianity.

Umayyad family after the massacre by the Abbasids in 750, he took flight across north Africa and seized power in Spain by defeating the emir of Cordoba. He is remembered as the builder of the great mosque at Cordoba and for the legendary battle with Charlemagne's rear guard at Roncesvalles in 778.

Roland
    (    -778), age ?
Harun al-Rashid
    (c.764-809), age c.11
Han Yu
    (768-824), age 7
Po Chu-i
    (772-846), age 3

of a despotic barbarian chief. He waged war for 40 years and established his authority over Western Europe. His empire, which he administered from Aachen, or Aix-la-Chapelle, in western Germany near the Belgian and Dutch borders, included the area which is now France, Germany, the Low Countries, Bavaria and northern Italy. He had married the daughter of the Lombard king of Italy, but nevertheless overthrew the kingdom and dispatched his father-in-law to a monastery.

Charlemagne could read and appreciate the practical value of learning, but he never learned to write. What is called a revival of learning at his court was a comparatively minor affair, with scholars such as Alcuin and Paul the Deacon in charge of instructing court officials and the nobility. There was some literary activity, and schools were established at various places throughout the empire for the instruction of the clergy. The level of achievement was certainly not high, but it was at least a beginning.

## 800

**Cynewulf,** age ?; Anglo-Saxon poet of Northumbria or Mercia, four of whose religious poems have survived. He treated such themes as the martyrdom of St. Juliana, Christ's ascension and the finding of the true cross.

**Alcuin** (Ealhwine), age 40; English scholar and ecclesiastic born in Yorkshire, a leading figure in the revival of learning at Charlemagne's court (781–790) and abbot of a monastery at Tours in 796. He wrote manuals of instruction in grammar and rhetoric.

**St. Leo III,** age c.25; Italian ecclesiastic; pope from 795–816. He established the temporal authority of the papacy over the city of Rome and built many churches. With his coronation of Charlemagne, he created the Holy Roman Empire.

**Roland,** age ?; French hero of the epic poem *The Song of Roland* (of the 12th century), who commanded the rear guard of Charlemagne's army returning from Spain in 778. According to legend, he was attacked by Saracens at Roncesvalles, in the Pyrenees, but stoutly refused to blow his horn. Historians believe the attackers were Basques, not Saracens, and that Roland was not Charlemagne's nephew but his commander on the Brittany border.

Harun al-Rashid
    (c.764-809), age c.36
Han Yu
    (768-824), age 32
Po Chu-i
    (772-846), age 28
Egbert
    (775?-839), age 25?
Louis I (Emperor)
    (778-840), age 22
al-Mamun
    (786-833), age 14
Shankara
    (788-820), age 12

# 800–825

In the year 800 the world from East to West appeared to be moving toward a more civilized way of life. Barbarism seemed for the moment in retreat. China was at peace under the T'ang emperors and enjoying the late phase of its golden age of literature; it was the age of Han Yu and Po Chu-i. In a peaceful India, Shankara was expounding the Vedanta philosophy; in Europe the Western Roman Empire had been restored, after a fashion, under Christian rulers; and in Baghdad Harun al-Rashid presided over a brilliant, luxurious court, into which wealth poured from every part of the vast Muslim dominions.

Harun al-Rashid is perhaps the only Muslim caliph well known outside Islam, as the ideal caliph of romance and legend. The fifth Abbasid caliph, he succeeded his brother in 786 at the age of 22, reigned 23 years and died at 45. His

**800**

Alcuin
  (735-804), age 65
Charlemagne
  (742-814), age 58
St. Leo III (Pope)
  (c.750-816), age c.50

**Harun al-Rashid,** age c.36; fifth and most famous Abbasid caliph of Baghdad (786–809), grandson of al-Mansur. Remembered for the splendor of his court, his patronage of art and learning and for prowling the streets of Baghdad in disguise. A powerful monarch, he controlled all of southwestern Asia and north Africa and sent embassies to Charlemagne and the T'ang emperor. He appears in the *Arabian Nights* as the ideal Muslim caliph.

**Han Yu** (Han wen-kung), age 32; Chinese essayist and poet, the foremost prose writer of the T'ang period and creator of the classic style of the prose essay. His simple straightforward style caused the artificial writing of the time to lose favor. He was also a court official and an opponent of Buddhism.

**Po Chu-I,** age?; Chinese poet and government official (at one time head of the war department) of the T'ang court. He won fame with his more than 3,000 poems, many of them short, satirical verses on current topics. His best-known poem is *The Everlasting Wrong,* about an

# 825–850

It was the custom of Frankish kings to divide their kingdoms among all their sons, thus destroying the unity that had been so hard to achieve. Charlemagne was prevented from following this custom only because he outlived all his sons but one. The empire passed intact to his third son, Louis I, called Louis the Pious, who in 814, at the age of 36,

**825**

reign was not altogether peaceful. He waged war with the Byzantine empress, Irene, leading his troops in person, and forced her to pay tribute. He faced many insurrections toward the end of his reign and was on an expedition to suppress a revolt in Khurasan when he died. None of this is remembered in the legends, however, which recall him spending his days and nights in the magical, mysterious city of Baghdad.

His relation to the *Arabian Nights* stories is not clear. One tradition casts him in the role of the husband of Scheherazade, but he sometimes appears in the stories as a romantic figure prowling incognito through the bazaars. Many of the stories are of course older than he and older even than Islam, although the present collection of 264 tales is in Arabic, and thoroughly Muslim in spirit. When and by whom he was introduced into the stories is a mystery, but the romantic Harun of Baghdad will no doubt be remembered after the historical caliph, confined to the prosaic world of official duties and practical affairs, has been forgotten.

emperor's grief over the murder of his concubine. He was partially paralyzed and arthritic in his later years.

**Egbert** (Echbryht), age 25?; king of the West Saxons 802–839. Driven into exile in 786 by Offa, king of Mercia, he spent his youth at the court of Charlemagne. Returning in 802, he conquered neighboring kingdoms and became the first ruler of all the English peoples. He was the grandfather of Alfred the Great.

**Louis I** (Louis the Pious), age 22; Holy Roman emperor and king of France and Germany from 814–840; third son and successor of Charlemagne. By arranging upon his death, for the division of the empire among his three sons, he imprudently fragmented the unified power that might have resisted the Norsemen.

**Shankara** (Sankara), age 12; Indian philosopher, founder of the most influential school of Vedanta. A native of Malabar, he wandered about India and died in the Himalayas. His exposition of the *Upanishads* and commentaries on the Vedanta philosophy are regarded as authoritative.

al-Mamun
(786-833), age 39
Yoshifusa
(804-872), age 21
Louis II of Germany
(804-876), age 21
Albumazar
(805-886), age 20
al-Kindi
(    -after 870), age ?
Basil I (Byzantine emperor)
(c.812-886), age c.13
Johannes Scotus Erigena
(810 or 815-877), age 10?
Charles the Bald
(823-877), age 2

became king of France and Germany and emperor of the West. Throughout his reign his four sons quarreled continually with each other and with him over the division of the realm. He was deposed several times by his impatient sons, but always regained his throne. When Louis the Pious died in 840, his sons Louis the German and Charles the Bald received the areas that are today Germany and France, while Lothair succeeded his father as emperor and received northern Italy and Lorraine. The fourth son did not survive his father. Lothair had three sons and in 855 divided his kingdom among them, retiring to a monastery near Trier where he died the same year. Lothair's son Louis II became emperor in 855. When he died in 875 his uncle, Charles the Bald, invaded Italy and was crowned emperor. Charles the Bald was then 52 and wore the crown only two years before his death in 877.

The first Norse raids, in the closing years of the eighth century, were sporadic, striking the coast of Ireland, the

**825**

Po Chu-i
    (772-846), age 53
Egbert
    (775?-839), age 50?
Louis I (Emperor)
    (778-840), age 47

**Abdullah al-Mamun,** age 39; seventh Abbasid caliph of Baghdad (813–833), son of Harun al-Rashid. He maintained a magnificent court noted for its intellectual attainments. A patron of philosophy and science, he was a rationalist with a critical attitude toward the Koran and little respect for narrow, orthodox Muslims. His scholars translated many books from the Greek.

**Yoshifusa,** age 21; Japanese noble who in 858 achieved for his family, the Fujiwara, complete ascendancy over the imperial family, which they maintained for three centuries. They tutored the emperor's children, married into the family, provided prime ministers and after 858 ruled as regents or dictators.

**Louis II** (Louis the German), age 21; king of Germany from 843–876.

# 850–875

The high-prowed Norse boats carrying 30 or 40 Vikings terrorized not only the coasts but also towns far inland. Ascending the rivers, they would make a surprise attack on an unsuspecting village or monastery and slip away downstream with their plunder. Growing bolder, they rode inland on stolen horses to pillage the countryside. No village or town was safe. About 840 the Danes joined in the attacks and every year raided the French coast. Nantes, Rouen and Bordeaux were left in flames. About 855 Norsemen ascended the Elbe, the Seine and the Loire in their boats, then struck inland and sacked and burned Amiens, Orleans and Paris. Large areas of Europe were reduced to chaos, as in the barbarian migrations centuries earlier.

Yet the Norse terror had its limitations, for there were

**850**

Hebrides, Northumbria and the Thames estuary. When first they struck Gaul, at Dorestal, Charlemagne was still alive and took steps to guard the coastal towns and river estuaries. Between 815 and 820 Norsemen attacked the lower Rhine and Seine, but this was only the beginning. Each spring larger numbers of Viking boats attacked the coasts and rivers; the Continent, with Charlemagne's empire disintegrating into a dozen pieces, increasingly unable to resist.

Grandson of Charlemagne and son of Louis the Pious, he is generally regarded as the founder of Germany; the Treaty of Verdun in 843 established a line behind which Germany and France evolved independently. In the famous Strasbourg Oath taken by Louis and Charles the Bald, each used his own vernacular, and these documents are believed to be the first written in French and German.

**Albumazar,** age 20; Arabic astronomer of Baghdad who made important contributions to astronomy and the study of tides, despite his superstitious astrological beliefs. He was the author of nearly 50 books, many of which were translated into Latin in the 15th century. He predicted the world would come to an end when all the planets are in conjunction in Pisces.

al-Kindi
( -after 870), age ?
Basil I (Byzantine emperor)
(c.812-886), age c.38
Johannes Scotus Erigena
(810 or 815-877), age 35?
Charles the Bald
(823-877), age 27
Rurik
( -879), age ?
Arpad
( -907), age ?
Alfred the Great
(849-899), age 1

islands of security beyond the reach of the raiders; the safest place was the royal court, protected by men-at-arms, for the Vikings, with their hit-and-run tactics, seldom consented to open battle. Charles the Bald had acquired a taste for learning and in 847 invited Johannes Scotus Erigena to Paris to take charge of the court school. Little is known of the life of this Christian philosopher except that he was born about 815, but some connection with the Irish scholars of the eighth century may be assumed. He was the most learned man of his time and a subtle thinker. In asserting that the function of philosophy is to define and analyze rather than to construct metaphysical propositions, he takes a place among 20th-century philosophers, yet his Neoplatonism links him with the ancients. He demonstrated that it was still possible in a lawless age to philosophize; John the Scot, born in Ireland, found a safe place to speculate, argue and write his books. He died in 877, the same year as his protector.

# 850

Yoshifusa
    (804-872), age 46
Louis II of Germany
    (804-876), age 46
Albumazar
    (805-886), age 45

**al-Kindi,** age ?; Arab philosopher born in Basra, the first outstanding Islamic philosopher and one of the first scholars in the Middle East to become familiar with Aristotle. Well known to medieval scholastics, he wrote treatises on mathematics, music, physics, medicine and astrology, most of which have been lost. He attempted to harmonize the views of Plato and Aristotle with one another, and both with Islam.

**Basil I** (Basil the Macedonian), age c.38; Byzantine emperor from 867–886, founder of the Macedonian dynasty (867–1056). A treacherous but able man, he gained the throne at the age of 56 by murdering his predecessor. He recovered territory lost to the Arabs, reoccupied Venice and Tarentum in Italy and regained control of the Mediterranean. He reformed Justinian's code by adding the *Basilica,* which gave more protection to the poor. His reign was the prelude to an age of

# 875–900

Egbert, the grandfather of Alfred the Great, was king of Wessex from 802–839. He ended the long overlordship of Mercia and made Wessex the strongest English kingdom. His son Ethelwulf, king from 839–858, was not a soldier, but a pious man devoted to the Church. He could not cope with the Viking raids which began almost immediately after his accession. He married Osburh, descended from Jutish royalty, and had five sons and a daughter. On his return from a pilgrimage to Rome after his wife's death in 855, he brought back to Wessex a 13-year-old bride, daughter of Charles the Bald. He lived only two years longer and was succeeded by his eldest surviving son, Ethelbald, who reigned from 858–860 and married his stepmother, to the horror of the Church. He was succeeded by his next brother, Ethelbert, who had a comparatively peaceful reign of six years, from 860–866. After Ethelbert's death, Ethelwulf's third son, Ethelred, became king; Alfred, then 17, was his chief lieutenant and second in command. Both were resolute young men.

# 875

splendor and power for the empire.

**Johannes Scotus Erigena,** age 35?; Irish theologian, first great philosopher of the Christian Middle Ages. Combining Neoplatonism with Christian doctrines, he verged on heresy and opposed Augustine's strict views on predestination, taking a democratic stand in favor of the eventual salvation of all souls.

**Charles the Bald,** age 27; king of France from 840–877 as Charles I, and Holy Roman emperor from 875–877 as Charles II; fourth son of Louis the Pious, half-brother of Louis the German and grandson of Charlemagne. The Treaty of Verdun in 843, granting him recognition as king of the West Franks, is regarded as the beginning of modern France. Bordeaux, Rouen and parts of Paris were pillaged by Norsemen during his reign.

Rurik
( -879), age ?
Arpad
( -907), age ?
Alfred the Great
(849-899), age 26
Harold I of Norway
(850?-933), age 25?
Rollo
(c.860-930/931), age c.15
Leo VI (Byzantine emperor)
(862/866-912), age c.9
Ubaydullah
( -934), age ?
al-Farabi
(870-950), age 5

The Danes, not satisfied with raiding the coasts, resolved about this time to conquer England and settle there. Led by Ivar the Boneless and his brother, a large force landed in 865 in East Anglia, rode north on stolen horses to Yorkshire, captured the town of York and set up a puppet English king in Northumbria. They plundered the country all around, living on the crops and livestock. In the fall of 869, four years after landing, they rode back to East Anglia and defeated and killed King Edmund—on November 20, a day still observed as St. Edmund's Day. In December 870 they marched toward Wessex. Early in January 871 Ethelred and Alfred marched out on the Berkshire Downs with their main army to meet them, and in a day-long battle defeated the Danes and killed many of their warriors. Toward the end of March, Ethelred and Alfred again gave battle. After another all-day struggle, the English suddenly gave way and withdrew. Ethelred, it is believed, had been wounded.

In the meantime, another large body of Danes had crossed from the Continent to join the fighting. Then, about April 23, the news spread through towns and villages that the king was dead. Alfred was 22. The future of the English people depended upon his leadership, strength, will and sagacity. What followed, in his reign of 28 years, accounts for his title of Alfred the Great.

## 900

Louis II of Germany
   (804-876), age 71
Albumazar
   (805-886), age 70
Basil I (Byzantine emperor)
   (c.812-886), age c.63
Johannes Scotus Erigena
   (810 or 815-877), age 60?
Charles the Bald
   (823-877), age 52

**Rurik,** age ?; Scandanavian chieftain, reputedly the founder of the Russian empire. He conquered Novgorod and established himself as grand prince in 862. The house of Rurik ruled until 1598.

**Arpad,** age ?; Magyar chief considered the founder of Hungary. Dislodged from their homeland by wild Turkish tribes, the Magyars moved west, and Arpad led them (875–890) to the Danube, then to Transylvania and onto the Hungarian plain. The Arpad dynasty ruled to 1301.

**Alfred the Great,** age 26; king of the West Saxons from 871–899 and

# 900–925

Historians disagree on whether the Holy Roman Empire was founded in 800 or 962, as well as on which German kings were emperors and which were not. It should therefore be borne in mind that the following account is not a universally accepted one.

After Charles the Bald had invaded Italy and made himself emperor in 875—following the death of Emperor Louis II, son of Lothair (brother of Charles the Bald)—he lived only two years. The next emperor, after a period of four years without one, was Charles III or Charles the Fat *(Charles le Gros),* who ruled from 881–887. He was the son of Louis the German (brother of Charles the Bald) and king of part of Germany from 876-887. On the death of his brother Carloman in 884, joint ruler of France with their brother Louis III from

## 900

Arpad
   (    -907), age ?
Harold I of Norway
   (850?-933), age 50?

**Rollo or Rolf or Hrolf** (Rolf the Ganger), age c.40; Norse chieftain and first duke of Normandy. He invaded northwest France (890–910) and received Rouen and some of its adjacent territory by treaty with Charles the Simple of France.
**Leo VI** (Leo the Wise), age c.34; Byzantine emperor from 886–912, son and successor of Basil I and son of Michael III's mistress, whom his father married after killing Michael. He maintained a strong, efficient administration, although the Arabs renewed their attacks and conquered Sicily in 907. He completed the modernization of Justinian's laws. A scholar, he wrote on theological submects and tried without success to mend the schism between the Eastern and Western churches.
**Ubaydullah** (Said ibn Husain), age ?; founder of the Fatimid caliphate in north Africa and Egypt, which ruled from 909–1171. A Shi'ite religious leader in Syria who claimed descent from Fatima and Ali, he

sovereign of all England after 886. He compelled the Danes to withdraw in 897 by organizing the first English fleet. He promoted learning and commissioned Anglo-Saxon translations of classical works.

**Harold I** (Harold the Fairhaired), age 25?; king of Norway from 860–930. By uniting all of Norway in a single kingdom in 872, he caused a wholesale emigration of defeated earls, to the peril of the rest of Europe. He abdicated in 930 in favor of his eldest son, Eric Bloodaxe, but after his death in 933, Norway was again split into petty kingdoms by his 20 sons.

879–882 and sole ruler from 882–884, Charles the Fat became king of all France as Charles II, but he was deposed by Arnulf in 887. Arnulf was the illegitimate son of Carloman and nephew of Charles the Fat. Arnulf was elected king of Germany in 887 and was emperor from 887–899. The next emperor, though uncrowned, was Louis III or Louis the Child, son of Arnulf. He was king of Germany from 899–911, from the age of 6 to 18, during which time the government was in the hands of the archbishop of Mainz. He was the last of the Carolingians to rule in Germany. Conrad I, or Conrad of Franconia, followed. As duke of Franconia, he was elected to succeed Louis the Child by Franconian, Bavarian, Saxon and Swabian nobles and ruled 911–918. Conrad named Henry the Fowler, duke of Saxony, to succeed him, although they had been enemies. Henry was elected in 919 as Henry I. He restored royal authority over the dukes, made important military reforms and secured the consent of the nobles for the succession of his son Otto, thus establishing the Saxon line of German kings.

went to north Africa after a follower fomented rebellion among the Berber tribes, and established a caliphate independent of the Abbasids in Baghdad. His realm included Tunisia, Sicily and parts of Algeria and Libya. He reigned from 909–934.

**al-Farabi,** age 30; Arab philosopher born in Transoxiana of Turkish descent. He helped introduce Aristotle's philosophy to the Arabs and continued the effort to reconcile Greek philosophy with Islam. He wrote a *Catalog of Sciences*, drawn largely from Aristotle; and *The Perfect City*, based on Plato's *Republic*. His Neoplatonic writings influenced Avicenna and Averroes.

**Henry I** (Henry the Fowler), age 24?; duke of Saxony from 912–936 and king of Germany from 919–936, first of the Saxon line of German kings; also Holy Roman emperor, although never crowned. He strengthened the empire and defeated the Hungarians and Danes, and was the father of Otto the Great.

# 900

Rollo
　(c.860-930/931), age c.40
Leo VI (Byzantine emperor)
　(862/866-912), age c.34
Ubaydullah
　(　　-934), age ?
al-Farabi
　(870-950), age 30
Henry I of Germany
　(876?-936), age 24?
Saadia ben Joseph
　(882 or 892-942), age 18?
Abd ar-Rahman III
　(891-961), age 9

# 925

Saadia ben Joseph
　(882 or 892-942), age 43?
Abd ar-Rahman III
　(891-961), age 34
Constantine VII (Byzantine
　emperor) (905-959), age 20
Moizz
　(　　-975), age ?
Otto I (Holy Roman emperor)
　(912-973), age 13
St. Bernard of Menthon
　(923-1008), age 2

# 925–950

While Europe struggled through difficult times and advanced toward more stable conditions, the rest of the world had also undergone changes. The T'ang dynasty of China had collapsed under a series of weak emperors; the Abbasid caliphate in Baghdad grew steadily weaker. Yet under the new Macedonian dynasty (867–1056), the Byzantine Empire was revived and strengthened, regaining some of its lost territories—Greece, Asia Minor, parts of Syria and southern Italy were recovered. Control of the Mediterranean, which had been lost to the Arabs, was also regained. Arts and letters flourished in the first half of the 10th century, during the reign of Constantine VII. The empire's generals boasted that they could field an army of 140,000.

On the far side of Europe, Spain had also experienced a

## 925

Harold I of Norway
  (850?-933), age 75?
Rollo
  (c.860-930/31), age c.65
Ubaydullah
  (    -934), age ?
al-Farabi
  (870-950), age 55
Henry I of Germany
  (876?-936), age 49?

**Saadia ben Joseph,** age 43?; Jewish scholar born in Egypt, an outstanding figure of early medieval Judaism and head of the great Jewish academy in Baghdad. He wrote commentaries, religous and grammatical works and translated the Old Testament into Arabic. Influenced by Aristotle, he was concerned with rational foundations of faith.

**Abd ar-Rahman III,** age 34; emir (912–929) and first caliph (929–961) of Cordoba, grandson of Abd ar-Rahman I. He brought the caliphate to the height of its power and made Cordoba one of the great cities of the West, the most advanced center of culture and learning in Europe. He

# 950–975

The T'ang dynasty of China had collapsed in 907 and was followed by a period of disorder called the Age of the Five Dynasties (907–960). A general, Chao K'uang-yin, consolidated several warring states and founded the Sung dynasty, which ruled for three centuries, from 960–1279. Not

## 950

remarkable renascence under the Moors and had become the most advanced region of Western Europe. Immediately after the Moorish conquest, Spain was ruled by emirs appointed by the caliph at Damascus—until the massacre of the Umayyad family in 750. Abd ar-Rahman I, the only member of the family to escape, founded an independent emirate in Spain, which developed into the caliphate of Cordoba. In the north some regions remained Christian. Asturias was expanded under the rule of a Visigothic chieftain, whose son-in-law, Alfonso I, became in 739 the first king of Leon and Asturias. In the 10th century the region of Navarre became independent under Sancho I, who reigned from 905–925; and in 932 Castile was made an independent kingdom under Fernan Gonzalez. Except for these small northern states, Spain was ruled by the Moors. In the long reign of Abd ar-Rahman III, emir from 912–929 and caliph of Cordoba from 929–961, Spain became a highly civilized, prosperous state, all the more splendid in contrast to the darkness north of the Pyrenees.

seized part of Morocco from the Fatimids and defeated the Christian kings of Leon and Navarre.

**Constantine VII,** age 20; Byzantine emperor from 913–959, son of Leo VI. During the regency of his mother, an ambitious admiral named Romanus seized power and retained it until Constantine was nearly 40. Even then Constantine preferred philosophy and letters to governing the empire. While he wrote a biography of Basil I, his grandfather, his beautiful daughter-in-law Theophano put power in the hands of her lovers, whom she chose from among the most able generals.

Moizz
( -975), age ?
Otto I (Holy Roman emperor)
(912-973), age 38
St. Bernard of Menthon
(923-1008), age 27
Chao K'uang-yin
(923-976), age 27
Brian Boru
(926?-1014), age 24?
Firdausi
(c.940-1020), age c.10
Hugh Capet
(938/940-996), age c.10
Sylvester II (Pope)
(940 or 945-1003), age 5?

so powerful militarily nor so extensive territorially as the T'ang empire, the Sung empire yet achieved lasting prosperity and security. Education and literacy were increased through the use of printing, and Confucianism was revived. Gunpowder and the magnetic compass came into use, and trade was established with India and Persia. The Sung period is especially noted for landscape painting. The famous novel *All Men Are Brothers* is also from this period.

In the meantime in north Africa, the Shi'ite Fatimid caliphate had become, under Moizz, the strongest Muslim power. Islam was now divided into three major caliphates, with capitals at Baghdad, Cordoba and, after 973, Cairo.

In Western Europe Otto I succeeded his father, Henry the Fowler, as king of Germany in 936. He was only 22—a powerful, red-haired soldier with no intellectual interests. He saw himself as the heir of Charlemagne, as one destined to restore and enlarge the empire. Crowned Holy Roman emperor in 962, he deposed the pope a year later and tried

## 950

al-Farabi
   (870-950), age 80
Abd ar-Rahman III
   (891-961), age 59
Constantine VII (Byzantine
   emperor) (905-959), age 45

**Moizz** (al-Mu'izz), age ?; fourth Fatimid caliph of North Africa (953–975). With the aid of his general Jauhr he greatly increased the power of the caliphate and conquered Egypt, Palestine and southern Syria, including Tyre and Damascus. In 969 he built the city of Cairo and in 973 made it his capital; the transference of Palestine and the Holy Land from Abbasid to Fatimid control had significant consequences.

**Otto I** (Otto the Great), age 38; king of the Germans from 936–973 and Holy Roman emperor from 962–973, son of Henry the Fowler. He annexed northern Italy and restored to the empire its former power. The long struggle between popes and emperors began when he deposed John XII and installed Pope Leo VIII.

# 975–1000

Otto III, king of Germany and Holy Roman emperor, was a handsome, brilliant and able young man who died suddenly at the age of 22. Succeeding his father, Otto II, at the age of three, he was under the regency of his mother, Theophano, until the age of 11, and the regency of his paternal grandmother and the archbishop of Mainz until he was 16, when he assumed control of the government. In him the Holy Roman Empire and the Byzantine Empire were united— he was the grandson of Otto the Great; great grandson of

## 975

to make the Church subservient to the imperial power. He opened negotiations for an alliance with the Byzantine Empire, but succeeded only in arranging a marriage between his son, later Otto II, and Theophano, granddaughter of Emperor Constantine VII and daughter of Romanus II. She brought Byzantine refinement to the German court and after the death of her husband ruled ably as regent for her son, Otto III, until her death in 991.

**St. Bernard of Menthon,** age 27; French priest born in Menthon, Savoy; archdeacon of Aosta in the Italian Alps. Although his fame rests on the hospices he built for travelers at the two St. Bernard passes in the Alps, it has been eclipsed by that of the dogs who since the 17th century have been rescuing travelers lost in the snow.

**Chao K'uang-yin,** age 27; emperor of China from 960–976, founder of the Sung dynasty (960–1279). A general of the preceding dynasty, he usurped the throne and began to reunite China after a period of near anarchy known as the Age of the Five Dynasties (907–960). His successors finished the tasks of unification and of strengthening the central government, and the Sung period became one of the great ages of Chinese civilization.

Brian Boru
   (926?-1014), age 49?
Firdausi
   (c.940-1020), age c.35
Hugh Capet
   (938/940-996), age c.35
Sylvester II (Pope)
   (940 or 945-1003), age 30?
Eric the Red
   (10th cent.), age ?
Vladimir I
   (956-1015), age 19
Basil II (Byzantine emperor)
   (c.958-1025), age c.17
Sweyn I
   (c.960-1014), age c.15
Leif Ericson
   (fl. 1000), age ?
Michinaga
   (966-1027), age 9
Olaf I
   (964 or 969-1000), age 6?
Mahmud of Ghazni
   (971?-1030), age 4?

Constantine VII; and descendant of Basil I, founder of the Macedonian dynasty. He was carefully brought up, given a Greek education by his mother and tutored by Gerbert of Aurillac, abbot of the monastery of Bobbio and the most learned man of the time. From the age of 16 he cherished the dream of fusing the two empires, reconstituting the empire of Constantine the Great with Rome as its capital. His tutor may have joined in these schemes, or encouraged them, or indeed have conceived them, for when he was made pope in 999 he took the name Sylvester II, after the bishop of Rome in the time of Constantine. Perhaps for a while sober men could believe that the dream of the Church would be realized, and East and West rejoined. But nothing was accomplished, for although Otto had ability, he was

Otto left hardly a ripple in history, but his tutor is remembered for his great learning. Sylvester II studied mathematics and astronomy in Muslim Spain in his youth and is said

## 975

Moizz
( -975), age ?
St. Bernard of Menthon
(923-1008), age 52
Chao K'uang-yin
(923-976), age 52

**Brian Boru,** age 49?; national hero and king of Ireland from 1002–1014. His victory in 1014 over the Danes at Clotarf, near Dublin, ended the Norse threat, but he was killed while waiting in his tent for news of the battle. If the dates are correct, he would have been 88.

**Firdausi** (Abul Kasim Mansur), age c.35; Persian epic poet born in Khurasan of a land-owning family. He was the author of the *Shah Namah* (Book of Kings), a famous epic poem containing 60,000 rhyming couplets (seven times longer than the Iliad) on the deeds of Persian kings and heroes, legendary and historical. It was published in 1010 after 35 years of labor. Its best-known story is *Sohrab and Rustum*, retold in English verse by Matthew Arnold.

**Hugh Capet,** age c.35; king of France from 987–996, first of the Capetian dynasty, which succeeded the Carolingian. By force of arms he maintained a strong centralized government and kept the feudal lords subservient.

**Sylvester II** (Gerbert of Aurillac), age 30?; first French pope (999–1003). A mathematician and natural scientist, he tutored the future

# 1000–1025

As European monarchs grew stronger and successfully repelled the Viking raiders, those adventurous seamen turned their energies elsewhere. Long sea voyages to the west provided an outlet for their qualities of daring and hardiness. Eric the Red is the first familiar name in this new enterprise. He sailed west from Iceland, which had been settled by Norsemen a century earlier, and discovered and explored Greenland (982–85). Settlements established in southern Greenland remained for several centuries and reached a population estimated at over 10,000. Eric's son, Leif Ericson, was commissioned by King Olaf I to introduce Christianity. It was on one of his journeys to Greenland that he is said to have discovered America, about 1000. If settlements were made in North America, they failed to survive. Consequently, though Leif Ericson may have preceded

## 1000

to have introduced Arabic numerals in Europe, where their first recorded use was in 976; but whether he did or not, his accomplishments as teacher and writer were more solid than those of his pupil. He died a year after Otto at the age of 58.

emperor, Otto III, who caused him to be made pope. Popularly believed to be a magician in league with the devil because of his wide learning, he is said to have introduced Arabic numerals in the West and invented the pendulum clock.

**Eric the Red,** age ?; Norweigian navigator who, sailing from Iceland, discovered and explored (982–985) the coast of Greenland, which he called Greenland to attract colonists. He is the subject of the Icelandic saga *Eric the Red*.

**Basil II,** age c.17; Byzantine emperor from 976–1025, son of Theophano and grandson of Constantine VII. Nominal ruler in 963 at age 5 under the regency of his mother, he assumed power at 18 and proved to be an indomitable soldier. He extended the frontiers, conquered the Bulgars and made the empire the strongest power in the East. Uneducated and capable of great cruelty, he returned 15,000 Bulgarian prisoners in 1014, blinded and with their hands cut off. At the sight, the czar of the Bulgars took ill and died.

Vladimir I
(956-1015), age 44
Sweyn I
(c.960-1014), age c.40
Leif Ericson
(fl. 1000), age ?
Michinaga
(966-1027), age 34
Olaf I
(964 or 969-1000), age 31?
Mahmud of Ghazni
(971?-1030), age 29?
Stephen I
(975-1038), age 25
Murasaki Shikibu
(c.978-1031?), age c.22
Avicenna
(980-1037), age 20
al-Hakim
(985-1021), age 15
Canute II
(994-1035), age 6

Columbus, his discovery had no lasting results.

Just as the Norsemen were adopting more peaceful ways, so were the Hungarians in central Europe, who had been as great a terror to settled peoples as the Vikings. In the mid-10th century they ravaged central Germany, Lorraine and Burgundy; and in the spring of 955, 100,000 horsemen are reported to have besieged Augsberg. A decisive defeat administered by Otto the Great put an end to the raids, and in 970 the Hungarian chief Geza and 5,000 of his warriors were baptized. It was his son, Wajk, who became St. Stephen, the first king and patron saint of Hungary.

While Europe was still feeling its way out of barbarism, a state of high civilization had already been attained in the Far East, in Japan. The refinement of court life during the Fujiwara period was vividly described by Lady Murasaki in the famous novel *Tale of Genji,* which for its realism and complicated plot has been called the best narrative work ever written by a woman. It would be 600 years before Europe produced anything comparable, and 800 before a European woman would.

# 1000

St. Bernard of Menthon
  (923-1008), age 77
Brian Boru
  (926?-1014), age 74?
Firdausi
  (c.940-1020), age c.60
Sylvester II (Pope)
  (940 or 945-1003), age 55?
Basil II (Byzantine emperor)
  (c.958-1025), age c.42

**Vladimir I** (the Great), age 44; first Christian ruler (grand prince) of Russia (980–1015). He established Greek Orthodox Christianity as the official religion and built monasteries and churches in the Byzantine or "onion-bulb" style.

**Sweyn I** (Sweyn Forkbeard), age c.40; king of Denmark from 986–1014, son of Harold Bluetooth and father of Canute the Great. In 994 his Viking fleet ravaged the coast of England and extorted tribute. Each year after 1002 he sent plundering expeditions to England and in 1013 he attempted to conquer it. He captured London in 1014, as Ethelred the Unready fled to Normandy.

**Leif Ericson** (or Ericsson), age ?; Norwegian mariner, son of Eric the Red. Sailing westward (as related in an Icelandic saga) he landed on a coast which he called Vinland, believed to be Labrador, Newfoundland, or New England.

**Michinaga,** age 34; Japanese regent and dictator from 998–1027, head of the Fujiwara clan, which dominated and manipulated the imperial family. Four of his daughters married emperors. It was the classical age of Japanese culture; the elegant, refined court left practical politics to the Fujiwara and devoted its time to poetry and banqueting.

**Olaf I** (Olaf Tryggvesson), age 31?; king of Norway from 995–1000, great-grandson of Harold I. He sought to convert Norway to Christianity and to unite Scandanavia into one kingdom, but, waylaid at sea by the combined Danish and Swedish fleets, he jumped overboard and disappeared. His heroic deeds are recounted in many Norse sagas.

**Mahmud of Ghazni,** age 29?; Muslim sultan of Ghazni from 999–1030, son of a Turkish slave. A great conqueror, he extended the boundaries of his small kingdom in central Afghanistan west to the Tigris and east to the Ganges. He terrorized northern India by looting, destroying

# 1025–1050

Edwin the Elder, son of Alfred the Great, succeeded his father in 899 and reigned until 924. He was succeeded by each of his three sons in turn: Athelstan, Edmund the Magnificent and Edred. Then came Edwy, the eldest son of Edmund the Magnificent, and Edgar the Peaceful, his younger brother, who was succeeded in turn by his two sons, Edmund the Martyr and Ethelred the Unready. The latter reigned from 978–1016 and was the great-great-grandson of Alfred the Great. By this time the Danes had become troublesome again. Ethelred was forced to pay tribute, but this did not stop the raids; as the coasts were ravaged, the interior was plundered by Danes who had come to stay. England was in chaos and an easy conquest for Sweyn Forkbeard in 1014. Ethelred fled to the court of his wife's brother, the duke of Normandy. Sweyn's triumph, however, was brief, for he died the same year, and the English nobles recalled Ethelred. Sweyn's son Canute, then 20, was forced

# 1025

temples and making forcible conversions to Islam. His conquests were not permanent, but parts of India remained Muslim. He was the patron, though ungenerous, of Firdausi.

**Stephen I** (St. Stephen), age 25; first king of Hungary (1001–1038), of the Arpad dynasty. Son of the duke of Hungary, he was converted to Christianity as a youth. For his coronation in 1001 Pope Sylvester II sent a crown, which remained the sacred symbol of Hungarian nationality for 900 years. He was granted the title of Apostolic Majesty and is the patron saint of Hungary.

**Murasaki Shikibu** (Lady Murasaki), age c.22; Japanese novelist and court figure of the Fujiwara period, author of the famous *Tale of Genji (Genji Monogatari),* which is an account of the life and romantic adventures of Prince Genji. Written in a subtle, sensitive manner, it is highly praised by Western critics. Lady Murasaki's diary for the years 1007–1010, revealing more details of court life, is also extant.

**Avicenna** (ibn-Sina), age 20; Persian philosopher and physician born near Bokhara. The most famous philosopher of medieval Islam, he was, like his predecessors, influenced by Aristotle and the Neoplatonists. Latin translations of his work stimulated European interest in Aristotle, while his *Canon of Medicine* was widely used as a standard textbook both in the Middle East and Europe.

**al-Hakim,** age 15; sixth Fatimid caliph of north Africa and Egypt (996–1021); called the Mad Caliph. He reversed the policy of religious toleration practiced by the Abbasids, persecuting Jews and Christians, destroying the Church of the Holy Sepulcher in Jerusalem and prohibiting pilgrimages to the Holy Land. In 1020 this unstable ruler declared himself an incarnation of God, and a year later he was assassinated, at 36. The First Crusade began 75 years later.

# 1025

Canute II
  (994-1035), age 31
Edward the Confessor
  (1002/1003-1066), age c.23
St. Leo IX (Pope)
  (1002-1054), age 23
Macbeth
  (      -1057), age ?
Robert Guiscard
  (c.1015-1085), age c.10
St. Gregory VII (Pope)
  (1020?-1085), age 5?

to flee, but he returned in 1015 with a great fleet and a powerful army to reconquer England. London was still holding out in 1016 when Ethelred died. The English nobles elected Canute king; Edmund Ironside, Ethelred's son, was simultaneously proclaimed king by the people of London. A treaty was concluded, dividing the rule between Edmund and Canute; but in November, at the age of 36, Edmund Ironside died, leaving Canute and the Danes in control.

The period of turbulence ended suddenly, and was followed by an era of peace during which England slowly recovered from its devastation. Canute reigned 19 years and died at the age of 41. He was succeeded by his two incompetent sons, Harold I or Harold Harefoot (1035–40), and Hardecanute (1040–42), his son by Emma of Normandy, the widow of Ethelred. The real force in the government was the Danish earl Godwin. After the death of Hardecanute, Ethelred's younger son, Edward, was recalled from Normandy and crowned king, with the blessing of Godwin, whose daughter he married. So ended the period of the Danish conquest. Edward the Confessor reigned 24 years, and then the period of the Norman Conquest began.

# 1050

# 1025

Basil II (Byzantine emperor)
  (c.958-1025), age c.67
Michinaga
  (966-1027), age 59
Mahmud of Ghazni
  (971?-1030), age 54?
Stephen I of Hungary
  (975-1038), age 50
Murasaki Shikibu
  (c.978-1031?), age c.47
Avicenna
  (980-1037), age 45

**Canute II** (Canute the Great), age 31; king of the Danes from 1018–1035 and king of England from 1016–1035, son of Sweyn Forkbeard. After his father's sudden death in 1014, Canuet had to reconquer England. Edmund Ironsides' death in 1016 left him in full control of the country and added England to his empire, which included Norway and Denmark (ruled by his sons), the coasts of the Baltic states and Poland. He was a strong supporter of the church and popular with his English subjects.

**Edward the Confessor,** age c.23; king of England from 1042–1066, son of Ethelred the Unready and the last of the Anglo-Saxon line. A cousin of William the Conqueror, he was recalled from Normandy and

# 1050–1075

Three men hoped to succeed Edward the Confessor as king of England: Harold Hardrada, king of Norway; Harold, son of Godwin; and William, duke of Normandy. William, as the king's cousin, seemed to have the best chance, for Edward had no heirs more closely related. It was generally believed that he had promised William the crown. Moreover, when Godwin's son Harold visited Normandy in 1064, William extracted from him an oath to support his own claim. Late in 1065 the king was seriously ill, however, and Harold—his chief minister since Godwin's death in 1053—was with him. It appears that at the last moment Edward designated Harold as his successor, and on the day after the king's death he was crowned Harold II. He was king January 6 to October 14. In September of the same year, 1066, Harold III of Norway, Harold Hardrada, set sail with a great fleet

# 1050

Edward the Confessor
  (1002/03-1066), age c.48

**Macbeth,** age ?; king of Scotland from 1040–1057, son of the governor of the province of Moray. In 1040 he became king after killing Duncan I in battle. Seventeen years later he was killed in the battle of

placed on the throne after the death of Canute's son. A devout Christian, he built monasteries which served as inns for travelers as well as centers of learning; codified the Anglo-Saxon laws; and founded Westminster Abbey, in which he was buried. He was canonized in 1161.

**St. Leo IX** (Bruno of Egisheim), age 23; German ecclesiastic born in Alsace; pope from 1049–1054. A bishop at 27, he was elected pope through the influence of Emperor Henry III, to whom he was related. With Cardinal Archdeacon Hildebrand (later Pope Gregory VII) to assist him, he vigorously suppressed heresy and defended clerical celibacy. The bitterness between the Eastern and Western churches culminated in 1054 in a formal schism, as Leo and the patriarch of Constantinople excommunicated one another.

with the intention of conquering England. Harold II was in the south, preparing for an expected attack from Normandy; he hurried north and met the invaders at Stamford Bridge, near York. In a great battle on September 25, Harold Hardrada was killed and his army destroyed. Twenty-five ships carried away the survivors of an army that had come in 300.

Nineteen days later the battle of Hastings was fought. William had slipped across the channel and landed at Pevensey September 27. The size of his army is not known, although the numbers actually engaged at Hastings were not large. Harold hurried south and camped nine miles from Hastings, on the edge of a forest, with sloping ground all around. Early on Saturday morning, October 14, the Normans made a surprise attack. Time after time they were beaten back, until, as dusk was falling, Harold II was killed by an arrow. William was crowned on Christmas Day in Westminster Abbey. Although his reign was frequently troubled by revolts of rebellious Saxons, he eventually restored peace and order to England, where his descendants still wear the crown.

Lumphanan by Duncan's son, who became Malcolm III. Lady Macbeth, whose name was Gruoch, was a granddaughter of Kenneth III, who had been overthrown by Malcolm II, ancestor of Duncan. Shakespeare's source for his play *Macbeth* was Holinshed's *Chronicles*.

## 1050

Macbeth
    (    -1057), age ?
Robert Guiscard
    (c. 1015-1085), age c.35
St. Gregory VII (Pope)
    (1020?-1085), age 30?
William I of England
    (1027/28-1087), age c.23
Alp Arslan
    (1029-1072), age 21
St. Anselm
    (1033-1109), age 19
The Cid
    (1040?-1099), age 10?
Pope Urban II
    (c.1042-1099), age c.8
Malik Shah
    (    -1092), age ?
Alexius I Comnenus
    (1048-1118), age 2

## 1075

St. Anselm
    (1033-1109), age 42

Pope Leo IX
(1002-1054), age 48

Robert Guiscard, age c.35; Norman adventurer, conqueror of southern Italy. He captured Rome in 1084 and delivered Pope Gregory VII from the Castel Sant' Angelo, where he had taken refuge from the emperor Henry IV.

St. Gregory VII (Hildebrand), age 30?; Benedictine monk born in Tuscany, one of the greatest of popes (1073–1085). Upholding the supremacy of the church over kings and emperors, he excommunicated Henry IV, Holy Roman emperor, who stood for three days in penance at Canossa in 1077. Subsequently deposed by the Emperor's forces, Gregory retired to Salerno in 1084 under the protection of Robert Guiscard and died the following year.

William I (William the Conqueror), age c.23; duke of Normandy from 1035–1087 and king of England from 1066–1087. He invaded

# 1075–1100

The 11th century was a period of reawakening in Europe, the beginning of a Christian counteroffensive against Islam on two fronts—in the Holy Land and in Spain. For three centuries the small Christian kingdoms of northern Spain, Leon, Navarre and Castile had retained their independence, and now they began to enlarge their territory. Sancho III, king of Navarre from 1000–1035, seized part of Aragon from the Moors. His second son, Ferdinand I of Castile and Leon, who ruled from 1033–1065, acquired more territory and gained control of what is now northern Portugal. In 1056 he proclaimed himself emperor of Spain, although the Muslims still held most of the country.

The reconquest was hastened by the collapse of the caliphate of Cordoba. Hisham III, who reigned from 1027–1031, was the last caliph. After his death, the country broke up into small Muslim kingdoms. Granada, Seville, Toledo, Sar-

Robert Guiscard
(c.1015-1085), age c.60
Pope Gregory VII
(1020?-1085), age 55?
William I of England
(1027/28-1087), age c.48

St. Anselm, age 42; Christian theologian and philosopher born in Italy, archbishop of Canterbury from 1093–1109. Called the founder of scholasticism, he is famous for his ontological proof of the existence of God, which follows this line of reasoning: Since what exists in reality as well as in the mind is greater than what exists in the mind alone, and since the mind can conceive the idea of a being greater than anything else, it follows that this being must exist in reality as well as in the

England on the death of Edward the Confessor, and the installation of Harold II as king, defeated Harold II in the battle of Hastings in 1066 and was crowned in Westminster Abbey on Christmas Day. He refused to pay homage to the pope and organized the church as a dependency of the English crown.

**Alp Arslan** (Conquering Lion), age 21; sultan of the Seljuk Turks from 1063–1072; great-grandson of Seljuk, the tribal ancestor, and son of Togrul Beg, who conquered Persia and entered Baghdad in 1055. Alp Arslan added Georgia and Armenia to the realm of the Seljuks (1064–1065); he defeated and took prisoner Romanus IV, the Byzantine emperor (1071); and gained control of Jerusalem. He was succeeded by his son, Malik Shah.

# 1075

The Cid
(1040?-1099), age 35?
Pope Urban II
(c.1042-1099), age c.33
Malik Shah
(    -1092), age ?
Alexius I Comnenus
(1048-1118), age 27
Henry IV (Emperor)
(1050-1106), age 25
Omar Khayyam
(    -1123), age ?
al-Ghazzali
(1058-1111), age 17
Godfrey of Bouillon
(1060/61-1100), age c.15

agossa and Valencia became capitals of independent states; together they might have offered effective resistance, but individually they were no match for the resurgent Christian kingdoms. With the advantage on the Christian side, the son of Ferdinand, Alfonso el Bravo—who was Alfonso VI of Leon and Alfonso I of Castile and reigned from 1065–1109— continued the offensive with the assistance of the Cid (el Cid Campeador) and his celebrated feats of arms. Alfonso's capture of Toledo in 1085 put him deeply into central Spain, south of modern Madrid and only 150 miles from Cordoba. Alarmed at his advances, the Moors called for aid from Yusuf ibn-Tashfin, the Berber emir of north Africa, who led an army into Spain and defeated Alfonso in 1086. Alfonso still held Toledo and established his capital there. This Christian outpost in the heart of Muslim Spain had immense significance for northern Europe. It was a meeting place of the two cultures and a channel of communication through which the civilizing influence of Muslim Spain passed to the northern countries, hastening their technological as well as intellectual development.

# 1100

mind, or it is not greater than anything else.

**The Cid** (el Cid Campeador, the Lord Champion), Rodrigo Diaz de Vivar, age 35?; Spanish soldier and hero born near Burgos, famous for his exploits against the Moors. As a soldier of fortune in his later years, he served both Spaniards and Arabs. He is the subject of many legends and stories, of Corneille's drama and of Massenet's opera.

**Urban II** (Odo or Eudes de Chatillon), age c.33; French ecclesiastic;

al-Ghazzali
(1058-1111), age 42
Godfrey of Bouillon
(1060/61-1100), age c.40
Tancred
(1076/78-1112), age c.22

123

pope from 1088–1099. He vigorously asserted the supremacy of the church and excommunicated Emperor Henry IV and Philip I of France. In 1095 he preached the sermon that launched the First Crusade.

**Malik Shah,** age ?; sultan of the Seljuk Turks from 1072–1092, son of Alp Arslan. He consolidated and ably administered his great empire, as Seljuk power in the Middle East reached its zenith. He founded the University of Baghdad and appointed a panel of astronomers, which included Omar Khayyam, to reform the calendar.

**Alexius I Comnenus,** age 27; Byzantine emperor from 1081–1118, nephew of Isaac I, who founded the Comnenus dynasty, which succeeded the Macedonian. Following a series of weak monarchs, he restored military power and prestige to the empire and withstood attacks from Scythians, Seljuks and Normans (under Robert Guiscard). When the armies of the First Crusade arrived, he persuaded them—in exchange for money, supplies and transportation—to promise to return to him all former Byzantine territories that they might recon-

# 1100–1125

From 1096 to 1270 there were eight crusades—not counting the Children's Crusade of 1212—undertaken for the recovery of the Holy Land from the Muslims. Since 637, when the caliph Omar I took it from the Byzantine emperor, Palestine had been a part of Islam. However, both the Umayyad and Abbasid caliphs practiced a policy of toleration and permitted Christian pilgrims to come and go freely. In the 10th century the Fatimid caliphate of north Africa expanded eastward; about 969 Moizz, the fourth caliph, took Egypt, Syria and Palestine from the Abbasids. With the accession of the sixth caliph in 996, trouble began. A fanatical Muslim, al-Hakim suppressed Jews and Christians and forbade pilgrimages to the Holy Land. A further provocation occurred when the Seljuk Turks invaded the Near East under Alp Arslan. They defeated and took prisoner the Byzantine emperor Romanus IV in 1071 and captured Damascus and

St. Anselm
   (1033-1109), age 67
Alexius I (Byzantine emperor)
   (1048-1118), age 52
Henry IV (Emperor)
   (1050-1106), age 50
Omar Khayyam
   (    -1123), age ?

**al-Ghazzali,** age 42; Persian philosopher and theologian born in Khurasan. Regarded as the philosopher of Sufism, he endeavored to reconcile mysticism with orthodox Islam. He taught at Baghdad from 1091–1095, but abandoned the post for 10 years of wandering. His works were well known and influential in medieval Europe.

**Godfrey of Bouillon,** age c.40; French nobleman, duke of Lower Lorraine, leader in the First Crusade. He is the romantic hero of legend and story whose capture of Jerusalem on July 15, 1099, with an army of 20,000 is related in Tasso's *Jerusalem Delivered*.

quer, which they sometimes did. His biography was written by his learned daughter, Anna Comnenus.

**Henry IV,** age 25; king of Germany and Holy Roman emperor from 1056–1106. Excommunicated by Gregory VII for claiming it was the king's right to appoint bishops, he stood three days barefoot at the castle of Canossa in 1077 before being granted absolution. In 1084 he deposed Gregory by force and appointed Clement III. He was himself deposed and imprisoned in 1105 by an impatient son, but he escaped and died the following year.

**Omar Khayyam,** age ?; Persian poet and scientist born in Khurasan, son of a tentmaker. A notable mathematician of his time, the author of treatises on algebra and one of the eight men appointed by Sultan Malik Shah to reform the calendar, he is remembered today for the *Rugaiyat* (Quatrains), freely translated into English and rearranged by Edward FitzGerald (published in 1859). The hedonism of the poem is not typical of Persian poetry. One very famous line is: "The Moving Finger writes; and having writ/Moves on."

# 1100

Peter Abelard
    (1079-1142), age 21
St. Bernard of Clairvaux
    (1090/91-1153), age c.10
Conrad III of Germany
    (1093-1152), age 7

Jerusalem from the Fatimids. Pilgrimages were again forbidden.

A fever of religious enthusiasm swept through Europe after Pope Urban II preached his famous sermon in November 1095. Many hasty, ill-equipped expeditions set out and ended disastrously. The main armies, after careful preparations for a long campaign, left in the summer and fall of 1096. The principal leaders were Gidfrey of Bouillon; Bohemond, the son of Robert Guiscard; Tancred, Bohemond's nephew; Baldwin, brother of Godfrey; and Raymond, count of Toulouse. The combined armies numbered about 100,000 men. They captured Nicaea in May 1097; Antioch in June 1098, after a 7-month seige; and, in the summer of 1099, an army of 20,000 advanced on Jerusalem.

In 1098 the Fatimids, taking advantage of Seljuk weakness after the death in 1092 of Malik Shah, the patron of Omar Khayyam, had recovered Jerusalem and southern Syria. It was the Fatimids that the Crusaders defeated and slaughtered when they captured the city on July 15, 1099. Jerusalem remained Christian for 88 years.

# 1125

**Tancred,** age c.22; Norman hero of the First Crusade, nephew of Robert Guiscard. He joined his cousin, Bohemond, and assisted in the capture of Nicaea and Tarsus and in the seven-month siege of Antioch (which Bohemond kept as his prize). He also aided in the capture of Jerusalem. His valorous deeds are celebrated by Tasso in *Jerusalem Delivered*.

**Peter Abelard,** age 21; French philosopher, theologian and teacher. Best remembered for his tragic romance, his letters to Heloise and his autobiographical *Historia calamitatum,* an account of his misfortunes.

St. Bernard of Clairvaux
    (1090/91-1153), age c.35
Conrad III of Germany
    (1093-1152), age 32
Geoffrey of Monmouth
    (c.1100 1154), age c.25
Peter Lombard
    (1100-1160), age 25
Pope Adrian IV
    (1100-1159), age 25

## 1100

Neither a strict realist (believing that universals such as truth or beauty have a real existence) nor an extreme nominalist (to whom universals

# 1125–1150

The Guelph and Ghibelline political factions of medieval Italy had their origin in the rivalry between two German princely families: the Welfs and the Hohenstaufens. Welf in German became Guelph in Italian; and Waiblingen (an estate belonging to the Hohenstaufens), after losing something in translation, became Ghibelline in Italian. In the long struggle between popes and emperors, the Guelphs were the papal party; the Ghibellines, most numerous in the northern cities of Pisa, Arezzo and Verona, were the imperial party. The poet Dante was a Guelph; the Montefeltro family of Urbino and the Visconti family of Milan were Ghibellines.

The rivalry began during the reign of Emperor Henry IV (1056–1106) and continued with increased bitterness be-

## 1125

Peter Abelard
(1079-1142), age 46

**St. Bernard of Clairvaux,** age c.35; French ecclesiastic and writer, the most influential churchman of his time and principal opponent of Abelard's rationalistic theology. He founded a monastery at Clairvaux, where he remained as abbot until his death. His preaching launched the Second Crusade.

**Conrad III,** age 32; king of Germany from 1138–1152 and founder of the Hohenstaufen dynasty of Holy Roman emperors, although he was never crowned emperor himself. In 1138 the conflict which was known

are no more than the names assigned to them), he was a precursor of the moderate realism of Thomas Aquinas.

Arnold of Brescia
 (1090 or 1100-1155),
 age 25?
Alfonso I of Portugal
 (1109/12-1185), age c.16
Gerard of Cremona
 (1114-1187), age 11
John of Salisbury
 (1110/15-1180), age c.10
Thomas a Becket
 (1118-1170), age 7
Attar
 (1119-1229), age 6
Eleanor of Aquitaine
 (1122-1204), age 3
Frederick I (Emperor)
 (1122/23-1190), age c.2

tween the Guelph Henry the Proud and his son, Henry the Lion, and the Hohenstaufen emperor Conrad III. Both families were originally from Swabia, in southern Germany, and the Welfs (ancestors of the British royal family through the houses of Brunswick and Hanover) traced their descent to Welf, count of Swabia, whose daughter Judith had married Louis the Pious, son of Charlemagne. The most famous Welf was Henry the Lion, who lost his possessions by defying the emperor Frederick Barbarossa.

The most famous Hohenstaufens, who derived their name from their ancestral castle at Staufen in Swabia, were Conrad III, Frederick Barbarossa and Frederick II. The Hohenstaufen emperor Conrad III, with Louis VII of France, led the unsuccessful Second Crusade to the Holy Land (1147–1149), but he is chiefly remembered as the founder of the Hohenstaufen line of emperors. The Guelph–Ghibelline controversy died out in Italy in the 15th century.

in Italy from the 12th to the 15th century as the Guelph-Ghibelline struggle began with Henry the Proud, duke of Bavaria and Saxony; it continued with the latter's son, Henry the Lion. Conrad was the leader, with Louis VII of France, of the Second Crusade, 1047–1049.

**Geoffrey of Monmouth,** age c.25; English ecclesiastic and chronicler; author of a history of early British kings (*Historia regum Britanniae*, compiled from sources now lost), which traces their descent from the Trojans and contains the first large collection of Arthurian legends.

Alfonso I of Portugal
 (1109/12-1185), age c.41
Gerard of Cremona
 (1114-1187), age 36
John of Salisbury
 (1110/15-1180), age c.35
Thomas a Becket
 (1118-1170), age 32

**1125**

**Peter Lombard,** age 25; Italian theologian and bishop of Paris. His *Four Books of Sentences,* a collection of opinions of early fathers of the church, was widely used in medieval theological schools and the subject of many commentaries by eminent philosophers.

**Adrian IV** (Nicholas Breakspear), age 25; English ecclesiastic born near St. Albans; pope from 1154–1159, the only Englishman to become pope. He crowned Frederick I emperor in 1155, but was soon at odds with him over the church's claim of the exclusive right to name archbishops. Historians are in dispute over whether he did or did not

# 1150–1175

As early as the ninth century, reports had reached northern Europe of the wonders of Cordoba: its beautiful buildings, public baths, hospitals and libraries, its fine ceramics and carpets and its craftsmanship in marble and gold. Christian monks were not an uncommon sight in the streets of Cordoba—monasteries in the vicinity, where travelers could obtain food and lodging, were tolerated by the Moors—but there was not a significant amount of trade or communication between Muslim and Christian Europe.

Some scholars, including Gerbert of Aurillac, had already made their way to Spain in the 10th century, but their number was not large until the fall of Toledo to the Christians in 1085. Then the stream of scholars swelled, and the translation of Arabic books began in earnest. Gerard of Cremona is said to have spent 50 years in Cordoba and Toledo, translating 60 books. Other scholars came and went each

**1150**

**Alfonso I,** age c.41; first king of Portugal (1139–1185), son of the count of Portugal. In 1128 he exiled his mother and her Spanish lover,

grant Henry II permission to occupy Ireland as a papal fief.

**Arnold of Brescia** (Arnaldo da Brescia), age 25?; Italian monk and reformer, possibly a pupil of Abelard's in Paris and an early champion of liberty and democratic rights. He headed a popular movement in Rome that set up a republican government and was powerful enough to force Pope Eugenius III briefly into exile. He was idolized by the people, but condemned by Bernard of Clairvaux and forced into exile by Adrian IV; arrested by order of Frederick I, he was returned to Rome, tried and executed by the secular authorities.

Attar
(1119-1229), age 31
Eleanor of Aquitaine
(1122-1204), age 28
Frederick I (Emperor)
(1122/23-1190), age c.27
Averroes
(1126-1198), age 24
Henry the Lion
(1129-1195), age 21
Henry II of England
(1133-1189), age 17
Moses Maimonides
(1135-1204), age 15
Saladin
(1137/38-1193), age c.12
Chretien de Troyes
(fl. 1170), age ?
Yoritomo Minamoto
(1147/48-1199), age c.2

year. The debt of Christian Europe to Muslim science is most evident in astronomy, particularly in the names of the stars. Not only do the seven stars of the Big Dipper bear Arabic names (Alkaid, Mizar, Alioth, Megrez, Phecda, Merak and Dubhe), but in tables of stars of lesser magnitude, Arabic names predominate: Sadalsuud, Albali, Suhail, Hadar, Saak, Mirzam etc.

More curious is the fact that all first-magnitude stars with common Arabic names may be seen at one particular season of the year. They follow one another across the sky in a steady procession, beginning with Vega, Deneb and Altair, and continuing with Fomalhaut, Aldebaran, Betelguese and Rigel. Vega, Deneb and Rigel are overhead in August and early September. At midnight in September Betelguese and Rigel come into view, but the next first-magnitude stars to appear, Sirius and Procyon, are not visible until midnight the first of November. They bear Latin and Greek names, because by this time the traveling scholars, anxious to get home before the first snow, were well on their way. Traveling was hazardous, and there were bears and wolves in the Pyrenees.

who had ruled since the death of his father in 1112, and began to fashion an independent kingdom. He won victories over the Moors and

St. Bernard of Clairvaux
(1090/91-1153), age c.60
Conrad III of Germany
(1093-1152), age 57
Geoffrey of Monmouth
(c.1100-1154), age c.50
Peter Lombard
(1100-1160), age 50
Pope Adrian IV
(1100-1159), age 50
Arnold of Brescia
(1090 or 1100-1155),
age 50?

in 1139 proclaimed himself king. He took Lisbon from the Moors in 1147 and won papal recognition as an independent sovereign in 1179.

**Gerard of Cremona,** age 36; Italian scholar, one of the first and most famous translators of Arabic works into Latin. A member of the College of Translators in Toledo, Spain—founded by Archbishop Raymond—he translated Aristotle, Euclid, Hippocrates, Galen, al-Kindi, Avicenna and the *Almagest,* helping to dispel the darkness of medieval Europe.

**John of Salisbury,** age c.35; English ecclesiastic and scholastic philosopher born in Salisbury. He studied in Paris under Abelard and served as secretary to the archbishop of Canterbury (both Becket and his predecessor). The author of *Policraticus,* which contains a description of an ideal state ruled by clergy, as well as biographies of Becket and St. Anselm, he was in the cathedral when Thomas a Becket was murdered.

**Thomas a Becket,** age 32; English prelate of Norman parentage born in London. As archbishop of Canterbury he was renowned for his zeal in upholding the law of the church. He left England in 1164 to escape the jurisdiction of lay courts and returned in 1170 after a reconciliation had been forced upon Henry II. On Dec. 29, he was murdered in the cathedral by four knights of the court. He is the subject of T. S. Eliot's verse play *Murder in the Cathedral.*

**Attar** (Farid ud-Din), age 31; Persian Sufi poet, a druggist by trade, born in Nishapur. An expounder of Sufi doctrines, he is best known for *Mantiq ut Tair (Language of Birds),* an allegorical poem of 4,600 couplets. He also wrote about the lives of the Sufis and is said to have lived 110 years.

**Eleanor of Aquitaine,** age 28; duchess of Aquitaine, who succeeded her father in 1137 at the age of 15. She married Louis VII of France

# 1175–1200

The opportunity offered by the decline of both the Seljuk empire and the Fatimid caliphate in the Near East was seized by an upstart conqueror named Nur ad-Din, the son of Zangi, a chieftain of Turkish descent. He continued his father's conquests and established himself as sultan of Syria, becoming the principal opponent of the Christians in the Second Crusade. His next target was Egypt, to which the Fatimids still clung, and which his general, Shirkuh, conquered 1164–1168. Shirkuh was made vizier at Cairo and at his death in 1169 was succeeded by his nephew, Saladin, an ambitious and shrewd man of Kurdish descent. The Shi'ite caliph retained a shadow of prestige as spiritual leader, but in 1171 Saladin ordered his name dropped from the Friday prayers and that of the Abbasid Sunni caliph substituted. The Fatimid caliphate was thus abolished, even before the death of Adid,

and accompanied him on the Second Crusade. Accused of adultery and divorced in 1152, she married Henry of Anjou (later Henry II of England), inaugurating 400 years of contention over Aquitaine. She was not only the wife of two kings but also the mother of two: Richard the Lion-Hearted and John.

**Frederick I, or Frederick Barbarossa,** (red beard), age c.27; king of Germany and Holy Roman emperor from 1152–1190 and king of Italy from 1155–1190. He ruled a peaceful and prosperous Germany but failed in his long struggle to subjugate northern Italian cities. The rout of his mounted knights at Legnano by an infantry army made 1176 a significant date in military history; and 1177 became a significant date in the history of the papacy when he courteously held the pope's stirrup. He departed on the Third Crusade in 1189 and drowned while crossing a river in Asia Minor.

**Averroes, or ibn-Rushd,** age 24; Spanish-Arabian philosopher born in Spain, physician to the caliph of Morocco. His commentaries on Aristotle and his attempt to reconcile religion and philosophy strongly influenced the development of Christian scholasticism. He is the author of the theory of the "double truth," regarding religion as an allegorical world view held by the ordinary man unable to grasp the truths of philosophy.

**Henry the Lion,** age 21; duke of Saxony from 1139–1180 and of Bavaria from 1156–1180, son of Henry the Proud, of the house of Welf (Guelph). A powerful lord whose possessions extended from the North Sea to the Adriatic, he engaged in a long, complicated struggle with Conrad III, king of Germany, of the house of Hohenstaufen (Ghibelline). After being deprived of his possessions in 1180 by Emperor Frederick I, he spent much time in England. His second wife was the daughter of Henry II.

# 1175

Henry II of England
(1133-1189), age 42
Moses Maimonides
(1135-1204), age 40
Saladin
(1137/38-1193), age c.37
Chretien de Troyes
(fl. 1170), age ?
Yoritomo Minamoto
(1147/48-1199), age c.27
Richard I of England
(1157-1199), age 18
Pope Innocent III
(1160/61-1216), age c.14
Wolfram von Eschenbach
(1165 or 1170-1220), age 10?
Philip II of France
(1165-1223), age 10
Genghis Khan
(1162 or 1167-1227), age 8?
John of England
(1167-1216), age 8
St. Dominic
(1170-1221), age 5
Walther von der Vogelweide
(1170-1230), age 5

the 14th and last Fatimid caliph, in the same year. Saladin's growing power and influence alarmed Nur ad-Din, but before he could move against his vizier he died, in 1174, leaving Saladin sultan of Egypt and soon of Syria as well.

This was the Muslim encountered by the Christians of the Third Crusade. He had expanded his realm east, west and north. In 1187 he captured Jerusalem, ending the Latin Kingdom established with the victories of the First Crusade. The crusade to recover Jerusalem a second time was led by the emperor Frederick Barbarossa, Philip II of France and Richard the Lion-Hearted. They left in the spring and summer of 1190. Frederick Barbarossa, the one most feared by Saladin, drowned in Asia Minor in June, and the German army dispersed. Philip and Richard arrived at Acre in the spring of 1191 and captured the city in July. They quarreled, however, and Philip returned home. Richard continued the war until October 1192, when he concluded a truce with Saladin which permitted pilgrimages to Jerusalem. Accepting this partial success, Richard departed for England.

# 1200

**Alfonso I of Portugal**
(1109/12-1185), age c.66
**Gerard of Cremona**
(1114-1187), age 61
**John of Salisbury**
(1110/15-1180), age c.60
**Attar**
(1119-1229), age 56
**Eleanor of Aquitaine**
(1122-1204), age 53
**Frederick I (Emperor)**
(1122/23-1190), age c.52
**Averroes**
(1126-1198), age 49
**Henry the Lion**
(1129-1195), age 46

**Henry II** (Henry Plantagenet), age 42; king of England from 1154–1189, first of the Plantagenet kings; son of Geoffrey Plantagenet, count of Anjou, and of Matilda, daughter of Henry I of England; great-grandson of William the Conqueror and husband of Eleanor of Aquitaine. He inherited extensive territories in France, which together with England formed a sizable Angevin empire. After the murder and canonization (in 1172) of Becket, he was compelled to walk barefoot through the streets and submit to a flogging by the monks of Canterbury. He was succeeded by his son, Richard the Lion-Hearted.

**Moses Maimonides** (Moses ben Maimon), age 40; Jewish philosopher born in Spain; physician to Saladin, the sultan of Egypt. He wrote *Guide for the Perplexed,* an elucidation of religious and metaphysical problems, and attempted to reconcile Judaism with Aristotle.

**Saladin** (Salah-al-Din), age c.37; sultan of Egypt and Syria from 1175–1193, of Kurdish descent. He succeeded his uncle in 1169 as vizier at Cairo for Nur ad-Din of Aleppo, sultan of Syria and Egypt; after the death of Nur ad-Din in 1174, he proclaimed himself sultan. He is famous for his courageous resistance to the Crusaders led by Richard the Lion-Hearted and for Sir Walter Scott's portrayal of him in *The Talisman.*

# 1200–1225

In the 13th century the Mongols, riding out of the Asian steppes, cut a swath through history as they built an empire on terror and cruelty. Upon the death of Genghis Khan in 1227, the empire was divided among the sons of his favorite wife. Juji or Juchi, the eldest, died before his father, but his son, Batu Khan, became ruler of the Golden Horde in southern Russia. Jagatai, the second son, received the khanate of Turkestan. Ogadai, the third son, received the khanate of east Asia, with a capital at Karakorum, and the title of the Great Khan. Tului, the youngest son, is least

## 1200

**Chretien de Troyes** (Christian of Troyes), age ?; French poet, originator of the medieval courtly romance. He wrote five romances on the Arthurian legend (including the story of the Holy Grail), which were widely translated and imitated.

**Yoritomo Minamoto,** age c.27; first shogun (dictator) of Japan (1192–1199). Upon the decline of the Fujiwara family, the landowning families of Minamoto and Taira contended for power. Yoritomo crushed his enemies, eliminated many members of his own family and in 1192 assumed the title of shogun. He established a centralized feudal system controlled by a military dictatorship, which ruled Japan for seven centuries.

**Richard I** (Richard the Lion-Hearted), age 18; king of England from 1189–1199, third son of Henry II. He joined the Third Crusade in 1191 and recovered parts of the Holy Land. Returning home, he was seized in Austria and held for ransom by Emperor Henry VI, who demanded 100,000 pounds and his kingdom. Home in 1194, he stayed two months and returned to the wars. He was mortally wounded at 42 by an arrow in the shoulder.

Pope Innocent III
   (1160/61-1216), age c.39
Wolfram von Eschenbach
   (1165 or 1170-1220),
   age 35?
Philip II of France
   (1165-1223), age 35
Genghis Khan
   (1162 or 1167-1227),
   age 33?
John of England
   (1167-1216), age 33
St. Dominic
   (1170-1221), age 30
Walther von der Vogelweide
   (1170-1230), age 30
Robert Grosseteste
   (c.1175-1253), age c.25
Snorri Sturluson
   (1178/79-1241), age c.22
St. Francis of Assisi
   (1182-1226), age 18
Sadi
   (1184 or 1194-1282 or 1292),
   age 16?
Ogadai
   (1185-1241), age 15
St. Albertus Magnus
   (1193 or 1205/06-1280),
   age 7?
Frederick II (Emperor)
   (1194-1250), age 6

known, but his three sons—Mangu Khan, Kublai Khan and Hulagu Khan—were conquerors, like their grandfather. After the third generation, the Mongol Empire declined, disintegrated and finally disappeared, but its reputation for barbaric cruelty survived.

Savagery, however, was not solely the prerogative of the Mongols. In Europe from 1198 to 1208, there were two Holy Roman emperors: the Guelph Otto IV, duke of Bavaria and Saxony and son of Henry the Lion; and the Hohenstaufen Philip, duke of Swabia. The latter was one of the leaders of the infamous Fourth Crusade (1202–1204). The other leaders were the aged and nearly blind doge of Venice, Enrico Dandolo; Baldwin IX, count of Flanders; and other French and Flemish nobles. Launched by Pope Innocent III to recover the Holy Land and explore the possibility of unifying the Eastern and Western churches, the Fourth Crusade went astray. Taking sides in a Byzantine factional dispute, the leaders besieged and captured Constantinople. For three days in April 1204 they sacked the city, destroying irreplacable treasures, priceless art and monuments in a display of barbarism not surpassed by the Mongols. The Latin Empire of

Attar
(1119-1229), age 81
Eleanor of Aquitaine
(1122-1204), age 78
Moses Maimonides
(1135-1204), age 65

**Innocent III** (Giovanni Lotario de Conti), age c.39; Italian ecclesiastic of noble birth; pope from 1198–1216. Emulating the zeal of Gregory VII in his defense of the church's prerogatives, he deposed two European monarchs and forced their submission. Under him the papacy reached the zenith of its temporal power.

**Wolfram von Eschenbach,** age 35?; German epic poet and minnesinger. He is the author of *Parzival,* a long poem on the legend of the Holy Grail, based in part on Chretien de Troyes' *Perceval,* and the source of Wagner's *Parsifal*.

GENGHIS KHAN
Mongol chieftain
1162 or 1167-1227

**Genghis Khan** (Temujin), age 33?; Mongol chieftain born near Lake Baikal. He invaded northern China and Korea, plundered northern India and overran Iran, Iraq and southern Russia, creating an empire that extended from Hungary to Korea. He was the grandfather of Kublai Khan.

# 1225 – 1250

After the capture of Toledo from the Moors in 1085, the Christian reconquest of Spain proceeded slowly until the 13th century, when a new offensive by the Christian kingdoms delivered a series of crushing blows to the Muslims.

Constantinople was established, and Baldwin was crowned emperor in the Church of Santa Sophia as Baldwin I. The sacking of this Christian city horrified Europe, caused the papacy to lose prestige and dealt Constantinople a blow from which it never fully recovered.

**Philip II** (Philip Augustus), age 35; king of France from 1180–1223, called one of the greatest monarchs of the Middle Ages. He departed on the Third Crusade in 1190 with Richard the Lion-Hearted, but quarreled with him and returned. The English territories in France that he seized were retaken by Richard, but after Richard's death in 1099 Philip took Normandy, Brittany, Anjou and other provinces from King John, doubling the size of his kingdom. France became a leading power, as trade flourished and towns grew.

**John** (John Lackland), age 33; king of England from 1199–1216, brother and successor of Richard the Lion-Hearted. An unpopular, tyrannical monarch, he lost the English possessions in France and was forced by his feudal barons to sign the Magna Carta in 1215.

**St. Dominic** (Domingo de Guzman), age 30; Spanish priest born in Castile. He preached ten years in southern France against the Albigensian heresy and founded, at Toulouse in 1215, an order of preaching friars known as the Dominicans or Black Friars (from their black hooded coats), which acquired great power and influence.

**Walther von der Vogelweide,** age 30; German poet and minnesinger, called the greatest lyric poet of the Middle Ages. He lived as a wandering singer, going from court to court, and is famous for his series of love songs *Unter der Linden.*

**Robert Grosseteste** (great head), **Robert of Lincoln,** age c.25; English prelate and scholar born in Suffolk and one of the most learned men of the Middle Ages. As the first rector of the Franciscan school at Oxford, he made it into an important center of learning that profoundly influenced medieval thought. Roger Bacon was among his pupils. He wrote commentaries on Aristotle and treatises on various scientific subjects.

**Snorri Sturluson,** age c.22; Icelandic historian and statesman, author of a poetical chronicle of early Norse kings, but better known for the *Younger* or *Prose Edda,* a compendium of Norse mythology. He was assassinated by political enemies.

St. Francis of Assisi
(1182-1226), age 43
Sadi
(1184 or 1194-1282
or 1292), age 41?
Ogadai
(1185-1241), age 40
St. Albertus Magnus
(1193 or 1205/06-1280),
age 32?
Frederick II (Emperor)
(1194-1250), age 31
Batu Khan
( -1255), age ?
Jalal ud-Din Rumi
(1207-1273), age 18
Simon de Montfort
(1208?-1265), age 17?
Louis IX of France
(1214-1270), age 11
Roger Bacon
(c.1214-1294), age c.11
Kublai Khan
(1215/16-1294), age c.10
Hulagu Khan
(1217-1265), age 8
Rudolf I (Emperor)
(1218-1291), age 7
Alexander Nevski
(1220-1263), age 5
St. Bonaventura
(1221-1274), age 4

In July 1212, the armies of Alfonso VIII of Castile, Pedro II of Aragon and Sancho VII of Navarre converged on the Moorish army at Navas de Tolosa, near Toledo, and won an overwhelming victory. The offensive was continued by Ferdinand el Bravo. Crowned king of Castile and Leon in 1230 as Ferdinand III, he devoted his energy for the next twenty years to fighting the Moors. In another joint effort of Castile and Aragon, Ferdinand took Cordoba in 1236. It was no longer the capital, but it was the greatest city. As the former seat of Moorish power, its capture was a great symbolic loss. The great mosque, begun in the eighth century, one of the glories of Muslim architecture, was made a Christian cathedral. In 1248 Ferdinand captured Seville, and the Christian advance continued until the end of the century. Armies of Castile and Aragon took Gibraltar, where Tarik had landed in 711, in 1296. The Moors still held the region around Cadiz, a small part of what is now Portugal, and the kingdom of Granada, which was the last holdout. The Moors were not expelled from Granada until 1492.

## 1225

Attar
   (1119-1229), age 106
Genghis Khan
   (1162 or 1167-1227),
   age 58?
Walther von der Vogelweide
   (1170-1230), age 55
Robert Grosseteste
   (c.1175-1253), age c.50
Snorri Sturluson
   (1178/79-1241), age c.47

**St. Francis of Assissi** (Giovanni Francesco Bernardone), age 43; Italian friar, founder of the Franciscan order. Son of a wealthy merchant, he took vows of poverty at an early age and founded his order, known originally as the Gray Friars in 1209; in 1212 established the Order of Poor Ladies (Poor Clares). The *Little Flowers of St. Francis* is a collection of stories and legends of later date.

**Sadi, or Saadi** (Muslih ud-Din), age 41?; Persian Sufi poet born at Shiraz, one of the most celebrated and popular poets of his country. He wrote moralistic and epigramatic prose on the ways of dervishes and kings, and lyrical poetry of beauty and warmth. Goethe, Emerson and Thoreau were among his admirers. His best-known works are the *Bustan* (Garden of fruits) and the *Gulistan* (Rose garden); some familiar lines are: "Conclude not that there is a fire in the hovel of thy indigent neighbor. The smoke that thou seest issuing from the chimney is the sigh of his heart."

**Ogadai,** age 40; Mongol khan, third son of Genghis Khan. He built a great palace at Karakorum in Mongolia; began to consolidate the empire; and sent his nephew. Batu Khan, to conquer Europe in 1237. He died in 1241 and in 1251 his line of the family was supplanted by Mangu Khan and Kublai Khan, grandsons of Genghis Khan.

## 1250

# 1250–1275

As Christian Europe pushed back its geographical frontiers in Spain and in the East, its intellectual frontiers were

Spain's political and cultural preeminence in the 15th and 16th centuries can be attributed to its Moorish heritage. The Christians of Spain enjoyed an early advantage over the rest of Europe as the heirs of an advanced Islamic civilization. Their court and their manners were models to be imitated, their craftsmanship and technology matter to be learned and their wealth a blessing to be envied. They got by far the best of the bargain; when the Moors took Spain from the Visigoths, it was a poor, uncivilized country; when they gave it back to the Spaniards, it was wealthy beyond belief.

**1250**

**St. Albertus Magnus** (Count Albert von Bollstadt), age 32?; German scholastic philosopher, theologian and scientist, born in Swabia of a noble family. He was popularly believed to be a magician because of his extensive knowledge of chemistry and the physical sciences, and was the teacher of Thomas Aquinas. He was canonized in 1932.

**Frederick II,** age 31; king of Germany and Holy Roman emperor from 1215–1250; also known as Frederick I, king of Sicily from 1198–1250; the grandson of Frederick Barbarossa. A generally enlightened and skeptical monarch, he lived in Palermo, Sicily, at a court of Oriental splendor, and promoted literature and science (sometimes by means of inhuman experiments on his subjects). He was excommunicated three times.

**Batu Khan,** age ?; Mongol conqueror, grandson of Genghis Khan. Sent by his uncle Ogadai, the great khan, to invade Europe, he plundered Moscow and conquered Russia, Poland and Hungary. In 1241, as he was preparing to invade Germany, he was recalled by the death of Ogadai. He founded the Mongol state of the Golden Horde, or the Western Kipchak khanate, and lived in splendor at his capital on the Volga River.

Jalal ud-Din Rumi
(1207-1273), age 43
Simon de Montfort
(1208?-1265), age 42?
Louis IX of France
(1214-1270), age 36
Roger Bacon
(c.1214-1294), age c.36
Kublai Khan
(1215/16-1294), age c.35
Hulagu Khan
(1217-1265), age 33
Rudolf I (Emperor)
(1218-1291), age 32
Alexander Nevski
(1220-1263), age 30
St. Bonaventura
(1221-1274), age 29
St. Thomas Aquinas
(1225-1274), age 25
Michael VIII (Byzantine
emperor) (1234-1282),
age 16
Pope Boniface VIII
(1235-1303), age 15
Edward I of England
(1239-1307), age 11
Giovanni Cimabue
(c.1240-1302), age c.10
Alexander III of Scotland
(1241-1286), age 9

also expanding. Scholasticism, the philosophy of the schools, engaged the attention of the leading medieval thinkers. Their concern was to reconcile Christian faith with reason, to give faith a rational foundation and content. The Christian articles of belief were their starting point; these they accepted as absolutely and eternally true, and then proceeded to

**1275**

demonstrate that they were also rational, not contradictory to but in harmony with human reason.

The early scholastics were influenced by St. Augustine, the first important Christian philosopher; by the Neoplatonists; and by the Greek philosophers as transmitted to them by Boethius, whose translations and commentaries were their first introduction to Plato and Aristotle. Johannes Scotus Erigena is recognized as the first outstanding thinker of the Middle Ages, but his views were not altogether orthodox. St. Anselm (1033–1109) is called the first scholastic philosopher, for he formulated the basic premise of scholasticism in asserting that reason is the means toward a more complete understanding of faith. He was followed by such subtle thinkers as Peter Abelard, Albertus Magnus, Roger

## 1250

Robert Grosseteste
(c.1175-1253), age c.75
Sadi
(1184 or 1194-1282 or
1292), age 66?
St. Albertus Magnus
(1193 or 1205/06-1280),
age 57?
Frederick II (Emperor)
(1194-1250), age 56
Batu Khan
(      -1255), age ?

**Jalal ud-Din Rumi,** age 43; Persian poet born in Balkh, called the greatest of the Sufi poets. He lived in Asia Minor, where he founded a Sufi sect which is still in existence. His many beautiful lyrics, employing the familiar symbolism of rose and nightingale, moth and candle flame, expound Sufi doctrines when interpreted allegorically. (The name *Sufi* comes from the Arabic *suf,* a woolen cloak.)

**Simon de Montfort, Earl of Leicester,** age 42?; English statesman and soldier and leader in the Barons' War (1263–1265). After defeating King Henry III's army and capturing the king himself at the battle of Lewes in 1264, he summoned a meeting of parliament in 1265 that included the commons as well as the nobles—the first modern British parliament.

**Louis IX** (St. Louis), age 36; king of France from 1226–1270 and one of France's greatest monarchs, called the perfect knight—chivalrous, just and courageous. His long reign, a time of peace and prosperity, saw the completion of the great Gothic cathedrals at Chartres, Rheims and Paris. He died of the plague in Tunis.

KUBLAI KHAN
Khan of the Mongols
1215/16-1294

**Kublai Khan,** age c. 35; khan of the Mongols from 1260–1294, grandson of Genghis Khan and founder of the Mongol dynasty in China in 1280. He made an unsuccessful effort to conquer Japan and southeast

Bacon, St. Bonaventura, St. Thomas Aquinas, John Duns Scotus and William of Ockham. By the 13th century the works of Arabian and Jewish philosophers were known to the Christians; such thinkers as Moses Maimonides, Avicenna, Averroes, al-Kindi and al-Farabi also influenced Christian thinking, for they were concerned with much the same problem within the philosophical frameworks of their own religions.

In the famous controversy between nominalists and realists, the former appear to have won, for, partly due to the influence of William of Ockham, nominalism became predominant in the 14th century, just as scholasticism began to decline.

# 1275

Asia. His court of legendary splendor at Cambaluc (Peking) was visited by Marco Polo 1275–92; the palace is featured in Coleridge's famous poem *Kubla Khan*.

**Roger Bacon,** age c.36; English philosopher, scientist and Franciscan friar. He taught at Oxford University and the University of Paris, but his advanced views, urging observation and experimentation in science, brought him misfortune. Imprisoned twice (for 10 and 14 years), he died in obscurity, and his encyclopedic *Opus majus* was not published until 1733.

**Hulagu Khan,** age 33; Mongol ruler, granson of Genghis Khan, brother of Mangu Khan and Kublai Khan and cousin of Batu Khan. Sent by Mangu, the great Khan, to quell a rebellion in Persia, he laid siege to Baghdad, sacked and burned the city and executed the last Abbasid caliph. He broke Seljuk power in Persia, adopted Islam and established a khanate that ruled to 1335.

**Rudolf I of Hapsburg,** age 32; king of Germany and Holy Roman emperor from 1273–1291, the first of the Hapsburg line, whose name comes from the castle of Habsburg or Habichtsburg (hawk's castle) built in 1028 in what is now Switzerland.

**Alexander** (or Aleksandr) **Nevski,** age 30; Russian prince and national hero who defeated the invading Swedes in a great battle on the Neva River in 1240. Upon his father's death in 1246 he became the grand duke of Kiev and Novgorod, vassal of the Golden Horde.

**St. Bonaventura** (Giovanni di Fidanza), age 29; Italian scholastic philosopher born in Tuscany; professor of theology in Paris after 1253 and general of the Franciscan order after 1257. Four hundred years before John Locke, he declared the mind to be a blank tablet receiving impressions through the senses, but he maintained that knowledge of God, which is the prime object of inquiry, is independent of the senses. He appears in Dante's *Divine Comedy*.

**St. Thomas Aquinas** (the Angelic Doctor), age 25; Italian Dominican scholastic philosopher born of a noble family near Aquino in southern Italy. Called the most brilliant of the scholastics, he taught at the University of Paris from 1252–1261 and systemized Catholic theology on rational principles, declaring there could be no contradiction between theology and science because truth is indivisible. In 1879 Pope Leo XIII declared Thomism the official Catholic philosophy.

Michael VIII (Byzantine
emperor) (1234-1282),
age 41
Pope Boniface VIII
(1235-1303), age 40
Edward I of England
(1239-1307), age 36
Giovanni Cimabue
(c.1240-1302), age c.35
Alexander III of Scotland
(1241-1286), age 34
Marco Polo
(1254-1324), age 21
Duccio di Buoninsegna
(c.1255-1319), age c.20
Francesca da Rimini
(    -1285?), age ?
Osman
(1259-1326), age 16
Meister Eckhart
(c.1260-1327), age c.15
Dante Alighieri
(1265-1321), age 10
John Duns Scotus
(1265/66-1308), age c.10
Philip IV of France
(1268-1314), age 7
Robert I of Scotland
(1274-1329), age 1

# 1275–1300

The Sung dynasty of China may be divided into two periods, that of Sung proper (960-1127) and of Southern Sung (1127-1279). Before 1127 the capital was at Kaifeng, north of the Yangtze River, but in that year the Kin Tatars invaded the Yellow River Valley, seized the capital and carried off the emperor. The Sung dynasty was then reestablished south of the Yangtze River, with the capital at Hangchow, by members of the imperial family. The southern Sung empire continued to prosper for a century and a half. The north remained in the hands of the Tatars until it was conquered by Genghis Khan (1213-1215) and incorporated into the Mongol khanate, with its capital at Karakorum. Not until Kublai Khan succeeded his brother Mangu Khan in 1260 as the Great Khan was the southern Sung empire seriously threatened. The Sung dynasty fell not from internal weakness, but because of the superior military force of its foes. After many years of war, Kublai Khan defeated the Sung

## 1275

Sadi
    (1184 or 1194-1282 or
    1292), age 91?
St. Albertus Magnus
    (1193 or 1205/06-1280),
    age 82?
Roger Bacon
    (c.1214-1294), age c.61
Kublai Khan
    (1215/16-1294), age c.60
Rudolf I (Emperor)
    (1218-1291), age 57

**Michael VIII Palaeologus,** age 41; Byzantine emperor from 1261–1282, first emperor of the last Byzantine dynasty. He recaptured Constantinople from the Western Christians and expelled Baldwin II. An able soldier and ruler, he restored and strengthened the empire, but the devastation caused by the Latin emperors had set it permanently on the road to decline. Deprived of its monopoly of trade, it was unable to recover.

**Boniface VIII** (Benedetto Caetani), age 40; Italian ecclesiastic; pope from 1294–1303 and founder of the University of Rome. Boniface claimed papal supremacy in temporal as well as spiritual affairs, but could not enforce his claim. Conflict with Philip IV of France resulted in his imprisonment and death.

**Edward I** (Longshanks), age 36; king of England from 1272–1307. He conquered Wales in 1284, but is remembered for his long struggle to annex Scotland. He defeated Willaim Wallace at Falkirk in 1298 and had him hanged in 1305, but died two years later while marching north to fight Robert Bruce. His agreement to obtain the consent of Parliament before taxing his subjects extablished the principle of "no taxation without representation."

**Giovanni Cimabue** (Cenni di Pepo), age c.35; Italian painter and mosaicist born in Florence, called the herald of the Renaissance. He modified the stylized Byzantine tradition and achieved a more natural style of painting. He was Giotto's teacher.

**Alexander III,** age 34; king of Scotland from 1249–1286. He ascended to the throne at the age of eight, and at 10 was the husband of the daughter of Henry III of England. He was succeeded by his granddaughter Margaret, the Maid of Norway, whose engagement before her death at 7 to the son of Edward I (Longshanks) served as Edward's pretext for meddling in Scottish affairs.

emperor decisively in 1279, established the Mongol or Yuan dynasty of China (1280-1368) and moved his capital from Karakorum to Cambaluc (now Peking). There he lived in legendary luxury and splendor in a magnificent palace. On his hunting expeditions, he took along a great tent made of leopard skins and lined with ermine and sable.

Chinese scholarship and Confucianism declined, but trade and commerce flourished. Roads and canals were extended and improved, and caravan routes across Asia connected East and West. Gunpowder and printing were introduced into Europe at this time. It was an alien rule, however, unpopular with the native Chinese, and lasted less than a century. In 1368 the Ming dynasty restored native rule.

In western Asia the restoration of the Byzantine Empire and the expulsion of Baldwin II in 1261 by Michael VIII promised better days for Constantinople. The empire had lost much territory under the Latins and was nearly bankrupt, and, most serious of all, had lost to Venice its monopoly of trade. Nevertheless, the new dynasty brought new life, and the empire survived another two centuries.

# 1300

MARCO POLO
Venetian traveler
1254-1324

**Marco Polo,** age 21; Venetian traveler famous for his visit to the East. Departing in 1271 on an overland expedition with his father and uncle, he arrived at Cambaluc in 1275 and entered the diplomatic service of Kublai Khan. He returned to Venice in 1295 and related his adventures in *The Book of Marco Polo.*

**Duccio di Buoninsegna,** age c.20; Italian painter born in Siena; the last outstanding representative of Italian-Byzantine formalism before it was modified by the naturalism of the Renaissance. His most famous work is *Maesta,* the altarpiece for the cathedral of Siena.

**Francesca da Rimini,** age ?; tragic Italian beauty, daughter of Guido da Polenta of Ravenna. She has been immortalized in Dante's *Inferno* (Canto V) and is the subject of two operas, a drama by D'Annunzio, a painting by Ingres, a symphonic poem by Tchaikovsky and a poem by Leigh Hunt. Married by proxy to hunchbacked Giovanni Malatesta of Rimini, she fell in love with his handsome brother Paolo. Surprised by Giovanni, the lovers were killed with one sweep of the sword.

Osman
 (1259-1326), age 41
Meister Eckhart
 (c.1260-1327), age c.40
Dante Alighieri
 (1265-1321), age 35
John Duns Scotus
 (1265/66-1308), age c.35
Philip IV of France
 (1268-1314), age 32
Robert I of Scotland
 (1274-1329), age 26
Giotto
 (1266 or 1276-1337), age 24?
Orkhan
 (1279 or 1288-1359 or 1362), age 21?
Simone Martini
 (c.1283-1344), age c.17
Ockham
 (1285 or 1300-1349), age 15?

# 1300–1325

If Margaret, the Maid of Norway, had not died in 1290, at the age of seven, England and Scotland might have merged peacefully into one kingdom, and the world would never have heard of William Wallace or Robert Bruce. Her father was the king of Norway and her grandfather was Alexander III, king of Scotland from 1249–1286 and a descendant of Malcolm III, who defeated and killed Macbeth.in 1059. Upon his death Margaret became queen of Scotland at the age of three. At four she was betrothed to Prince Edward, son of Edward I (Longshanks) of England; at seven she died, under somewhat mysterious circumstances.

An Anglo-Norman, John de Baliol, one of 13 claimants for the Scottish throne, was crowned in 1292, after first acknowledging the overlordship of Edward I of England. Angered by thus being delivered over to England, the Scots revolted and William Wallace emerged as their leader. De-

## 1300

Pope Boniface VIII
  (1235-1303), age 65
Edward I of England
  (1239-1307), age 61
Giovanni Cimabue
  (c.1240-1302), age c.60
Marco Polo
  (1254-1324), age 46
Duccio di Buoninsegna
  (c.1255-1319), age c.45

**Osman** (Othman), age 41; founder of the Ottoman Turkish Empire. Succeeding his father Ertogrul as ruler of a small Turkish state in Asia Minor, Osman conquered adjacent territory and assumed the title of emir in 1299. He was succeeded by a series of warlike sultans who forged a powerful empire that lasted until 1918.

**Meister Eckhart** (Johannes Eckhardt), age c.40; German mystic and theologian, the first to write philosophy in German, born in Hochheim. He studied and taught at Paris, Strasbourg and Cologne and held various offices in the Dominican order. As a pantheist he verged on heresy, and some of his propositions were condemned by the pope after his death. His fervent preaching and writing initiated a popular mystical movement in Germany.

DANTE ALIGHIERI
Italian poet
1265-1321

**Dante Alighieri,** age 35; Italian poet born in Florence, one of the great figures of world literature. A supporter of the Guelph faction in politics, he was banished from Florence in 1302, led a wandering life and died at Ravenna. He wrote *La Vita Nuova* and *Commedia (The Divine Comedy)* in Italian, in addition to numerous works in Latin.

feated at the battle of Falkirk in 1298, he went into hiding and waged guerrilla warfare until he was betrayed and captured, taken to London, tried for treason and hanged in 1305.

Robert Bruce, earl of Caddick, was descended from a Norman duke, Robert de Brus, who was with William the Conqueror at Hastings. The family was granted fiefs in Scotland and produced a long line of Robert the Bruces. The fifth Robert the Bruce married the niece of Malcolm IV (the great-grandson of Malcolm III). Thus the famous Robert Bruce, grandson of the sixth Robert the Bruce, was descended from the slayer of Macbeth. His coronation in March 1306, in defiance of Edward I, resulted in a struggle that continued until 1328, when the English acknowledged Scottish independence. Robert Bruce was succeeded in 1329 by his son, David II. After a troubled and unhappy reign, he was followed by his nephew, Robert II, the son of Robert Bruce's daughter and the founder of the Stuart line of Scottish kings, who turned the tables on the English and in 1603 inherited the English throne.

# 1325

**John Duns Scotus** (Doctor Subtilis), age c.35; Scottish scholastic philosopher and teacher and a leader of the Franciscan opposition to Thomism. Banished from Paris for taking the side of Boniface VIII against the king, he was unpopular with the humanists because of his opposition to their classical studies. They coined the word *dunce* in retaliation.

**Philip IV** (Philip the Fair), age 32; king of France from 1285–1314, grandson of Louis IX. His reign marked the beginning of the decline of the papacy as a temporal power. After forcibly deposing Boniface VIII, he secured control by requiring Clement V to transfer his residence to Avignon in France.

**Robert I** (Robert Bruce), age 26; king of Scotland from 1306–1329 and national hero. He routed the army of Edward II at Bannockburn in 1314 and in 1328 secured recognition of Scottish independence from Edward III. He lived in seclusion in his last years at Cardross Castle, on the Firth of Clyde, and died of leprosy.

**Giotto** (Giotto di Bondone), age 24?; Florentine painter, architect and sculptor; the most important Italian artist before the Renaissance. A pupil of Cimabue and friend of Dante, he is known for his frescoes and altarpieces in Rome, Padua and Florence.

**Orkhan,** age 21?; Ottoman Turkish sultan from 1326–1359?, son and successor of Osman and the real organizer of the empire. He conquered large parts of Asia Minor, crossed the Bosporus and gained a foothold in Europe, assumed the title of sultan and married the daughter of the Byzantine emperor. He also instituted the military corps of Janissaries, Christian boys reared as Muslims and trained as soldiers, who formed the core of his army.

Simone Martini
(c.1283-1344), age c.42
Ockham
(1285 or 1300-1349),
age 40?
Ala ad-Din
(fl. 1330-40), age ?
Johannes Tauler
(c.1300-1361), age c.25
Petrarch
(1304-1374), age 21
Edward III of England
(1312-1377), age 13
Giovanni Boccaccio
(1313-1375), age 12
Murad I of Turkey
(1319 or 1326-1389),
age 6?
Hafiz
(c.1320-1389), age c.5
John Wycliffe
(1320/30-1384), age 5?

# 1325–1350

What the Arabs had repeatedly tried but failed to accomplish—to gain a foothold in eastern Europe—the Ottoman Turks, after their phenomenal rise in the 14th century, appeared to do with little effort. The destruction of Byzantine power by the Christian Crusaders and the loss of the trade which was the source of the empire's prosperity opened the way for Asiatic penetration into Europe. The barrier, if not down, was no longer so formidable.

Both the Seljuk and the Ottoman or Osmanli Turks belonged to the Oghuz family of Turkish-speaking peoples. Originally nomadic, in the sixth century they occupied an area in central Asia extending from Mongolia in the southwest to the Caspian and Black seas. About 900 they began migrating farther southwest. As they moved into the Middle East, they adopted the Muslim faith and were employed as mercenaries by the Abbasid caliphs. In the 11th century a

## 1325

Osman
   (1259-1326), age 66
Meister Eckhart
   (c.1260-c.1327), age c.65
Robert I of Scotland
   (1274-1329), age 51
Giotto
   (1266 or 1276-1337),
   age 49?
Orkhan
   (1279 or 1288-1359 or
   1362), age 46?

**Simone Martini,** age c.42; Italian painter born in Siena, a follower of Duccio, whose technique he softened and refined. His most famous work is the equestrian portrait of the condottiere Guidoriccio da Folignano in his gaudy coat, a fresco in Palazzo Pubblica, Siena. He was a friend of Petrarch's.

**Ockham** (William of Ockham or Occam; Doctor Invincibilis), age 40?; English scholastic philosopher of the Franciscan order. A nominalist, he held that universals have no real existence but are merely abstract terms, a conclusion in agreement with the principle of the famous Occam's Razor (Entities must not be unnecessarily multiplied). In his *Dialogues,* in 1343, he suggested the separation of church and state.

**Ala Ad-Din** (Aladdin), age ?; Turkish prince, son of Osman and

fresh wave of Seljuks, led by Togrul and Alp Arslan, swept into western Asia, captured Baghdad in 1055 and defeated the Byzantine emperor, thus opening up Asia Minor to Turkish settlement. Seljuk power peaked quickly and then declined in the early 12th century, as their empire disintegrated into small Turkish states.

In the 13th century, a minor Turkish tribe that had settled in Asia Minor on the Byzantine border began to enlarge its territory, absorbing other Turkish states. In the 14th century, under Osman, Orkhan, Murad I and Bajazet I, the tribe continued to expand at the expense of the Byzantine Empire. At the close of the century, they had already occupied parts of the Balkans in Europe. Under Muhammad II, sultan from 1451–1481, they captured Constantinople and made it their capital. Under Suleiman the Magnificent, sultan from 1520–1566, they captured Budapest and threatened Vienna, which only narrowly escaped. Compared to the Ottoman Empire in its greatest period, the European countries were pitifully weak, and their monarchs were regarded by the Turkish sultans as inferior.

# 1350

younger brother of Orkhan, whom he aided in organizing the empire. In 1330 he began the formation of the Janissaries *(yeni cheri*—that is, new troops). Taken from their parents when young, the boys were trained in strict military discipline and proved to be fierce and dauntless fighters.

**Johannes Tauler,** age c.25; German Dominican friar, one of the great preachers of the Middle Ages and a disciple of Eckhart's. His eloquent sermons, strictly adhering to orthodox Catholicism, were widely circulated and helped to popularize the Friends of God movement.

**Petrarch** (Francesco Petrarca), age 21; Italian poet and scholar, known for his sonnets and odes in the vernacular. The foremost humanist of his time, he searched for old manuscripts in an effort to revive the spirit of classical antiquity.

Edward III of England
  (1312-1377), age 38
Giovanni Boccaccio
  (1313-1375), age 37
Murad I of Turkey
  (1319 or 1326-1389),
  age 31?
Hafiz
  (c.1320-1389), age c.30
John Wycliffe
  (1320/30-1384), age 30?
Chu Yuan-chang
  (1328-1398), age 22
Edward the Black Prince
  (1330-1376), age 20
William Langland
  (c.1332-c.1400), age c.18
Jean Froissart
  (1333 or 1337/39-1400/10),
  age 17?
Tamerlane
  (c.1336-1405), age c.14
Geoffrey Chaucer
  (1340/45-1400), age c.10
John of Gaunt
  (1340-1399), age 10
Bajazet I of Turkey
  (1347-1403), age 3

# 1350–1375

Soon after the death of Kublai Khan in 1294, the Mongol or Yuan dynasty of China declined. Revolts and unrest among the peasants, coupled with continual dynastic rivalries, progressively weakened the empire. Chu Yuan-chang, a leader of the insurgents, emerged in the mid-14th century; he captured the provincial capital of Nanking in 1356 and set up his own government. In 1368 he marched on Peking and met little resistance from the last Mongol emperor, Toghan Temur. Peking fell in September 1368 and the native Chinese Ming dynasty was established. It ruled until 1644.

The emperors of the Ming dynasty reestablished orderly government, reformed the educational and judicial systems and created a favorable environment for the development of a high civilization, which ranks with the periods of the T'ang (618–907) and Sung (960–1279) dynasties as one

## 1350

Orkhan
   (1279 or 1288-1359 or
   1362), age 71?
Johannes Tauler
   (c.1300-1361), age c.50
Petrarch
   (1304-1374), age 46

**Edward III,** age 38; king of England from 1327–1377. He brought on the Hundred Years' War by laying claim to the French throne and demanding the abdication of Philip VI, whom he defeated in the famous Battle of Crecy in 1346. He introduced the weaving industry and forbade the export of raw wool. Senile in his last years, he let the government slip into the hands of his mistress and his fourth son, John of Gaunt.

GIOVANNI BOCCACCIO
Italian writer and humanist
1313-1375

**Giovanni Boccaccio,** age 37; Italian writer and humanist, born in Paris, the illegitimate son of a traveling Florentine merchant and a Parisian's daughter. He wrote novels and verse and won fame with the *Decameron,* a collection of 100 tales much admired by later writers.

**Murad I,** age 31?; Ottoman sultan from 1359 or 1362 to 1389, son and successor of Orkhan. Turkish power continued to grow as he conquered Macedonia and settled Turks there and moved his capital to Adrianople (Edirne) in Europe. He also won new territory in Asia Minor and forced Byzantine Emperor John V to pay tribute. He was assassinated in his tent after a battle with the Serbs.

**Hafiz** (Shams ad-Din Muhammad), age c.30; Persian lyric poet born in Shiraz, author of the *Divan,* a collection of more than 500 short odes or ghazels. He was much admired by Emerson, who compared him to Pindar and Horace and translated some of his poems from the German. His tomb near Shiraz is a shrine for pilgrims.

of China's greatest ages. Of its 17 emperors, the most outstanding were Yung Lo, who reigned from 1403–1424; Chia Ching, emperor from 1522–1566 who granted Macao to the Portuguese in 1557; and Wan Li, emperor from 1573–1620. The Ming period is known for its bronze vases and delicate porcelain ware, highly prized by collectors. Until about 1700 porcelain was made only in China. Fine landscape painting was also characteristic of the age; Tai Chih, who flourished about 1450, is especially famous for his landscapes in black ink.

Although the Ming period had no writers to equal those of the classic age of T'ang literature, the novel and drama flourished and commentaries on Confucianism were produced. The foremost Ming philosopher was Wang Yang-ming (1472–1528), a neo-Confucian who, like the famous Chu Hsi (1130–1200) of the Sung period, endeavored to reinforce Confucian ethics with a metaphysical foundation. An idealist, he maintained that there exists as an integral part of every human mind a faculty promoting right conduct, which the individual can discover within himself.

# 1375

JOHN WYCLIFFE
English religious reformer
1320/30-1384

**John Wycliffe,** age 30?; English theologian and religious reformer, called the "morning star of the Reformation." He maintained that the scripture, rather than the papacy, was the ultimate authority and he initiated the first complete translation of the Bible into English (which was completed by others). He was condemned as a heretic but not sentenced until 30 years after his death, when his body was disinterred and burned.

**Chu Yuan-chang** (Hung Wu), age 22; emperor of China from 1368–1398, founder of the Ming dynasty (1368–1644). A former Buddhist monk and the son of a poor peasant, he gained control over the insurgent groups that sprang up under the weak successors of Kublai Khan. As their leader he attacked and captured Peking, as the Mongols withdrew to Mongolia. Proclaimed emperor, he established his capital at Nanking and set about restoring a traditional Chinese culture.

**Edward the Black Prince,** age 20; prince of Wales and duke of Cornwall, eldest son of Edward III. Conspicuous in battle for his courage and his black armor, he commanded the right wing at Crecy and was in full command at Poitiers. He contracted an illness while campaigning in Spain and died one year before his father. The throne passed to his son, Richard II, aged 10.

William Langland
(c.1332-c.1400), age c.43
Jean Froissart
(1333 or 1337/39-1400/10),
age 42?
Tamerlane
(c.1336-1405), age c.39
Geoffrey Chaucer
(1340/43-1400), age c.35
John of Gaunt
(1340-1399), age 35
Bajazet I of Turkey
(1347-1403), age 28
Wat Tyler
(       -1381), age ?
Margaret of Denmark
(1353-1412), age 22
John I of Portugal
(1357-1433), age 18
Yung Lo
(1359-1424), age 16
Hubert van Eyck
(1366 or 1370-1426), age 9?
Richard II of England
(1367-1400), age 8
Henry IV of England
(1367-1413), age 8
John Huss
(1369/73-1415), age 6?
Jan van Eyck
(1370 or 1385-1440), age 5?

# 1375–1400

The famous War of Roses (1455–1485) between the English noble families of York and Lancaster followed immediately the Hundred Years' War (1337–1453) and had its origins in the family rivalries and vendettas of that earlier period. The two contending factions in the War of Roses were descended from the sons of Edward III: Edward the Black Prince, the eldest; John of Gaunt, the fourth son; and Edmund of Langley, the fifth son. If the Black Prince had not died before his father, there would probably have been no War of Roses.

The Black Prince was an indomitable soldier, whose victories in France resulted in impressive territorial gains, but when he became ill and John of Gaunt took command, most of what had been gained was lost. John of Gaunt was more successful in domestic affairs. His marriage to Blanche, daughter of Henry the duke of Lancaster, gave him possession, after her father's death in 1361, of the Lancaster hold-

## 1375

Edward III of England
  (1312-1377), age 63
Giovanni Boccaccio
  (1313-1375), age 62
Murad I of Turkey
  (1319 or 1326-1389),
  age 56?
Hafiz
  (c.1320-1389), age c.55
John Wycliffe
  (1320/30-1384), age 55?
Chu Yuan-chang
  (1328-1398), age 47
Edward the Black Prince
  (1330-1376), age 45

**William Langland,** age c.43; English poet. He studied for the priesthood, but led a wandering life and wrote a long allegorical poem, *The Vision of William Concerning Piers the Ploughman,* which, while attacking corruption and exposing ignorance, presented a vision of an ideal society based on the Christian virtues.

**Jean Froissart,** age 42?; French chronicler and courtier, secretary to the queen of England in 1361. He traveled widely (meeting Chaucer and Petrarch) and wrote *Chronicles of France, England, Scotland, and Spain,* which covered the years 1325–1400.

**Tamerlane** (Timur the Lame), age c.39; Mongol conqueror born in Samarkand, son of a Turkish chieftain. Claiming descent from Genghis Khan, he embarked on a senseless and brutal career of conquests; his army of Turks and Mongols overran Persia, Armenia, Georgia, Mesopotamia, Syria and northern India. In 1402 he invaded Asia Minor and met and defeated the army of Bajazet I, taking the Turkish sultan prisoner. His empire fell apart after his death. He is the subject of a play by Christopher Marlowe.

**John of Gaunt** (Ghent), age 35; duke of Lancaster, fourth son of Edward III of England, brother of the Black Prince and ruler of England during the years of his father's senility. He was the father of Henry IV (Bolingbroke) and ancestor, through his illegitimate son John Beaufort, of the kings and queens of the houses of Tudor, Stuart, Hanover and Saxe-Coburg-Gotha.

**Bajazet I** (or Beyazid), age 28; Ottoman sultan from 1389–1402, son and successor of Murad I. He strangled his younger brother Yacob to secure his rule before overrunning southeastern Europe and the greater

ings, making him the wealthiest man in England. His brother's continued illness and his father's senility presented other opportunities. He allied himself with Alice Perrers, the king's mistress, and became virtual ruler of England. The Black Prince died in 1376 at the age of 46; Edward III died in June 1377 and was succeeded by the son of the Black Prince, Richard II, who was 10. During Richard's minority the government was administered by the duke of Lancaster—John of Gaunt—and the duke of Gloucester. Richard assumed control in May 1389 at the age of 22.

Family quarrels and rivalry between Richard II and his cousin Henry Bolingbroke, son of John the Gaunt, led to Bolinbroke's banishment in 1398 for ten years. When John of Gaunt died the following year, Richard confiscated the rich Lancaster estates. There was nothing for Henry to do but try to recover the family possessions. He returned to England in July 1399, while Richard was absent in Ireland, raised an army from among the king's enemies and captured Richard in August. Richard abdicated, but that did not save his life. He was imprisoned and died—or perhaps was murdered—the following year.

# 1400

part of Asia Minor. A Christian army of Poles, Hungarians and French under Sigismund, king of Hungary, attempted to stop him in 1396 but was defeated at Nicopolis. He was defeated and taken prisoner in 1402 by Tamerlane and died a year later in camp.

GEOFFREY CHAUCER
English author
1340/45-1400

**Geoffrey Chaucer,** age c.35; English poet born in London, the first outstanding poet of the English language. He held minor government posts and was a member of Parliament in 1386, but at other times he was near poverty. He is the author of *The Canterbury Tales,* 23 stories in verse told by pilgrims.

**Margaret of Denmark** (Margrete), age 22; queen of Denmark, Norway and Sweden; daughter of the king of Denmark, she married the

John I of Portugal
(1357-1433), age 43
Yung Lo
(1359-1424), age 41
Hubert van Eyck
(1366 or 1370-1426),
age 34?
Richard II of England
(1367-1400), age 33
Henry IV of England
(1367-1413), age 33
John Huss
(1369/73-1415), age 31?
Jan van Eyck
(1370 or 1385-1440),
age 30?
Filippo Brunelleschi
(1377-1446), age 23
Lorenzo Ghiberti
(1378-1455), age 22
Thomas a Kempis
(1379/80-1471), age c.20
Donatello
(1386-1466), age 14
Fra Angelico
(1387 or 1400-1455),
age 13?
Henry V of England
(1387-1422), age 13

king of Norway. After the death of both monarchs and of her son Olaf, she defeated the Swedish king in battle and effected a union of the three countries (the Kalmar Union, 1397). Until her death in 1412, she ruled, autocratically, the most extensive kingdom in Europe.

**Wat** (Walter) **Tyler,** age ?; English rebel, a roof tiler by trade, leader

# 1400–1425

Edward III of England failed to make good his claim to the throne of France and thereby failed to create a powerful Anglo-French kingdom which would certainly have changed the course of European history. His great-grandson, Henry V, came much closer to success, for at the age of 35 he was recognized as heir apparent to the French throne by virtue of his military successes and his marriage to Catherine, daughter of Charles VI.

Henry was the handsome and reckless Prince Hal of Shakespeare's *Henry IV.* He succeeded his father as king of England in 1413 at the age of 26 and immediately resolved to regain the lands England had lost in France. The winds were favorable as he crossed the channel in 1415 with an army of archers estimated at 5,000, landed in Picardy and seized the port of Harfleur. Marching toward Calais the English were intercepted in a narrow valley near the village of

William Langland
(c.1332-c.1400), age c.68
Jean Froissart
(1333 or 1337/39-1400/10),
age 67?
Tamerlane
(c.1336-1405), age c.64
Geoffrey Chaucer
(1340/43-1400), age c.60
Bajazet I of Turkey
(1347-1403), age 53

**John I** (Joao), **John the Great,** age 43; king of Portugal from 1385–1433. His long and prosperous reign marked the beginning of Portuguese overseas expansion. His wife was the daughter of John of Gaunt and his third son was Prince Henry the Navigator.

**Yung Lo,** age 41; emperor of China from 1403–1424, third emperor of the Ming dynasty and son of Hung Wu (Chu Yuan-chang); called one of the greatest Chinese emperors. Although he maintained pressure on the Mongols in the north, his reign was mostly peaceful, devoted to the expansion of trade and consolidation of the empire. In 1421 he transferred the capital from Nanking to Peking and built the Forbidden City (his residence) inside the Imperial City (the residence of his officials).

of the Peasants' Revolt of 1381. Attempts by the government to hold down rising wages and restrict the mobility of laborers, plus the imposition of a poll tax, led to a general uprising and a march on London, where many houses, including John of Gaunt's, were plundered and burned. Richard II yielded to some of their demands, but after Wat Tyler was killed by the Lord Mayor of London he revoked most of the concessions.

Janos Hunyadi
   (1385/87-1456), age c.13
Muhammad I of Turkey
   (1387/89-1421), age c.13
Cosimo de' Medici
   (1389-1464), age 11
Henry the Navigator
   (1394-1460), age 6
Michelozzo
   (1396-1472), age 4

Agincourt by a French force of 25,000 heavily armed infantry and cavalry. The ground was muddy from recent heavy rains, and the French cavalry became mired in the mud, making easy targets for the English archers. According to Shakespeare (Henry V, Act 4, Scene 8) the English lost 29 men and the French 10,000, which is surely an exaggeration; however, the battle of Agincourt on Oct. 25, 1415, is recorded in history as one of England's greatest victories. It made young Henry into a hero.

Henry captured Rouen in 1419, gaining control of Normandy. In 1420 he concluded a peace treaty with Charles VI by which he obtained the king's daughter in marriage and the right of succession to the French throne. He was married June 2, 1420 and returned to England the following year with his queen.

Resuming his wars in 1421 against French opposition, he fell ill and died Aug. 31, 1422 at the age of 35. He was succeeded by his infant son, Henry VI, during whose unhappy reign the French recovered their lands and their independence with the aid of Joan of Arc.

**Hubert van Eyck,** age 34; Flemish painter, the first Flemish realist. He collaborated with his brother Jan on the famous altarpiece in the Church of St. Bavon in Ghent.

**Richard II,** age 33; king of England from 1377–1399, last of the Plantagenet kings; grandson of Edward III and son of the Black Prince. Contention with Henry Bolingbroke, his cousin, led to war and to Richard's defeat and capture by Bolingbroke's army. He died in prison (possibly murdered) in 1400. His story is told by Shakespeare in *Richard II*.

**Henry IV** (Bolingbroke), age 33; king of England from 1399–1413;

Donatello
   (1386-1466), age 39
Fra Angelico
   (1387 or 1400-1455),
   age 38?
Janos Hunyadi
   (1385/87-1456), age c.38
Cosimo de' Medici
   (1389-1464), age 36
Henry the Navigator
   (1394-1460), age 31

# 1400

Margaret of Denmark
(1353-1412), age 47

grandson of Edward III and son of John of Gaunt. The first of the house of Lancaster, he was acclaimed king by Parliament after he deposed Richard II. His succession and reign are the subject of Shakespeare's *Henry IV,* Parts I and II.

**John Huss** (Jan Hus), age 31?; Bohemian religious reformer and rector of the University of Prague. Influenced by the writings of John Wycliffe, Huss attacked abuses practiced by the clergy and won a large following. Excommunicated in 1410, he was tried for heresy and burned at the stake in 1415. The rebellion of his followers, known as the Hussite Wars, continued from 1419 to 1436.

JAN VAN EYCK
Flemish painter
1370 or 1385-1440

**Jan van Eyck,** age 30?; founder, with his brother Hubert, of the Flemish school of painting. His works are known for their realism; an example is the *Madonna of Chancellor Rolin*, in the Louvre. He was the court painter to the duke of Burgundy.

**Filippo Brunelleschi,** age 23; first great architect of the Italian Renaissance. His masterpiece, the brick dome of Santa Maria del Fiore Cathedral in Florence, rivals St. Peter's in its dimensions.

**Lorenzo Ghiberti,** age 22; Italian sculptor best known for the huge bronze doors, which depict Biblical scenes, of the baptistery of San Giovanni in Florence.

**Thomas a Kempis** (Thomas Hamerken), age c.20; German priest and writer born in Prussia. He entered a monastery in the Netherlands in 1407 and wrote the *Imitation of Christ* (in Latin), which has been translated into every major language.

**Henry V,** age 13; king of England from 1413–1422, son of Henry IV; remembered for his celebrated victory over the French in the battle of Agincourt in 1415. He married the daughter of Charles VI of France in 1420 and became heir apparent to the French throne, but died two years later and was succeeded by his infant son, Henry VI. The subject of Shakespeare's *Henry V*, he also appears in *Henry IV* as Prince Hal.

**Muhammad I,** age c.13; Ottoman sultan from 1413–1421, youngest son of Bajazet I. From 1402–1413 the Turkish empire neared collapse as he and his brothers fought over the succession. Muhammad emerged victorious and reunited the empire in preparation for further expansion; Tamerlane's conquests had checked only temporarily the growth of Ottoman power. He was succeeded by his son Murad II.

Michelozzo
(1396-1472), age 29
Johann Gutenberg
(1397/1400-1468),
age c.25
Luca della Robbia
(1399/1400-1482),
age c.25
Rogier van der Weyden
(1399/1400-1464),
age c.25
Masaccio
(1401-1428), age 24
Nicholas of Cusa
(1401-1464), age 24
Charles VII of France
(1403-1461), age 22
Murad II of Turkey
(1403-1451), age 22
Constantine XI
(Byzantine emperor)
(1404-1453), age 21
Fra Filippo Lippi
(1406-1469), age 19
Sir Thomas Littleton
(1407 or 1422-1481),
age 18?
Dirk Bouts
(1410/20-1475), age c.15
Joan of Arc
(1412-1431), age 13
Jami
(1414-1492), age 11
Pope Sixtus IV
(1414-1484), age 11
Sir Thomas Malory
(fl. 1470), age ?
Piero della Francesca
(1420-1492), age 5
Tomas de Torquemada
(1420-1498), age 5
Henry VI of England
(1421-1471), age 4
John Paston
(1421-1466), age 4
William Caxton
(1422-1491), age 3
Andrea del Castagno
(1423-1457), age 2
Louis XI of France
(1423-1483), age 2

# 1425–1450

Cimabue was first: a solitary artist among kings, statesmen and churchmen. Giotto followed, and after him came a torrent of Italian painters, sculptors and architects, who preempted the places of honor customarily reserved for politicians and generals. For the Italian Renaissance arrived at a gallop; the artists appeared not one by one, but in swarms. Scarcely had Duccio di Buoninsegna (c. 1255–1319) painted his last altarpiece in the Italian-Byzantine style, when, hard on the heels of Giotto (1276?–1337) came among others: Brunelleschi (1337–1446), Ghiberti, Donatello, Fra Angelico, Michelozzo, Masaccio, Fra Filippo Lippi, Piero della Francesca, Andrea del Castagno, Gentile and Giovanni Bellini, Andrea Mantegna, Verrocchio, Botticelli, Bramante, Il Perugino, Leonardo da Vinci, Michelangelo, Il Giorgione, Raphael, Andrea del Sarto and Titian.

## 1425

John I of Portugal
  (1357-1433), age 68
Hubert van Eyck
  (1366 or 1370-1426),
  age 59?
Jan van Eyck
  (1370 or 1385-1440),
  age 55?
Filippo Brunelleschi
  (1377-1446), age 48
Lorenzo Ghiberti
  (1378-1455), age 47
Thomas a Kempis
  (1379/80-1471), age c.45

**Donatello,** age 39; Italian sculptor born in Florence, called the father of modern sculpture. Dramatic realism characterized his work, as in the bronze equestrian statue *Gattamelata* in Padua, and *Judith and Holofernes* in Florence.

**Fra Angelico** (Guido di Pietro, or Giovanni da Fiesole), age 38?; Italian painter born in Tuscany, a monk in the Dominican monastery at Fiesole after 1407. His religious paintings are known for their intense pink and blue colors.

**Janos Hunyadi,** age c.38; Hungarian soldier and national hero who repulsed the first Turkish thrust into central Europe. As voivode (governor) of Transylvania, he won several victories over Murad II (1437–1438 and 1441–1443), but was overwhelmingly defeated at Varna in 1444, when the king of Hungary was killed. In 1456 he defeated the Turkish fleet in the Danube River, breaking the siege of Belgrade.

**Cosimo de' Medici,** age 36; Florentine banker, statesman and patron of the arts; son of Giovanni de' Medici, who was the founder of the family and made a fortune as a merchant. Cosimo was virtual ruler of the Florentine republic from 1434–1464 and the founder of the Medici Library.

**Henry the Navigator** (Henrique), age 31; Prince Henry of Portugal, third son of John I. He made no voyages himself, but actively promoted exploration and discovery; he organized expeditions to the African coast, established a school of navigation, improved the compass and introduced new methods of shipbuilding.

**Michelozzo** (Michelozzo di Bartolommeo), age 29; Italian architect born in Florence. The second most important figure (after Brunelleschi) in establishing the Renaissance style, he designed villas for the Medici family and built the great Medici-Riccardi palace. He also rebuilt the Church of San Marco in Florence.

Such a showering of creative ability upon a few generations in Italy has sometimes been regarded as a mystery beyond understanding, although there is a matter-of-fact explanation for the burgeoning artistry of the period. Rising prosperity in Europe had brought a wave of new construction; hundreds of churches, chapels, monasteries and ducal palaces, recently built, remained undecorated, and the means were at hand to pay for their decoration. It was a time when the artist's trade flourished, and the place was propitious; the dry, sunny climate of Italy was especially suitable for fresco painting and church decorating. Ambitious men were quick to seize the opportunity these circumstances offered and chose the artist's profession for its material rewards. It has often been observed in the history of culture that musicians, philosophers, dramatists, novelists, poets and scientists, as well as artists, come more often in throngs than singly, a phenomenon due not so much to the random concentration of a certain kind of creative ability in one time and place as to external circumstances, which foster the development of that ability over others.

# 1450

JOHANN GUTENBERG
German inventor
1397/1400-1468

**Johann Gutenberg,** age c.25; German inventor of a printing press with movable type. The first printed Bible, usually credited to him, may actually have been printed by others because of his difficulties with creditors and money lenders.

**Luca della Robbia,** age c.25; Italian sculptor and ceramicist born in Florence. Famous for the *Singing Galleries,* done in marble high relief for the Florence cathedral, he is also remembered for the glazed terra cotta reliefs and figures known as Della Robbia ware, which he and his nephew, Andrea della Robbia, produced in large numbers.

**Rogier van der Weyden,** age c.25; Flemish painter of portraits and Biblical subjects, and the successor of Jan van Eyck as leader of the Flemish school. Less objective than his predecessor, he skillfully ex-

Fra Filippo Lippi
  (1406-1469), age 44
Sir Thomas Littleton
  (1407 or 1422-1481),
  age 43?
Dirk Bouts
  (1410/20-1475),
  age c.40
Jami
  (1414-1492), age 36
Pope Sixtus IV
  (1414-1484), age 36
Sir Thomas Malory
  (fl. 1470), age ?
Piero della Francesca
  (1420-1492), age 30
Tomas de Torquemada
  (1420-1498), age 30
Henry VI of England
  (1421-1471), age 29
John Paston
  (1421-1466), age 29
William Caxton
  (1422-1491), age 28
Andrea del Castagno
  (1423-1457), age 27
Louis XI of France
  (1423-1483), age 27
Gentile Bellini
  (1429-1507), age 21

pressed emotions in a highly individual style.

**Masaccio** (Tommaso Guidi), age 24; Florentine painter, considered one of the founders of modern art, who had great influence on Michelangelo and Raphael. He died at 27, but in the *Life of St. Peter* frescoes (painted for the Church of Santa Maria del Carmine in Florence), including the notable *Tribute Money*, he achieved one of the masterpieces of Italian painting.

**Nicholas of Cusa,** age 24; German ecclesiastic, philosopher and mathematician born in Kues (Cusa), near Trier, the son of a fisherman. A cardinal and bishop, he was one of the first to break away from the intellectualism of the scholastics, maintaining that God can be approached only through direct intuition. His chief claim to distinction is his conclusion, some 20 years before Copernicus was born, that the earth rotates on its axis and revolves about the sun.

**Charles VII,** age 22; king of France from 1422–1461. On his father's death, according to treaty, the French throne passed to the infant Henry VI, king of England. The English already held northern France and were besieging Orleans, when, with the aid of Joan of Arc, the tide was turned. Charles was crowned in 1429, with Joan of Arc at his side, and entered Paris in 1436. By 1453, after the last battle of the Hundred Years' War, the French had recovered all their territories except Calais.

**Murad II,** age 22; Ottoman sultan from 1421–1451, son and successor of Muhammad I. With the complete subjugation of the Balkans as his aim, he seized Salonika, invaded Greece and waged a series of wars with the Hungarians. After many setbacks and discouragements, he won a great victory over the Christians at Varna in 1444. His ardor for conquest subsided during the last years of his reign.

**Constantine XI Palaeologus,** age 21; last Byzantine emperor (1448–1453). With their hold on Asia Minor and their conquest of the Bal-

# 1450–1475

After the Western occupation of Constantinople (1204–1261), the Byzantine Empire never recovered even a fraction of its former power. After having served so long as the guardian of Europe, protecting the continent's eastern flank from Asiatic penetration, it found itself so reduced that it

kans, the Turks had isolated Constantinople. Constantine appealed to the West and proclaimed the union of the Eastern and Western churches, but to no avail. With courage and resolution, his 8,000 Greek and Venetian defenders withstood for two months the siege of Muhammed II and his 150,000 Turks. Constantine was killed at one of the gates of the city, and what was left of the great Eastern Roman Empire fell with Constantinople on May 29, 1453.

JOAN OF ARC
French national heroine
1412-1431

**Joan of Arc** (Jeanne d'Arc), age 13; French national heroine of peasant origin. In 1428 she persuaded the dauphion (later Charles VII) of her divine mission and was given command of an army. She ended the siege of Orleans and forced the English to retreat. Falling into their hands in 1430, she was tried for heresy and sorcery and burned at the stake. She was canonized in 1920.

Giovanni Bellini
  (1430-1516), age 20
Muhammad II of Turkey
  (1430-1481), age 20
Francois Villon
  (1431-after 1463), age 19
Pope Alexander VI
  (1431-1503), age 19
Andrea Mantegna
  (1431-1506), age 19
Charles the Bold
  (1433-1477), age 17
Marsilio Ficino
  (1433-1499), age 17

Andrea del Verrocchio
  (1435-1488), age 15
Hugo van der Goes
  (c.1440-1482), age c.10
Ivan III of Russia
  (1440-1505), age 10
Matthias Corvinus
  (1440-1490), age 10
Edward IV of England
  (1442-1483), age 8
Pope Julius II
  (1443-1513), age 7
Sandro Botticelli
  (1444/45-1510), age c.6
Bramante
  (1444-1514), age 6
Il Perugino
  (1445/50-1523), age c.4
Bajazet II of Turkey
  (1447-1513), age 3
Domenico Ghirlandajo
  (1449-1494), age 1
Lorenzo de' Medici
  (1449-1492), age 1

could not save its own territory; the Ottoman Turks took Asia Minor, the Greek islands and the Balkans. Several times the city itself had only narrowly escaped capture. In 1403 the end appeared to be in sight, when Bajazet I blockaded Constantinople and prepared for a siege; but the city was inadvertently saved by Tamerlane, who defeated and captured Bajazet and held him prisoner for the rest of his life.

The last Byzantine emperor, named Constantine like the

# 1475

# 1450

first, was 44 years old when he succeeded his brother, John VIII, in 1448. The empire he inherited consisted of little more than the city and its suburbs. In 1451 Muhammad II became sultan of the Ottoman Turks and immediately prepared for a siege. He gathered a force of 250,000, encircled the city and closed the Bosporus. Proceeding deliberately with his preparations, he was ready early in April 1453. Constantine XI had a determined force of 8,000 or 9,000 defenders and walls that were said to be impregnable. The first attack, launched April 18, was repulsed with heavy

Lorenzo Ghiberti
(1378-1455), age 72
Thomas a Kempis
(1379/80-1471), age c.70
Donatello
(1386-1466), age 64
Fra Angelico
(1387 or 1400-1455),
age 63?
Janos Hunyadi
(1385/87-1456), age c.63
Cosimo de' Medici
(1389-1464), age 61
Henry the Navigator
(1394-1460), age 56
Michelozzo
(1396-1472), age 54
Johann Gutenberg
(1397/1400-1468),
age c.50
Luca della Robbia
(1399/1400-1482),
age c.50
Rogier van der Weyden
(1399/1400-1464),
age c.50
Nicholas of Cusa
(1401-1464), age 49
Charles VII of France
(1403-1461), age 47
Murad II of Turkey
(1403-1451), age 47
Constantine XI
(Byzantine emperor)
(1404-1453), age 46

**Fra Filippo Lippi,** age 44; Italian painter of religious subjects born in Florence, orphaned in early childhood and adopted by Carmelite friars. His best-known works are two frescoes in the cathedral at Prato, *Life of John the Baptist* and *Life of St. Stephen*. He was released from his vows at 56 to marry a nun with whom he had eloped. His story is told by Robert Browning.

**Sir Thomas Littleton,** age 43?; English jurist remembered for his summation of English land and estate law entitled *Tenures*. Written in legal French in 1481, it was the earliest printed work on English law. As expanded by Sir Thomas Coke in *Coke upon Littleton*, it remained a standard textbook for many years.

**Dirk** (or Dierik) **Bouts,** age c.40; Dutch painter born in Haarlem, regarded as second only to Jan van Eyck among 15th-century Dutch and Flemish painters. He is best known for his altarpieces. A *Madonna* and a *Portrait of a Man* are in the Metropolitan Museum, New York.

**Jami** (Nur ad-Din Abd ar-Rahman ibn Ahmad), age 36; Persian poet born in Jam, in Khurasan, the last of the great Sufi poets. Singing of love, nightingales and rose gardens, the Sufis closed their eyes to the beauty of the world and in mystical contemplation searched for the beauty which, in Jami's familiar lines, "through the forms of earthly beauties shines/Obscured, as through a veil."

**Sixtus IV** (Francesco della Rovere), age 36; Italian Franciscan friar, general of the order after 1464, cardinal after 1467 and pope from 1471-1484. As pope he was embroiled in Italian politics and waged war with Florence from 1478-1480. He is remembered as the builder of the Sistine Chapel and for admitting to the Papal States Jews expelled from Spain.

**Sir Thomas Malory,** age ?; English author and translator; believed to be of knightly birth, although some sources identify him with a confirmed criminal who spent much time in prison. He is said to have written his *Book of King Arthur and the Noble Knights of the Round Table* while in prison (1469–70). The title *Le Morte d'Arthur* was given it by William Caxton, who printed it in 1485.

losses. Repeated attacks in April and early May also failed. A final effort was decided upon, with the last and best reserves, 12,000 Janissaries. It is said that Constantine was informed of the impending attack, and that on the preceding evening a solemn High Mass was celebrated in the Church of Santa Sophia, the last one for the old church. At 1 a.m. on Tuesday, May 29, 1453, the attack began, and at dawn the Turks were within the city. The body of Constantine XI was found among the dead at one of the gates.

**Piero della Francesca,** age 30; Italian painter and mathematician born in Umbria; the leading realist of his time. His most famous works are frescoes: *Story of the True Cross,* in Arezzo; the majestic *Resurrection,* in the San Sepoltro town hall; and *Baptism of Christ,* in the National Gallery, London. In his last years he wrote a treatise on geometry.

**Tomas de Torquemada,** age 30; Spanish Dominican monk, organizer of the Inquisition. He was appointed inquisitor general by Ferdinand and Isabella in 1483 and grand inquisitor by Pope Innocent VIII in 1487. He was notorious for his severity and cruelty.

**Henry VI,** age 29; king of England from 1422–1461 and again in 1470–1471, son of Henry V of the house of Lancaster. He lost the English possessions in France, and in later years suffered periods of mental derangement. Deposed in 1461 by the duke of York (Edward IV), he was rescued from prison and restored to the throne in October of 1470 for seven months. Deposed again, he was imprisoned in the Tower of London and murdered. He is the subject of Shakespeare's *Henry VI, Parts I, II* and *III.*

**John Paston,** age 29; English gentleman, prolific letter writer and member of a well-to-do Norfolk family who saved every scrap of family and business correspondence. The famous Paston letters are a mine of information on the manners, morals and customs of England during the reigns fo Henry VI, Edward IV and Richard III.

**Andrea del Castagno,** age 27; Italian painter born in Castagno, near Florence. Influenced by Masaccio, whose realism he imitated, he is best known for the frescoes painted for the convent of Sant' Apollonia in Florence, which include giant figures of famous men and women: Dante, Petrarch and others. *The Youthful David* is in the National Gallery, Washington, D.C.

**Louis XI,** age 27; king of France from 1461–1483, son of Charles VII, whom he tried unsuccessfully to dethrone. He weakened the power of the nobles through bribery, intrigue and treachery; consolidated royal power; and laid the foundations for absolute monarchy in France, the cause of much subsequent woe. His chief antagonist was Charles the

Pope Alexander VI
(1431-1503), age 44
Andrea Mantegna
(1431-1506), age 44
Charles the Bold
(1433-1477), age 42
Marsilio Ficino
(1433-1499), age 42
Andrea del Verrocchio
(1435-1488), age 40
Hugo van der Goes
(c.1440-1482), age c.35
Ivan III of Russia
(1440-1505), age 35
Matthias Corvinus
(1440-1490), age 35
Edward IV of England
(1442-1483), age 33
Pope Julius II
(1443-1513), age 32
Sandro Botticelli
(1444/45-1510), age c.31
Bramante
(1444-1514), age 31
Il Perugino
(1445/50-1523), age c.29
Bajazet II of Turkey
(1447-1513), age 28
Domenico Ghirlandajo
(1449-1494), age 26
Lorenzo de' Medici
(1449-1492), age 26
Hieronymous Bosch
(c.1450-1516), age c.25
John Cabot
(1450-1498), age 25
Bartholomeu Dias
(1450-1500), age 25
Huayna Capac
(1450?-1525), age 25?

Bold, duke of Burgundy, whose territories he incorporated into France after the duke's death.

WILLIAM CAXTON
First English printer
1422-1491

**William Caxton,** age 28; first English printer. He printed in English in 1475 (while in partnership in Bruges, Belgium) a popular medieval romance, *The Recuyell of the Historyes of Troye*. Establishing a press in England at Winchester in 1477, he was the first to print a book in England, *Dictes & Sayings of the Philosophres*.

**Gentile Bellini,** age 21; Italian painter born in Venice, official painter to the Venetian republic and to the court of the Turkish sultan in Constantinople. He collaborated with his brother on frescoes in the doge's palace in Venice.

**Giovanni Bellini,** age 20; Italian painter and first of the great Venetian painters, brother of Gentile and teacher of Giorgione and Titian. His most notable works are: *Transfiguration, Earthly Paradise* and *Feast of the Gods*.

**Muhammad II** (the Great), age 20; sultan of Turkey from 1451–1481, son and successor of Murad II. Two years after his accession he captured Constantinople and made it his capital. His siege of Belgrade in 1456 failed, but he took Serbia, Albania, the Greek islands and Otranto, in Italy. With all of Asia Minor in his possession as well as the Balkans as far as the Hungarian frontier and all the Muslim lands of Africa and Asia, he was supreme in the eastern Mediterranean and ready to thrust deeper into Europe.

**Francois Villon,** age 19; French poet, whose name is uncertain, born in or near Paris of a poor family. Adopted by Guillaume de Villon, a priest, he was educated at the University of Paris. After an arrest for brawling he led a vagabond life, was several times imprisoned for theft and robbery, narrowly escaped hanging and was banished from Paris in 1463. One of the greatest of medieval poets and the first French lyric poet, his verse includes the famous line: "But where are the snows of yesteryear?"

# 1475

Christopher Columbus
(1451-1506), age 24
Isabella I of Castile
(1451-1504), age 24
Ludovico Sforza
(1451/52-1508), age c.24
Ferdinand II of Aragon
(1452-1516), age 23
Leonardo da Vinci
(1452-1519), age 23
Richard III of England
(1452-1485), age 23
Girolamo Savonarola
(1452-1498), age 23
Alfonso de Albuquerque
(1453-1515), age 22
Amerigo Vespucci
(1451 or 1454-1512),
age 21
Henry VII of England
(1457-1509), age 18
Maximilian I (Emperor)
(1459-1519), age 16
Pedro Cabral
(1460/67-1520/26),
age 15?
Vasco da Gama
(1460 or 1469-1524),
age 15?
Juan Ponce de Leon
(1460-1521), age 15
John Skelton
(1460-1529), age 15
Louis XII of France
(1462-1515), age 13
Piero di Cosimo
(1462-1521), age 13
Pico della Mirandola
(1463-1494), age 12
Desiderius Erasmus
(1466-1536), age 9
Selim I of Turkey
(1467-1520), age 8
Pope Paul III
(1468-1549), age 7
Emanuel I of Portugal
(1469-1521), age 6
Niccolo Machiavelli
(1469-1527), age 6
Edward V of England
(1470-1483), age 5

## 1450

## 1475

# 1475–1500

The Portuguese were the first modern Europeans to venture far in the open sea, and Henry the Navigator was the first Portuguese to promote such voyages. He did not live to see the epoch-making voyage of Bartholomeu Dias in 1487–1488, which inaugurated the age of exploration, but it was truly the culmination of his efforts. As a young man, in 1418, Prince Henry of Portugal took up residence at Cape St. Vincent, on the southwestern coast of Portugal, established a school of navigation and promoted voyages down the African coast. In 1433 his captains reached Cape Bojador, just south of the Canary Islands; they reached Cape Verde in 1444; by 1460, the year of Henry's death, they had nearly reached the equator. In 1484 Diogo Cam discovered the mouth of the Congo River (five degrees south of the equator); in 1487–1488 Dias reached the southern end of Africa and saw the open sea extending eastward. Thereafter, however, the Portuguese were not alone on the high seas.

Luca della Robbia
(1399/1400-1482),
age c.75

Sir Thomas Littleton
(1407 or 1422-1481),
age 68?

Dirk Bouts
(1410/20-1475), age c.65

**Alexander VI** (Rodrigo Lanzol Borgia), age 44; Spanish ecclesiastic; pope from 1492–1503; father of Cesare and Lucrezia Borgia. One of the most disreputable popes, he lived a life of luxury and pleasure and used the office to enrich his family. He instituted a censorship of books in 1501 and was the patron of Raphael and Michelangelo.

**Andrea Mantegna,** age 44; Italian painter and engraver of the Paduan school; court painter of the Gonzaga family of Mantua. His many masterpieces include *Death of the Virgin,* now in Madrid; and *Crucifixion* and *Parnassus,* in the Louvre. He married the sister of Gentile and Giovanni Bellini.

Matthias Grunewald
  (1470/80-1528), age c.5
Albrecht Durer
  (1471-1528), age 4
Lucas Cranach
  (1472-1553), age 3
Guidobaldo da Montefeltro
  (1472-1508), age 3
Nicolaus Copernicus
  (1473-1543), age 2
Ludovico Ariosto
  (1474-1533), age 1
Isabella d'Este
  (1474-1539), age 1

Christopher Columbus was next, in 1492, sponsored by the Spanish. The Italian John Cabot, sailing under the English flag, discovered Nova Scotia and Newfoundland in 1497–1498. Also in 1497–1498 came the long-awaited voyage around Africa by Vasco da Gama, the Portuguese explorer, making him the first man to reach the East by sea.

In 1499–1500 the Spaniards Alonso de Ojeda and Vicente Yanez Pinzon, in separate expeditions, explored the South American coast, In 1500 the Portuguese sent another expedition east around the Cape of Good Hope, but Pedro Alvares Cabral touched the coast of Brazil first and claimed it for Portugal. In 1501 the Portuguese explorer Gaspar Corte-Real explored the coast of Canada; in 1513 the Spaniard Ponce de Leon discovered Florida; and in 1519–1521 came the greatest voyage of all, as the Portuguese Ferdinand Magellan crossed the Atlantic, rounded South America and crossed the Pacific to the Philippines, where he died. When one ship, the *Victoria,* commanded by Juan Sebastian del Cano, completed the voyage around Africa from east to west, the seven seas had all been conquered.

# 1500

**Charles the Bold,** age 42; last duke of Burgundy (1467–1477), son of Philip the Good. To resist the aggression of Louis XI of France, he formed an alliance of nobles and defeated the king in 1465 near Paris. Eager to restore the ancient kingdom of Burgundy, he waged war intermittently with Louis XI until his final defeat and death in 1477, when Burgundy became a part of France.

**Marsilio Ficino,** age 42; Italian philosopher. A major figure in the Platonic revival of the Renaissance, he participated in Cosimo de' Medici's attempt to establish an academy in Florence modeled after that of Plato in ancient Greece. He translated the *Dialogues* and wrote

Henry VII of England
  (1457-1509), age 43
Maximilian I (Emperor)
  (1459-1519), age 41
Pedro Cabral
  (1460/67-1520/26),
  age 40?
Vasco da Gama
  (1460 or 1469-1524), age 40?

# 1475

*Theologia Platonica.* All souls, he maintained, possess a natural desire for truth and virtue.

**Andrea del Verrocchio,** age 40; Florentine sculptor and painter, one of the masters of the early Renaissance. The work for which he is best known is the great bronze equestrian statue in Venice of the condottiere Bartolommeo Colleone, which rivals Donatello's *Gattamelata* in Padua. He established an acedemy in Florence where he taught Leonardo and Il Perugino, among others. A notable painting is the *Baptism of Christ* in the Uffizi Gallery.

**Hugo van der Goes,** age c.35; Flemish painter of religious subjects born near Ghent. His best-known work is the altarpiece *Adoration of the Shepherds,* commissioned by a Florentine banker and now in the Uffizi Gallery in Florence. He retired to a monastery near Brussels in 1475 and continued to paint until overcome by melancholia in 1481. He died the following year.

**Ivan III Vasilievich** (Ivan the Great), age 35; grand duke of Muscovy from 1462–1505, sovereign of all Russia. He married the niece of the last Byzantine emperor and claimed succession to the guardianship of Orthodox Christianity. He added the two-headed eagle of Byzantium to the arms of Muscovy as a symbol of Holy Russia.

**Matthias Corvinus** (Matyas Hollos), age 35; king of Hungary from 1458–1490 and of Bohemia from 1478–1490, second son of Janos Hunyadi. He stood firm against the Turks throughout his long reign, and also waged war with Bohemia and the Holy Roman emperor. He seized Vienna in 1485 and made it his capital. During his reign Hungary enjoyed its last great age before falling to the Turks.

**Edward IV,** age 33; king of England from 1461–1470 and again from 1471–1483; first of the house of York. The Battle of Mortimer's Cross in 1461 convinced Parliament that Henry VI was a usurper and Edward the rightful king. Edward was forced into exile in 1470, but after the victory at Tewkesbury he regained the throne.

**Julius II** (Giuliano della Rovere), age 32; Italian ecclesiastic and military commander; pope from 1503–1513. He extended the boundaries of the Papal States and restored the power of the papacy using both diplomacy and war (in personal command of the troops). Probably the world's greatest art patron, he commissioned Bramante to design a new St. Peter's Basilica, Michelangelo to paint the ceiling of the Sistine Chapel and Raphael to fresco walls in the Vatican and paint the famous altarpiece, the *Sistine Madonna.*

SANDRO BOTTICELLI
Italian painter
1444/45-1510

**Sandro Botticelli,** age c.31; Italian painter born in Florence, pupil of

Fra Filippo Lippi. A Neoplatonist in his youth, he later became a supporter of Savonarola's and painted only religious subjects. Two famous early works are *Primavera* and *Birth of Venus*, both extravagantly praised by critics and both in the Uffizi Gallery in Florence.

BRAMANTE (Donato
d'Agnolo)
Italian architect
1444-1514

**Bramante** (Donato d'Agnolo), age 31; Italian architect born near Urbino. He designed the Belvedere Courtyard in the Vatican and drew up plans for the new St. Peter's, which were considerably altered by succeeding architects.

**Il Perugino** (Pietro Vannucci), age c.29; Italian painter born near Perugio, leader of the Umbrian school. He studied under Verrocchio and taught Raphael. Among his outstanding religious works are the frescoes in the Sistine Chapel of the Vatican depicting *Christ Delivering the Keys to St. Peter*.

**Bajazet II,** age 28; sultan of Turkey from 1481–1512, son and successor of Muhammad II. Ottoman power continued to increase as he waged war with Hungary, Poland and Venice, as well as Persia and Egypt. He built many mosques, including the magnificent mosque of Bajazet in Constantinople (1505). He was forced to abdicate in 1512.

**Domenico Ghirlandajo,** age 26; Italian painter born in Florence of a famous family of painters. A realist influenced by Masaccio and Castagno, he was called to Rome by Sixtus IV to help decorate the Sistine Chapel, where he painted *The Calling of St. Peter and Andrew*. He was the teacher of Michelangelo.

**Hieronymous Bosch** (Hieronymous van Aeken), age c.25; Flemish painter born in Hertogenbosch (now in the Netherlands). Called a forerunner of surrealism, he is known for the bizarre distortions of his paintings, which are filled with monsters and devils and strange animals. The famous *Garden of Earthly Delights,* in the Prado, was taken to Spain by Philip II.

**John Cabot** (Giovanni Caboto), age 25; Italian navigator and explorer born in Genoa. He settled in Bristol, England, in 1484 and, under the aegis of Henry Tudor, discovered the North American continent 1497–1498. He is believed to have touched Newfoundland and Nova Scotia, and sailed south to Chesapeake Bay.

**Bartholomeu Dias,** age 25; Portuguese navigator who opened the way to the East. He reached the southern tip of Africa and discovered the Cape of Good Hope, 1487–1488.

**Huayna Capac,** age 25?; Inca of Peru from 1487–1525. The last

Juan Ponce de Leon
    (1460-1521), age 40
John Skelton
    (1460-1529), age 40
Louis XII of France
    (1462-1515), age 38
Piero di Cosimo
    (1462-1521), age 38
Desiderius Erasmus
    (1466-1536), age 34
Selim I of Turkey
    (1467-1520), age 33
Pope Paul III
    (1468-1549), age 32
Emanuel I of Portugal
    (1469-1521), age 31
Niccolo Machiavelli
    (1469-1527), age 31
Matthias Grunewald
    (1470/80-1528), age c.30
Albrecht Durer
    (1471-1528), age 29
Lucas Cranach
    (1472-1553), age 28
Guidobaldo da Montefeltro
    (1472-1508), age 28
Nicolaus Copernicus
    (1473-1543), age 27
Ludovico Ariosto
    (1474-1533), age 26
Isabella d'Este
    (1474-1539), age 26
Vasco Nunez de Balboa
    (1475-1517/19), age 25
Cesare Borgia
    (1475/76-1507), age c.25
Pope Leo X
    (1475-1521), age 25
Michelangelo
    (1475-1564), age 25
Thomas Wolsey
    (1472/75-1530), age c.25
Alfonso I d'Este
    (1476-1534), age 24
Francisco Pizarro
    (1470 or 1475/76-1541),
    age 24?
Il Giorgione
    (1477/78-1511), age c.23
Baldassare Castiglione
    (1478-1529), age 22

emperor before the arrival of the Spanish, he ruled an empire extending 3,000 miles north and south from his capital at Cuzco. His division of the empire between his sons, Atahualpa and Huascar, led to war between them. The Spanish were already on the continent when he died.

LORENZO DE' MEDICI
Italian statesman
1449-1492

**Lorenzo de' Medici** (Il Magnifico), age 26; Italian statesman, ruler of Florence from 1478–1492 and one of the most famous figures of Renaissance Italy. A patron of art and literature and the grandson of Cosimo de' Medici, he inherited great wealth from the Medici family of merchants and bankers.

CHRISTOPHER COLUMBUS
Italian navigator and explorer
1451-1506

**Christopher Columbus** (Cristoforo Colombo), age 24; Italian navigator and explorer born in Genoa. He sailed west with three ships equipped by Ferdinand and Isabella and sighted one of the Bahama islands on Oct. 12, 1492. He sailed along the northern coasts of Cuba and Haiti and left a colony of 40 men on Haiti.

**Isabella I,** age 24; queen of Castile from 1474–1504. She married

Ferdinand II of Aragon (who became Ferdinand V of Castile) in 1469 and from 1479 to 1504 they ruled jointly over the two kingdoms, the union of which laid the foundation of Spanish power. She initiated the Inquisition and sponsored Christopher Columbus' voyages.

**Ludovico Sforza,** age c.24; duke of Milan from 1494–1499 (regent from 1480–1494), called *Il Moro* (the Moor) for his swarthy visage. He was a member of the powerful Sforza family and one of the wealthiest princes of Renaissance Italy. He married Beatrice d'Este and maintained the most magnificent court in Europe, with Leonardo da Vinci as a longtime resident. After his defeat and capture in 1500 by Louis XII, he was imprisoned in the castle of Loches, France, where he died eight years later.

**Ferdinand II,** age 23; king of Aragon from 1479–1516 and joint ruler of Aragon-Castile from 1479–1504. He organized the Inquisition in 1480, took Granada from the Moors and expelled the Jews in 1492. He was sole ruler from 1506–1516 as king of Aragon and regent of Castile for his daughter.

LEONARDO DA VINCI
Italian painter, sculptor,
architect and engineer
1452-1519

**Leonardo da Vinci,** age 23; Italian painter, sculptor, architect and engineer, born in Tuscany, the illegitimate son of a peasant girl; pupil and assistant of Verrocchio in his youth. Among his patrons were Lorenzo de' Medici, Ludovico Sforza, Cesare Borgia, Louis XII and Francis I of France and Pope Leo X. His best known works, and perhaps the world's most celebrated paintings, are *The Last Supper,* a fresco in Milan, and *Mona Lisa,* in the Louvre.

**Richard III,** age 23; king of England from 1483–1485, last of the house of York and younger brother of Edward IV. He usurped the throne after Edward's death and confined young Edward V, his nephew, in the Tower of London, but was defeated and killed two years later in the Battle of Bosworth Field by the forces of Henry Tudor, earl of Richmond. The story is told in Shakespeare's *Richard III.*

**Girolamo Savonarola,** age 23; Italian Dominican monk and reformer. He denounced Pope Alexander VI (Borgia) and the Florentine nobles for corruption and immorality and won popular support for his crusade to establish an ideal Christian state. He ruled Florence as virtual dicta-

Pope Clement VII
(1478-1534), age 22
Sir Thomas More
(1478-1535), age 22
Albrecht Altdorfer
(c.1480-1538), age c.20
Lucrezia Borgia
(1480-1519), age 20
Ferdinand Magellan
(1480-1521), age 20
Montezuma
(1480?-1520), age 20?
Giovanni da Verrazano
(1480/85-1527/28),
age 20?
Babur
(1483-1530), age 17
Martin Luther
(1483-1546), age 17
Raphael
(1483-1520), age 17
Huldreich Zwingli
(1484-1531), age 16
Catherine of Aragon
(1485-1536), age 15
Hernando Cortes
(1485-1547), age 15
Andrea del Sarto
(1486-1530/31), age 14
Pedro de Alvarado
(1486-1541), age 14
Miles Coverdale
(1488-1569), age 12
Thomas Cranmer
(1489-1556), age 11
Antonio de Mendoza
(1485/90-1552), age 10?
Titian
(1477 or 1487/90-1576),
age 10?
Jacques Cartier
(1491-1557), age 9
Henry VIII of England
(1491-1547), age 9
St. Ignatius of Loyola
(1491-1556), age 9
Pietro Aretino
(1492-1556), age 8
William Tyndale
(1492/94-1536), age c.8

tor from 1494–1496. Excommunicated and imprisoned, he was tried for sedition and heresy in 1498, and was tortured, hanged and burned.

AMERIGO VESPUCCI
Italian merchant and
explorer
1451 or 1454-1512

**Amerigo Vespucci,** age 21?; Italian merchant and explorer. He ac-

# 1500 – 1525

In 1509, at the age of 18, Henry VIII succeeded his father, and England was provided with a legitimate male heir to the throne. For a number of years a delicate situation had existed. When the War of Roses ended in 1485 with the death of Richard III, there was no male heir of the royal house of York or of Lancaster. Henry Tudor, the earl of Richmond, who defeated Richard at Bosworth Field, was acknowledged king by Parliament and crowned as Henry VII. But who was Henry Tudor and what were his antecedents?

It is an extraordinary fact, and one in which the English take pride, that the royal family is descended in an unbroken line from William the Conqueror. The name of the ruling house has changed from time to time—Plantagenet, Lancaster, York, Tudor, Stuart, Hanover and so on—but the

companied the Spanish expedition of Alonso de Ojeda (1499–1500) that discovered the mainland of South America and explored its northern coast. His accounts and maps of the expedition were published in 1507 by a German cartographer, Martin Waldseemueller, who called the new continent *America*.

**Alfonso de Albuquerque,** age 22; Portuguese soldier and statesman, founder of the Portuguese empire in the East. Succeeding Almeida in 1509, he captured Goa in 1510, built forts along the coasts and secured for Portugal the control of the spice trade.

**Conte Giovanni Pico della Mirandola,** age 12; Italian philosopher and scholar, friend of Ficino's. In Florence, under the patronage of Lorenzo de' Medici, he became famous as a Platonist and humanist, but ran afoul of the church in his endeavor to combine Greek and Christian ideas. After being arrested and forced to retract some of his propositions, he joined the followers of Savonarola. He is said to have been extremely handsome.

**Edward V,** age 5; king of England April-June 1483, son of Edward IV and his successor at the age of 13. He was imprisoned with his younger brother, the duke of York, in the Tower by his uncle Richard, duke of Gloucester and murdered.

# 1500

Paracelsus
(1493?-1541), age 7?
Correggio
(1494-1534), age 6
Francis I of France
(1494-1547), age 6
Lucas van Leyden
(1494-1533), age 6
Francois Rabelais
(1490 or 1494/95-
1553), age 6?
Hans Sachs
(1494-1576), age 6
Juan Rodriguez Cabrillo
(      -1543), age ?
Huascar
(1495?-1533), age 5?
Gustavus I of Sweden
(1496-1560), age 4
Suleiman I of Turkey
(1494/96-1566), age c.4
Hans Holbein
(1497/98-1543), age c.3
Melanchthon
(1497-1560), age 3

family has remained the same. A change in the name of the house simply means that descent has passed through a daughter instead of a son. This continuity was maintained after the War of Roses, but only by somewhat questionable means, until the birth of a son to Henry VII made it undeniably valid. Henry Tudor or Henry VII was descended from John of Gaunt and through him from Edward III, and would thus appear to be of the royal family. But his descent came through John Beaufort, the illegitimate son of John of Gaunt, and this caused considerable uneasiness. Fortunately, a remedy was at hand in the person of Elizabeth of York, eldest daughter of Edward IV. This was a legitimate line, for Edward IV was the son of Richard, duke of York; Richard was the grandson of Edmund of Langley, the fifth son of Edward III. Therefore no time was lost in arranging the wedding. Henry and Elizabeth were married in January 1486, and the country breathed a sigh of relief, for the royal family could then trace its descent through Elizabeth and disregard the bastard line.

# 1525

# 1500

Gentile Bellini
(1429-1507), age 71
Giovanni Bellini
(1430-1516), age 70
Pope Alexander VI
(1431-1503), age 69
Andrea Mantegna
(1431-1506), age 69
Ivan III of Russia
(1440-1505), age 60
Pope Julius II
(1443-1513), age 57
Sandro Botticelli
(1444/45-1510), age c.56
Bramante
(1444-1514), age 56
Il Perugino
(1445/50-1523), age c.54
Bajazet II of Turkey
(1447-1513), age 53
Hieronymous Bosch
(c.1450-1516), age c.50
Bartholomeu Dias
(1450-1500), age 50
Huayna Capac
(1450?-1525), age 50?
Christopher Columbus
(1451-1506), age 49
Isabella I of Castile
(1451-1504), age 49
Ludovico Sforza
(1451/52-1508), age c.49
Ferdinand II of Aragon
(1452-1516), age 48
Leonardo da Vinci
(1452-1519), age 48
Alfonso de Albuquerque
(1453-1515), age 47
Amerigo Vespucci
(1451 or 1454-1512),
age 46?

**Henry VII** (Henry Tudor), age 43; king of England from 1485–1509, first of the house of Tudor. As the exiled earl of Richmond (great-grandson of John Beaufort, the illegitimate son of John of Gaunt) he invaded England from Brittany, defeated Richard III at Bosworth Field and was acknowledged king. He was the father of Henry VIII.

**Maximilian I,** age 41; Holy Roman emperor from 1493–1519 and king of Germany from 1486–1519, born in Germany, a descendant of Rudolf I of Hapsburg. Marriage diplomacy, rather than military success, was the secret of Hapsburg expansion. Maximilian's marriage to Mary of Burgundy brought him the Low Countries; the marriage of his son Philip to the heiress of Ferdinand and Isabella brought the Spanish dominions; and the marriage of his grandson Ferdinand to Anne of Bohemia and Hungary assured Hapsburg succession in those countries. His grandson Charles V fell heir to half of Europe.

**Pedro Alvares Cabral,** age 40?; Portuguese navigator. Sent by Emanuel I with 13 ships and 1,000 men to establish trade with the East Indies, he steered off his course to the west, touched the coast of Brazil and claimed it for Portugal in April 1500 before continuing east around the Cape of Good Hope.

**Vasco da Gama,** age 40?; Portuguese navigator, the first to reach the East by rounding Africa. He sailed from Lisbon in July 1497 and arrived at Calicut, on the west coast of India, in May 1498. He is the subject of Camoens' epic poem *The Lusiads*.

**Juan Ponce de Leon,** age 40; Spanish explorer. He accompanied Columbus on his second voyage in 1493. He was the governor of Puerto Rico after 1510 and the founder of San Juan in 1511. In 1513 he sailed with three ships to search for the fabulous island of Bimini and the Fountain of Youth, and discovered Florida instead.

**John Skelton,** age 40; English poet and satirist born in Norfolk, tutor of Prince Henry before he became Henry VIII. His rude, original, sometimes obscene verses, with short lines and repeated rhymes, attacked the court, the clergy and Cardinal Wolsey; as he said, "Though my rime be ragged,/Tattered and jagged,//If ye take well therewith,/It hath in it some pith."

**Louis XII** (Father of the People), age 38; king of France from 1498–1515. Son of the duke of Orleans, he gained the French throne by his marriage to the crippled daughter of Louis XI. Attempting to assert hereditary claims in Italy (based on his descent from the Visconti family, rulers of Milan before the Sforzas), he captured Ludovico Sforza in 1500 and imprisoned him in France. He was popular at home for his mild and just rule.

**Piero di Cosimo,** age 38; Italian painter born in Florence. He assisted in decorating the Sistine Chapel, but is better known for his mythological scenes and a series depicting the life of primitive man, including *Hunting Scene* (Metropolitan Museum, New York) and *Discovery of Wine* (Fogg Museum, Cambridge). A wild, romantic innocence—anticipating 19th-century Romanticism—pervades some of his work, as in *Death of Procris* (National Gallery, London).

**Desiderius Erasmus** (Gerhard Gerhards), age 34; Dutch scholar and humanist, a leader in the revival of learning in northern Europe. He opposed the Reformation and advocated reform within the Catholic Church. He is the author of *Praise of Folly*.

**Selim I** (Selim the Grim), age 33; sultan of Turkey from 1512–1520 and son of Bajazet II, whom he dethroned. He proclaimed himself successor to the caliphs as guardian of the holy cities of Mecca and Medina, and in the interests of religious orthodoxy killed 40,000 Shi'ites. He wrote poetry in Persian.

**Paul III** (Alessandro Farnese), age 32; Italian ecclesiastic born in

Tuscany; pope from 1534–1549. An astute and energetic statesman, he hoped to reconcile the Protestants and reform the Catholic Church. He approved the formation of the Jesuits in 1540 and convened the Council of Trent in 1545. He also used his office to enrich his family, carving the duchy of Parma and Piacenza out of papal lands for his illegitimate son, Pier Luigi Farnese. He began construction of the Farnese palace in Rome.

**Emanuel I** (Emanuel the Fortunate), age 31; king of Portugal during its golden age of expansion and prosperity (1495–1521). During his reign Brazil was discovered and claimed in 1500, Goa occupied, in 1510, and commercial relations established with Persia and China. All Jews (Sephardim) were expelled in 1497–1498.

NICCOLO MACHIAVELLI
Italian writer and statesman
1469-1527

**Niccolo Machiavelli,** age 31; Italian writer and statesman; diplomat for the Florentine republic until 1512, when the Medici regained power and dismissed him. He retired to his country estate and wrote *Il Principe (The Prince); Discourses of the First Ten Books of Livy;* and *History of Florence.* He also wrote comedies.

**Matthias Grunewald,** age c.30; German painter born in Wurzburg, court painter and architect to two archbishops of Mainz. Called the last great German Gothic painter, he is noted for the violences and passion of his religious subjects, as in the *Crucifixion* of the Isenheim altarpiece.

**Albrecht Duerer,** age 29; German painter and engraver born in Nurnberg, famous for his woodcuts; the first outstanding artist of the German Renaissance. He visited Italy in 1505–1507 and introduced southern naturalism into the German Gothic style.

**Lucas Cranach, the Elder** (Lucas Mueller), age 28; German painter and engraver; court painter to the elector of Saxony at Wittenberg. He also engaged in large-scale production and employed many assistants. He was a friend of Martin Luther's, whose portrait he painted.

**Guidobaldo da Montrefeltro,** age 28; Italian nobbleman, duke of Urbino, whose court was immortalized by Castiglione as the scene of the polite conversations described in *The Book of the Courtier.* Though left an invalid by an illness at 20, the duke was admired in other respects as the ideal Renaissance prince. He married Elizabeth Gonzaga, the ''my Lady Duchess'' of the conversations.

**Nicolaus Copernicus** (Nikilaj Kopernik), age 27; Polish ecclesiastic and astronomer (born in Prussian Poland), originator of the Copernican system, which holds that the earth rotates on its axis and the planets circle the sun. An orthodox Christian and canon at the cathedral of Frauenburg (appointed by his uncle, the bishop), to whom astronomy was a second interest, he completed his book *De revolutionibus orbium coelestium* about 1530, but prudently its publication until 1543, the year of his death.

Giovanni da Verrazano
  (1480/85-1527/28),
  age 45?
Babur
  (1483-1530), age 42
Martin Luther
  (1483-1546), age 42
Huldreich Zwingli
  (1484-1531), age 41
Catherine of Aragon
  (1485-1536), age 40
Hernando Cortes
  (1485-1547), age 40
Andrea del Sarto
  (1486-1530/31), age 39
Pedro de Alvarado
  (1486-1541), age 39
Miles Coverdale
  (1488-1569), age 37
Thomas Cranmer
  (1489-1556), age 36
Antonio de Mendoza
  (1485/90-1552), age 35?
Titian
  (1477 or 1487/90-1576),
  age 35?
Jacques Cartier
  (1491-1557), age 34
Henry VIII of England
  (1491-1547), age 34
St. Ignatius of Loyola
  (1491-1556), age 34
Pietro Aretino
  (1492-1556), age 33
William Tyndale
  (1492/94-1536),
  age c.33
Paracelsus
  (1493?-1541), age 32?
Correggio
  (1494-1534), age 31
Francis I of France
  (1494-1547), age 31
Lucas van Leyden
  (1494-1533), age 31
Francois Rabelais
  (1490 or 1494/95-1553),
  age 31?
Hans Sachs
  (1494-1576), age 31
Juan Rodriguez Cabrillo
  (     -1543), age ?

**Ludovico Ariosto,** age 26; Italian epic poet born in north Italy, near Parma. He entered the diplomatic service of Cardinal d'Este and wrote *Orlando Furioso,* an epic poem based on the legends of Charlemagne and Roland whose heroic protagonist is the founder of the house of Este. He also wrote comedies.

**Isabella d'Este,** age 26; Italian beauty of the noble family of Este, celebrated art patrons and rulers of Ferrara from 1240–1597 and of Modena from 1288–1706. At 16 she married Giovanni Francesco Gonzaga, the marquis of Mantua, and enjoyed the unique distinction of having her portrait painted by both Leonardo da Vinci and Titian.

**Vasco Nunez de Balboa,** age 25; Spanish explorer. He sailed in 1500 with a trading expedition to the northern coast of South America. In 1513 he won lasting fame by leading an exploring party across the Isthmus of Panama to the shore of the Pacific Ocean, which he claimed for Spain. He was subsequently accused of sedition and executed.

**Cesare Borgia,** age c.25; Italian ecclesiastic and soldier, illegitimate son of Rodrigo Borgia (later Pope Alexander VI); cardinal from 1493–1498. Given the duchy of Romagna by his father, he enlarged his realm through aggression and intrigue. Described as cruel and treacherous, with a violent temper, he is said to have been Machiavelli's model for *The Prince*.

**Leo X** (Giovanni de' Medici), age 25; Italian ecclesiastic; pope from 1513–1521. The son of Lorenzo the Magnificent, he was made cardinal at 13 and pope at 37, and is remembered for his excommunication of Martin Luther in 1520. He made Rome the cultural capital of Europe but depleted the papal treasury. After an assassination plot against him miscarried in 1517, he appointed 31 new cardinals to replace those imprisoned and executed. Raphael painted his portrait in the company of two of his new cardinals (Pitti Palace, Florence).

**Michelangelo Buonarroti,** age 25; Italian sculptor, painter and architect, born in Tuscany; one of the great Italian masters. A student at the Medici academy of sculpture at 14, he is famous for the great marble statues of *David* and *Moses* and equally famous for painting the ceiling of the Sistine Chapel. As chief architect of St. Peter's after 1546, he designed the great central dome.

**Thomas Wolsey,** age c.25; English prelate and statesman; archbishop of York after 1514 and cardinal after 1515. As lord chancellor from 1515 to 1529, he was in virtual control of the government, with a court that rivaled the king's in splendor. He fell from favor over the affair fo Catherine of Aragon's divorce, was accused of high treason and arrested, but died on the way to London.

FRANCISCO PIZARRO
Spanish explorer and
conqueror
1470 or 1475/76-1541

**Francisco Pizarro,** age 24?; Spanish explorer and conqueror of Peru. Landing in 1532 with 180 men, he overcame and executed the Inca, Atahualpa, in 1533 and founded a new capital of Peru at Lima in 1535. He was assassinated in 1541 by members of his own party.

**Alfonso I d'Este,** age 24; duke of Ferrara from 1505–1534, brother of Isabella and Beatrice and third and last husband of Lucrezia Borgia. His family was one of the oldest in Italy, having ruled in Tuscany in Carolingian times; the German branch were ancestors of the British royal family.

**Il Giorgione** (Giorgio Barbarelli), age c.23; Italian painter of the Venetian school, a pupil of Bellini's. The famous languorous nudes in green landscapes—*Concert Champetre* in the Louvre and *Sleeping Venus* in Dresden—are probably his works, although they are sometimes attributed to Titian, whom he strongly influenced. He died of the plague in 1511.

**Baldassare Castiglione,** age 22; Italian writer and diplomat born near Mantua. He wrote *The Book of the Courtier,* an account of conversations among courtiers and ladies at Urbino concerning the qualities of mind and body that make a perfect courtier. He was a friend of Raphael's.

**Clement VII** (Giulio de' Medici), age 22; Italian ecclesiastic born in Florence; pope from 1523–1524; illegitimate son of the younger brother of Lorenzo de' Medici and cousin of Leo X. His hostility to Charles V resulted in the sacking of Rome by the imperial troops in 1527 and the pope's imprisonment. He later made peace and crowned Charles emperor. His refusal to sanction Henry VIII's divorce led to the establishment of the Church of England.

**Sir Thomas More,** age 22; English statesman and writer; More became lord chancellor in 1529, succeeding Thomas Wolsey. He clashed with Henry VIII and resigned in 1532, after refusing to acknowledge the authority of the king over the church. Accused of high treason, he was imprisoned and beheaded. He is the author of *Utopia,* describing a perfect society on an imaginery island—hence adding the word *utopian* to the English language—and the subject of Robert Bolt's drama *A Man for All Seasons.* He was canonized in 1935.

**Albrecht Altdorfer,** age c.20; German painter, engraver and architect; founder of the Danube school and one of the earliest to paint pure landscape. His *Danube Landscape at Regensburg* may be the first European picture with nature as its sole subject. He also painted *St. George* against a deeply wooded landscape and *Victory of Alexander at Arbela,* which Napoleon carried off to Paris but which is now in the Alte Pinakothek, in Munich.

FERDINAND MAGELLAN
Portuguese navigator
1480-1521

**Ferdinand Magellan,** age 20; Portuguese navigator. In 1519, in the

Huascar
    (1495?-1533), age 30?
Gustavus I of Sweden
    (1496-1560), age 29
Suleiman I of Turkey
    (1494/96-1566), age c.29
Hans Holbein
    (1497/98-1543), age c.28
Melanchthon
    (1497-1560), age 28
Atahualpa
    (1500?-1533), age 25?
Benvenuto Cellini
    (1500-1571), age 25
Charles V (Emperor)
    (1500-1558), age 25
Hernando de Soto
    (c.1500-1542), age c.25
Manco Capac
    (1500?-1544), age 25?
Pope Gregory XIII
    (1502-1585), age 23
Il Bronzino
    (1503-1572), age 22
Pier Luigi Farnese
    (1503-1547), age 22
Ferdinand I (Emperor)
    (1503-1564), age 22
Il Parmigianino
    (1503-1540), age 22
Sir Thomas Wyatt
    (1503-1542), age 22
John Knox
    (1505 or 1513/15-1572),
    age 20?
St. Francis Xavier
    (1506-1552), age 19
Anne Boleyn
    (1507-1536), age 18
Humayun
    (1507/08-1556), age c.17
Andrea Palladio
    (1508 or 1518-1580),
    age 17?
John Calvin
    (1509-1564), age 16
Francisco de Coronado
    (1510-1554), age 15
Giorgio Vasari
    (1511-1574), age 14

service of Emperor Charles V, he sailed west with five vessels, making for the Spice Islands. He rounded the tip of South America, crossed the broad Pacific and discovered the Phillipine Islands in 1521, where he was killed by natives. One ship completed the voyage around the world in 1522, proving the Americas to be a New World separate from Asia.

**Lucrezia Borgia,** age 20; beautiful Italian noblewoman, daughter of Rodrigo Borgia (Pope Alexander VI), sister of Cesare Borgia and duchess of Ferrara. Modern historians believe she has been the victim of malicious gossip and that charges of poison plots and incest are unfounded, though perpetuated by Victor Hugo's drama and Donizetti's opera. At 21 she married her third husband, Alfonso d'Este, and maintained a brilliant court at Ferrara, far from the intrigues of her family.

**Montezuma,** age 20?; Aztec emperor (c.1502–1520) at the time of the Spanish conquest of Mexico. A warlike despot, he did not fear the Spaniards, believing them to be descendants of the Aztec god, and admitted them to his palace. He was seized and held hostage by Cortes and killed in a native uprising the following year.

# 1525–1550

Michelangelo was only eight years older than Martin Luther, a fact that shows clearly the relationship between the Renaissance and the Protestant Reformation. Historians have generally treated the two as distinct historical periods, when actually they were nearly simultaneous. The Reformation may be seen as one phase of the reawakening experienced by Europe in the 15th and 16th centuries. Both it and the Renaissance were expressions of the new humanist attitude that rejected artificial and formal restraints of whatever kind and urged a return to the simplicity and purity of classicism.

It was no accident that the clamor for ecclesiastical reform reached a climax in the pontificates of the Medici popes, Leo X (1513-21) the Clement VII (1523-39). They had taken few precautions to conceal their crimes, the odor of

RAPHAEL
Italian painter
1483-1520

**Raphael** (Raffaello Santi), age 17; Italian painter born in Urbino, a humanist and Neoplatonist. In his short life of 37 years he created scores of masterpieces, including the *Madonna of the Chair* and the *Sistine Madonna*. Among his frescoes in the Vatican palace are the famous *School of Athens* and *Parnassus*. He succeeded Bramante in 1514 as chief architect of St. Peter's. His funeral mass was celebrated in the Vatican.

Gerhardus Mercator
  (1512-1594), age 13
St. Theresa
  (1515-1582), age 10
Mary I of England
  (1516-1558), age 9
Tintoretto
  (1518-1594), age 7
Catherine de Medicis
  (1519-1589), age 6
Cosimo I de' Medici
  (1519-1574), age 6
Pieter Brueghel
  (1520 or 1525-1569),
  age 5?
Pope Sixtus V
  (1521-1590), age 4
Luiz Vaz de Camoens
  (1524-1580), age 1
Pierre de Ronsard
  (1524-1585), age 1
Selim II of Turkey
  (c.1524-1574), age c.1

which, wrote a contemporary, hung like a poisonous fog over Rome. A great public outcry was raised against the deeds of the hierarchy. Charges of simony, nepotism, waste, extravagance, thievery and immorality were hurled by religious zealots who appeared in the streets and squares of Rome, alleging the pope to be the Antichrist. The suffering and misery caused by the sacking of Rome in 1527 by the army of Charles V simply intensified the cries for reform.

In the north, decisive action had already been taken to save the church from its enemies. A 34-year-old priest, Martin Luther, formally initiated the German Reformation when, in defiance of ecclesiastical authorities, he attacked the sale of indulgences and nailed his 95 theses to the church door at Wittenberg, on Oct. 31, 1517. Luther's assertion of the primacy of individual faith grounded on the eternal truths of the Bible, and his claim that the Bible rather than the church is the ultimate source of religious authority, gave birth to a new church, altered profoundly the medieval way of life and ushered in the modern era.

# 1525

Huayna Capac
   (1450?-1525), age 75?
John Skelton
   (1460-1529), age 65
Desiderius Erasmus
   (1466-1536), age 59
Pope Paul III
   (1468-1549), age 57
Niccolo Machiavelli
   (1469-1527), age 56
Matthias Grunewald
   (1470/80-1528), age c.55
Albrecht Durer
   (1471-1528), age 54
Lucas Cranach
   (1472-1553), age 53
Nicolaus Copernicus
   (1473-1543), age 52
Ludovico Ariosto
   (1474-1533), age 51
Isabella d'Este
   (1474-1539), age 51
Michelangelo
   (1475-1564), age 50
Thomas Wolsey
   (1472/75-1530), age c.50
Alfonso I d'Este
   (1476-1534), age 49
Francisco Pizarro
   (1470 or 1475/76-1541),
   age 49?
Baldassare Castiglione
   (1478-1529), age 47
Pope Clement VII
   (1478-1534), age 47
Sir Thomas More
   (1478-1535), age 47
Albrecht Altdorfer
   (c.1480-1538), age c.45

**Giovanni da Verrazano,** age 45?; Italian navigator and explorer born near Florence. Commissioned by Francis I of France to search for a westward route to China, he explored the North American coast from the Carolinas to Maine and is believed to have been the first Italian to enter New York Bay (1524), an event commemorated 440 years later by the opening of the Verrazano-Narrows Bridge.

**Babur** (Zahir ud-Din Muhammad), age 42; Mongol emperor of India from 1526–1530 and founder of the Mogul dynasty (1526–1857). A descendant of Tamerlane and ruler of Fergana, in central Asia, he led an army across the Indus River and defeated the sultan of Delhi, whose huge army included 100 war elephants. He organized an efficient administration and wrote his memoirs. He was succeeded by his son Humayun.

MARTIN LUTHER
German religious reformer
1483-1546

**Martin Luther,** age 42; religious reformer, leader of the Protestant Reformation in Germany. He was ordained a priest in 1507; was a professor at Wittenberg after 1511; posted his theses on the church door in 1517; and was excommunicated in 1520. The long-term results were the rise of the middle class, the growth of democratic institutions and the modern secular state.

**Huldreich Zwingli** (or Ulrich), age 41; Swiss Protestant reformer. By his preaching and introduction of Protestant practices in his own church, he peacefully established the Reformation in Zurich. He was killed in 1531 while accompanying Zurich troops as chaplain in a war with the Catholic cantons.

**Catherine of Aragon,** age 40; first wife of Henry VIII of England (married 1509); daughter of Ferdinand and Isabella of Spain and mother of Mary I. After the archbishop of Canterbury, Thomas Cranmer, had declared the marriage null in 1533, enabling Henry to marry Anne Boleyn, Pope Clement VII declared the first marriage valid, leading to a schism between the king and the Catholic Church and the establishment of the Church of England. Catherine, in confinement, occupied herself with religious devotion and died in 1536 after a long illness.

**Hernando Cortes,** age 40; Spanish explorer and conqueror of the Aztec empire in Mexico. He landed with 600 men, marched inland and entered what is now Mexico City without opposition in 1519. He took Montezuma hostage and gained control of the city in 1521.

**Andrea del Sarto,** age 39; Italian painter born in Florence, known as a master of chiaroscuro; court painter to Francis I (1518–1519). Given money to buy paintings in Italy for the court, he never returned to Paris but instead built a house for his beautiful wife, who posed for his madonnas. He escaped punishment, but his wife's infidelity made it a house of tears. Robert Browning told his story in verse.

**Pedro de Alvarado,** age 39; Spanish conquistador, second in command to Cortes in the conquest of Mexico. He conquered and colonized Guatemala and became its first governor. Lured by stories of the fabulous Seven Cities of Cibola, he planned an expedition but was killed in an Indian rebellion in Mexico, known as the Mixton War. His wife succeeded him as governor of Guatemala.

**Miles Coverdale,** age 37; English translator of the Bible, born in Yorkshire. In sympathy with Lutheranism, he preached against confession and image worship and undertook a translation of the Bible. Completed in 1535, it was dedicated to Henry VIII. Much of its phraseology was incorporated into the King James version (1611).

**Thomas Cranmer,** age 36; English prelate, first Anglican archbishop of Canterbury. He won the favor of Henry VIII by nullifying the king's marriage to Catherine of Aragon on the pretext of a prior marriage. He revised the *Book of Common Prayer* and placed an English Bible in every church. After the accession of Mary I he was accused of treason, convicted of heresy and burned at the stake.

**Antonio de Mendoza,** age 35?; Spanish colonial administrator, first viceroy of New Spain (Mexico) from 1535–1550 and viceroy of Peru in 1551–1552. Of aristocratic birth, he was an able and just governor who improved the condition of the Indians, promoted religion and education and laid a solid foundation for prosperity by developing industry and agriculture. He encouraged exploration to the north and brought the first printing press to America in 1535.

**Titian** (Tiziano Vecelli), age 35?; Italian painter of the Venetian school and one of the supreme masters of the High Renaissance. He studies under the aged Giovanni Bellini and worked with Il Giorgione, painting religious and mythological subjects in sumptuous style with glowing colors. Unexcelled as a portraitist, he was court painter to Emperor Charles V and his son Philip II. Some of his celebrated works include *The Resurrection of Christs, Venus and Adonis* (now in the Prado) and *Sacred and Profane Love* (in the Borghese Gallery in Rome).

**Jacques Cartier,** age 34; French navigator and explorer. He made three voyages between 1534 and 1542 in the service of Francis I, in search of a northwest passage to the East. He discovered the St. Lawrence River (which he named) and ascended to the current site of Montreal. Colonization efforts failed, but his discoveries were made the basis of French claims in Canada.

**Henry VIII,** age 34; king of England from 1509–1547 and king of Ireland from 1541–1547, of the house of Tudor. Henry was a popular monarch whose reign was comparatively peaceful except for his marital affairs; these caused the downfall and execution of several ministers, the establishment of the Church of England and intricate problems of succession. His six wives gave birth to two girls (later Mary I and Elizabeth I) and one boy (Edward VI). He divorced two of his wives, two were beheaded, one died in childbirth and one outlived him. He closed English monasteries and confiscated their property. He was succeeded by his son (by Jane Seymour), Edward VI, age 10, who died of consumption at 16.

**Saint Ignatius of Loyola,** age 34; Spanish ecclesiastic, founder of the Jesuit order. He abandoned a military career at 31, adopted an ascetic life and made a barefoot pilgrimage to Jerusalem. With Francis Xavier and five others, he founded the Society of Jesus, approved by the pope in 1540, to convert infidels and couteract the Protestant Reformation.

**Pietro Aretino,** age 33; Italian playwright and satirist and master of coarse invective, famous for his derisive attacks, which were commissioned, on famous contemporaries. Both Leo X and Celment VII were

# 1550

Humayun
(1507/08-1556),
age c.42
Andrea Palladio
(1508 or 1518-1580),
age 42?
John Calvin
(1509-1564), age 41
Francisco de Coronado
(1510-1554), age 40
Giorgio Vasari
(1511-1574), age 39
Gerhardus Mercator
(1512-1594), age 38
St. Theresa
(1515-1582), age 35
Mary I of England
(1516-1558), age 34
Tintoretto
(1518-1594), age 32
Catherine de Medicis
(1519-1589), age 31
Cosimo I de' Medici
(1519-1574), age 31
Pieter Brueghel
(1520 or 1525-1569),
age 30?
Pope Sixtus V
(1521-1590), age 29
Luiz Vaz de Camoens
(1524-1580), age 26
Pierre de Ronsard
(1524-1585), age 26
Selim II of Turkey
(c.1524-1574), age c.26
Raphael Holinshed
(c.1525-1580), age c.25
Giovanni Palestrina
(1525/26-1594),
age c.25
Philip II of Spain
(1527-1598), age 23
Paolo Veronese
(1528-1588), age 22
Ivan IV of Russia
(1530-1584), age 20
Hiawatha
(fl. 1550-70), age ?
Elizabeth I of England
(1533-1603), age 17
Michel de Montaigne
(1533-1592), age 17

his patrons, and Titian painted his portrait. His mediocre plays have been forgotten.

**William Tyndale,** age c.33; English religious reformer and translator of the New Testament (1525) and the Pentateuch. He smuggled 3,000 copies of the New Testament from Germany into England; thcy were confiscated, however, by Cardinal Wolsey. Arrested in Flanders, he was imprisoned, strangled and burned at the stake. His translations formed the basis of the King James version.

**Philippus Aureolus Paracelsus** (Theophrastus Bombastus Hohenheim), age 32?; Swiss physician and alchemist whose reputation for charlatanism has overshadowed his important contributions to medicine. Rejecting the humoral theory of disease in vogue since Galen, which related illness to an excess or deficiency of certain bodily fluids, he proposed specific chemical remedies for specific disease. He is called the father of chemotherapy.

**Correggio** (Antonio Allegri), age 31; Italian painter born in Correggio. Of his many paintings in churches and convents in northern Italy (Parma, Modena, Correggio), the best known is the *Assumption of the Virgin* in the Parma cathedral. He also painted mythological subjects, such as *Mercury Instructing Cupid,* now in the National Gallery, London.

**Francis I,** age 31; king of France from 1515–1547; an ambitious and powerful monarch, patron of art and literature, and builder of Fontainebleau Castle. In 1520, amid great pomp and pageantry on a plain near Calais, the famous Field of the Cloth of Gold, he conferred with Henry VIII. He was intermittently at war with Charles V.

**Lucas Van Leyden,** age 31; Dutch painter and engraver of genre and religious subjects, among them *The Milkmaid, The Chess Players* and *The Worship of the Golden Calf*—the last is now in the Museum of Fine Arts in Boston. A child prodigy, he produced masterpieces at 12 and 14.

**Francois Rabelais,** age 31?; French writer born near Tours, son of a country lawyer. He entered a monastery in his early youth and became a priest; traveled in France and Italy; and studied, taught and practiced medicine at various times. He is famous for two novels of satire and broad humor, *Pantagruel* (1532) and *Gargantua* (1534), both immediately popular, but condemned by the theological faculty of the University of Paris for sacrilege and obscenity.

**Hans Sachs,** age 31; German *meistersinger* born in Nurnberg. A prolific writer of songs, plays, poems and fables, he is best known for his poem on Martin Luther, *The Nightingale of Wittenberg*. He is the subject of Wagner's opera *Die Meistersinger von Nurnberg*.

**Juan Rodriguez Cabrillo,** age ?; Portuguese soldier and explorer in the service of Spain; discoverer of California. He was second in command on the expedition of Pedro de Alvarado in 1541, which explored the west coast of Mexico, and assumed command after Alvarado's death and continued northward. He discovered San Diego Bay on Sept. 28, 1542, and sailed north past San Francisco Bay. He also discovered Catalina Island and died on San Miguel Island, off Santa Barbara.

**Huascar,** age 30?; Inca of Peru, eldest son of Huayna Capac, who at his death in 1525 had divided the empire, which he had greatly expanded, between Huascar and his younger half-brother, Atahualpa. This led to war between the brothers and to the defeat and imprisonment of Huascar shortly before the arrival of the conquistadors, who then took the empire from Atahualpa.

**Gustavus I** (Gustavus Vasa), age 29; king of Sweden from 1523–1560, founder of the Vasa dynasty and father of modern Sweden. An officer of noble birth, he led an army of peasants against the Danes and drove them from the country, terminating the Kalmar Union. He confiscated the property of the Catholic Church and made Protestantism the state religion.

**Suleiman I** (Suleiman the Magnificent), age c.29; Ottoman sultan from 1520–1566, son and successor of Selim the Grim. During his reign the Turkish penetration into Europe reached its farthest point. Controlling thie Middle East, north Africa and the Balkans, he invaded Hungary and captured Buda and Pest. His siege of Vienna in 1529 failed. He also added Rhodes, Tabriz and Baghdad to his empire.

**Hans Holbein, the Younger,** age c.28; German painter and engraver born in Augsburg, son of Hans Holbein the Elder, also a painter. A book illustrator and painter of religious subjects, he is best known today for his portraits of such famous people as Erasmus, Thomas More and Henry VIII and his wives.

**Melanchthon** (Philipp Schwarzert), age 28; German scholar, professor of Greek and theology at Wittenberg and a major figure in the Reformation. He drew up the Augsburg Confession and assumed leadership of the Protestant movement during Luther's confinement in Wartburg Castle. He favored a reconciliation of differences to preserve the unity of Christianity.

**Atahualpa,** age 25?; Inca of Peru, son of Huayna Capac and half-brother of Huascar. The empire was divided at their father's death, and in 1532 Atahualpa invaded Huascar's realm, defeating and imprisoning him just as Francisco Pizarro arrived on the scene. The ensuing tangle of intrigue, treachery and murder ended with Atahualpa, the emperor, being accused of conspiring against Pizarro, an illegal intruder, and being executed for it.

BENVENUTO CELLINI
Italian goldsmith and
    sculptor
1500-1571

**Benvenuto Cellini,** age 25; Italian goldsmith and sculptor born in Florence. He produced jewelry, medallions and gold and enamel saltcellars for princes and popes (Francis I, Clement VII and the Medici family). He also executed the famous bronze sculpture *Perseus with the Head of Medusa,* now in the National Museum in Florence. His autobiography inspired an opera by Berlioz.

**Charles V,** age 25; Holy Roman emperor from 1519–1556, of the house of Hapsburg, king of Spain from 1516–1556 as Charles I. As grandson of Ferdinand and Isabella and of Emperor Maximilian I, he inherited a vast realm that included the Netherlands, Flanders, Spain, Spanish America, Austria, Germany, Naples and Sicily. The rise of Protestantism, religious disputes and wars, the ambitions of Francis I and the Turkish threat allowed him no time for relaxation. He gave up the Netherlands and Spain to his son, Philip II, and the imperial crown to his brother, Ferdinand I, and retired in 1557 to a monastery in Spain where he died the following year. His abdication speech has been preserved.

William I of Orange
    (1533-1584), age 17
Nobunaga
    (1534-1582), age 16
Sir Martin Frobisher
    (1535?-1594), age 15?
Toyotomi Hideyoshi
    (1536-1598), age 14
Faustus Socinus
    (1539-1604), age 11
Sir Francis Drake
    (1540/45-1596),
    age c.10
Akbar the Great
    (1542-1605), age 8
Iyeyasu
    (1542-1616), age 8
St. John of the Cross
    (1542-1591), age 8
Mary, Queen of Scots
    (1542-1587), age 8
William Byrd
    (1543-1623), age 7
Torquato Tasso
    (1544-1595), age 6
Alessandro Farnese
    (1545-1592), age 5
Murad III of Turkey
    (1546-1595), age 4
Tycho Brahe
    (1546-1601), age 4
Mateo Aleman
    (1547-1610/14), age 3
Miguel de Cervantes
    (1547-1616), age 3
John of Austria
    (1545/47-1578), age c.3
Giordano Bruno
    (1548-1600), age 2
El Greco
    (1541 or 1548-1614?),
    age 2?

**Hernando de Soto,** age c.25; Spanish explorer. He led an expedition of 1,000 men to Florida in 1539 in search of a rich empire believed to exist in the interior. He explored the area comprising present-day Georgia, North and South Carolina, Tennessee, Alabama, Mississippi, Arkansas, Oklahoma and north Texas. He discovered the Mississippi River in 1541, into which his weighted corpse was sunk the following year when he died of fever.

**Manco Capac,** age 25?; Inca of Peru, third son of Huayna Capac and brother of Huascar. He put up the stoutest resistance to Pizarro of all his family; he raised a huge army and laid siege to Cuzco. The siege failed, but for the next ten years he waged guerrilla warfare against the Spanish, until he was treacherously murdered.

**Gregory XIII** (Ugo Buoncompagni), age 23; Italian ecclesiastic; pope from 1572–1585. He built colleges and churches in an effort to restore Catholic supremacy and took a leading part in the Councilof Trent (1562–63). He reformed the calendar in 1582, replacing the Julian calendar with the modern Gregorian.

**Il Bronzino** (Agnolo di Cosimo di Mariano), age 22; Florentine mannerist painter; court painter to Cosimo I, duke of Tuscany. He developed a court painting style which titillated while pretending to moralize, as in *Venus, Cupid, Folly, and Time*. His best-known work is *Portrait of a Young Man,* in the Metropolitan Museum of Art in New York.

**Pier Luigi Farnese,** age 22; scion of an ancient Italian family; illegitimate son of Pope Paul III. His only claim to fame is that he was the first duke of Parma and Piacenza, a duchy created for him by his father cout of papal dominions. The Farnese took their name from the castle of Farneto in the 12th century and ruled Parma from 1545–1731. He was reputedly a vicious, bad-tempered man.

**Ferdinand I,** age 22; Holy Roman emperor from 1556–1564, younger brother of Charles V, who left him all his German territories. He was the founder of the Austrian branch of the Hapsburgs.

# 1550–1575

The Tudors of England and the Hapsburgs of the Continent occupied the center of the historical stage for the greater part of the 16th century. After the death of Henry VIII in 1547 and the retirement of Charles V in 1556, the drama revolved around Philip II of Spain and the Netherlands and Mary and Elizabeth of England. Philip never gave up the hope that England might be returned to Roman Catholicism. He believed his marriage to Mary I, queen of England from 1553–1558, would accomplish that end and also add the rich domain of England to the Hapsburg dominions. He was bitterly disappointed. Mary, the daughter of Catherine of Aragon and granddaughter of Ferdinand and Isabella, was brought up as a Roman Catholic and dutifully married her relative, who was the great-grandson of Ferdinand and Isabella and 11 years her junior. They were wed in 1554, one

**Il Parmigianino** (Francesco Mazzola), age 22; Italian mannerist painter born in Parma; a pupil of Correggio's. His best-known works are *The Vision of St. Jerome* (National Gallery, London) and *The Madonna with the Long Neck* (Uffizi, Florence). He also painted portraits of Columbus and Vespucci. Poverty-stricken in his last years, he became an eccentric.

**Sir Thomas Wyatt,** age 22; English poet and courtier. Suspected of being a lover of Anne Boleyn, he was briefly imprisoned in the Tower in 1536, then knighted in 1537 and made ambassador to the court of Charles V from 1537–1539. He translated Petrarch's sonnets and is credited with introducing the sonnet into English verse. Wyatt also wrote love lyrics and metrical paraphrases of the Psalms, published as *Certayne Psalmes*. He died of fever at 39.

**John Knox,** age 20?; Scottish religious reformer, founder of Scottish Presbyterianism. He joined Protestant nobles in opposing the Catholic monarch Mary, Queen of Scots, and her mother and regent, Mary of Guise. He published such tracts as *The First Blast of the Trumpet against the Monstrous Regiment of Women.* The issue was not religious liberty, but their desire for the establishment of Presbyterianism instead of Catholicism as the state religion.

**St. Francis Xavier,** age 19; Jesuit missionary born near Pamplona, Spani, of a noble Basque family. After assisting St. Ignatius in founding the Jesuit order, he was sent by John III of Portugal to Goa in 1541 as a missionary, and remained in the East until his death at 46. He is called the Apostle of the Indies.

**Anne Boleyn,** age 18; second wife of Henry VIII of England, mother of Elizabeth I and daughter of Sir Thomas Boleyn, earl of Wiltshire. The mistress of Henry VIII after 1527 and his wife after 1533, in 1536 she was accused of adultery with five men and conspiracy against the king. Convicted of high treason, she was beheaded on May 19, 1536. On May 20 Henry married Jane Seymour.

year after she became queen. The English Parliament refused, however, to crown Philip, and he left England the same year. Mary had no children, and after her death in 1558 Philip tried again and made an offer of marriage to her half-sister, Queen Elizabeth. This time he was refused, possibly because of his spindly legs.

Many years later Philip attempted to gain his end by war and prepared a great armada for the invasion of England, but fortune favored the English with a violent storm which destroyed Philip's fleet in 1588. The Spanish naval power was formidable, however; it had won a great victory at Lepanto in 1571, when a Christian fleet commanded by Don Juan of Austria, Philip's half brother, destroyed the Turkish fleet.

It was in Philip's long reign that the first signs of the decline of Spain appeared, while Elizabeth's reign marked the beginning of a strong, unified England. The center of power and prosperity was shifting from southern to northern Europe. The reign of Elizabeth is remembered as the golden age of English drama, but also for the imprisonment and execution of her cousin Mary, Queen of Scots.

# 1550

Lucas Cranach
   (1472-1553), age 78
Michelangelo
   (1475-1564), age 75
Miles Coverdale
   (1488-1569), age 62
Thomas Cranmer
   (1489-1556), age 61
Antonio de Mendoza
   (1485/90-1552), age 60?
Titian
   (1477 or 1487/90-1576),
   age 60?
Jacques Cartier
   (1491-1557), age 59
St. Ignatius of Loyola
   (1491-1556), age 59
Pietro Aretino
   (1492-1556), age 58
Francois Rabelais
   (1494/95-1553), age 56?
Hans Sachs
   (1494-1576), age 56
Gustavus I of Sweden
   (1496-1560), age 54
Suleiman I of Turkey
   (1494/96-1566), age c.54
Melanchthon
   (1497-1560), age 53
Benvenuto Cellini
   (1500-1571), age 50
Charles V (Emperor)
   (1500-1558), age 50
Pope Gregory XIII
   (1502-1585), age 48
Il Bronzino
   (1503-1572), age 47
Ferdinand I (Emperor)
   (1503-1564), age 47
John Knox
   (1505 or 1513/15-1572),
   age 45?
St. Francis Xavier
   (1506-1552), age 44

**Humayun,** age c.42; emperor of India from 1530–1556, second of the Mogul dynasty, son and successor of Babur. Distracted by the pleasures of his court, he neglected military defenses, lost several battles as enemies overran Bengal and was driven from India. He took refuge in Persia in 1544, and it was not until 1555 that he mobilized an army and recovered his kingdom. He was succeeded by his son, Akbar the Great.

**Andrea Palladio,** age 42?; Italian architect born in or near Padua. He blended features of the Roman temple with early Renaissance style to create formal, symmetrical designs. Famous for villas near Vicenza, palaces on the Grand Canal and churches in Venice. *(San Giorgio Maggiore* and *Il Redentore),* he influenced Inigo Jones and Christopher Wren in England and inspired the Georgian style of the 18th century (often called Colonial in America).

JOHN CALVIN
French theologian
1509-1564

**John Calvin** (Jean Chauvin), age 41; French theologian born in Picardy, leader of the authoritarian branch of Protestantism, deriving its inspiration from the Old Testament. He established a theocratic government in Geneva, which he dominated for 20 years. Calvin systemized Protestant theology, rejecting the belief in human perfectability and maintaining that all men are not created on an equal footing, some being destined for eternal life, others foreternal damnation. He caused Michael Servetus to be burned at the stake over a doctrinal dispute. Calvin also introduced congregational singing.

**Francisco Vasquez de Coronado,** age 40; Spanish explorer born in Salamanca. He went to Mexico at 25 and became governor of the province of Nueva Galicia at 29. Lured by stories of the Seven Cities of Cibola and the fabulously rich kingdom of Quivira, he set out Feb. 23, 1540, with a large party (300 Spaniards and many Indians). His party discovered the Grand Canyon and were the first Europeans to see herds of bison on the Great Plains. They found the Seven Cities (Zuni pueblos in New Mexico) and they found Quivira (a Wichita Indian village in western Kansas), but no gold.

**Giorgio Vasari,** age 39; Italian architect and painter born in Arezzo, famous as the first modern art historian and critic. His *Lives of the*

*Artists* (1550) contains biographies of painters, architects and sculptors from Cimabue to Michelangelo. He studied under Andrea del Sarto and Michelangelo and designed the Uffizi Palace in Florence.

**GERHARDUS MERCATOR**
Flemish geographer and
cartographer
1512-1594

**Gerhardus Mercator** (Gerhard Kremer), age 38; Flemish geographer and cartographer, inventor in 1568 of the Mercator system of projection widely used in mapmaking, which is accurate at the equator but distorts high latitudes and cannot indicate the poles.

**St. Theresa** (Theresa of Avila), age 35; Spanish Carmelite nun and mystic, born of a wealthy family. In 1562 she founded her first convent, St. Joseph's in Avila, of the Reformed, or Barefoot, Carmelite order. Thereafter she traveled widely, founding other convents in collaboration with St. John of the Cross. She also wrote books on the religious life and was made Doctor of the Church in 1970 by Pope Paul VI.

**Mary I** (Mary Tudor, called Bloody Mary), age 34; queen of England and Ireland from 1553–1558, daughter of Henry VIII and Catherine of Aragon. She married Philip II of Spain in 1554, reestablished the Roman Catholic Church and executed 300 Protestants as heretics. During her reign Calais was lost to the French.

**Tintoretto** (Jacobo Robusti), age 32; Italian painter of the Venetian school, creator of the spectacular *Last Supper* for Palladio's San Giorgio Maggiore church in Venice. He is also known for the spectacular dimensions of his paintings; *Paradise,* a canvas painted for the ducal palace, measures 34 feet x 74 feet.

**Catherine de Medicis** (de' Medici in Italian; de Medicis in French), age 31; queen of France, born in Italy; daughter of Lorenzo de' Medici, duke of Urbino (not Lorenzo the Magnificent, but the nephew of Pope Leo X). At 14 she married Henry, second son of Francis I, and became queen on his accession as Henry II in 1547. Of their four sons, three were kings. She controlled the government during the reign of Charles IX, her second son, and is blamed for the St. Bartholomew's Day Massacre of French Protestants in 1572.

**Cosimo I de' Medici,** age 31; duke of Florence from 1537–1569 and

Elizabeth I of England
   (1533-1603), age 42
Michel de Montaigne
   (1533-1592), age 42
William I of Orange
   (1533-1584), age 42
Nobunaga
   (1534-1582), age 41
Sir Martin Frobisher
   (1535?-1594), age 40?
Toyotomi Hideyoshi
   (1536-1598), age 39
Faustus Socinus
   (1539-1604), age 36
Sir Francis Drake
   (1540/45-1596),
   age c.35
Akbar the Great
   (1542-1605), age 33
Iyeyasu
   (1542-1616), age 33
St. John of the Cross
   (1542-1591), age 33
Mary, Queen of Scots
   (1542-1587), age 33
William Byrd
   (1543-1623), age 32
Torquato Tasso
   (1544-1595), age 31
Alessandro Farnese
   (1545-1592), age 30
Murad III of Turkey
   (1546-1595), age 29
Tycho Brahe
   (1546-1601), age 29
Mateo Aleman
   (1547-1610/14), age 28
Miguel de Cervantes
   (1547-1616), age 28
John of Austria
   (1545/47-1578), age c.28
Giordano Bruno
   (1548-1600), age 27
El Greco
   (1541 or 1548-1614?),
   age 27?
John Napier
   (1550-1617), age 25
Boris Godunov
   (1551/52-1605), age c.24

grand duke of Tuscany from 1569–1574; great-great-grandson of the brother of the first Cosimo de' Medici (1384–1464). A despotic and aggressive ruler, he doubled the territory of Tuscany and increased its power and prosperity. He built the Uffizi Palace and was the patron of Bronzino.

**Sixtus V** (Felice Peretti), age 29; Italian ecclesiastic; pope for five years (1585–1590) at the end of a long career in the church, which began when he entered the Franciscan order at 12. He rebuilt churches in Rome, improved the streets and erected new monuments. He built the Lateran Palace and the Vatican Library and sanctioned Philip II's attempt to conquer England to restore Catholicism.

PIETER BRUEGHEL (the Elder)
Flemish painter
1520 or 1525-1569

**Pieter Brueghel, the Elder,** age 30?; Flemish painter of landscapes and scenes of peasant life; founder of a large family of painters. Known for his *Hunters Return in the Snow* and other popular winter scenes.

**Luiz Vaz de Camoens** (Camoes), age 26; Portugal's greatest poet, author of *The Lusiads,* an epic poem on Portuguese history and the voyage of Vasco da Gama. The son of an impoverished noble family, he was banished from court over a love affair and spent 16 years in India as soldier and adventurer. After enduring imprisonment, shipwreck and the loss of an eye, he was restored to honor and favor at court upon publication of his poem.

**Pierre de Ronsard,** age 26; French lyric poet, court poet to Charles IX. Rejecting medieval traditions, he wrote sonnets and odes in imitation of classical models, boasting that he rivaled Pindar and surpassed Horace. He was admired by the Elizabethans.

**Selim II,** age c.26; sultan of Turkey from 1566–1574, son and successor of Suleiman the Magnificent. On Oct. 7, 1571, off the coast of Greece, the great naval battle of Lepanto was fought between Turks and Christians. With 200 galleys and 30,000 fighting men, the fleets of Spain, Venice and the Papal States sank the Turkish fleet, killing or capturing 15,000 Turks and liberating 10,000 Christian galley slaves. Among the wounded Christians was Cervantes. The battle is said to have marked the beginning of the decline of the Ottoman Empire.

**Raphael Holinshed,** age c.25; English chronicler who continued the project begun by Reginald Wolfe, the queen's printer, and compiled from many sources the *Chronicles of England, Scotland, and Ireland* (published in 1578); they were Shakespeare's source for his historical plays and for *Cymbeline, King Lear* and *Macbeth.*

**Giovanni Palestrina,** age c.25; foremost Italian Renaissance composer; choirmaster in the Vatican. He composed mostly religious choral works: masses, motets and litanies.

**Philip II,** age 23; king of Spain from 1556–1598, son of Emperor Charles V; also ruler of Naples, Sicily and the Netherlands. He married four times, the second time (1554) to Mary I, queen of England; after her death, his offer of marriage was refused by Elizabeth I of England. Naval supremacy passed to England after the defeat of the Armada in 1588, and the decline of commerce is attributed to his restrictive policies. He vigorously supported the Catholic Church and suppressed Protestantism.

**Paolo Veronese** (Paolo Cagliari), age 22; Italian painter of the Venetian school, born in Verona, the last representative of High Renaissance style. He painted both religious and secular frescoes and restored and decorated the doge's palace. Familiar works include *Supper at Emmaeus* and *Marriage at Cana,* both in the Louvre.

**Hiawatha,** age ?; chief of the Onondaga Indians of North America, credited with organizing the Five Nations of the Iroquois into a confederation for mutual protection. Possibly a shaman, he was said to possess miraculous powers against evil spirits and to have introduced medicine and agriculture. His story was romanticized by Longfellow in *The Song of Hiawatha.*

IVAN THE TERRIBLE
First czar of Russia
1530-1584

**Ivan IV Vasilievich** (Ivan the Terrible), age 20; grand duke of Muscovy

Sir Edward Coke
  (1552-1634), age 23
Richard Hakluyt
  (1552-1616), age 23
Sir Walter Raleigh
  (c.1552-1618), age c.23
Edmund Spenser
  (1552/53-1599), age c.23
Henry IV of France
  (1553-1610), age 22
Sir Fulke Greville
  (1554-1628), age 21
Richard Hooker
  (1554?-1600), age 21?
John Lyly
  (c.1554-1606), age c.21
Sir Philip Sidney
  (1554-1586), age 21
Abbas I of Persia
  (1557-1628), age 18
Thomas Kyd
  (1557/58-1594/95),
  age c.18
George Peele
  (1558?-1597), age 17?
Jacobus Arminius
  (1560-1609), age 15
Annibale Carracci
  (1560-1609), age 15
Robert Greene
  (c.1560-1592), age c.15
Sir Francis Bacon
  (1561-1626), age 14
Samuel Daniel
  (1562-1619), age 13
Lope de Vega
  (1562-1635), age 13
Ferenc Esterhazy
  (1563-1594), age 12
Michael Drayton
  (1563-1631), age 12
Galileo Galilei
  (1564-1642), age 11
Christopher Marlowe
  (1564-1593), age 11
William Shakespeare
  (1564-1616), age 11
James I of England
  (1566-1625), age 9
Muhammad III of Turkey
  (c.1566-1603), age c.9

beginning at the age of three under the regency of his mother (1533–1547); czar of Russia from 1547–1584, the first to assume that title. He broke the power of the Tatars; conquered Kazan, Astrakhan and Siberia; suppressed the powerful nobles by torture, exile and execu-

# 1575–1600

The golden age of English drama is generally placed between 1580 and 1642. The cause of its termination is known—the closing of London theaters by the Puritan Parliament—but the circumstances surrounding the beginning are less clear. Thomas Kyd (1557–1595) apparently opened the era with *The Spanish Tragedy* and was followed closely by Christopher Marlowe (1564–1593), Robert Greene (1560–1592), George Peele (1558–1598) and then Shakespeare. Suddenly, within a single decade, mature, first-rate plays were being written and produced.

Among the probable causes for this sudden outburst of blank-verse drama, the most conspicuous is the fact that Seneca's plays were translated and published in England

tion; and established an autocratic government. Mentally unbalanced after 1560, he was subject to violent fits of temper (during one of which he killed his eldest son), followed by tearful remorse. He is the prototype of many Russian fictional characters.

Thomas Campion
    (1567-1620), age 8
Samuel de Champlain
    (1567-1635), age 8
Claudio Monteverdi
    (1567-1643), age 8
Thomas Nashe
    (1567-1601), age 8
Tommaso Campanella
    (1568-1639), age 7
Jahangir
    (1569-1627), age 6
Guy Fawkes
    (1570-1606), age 5
Johannes Kepler
    (1571-1630), age 4
Thomas Dekker
    (1570/72-1632), age c.3
Caravaggio
    (1565 or 1573-1609/10),
    age 2?
John Donne
    (1572/73-1631), age c.2
Inigo Jones
    (1573-1652), age 2
Ben Jonson
    (1572/73-1637), age c.2
William Laud
    (1573-1645), age 2

between 1559 and 1581. It is fairly certain that without the revival of interest in classical drama—that is, the Latin tragedies of Seneca and the comedies of Terence and Plautus—there would have been no Elizabethan drama. Signs of dependence are obvious; the Roman dramatists were closely imitated, sometimes to the extent of borrowing a whole plot and characters, as in Shakespeare's *Comedy of Errors.*

A second probable cause is that playwriting had become profitable, as Shakespeare's retirement at 48 would seem to indicate. The dependence of the dramatists on court patronage is fairly certain, since there was no popular theater in 1580, and in fact theatrical performances were forbidden by the civic authorities of London, who regularly imprisoned actors on charges of vagrancy. The first public performances, necessarily outside the city walls, and usually in inn yards, were not likely to offer sufficient rewards to attract much talent. Nor were hostlers and innkeepers and lodgers at the

Titian
   (1477 or 1487/90-1576),
   age 85?
Hans Sachs
   (1494-1576), age 81
Pope Gregory XIII
   (1502-1585), age 73
Andrea Palladio
   (1508 or 1518-1580),
   age 67?
Gerhardus Mercator
   (1512-1594), age 63
St. Theresa
   (1515-1582), age 60
Tintoretto
   (1518-1594), age 57
Catherine de Medicis
   (1519-1589), age 56
Pope Sixtus V
   (1521-1590), age 54
Luiz Vaz de Camoens
   (1524-1580), age 51
Pierre de Ronsard
   (1524-1585), age 51
Raphael Holinshed
   (c.1525-1580), age c.50
Giovanni Palestrina
   (1525/26-1594), age c.50
Philip II of Spain
   (1527-1598), age 48
Paolo Veronese
   (1528-1588), age 47
Ivan IV of Russia
   (1530-1584), age 45

inn the most appreciative audience. What else but the prospect of court patronage could have persuaded such men as Thomas Nashe, Thomas Dekker, Ben Jonson and the rest

ELIZABETH I
Queen of England
1533-1603

**Elizabeth I,** age 42; queen of England and Ireland from 1558–1603 and the last of the Tudors; daughter of Henry VIII and Anne Boleyn. Imprisoned at 21 in the Tower of London by her half-sister, Mary I, for her Protestant sympathies, she became queen at 25 after Mary's death. Vain and capricious, but popular with her subjects, she built a strong navy, reestablished the Church of England and suppressed Roman Catholics. She declined a marriage offer from Philip II of Spain and defeated his armada (assisted by a violent storm). Her reign was one of England's great periods and the golden age of English literature.

**Michel Eyquem de Montaigne,** age 42; French writer born in Bordeaux of a noble merchant family. He gave up public office at 37 and retired to his family estate to read Plutarch and write his *Essais*. He invented a new literary form, the informal, personal essay of a skeptical nature, oriented to the new humanistic morality (or heresy) of toleration of human error, both in oneself and others. He was the mayor of Bordeaux from 1581–1585.

**William I** (William the Silent), age 42; founder of the Dutch Republic and first stadtholder, 1579–1584. As commander of the imperial army and governor of northern Holland, he opposed the persecution of Protestants by Philip II and led the War of Liberation against Spain (1567–1576). He was assassinated by a religious fanatic.

**Nobunaga,** age 41; Japanese warlord and statesman of the Taira clan; he restored order and began the reunification of Japan after a period of anarchy and feudal war. Though he never held the title of shogun, he was the actual ruler from 1568–1582. He was assassinated by a discontented general.

**Sir Martin Frobisher,** age 40?; English mariner born in Yorkshire, commander of an expedition in search of a northwest passage to the East in 1576. He discovered Frobisher Bay in Canada and returned the following year to search for gold, without success. He commanded the *Triumph* in the battle with the Spanish Armada in 1588 and was knighted the same year.

**Toyotomi Hideyoshi,** age 39; Japanese general and dictator, son of a poor woodcutter. He rose from common soldier to chief lieutenant of

to compete? Elizabethan drama appears to be well-named, for it is quite possible that it was inspired by Elizabeth's fondness for drama—and she was one who could afford to pay well.

Nobunaga and ruled as dictator after Nobunaga's death in 1582. He finished the task of unifying and pacifying Japan after a century of disorder. He froze the class structure and erected many buildings and monuments in his capital of Osaka.

**Faustus Socinus** (Fausto Sozzini), age 36; Italian religious reformer, organizer of modern Unitarianism and founder of Socinianism. In Poland from 1579–1604, he brought the anti-Trinitarian groups together and formed the Polish Brethren. Opposed by both Roman Catholics and Protestants, he denied the natural depravity of man and held that no doctrine contrary to reason or progress should be accepted.

SIR FRANCIS DRAKE
English navigator and
    privateer
1540/45-1596

**Sir Francis Drake,** age c.35; English navigator and privateer, first Englishman to sail around the world (1577–1580). He engaged in piracy 1570–1572 against Spanish ships and settlements in the West Indies, under license from the queen, and was knighted in recognition of his services. He commanded one-third of the fleet that destroyed the Armada. Drake died of dysentery at sea.

**Akbar the Great,** age 33; third Mogul emperor of India (1556–1605), grandson of Babur. He expanded and consolidated the empire and maintained splendid courts in three cities, which were centers of arts and letters, although he himself was illiterate. His attempt to found a new religion by incorporating elements of other faiths was not successful. He was succeeded by his son Jahangir.

**Iyeyasu,** age 33; Japanese general and dictator, founder of the Tokugawa Shogunate, which ruled until 1867. As an aide to Nobunaga and Hideyoshi, he helped unify Japan. Upon the latter's death in 1598, he became one of four regents. In a great battle in 1600 he eliminated his fellow regents and assumed complete control of the government. Named shogun by the emperor in 1603, he established his capital at Yedo (modern Tokyo). His mausoleum has become a famous shrine.

**St. John of the Cross** (Juan de Yepes y Alvarez), age 33; Spanish monk, mystic and poet, born in Avila; friend of St. Theresa, whom he assisted in founding Barefoot Carmelite monasteries. He was imprisoned in 1577–1578 for his excessive zeal in promoting reforms in the Carmelite order. Considered one of the foremost Spanish lyric poets,

Abbas I of Persia
    (1557-1628), age 43
Jacobus Arminius
    (1560-1609), age 40
Annibale Carracci
    (1560-1609), age 40
Sir Francis Bacon
    (1561-1626), age 39
Samuel Daniel
    (1562-1619), age 38
Lope de Vega
    (1562-1635), age 38
Michael Drayton
    (1563-1631), age 37
Galileo Galilei
    (1564-1642), age 36
William Shakespeare
    (1564-1616), age 36
James I of England
    (1566-1625), age 34
Muhammad III of Turkey
    (c.1566-1603), age c.34
Thomas Campion
    (1567-1620), age 33
Samuel de Champlain
    (1567-1635), age 33
Claudio Monteverdi
    (1567-1643), age 33
Thomas Nashe
    (1567-1601), age 33
Tommaso Campanella
    (1568-1639), age 32
Jahangir
    (1569-1627), age 31
Guy Fawkes
    (1570-1606), age 30
Johannes Kepler
    (1571-1630), age 29
Thomas Dekker
    (1570/72-1632),
    age c.28
Caravaggio
    (1565 or 1573-1609/10),
    age 27?
John Donne
    (1572/73-1631), age c.27

he is best known for *The Dark Night of the Soul* and *The Ascent of Mount Carmel*. He was canonized in 1726 and made a Doctor of the Church in 1926.

MARY STUART
Queen of Scotland
1542-1587

**Mary, Queen of Scots** (Mary Stuart), age 33; queen of Scotland from 1542–1567, succeeding her father, James V, when she was only six days old. Brought up at the French court as a Roman Catholic, she married the king's son (later Francis II), and after his death in 1560 returned to Scotland as queen. Forced to abdicate in 1567 by intrigues among the Protestant nobles, she fled to England, only to be imprisoned for 19 years by her second cousin, Elizabeth, and finally executed. She is a popular subject of fiction and drama.

**William Byrd,** age 32; English composer and organist famous for his sacred music. He composed anthems for the Anglican Church and masses and motets for the Roman Catholic Church. A favorite of Queen Elizabeth's in 1575, he was granted (jointly with another organist) a 21-year monopoly for printing and selling music in England.

**Torquato Tasso,** age 31; Italian poet born in Sorrento. Under the patronage of the Este family, he wrote a heroic epic poem on the First Crusade, *Jerusalem Delivered,* whose stirring battle scenes, valorous knights and beautiful infidels made it immediately popular. Suffering delusions of persecution, he was confined to an asylum from 1579–1586. He is the subject of Byron's *The Lament of Tasso* and Goethe's drama.

**Alessandro Farnese,** age 30; Italian general and statesman, duke of Parma from 1586–1592; grandson of Pier Luigi Farnese, grandson of Charles V (whose illegitimate daughter, Margaret of Parma, was Alessandro's mother), nephew of Philip II and nephew of John of Austria. He distinguished himself at Lepanto under John of Austria and succeeded him as governor of the Netherlands in 1578.

**Murad III,** age 29; sultan of Turkey from 1574–1595, son and successor of Selim II. While his generals won victories in Persia and Georgia and resumed war with Austria, he was primarily occupied with his harem. Historians see the spread of corruption in his government as the beginning of Turkish decline.

**Tycho Brahe,** age 29; Danish astronomer born in Sweden. For 20 years he worked in an observatory built for him by Frederick II on the island of Hven. His importance lies in his introduction of precision into astronomical observations. It was his accuracy in calculating the length of the year that resulted in the adoption of the new Gregorian calendar. He went to Bohemia in 1597, where Kepler worked as his assistant and based his laws of planetary motion on Brahe's precise observations of the positions of planets and stars.

**Mateo Aleman,** age 28; Spanish novelist born in Seville, known for one picaresque novel, *Guzman de Alfarache,* published in two parts in

1599 and 1604 and translated into English, French and Latin. He lived an unconventional life and finally emigrated to Mexico City and became a printer.

MIGUEL DE CERVANTES
SAAVEDRA
Spanish novelist
1547-1616

**Miguel de Cervantes Saavedra,** age 28; Spanish novelist, son of an impoverished apothecary and famous for a single work, *Don Quixote de la Mancha.* After several years in the army, five years as a captive of pirates in Algiers and long years of struggle to support his family, at 58 he produced his masterpiece, *Don Quixote,* called the first modern novel and one of the world's greatest. He and Shakespeare died the same day.

**John of Austria** (Juan de Austria), age c.28; Spanish admiral born in Ratisbon, illegitimate son of Emperor Charles V and Barbara Blomberg. He is famous as the supreme commander of the Christian fleet that defeated the Turks at Lepanto in 1571. He was governor general of the Netherlands from 1576–1578.

**Giordano Bruno,** age 27; Italian philosopher born in Nola, a Dominican friar until he reached the age of 28. He carried Copernican cosmology a step further and suggested that the stars are also suns, with their own satellite systems. Arrested by the Inquisition in Venice 1592, he was imprisoned seven years and burned at the stake in Rome. His metaphysics influenced Spinoza and Leibniz.

**El Greco** (Kyriakos Theotokopoulos), age 27?; painter of the Castilian school born in Crete; he studied in Venice and settled in Toledo in 1576. His strangely illuminated distortions, influenced by Spanish mysticism, were not popular in his own time, but are highly praised by modern critics. One familiar work is the *View of Toledo,* in the Metropolitan Museum of Art in New York.

**John Napier,** age 25; Scottish mathematician and laird of Merchiston Castle near Edinburgh. He invented logarithms, wrote the first logarithm table in 1614 and introduced the use of the decimal point.

**Boris Fedorovich Godunov,** age c.24; regent of Russia from 1584–1598 for his brother-in-law, Fedro I, the mentally deficient son of Ivan the Terrible; czar from 1598–1605. He issued an edict in 1587 forbidding the transfer or sale of serfs, thus binding them to the soil, and introduced the practice of banishing political dissidents to Siberia. He is the subject of a drama by Pushkin and an opera by Mussorgsky.

**Sir Edward Coke,** age 23; English jurist known for his compilation of law, *Institutes of the Laws of England* (including *Coke Upon Littleton*), 1628–1644. Chief justice of the King's Bench from 1613–1616 and a member of Parliament after 1620, he was a lifelong political rival of Francis Bacon.

**Richard Hakluyt,** age 23; English geographer and clergyman. Educated for the ministry, he took time from his career in the church to

Inigo Jones
(1573-1652), age 27
Ben Jonson
(1572/73-1637),
age c.27
William Laud
(1573-1645), age 27
Will Adams
(1564 or 1575-1620),
age 25?
Jakob Boehme
(1575-1624), age 25
Henry Hudson
(1575?-1611), age 25?
John Carver
(c.1576-1621), age c.24
Robert Burton
(1577-1640), age 23
Baron De La Warr
(1577-1618), age 23
Peter Paul Rubens
(1577-1640), age 23
William Harvey
(1578-1657), age 22
John Fletcher
(1579-1625), age 21
George Calvert
(c.1580-1632), age c.20
Frans Hals
(1580/85-1666), age c.20
Massasoit
(1580?-1661), age 20?
Peter Minuit
(1580-1638), age 20
John Smith
(1580-1631), age 20
John Webster
(1575 or 1580-1625?),
age 20?
St. Vincent de Paul
(1580/81-1660), age c.19
Hugo Grotius
(1583-1645), age 17
Lord Herbert of Cherbury
(1583-1648), age 17
Francis Beaumont
(1584-1616), age 16
John Cotton
(1584-1652), age 16
Miles Standish
(c.1584-1656), age c.16

gather information on English explorations and wrote a complete account called *The Principal Navigations, Voyages, and Discoveries of the English Nation* (1589).

SIR WALTER RALEIGH
English navigator
c.1552-1618

**Sir Walter Raleigh,** age c.23; English navigator and favorite of Queen Elizabeth. He explored the North American coast from Florida to North Carolina in 1584 and named it *Virginia,* but failed in colonization efforts. Charged with conspiracy after the death of Elizabeth in 1603, he was sent to the Tower, where he lived with his wife and son for 13 years (and wrote a history of the world). He was released in 1616 to undertake another expedition and beheaded two years later. Raleigh is credited with introducing tobacco and the potato into England and Ireland.

EDMUND SPENSER
English poet
1552/53-1599

**Edmund Spenser,** age c.23; English poet born in London. Richly talented, he was a friend of Philip Sidney and Walter Raleigh, but was disappointed in his efforts to obtain patronage and court preferment—a castle in Ireland and 50 pounds a year was hardly enough. His castle was burned in 1598 by Irish insurgents, causing the death of his youngest child; he died in London three months later at 46. His major work, *The Faerie Queen,* is an allegory in defense of Protestantism and Puritanism.

**Henry IV** (Henry of Navarre), age 22; king of France from 1589–1610, first of the house of Bourbon. Son of Anthony of Bourbon (duke of Vendome and king of Navarre), he inherited the French throne by marrying the sister of Francis II, Charles IX and Henry III—all children of Henry II and Catherine de Medicis. He pacified the kingdom, terminated religious wars and signed the Edict of Nantes in 1598, which guaranteed religious freedom. He also encouraged the colonization of America. Henry IV was assassinated by a religious zealot and succeeded by his son Louis XIII.

**Sir Fulke Greville,** age 21; first Baron Brooke, English poet and statesman, friend of Sir Philip Sidney's and favorite of Queen Elizabeth's. He held a number of important offices and wrote sonnets and tragedies, but is best known as the author of *The Life of the Renowned Sir Philip Sidney*.

**Richard Hooker,** age 21?; English theologian and clergyman born in Exeter, author of *Of the Laws of Ecclesiastical Polity* (in eight books). An influential treatise on church government, it was admired for its prose style and important for its bearing on civil government, thanks to Hooker's clear distinction between the laws of the state and the law of nature.

**John Lyly,** age c.21; English dramatist and prose writer whose romance in two parts—*Euphues, the Anatomy of Wit* (1579) and *Euphues and His England* (1580)—gave currency to the term *euphuism*. Its affected, artificial style was ridiculed by Shakespeare, though the work was very influential in its time.

**Sir Philip Sidney,** age 21; English courtier and favorite of Queen Elizabeth's, greatly admired as the ideal English aristocrat. Diplomat, poet, scholar and heroic cavalry commander, he was mortally wounded fighting the Spanish in Holland died at 32. He is popularly remembered for surrendering his water flask to a foot soldier.

**Thomas Kyd,** age c.18; influential English dramatist born in London, author of *The Spanish Tragedy* (1586), a melodramatic story of revenge, highly successful in its time. He is believed to have written a Hamlet play used by Shakespeare as the basis of his tragedy. Accused of holding unorthodox religious and moral views, he was imprisoned in 1593 and died in poverty soon after his release.

**George Peele,** age 17?; English dramatist, poet and actor, one of the Elizabethans who lived recklessly and died young. He was raised in an orphanage (where his father was bookkeeper) and educated at Oxford. His best-known play is *The Old Wives' Tale*, which is believed to be the source of Milton's *Comus*.

**Robert Greene,** age c.15; English dramatist and prose writer and the author of popular romances, one of which suggested the plot of Shakespeare's *A Winter's Tale*. He is believed to have collaborated with Shakespeare on *Henry VI*. Greene also wrote tracts and pamphlets, including a series on the London underworld. He lived a bohemian life and died in poverty. His best-known play is *The Honourable History of Friar Bacon and Friar Bungay*.

**Ferenc Esterhazy,** age 12; first of the famous Magyar Esterhazy family of Hungary. His name was Ferenc Zerhazy, but after being made baron of Galanta (now a town in Czechoslovakia) he took the name Esterhazy. The family was noted for its wealth and its patronage of artists, including the composer Joseph Haydn.

**Christopher Marlowe,** age 11; English dramatist, son of a shoemaker and Shakespeare's closest rival. His best-known works are *Dr. Faustus, The Jew of Malta* and *Edward II*. He also translated Book I of Lucan's *Pharsalia*. An atheist and a familiar figure in the London underworld, he was fatally stabbed at 29 in a tavern brawl.

# 1600

Cornelis Jansen
   (1585-1638), age 15
Duc de Richelieu
   (1585-1642), age 15
John Ford
   (c.1586-after 1638),
   age c.14
Thomas Hooker
   (c.1586-1647), age c.14
Thomas Hobbes
   (1588-1679), age 12
John Winthrop
   (1588-1649), age 12
Ahmed I of Turkey
   (1589-1617), age 11
William Bradford
   (1590-1657), age 10
Robert Herrick
   (1591-1674), age 9
Anne Hutchinson
   (1591-1643), age 9
Shah Jahan
   (1592-1666), age 8
George Herbert
   (1593-1633), age 7
Izaak Walton
   (1593-1683), age 7
Gustavus II of Sweden
   (1594-1632), age 6
Nicolas Poussin
   (1593/94-1665), age c.6
Thomas Carew
   (1595?-1639?), age 5?
Pocahontas
   (1595?-1617), age 5?
Kiliaen Van Rensslaer
   (1595?-1644), age 5?
Rene Descartes
   (1596-1650), age 4
Michael Romanov
   (1596-1645), age 4
Giovanni Bernini
   (1598-1680), age 2
John Alden
   (c.1599-1687), age c.1
Francesco Borromini
   (1599-1667), age 1
Oliver Cromwell
   (1599-1658), age 1
Anthony Van Dyck
   (1599-1641), age 1
Velazquez
   (1599-1660), age 1

# 1600–1625

When the first French and English colonies were planted in North America, it was no longer an unknown continent. For nearly a century it had been periodically penetrated from the north, the south and the west. Prominent among the explorers were Ponce de Leon in Florida (1513); the Spanish conquistadors in Mexico (1519–1536); Jacques Cartier on the St. Lawrence River (1534–1535); De Soto in the lower Mississippi valley and the southeastern states (1539–1542); and Coronado in the southwest as far as Texas, Oklahoma and Kansas, searching for the Seven Cities (1540–1542). As late as the early 17th century, however, the eastern seaboard was still a largely unexplored wilderness. Beginning about 1599 the French had established fur-trading posts along the St. Lawrence River, and in 1608 Samuel de Champlain established the first permanent settlement on the site of Quebec. He was governor of the colony from 1616–1629 and 1634–1635 and was buried there.

## 1600

Elizabeth I of England
   (1533-1603), age 67
Faustus Socinus
   (1539-1604), age 61
Akbar the Great
   (1542-1605), age 58
Iyeyasu
   (1542-1616), age 58
William Byrd
   (1543-1623), age 57
Tycho Brahe
   (1546-1601), age 54
Mateo Aleman
   (1547-1610/14), age 53
Miguel de Cervantes
   (1547-1616), age 53
Giordano Bruno
   (1548-1600), age 52
El Greco
   (1541 or 1548-1614?),
   age 52?
John Napier
   (1550-1617), age 50
Boris Godunov
   (1551/52-1605), age c.49
Sir Edward Coke
   (1552-1634), age 48

**Abbas I** (Abbas the Great), age 43; shah of Persia from 1586–1628. He recovered extensive territory from the Turks and restored Persian power, besieging and capturing Baghdad in 1623. He built splendid palaces and mosques in his capital of Estaban and sent ambassadors to European countries. At his death Persia extended from the Tigris to the Indus.

**Jacobus Arminius** (Jacob Harmensen), age 40; Dutch Protestant theologian, professor at Leiden. He rejected Calvin's strict predestination in favor of universal salvation, or salvation by free choice. Arminianism was adopted by Methodists in America and Wesleyans in Britain. Attempts to bring him to trial failed, and he died peacefully.

**Annibale Carracci,** age 40, Italian painter born in Bologna of a family of painters that included his cousin Ludovico (founder of an academy of painting) and his brother Agostino. They attempted to revive the natural simplicity of the early Renaissance. Annibale's paintings include *Quo vadis, Domine?* (National Gallery, London) and *Fishing Scene* (Louvre), a classic landscape anticipating Poussin.

**Sir Francis Bacon,** age 39; English statesman and writer; lord chancellor from 1618–1621. He confessed to corrupt practices and the acceptance of bribes and was fined and banished from Parliament and court. He is the author of *The New Atlantis* and *Novum organum,* but is better known for his *Essays* on practical wisdom, opening with the famous line, *"What is truth?* said jesting Pilate, and would not stay for an answer."

**Samuel Daniel,** age 38; English poet and historian; tutor of noble children. He was the author of a history of England, tragicomedies and masques for the court of James I and a collection of sonnets to *Delia.* Coleridge called him a major poet for the simplicity of his diction.

**Lope de Vega** (Lope Felix de Vega Carpio), age 38; Spanish dramatist

English claims in North America were based on the discoveries of John Cabot in 1497–1498, but a century passed before colonization began. An unsuccessful attempt was made in 1583 in Newfoundland, where the severe cold sent the colonists back to England the same year. Not until 1607, in the reign of James I, was a permanent settlement made, at Jamestown, Va. Even in this milder climate, the hardships and privations were so acute that only the providential arrival of Lord Delaware in 1610, with new settlers and fresh supplies, saved the colony from extinction. The second permanent English settlement was Plymouth Colony in Massachusetts, on Cape Cod Bay, established in 1620 by John Carver and the Pilgrims, and carried through difficult times by the second governor, William Bradford.

By the time Massachusetts Bay Colony was established on the site of Boston in the summer of 1630, the risks and many of the hardships had been eliminated. Gov. John Winthrop arrived with about 1,800 colonists and proceeded to establish a prosperous, flourishing community. Colonization of the Atlantic seaboard continued steadily, and by 1790 there were 3,929,214 people in the United States.

# 1625

born in Madrid. He served in the armada in his youth and, turning to writing, singlehandedly created Spanish national drama; he is said to have written 1800 plays, 430 of which are extant, ranging from tragedy to melodrama and farce. He became a priest at 52, after the death of his second wife, and a doctor of theology at 65.

**Michael Drayton,** age 37; English poet, son of a prosperous tradesman of Warwickshire. A versatile and prolific poet, he wrote lyrics, satires, pastorals, popular ballads and plays in collaboration with Thomas Dekker and John Webster. His major work is the seldom-read, 15,000-line topographical tour of the English countryside, *Poly-Olbion*. A familiar line from the *Ballad of Agincourt* is, "Fair stood the wind for France."

GALILEO GALILEI
Italian physicist and
astronomer
1564-1642

**Galileo Galilei,** age 36; Italian physicist and astronomer born in Pisa. He was a professor of mathematics at the universities of Pisa, Padua and Florence and mathematician extraordinary to Cosimo II, the grand duke of Tuscany. The first outstanding experimental physicist since

Massasoit
(1580?-1661), age 45?
Peter Minuit
(1580-1638), age 45
St. Vincent de Paul
(1580/81-1660),
age c.44
Hugo Grotius
(1583-1645), age 42
Lord Herbert of Cherbury
(1583-1648), age 42
John Cotton
(1584-1652), age 41
Miles Standish
(c.1584-1656), age c.41
Cornelis Jansen
(1585-1638), age 40
Duc de Richelieu
(1585-1642), age 40
John Ford
(c.1586-after 1638),
age c.39
Thomas Hooker
(c.1586-1647),
age c.39
Thomas Hobbes
(1588-1679), age 37

# 1600

Richard Hakluyt
   (1552-1616), age 48
Sir Walter Raleigh
   (c.1552-1618), age c.48
Henry IV of France
   (1553-1610), age 47
Sir Fulke Greville
   (1554-1628), age 46
Richard Hooker
   (1554?-1600), age 46?
John Lyly
   (c.1554-1606), age c.46

Archimedes and the principal founder of modern science, he discovered the first two of Newton's three laws of motion (the law of uniform motion and the law of acceleration). He also discovered that moonlight is reflected light. Galileo accepted the Copernican system and narrowly escaped the church's persecution with his life. He died at 78, after five years of blindness.

WILLIAM SHAKESPEARE
English dramatist
1564-1616

**William Shakespeare,** age 36; English dramatist and poet born in Stratford-upon-Avon, the son of a small merchant. He married Anne Hathaway, eight years his senior, in 1582 and had three children. Besides the 37 or 38 well-known plays, he wrote two narrative poems, *Venus and Adonis* and *The Rape of Lucrece,* and 154 sonnets. *The Tempest* (1611) was his last play, except for occasional collaborations. He retired to Stratford in 1612 and died four years later, aged 52.

**James I,** age 34; king of England and Ireland from 1603–1625, first of the house of Stuart; son of Mary, Queen of Scots, and Henry Stewart, Lord Darnley; great-great-grandson of Henry VII; also king of Scotland from 1567–1625 as James VI. He authorized a new translation of the Bible, was the patron of Shakespeare's Globe Theatre and had literary ambitions of his own. His best-known work is a tract on the evils of tobacco. He encouraged the colonization of North America.

**Muhammad III,** age c.34; sultan of Turkey from 1595–1603, son and successor of Murad III. During his reign war continued in Hungary and in Persia, where Tabriz was lost to Abbas I. The momentum of Turkish conquest appeared spent. He was succeeded by his son Ahmed I.

**Thomas Campion,** age 33; English poet and composer; a London physician by profession. He wrote words and music for court entertainments, Latin epigrams and elegies and a text on musical counterpoint. He is chiefly known for his graceful lyrics, many of which were set to music and published in a series of popular songbooks.

**Samuel de Champlain,** age 33; French explorer who established a permanent settlement at Quebec in 1608 and laid the foundations of lasting friendly relations with the Indians of Canada, whom he described in *The Savages* (1603). He also discovered Lake Champlain.

**Claudio Monteverdi,** age 33; Italian composer born in Cremona, the first outstanding operatic composer. *Orfeo,* produced in 1607, established opera as a serious art form. He was ordained a priest in 1633.

**Thomas Nashe,** age 33; English pamphleteer, novelist and dramatist deeply involved, as an ardent anti-Puritan, in the religious and literary controversies of his time. In 1596 he finished the *Tragedy of Dido,* left unfinished by his friend Christopher Marlowe. His romance *The Unfortunate Traveller* or *The Life of Jack Wilton* (1594) was a forerunner of the realistic adventure novels of Defoe and Smollett.

**Tommaso Campanella,** age 32; Italian Renaissance philosopher and Dominican monk and the author of over 80 books, including *City of the Sun,* a description of a utopian society. He was imprisoned in Naples 27 years (1599–1626) on charges of heresy and conspiracy.

**Jahangir,** age 31; fourth Mogul emperor of India (1605–1627), son and successor of Akbar. Agents from the British East India Company arrived (1609–1611) and were granted trading privileges. He was succeeded by his son Shah Jahan.

**Guy Fawkes,** age 30; English conspirator born in York. A Protestant by birth, he turned Roman Catholic and served in the Spanish army in Flanders. He is remembered for his part in the Gunpowder Plot, a scheme to blow up the houses of Parliament to protest the anti-Catholic laws of James I. On the night of Nov. 4, 1605, he was caught in the cellar of the House of Lords with 36 barrels of gunpowder. He was executed with his fellow conspirators.

**Johannes Kepler,** age 29; German astronomer born in Wurttemberg; imperial mathematician and court astronomer to Rudolf III, Holy Roman emperor. He is famous for his three laws of planetary motion, which state, first, that the planets describe ellipses, rather than circles, around the sun; second, that the closer a planet approaches the sun, the faster it moves; and third, that there is a direct ration between the square of the time required for a planet to orbit the sun and the cube of its mean distance from the sun. He believed the sun to be the center of the universe.

**Thomas Dekker,** age c.28; prolific English dramatist and pamphleteer born in London. He was employed by Philip Henslowe, a theater manager, to write plays in collaboration with others—including Ben Jonson, who later made him the object of his satirical play *The Poetaster*. His plays have contemporary characters and settings and afford glimpses of everyday Elizabethan London. The best-known are *The Shoemaker's Holiday,* a domestic comedy, and *Old Fortunatus.*

**Caravaggio** (Michelangelo Merisi), age 27?; Italian painter of genre and religious subjects born in Caravaggio, a village in Lombardy. He rejected the classical idealization of subject and painted realistically from life, using mostly plebian types, with dramatic emphasis on light and shadow as in *Supper at Emmaeus* (in the National Gallery in London) and *Calling of St. Matthew* (in Rome).

**John Donne,** age c.27; English poet and Anglican clergyman born in London, remembered today for his poetry ("Go and catch a falling star. . . ."), but known in his time as an eloquent preacher and dean of St. Paul's. His prose work, *Devotions upon Emergent Occasions,* contains the famous lines: "No man is an illand, intire of it selfe . . . any man's death diminishes me, because I am involved in mankinde; and therefore never send to know for whom the bell tolls; it tolls for thee."

**Inigo Jones,** age 27; English architect born in London. He visited Italy to study Palladio's architecture and returned to design the royal banquet hall at Whitehall Palace in London (1619–1622), which inspired the Georgian style of English architecture. He also reconstructed St. Paul's Cathedral.

**Ben Jonson,** age c.27; English dramatist, poet and actor; son of a clergyman and stepson (after his father's death) of a bricklayer. An influential writer of his time and favorite of James I, he produced entertainments (masques) for the court. He is best remembered for his satirical comedies *Volpone, The Alchemist* and *Bartholomew Fair* and for the song "To Celia" ("Drink to me only with thine eyes. . .").

**William Laud,** age 27; English prelate; archbishop of Canterbury from 1633–1645. An ardent supporter of Charles I and of absolutism

# 1625

John Winthrop
(1588-1649), age 37
William Bradford
(1590-1657), age 35
Robert Herrick
(1591-1674), age 34
Anne Hutchinson
(1591-1643), age 34
Shah Jahan
(1592-1666), age 33
George Herbert
(1593-1633), age 32
Izaak Walton
(1593-1683), age 32
Gustavus II of Sweden
(1594-1632), age 31
Nicolas Poussin
(1593/94-1665),
age c.31
Thomas Carew
(1595?-1639?), age 30?
Kiliaen Van Rensslaer
(1595?-1644), age 30?
Rene Descartes
(1596-1650), age 29
Michael Romanov
(1596-1645), age 29
Giovanni Bernini
(1598-1680), age 27
John Alden
(c.1599-1687), age c.26
Francesco Borromini
(1599-1667), age 26
Oliver Cromwell
(1599-1658), age 26
Anthony Van Dyck
(1599-1641), age 26
Velazquez
(1599-1660), age 26
Calderon de la Barca
(1600-1681), age 25
Charles I of England
(1600-1649), age 25
Claude Lorrain
(1600-1682), age 25
Baltasar Gracian
(1601-1658), age 24
Louis XIII of France
(1601-1643), age 24
Jules Mazarin
(1602-1661), age 23

in religion and government, he was a bitter enemy of Calvinism and Puritanism. With England on the brink of civil war in 1641, he was impeached by the Long Parliament and imprisoned in the Tower. He was convicted of high treason and executed in 1645.

**Will Adams** (Anjin Sama), age 25?; English mariner, the first Englishman to visit Japan. As pilot for five Dutch vessels bound for the Indies, he encountered rough weather, and his ship was blown off course and onto the coast of Japan in 1600. He was taken to Iyeyasu and retained as a maritime adviser. He married a Japanese girl, was given an estate and remained all his life, supervising shipbuilding and promoting trade.

**Jakob Boehme,** age 25; German shoemaker and mystic born in Prussia. With only a rudimentary education and his visions to guide him, and the Bible and Paracelsus as his sources, he constructed an unorthodox theology that pictured God not as the beneficent Father, but rather as the primordial source of both good and evil. He gained many followers in Germany and Holland and influenced Hegel and Schopenhauer.

**Henry Hudson,** age 25?; English navigator and explorer. On his third voyage in search of a northwest passage to the East, in 1609, he discovered the Hudson River and ascended to the site of Albany. On his fourth voyage (1610–1611) he discovered Hudson Bay, where he was abandoned in a small boat with his son and seven others by a mutinous crew, who returned to England, where they were imprisoned.

**John Carver,** age c.24; first governor of Plymouth Colony in New England and principal organizer of the voyage of the *Mayflower*. A wealthy London merchant, he arranged financial backing, chartered the vessel and equipped it. He sailed from Plymouth, England, on Sept. 16, 1620 (after an earlier departure from Southampton) with 101 colonists; sighted land Nov. 19; and landed at Plymouth Dec. 26. He died of a stroke in 1621 and was succeeded by William Bradford.

**Robert Burton,** age 23; English clergyman and scholar, vicar at St. Thomas's, Oxford, from 1616–1640. A scholarly bachelor, he is remembered for *The Anatomy of Melancholy,* an exhaustive exploration of the causes, effects and cures of the various kinds of melancholy. Written in a quaint prose style and displaying extraordinary erudition, it was admired by John Milton and Charles Lamb.

PETER PAUL RUBENS
Flemish painter and
  diplomat
1577-1640

**Peter Paul Rubens,** age 23; Flemish painter and diplomat. The most popular artist of his time, he painted portraits and decorated palaces for the royalty of France, Spain and England. He set up a workshop, employing many assistants, and produced more than 2,000 paintings.

*Descent from the Cross* (in the cathedral at Antwerp) and *Venus and Adonis* (in the Metropolitan Museum of Art in New York) are among his most famous masterpieces. Also famous are his "Rubensesque"—rather plump—nudes.

**Thomas West, Third Baron de la Warr** (Lord Delaware), age 23; first British colonial governor of Virginia (1610–1618). He arrived at Jamestown in 1610 with three ships, carrying desperately needed supplies and 150 new settlers, just as the original settlers were preparing to abandon the colony. He reestablished Jamestown on a sound basis and returned to England in 1611. A state, river, bay and Indian tribe were named for him.

**William Harvey,** age 22; English physician and anatomist; physician to James I, Charles I and Francis Bacon. He is known for his discovery of the circulation of the blood and the function of the heart as pump, first stated in his lectures in 1616 and later published, in Latin, in *Essay on the Motion of the Heart and the Blood.*

**John Fletcher,** age 21; English dramatist, son of an eminent clergyman. His plays, written in collaboration with Francis Beaumont (*The Maid's Tragedy, A King and No King* and about 50 others), were more popular with contemporaries than Shakespeare's, with whom he probably collaborated on *Henry VIII* and *Two Noble Kinsmen.*

**George Calvert, First Baron Baltimore,** age c.20; English statesman and colonizer in North America; secretary of state and member of the privy council until 1625. After an unsuccessful attempt to establish a colony in Newfoundland, he was granted territory north of the Potomac River, but died before the formalities were completed. The grant passed to his sons and grandsons, who were governors and proprietors of Maryland until 1715.

**Frans Hals,** age c.20; Dutch portrait and genre painter born in Antwerp. He settled in Haarlem and became a highly successful painter of middle-class merchants and officials, both individually and in groups. Two famous works are *Laughing Cavalier* and *La Bohemienne.*

POCAHONTAS
American Indian
1595?-1617

**Pocahontas** (Matoaka), age 5?; American Indian beauty daughter of Powhatan, Algonquin chief. She is famous for having saved the life of Capt. John Smith at the age of 13. At 17 or 18 she was taken prisoner and held hostage at Jamestown, where she was converted to Christianity, baptized as Rebecca and married to John Rolfe, the colonist who discovered how to cure tobacco. She accompanied her husband to England in 1615, was introduced at court to James I and died the following year. Her son Thomas was educated in England, became wealthy upon his return to America and is claimed as an ancestor by many prominent Virginians.

Abel Tasman
(1603-1659), age 22
Roger Williams
(1603-1683), age 22
Giacomo Carissimi
(1604/05-1674), age c.21
Sir Thomas Browne
(1605-1682), age 20
Philip IV of Spain
(1605-1665), age 20
Pierre Corneille
(1606-1684), age 19
Rembrandt
(1606-1669), age 19
Edmund Waller
(1606-1687), age 19
John Milton
(1608-1674), age 17
Murad IV of Turkey
(1609/12-1640), age c.16
Sir John Suckling
(1609-1642), age 16
Peter Stuyvesant
(1592 or 1610-1672),
age 15?
Anne Bradstreet
(c.1612-1672), age c.13
Samuel Butler
(1612-1680), age 13
Richard Crashaw
(1612/13-1649), age c.12
La Rochefoucauld
(1613-1680), age 12
Jeremy Taylor
(1613-1667), age 12
Bartolome Murillo
(1617-1682), age 8
Aurangzeb
(1618-1707), age 7
Abraham Cowley
(1618-1667), age 7
Richard Lovelace
(1618-1657/58), age 7
Charles Le Brun
(1619-1690), age 6
Frontenac
(1620-1698), age 5
La Fontaine
(1621-1695), age 4
Andrew Marvell
(1621-1678), age 4

## 1600

**JOHN SMITH**
English colonist and soldier
1580-1631

**John Smith,** age 20; English colonist, soldier and adventurer who fought the Turks in Transylvania before sailing to America. He arrived

## 1625 – 1650

James I of England, son of Mary, Queen of Scots, succeeded his third cousin Elizabeth in 1603 and was succeeded in 1625 by his second son, Charles I, whose reign covered all but one year of the second quarter of the century. Charles I is remembered as the slim, elegant figure in hunting dress and cavalier hat in the portrait by Anthony van Dyck. In a country committed to Parliamentary government, he insisted on absolute power. He dissolved three Parliaments in four years, and for ten years governed without a Parliament. After many years of controversy, civil war (the Great Rebellion) broke out in 1642 between the Royalists and the Parliamentarians. A series of Royalist defeats led to Charles' surrender to the Scottish army in May 1646 and in June 1647, he was delivered to the English Parliament. A Rump Parliament, from which all moderate members had been forcibly ejected, in what is known as Pride's Purge, ordered

## 1625

Sir Edward Coke
    (1552-1634), age 73
Sir Fulke Greville
    (1554-1628), age 71
Abbas I of Persia
    (1557-1628), age 68
Sir Francis Bacon
    (1561-1626), age 64
Lope de Vega
    (1562-1635), age 63

**Massasoit** (Ousmequin), age 45?; American Indian chief of the Wampanoag tribe, which occupied the greater part of what is now Massachusetts. A powerful and honorable chief, he negotiated a peace treaty in 1621 with the Plymouth colonists, strictly observed it and remained friendly all his life. He was the father of Metacomet (King Philip).

**Peter Minuit,** age 45; Dutch colonial administrator born in Germany, called the founder of New York City. He was sent to America in 1626 by the Dutch West India Company as director general of the settlement, which had been established in 1624. He purchased Manhattan Island for $24 worth of trinkets, built a fort on the southern end of the

with the first colonists in May 1607 at Jamestown, Va., and made the acquaintance of Chief Powhatan and his beautiful daughter Pocahontas. As president of the colony's governing council in 1608–1609, he carried Jamestown through a period of hardship and privation. He returned to England in 1609 and later made trading expeditions to New England, and wrote many books about America and his adventure.

**John Webster,** age 20?; English dramatist, son of a tailor. Two of his plays, *The White Devils* and *The Duchess of Malfi,* are practically equal to Shakespeare's. He wrote many plays in collaboration with others, including *Appius and Virginia,* about ancient Rome.

**Francis Beaumont,** age 16; English dramatist, the dominant partner in collaboration with John Fletcher on more than 50 popular plays. He died at 32.

**Ahmed I,** age 11; sultan of Turkey from 1603–1617, son and successor of Muhammad III. The rise of Europe and the decline of Turkey was manifested in the signing of the Treaty of Szitvatork in 1606, whereby the Holy Roman emperor, as king of Hungary, ceased paying annual tribute to the sultan of Turkey.

## 1625

Earl of Shaftesbury
 (1621-1683), age 4
Moliere
 (1622-1673), age 3
Henry Vaughan
 (1622-1695), age 3
Blaise Pascal
 (1623-1662), age 2
George Fox
 (1624-1691), age 1
John III Sobieski
 (1624-1696), age 1

the king brought to trial. Charles denied the legality of the court and refused to plead. On Jan. 27, 1649 he was condemned as a tyrant, murderer and enemy of the nation, and was hanged three days later.

In Italy, the Renaissance having come to a close, a new art style, the baroque, had come into favor. Bernini and Borromini were the most successful exponents of baroque, which combined monumentalism with profuse decoration. Italian art in general, however, appeared to be in decline, not from lack of talent but from lack of money. Italian commerce and industry were losing the Mediterranean markets to Dutch and English competitors. Rome's population was shrinking, and houses stood empty along the busiest streets. Even as Bernini and Borromini were transforming Rome into a baroque city with new churches, fountains and palaces, the papal treasury teetered on the edge of bankruptcy. Young artists complained they could not find work, and as the center of European art shifted to Paris and northern cities, many of them migrated with the trend, in search of lucrative commissions.

## 1650

island, calling it Fort Amsterdam. Around the fort the settlement of New Amsterdam (later New York) grew up.

**St. Vincent de Paul,** age c.44; French priest born in Gascony, famous for his charitable works. Regarded as the founder of organized charity in France, he inspired many of the nobility to assist the poor of Paris; he founded such organizations as the Lazarists and the Sisters of Charity. The organization bearing his name was founded in Paris in 1833 in his honor.

**Hugo Grotius** (Huig de Groot), age 42; Dutch jurist and statesman and the author of *De jure belli et pacis,* generally regarded as the foundation of international law. Imprisoned by Calvinists, he escaped to

Edmund Waller
 (1606-1687), age 44
John Milton
 (1608-1674), age 42
Peter Stuyvesant
 (1592 or 1610-1672),
 age 40?
Anne Bradstreet
 (c.1612-1672),
 age c.38

# 1625

Michael Drayton
(1563-1631), age 62
Galileo Galilei
(1564-1642), age 61
James I of England
(1566-1625), age 59
Samuel de Champlain
(1567-1635), age 58
Claudio Monteverdi
(1567-1643), age 58
Tommaso Campanella
(1568-1639), age 57
Jahangir
(1569-1627), age 56
Johannes Kepler
(1571-1630), age 54
Thomas Dekker
(1570/72-1632), age c.53
John Donne
(1572/73-1631), age c.52
Inigo Jones
(1573-1652), age 52
Ben Jonson
(1572/73-1637), age c.52
William Laud
(1573-1645), age 52
Robert Burton
(1577-1640), age 48
Peter Paul Rubens
(1577-1640), age 48
William Harvey
(1578-1657), age 47
John Fletcher
(1579-1625), age 46
George Calvert
(c.1580-1632), age c.45
Frans Hals
(1580/85-1666), age 45
John Smith
(1580-1631), age 45
John Webster
(1575 or 1580-1625?),
age 45?

France and became the Swedish ambassador.

**Lord Herbert of Cherbury** (Edward Herbert), age 42; English philosopher, poet and diplomat; elder brother of George Herbert, the poet. He maintained that there is a universal natural religion (the source of the many varieties) based on the inner nature of man, and that all men possess an intuitive knowledge of the existence of God. He is called the forerunner of the deists.

**John Cotton,** age 41; Puritan clergyman born in Derbyshire, England, in whose honor the city of Boston was named. From 1612 to 1633 he was the influential vicar of St. Botolph's in Boston, Lincolnshire. He sailed to Massachusetts in 1633 and with John Winthrop established a theocratic state which, in a spirt of benevolent paternalism, forbade free speech, free thought and freedom of religion. He caused the expulsion of Roger Williams from the colony. His daughter married Increase Mather and was the mother of Cotton Mather.

**Miles** (or Myles) **Standish,** age c.41; American colonist born in England. A soldier in his youth, he sailed with the Pilgrims in the *Mayflower* in 1620 and became the military leader of the colony at Plymouth and served on the governing council for 29 years. The story of his courtship of Priscilla Mullens is believed to be fictional.

**Cornelis Jansen,** age 40; Dutch Roman Catholic theologian, professor at Louvain University and bishop of Ypres. His *Augustinus* (published two years after he died of the plague at 53) attacked Jesuit teachings as contrary to those of St. Augustine on grace and predestination. He declared that Christ did not die for all mankind but for a small number of the elect—those predestined for salvation. The Jansenist movement centered in the Port-Royal convent near Paris, with Pascal among its defenders.

**Duc de Richelieu** (Armand Jean du Plessis), age 40; French cardinal and statesman born in Paris; chief minister to Louis XIII from 1624–1642 and in actual control of the government. Through intrigues and shrewd statesmanship, he made France the strongest power in Europe. He instituted domestic espionage and founded the French Academy. He was succeeded by Mazarin.

**John Ford,** age c.39; English dramatist born in Devonshire, the most important playwright during the reign of Charles I. His best-known plays are *'Tis Pity She's a Whore* (a tragedy dealing with incest); *Broken Heart;* and *The Witch of Edmonton,* written in collaboration with Thomas Dekker and William Rowley.

**Thomas Hooker,** age c.39; Puritan clergyman born in England. To escape charges of nonconformism he went first to Holland and then to America with John Cotton in 1633. After three years as pastor at Newton (now Cambridge), he moved with many of his congregation to Connecticut, where they founded Hartford. He assisted in drafting the Fundamental Articles of Connecticut.

**Thomas Hobbes,** age 37; English materialist philosopher, son of a clergyman. He is famous as the author of *Leviathan,* in which he formulated the social-contract theory and described human life as "nasty, brutish, and short," a "war of each against all," requiring an absolute monarch to maintain order and peace. He was a friend of William Harvey and Ben Jonson and of Galileo, whom he met in Italy.

**John Winthrop,** age 37; first governor of Massachusetts Bay Colony, born in Suffolk, England, of a landowning family. He studied and practiced law in London and was a member of the company that obtained a charter from Charles I for a settlement in Massachusetts. He sailed April 8, 1630 with about 1800 Puritans in the *Arbella* and other ships, arrived June 12 and established a settlement that became Boston on the Shawmut peninsula. He served as governor 12 times and was largely responsible for the success and prosperity of the colony, although he did not believe in democracy or religious freedom.

**William Bradford,** age 35; governor of Plymouth Colony, born in Yorkshire, England. A member of the separatist congregation at Scrooby called the Brownists, he went with the group in 1609 to Holland and in 1620 sailed with them to America on the *Mayflower*. He was elected governor after the death of John Carver in 1621 and continued to serve most of his life. He maintained friendly relations with the Indians; developed fishing, trade and agriculture; and managed to keep Plymouth independent of Massachusetts Bay Colony. His *History of Plymouth Plantation* is the principal source of information on the colony.

**Robert Herrick,** age 34; English lyric poet born in London, one of the cavalier poets. He was the vicar of Dean Prior in Devonshire from 1629–1647 and 1662–1674, having been deprived of the office in the intervening 15 years because of his royalist sympathies. Many of his poems are well known: *To the Virgins, to Make Much of Time; Corinna's Going a-Maying;* and *The Night Piece to Julia.* One familiar line is: "Gather ye rosebuds while ye may."

**Anne Hutchinson,** age 34; religious nonconformist in New England, born Anne Marbury in Lincolnshire, England. She emigrated to Boston in 1634 with her husband and 13 children and was banished from the colony in 1637 for holding and teaching heretical views. She settled in what is now the Bronx, New York City, where she and her family were massacred by Indians in 1643.

**Shah Jahan,** age 33; fifth Mogul emperor of India (1628–1658), grandson of Akbar. His reign constituted the golden age of Indian Muslim architecture. The famous Taj Mahal at Agra was built 1632–1647 as a mausoleum for his favorite wife. He also built the Pearl Mosque at Agra, the Great Mosque at Delhi and the Peacock Throne.

**George Herbert,** age 32; English poet and clergyman born in Wales of a noble family, younger brother of Lord Herbert. One of the metaphysical poets, he was a country parson in Wiltshire the last three years of his short life. His devotional poems, published posthumously, are noted for their precise diction. Izaak Walton wrote his biography.

**Izaak Walton,** age 32; English writer and businessman. Retiring from his London business in 1644, he published biographies of John Donne, Richard Hooker and others, but is remembered for his masterpiece in praise of fishing and the English countryside, *The Compleat Angler; or The Contemplative Man's Recreation* (1653).

**Gustavus II** (Gustavus Adolphus), age 31; king of Sweden from 1611–1632, called the Lion of the North. A brilliant general, he saved the Protestant cause in Germany in the Thirty Years' War, cut off Russian access to the Baltic Sea and laid the foundation of modern Sweden. Killed in battle at 38, he was succeeded by his daughter Christina.

**Nicolas Poussin,** age c.31; French painter born in Normandy of a peasant family. He settled in Rome in 1624 and painted landscapes and classical themes which are praised for their exceptional harmony and clarity. Called the founder of the French classical school, he influenced David and Ingres. Some of his famous works are *Funeral of Phocion* and *Orpheus and Eurydice* (both in the Louvre) and *The Rape of the Sabine Women* (in the Metropolitan Museum of Art in New York).

**Thomas Carew,** age 30?; one of the English cavalier poets, best known for his short love lyrics, many of which were set to music. After a short diplomatic career, he became a court official of Charles I, who presented him with an estate. He was a friend of Ben Jonson and John Suckling.

# 1650

Samuel Butler
(1612-1680), age 38
La Rochefoucauld
(1613-1680), age 37
Jeremy Taylor
(1613-1667), age 37
Bartolome Murillo
(1617-1682), age 33
Aurangzeb
(1618-1707), age 32
Abraham Cowley
(1618-1667), age 32
Richard Lovelace
(1618-1657/58), age 32
Charles Le Brun
(1619-1690), age 31
Frontenac
(1620-1698), age 30
La Fontaine
(1621-1695), age 29
Andrew Marvell
(1621-1678), age 29
Earl of Shaftesbury
(1621-1683), age 29
Moliere
(1622-1673), age 28
Henry Vaughan
(1622-1695), age 28
Blaise Pascal
(1623-1662), age 27
George Fox
(1624-1691), age 26
John III Sobieski
(1624-1696), age 26
Jan De Witt
(1625-1672), age 25
Christina of Sweden
(1626-1689), age 24
Jacques Bossuet
(1627-1704), age 23
Robert Boyle
(1627-1691), age 23
John Bunyan
(1628-1688), age 22
Marcello Malpighi
(1628-1694), age 22
Jacob van Ruisdael
(1628/29-1682),
age c.22
Christian Huygens
(1629-1695), age 21

**Kiliaen Van Rensselaer,** age 30?; Dutch gem merchant born in Amsterdam, one of the organizers, in 1621, of the Dutch West India Company, which colonized New Netherland (New York). Under the patroon system, adopted to encourage settlement, he bought through agents a large tract of land along the Hudson River near Albany (comprising three present-day New York state counties) which became the foundation of the first great American fortune.

RENE DESCARTES
French philosopher and
    mathematician
1596-1650

**Rene Descartes,** age 29; French philosopher and mathematician of a noble family, called the founder of modern philosophy. An officer in foreign armies (Nassau and Bavaria) in his youth, in 1637 he published the famous *Discourse on Method,* in which he proposed to dismiss the chaos of ancient and medieval ideas and make a fresh beginning, applying mathematical precision to metaphysics. He lived in Holland from 1629–1649 and spent his last year in Stockholm (where he died of pneumonia) instructing Queen Christina in philosophy.

**Michael Romanov** (Mikhail Fedorovich), age 29; czar of Russia from 1613–1645, first of the house of Romanov. He was the grand-nephew of Anastasia Romanovna, first wife of Ivan the Terrible and daughter of Roman Yurievich Kobyla; the latter took the name Romanov, but was a descendant of Andrew Kobyla, a German nobleman who emigrated from Prussia in the 14th century. Michael restored order after a period of anarchy and war.

**Giovanni Lorenzo Bernini,** age 27; Italian baroque sculptor, architect and painter, born in Naples. The dominant figure in Italian art for half a century—with Pope Boniface VIII, Pope Alexander VII and Queen Christina of Sweden among his patrons—he decorated the interior of the recently completed St. Peter's Basilica and designed the great circular piazza and colonade in front of the church. His most famous sculpture is *The Ecstasy of St. Teresa,* in colored marble, bronze and stucco.

**John Alden,** age c.26; Puritan settler in Plymouth Colony, famous for two things. He won immortality through a romantic story, retold in verse by Longfellow in *The Courtship of Miles Standish* (1858), and, at 88, he was the last survivor of the Pilgrims who arrived on the *Mayflower*. He married Priscilla, whose last name was Mullens, and lived in nearby Duxbury all his life.

**Francesco Borromini,** age 26; Italian architect born in Lombardy, master of the baroque style. He worked with Bernini on St. Peter's and succeeded him as chief architect in 1644. The church of San Carlo alle Quattro Fontane in Rome is one of his masterpieces. He committed suicide at 68 in a period of depression.

**Oliver Cromwell,** age 26; English soldier and statesman. An enthusiastic supporter of the Puritan cause in the civil war, he assumed leadership by virtue of his military ability. As Lord Protector from 1653–1658, he enforced strict laws against the theater, dancing and other amusements. When he died of the ague at 59, he was buried in Westminster Abbey, only to be disinterred three years later and hung on a gallows as a regicide.

**Anthony Van Dyck** (or Van Dyke), age 26; Flemish painter of portraits and religious subjects born in Antwerp, son of a merchant. He entered the workshop of Rubens and won early fame and popularity for his graceful portraits of aristocrats. The court painter to Charles I of England 1632–1641, he was knighted in 1632. His most famous work is *Charles I in Hunting Dress* in the Louvre.

**Diego Rodriguez de Silva y Velazquez,** age 26; world-renowned Spanish painter born in Seville, son of a lawyer; court painter to Philip IV of Spain from 1623–1660. A master of chiaroscuro, he portrayed the life of his times with simple, impressive naturalism. Famous paintings include *Los Borrachos* (The Drinkers), *The Tapestry Weavers* and *The Surrender of Breda,* all in the Prado in Madrid. He painted many full-length portraits of Philip IV and his son, Don Baltasar Carlos.

**Pedro Calderon de la Barca,** age 25; Spanish dramatist born in Madrid, son of a government official. He wrote about 120 three-act plays, including a series for the royal theater, and was knighted by Philip IV in 1637. Ordained a priest in 1651, he then wrote over 70 one-act religious plays. His best-known play is *Life is a Dream,* generally ranked among the best European plays.

**Charles I,** age 25; king of England, Scotland and Ireland from 1625–1649; second son of James I, of the house of Stuart. His autocratic rule caused large migrations to America and brought on the Great Rebellion. After the destruction of the royalist army at Nasby in 1645, he was captured and brought to trial in 1649; condemned by a court of 67 judges as a tyrant and enemy of the country, he went courageously to his execution.

**Claude Lorrain** (Claude Gellee), age 25; French landscape painter born in Lorraine; founder of the romantic school of landscape painting. His idyllic scenery and brilliant atmospheric effects outshine the insignificant figures in his paintings. Two examples are the famous *Seaport at Sunset* (in the Museum of Fine Arts in Boston) and *Cephalus and Procris* (in the National Gallery in London).

**Baltasar Gracian,** age 24; Spanish writer, preacher and educator; rector of Jesuit college at Terragona. He wrote a three-part philosophical novel, *El Criticon (The Critic),* which examines civilization from the point of a view of a savage. Darkly pessimistic, he saw the majority of men blindly driven by forces within them, and only a few exceptional individuals living by the light of reason. He was highly praised by Schopenhauer.

**Louis XIII,** age 24; king of France from 1610–1643, born in Fontainebleau Castle. Of a retiring nature, he was dominated by his mother, Marie de Medicis, in his youth and by Richelieu and Mazarin in later years. It was a period in which there was an inordinate growth of centralized royal power. He was the father of Louis XIV.

**Jules Mazarin** (Giulio Mazarini), age 23; French statesman and cardinal born in Italy of Sicilian parentage. He entered the service of Richelieu and became a naturalized French citizen in 1639, and a cardinal in 1641. As chief minister (after Richelieu's death in 1642), he laid the foundation of the powerful monarchy of Louis XIV. He amassed a great private fortune and died at 59.

**Abel Janszoon Tasman,** age 22; Dutch navigator and discoverer of New Zealand. In the service of the Dutch East India Company, he made exploring voyages in the Pacific and touched the Philippines, Taiwan and Japan. In 1642 he sailed south from Java, around Australia, and discovered Tasmania, New Zealand and the Tonga and Fiji islands.

# 1650

Charles II of England
(1630-1685), age 20
Richard Cumberland
(1631-1718), age 19
John Dryden
(1631-1700), age 19
John Locke
(1632-1704), age 18
Jean-Baptiste Lully
(1632-1687), age 18
Baruch Spinoza
(1632-1677), age 18
Jan Vermeer
(1632-1675), age 18
Sir Christopher Wren
(1632-1723), age 18
James II of England
(1633-1701), age 17
Samuel Pepys
(1633-1703), age 17
King Philip
(        -1676), age ?
Nicolas Boileau
(1636-1711), age 14
Jacques Marquette
(1637-1675), age 13
Meindert Hobbema
(1638-1709), age 12
Louis XIV of France
(1638-1715), age 12
Nicolas de Malebranche
(1638-1715), age 12
Shun Chih
(1638-1661), age 12
Increase Mather
(1639-1723), age 11
Jean Baptiste Racine
(1639-1699), age 11
William Wycherley
(1640?-1716), age 10?
Muhammad IV of Turkey
(1641-1691), age 9
Isaac Newton
(1642-1727), age 8
Sieur de La Salle
(1643-1687), age 7
William Penn
(1644-1718), age 6
Louis Jolliet
(1645-1700), age 5
Captain William Kidd
(c.1645-1701), age c.5

**Roger Williams,** age 22; clergyman and teacher born in London, founder of the colony of Rhode Island. He emigrated to Massachusetts Bay Colony in 1631, but was banished in 1635 for insisting that civil magistrates had no jurisdiction in matters of religion or conscience. He purchased land from the Narragansett Indians and founded Providence, which became a haven for refugees from religious persecution, in 1636.

**Giacomo Carissimi,** age c.21; Italiam composer, favorite of the nobility of Rome, where he spent most of his life as *kapellmeister*. He composed chamber cantatas, masses, motets and oratorios, including *Jephtha* and *Baltazar*. He was the teacher of Alessandro Scarlatti.

**Sir Thomas Browne,** age 20; English physician and writer born in London. He is noted for his rich and complex prose style in *Religio medici* (The Religion of a Doctor) and *Hydriotaphia; or Urn Burial*, on death, immortality and burial customs. He was knighted by Charles II for his antiquarian scholarship.

**Philip IV,** age 20; king of Spain from 1621–1665, grandson of Philip II and great-grandson of Charles V. His reign was a period of decline, impoverishment and unsuccessful foreign wars; Portugal and Holland were lost. He is remembered mostly for his patronage of Velazquez and Calderon.

**Pierre Corneille,** age 19; French dramatist born in Rouen. He studied law and held office in municipal government. His most popular plays were *Le Cid, Horace, Cinna* and *Polyeucte*. He is regarded as the creator of French classical tragedy.

**Murad IV,** age c.16; Ottoman sultan from 1623–1640, nephew and successor of the insane Mustafa I. He is called the last of the warlike sultans; after he recovered Baghdad from the Persians, Turkish expansion ceased. A vigorous and ruthless ruler, he had many people killed on suspicion of conspiracy, including the Greek patriarch of Constantinople.

**Sir John Suckling,** age 16; English lyric poet and courtier, one of the cavalier poets; the son of a prominent court official, from whom he inherited a large fortune. He is remembered for his wit, extravagance and gallantry and as the inventor of cribbage. When efforts to save Charles I and the royalist cause failed, he fled to France, where, it is

# 1650–1675

After the execution of Charles I in 1649, the English Rump Parliament abolished the House of Lords and the title and office of king and established a republican form of government, with Oliver Cromwell as chief executive. In 1660, 11 years after the death of Charles, the monarchy was restored and his son was crowned as Charles II. A public clamor for the return of the Stuart kings had arisen after Oliver Cromwell's death in 1658, when his son Richard proved incapable of governing. In the period known as the Restoration (1660–1688), a light-hearted reaction against the restrictions of the Puritan decade was manifested in freer man-said, he chose suicide at 33 in preference to poverty. Some familiar lines are: "Why so pale and wan, fond lover?/Prithee why so pale?"

**Richard Crashaw,** age c.12; English poet, one of the metaphysical poets influenced by John Donne. Son of a Puritan poet and clergyman, he went to the continent at the outbreak of civil war, was converted to Roman Catholicism and became secretary to Cardinal Palotta. His religious poems were collected in *Steps to the Temple* (1646). He died of a fever at 36.

REMBRANDT
Dutch painter and etcher
1606-1669

**Rembrandt** (Rembrandt Harmensz van Rijn), age 19; foremost Dutch painter and etcher, born in Leiden, the son of a miller. Early popularity as a portrait painter in Amsterdam (1631–1642) was followed, after the death of his wealthy wife, by financial difficulties and loss of favor. Neglected and poor in his last years, he left over 700 paintings (and 300 etchings), of which *The Night Watch* (or *The Military Company of Captain Frans Banning Cocq*) and *The Syndics of the Cloth Guild* are world-renowned masterpieces.

# 1650

Jean de La Buyere
  (1645-1696), age 5
Baron von Leibniz
  (1646-1716), age 4
Nathaniel Bacon
  (1647-1676), age 3
Pierre Bayle
  (1647-1706), age 3
Denis Papin
  (1647-c.1712), age 3

ners and a hedonistic spirit, accompanied by a certain amount of licentiousness. The theaters were reopened and English drama entered a second brilliant period. The Restoration playwrights George Etherege, William Wycherley and William Congreve wrote brilliant comedies of manners which helped people forget the dour Puritans.

This quarter century saw the publication of John Milton's great poems, *Paradise Lost* and *Paradise Regained,* which evoked the ethos of an earlier time. It saw the rise of modern chemistry and physics in the work of Robert Boyle and Christian Huygens, and it saw Queen Christina abdicate the throne of Sweden to join the social and cultural life of Rome.

Charles II was notorious for his extravagance and chronic need of money, the consequences of which were felt as far away as America. In exchange for financial assistance from

# 1675

Louis XIV, Charles made an alliance with France which drew England into war with the Netherlands. In the course of that war, a number of English vessels entered New York

Inigo Jones
(1573-1652), age 77
William Harvey
(1578-1657), age 72
Frans Hals
(1580/85-1666), age c.70
Massasoit
(1580?-1661), age 70?
St. Vincent de Paul
(1580/81-1660), age c.69
John Cotton
(1584-1652), age 66
Miles Standish
(c.1584-1656), age c.66
Thomas Hobbes
(1588-1679), age 62
William Bradford
(1590-1657), age 60
Robert Herrick
(1591-1674), age 59
Shah Jahan
(1592-1666), age 58
Izaak Walton
(1593-1683), age 57
Nicolas Poussin
(1593/94-1665), age c.56
Rene Descartes
(1596-1650), age 54
Giovanni Bernini
(1598-1680), age 52
John Alden
(c.1599-1687), age c.51
Francesco Borromini
(1599-1667), age 51
Oliver Cromwell
(1599-1658), age 51
Velazquez
(1599-1660), age 51
Calderon de la Barca
(1600-1681), age 50
Claude Lorrain
(1600-1682), age 50
Baltasar Gracian
(1601-1658), age 49
Jules Mazarin
(1602-1661), age 48
Abel Tasman
(1603-1659), age 47

**Edmund Waller,** age 44; English poet known for the smoothness and polish of his verses and for his political adaptability. As a royalist, he devised Waller's Plot to save Charles I; when it failed, he wrote a panegyric to Cromwell, and then, when the wind changed again, a eulogy of Charles II. He was a member of Parliament from 1661–1687.

JOHN MILTON
English poet
1608-1674

**John Milton,** age 42; English poet born in London of a middle-class family. Between the works of his youth—*L'Allegro, Il Penseroso and Lycidas*—and the great poems of his later years—*Paradise Lost, Paradise Regained* and *Samson Agonistes*—he wrote, in the 20-year period from 1640–1660, many tracts in defense of the Puritan cause, and served as a member of Cromwell's government. He was totally blind at 44. One very famous line is, "They also serve who only stand and wait."

**Peter Stuyvesant,** age 40?; one-legged Dutch colonial administrator born in the Netherlands; director general from 1647–1664 of the Dutch West India Company colony of New Netherland. An efficient but despotic governor, he was so unpopular that when an English fleet sailed into New York Bay in 1664, the settlers would not fight and the colony passed uncontested to the English. He retired to his Manhattan farm (*bouwerij* in Dutch) and was buried there, where St. Mark's-in-the-Bouwerie now stands.

**Anne Bradstreet,** age c.38; first woman poet in America, born in Northampton, England. She emigrated to Massachusetts in 1630 with her father, Thomas Dudley, and husband, Simon Bradstreet (both of whom became governors of the colony); she raised a family of eight children, and wrote poetry. Her first volume, *The Tenth Muse Lately Sprung up in America,* was published in London in 1650.

**Samuel Butler,** age 38; English satirical poet known for *Hudibras,* a mock-heroic poem attacking the Puritans for their hypocrisy and self-esteem. The Puritan officer Sir Samuel Luke, for whom he served as aide in the civil war, was his model for Sir Hudibras.

**Francois, duc de La Rochefoucauld,** age 37; French writer born in Paris of an ancient noble family. He took a leading part in the struggle of the nobility against the encroachments of royal power, but is remembered as a frequenter of the most fashionable salons, a lover of the most noble women and the author of witty epigrams published as

Bay, ousted Peter Stuyvesant and made New Amsterdam an English colony—calling it New York in honor of the king's brother, the duke of York, later James II.

1675

*Reflexions ou sentences et maximes morales* (1655). One famous line states: "There are many people who would never have been in love if they had never heard love spoken of."

**Jeremy Taylor,** age 37; English clergyman and theological writer. He was chaplain to Charles I, who gave him his watch and some jewels before he was executed. He took refuge in Wales, where he wrote his literary masterpieces: *Holy Living* (1650), *Holy Dying* (1651) and *The Golden Grove* (1655). He was appointed bishop in Ireland after the Restoration.

**Bartolome Esteban Murillo,** age 33; Spanish painter born in Seville, where he enjoyed great popularity all his life, painting for churches and monasteries. He also painted genre scenes and portraits, but is best known for the warm, sweet piety of his religious pictures. Some famous works are *Birth of the Virgin* (in the Louvre) and *Return of the Prodigal* (in the National Gallery in Washington).

**Aurangzeb,** age 32; emperor of India from 1658–1707, of the Mogul dynasty, son of Shah Jahan, whom he dethroned and kept imprisoned the last eight years of his life. He also caused the death of his three brothers. A fanatical Muslim, he persecuted Hindus and destroyed temples, causing frequent and widespread rebellions. Under his rule the empire reached its greatest extent, but collapsed soon after his death.

**Abraham Cowley,** age 32; English poet born in London who published his first volume of verses at 15. As secretary to the queen of England in Paris, he transmitted her letters to Charles I in cipher. He is said to have introduced in England the informal, intimate essay, originated in France by Montaigne and practices by Charles Lamb. Influenced by John Donne, he wrote love lyrics, odes and elegies.

**Richard Lovelace,** age 32; English lyric poet, one of the cavalier poets, born in Kent of an aristocratic family. A favorite at the court of Charles I and an ardent royalist, he was imprisoned twice during the civil war, lost his fortune and died in poverty at an early age. He is remembered especially for the lyric poems *To Althea, from Prison* and *To Lucasta, Going to the Wars*. Two famous lines are, "Stone walls do not a prison make/Nor iron bars a cage."

**Charles Le Brun,** age 31; French painter and decorator to Louis XIV. In Fontainebleau Castle he painted a series on the life of Alexander the Great, and spent 18 years designing the furnishings and supervising the decoration of the palace of Versailles. Dictator of the arts for two decades, he set the style with his courtly grand manner. One famous work is *Chancellor Seguier,* in the Louvre.

**Frontenac** (Louis de Buade, comte de Palluau et de Frontenac), age 30; French soldier and colonial governor. As governor of New France (Canada) from 1672–1682 and again from 1689–1698, he sponsored the explorations of Jolliet, Marquette and La Salle, whereby the French acquired Louisiana and the Mississippi Valley. He established and maintained peaceful relations with the Indians.

**Jean de la Fontaine,** age 29; French poet and writer born in Chateau-Thierry of a middle-class family. His reputation rests on his animal fables in verse, taken from Aesop. Published in 12 books (1668–1694), his *Selected Fables in Verse* contain 230 fables and won immediate

Richard Cumberland
(1631-1718), age 44
John Locke
(1632-1704), age 43
Jean-Baptiste Lully
(1632-1687), age 43
Baruch Spinoza
(1632-1677), age 43
Jan Vermeer
(1632-1675), age 43
Sir Christopher Wren
(1632-1723), age 43
James II of England
(1633-1701), age 42
Samuel Pepys
(1633-1703), age 42
King Philip
(     -1676), age ?
Nicolas Boileau
(1636-1711), age 39
Jacques Marquette
(1637-1675), age 38
Meindert Hobbema
(1638-1709), age 37
Louis XIV of France
(1638-1715), age 37
Nicolas de Malebranche
(1638-1715), age 37
Increase Mather
(1639-1723), age 36
Jean Baptiste Racine
(1639-1699), age 36
William Wycherley
(1640?-1716), age 35?
Muhammad IV of Turkey
(1641-1691), age 34
Isaac Newton
(1642-1727), age 33
Sieur de La Salle
(1643-1687), age 32
William Penn
(1644-1718), age 31
Louis Jolliet
(1645-1700), age 30
Captain William Kidd
(c.1645-1701), age c.30
Jean de La Bruyere
(1645-1696), age 30

# 1650

Roger Williams
  (1603-1683), age 47
Giacomo Carissimi
  (1604/05-1674), age c.46
Sir Thomas Browne
  (1605-1682), age 45
Philip IV of Spain
  (1605-1665), age 45
Pierre Corneille
  (1606-1684), age 44
Rembrandt
  (1606-1669), age 44

success throughout Europe.

**Andrew Marvell,** age 29; English poet and pamphleteer, assistant to John Milton in his government post. Known in his time as a wit and satirist and defender of republican principles, he is remembered for a few poems of high quality, including *An Horatian Ode upon Cromwell's Return from Ireland, The Garden* and *To His Coy Mistress*—from which came the familiar lines: "Had we but world enough, and time,/This coyness, Lady, were no crime."

**Earl of Shaftesbury** (Anthony Ashley Cooper, first Baron Ashley and first earl of Shaftesbury), age 29; English statesman born in Hampshire, son of a baronet. He survived a long political career through dangerous times and held high office under both Cromwell and Charles II. He is remembered for securing passage of the Habeas Corpus Act in 1679, and as Achitophel, the object of Dryden's savage satire in *Absalom and Achitophel.* He was a friend of John Locke's and grandfather of the third earl of Shaftesbury, a moral philosopher.

**Moliere** (Jean Baptiste Poquelin), age 28; French dramatist and actor born in Paris, son of a well-to-do bourgeois. He toured the provinces for many years with an acting company and in 1658 won acclaim in Paris and patronage from Louis XIV. After 15 triumphant years of writing, producing and acting in his own plays, he made a grand exit in the best tradition of the theater. In February 1673, playing the last scene of *The Imaginary Invalid,* he suffered a hemorrhage of the lungs. He finished the scene, acknowledged the applause and collapsed behind the curtain. Carried to his house, he died within a few hours. His dramatic comedies—*The Miser, The Misanthrope, Tartuffe, School for Wives*—have never been surpassed.

**Henry Vaughan,** age 28; English poet born in South Wales, where he practiced medicine all his life. Influenced by George Herbert, he published two volumes of religious poetry (1650 and 1655) and some secular verse, but his genius was not recognized until the 19th century. One very famous line is, "I saw Eternity the other night".

BLAISE PASCAL
French philosopher and
  scientist
1623-1662

**Blaise Pascal,** age 27; French philosopher and scientist; a mathematical prodigy as a boy. He invented the first mechanical adding machine, but is more famous for *The Provincial Letters* in defense of Jansenism and *Pensees,* a collection of thoughts on religion and other subjects published after his death from manuscript notes. He distrusted human reason unsupported by faith and mystical revelation. Shy and sickly, he died at 39. One famous line is, "The heart has its reasons which reason cannot know."

**George Fox,** age 26; English religious leader born in Leistershire, founder of the Society of Friends (Quakers), originally called the Friends of Truth. An apprentice shoemaker, he began preaching in 1647 the doctrine that truth is discoverable by an inner light emanating from the

Holy Spirit, and won many followers. His *Journal*, revised by William Penn and others, was published in 1694.

**John III Sobieski,** age 26; king of Poland from 1674–1696. A soldier from his youth, he was made commander-in-chief of the Polish army in 1665 and elected king in 1674. With an army of 20,000 he routed an Ottoman Turkish force three times as large, raised the siege of Vienna in 1683 and ended the Turkish threat in Europe. He has been called "the savior of Christendom."

**Jan De Witt,** age 25; Dutch statesman; leader of Parliament in opposition to the house of Orange and Grand Pensionary of Holland (chief executive) from 1653–1672. Under his government the Dutch achieved commercial and maritime supremacy and enjoyed a golden age of art and literature, but popular sentiment turned against him and looked to William III of Orange for leadership in resisting the French invasion. He was killed by an angry mob while visiting his brother Cornelis in prison.

**Christina,** age 24; queen of Sweden from 1632–1654, succeeding her father, Gustavus Adolphus, at the age of six. She invited Descartes to Stockholm in 1649; she preferred the study of philosophy to politics. She refused to marry and abdicated in 1654 in favor of her cousin, Charles X. Settling in the Farnese palace in Rome in 1655, she embraced Roman Catholicism and became the center of the city's social and cultural life, numbering Bernini among her friends.

**Jacques Benigne Bossuet,** age 23; French prelate born in Dijon, famous for his oratory. Bossuet was tutor to the dauphin (Louis XIV's son, who never became king) and bishop of Meaux after 1681. For his pupil he wrote his *Discourse on Universal History,* but is better knwon for his eloquent *Funeral Orations,* published in 1689. A formidable polemicist, he attacked Fenelon, the Jesuits and the Protestants.

**Robert Boyle,** age 23; British physicist and founder of modern chemistry; born in Lismore Castle, Ireland, seventh son of the last earl of Cork. He engaged in scientific research at Oxford and was the first to distinguish between elements and compounds. He was also one of the founders of the Philosophical College, which became known as the Royal Society of London.

**John Bunyan,** age 22; English writer and layman preacher born in Bedford, son of a tinsmith. He won a large following among the common people and was imprisoned (1660–1672) by the restored monarchy for preaching without a license. His masterpiece, *Pilgrim's Progress* (Part I of which was published in 1678), gained immediate popularity and has remained a classic.

**Marcello Malpighi,** age 22; Italian anatomist, professor of medicine at the University of Bologna from 1666–1691. A pioneer in the use of the microscope, he discovered the movement of the blood through the capillaries, supplementing Harvey's discovery. The Malpighian tufts, corpuscles, layer and tubes are all named for him, indicating the extent of his wide-ranging investigations.

**Jacob van Ruisdael,** age c.22; foremost Dutch landscape painter and etcher, born in Haarlem. His forest and mountain scenes and panoramic views of the Dutch countryside are notable for their realism. He studied and practiced medicine in Amsterdam late in life and returned to Haarlem in 1681 to die in the almshouse. He was the teacher of Hobbema. Two famous works are *Extensive Landscape* (in the National Gallery in London) and *The Jewish Cemetery* (in the Detroit Institute of Art).

**Christian Huygens,** age 21; Dutch physicist, astronomer and mathematician; born at The Hague, son of the poet and diplomat Constantijn Huygens. He invented a new method of grinding lenses and built a

# 1675

Baron von Leibniz
    (1646-1716), age 29
Nathaniel Bacon
    (1647-1676), age 28
Pierre Bayle
    (1647-1706), age 28
Denis Papin
    (1647-c.1712), age 28
Duke of Marlborough
    (1650-1722), age 25
William III of England
    (1650-1702), age 25
Fenelon
    (1651-1715), age 24
William Randolph
    (c.1651-1711), age c.24
Chikamatsu Monzaemon
    (1653-1725), age 22
K'ang-hsi
    (1654-1722), age 21
Edmund Halley
    (1656-1742), age 19
Fontenelle
    (1657-1757), age 18
Frederick I of Prussia
    (1657-1713), age 18
Cadillac
    (1658-1730), age 17
Henry Purcell
    (1659-1695), age 16
Alessandro Scarlatti
    (1659/60-1725), age c.16
Daniel Defoe
    (1659/60-1731), age c.15
George I of Great Britain
    (1660-1727), age 15
Sieur d'Iberville
    (1661-1706), age 14
Cotton Mather
    (1663-1728), age 12
Thomas Newcomen
    (1663-1729), age 12
Matthew Prior
    (1664-1721), age 11
Queen Anne
    (1665-1714), age 10
Jonathan Swift
    (1667-1745), age 8
Francois Couperin
    (1668-1733), age 7
Giovanni Battista Vico
    (1668-1744), age 7

telescope more powerful than any yet produced. He also developed the wave theory of light. He worked in Paris from 1666–1681 at the invitation of Louis XIV.

**Charles II,** age 20; king of England, Scotland and Ireland from 1660–1685, second son of Charles I. He lived in Paris from 1646–1648 with Thomas Hobbes as his tutor. He made a futile attempt to save his father's life by sending Parliament a blank sheet of paper with his signature. His extravagant, pleasure-loving nature set the tone of the popular reaction against the Puritan decades. Two events for which his reign is remembered are the plague in 1665 and the great London fire in 1666. Having no legitimate children (but many mistresses, including the actress Nell Gwyn), he was succeeded by his brother James II.

# 1675–1700

While the English were advancing a step at a time toward constitutional monarchy and parliamentary government, the French continued to dance to the tune of an unchallenged monarchy. Louis XIV reigned 73 years as the living symbol of absolute power. While some Englishmen had begun to believe that kings exist for their subjects and that the aim of government should be the happiness of the greatest number, no such thoughts were expressed by the French nobility. The aristocracy was its own end. In Louis XIV's reign (1643–1715), French culture attained a pinnacle of refinement. It was the age of the classical drama of Racine and Corneille and of excellence in painting, music and philosophy—all subsidized by the king. Yet along with the highly cultivated aristocracy in powdered wigs and silks and satins and gold-buckled shoes there existed the hard-working, half-starved peasantry in their homespuns. It is no more para-

Thomas Hobbes
   (1588-1679), age 87
Izaak Walton
   (1593-1683), age 82
Giovanni Bernini
   (1598-1680), age 77
John Alden
   (c.1599-1687), age c.76
Calderon de la Barca
   (1600-1681), age 75

**Richard Cumberland,** age 44; English philosopher born in London, bishop of Peterborough from 1691–1718. Called the founder of utilitarianism, he is best known for *De legibus naturae* (1672), an inquiry into the laws of nature in which he rejected Hobbes' conception of human life as a war of each against all; he proposed the idea of the common good and universal benevolence as both more rational and more natural.

**John Locke,** age 43; English philosopher born in Somerset, son of a lawyer who joined the Parliamentary army in the civil war. He was the founder of modern empiricism, to which he gave systematic expression in his *Essay Concerning Human Understanding* (1690). Of his *Two Treatises on Government,* the second, called *Essary Concerning*

**John Dryden,** age 19; English poet, dramatist and critic, foremost English writer of the last quarter of the 17th century. He wrote broad comedies *(The Rival Ladies; Marriage a la Mode)*, tragic drama *(All for Love,* on Anthony and Cleopatra), criticism and political satire *(Absalom and Achitophel).* Primarily a poet for his own age, he made poetry of contemporary issues and events.

**Shun Chih,** age 12; emperor of China from 1644–1661, first of the Ch'ing, or Manchu, dynasty. Placed on the throne at the age of six by his father, Ch'ung Te, ruler of Manchuria, after the Manchus captured Peking in 1644, he died at 23 and was succeeded by his son, K'ang-hsi. The Manchus ruled from 1644–1912.

## 1675

William Congreve
    (1670-1729), age 5
Bernard Mandeville
    (1670?-1733), age 5?
Joseph Addison
    (1672-1719), age 3
Peter I of Russia
    (1672-1725), age 3
Richard Steele
    (1672-1729), age 3

doxical that an extremely high level of culture should co-exist with a depressed standard of living than that the cultural level should sink as the general standard of living rises. But however splendid the view from the castle, the French aristocracy was merely postponing the hour of revolution and regicide. They would pay, not a little at a time like the English, but all at once.

During Frontenac's term as governor of New France, French colonial expansion proceeded vigorously. While the English were confined to the Atlantic coastal strip, the French penetrated the heart of the continent and laid claim to the entire Mississippi Valley. Jolliet, Marquette and La Salle descended the Mississippi River; Sieur d'Iberville established a colony in Louisiana; and Bienville founded Mobile and New Orleans.

The last quarter of the 17th century was also notable for the planting of William Penn's colony in America and the founding of the city of Philadelphia. Glimmerings of the industrial age appeared, in the form of Denis Papin's design for a steam engine.

## 1700

JOHN LOCKE
English philosopher
1632-1704

Edmund Halley
    (1656-1742), age 44
Fontenelle
    (1657-1757), age 43
Frederick I of Prussia
    (1657-1713), age 43
Cadillac
    (1658-1730), age 42
Alessandro Scarlatti
    (1659/60-1725), age c.41

# 1675

Claude Lorrain
  (1600-1682), age 75
Roger Williams
  (1603-1683), age 72
Sir Thomas Browne
  (1605-1682), age 70
Pierre Corneille
  (1606-1684), age 69
Edmund Waller
  (1606-1687), age 69
Samuel Butler
  (1612-1680), age 63
La Rochefoucauld
  (1613-1680), age 62
Bartolome Murillo
  (1617-1682), age 58
Aurangzeb
  (1618-1707), age 57
Charles Le Brun
  (1619-1690), age 56
Frontenac
  (1620-1698), age 55
La Fontaine
  (1621-1695), age 54
Andrew Marvell
  (1621-1678), age 54
Earl of Shaftesbury
  (1621-1683), age 54
Henry Vaughan
  (1622-1695), age 53
George Fox
  (1624-1691), age 51
John III Sobieski
  (1624-1696), age 51
Christina of Sweden
  (1626-1689), age 49
Jacques Bossuet
  (1627-1704), age 48
Robert Boyle
  (1627-1691), age 48
John Bunyan
  (1628-1688), age 47
Marcello Malpighi
  (1628-1694), age 47
Jacob van Ruisdael
  (1628/29-1682), age c.47
Christian Huygens
  (1629-1695), age 46
Charles II of England
  (1630-1685), age 45
John Dryden
  (1631-1700), age 44

*the True Original Extent and End of Civil Government* (1690), written to justify and make respectable the Glorious Revolution of 1688, contains ideas and phrases echoed in the American Declaration of Independence.

**Jean-Baptiste Lully** (Giovanni Battista Lulli), age 43; French composer born in Florence, Italy, of a humble family and taken to Paris as a servant at 14. Self-taught, he became a court musician at 20 and, in 1653, court composer to Louis XIV, for whom he composed masques, ballets and operas. His most-famous song is *Au Clair de la Lune*.

BARUCH SPINOZA
Dutch philosopher
1632-1677

**Baruch Spinoza,** age 43; Dutch philosopher born in Amsterdam of Portuguese-Jewish descent. A pantheist and a strict determinist, he held that man's only freedom is intellectual freedom and that domination by the passions is human bondage. He refused a chair of philosophy at the University of Heidelberg, rejected Louis XIV's offer of patronage and supported himself as a grinder of optical lenses. Spinoza risked his life in protesting the murders of Jan and Cornelis De Witt.

**Jan Vermeer,** age 43; Dutch painter born in Delft. Unrecognized as an important artist until long after his death, he supported himself as an art dealer. He painted about 40 pictures: landscapes, Dutch interiors and portraits, including *View of Delft* (in the Hague) and *Girl Reading* (in Dresden).

SIR CHRISTOPHER WREN
English architect
1632-1723

**Sir Christopher Wren,** age 43; English architect born in Wiltshire, son of a prominent clergyman. A professor of astronomy at Oxford before turning to architecture, he designed and rebuilt 52 London churches after the great fire of 1666. He also designed the new St. Paul's Cathedral; the library of Trinity College, Combridge; the chapel of Queen's College, Oxford; Chelsea Hospital and Kensington Palace. He was knighted in 1673.

**James II,** age 42; king of England, Scotland and Ireland from 1685–1688, son of Charles I and brother of Charles II. His Catholic sympathies aroused fears that he would reestablish Roman Catholicism and prompted English nobles to offer the throne to William of Orange, whose wife was James' daughter. He fled to France in 1688 but in 1689 landed an army in Ireland, only to be defeated by William at the Battle of the Boyne in 1690. New Amsterdam was renamed New York in 1664, when he was the duke of York, in his honor.

**Samuel Pepys,** age 42; English naval official, son of a London tailor. Secretary of the admiralty from 1684–1689 and author of *Memoirs Relating to the State of the Royal Navy* (1690), he is more often remembered for the famous secret diary of the years 1660–1669, written in code and shorthand, revealing the details of everyday life in his time. It was not published until 1825.

**King Philip** (Metacomet), age ?; American Indian chief of the Wampanoag tribe, son of Massasoit. King Philip's War erupted in June 1675. Towns were burned and women and children killed in a general uprising of Wampanoags, Nipmucks and Narragansetts. In August 1676, Philip was killed by a traitorous Indian and his head exposed on a pole in Plymouth. The result was the extermination of Indian tribal life in New England. The survivors vanished from the woods, leaving the way open for settlers.

**Nicolas Boileau-Despreaux,** age 39; French literary critic and poet whose *L'Art poetique* (1674), a treatise in verse on the principles of classicism in literature established him as the leading critic of his time. His opinions were accepted as law in the 18th century, but denigrated by 19th-century Romantics. His best-known satire, in the style of Juvenal, is Satire X, on women.

**Jacques Marquette** (Pere Marquette), age 38; French Jesuit missionary and explorer born in Laon, France. Sent to New France in 1666 as a missionary to Indians in the northern Great Lakes region, he was appointed by Frontenac in 1673 to accompany Louis Jolliet on an expedition to find the great river said to flow south. The party of seven reached the Mississippi on June 17 and descended as far as the Arkansas River. His journal of the voyage was published in 1681.

**Meindert Hobbema,** age 37; Dutch landscape painter born in Amsterdam, pupil of Jacob van Ruisdael. He painted woodland scenes, country villages and old castles. Only after he died in poverty was he recognized as a master. Familiar works include *The Mill* (in the Louvre) and *Entrance to a Village* (in the Metropolitan Museum of Art.

**Louis XIV** (The Sun King), age 37; king of France from 1643–1715, of the house of Bourbon. He was king at the age of five and in personal charge of the government at 23. In his reign of 73 years, the longest in European history, France attained the zenith of its military power and the French court reached an unprecedented level of culture and refinement. But the condition of the poor grew steadily worse, and the revocation of the Edict of Nantes, which had guaranteed religious freedom, in 1685 caused thousands to emigrate.

**Nicolas de Malebranche,** age 37; French philosopher born in Paris. A secular priest, he studied Descartes for 10 years and published *Recherche de la Verite* (Search for Truth), which is said to have influenced Leibniz and Berkeley, in 1674; it is little read today. He held that knowledge of the external world is possible only through God.

**Increase Mather,** age 36; American Puritan clergyman born in Dorchester, Mass.; pastor of North Church in Boston for 58 years. Succeeding John Cotton as the spiritual shepherd of Massachusetts Bay Colony, he married his predecessor's daughter and named his son Cotton. The author of religious tracts, political pamphlets and a short history of King Philip's War, he was president of Harvard from 1685–1701.

Daniel Defoe
(1659/60-1731),
age c.40
George I of Great Britain
(1660-1727), age 40
Sieur d'Iberville
(1661-1706), age 39
Cotton Mather
(1663-1728), age 37
Thomas Newcomen
(1663-1729), age 37
Matthew Prior
(1664-1721), age 36
Queen Anne
(1665-1714), age 35
Jonathan Swift
(1667-1745), age 33
Francois Couperin
(1668-1733), age 32
Giovanni Battista Vico
(1668-1744), age 32
William Congreve
(1670-1729), age 30
Bernard Mandeville
(1670?-1733), age 30?
Joseph Addison
(1672-1719), age 28
Peter I of Russia
(1672-1725), age 28
Richard Steele
(1672-1729), age 28
Antonio Vivaldi
(c.1675-1741),
age c.25
Sir Robert Walpole
(1676-1745), age 24
Viscount Bolingbroke
(1678-1751), age 22
Sieur de Bienville
(1680-1768), age 20
Charles XII of Sweden
(1682-1718), age 18
George II of Great Britain
(1683-1760), age 17
Philip V of Spain
(1683-1746), age 17
Jean Philippe Rameau
(1683-1764), age 17
Edward Young
(1683-1765), age 17
Jean Antoine Watteau
(1684-1721), age 16

**Jean Baptiste Racine,** age 36; French dramatist of middle-class parentage, orphaned at four and educated at Port-Royal in the school established for destitute boys. His classic tragedies *(Britannicus, Phedre, Athalie* and others) won him the patronage of Louis XIV and a secure place among the greatest French dramatists. He was a friend of Moliere, whose company produced his first two plays.

**William Wycherley,** age 35?; English Restoration dramatist whose first play, *Love in a Wood* (1671), won the favor of the duchess of Cleveland, mistress of Charles II, and assured his success. His two masterpieces, *The Country Wife* (1674) and *The Plain Dealer* (1676), are witty and well constructed, but reflect the age's vulgarity. Imprisonment for debt, a pension from James II and friendship with Alexander Pope occupied his later years.

**Muhammad IV,** age 34; Ottoman Turkish sultan from 1648–1687, son and successor of Ibrahim, whom the Janissaries deposed. During his reign disorder and corruption spread, although the empire was strengthened briefly by the efforts of an Albanian nobleman as grand vizier. His son-in-law, Kara Mustafa, led the Turks, allied with the Hungarians, in the siege of Vienna (1683), which failed. After a defeat by the Christians in 1687, Muhammad was deposed.

SIR ISAAC NEWTON
English physicist, astronomer
and mathematician
1642-1727

**Sir Isaac Newton,** age 33; English physicist, astronomer and mathematician, one of the founders of modern science. From the third of Kepler's laws of planetary motion, he derived the law of gravitation: all bodies in the universe have a mutual attraction for one another, with a force directly proportional to the product of their masses and inversely proportional to the squares of the distance between them. Professor of mathematics at Cambridge from 1669–1699, he was knighted in 1705. The poet wrote in tribute: "Nature and nature's laws lay hid in night:/God said, Let Newton be! and all was light."

**Robert Cavelier,** Sieur de La Salle, age 32; French explorer born in Rouen. With a party of French and Indians and one Italian, he descended the Mississippi River to the Gulf of Mexico, arriving April 9, 1682. He claimed the entire valley for Louis XIV and called it Louisiana. In 1684 he sailed from France with four ships to establish a colony at the mouth of the Mississippi. He landed by error on the Texas shore and was killed in a mutiny before he found the river.

**William Penn,** age 31; English Quaker, son of Adm. Sir William Penn; imprisoned several times for activity in behalf of religious liberty. In 1681 he obtained from Charles II a grant of land in America in payment of a large debt owed his father. He sailed in 1682, made peace treaties with the Indians, organized the government of the colony of Pennsylvania—which guaranteed religious freedom—and laid out and named the city of Philadelphia. He returned to England in 1684.

**Louis Jolliet** (or Joliet), age 30; French Canadian explorer born in Quebec. Appointed by Frontenac to lead an expedition in search of the great river reported by the Indians, he left the Michigan shore on May 17, 1673 with five woodsmen and Father Marquette, crossed Lake Michigan, ascended the Fox River, descended the Wisconsin River and on June 17 entered the Mississippi. They floated down to the mouth of the Arkansas River before turning back.

**William Kidd,** (Captain Kidd), age c. 30; British pirate born in Scotland. A respectable shipowner and sea captain until the age of 52, he engaged in piracy only two years (1697–1699) before turning himself in, expecting a pardon. Kidd has acquired a reputation as the most bloodthirsty of all pirates. He was hanged in England in 1701. Stories of immense treasure he had buried somewhere along the Atlantic coast inspired Edgar Allan Poe's story, *The Gold Bug.*

**Jean de La Bruyere,** age 30; French writer born in Paris, tutor and later secretary to Louis de Bourbon, a relative of the king. He won fame with *Les 'Caracteres' de Theophraste* (1688), a translation of Theophrastus with added character sketches of his own contemporaries and ironic comments on social life and literature. It was reprinted nine times in his lifetime.

**Baron Gottfried Wilhelm von Liebniz,** age 29; German philosopher and mathematician, regarded in his time as a universal genius. Librarian and privy councillor to the duke of Brunswick (later elector of Hanover) from 1676–1716, he was the inventor of a calculating machine that could multiply, divide and extract square roots. He developed a system of metaphysics known as monadology and wrote *New Essays on Human Understanding* in rebuttal of Locke's *Essay* replying to Locke's arguments paragraph by paragraph (in French).

**Nathaniel Bacon,** age 28; American colonist of aristocratic birth, leader of Bacon's Rebellion in Virginia in 1676. A graduate of Cambridge and member of the governor's council, he sided with the frontiersmen in their protests against high taxes, favoritism and inadequate defenses against Indian attacks. The rebels captured Jamestown, burned it and forced Gov. Berkeley to take flight; Bacon's sudden death from malaria, in October 1676, ended the revolt.

**Pierre Bayle,** age 28; French philosopher, called the forerunner of 18th-century rationalism; professor of philosophy at Rotterdam from 1681–1693. After his dismissal on suspicion of religious skepticism, he wrote his *Dictionnaire Historique et Critique* (1697), in which he analyzed current beliefs and advocated freedom of thought. He strongly influenced the French encyclopedists.

**Denis Papin,** age 28; French physicist and mathematician, professor at Marburg University in Hesse. In 1690 he published the first design of a piston steam engine and drew plans for steam-driven carts and boats. He also invented the pressure cooker. He was a friend of Liebniz and an associate of Robert Boyle.

**Duke of Marlborough** (John Churchill, first duke of Marlborough), age 25; English general and statesman, one of the greatest military commanders in history, famous for his victory over the French at Blenheim in 1704. His influence with Prime Min. Godolphin and his wife's friendship with Queen Anne made him a powerful figure in the government. His sister Arabella was the mistress of James II. The Duke was one of Sir Winston Churchill's ancestors.

**William III** (William of Orange), age 25; king of England, Scotland

# 1700

Johann Sebastian Bach
(1685-1750), age 15
George Berkeley
(1685-1753), age 15
John Gay
(1685-1732), age 15
George Frederick Handel
(1685-1759), age 15
Domenico Scarlatti
(1685-1757), age 15
Gabriel Fahrenheit
(1686-1736), age 14
Henry Carey
(c.1687-1743), age c.13
Frederick William I
of Prussia
(1688-1740), age 12
Nadir Shah
(1688-1747), age 12
Alexander Pope
(1688-1744), age 12
Emanuel Swedenborg
(1688-1772), age 12
Montesquieu
(1689-1755), age 11
Samuel Richardson
(1689-1761), age 11
Joseph Butler
(1692-1752), age 8
Sir John Randolph
(c.1693-1737), age c.7
Lord Chesterfield
(1694-1773), age 6
Francis Hutcheson
(1694-1746), age 6
Voltaire
(1694-1778), age 6
Edward Braddock
(1695-1755), age 5
James Oglethorpe
(1696-1785), age 4
Giovanni Tiepolo
(1696-1770), age 4
Antonio Canaletto
(1697-1768), age 3
William Hogarth
(1697-1764), age 3
Abbe Prevost
(1697-1763), age 3
Jean-Baptiste Chardin
(1699-1779), age 1

and Ireland from 1689–1702, of the house of Stuart, ruling jointly with his wife, Mary II (both were grandchildren of Charles I); also stadtholder of the Netherlands from 1672–1702, succeeding Jan De Witt. Invited to assume the English crown by influential nobles who were dissatisfied with the despotism and Catholicism of James II, he landed in England in 1688 as James, his father-in-law and uncle, left for Paris. This event is known as the Glorious Revolution.

**Fenelon** (Francois de Salignac de La Mothe-Fenelon), age 24; French prelate and writer, remembered for his controversy with Bossuet over quietism (which Fenelon defended). Tutor to the grandson of Louis XIV and archbishop of Cambrai after 1695, he fell from favor after the pope condemned parts of his *Maxims of the Saints* (1697) as contrary to Christian teachings. In his novel *Telemaque* (1699) he declared that kings exist for their subjects, a point of view incomprehensible to the French monarch.

**William Randolph,** age c. 24; colonial planter born in Warwickshire, England, of the landed gentry; founder of the Randolph family of Virginia. He emigrated in 1673, amassed a fortune and became one of the leading planters and slave owners of Virginia. A member of the House of Burgesses from 1685–1699 and again from 1703–1710, speaker of the house from 1699–1702 and one of the founders of the College of William and Mary, he was the father of Sir John Randolph and the grandfather of Peyton Randolph.

**Chikamatsu Monzaemon,** age 22; Japanese dramatist, a significant figure in world literature, called the Shakespeare of Japan. He wrote over 100 plays, mostly for the puppet theater, including both historical romances and domestic comedies.

**K'ang-hsi** (Sheng-tzu), age 21; emperor of China from 1661–1722, of the Ch'ing (Manchu) dynasty, son and successor of Shun Chin. A

# 1700–1725

The 18th century opened with the reign of the last Stuart, Queen Anne (1702–1714). It was a period notable for intrigues on behalf of the Old Pretender; for the War of the Spanish Succession and Marlborough's victory at Blenheim; for the creation of Great Britain by the union of Scotland and England; and for Queen Anne furniture, a graceful modification of baroque. It was also the age of Alexander Pope's heroic couplets; Jonathan Swift's satires; Daniel Defoe's novels; the birth of periodical journals; and the classic age of English prose. But, most of all, it was a time when the middle class was coming into its own.

Defoe's novels, published between 1719 and 1723, were written for middle-class readers. He spoke for them when he said, through Robinson Crusoe's father, that what might be called the upper station of low life is the best state in the

vigorous and enlightened ruler, he conquered the feudal states of south China, annexed Taiwan (in 1683) and Tibet and established diplomatic relations with Russia. He encouraged arts and sciences and the production of fine Kingtehchen porcelain ware. His scholars compiled dictionaries and encyclopedias.

HENRY PURCELL
English composer and
organist
1659-1695

**Henry Purcell,** age 16; English composer and organist, called the foremost native-born English composer. The organist for many years at Westminster Abbey and the royal chapel, he composed music for masques and dramatic works and songs for public occasions, notably *Sound the Trumpets* for James II's birthday. His one opera, *Dido and Aeneas,* is sometimes called the best opera in English.

world and the most suited for human happiness; that peace and plenty are the handmaids of a middle fortune; that temperance, moderation, quietness, health, society and all agreeable diversions and pleasures are the blessings attending the middle state of life; that this way men pass silently and smoothly through the world and comfortably out of it.

His readers agreed. They might enjoy reading of such outlandish adventures as befell Robinson Crusoe, but they preferred the quiet and secure life, which had become possible in 18th-century England. The easy, informal prose style of Addison and Steele in the *Tatler* and *Spectator* was also consciously addressed to the middle class. The papers contained brief essays on fashions, manners and literature, sprinkled with anecdotes and moral reflections.

The 18th century believed in reason, moderation and common sense and felt that human affairs might be ordered in a rational manner through the exercise of these qualities and the avoidance of excesses. Apparently life had become pleasant and agreeable for a considerable number of people.

# 1700

Aurangzeb
(1618-1707), age 82
Jacques Bossuet
(1627-1704), age 73
Richard Cumberland
(1631-1718), age 69
John Dryden
(1631-1700), age 69
John Locke
(1632-1704), age 68
Sir Christopher Wren
(1632-1723), age 68
James II of England
(1633-1701), age 67
Samuel Pepys
(1633-1703), age 67
Nicolas Boileau
(1636-1711), age 64
Meindert Hobbema
(1638-1709), age 62
Louis XIV of France
(1638-1715), age 62
Nicolas de Malebranche
(1638-1715), age 62
Increase Mather
(1639-1723), age 61
William Wycherley
(1640?-1716), age 60?
Isaac Newton
(1642-1727), age 58
William Penn
(1644-1718), age 56
Louis Jolliet
(1645-1700), age 55
William Kidd
(c.1645-1701), age c.55
Baron von Leibniz
(1646-1716), age 54
Pierre Bayle
(1647-1706), age 53
Denis Papin
(1647-c.1712), age 53
Duke of Marlborough
(1650-1722), age 50
William III of England
(1650-1702), age 50
Fenelon
(1651-1715), age 49
William Randolph
(c.1651-1711),
age c.49

**Edmund Halley,** age 44; English astronomer born in London for whom Halley's Comet was named. He predicted that the comet, which had appeared in 1531, 1607 and 1682, would reappear in 1758, which it did (Halley was by then no longer alive). A friend of Isaac Newton, whose *Principia* he published at his own expense, he was appointed royal astronomer in 1721. His comet is due to appear again in 1985 or 1986.

**Bernard le Bovier de Fontenelle,** age 43; French writer, known as an interpreter of science, born in Rouen, the son of a lawyer. Secretary of the royal academy of sciences for 40 years and the author of an exposition of the Copernican system and a work on the origin of myths, he is called a precursor of the Enlightenment. He lived 99 years and 11 months.

**Frederick I,** age 43; first king of Prussia, from 1701–1713. Succeeding his father, Frederick William, as elector of Brandenburg in 1688, he assumed the title of king of Prussia in 1701 when Brandenburg and Prussia were reconstituted as the kingdom of Prussia. He was the grandfather of Frederick the Great.

**Antoine de la Mothe Cadillac,** age 42; French colonial governor born in Gascony, of the minor nobility; founder of Detroit. He obtained a grant of land where Detroit now stands after persuading the French government of its strategic advantage against the English, established a large French colony in 1701 and remained there 10 years as governor. After a short, troubled term as governor of Louisiana (1713–1716), he retired to Gascony.

**Alessandro Scarlatti,** age c. 41; Italian composer born in Sicily. He wrote *Pompeo* and 114 other operas and enjoyed the patronage of princes and cardinals in Rome, Florence, Venice and Naples. He was the father of Domenico Scarlatti.

**Daniel DeFoe** (originally Daniel Foe), age c. 40; English journalist and novelist born in London. He tried his hand at many occupations—hosiery merchant, operator of a brick and tile factory, pamphleteer, political spy, publisher of a news journal and hack writer—before becoming a novelist at the age of 60. After the success of *Robinson Crusoe* (1719), he wrote *Moll Flanders, A Journal of the Plague Year* and *Roxana*. He is called the first true English novelist.

**George I** (George Louis Wettin), age 40; king of Great Britain and Ireland from 1714–1727, first of the house of Hanover, and elector of Hanover from 1698–1727. He was the great-grandson of James I of England through James's daughter Elizabeth (who married the elector of the Palatinate) and her daughter Sophia (who married the elector of Hanover). The Act of Settlement, passed by Parliament in 1701, provided that succession should pass to the house of Hanover if both William III and Princess Anne died without heirs. He spent most of his time in Hanover and never learned the English language.

**Pierre Lemoyne, Sieur d'Iberville,** age 39; French Canadian naval officer and explorer; founder of the territory of Louisiana. He was born in Villa Marie (now in Montreal), one of 11 sons of the French colonist Charles Lemoyne and brother of Bienville. From 1686–1697 he led raids against British fur-trading posts, and in 1698 was appointed to establish a settlement in the lower Mississippi Valley. With colonists and supplies in four ships, he reached the Gulf of Mexico in 1699 and founded Old Biloxi (Ocean Springs, Miss.). He explored the Mississippi delta, discovering the true mouth of the river; he died of yellow fever in Havana at 45.

COTTON MATHER
American Puritan clergyman
and writer
1663-1728

**Cotton Mather,** age 37; American Puritan clergyman and writer, assistant pastor to his father, Increase Mather, at North Church in Boston for most of his life. At 60 he succeeded him as pastor. Often accused of narrow intolerance, he was nevertheless influential in promoting education and science through his writings, although his books on demonic possession are said to have contributed to the wave of hysteria preceding the Salem witch trials of 1692.

**Thomas Newcomen,** age 37; English inventor and blacksmith born in Devonshire. In 1705 he built the first practical, working steam engine (having improved the cumbersome engine patented by Thomas Savery in 1698). After further improvements in 1725 his engine was widely used for pumping water from mines, until replaced by James Watts's engine after 1769.

**Matthew Prior,** age 36; English poet and diplomat, prominent during Queen Anne's reign, particularly for helping to conclude the Treaty of Utrecht (1713), known as "Matt's Peace." He is better known for his light verse (*The City Mouse and the Country Mouse*) and satires (*Alma, or the Progress of the Mind,* 1718).

**Anne,** age 35; queen of England, Scotland and Ireland from 1702–1707 and queen of Great Britain and Ireland from 1707–1714, last of the house of Stuart; second daughter of James II and a sister of Mary II. Her reign saw the transition to parliamentary government, the growth of empire and the legislative union of England and Scotland, as 45 Scottish members were added to the House of Commons and 16 to the House of Lords. She married Prince George of Denmark, but none of her 17 children survived her. Succession passed to the house of Hanover and George I.

**Francois Couperin,** age 32; French composer, harpsichordist and organist; born in Paris of a famous family of musicians who for two centuries kept the position of organist at the Church of St. Gervais in the family. He is best known for his graceful, ornamental harpsichord pieces, such as *Les Papillons* and *La Voluptueuse.* He held the post at St. Gervais from 1685–1733 and was harpsichordist at the court of Louis XIV.

**Giovanni Battista Vico,** age 32; Italian philosopher and historian, called the first modern historian for his systematic method of historical research. His belief that the development of societies is the proper

George II of Great Britain
(1683-1760), age 42
Philip V of Spain
(1683-1746), age 42
Jean Philippe Rameau
(1683-1764), age 42
Edward Young
(1683-1765), age 42
Johann Sebastian Bach
(1685-1750), age 40
George Berkeley
(1685-1753), age 40
John Gay
(1685-1732), age 40
George Frederick Handel
(1685-1759), age 40
Domenico Scarlatti
(1685-1757), age 40
Gabriel Fahrenheit
(1686-1736), age 39
Henry Carey
(c.1687-1743),
age c.38
Frederick William I
of Prussia
(1688-1740), age 37
Nadir Shah
(1688-1747), age 37
Alexander Pope
(1688-1744), age 37
Emanuel Swedenborg
(1688-1772), age 37
Montesquieu
(1689-1755), age 36
Samuel Richardson
(1689-1761), age 36
Joseph Butler
(1692-1752), age 33
Sir John Randolph
(c.1693-1737),
age c.32
Lord Chesterfield
(1694-1773), age 31
Francis Hutcheson
(1694-1746), age 31
Voltaire
(1694-1778), age 31
Edward Braddock
(1695-1755), age 30
James Oglethorpe
(1696-1785), age 29

Chikamatsu Monzaemon
(1653-1725), age 47
K'ang-hsi
(1654-1722), age 46

subject of history, and that societies pass through similar periods in a certain order, made him a forerunner of Spengler and Toynbee. His importance was not recognized until the 19th century.

JONATHAN SWIFT
English writer and political
pamphleteer
1667-1745

**Jonathan Swift,** age 33; English writer and political pamphleteer born in Dublin of English parents; a distant cousin of John Dryden. He became a clergyman in 1695 and dean of St. Patrick's Cathedral in Dublin in 1713. His satires, *Battle of the Books* and *A Tale of a Tub,* are seldom read, but *Gulliver's Travels* became a children's classic after expurgation. He is extolled as a master of English prose.

**William Congreve,** age 30; English dramatist born in Yorkshire, son of a clergyman. He is famous for his comedies of manners—*The Old Bachelor, The Double Dealer, Love for Love* and *The Way of the World*—but his two immortal lines, "Nor Hell a fury like a woman scorn'd" and "Music hath charms to soothe the savage breast," are from his one tragedy, *The Mourning Bride.*

**Bernard Mandeville,** age 30?; Dutch physician born in Dordrecht who went to London to practice medicine and became an English writer. He is famous for *The Fable of the Bees, or Private Vices, Public Virtues* (1714), a satire in verse, based on the familiar theme that selfishness is the motivation of all human conduct. He is said to have influenced 19th-century utilitarians.

JOSEPH ADDISON
English essayist and
statesman
1672-1719

**Joseph Addison,** age 28; English essayist and statesman, born in

Wiltshire, son of a clergyman. Best known as an urbane prose stylist in essays contributed to the *Tatler* and *Spectator,* he also wrote an epic poem, *The Campaign,* celebrating the victory at Blenheim, and a successful play, *Cato.* He was a member of Parliament in 1708.

PETER THE GREAT
Czar of Russia
1672-1725

**Peter I** (Peter the Great), age 28; czar of Russia from 1682–1725, grandson of Michael Romanov. He developed industry and trade, introduced Western ideas and practices and transformed Russia into a major European power as well as a regimented police state. His victory over Charles XII at Poltava in 1709 gave him control of the Baltic Sea. He introduced Arabic numerals to Russia and built the new capital of St. Petersburg.

**Richard Steele,** age 28; British essayist and playwright born in Dublin, best known for his triweekly journal, the *Tatler* and, in association with Addison, the *Spectator.* A Whig member of Parliament, he was knighted by George I in 1715. He also managed the Drury Lane theater.

ANTONIO VIVALDI
Italian violinist and baroque
composer
c. 1675-1741

**Antonio Vivaldi,** age c. 25; Italian violinist and baroque composer, born in Venice, son of a violinist at St. Mark's. Ordained a priest in 1703, he taught and played the violin and composed prolifically: cantatas, concertos and operas. His music was much admired but neglected, after his death, until an early 20th-century revival. His best-known work is *The Four Seasons.*

Giovanni Tiepolo
(1696-1770), age 29
Antonio Canaletto
(1697-1768), age 28
William Hogarth
(1697-1764), age 28
Abbe Prevost
(1697-1763), age 28
Jean-Baptiste Chardin
(1699-1779), age 26
Baal-Shem-Tov
(1698/1700-1760),
age c.25
James Thomson
(1700-1748), age 25
Anders Celsius
(1701-1744), age 24
Francois Boucher
(1703-1770), age 22
Jonathan Edwards
(1703-1758), age 22
John Wesley
(1703-1791), age 22
Benjamin Franklin
(1706-1790), age 19
Comte de Buffon
(1707-1788), age 18
Henry Fielding
(1707-1754), age 18
Carlo Goldoni
(1707-1793), age 18
Linnaeus
(1707-1778), age 18
Charles Wesley
(1707-1788), age 18
William Pitt (the Elder)
(1708-1778), age 17
Samuel Johnson
(1709-1784), age 16
Julien de La Mettrie
(1709-1751), age 16
Wilhelm Friedemann Bach
(1710-1784), age 15
Louis XV of France
(1710-1774), age 15
Thomas Reid
(1710-1796), age 15
Ch'ien Lung
(1711-1799), age 14
David Hume
(1711-1776), age 14

**Sir Robert Walpole,** age 24; first earl of Oxford, British statesman; prime minister from 1715–1717 and 1721–1727 for George I and from 1727–1742 for George II. The king's frequent trips to Hanover and disinterest in English affairs made Walpole the most powerful man in England. His administration demonstrated the soundness of parliamentary government, as power shifted from the House of Lords to the House of Commons and the country prospered. He was the father of Horace Walpole.

**Henry St. John,** age 22; first Viscount Bolingbroke, English statesman and orator; member of Parliament (after 1701) and cabinet minister. He is remembered for his unsuccessful effort to secure the succession of the Old Pretender, James Francis Edward Stuart, son of James II. After a period of exile in France (1714–1723), he became a close friend of Pope and Swift and wrote philosophical treatises propounding ideas similar to those expressed by Pope in his *Essay on Man*.

**Jean Baptiste Lemoyne, Sieur de Bienville,** age 20; French Canadian colonial governor and founder of New Orleans; born in Villa Marie (Montreal), the younger brother of Iberville. He accompanied his brother to Louisiana and succeeded him as governor, serving in 1701–1712, 1718–1726 and 1733–1743. He founded Mobile in 1710 and New Orleans in 1718, making the latter the capital in 1722. After the introduction of slavery, he instituted the Code Noir (1724), which strictly regulated slave life. He retired in 1743 and spent his last years in Paris.

**Charles XII,** age 18; king of Sweden from 1697–1718, called the Alexander of the North. For nearly 20 years the terror of Europe, he is remembered for his rout of Peter the Great's army at Narva in 1700 and for the complete destruction of his own army in the three-day battle at Poltava in 1709. His favorite tactic was the frontal assault against superior forces, and he is said never to have asked his scouts about the enemy's numbers or fortifications, but only, "Where are they?" After many incredible adventures, he was killed at 36 while invading Norway.

**Jean Antoine Watteau,** age 16; French painter of Flemish origin, a leading exponent of the rococo style. He is known for his outdoor scenes imbued with a melancholy, autumnal air, and for his paintings of clowns and wandering actors. He died of tuberculosis at 37. One famous work is *Embarkation for Cythera,* in the Louvre.

# 1725–1750

The second quarter of the 18th century was the age of Walpole, the Whig prime minister from 1721 to 1742 for George I and George II. A brilliant statesman and sound administrator, Sir Robert Walpole dominated English political life for two decades. His aims were stability and prosperity at home and peace abroad, and he succeeded, at least, in keeping the upper classes prosperous. The poor remained poor. The population of England at that time has been estimated at about six million; London had perhaps 500,000 and such towns as Bristol, Manchester and Liverpool close

Horace Walpole
(1717-1797), age 8

Maria Theresa of Austria
(1717-1780), age 8

Thomas Gage
(1721-1787), age 4

Mme. de Pompadour
(1721-1764), age 4

Peyton Randolph
(1721-1775), age 4

Tobias Smollett
(1721-1771), age 4

Samuel Adams
(1722-1803), age 3

John Burgoyne
(1722-1792), age 3

Christopher Smart
(1722-1771), age 3

Sir William Blackstone
(1723-1780), age 2

Baron d'Holbach
(1723-1789), age 2

Sir Joshua Reynolds
(1723-1792), age 2

Adam Smith
(1723-1790), age 2

Immanuel Kant
(1724-1804), age 1

Friedrich Klopstock
(1724-1803), age 1

Pierre Laclede
(1724-1778), age 1

Frederick II of Prussia
(1712-1786), age 13

Francesco Guardi
(1712-1793), age 13

Marquis de Montcalm
(1712-1759), age 13

Jean Jacques Rousseau
(1712-1778), age 13

Denis Diderot
(1713-1784), age 12

Laurence Sterne
(1713-1768), age 12

Karl Philipp Bach
(1714-1788), age 11

Miklos Esterhazy
(1714-1790), age 11

Christoph Gluck
(1714-1787), age 11

Lord Monboddo
(1714-1799), age 11

Etienne de Condillac
(1715-1780), age 10

Claude Helvetius
(1715-1771), age 10

Thomas Gray
(1716-1771), age 9

Jean d'Alembert
(1717-1783), age 8

Jeffrey Amherst
(1717-1797), age 8

David Garrick
(1717-1779), age 8

to 50,000. Living conditions in the towns were primitive; there was no running water in the houses and no central heating. There were no sewers; the streets were narrow, unpaved and muddy and served as dumping grounds for garbage. The houses of the poor were ramshackle, often of one or two rooms, with only weatherboarding to keep out the cold. Sharing the house or the cellar with the domestic animals was not uncommon. In such conditions smallpox, typhoid and dysentery spread unchecked.

However, it is hazardous to make broad generalizations based on bits of information. While there is sufficient evidence to show that primitive, unsanitary conditions did exist, to what extent they were prevalent is more difficult to ascertain. It is possible that the worst conditions existed only at a

# 1750

# 1725

Isaac Newton
   (1642-1727), age 83
Chikamatsu Monzaemon
   (1653-1725), age 72
Edmund Halley
   (1656-1742), age 69
Fontenelle
   (1657-1757), age 68
Cadillac
   (1658-1730), age 67
Alessandro Scarlatti
   (1659/60-1725), age c.66
Daniel Defoe
   (1659/60-1731), age c.65
George I of Great Britain
   (1660-1727), age 65
Cotton Mather
   (1663-1728), age 62
Thomas Newcomen
   (1663-1729), age 62
Jonathan Swift
   (1667-1745), age 58
Francois Couperin
   (1668-1733), age 57
Giovanni Battista Vico
   (1668-1744), age 57
William Congreve
   (1670-1729), age 55
Bernard Mandeville
   (1670?-1733), age 55?
Peter I of Russia
   (1672-1725), age 53
Richard Steele
   (1672-1729), age 53
Antonio Vivaldi
   (c.1675-1741), age c.50
Sir Robert Walpole
   (1676-1745), age 49
Viscount Bolingbroke
   (1678-1751), age 47
Sieur de Bienville
   (1680-1768), age 45

certain time and place, as people from the country were crowding into towns not prepared to accommodate them. Whether life was painful for a tiny minority, a sizable proportion of the population or of the majority is not known. The

**George II** (George Augustus), age 42; king of Great Britain and Ireland from 1727–1760 and elector of Hanover from 1727–1760, son and successor of George I. The last British king to lead his troops in person, he defeated the French at Dettingen in 1743 in the War of the Austrian Succession. England was becoming a great commercial power as the colonial wars with France began in India and America. He was succeeded by his grandson George III.

**Philip V,** age 42; first Bourbon king of Spain (1700–1746), born in Versailles, grandson of Louis XIV. His accession precipitated the War of the Spanish Succession (1701–1714), in which all Europe was involved; the war was concluded with the Treaty of Utrecht, which deprived Spain of the Spanish Netherlands, Milan, Naples, Sardinia and Sicily. He was dominated by his second wife, Elizabeth Farnese.

**Jean Philippe Rameau,** age 42; French composer and musical theorist born in Dijon, the son of a church organist. He wrote important treatises on harmony, introducing the theory of chord inversion, and wrote over 20 operas, the best-known being *Hippolyte et Aricie* (1733) and *Castor et Pollux* (1737). He also wrote chamber music and harpischord pieces in an elegant rococo style.

**Edward Young,** age 42; English poet born in Hampshire, son of a country clergyman and himself rector in Hartfordshire from 1730–1765. Called the founder of the "graveyard school" of poetry, he is best known for his melancholy meditation in blank verse, *The Complaint, or Night-Thoughts on Life, Death, and Immortality* (1742–1745). A famous line is, "Procrastination is the thief of time."

JOHANN SEBASTIAN
BACH
German composer and
organist
1685-1750

**Johann Sebastian Bach,** age 40; German composer and organist born in Eisenach, Thuringia. Court organist at Weimar from 1708–1717, and thereafter musical director and choirmaster at various churches and courts, he was recognized as an organ virtuoso but unappreciated as a

picture may be overdrawn, for England was still a country of hamlets and villages; most people lived rural lives, which, however laborious they may have been, were surely less grim than those of the poor who lived in towns, of which we have abundant descriptions.

composer until long after his death. He married twice and had 20 children. Among his many famous works are the *Christmas Oratorio, The Passion of St. Matthew, Mass in B Minor* and *The Art of Fugue.* He died totally blind.

**George Berkeley,** age 40; Irish philosopher and churchman born in County Kilkenny; bishop of Cloyne from 1734–1752. The foremost modern idealist, he carried Locke's ideas further and developed a system of subjective idealism, affirming that external objects exist only as they are perceived in the mind. He is the author of *A Treatise Concerning the Principles of Humgn Knowledge* (1710).

**John Gay,** age 40; English poet and playwright born in Devonshire. Orphaned at 10 and apprenticed to a silk merchant in London, he won fame and patronage at 24 and wrote satires, burlesques, fables, ballads and mock-heroic poems. He is remembered for a single work, *The Beggar's Opera.* The drama of Macheath, the highwayman (Mack the Knife), inspired *The Threepenny Opera* of Bertolt Brecht and Kurt Weill two centuries later. He was a lifelong friend of Alexander Pope.

GEORGE FREDERICK
HANDEL
German-British composer
1685-1759

**George Frederick Handel,** age 40; German-British composer born in Halle, Brandenburg, the son of a barber. His first opera was produced in Hamburg when he was 20, the second in Florence at 23, the third in Venice at 24 and his fourth, *Rinaldo,* in London at 26. He left his position as court conductor to the elector of Hanover in 1712 and settled permanently in England, two years before his patron, George I, arrived. He wrote more than 40 operas and 20 oratorios, including *Esther, Israel in Egypt* and *Messiah* (1742). Handel became a naturalized British subject in 1726.

**Domenico Scarlatti,** age 40; Italian composer and harpsichord virtuoso born in Naples, son of Alessandro Scarlatti. Musical director to royalty all his life, including Ferdinand VI of Spain, he originated many features of modern keyboard technique (arpeggios and crossing

Comte de Buffon
(1707-1788), age 43
Henry Fielding
(1707-1754), age 43
Carlo Goldoni
(1707-1793), age 43
Linnaeus
(1707-1778), age 43
Charles Wesley
(1707-1788), age 43
William Pitt (the Elder)
(1708-1778), age 42
Samuel Johnson
(1709-1784), age 41
Julien de La Mettrie
(1709-1751), age 41
Wilhelm Friedemann Bach
(1710-1784), age 40
Louis XV of France
(1710-1774), age 40
Thomas Reid
(1710-1796), age 40
Ch'ien Lung
(1711-1799), age 39
David Hume
(1711-1776), age 39
Frederick II of Prussia
(1712-1786), age 38
Francesco Guardi
(1712-1793), age 38
Marquis de Montcalm
(1712-1759), age 38
Jean Jacques Rousseau
(1712-1778), age 38
Denis Diderot
(1713-1784), age 37
Laurence Sterne
(1713-1768), age 37
Karl Philipp Bach
(1714-1788), age 36
Miklos Esterhazy
(1714-1790), age 36
Christoph Gluck
(1714-1787), age 36
Lord Monboddo
(1714-1799), age 36

of the hands) and composed 500 short sonatas for the harpischord.

**Gabriel Daniel Fahrenheit,** age 39; German physicist born in Danzig. He devised the first alcohol thermometer in 1709 and the first mercury thermometer in 1714, and was the inventor of the Fahrenheit scale. He lived mostly in Holland and England.

**Henry Carey,** age c. 38; English poet and composer born in London, said to be the illegitimate son of the marquis of Halifax. He wrote mostly for the London stage—farces, burlesques and ballads—and is remembered chiefly for his songs. These are some familiar lines: "Of all the girls that are so smart/ There's none like pretty Sally;/ She is the darling of my heart,/ And she lives in our alley."

**Frederick William I,** age 37; king of Prussia from 1713–1740, son and successor of Frederick I and father of Frederick the Great. A coarse, illiterate man with no taste for art or culture, he is called the real founder of Hohenzollern power. His administrative and military reforms, strict economy and personal attention to the details of government made Germany a strong, centralized kingdom.

**Nadir Shah,** age 37; king of Persia from 1736–1747, born in Khurasan of Turkish descent. Called the last great Asiatic conqueror, he rose from obscurity, usurped the throne, defeated the Afghans and Turks, invaded Mogul India (1738–1739), captured and sacked Delhi and Lahore and carried off the Koh-i-noor diamond and the Peacock Throne. Two years after his assassination by officers of the guard, the dynasty collapsed.

ALEXANDER POPE
English poet
1688-1744

**Alexander Pope,** age 37; English poet born in London of a prosperous Roman Catholic family. Physically deformed, less than five feet tall and in frail health, he was at 25 the greatest living poet. He made a fortune with his translations of the *Iliad* and *Odyssey,* moved with his mother to an estate outside London and never married. Only in the works of Shakespeare and in the Bible are there a greater number of familiar lines. Among the best known are "Damn with faint praise"; "To err is human"; "Fools rush in where angels fear to tread"; "Hope springs eternal in the human breast"; and "A little learning is a dangerous thing." But some believe his best lines are those inscribed on the collar of the dog he presented to the king: "I am his Highness' dog at Kew,/ Pray tell me, sir, whose dog are you?"

**Emanuel Swedenborg** (Svedborg), age 37; Swedish scientist and religious writer born in Stockholm, son of a professor at Uppsala University. At 55 he began having visions and at 59 gave up his post as assessor on the royal board of mines to write religious books based on an allegorical interpretation of the Bible, which made him famous throughout Europe. His most well-known work is *Heaven and Hell*.

**Montesquieu** (Charles Louis de Secondat, Baron de La Brede et de Montesquieu), age 36; French political philosopher and lawyer born near Bordeaux. He wrote *The Persian Letters; Reflections on the Causes of the Greatness and Decline of the Romans* (in 1734, three years before Gibbon was born) and *The Spirit of Laws* (1748), his masterpiece. He found the origin of laws not in the arbitrary will of princes, but in the common experience and conditions of human life.

**Samuel Richardson,** age 36; English novelist born in Derbyshire. A successful and prosperous printer, he undertook his first novel, *Pamela: or Virtue Rewarded,* at 50. He also wrote *Clarissa* and *The History of Sir Charles Grandison;* all three are sentimental, moral, but realistic and popular novels. They were parodied by Henry Fielding and admired by Rousseau.

**Joseph Butler,** age 33; English theologian and moral philosopher, son of a retired linen draper. He preached at Rolls Chapel, London, and was later bishop of Bristol and bishop of Durham. His enduring works are the *Sermons on Human Nature* and the famous *Analogy of Religion, Natural and Revealed, to the Constitution and Course of Nature* (1736), which has been called the ablest and most reasonable argument for theism ever written.

**Sir John Randolph,** age c. 32; American lawyer and legislator born in Virginia, son of William Randolph. He was clerk of the House of Burgesses from 1718–1734 and speaker from 1734–1737. As colonial agent in England in 1732, he was knighted at the request of Sir Robert Walpole for his services in legislative matters, the only native Virginian to be knighted. He was the father of Peyton Randolph.

**Lord Chesterfield** (Philip Dormer Stanhope, fourth earl of Chesterfield), age 31; English statesman and man of letters born in London. During his long political career he held important offices under George II, but is remembered for *Letters to His Son,* published in 1774 by his widow (the illegitimate daughter of George I) and written 1737–1768 for his own illegitimate son, Philip Stanhope, instructing him in the proper behavior of a man of the world; they are known for their wit, cynicism and polished prose. He was a friend of Pope, Swift and Bolingbroke.

**Francis Hutcheson,** age 31; British philosopher born in County Down, Ireland; professor of moral philosophy at the University of Glasgow from 1729–1746. He believed in a moral sense that intuitively distinguishes right from wrong, and held that right action is that which benefits the whole of society. He was the first to use the phrase "the greatest good for the greatest number," anticipating the yet-unborn Jeremy Bentham.

VOLTAIRE (Francois Marie Arouet)
French writer
1694-1778

**Voltaire** (Francois Marie Arouet), age 31; French writer born in Paris,

Etienne de Condillac
  (1715-1780), age 35
Claude Helvetius
  (1715-1771), age 35
Thomas Gray
  (1716-1771), age 34
Jean d'Alembert
  (1717-1783), age 33
Jeffrey Amherst
  (1717-1797), age 33
David Garrick
  (1717-1779), age 33
Horace Walpole
  (1717-1797), age 33
Maria Theresa of Austria
  (1717-1780), age 33
Thomas Gage
  (1721-1787), age 29
Mme. de Pompadour
  (1721-1764), age 29
Peyton Randolph
  (1721-1775), age 29
Tobias Smollett
  (1721-1771), age 29
Samuel Adams
  (1722-1803), age 28
John Burgoyne
  (1722-1792), age 28
Christopher Smart
  (1722-1771), age 28
Sir William Blackstone
  (1723-1780), age 27
Baron d'Holbach
  (1723-1789), age 27
Sir Joshua Reynolds
  (1723-1792), age 27
Adam Smith
  (1723-1790), age 27
Immanuel Kent
  (1724-1804), age 26
Friedrich Klopstock
  (1724-1803), age 26
Pierre Laclede
  (1724-1778), age 26
Casanova
  (1725-1798), age 25
Robert Clive
  (1725-1774), age 25
George Mason
  (1725-1792), age 25
James Otis
  (1725-1783), age 25

author of *Candide*. An assimilator of ideas rather than an original thinker, he believed literature should be useful. He is best known for his attacks on the church and for his defense of John Locke's liberal political views.

**Edward Braddock,** age 30; British major general. He arrived in Virginia in 1755 as commander-in-chief of the British forces in North America and set out through the wilderness to retake Fort Duquesne (on the site of Pittsburgh) from the French. Unfamiliar with Indian warfare, he was ambushed while crossing the Monongahela River and lost two-thirds of his force in a bloody rout. After the fourth horse was shot from under him, he was mortally wounded and died four days later, on July 13, 1755.

**James Edward Oglethorpe,** age 29; English general and philanthropist born in London; founder of the colony of Georgia. In 1732 he sailed with 116 colonists, all unemployed men just out of debtor's prison, and, on Feb. 12, 1733, founded the city of Savannah. His subsequent attempts to prohibit run and slavery aroused opposition and led to his recall. In his later years he was a member of Samuel Johnson's circle.

**Giovanni Battista Tiepolo,** age 29; Italian painter borne in Venice, last great master of Venetian baroque. A painter of frescoes depicting allegorical and historical themes, he is especially famous for the Cleopatra frescoes in the Palazzo Labia in Venice and for the frescoes in the bishop's palace in Wurzburg and in the royal palace in Madrid, the latter painted for Charles III *(Apotheosis of Spain)*.

**Antonio Canaletto,** age 28; Italian painter famous for his Venetian scenes: *View of the Grand Canal, Regatta on the Grand Canal* and *Piazza San Marco*. He lived in England several years and painted views of London and the Thames, many of which are in the National Gallery in London.

WILLIAM HOGARTH
English painter and engraver
1697-1764

**William Hogarth,** age 28; English painter and engraver born in London, known as a pictorial satirist. He won fame and fortune from the sale of reproductions of his two series of paintings, *The Rake's Progress* and *The Harlot's Progress* (in the Sloan Museum in London). The *Marriage a la Mode* series, in the National Gallery, is considered his masterpiece. He also painted *Garrick as Richard III* and *Strolling Actresses Dressing in a Barn*.

**Abbe Prevost** (Antoine Francois Prevost d'Exiles), age 28; French writer born in Artois, son of a lawyer. He entered a Benedictine monastery early, but left at 31 for a life of adventure, supported by writing popular novels. He is remembered for one novel, *Manon Lescaut*, the story of a young man's passion for an amoral, frivolous young

# 1750

Thomas Gainsborough
(1727-1788), age 23

James Wolfe
(1727-1759), age 23

James Cook
(1728-1779), age 22

Horatio Gates
(1727/28-1806),
age c.22

Oliver Goldsmith
(1728 or 1730-1774),
age 22?

Niccolo Piccini
(1728-1800), age 22

Louis de Bougainville
(1729-1811), age 21

Edmund Burke
(1729-1797), age 21

Catherine II of Russia
(1729-1796), age 21

Sir William Howe
(1729-1814), age 21

G. E. Lessing
(1729-1781), age 21

Moses Mendelssohn
(1729-1786), age 21

Thomas Percy
(1729-1811), age 21

Baron von Steuben
(1730-1794), age 20

Josiah Wedgwood
(1730-1795), age 20

Henry Cavendish
(1731-1810), age 19

William Cowper
(1731-1800), age 19

Johann Christoph Bach
(1732-1795), age 18

Pierre de Beaumarchais
(1732-1799), age 18

Jean Honore Fragonard
(1732-1806), age 18

Warren Hastings
(1732-1818), age 18

Joseph Haydn
(1732-1809), age 18

Richard Henry Lee
(1732-1794), age 18

Francis Marion
(c.1732-1795), age c.18

David Rittenhouse
(1732-1796), age 18

George Washington
(1732-1799), age 18

Joseph Priestley
(1733-1804), age 17

Philip Schuyler
(1733-1804), age 17

Daniel Boone
(1734-1820), age 16

John Adams
(1735-1826), age 15

Johann Christian Bach
(1735-1782), age 15

Paul Revere
(1735-1818), age 15

Patrick Henry
(1736-1799), age 14

James Macpherson
(1736-1796), age 14

James Watt
(1736-1819), age 14

Edward Gibbon
(1737-1794), age 13

John Hancock
(1737-1793), age 13

Thomas Paine
(1737-1809), age 13

Ethan Allen
(1738-1789), age 12

John Copley
(1738-1815), age 12

Charles Cornwallis
(1738-1805), age 12

George III of Great Britain
(1738-1820), age 12

Benjamin West
(1738-1820), age 12

Grigori Potemkin
(1739-1791), age 11

John Rutledge
(1739-1800), age 11

James Boswell
(1740-1795), age 10

Marquis de Sade
(1740-1814), age 10

Haym Salomon
(1740-1785), age 10

Benedict Arnold
(1741-1801), age 9

woman. It inspired two operas: *Manon* by Massenet and *Manon Lescaut* by Puccini.

**Jean-Baptiste-Simeon Chardin,** age 26; French painter born in Paris, son of a carpenter. Called the greatest 18-century French artist after Watteau, he departed from the fashionable rococo style and painted simple still lifes and interiors without sentimentality. Two notable works are *Breakfast Table* (in the Louvre) and *Blowing Bubbles* (in the Metropolitan Museum of Art).

**Baal-Shem-Tov** (Israel ben Eliezer), age c. 25; Jewish religious teacher and healer born in the Ukraine; the founder of modern Hasidism. Of humble origin and occupation (a synagogue watchman and innkeeper), he won a large following among the Jews of Eastern Europe with his piety, humility and charity, his joyful approach to religious worship and his reputed power to work miracles. He is the subject of many legends and stories.

**James Thomson,** age 25; British poet born in Scotland, son of a clergyman; the first of two poets of the same name. His blank-verse poems, *The Seasons,* which center around descriptions of nature, prepared the way for the romantic poets. He also wrote plays and the famous ode, *Rule Brittanica.*

**Anders Celsius,** age 24; Swedish astronomer, professor at Uppsala University from 1730–1744 and first director of the Uppsala Observatory, from 1740–1744. He is remembered as the inventor of the centigrade (or Celsius) thermometer scale and for his studies of the Aurora Borealis.

**Francois Boucher,** age 22; French rococo painter born in Paris; court painter, a favorite of Mme. de Pompadour's and the most fashionable artist of his time. Elegant and frivolous, he is also known as a decorator of boudoirs and designer of tapestries. Examples of his paintings are *The Toilet of Venus* (in the Metropolitan Museum of Art) and *Diana Bathing* (in the Louvre). He was the teacher of Fragonard.

**Jonathan Edwards,** age 22; American clergyman and theologian born in Connecticut; pastor (1729–1750) of Northampton Church, the largest in Massachusetts Bay Colony. A strict Calvinist and powerful pulpit orator, he could stir his congregation to a state of religious frenzy and hysteria. He was the author of a treatise on freedom of the will (a concept he denied). He died five weeks after being inaugurated as president of the University of New Jersey (now Princeton University).

**John Wesley,** age 22; English evangelist, theologian and founder of Methodism; born in Epworth, Lincolnshire, the 15th child of a clergyman. He began open-air preaching in the fields near Bristol in 1739, rejecting Calvin's exclusiveness and declaring that all men, as children of God, might be saved through faith in Jesus Christ. He traveled on horseback throughout England, Scotland and Ireland, organizing Methodist societies, but had no intention of founding a new sect. The separation of Methodists from the Church of England occurred after his death. He married at 48, but separated from his wife and had no children.

**Benjamin Franklin,** age 19; American statesman, scientist and homespun philosopher, born in Boston, the 15th child (and 10th son) of a candlemaker. Apprenticed to his brother as a printer at 12, at 23 he was proprietor of a print shop in Philadelphia and publisher of the weekly *Pennsylvania Gazette.* He also published *Poor Richard's Almanac* (1732–1757) and served as deputy postmaster at Philadelphia (1737–1753), and deputy postmaster general for the colonies (1753–1774). He invented the Franklin stove, bifocal lenses and the lightning rod and helped draft the Declaration of Independence. He is called the patron saint of American small businessmen.

Charles Willson Peale
(1741-1827), age 9
Gebhard von Blucher
(1742-1819), age 8
Nathaniel Greene
(1742-1786), age 8
Edmund Cartwright
(1743-1823), age 7
Cagliostro
(1743-1795), age 7
Marquis de Condorcet
(1743-1794), age 7
Mme. Du Barry
(1743-1793), age 7
John Fitch
(1743-1798), age 7
Thomas Jefferson
(1743-1826), age 7
Antoine Lavoisier
(1743-1794), age 7
Jean Paul Marat
(1743-1793), age 7
William Paley
(1743-1805), age 7
Meyer Rothschild
(1743-1812), age 7
Elbridge Gerry
(1744-1814), age 6
Johann von Herder
(1744-1803), age 6
Chevalier de Lamarck
(1744-1829), age 6

John Jay
(1745-1829), age 5
Mikhail Kutuzov
(1745-1813), age 5
Henry Mackenzie
(1745-1831), age 5
Benjamin Rush
(1745-1813), age 5
Alessandro Volta
(1745-1827), age 5
Anthony Wayne
(1745-1796), age 5
Francisco Jose de Goya
(1746-1828), age 4
John Paul Jones
(1747-1792), age 3
Jeremy Bentham
(1748-1832), age 2
Jacques Louis David
(1748-1825), age 2
Vittorio Alfieri
(1749-1803), age 1
Johann Wolfgang von
Goethe
(1749-1832), age 1
Edward Jenner
(1749-1823), age 1
Marquis de Laplace
(1749-1827), age 1
Comte de Mirabeau
(1749-1791), age 1
John Stevens
(1749-1838), age 1

# 1750–1775

The industrial revolution, which transformed Britain from an agricultural to an industrial nation, began in the mid-18th century. The transition from hand labor to machine power occurred first in the textile industry, following a number of significant inventions. John Kay had invented the flying shuttle in 1733; in 1764 James Hargreaves invented the spinning jenny; in 1769 Sir Richard Arkwright invented the water frame for spinning; in 1779 Samuel Crompton invented the spinning mule; and in 1785 Edmund Cartwright invented the power loom. James Watt had perfected a steam engine in 1769, but factories continued to be run on water power until 1785, when a steam engine was first installed in a cotton factory. The British maintained their industrial advantage for many years by passing laws forbidding the export of machines or machine designs.

## 1750

Fontenelle
 (1657-1757), age 93
Viscount Bolingbroke
 (1678-1751), age 72
Sieur de Bienville
 (1680-1768), age 70
George II of Great Britain
 (1683-1760), age 67
Jean Philippe Rameau
 (1683-1764), age 67
Edward Young
 (1683-1765), age 67
Johann Sebastian Bach
 (1685-1750), age 65
George Berkeley
 (1685-1753), age 65
George Frederick Handel
 (1685-1759), age 65
Domenico Scarlatti
 (1685-1757), age 65
Emanuel Swedenborg
 (1688-1772), age 62
Montesquieu
 (1689-1755), age 61
Samuel Richardson
 (1689-1761), age 61
Joseph Butler
 (1692-1752), age 58
Lord Chesterfield
 (1694-1773), age 56

**Buffon** (Georges Louis Leclerc, comte de Buffon), age 43; French naturalist, the first to suggest that the earth was more than 6,000 years old. As director of the royal botanical gardens in Paris, he and his assistants produced the 44-volume *Histoire Naturelle,* a summary of the contemporary knowledge of nature.

**Henry Fielding,** age 43; English novelist and playwright born in Somersetshire of a middle-class family. At 30 he had written and produced 25 plays, including farces and adaptations from Moliere. However, his fame rests on two novels: *Joseph Andrews,* a parody of Richardson's *Pamela;* and *The History of Tom Jones, a Foundling* (1749), his masterpiece and one of the great English novels. He also practiced law and served as justice of the peace.

CARL LINNAEUS
Swedish botanist
1707-1778

**Linnaeus** (Carl von Linne), age 43; Swedish botanist, son of a Lutheran clergyman. Called the founder of modern taxonomy, he invented the

Simultaneously with the development of the factory system, Britain entered a trade war with France, joining the Seven Years' War (1756–1763) on the side of Prussia and Hanover against France, Austria, Spain, Russia and Sweden. William Pitt the Elder, who conducted the war for Britain, was less concerned with the central Continental issue of who should possess Silesia than with the four principal French trading areas: North America, the West Indies, Africa and India. Pitt's strategy began with a blockade of the French fleet in the ports of Brest and Toulon, while coordinated attacks were made on French trade. Through the heroism of James Wolfe, Quebec was captured in 1759, and with it the fur and fish trade. With the capture of Guadeloupe in the West Indies, the British secured the sugar trade; and with the capture of Dakar, the slave trade. Robert Clive's victories in India gave Britain the commercial advantage there. With the Treaty of Paris in 1763, Britain acquired the French empire in Canada, and obtained Florida from the Spanish; Britain was well on the way to becoming the strongest power in the world.

# 1775

binomial method of plant and animal classification (as in *Homo sapiens*) and was professor of medicine and botany at Uppsala University. He was granted a patent of nobility by Gustavus III in 1761.

WILLIAM PITT (the elder)
British statesman
1708-1778

**William Pitt** (the Elder), age 42; first earl of Chatham, British statesman; foreign minister from 1756–1761. Through his vigorous prosecution of the Seven Years' War, English armies defeated the French in India, Africa and Canada (in the French and Indian Wars) and laid the foundation of the British Empire in India. He formed a new ministry in 1766, but gout restricted his activity. He suffered an apoplectic stroke while addressing the House of Lords in 1778 and died a month later.

**Carlo Goldoni,** age 43; Italian dramatist born in Venice; the creator of modern Italian comedy. The buffoonery of *commedia dell' arte*, with

Johann Christoph Bach
  (1732-1795), age 43
Pierre de Beaumarchais
  (1732-1799), age 43
Jean Honore Fragonard
  (1732-1806), age 43
Warren Hastings
  (1732-1818), age 43
Joseph Haydn
  (1732-1809), age 43
Richard Henry Lee
  (1732-1794), age 43
Francis Marion
  (c.1732-1795), age c.43
David Rittenhouse
  (1732-1796), age 43
George Washington
  (1732-1799), age 43
Joseph Priestley
  (1733-1804), age 42
Philip Schuyler
  (1733-1804), age 42
Daniel Boone
  (1734-1820), age 41
John Adams
  (1735-1826), age 40
Johann Christian Bach
  (1735-1782), age 40
Paul Revere
  (1735-1818), age 40

# 1750

Voltaire
(1694-1778), age 56
Edward Braddock
(1695-1755), age 55
James Oglethorpe
(1696-1785), age 54
Giovanni Tiepolo
(1696-1770), age 54
Antonio Canaletto
(1697-1768), age 53
William Hogarth
(1697-1764), age 53
Abbe Prevost
(1697-1763), age 53
Jean-Baptiste Chardin
(1699-1779), age 51
Baal-Shem-Tov
(1698/1700-1760), age c.50
Francois Boucher
(1703-1770), age 47
Jonathan Edwards
(1703-1758), age 47
John Wesley
(1703-1791), age 47
Benjamin Franklin
(1706-1790), age 44

its stereotyped characters such as Harlequin and Pantaleone, eventually gave way to his comedies in the manner of Moliere, with lifelike characters and situations. He wrote over 150 comedies, including *The Mistress of the Inn* and *The Accomplished Maid*.

**Charles Wesley,** age 43; English evangelist and hymn writer, son of a clergyman and younger brother of John Wesley. In 1729 at Oxford he organized, with other earnest young men, the Holy Club, which became the first Methodist Society—so called, it is said, because of his regular, methodical habits. He wrote six or seven thousand hymns, including *Jesus, Lover of My Soul* and *Hark! the Herald Angels Sing*.

SAMUEL JOHNSON
English writer, critic and
lexicographer
1709-1784

**Samuel Johnson** (called Dr. Johnson), age 41; English writer, critic and lexicographer, born in Lichfield, son of a book dealer. He was blind in one eye and myopic in the other, corpulent and slovenly in appearance and habits; he suffered from involuntary muscular spasms, a melancholy disposition and a morbid fear of death. Yet he was blessed with extraordinary mental powers. He supported himself much of his life as a hack writer for booksellers. His greatest accomplishments were the *Dictionary of the English Language,* with 40,000 definitions and twice as many illustrative quotations; and *The Lives of the Poets,* in 10 volumes. Dr. Johnson is remembered from his depiction in Boswell's biography as the great conversationalist, imposing his critical opinions on his listeners and on the age.

**Julien Offray de La Mettrie,** age 41; French philosopher and physician born in St. Malo, known as a thorough materialist. He denied the existence of God or an immortal soul and declared that man is a machine, all his actions being determined physiologically, and that the pursuit of sensual pleasure is the aim of life. He is the author of *L'Homme machine* (1748).

**Wilhelm Friedemann Bach,** age 40; German composer and organist born in Weimar, eldest son of Johann Sebastian Bach. Known as "the Halle Bach," he was organist at Dresden from 1733–1746 and at Halle from 1746–1764. An accomplished organist and successful composer, he is said to have led a dissolute life and to have disappointed his father.

**Louis XV,** age 40; king of France from 1715–1774; great-grandson of Louis XIV, whom he succeeded at the age of five. He inherited an over-refined, luxurious court and an unstable economy. He lost Canada and India to the British, while burdensome taxation and periodical famine fostered discontent at home. Two famous mistresses, Mme. de Pompadour and Mme. du Barry, strongly influenced his policy-making.

**Thomas Reid,** age 40; Scottish philosopher and professor of moral philosophy at the University of Glasgow from 1764–1781 succeeding Adam Smith. Known as the founder of the common-sense school, he declared that the skepticism of Hume and the idealism of Berkeley neglect common sense and that external objects are real and self-evident and not mere representations presented by the senses. He wrote *An Inquiry into the Human Mind on the Principles of Common Sense* (1764).

**Ch'ien Lung** (Kao Tsung), age 39; Chinese emperor from 1736–1796, fourth of the Ch'ing or Manchu dynasty, grandson of K'ang-hsi. A strong and able ruler, he further extended China's boundaries, established friendly relations with Europe and traded with the United States, exchanging tea and silk for American furs. After a 60-year reign, he abdicated at 85 in favor of his son.

**David Hume,** age 39; Scottish philosopher and historian born in Edinburgh, youngest son of a prominent family. The foremost British skeptic, he carried Locke's empiricism to its logical conclusion and held that there is nothing in the mind but a succession of impressions—no underlying self. He is the author of *A Treatise of Human Nature* (1739–1740), *Dialogues Concerning Natural Religion*, a 6-volume *History of England* and an eight-page autobiography. One very famous line is "Reason is the slave of passion."

FREDERICK II (the Great)
King of Prussia
1712-1786

**Frederick II** (Frederick the Great), age 38; king of Prussia from 1740–1786, grandson of Frederick I and son of Frederick William I, who despised him for his effeminacy. He was a brilliant and able ruler under whom Prussia became a major power. An admirer of French culture and friend of Voltaire's, he wrote voluminously on many subjects and built *Sans Souci* palace.

**Francesco Guardi,** age 38; Italian painter born in Venice, son of a painter. He collaborated with his brothers Niccolo and Giovanni on paintings for Venetian churches, but is known particularly for his popular views of Venice and paintings of public events on the canals, done in a romantic, impressionist style. His famous works include *Ascent in a Balloon* (in Berlin) and *Doges' Palace* (in the National Gallery in London). He was the brother-in-law of Tiepolo.

# 1775

Patrick Henry
(1736-1799), age 39
James Macpherson
(1736-1796), age 39
James Watt
(1736-1819), age 39
Edward Gibbon
(1737-1794), age 38
John Hancock
(1737-1793), age 38
Thomas Paine
(1737-1809), age 38
Ethan Allen
(1738-1789), age 37
John Copley
(1738-1815), age 37
Charles Cornwallis
(1738-1805), age 37
George III of Great Britain
(1738-1820), age 37
Benjamin West
(1738-1820), age 37
Grigori Potemkin
(1739-1791), age 36
John Rutledge
(1739-1800), age 36
James Boswell
(1740-1795), age 35
Marquis de Sade
(1740-1814), age 35
Haym Salomon
(1740-1785), age 35
Benedict Arnold
(1741-1801), age 34
Charles Willson Peale
(1741-1827), age 34
Gebhard von Blucher
(1742-1819), age 33
Nathaniel Greene
(1742-1786), age 33
Edmund Cartwright
(1743-1823), age 32
Cagliostro
(1743-1795), age 32
Marquis de Condorcet
(1743-1794), age 32
Mme. Du Barry
(1743-1793), age 32
John Fitch
(1743-1798), age 32
Thomas Jefferson
(1743-1826), age 32

MARQUIS DE MONTCALM
French general
1712-1759

**Montcalm** (Marquis Louis Joseph de Montcalm de Saint-Veran), age 38; French general born near Nimes. Sent to America in 1756 as commander-in-chief of the French forces in New France (Canada), he won early victories over the British and defended Fort Carillon (Ticonderoga) against a force of 16,000. On the Plains of Abraham, at Quebec, on Sept. 13, 1759, the battle that ended French power in Canada was fought. Montcalm was mortally wounded, and Quebec was surrendered to the British.

**Jean Jacques Rousseau,** age 38; French writer and political theorist born in Geneva, Switzerland, son of a watchmaker of French descent. He ran away at 16 and met the wealthy Mme. de Warens, who kept him between his wanderings until he was 29. In Paris after 1741 he wrote *Discourse on the Sciences and Arts* and *Discourse on the Origin of Inequality,* advancing the view that man is by nature good, but corrupted by social institutions. He also wrote *The Social Contract; Julie, or the New Eloise* (a sentimental, moralizing romance); *Emile;* and his autobiography, *Confessions,* in two volumes. He became paranoiac in his later years.

LAURENCE STERNE
British novelist and
    clergyman
1713-1768

**Laurence Sterne,** age 37; British novelist and clergyman born in Ireland. He achieved success with *The Life and Opinions of Tristram Shandy,* a work of great significance to the development of the novel, noted for its eccentricity and odd humor. He is said to have driven his wife insane with his unconventional habits. He also wrote *A Sentimental Journey through France and Italy*.

**Denis Diderot,** age 37; French encyclopedist and writer; principal editor of the famous *Encyclopedie,* in 28 volumes, over which he labored for more than 20 years (1751–1772), assisted by Jean d'Alembert, Voltaire, Montesquieu, Rousseau, Buffon and others. A skeptic and materialist, he also wrote plays, novels and art criticism. He was invited to St. Petersburg by Catherine the Great (1773–1774).

**Karl Philipp Emanuel Bach,** age 36; German composer born in Weimar, third and most gifted son of Johann Sebastian Bach. Called "the Berlin Bach," he was harpischordist at the court of Frederick the Great (1740–1767) and musical director of Hamburg churches (1767–1788). Falling somewhere between the baroque and the classical in style, his 210 harpischord pieces, 12 symphonies, concertos, sonatas and oratorios influenced Haydn and Beethoven.

**Miklos Jozsef Esterhazy,** age 36; Hungarian prince of the Holy Roman Empire and wealthy art patron, whose palace, on the shore of Neuslieder Lake southeast of Vienna, was known as the Hungarian Versailles. Joseph Haydn was the conductor of Esterhazy's private orchestra from 1766–1790, composing chamber music, symphonies and operas for private performances in the palace.

**Christoph Willibald Gluck,** age 36; German operatic composer born in Bavaria. He wrote and produced Italian-style operas in various European cities. With *Orfeo ed Euridice* produced in Vienna in 1762, he abandoned this style and restored to opera its original character as music drama. He influenced Mozart and Wagner.

**James Burnett, Lord Monboddo,** age 36; Scottish jurist and pioneer anthropologist, a controversial figure in his time because of his alleged statement that men are descended from monkeys. The allegation was untrue, for he was not an evolutionist and merely said that man's nearest living relative and fellow member of the species *Homo* is the orangutan, "the man of the woods," whom he found to be gentle, affectionate and social by nature, with a sense of honor and decency. He wrote *Of the Origin and Progress of Language* in six volumes (1773–1792).

**Etienne Bonnot de Condillac,** age 35; French philosopher and Catholic priest born in Grenoble. A follower of John Locke and an exponent of sensationalism, he believed that all mental activity is the result of sense impressions and that there are no innate ideas. He attempted to reconcile this with Christian theology and Cartesian dualism of body and soul.

**Claude Adrien Helvetius,** age 35; French philosopher and philanthropist born in Paris. He retired at 36 from his post as farmer general (tax collector) to his country estate and wrote *De l'esprit (On the Spirit)* in 1758, which was condemned by the Sorbonne and publicly burned in 1759. Believing in the equal endowment of all men and attributing differences to education and circumstances, he saw self-interest as the sole human motive; the solution to all human problems could be achieved only, he thought, through the total identification of individual interests with those of society in general, as in an ant colony or an ideal communist state.

Antoine Lavoisier
(1743-1794), age 32
Jean Paul Marat
(1743-1793), age 32
William Paley
(1743-1805), age 32
Meyer Rothschild
(1743-1812), age 32
Elbridge Gerry
(1744-1814), age 31
Johann von Herder
(1744-1803), age 31
Chevalier de Lamarck
(1744-1829), age 31
John Jay
(1745-1829), age 30
Mikhail Kutuzov
(1745-1813), age 30
Henry Mackenzie
(1745-1831), age 30
Benjamin Rush
(1745-1813), age 30
Alessandro Volta
(1745-1827), age 30
Anthony Wayne
(1745-1796), age 30
Francisco Jose de Goya
(1746-1828), age 29
John Paul Jones
(1747-1792), age 28
Jeremy Bentham
(1748-1832), age 27
Jacques Louis David
(1748-1825), age 27
Vittorio Alfieri
(1749-1803), age 26
Johann Wolfgang von Goethe
(1749-1832), age 26
Edward Jenner
(1749-1823), age 26
Marquis de Laplace
(1749-1827), age 26
Comte de Mirabeau
(1749-1791), age 26
John Stevens
(1749-1838), age 26
Jouffroy d'Abbans
(1751-1832), age 24
James Madison
(1751-1836), age 24
Richard Sheridan
(1751-1816), age 24

THOMAS GRAY
English poet and scholar
1716-1771

**Thomas Gray,** age 34; English poet and scholar born in London. Indifferent to fame, he chose the quiet life of a Cambridge don and wrote a few poems of high quality, including *Elegy Written in a County Churchyard* (1751). Sometimes called the most perfect poem in the English language, it contains dozens of familiar lines, such as, "Far from the madding crowd's ignoble strife . . . ."

**Jean le Rond d'Alembert,** age 33; French mathematician and philosopher born in Paris, left as an infant on the steps of the Church of St. Jean le Rond (for which he was named) by his prominent unmarried parents. Co-editor, with Diderot, of the *Encyclopedie,* he wrote the preliminary essay on the progress of the sciences, and articles on mathematics, music, philosophy and literature.

**Jeffrey Amherst,** age 33; Baron Amherst, British general born in Kent for whom Amherst College was named. Sent to America in 1758, he became commander-in-chief in 1759 and captured Ticonderoga, but arrived too late to help Wolfe at Quebec. He took Montreal on Sept. 8. 1760, and was appointed governor general of British America. He returned to England in 1763 and refused to command British troops in the American Revolution. He was made a baron in 1776.

DAVID GARRICK
English actor
1717-1779

**David Garrick,** age 33; English actor born in Hereford. One of the greatest actors of all time, he abandoned the old-fashioned declamatory style, introducing to the stage a natural diction and manner. He became famous at 24 in the role of Richard III, and amassed a fortune in a long, successful career. He was a lifelong friend of Samuel Johnson.

**Horace Walpole,** age 33; fourth earl of Oxford; English writer born in London, the fourth son of Sir Robert Walpole. A bachelor of great wealth and the owner of Strawberry Hill estate, famous for its Gothic architecture, he wrote the first Gothic novel, *The Castle of Otranto* (1764), which inspired many imitators.

**Maria Theresa,** age 33; archduchess of Austria and queen of Hungary and Bohemia from 1740–1780, of the house of Hapsburg. She inherited from her father, Charles VI, Holy Roman emperor, the Austrian possessions but not the imperial crown. After her marriage to Francis, duke of Lorraine, he became emperor as Francis I. She was a generous patron of the arts and the mother of Marie Antoinette.

**Thomas Gage,** age 29; British general and colonial administrator born in Sussex. Sent to America in 1754, he served under Braddock and Amherst and was made commander-in-chief in 1763 and governor of Massachusetts in 1774. When he dispatched troops to confiscate military supplies at Lexington, the Revolutionary War began with the Battle of Lexington and Concord, April 19, 1775. He resigned and returned to England in October.

**Mme. de Pompadour** (Jeanne Antoinette Poisson, marquise de Pompadour), age 29; French beauty after whom a hair style is named; mistress of Louis XV of France. Of a middle-class family, she married at 20, met the king at 23, became his mistress at 24, and remained his confidante all her life. The king presented her with the estate of Pompadour and made her a duchess in 1752. Her meddling in state affairs is sometimes blamed for causing the Seven Years' War (1756–1763). She was the patroness of many artists.

**Peyton Randolph,** age 29; American political leader born in Williamsburg, Va., son of Sir John Randolph, and first president of the Continental Congress (1774, 1775). A personal friend of George Washington, he was king's attorney for Virginia from 1748–1766, a longtime member of the House of Burgesses and its speaker from 1766–1775. Illness and early death deprived him of a major role in the new republic.

**Tobias George Smollett,** age 29; British novelist born in Scotland. He began life as a surgeon's assistant in Glasgow and surgeon's mate on a British vessel. His first two novels, *Roderick Random* and *Peregrine Pickle,* are notable for their depiction of the rough sea life on 18th-century sailing ships. *The Expedition of Humphrey Clinker* is said to be his best novel and is sometimes called a classic.

**Samuel Adams,** age 28; American political leader born in Boston, a second cousin of John Adams. An unsuccessful businessman, he assumed leadership of the extremists in the Massachusetts legislature from 1765–1774 and in the Continental Congress from 1774–1781. He instigated the Boston Tea Party and with John Hancock organized the Sons of Liberty. His arrest was ordered by Gen. Gage, but he lived to become governor of Massachusetts from 1794–1797.

**John Burgoyne,** age 28; British general and playwright, remembered for his plan to defeat the colonies by invading New York from Canada. After early successes the plan miscarried, and his surrender at Saratoga on Oct. 17, 1777 marked a turning point in the war. He returned to England and wrote several successful plays, including *The Heiress,* produced in 1786.

**Christopher Smart,** age 28; English poet born in Kent. He went to London at 31, edited a humorous magazine, produced plays, wrote verse and translated the works of Horace. Three years later, in 1756,

# 1775

Fanny Burney
(1752-1840), age 23
George Rogers Clark
(1752-1818), age 23
Philip Freneau
(1752-1832), age 23
Edmund Jennings Randolph
(1753-1813), age 22
George Crabbe
(1754-1832), age 21
Pierre Charles L'Enfant
(1754-1825), age 21
Louis XVI of France
(1754-1793), age 21
Talleyrand
(1754-1838), age 21
Alexander Hamilton
(1755-1804), age 20
Louis XVIII of France
(1755-1824), age 20
Marie Antoinette
(1755-1793), age 20
John Marshall
(1755-1835), age 20
Gerhard von Scharnhorst
(1755-1813), age 20
Sarah Siddons
(1755-1831), age 20
Gilbert Stuart
(1755-1828), age 20
Aaron Burr
(1756-1836), age 19
William Godwin
(1756-1836), age 19
Henry Lee
(1756-1818), age 19
Wolfgang Amadeus Mozart
(1756-1791), age 19
Sir Henry Raeburn
(1756-1823), age 19
William Blake
(1757-1827), age 18
Antonio Canova
(1757-1822), age 18
Charles X of France
(1757-1836), age 18
Marquis de Lafayette
(1757-1834), age 18
George Vancouver
(1757-1798), age 18
James Monroe
(1758-1831), age 17

he was stricken with a mental disorder, which caused his confinement in asylums at various times. He is remembered chiefly for one highly praised, 240-line devotional poem, *Song to David* (1763). He died in debtor's prison at 49.

**Sir William Blackstone,** age 27; English jurist born in London, author of *Commentaries on the Laws of England* (four volumes; 1765–1769), the basic legal textbook in Britain for over a century. He became the first professor of English law at Oxford in 1758.

**Baron Paul Henri Dietrich d'Holbach,** age 27; French philosopher and encyclopedist born in Germany. He grew up in Paris and became, in retrospect, a typical 18th-century French philosopher—materialistic and antireligious. He contributed many articles to the *Encyclopedie* and wrote *Systeme de la Nature* (1770).

ADAM SMITH
Scottish economist
1723-1790

**Adam Smith,** age 27; Scottish economist born in Kirkcaldy, founder of the science of political economy. Author of *An Inquiry into the Nature and Causes of the Wealth of Nations* (1776), he thought it highly impertinent of kings and ministers to pretend to watch over the economy of private citizens.

IMMANUEL KANT
German philosopher
1724-1804

**Immanuel Kant,** age 26; German philosopher of Scottish and German descent born in Koenigsberg (now in the USSR), the son of a saddler. One of the world's greatest thinkers, he was a small, frail bachelor who lived an uneventful life. Professor of logic and metaphysics at Koenigsberg from 1770–1796 and author of *Critique of Pure Reason* (1781), he maintained that as our imperfect senses come in contact with reality, the world we know and live in is formed, which is the only world we shall ever know—although out there, beyond the wall of our sense impressions, there is something else. It fell to him to point out the faulty logic of Anselm's proof of the existence of God.

**Sir Joshua Reynolds,** age 27; English painter born near Plymouth, son of a clergyman. The most fashionable and popular painter of his time, he produced, with the help of assistants, nearly 2,000 paintings, including portraits of Samuel Johnson, Goldsmith, Burke, Garrick, Gibbon, Sterne, and Sarah Siddons. His studies of women and children *(The Strawberry Girl* and *Lady Penelope Boothby)* are also much admired. He was knighted in 1768. Reynolds was also a member of Samuel Johnson's circle.

**Friedrich Gottlieb Klopstock,** age 26; German poet and dramatist whose epic poem, *Messias (The Messiah)* four volumes, 1751–1773) was the first important work of modern German literature. He also wrote a dramatic trilogy in prose on Arminius (Hermann), the first century Germanic chieftain. Many of his odes were set to music by Beethoven, Schubert and others.

**Pierre Laclede,** age 26; French pioneer and fur trader; founder of St. Louis, Mo. He migrated to New Orleans from France in 1755 and, as a member of the company holding a monopoly on the fur trade, ascended the Mississippi River with his stepson, Rene Chouteau, then 15. He established a trading post on the west bank in 1764, calling it St. Louis in honor of Louis IX.

**Casanova** (Giovanni Giacomo [or Jacopo] Casanova de Seingalt), age 25; Italian gambler, police spy, celebrated lover and director of the French state lotteries, born in Venice of a family of actors. Of great personal charm, he was involved in a succession of intrigues in various capitals of Europe and won the confidence of many prominent people. At 60 he retired to the castle of his patron, Count Waldstein, in Bohemia, and wrote his memoirs in 12 volumes.

**Robert Clive** (Baron Clive of Plassey), age 25; British general and statesman born in Shropshire, founder of the British Empire in India. In a series of victories during the Seven Years' War (1756–1763), he destroyed French power in India and won sovereignty for the East India Company. Addicted to opium, he committed suicide at 49.

**George Mason,** age 25; wealthy American planter and statesman born in Fairfax County, Va,; one of the earliest opponents of British policies and the author of the Virginia Declaration of Rights, which was Jefferson's model for the Declaration of Independence. He helped draft the federal constitution, but refused to sign it because of its lack of a bill of rights and restrictions on states' rights.

**James Otis,** age 25; American political leader and lawyer born in Massachusetts. He resigned as king's advocate general in 1761 over abuses of the rights of the colonists, arguing that natural law and natural rights took precedence over acts of Parliament. He published *The Rights of the British Colonies Asserted and Proved* (1764) and became a leader of the radicals in the Massachusetts legislature. In a quarrel with a customs official in 1769, he was struck over the head and incapacitated. He later became insane.

**Thomas Gainsborough,** age 23; English painter born in Suffolk, a close rival of Sir Joshua Reynolds for public favor and preferred to him by the king. He employed no assistants and complained of being overburdened with portrait commissions when he would have rather painted landscapes. He painted George III, Sarah Siddons, Garrick, Richardson, Sterne, William Pitt, Edmund Burke and Robert Clive. His most famous picture is *The Blue Boy* (in the Huntington Gallery, San Marino, Calif.)

# 1775

Horatio Nelson
(1758-1805), age 17
Maxmilien de Robespierre
(1758-1794), age 17
Noah Webster
(1758-1843), age 17
Robert Burns
(1759-1796), age 16
Georges Danton
(1759-1794), age 16
William Pitt (the Younger)
(1759-1806), age 16
Friedrich von Schiller
(1759-1805), age 16
William Wilberforce
(1759-1833), age 16
Luigi Cherubini
(1760-1842), age 15
Camille Desmoulins
(1760-1794), age 15
Neithardt von Gneisenau
(1760-1831), age 15
Hokusai
(1760-1849), age 15
Comte de Saint-Simon
(1760-1825), age 15
Albert Gallatin
(1761-1849), age 14
August von Kotzebue
(1761-1819), age 14
Johann Gottlieb Fichte
(1762-1814), age 13
John Jacob Astor
(1763-1848), age 12
Charles Bulfinch
(1763-1844), age 12
Josephine
(1763-1814), age 12
Jean Paul Richter
(1763-1825), age 12
Benjamin Latrobe
(1764-1820), age 11
Ann Radcliffe
(1764-1823), age 11
Robert Fulton
(1765-1815), age 10
James Smithson
(1765-1829), age 10
Eli Whitney
(1765-1825), age 10
John Dalton
(1766-1844), age 9

**James Wolfe,** age 23; British army officer, second in command, after 1758, to Jeffrey Amherst in the French and Indian War. He was given command, with the rank of major general, of the campaign against Quebec. There, on the Plains of Abraham on Sept. 13, 1759, the battle that gave Canada to the British was won. Both Wolfe and Montcalm fell, mortally wounded. Wolfe appears in Thackeray's *Virginians*.

JAMES COOK
English mariner and
explorer
1728-1779

**James Cook** (Capt. Cook), age 22; English mariner and explorer, son of a farm laborer. On three voyages to the Pacific between 1768 and 1779, he visited Tahiti; discovered and claimed for Britain New Zealand and eastern Australia; discovered the Sandwich Islands (Hawaii); and charted the Pacific coast of North America from Oregon to the Bering Strait. He was killed by natives in Hawaii.

**Horatio Gates,** age c. 22; American Revolutionary general born in Essex, England. He served in the British army in the French and Indian War, but sided with the colonies in the Revolution. He was seen as Washington's rival for the supreme command after the victory at Saratoga in 1777; however, in 1780, after the disastrous defeat at Camden, S.C., he was relieved of his command and remained inactive for two years before being recalled. After the war he freed his slaves and moved to New York.

OLIVER GOLDSMITH
British poet, playwright
and novelist
1728 or 1730-1774

**Oliver Goldsmith,** age 22?; British poet, playwright and novelist, born in Ireland, son of a clergyman. A hack writer for most of his life, like his friend Samuel Johnson, he is remembered for a poem, a play and a novel: *The Deserted Village, She Stoops to Conquer* and *The Vicar of Wakefield*. These famous lines are his: "Princes and lords may flourish or may fade;/ A breath can make them, as a breath has made;/ But a bold peasantry, their country's pride,/ When once destroyed, can never be supplied."

**Niccolo Piccini,** age 22; Italian opera composer born in Bari. He composed more than 100 operas—Italian and French, serious and comic—and was summoned to Paris in 1776 by Marie Antoinette, where his presence provoked a feud between lovers of Italian-style opera and admirers of Gluck's music dramas. His well-known operas include *La Cecchina, Roland* and *Alys*.

**Louis Antoine de Bougainville,** age 21; French soldier and navigator born in Paris; leader of the first French expedition around the world (1766–1769). Accompanied by natural scientists and astronomers, he visited Tahiti, Samoa and other Pacific islands and published an account of the voyage in 1771. A tropical flowering vine, two straits and the largest of the Solomon Islands are named for him.

EDMUND BURKE
British statesman, orator
and writer
1729-1797

**Edmund Burke,** age 21; British statesman, orator and writer, born in Dublin, son of a lawyer. A longtime member of Parliament (1765–1794), he is remembered as a defender of the rights of the colonies (*On Conciliation with America,* 1775) and an enemy of the French Revolution (*Reflections on the Revolution in France,* 1790). He was much admired in his time as an orator and master of English prose.

CATHERINE THE GREAT
Empress of Russia
1729-1796

**Catherine II** (Catherine the Great), age 21; empress of Russia from

Thomas Malthus
  (1766-1834), age 9
Sequoyah
  (1766 or 1770-1843),
  age 9?
Mme. de Stael
  (1766-1817), age 9
Alexander Wilson
  (1766-1813), age 9
John Quincy Adams
  (1767-1848), age 8
Benajmin Constant
  (1767-1830), age 8
Maria Edgeworth
  (1767-1849), age 8
Andrew Jackson
  (1767-1845), age 8
Joachim Murat
  (1767-1815), age 8
Louis Antoine de
Saint-Just
  (1767-1794), age 8
August Wilhelm von
Schlegel
  (1767-1845), age 8
Vicomte de Chateaubriand
  (1768-1848), age 7
Francis II (Emperor)
  (1768-1835), age 7
Ivan Krylov
  (1768-1844), age 7
Duncan Phyfe
  (1768-1854), age 7
Friedrich Schleiermacher
  (1768-1834), age 7
Samuel Slater
  (1768-1835), age 7
Tecumseh
  (1768?-1813), age 7?
Viscount Castlereagh
  (1769-1822), age 6
De Witt Clinton
  (1769-1828), age 6
Baron Cuvier
  (1769-1832), age 6
Alexander von Humboldt
  (1769-1859), age 6
Sir Thomas Lawrence
  (1769-1830), age 6
Napoleon I
  (1769-1821), age 6
Michel Ney
  (1769-1815), age 6

1762–1796, born in Germany as Princess Sophia Augusta Frederica of Anhalt-Zerbst. Married to Peter III, the incompetent grandson of Peter the Great, she became sole ruler when a palace conspiracy deposed the czar six months after his coronation. She extended the frontiers of the empire and began the colonization of Alaska. She admired French culture and held liberal views.

**Sir William Howe,** age 21; British general, commander at the Battle of Bunker Hill (1775) and successor of Thomas Gage as commander-in-chief (October 1775). He captured New York City and won victories on Long Island and at White Plains and Brandywine, but his failure to join Burgoyne at Saratoga is blamed for Burgoyne's surrender. He resigned in 1778 and returned to England.

**Gotthold Ephraim Lessing,** age 21; German dramatist and critic, son of a Protestant clergyman. A leading exponent of the Enlightenment in Germany, he is known as the author of the first German drama of middle-class life, *Miss Sara Sampson* (1775); of a drama in verse, *Nathan the Wise,* urging tolerance; and of a famous essay on aesthetics, *Laocoon* (1766).

**Moses Mendelssohn,** age 21; German Jewish philosopher born in Dessau; the author of several works on metaphysics and aesthetics, translator of the Pentateuch and advocate of cultural assimilation of the Jews. A lifelong friend of Lessing's, he is said to have served as the model for *Nathan the Wise.* He was the grandfather of Felix Mendelssohn, the composer and pianist.

FRIEDRICH WILHELM,
BARON VON STEUBEN
Prussian officer
1730-1794

**Friedrich Wilhelm, Baron von Steuben,** age 20; Prussian officer born in Magdeburg; staff officer of Frederick the Great. He met Benjamin Franklin in Paris and went to America in 1777. Given charge of training the Continental Army, he received much credit for its performance and became a trusted adviser of Washington's. He remained in New York after the war and was granted a pension by Congress.

**Thomas Percy,** age 21; English antiquary and Protestant bishop of Dromore, Ireland (1782–1811), born in Shropshire. He is remembered for a collection in three volumes of English and Scottish ballads known as Percy's *Reliques (Reliques of Ancient English Poetry,* 1765), which aroused a romantic interest in early Anglo-Saxon and Celtic poetry. He is the author of the ballad *The Hermit of Warkworth* (1771).

**Josiah Wedgwood,** age 20; English potter born in Staffordshire of a family of potters. Beginning at the age of nine, he became a master potter and transformed the trade into a fine art. His most famous products were a glazed, cream-colored earthenware called queen's ware, of which he made a dinner service for Catherine the Great, and Jasper ware, of a delicate blue with Greek figures in white. He was the grandfather of Charles Darwin.

**Henry Cavendish,** age 19; English chemist and physicist, born in Nice of an aristocratic English family. A wealthy bachelor who devoted his life to science, he isolated and described hydrogen, analyzed the composition of water (some time before 1783) and calculated the density of the earth and of the atmosphere. He lived as a recluse, and most of his writings were published posthumously.

WILLIAM COWPER
English poet
1731-1800

**William Cowper,** age 19; English poet born in Hertfordshire, son of a clergyman. He is remembered for his long poem *The Task,* containing descriptions of English country life and rural beauty, and for the ballad *The Diverting History of John Gilpin.* Subject to periods of despondency, he attempted suicide in 1783 and was confined in an asylum for 18 months. This famous line is his: "God moves in a mysterious way,/ His wonders to perform."

Duke of Wellington
    (1769-1852), age 6
Ludwig van Beethoven
    (1770-1827), age 5
William Clark
    (1770-1838), age 5
G. W. F. Hegel
    (1770-1831), age 5
Friedrich Hoderlin
    (1770-1843), age 5
William Wordsworth
    (1770-1850), age 5
E. I. du Pont de Nemours
    (1771-1834), age 4
Robert Owen
    (1771-1858), age 4
Mungo Park
    (1771-1806), age 4
Sir Walter Scott
    (1771-1832), age 4
Sydney Smith
    (1771-1845), age 4
Richard Trevithick
    (1771-1833), age 4
Samuel Taylor Coleridge
    (1772-1834), age 3
Charles Fourier
    (1772-1837), age 3
David Ricardo
    (1772-1823), age 3
Friedrich von Schlegel
    (1772-1829), age 3
Nathaniel Bowditch
    (1773-1838), age 2
William Henry Harrison
    (1773-1841), age 2
Louis Philippe
    (1773-1850), age 2
Metternich
    (1773-1859), age 2
John Randolph
    (1773-1833), age 2
Meriwether Lewis
    (1774-1809), age 1
Elizabeth Ann Seton
    (1774-1821), age 1
Robert Southey
    (1774-1843), age 1

# 1775–1800

George Washington was not by nature a political man. He was not a good public speaker nor exceptionally brilliant and, in fact, held a very modest opinion of his own abilities. Nor was he interested in such abstractions as the natural rights of man or social contracts; that was Jefferson's domain. He was descended from fairly prosperous landowners of Northamptonshire, England. His father, a Virginia tobacco planter, died when he was 11, leaving little property to his six children by his second wife. It was through his older half-brother, Lawrence, son of his father's first marriage, that George became the wealthy proprietor of Mount Vernon, the estate on the Potomac River 15 miles south of the site of the future capital. Lawrence had married a daughter of the Fairfax family, the largest landowners of Virginia, and in 1743 had built the wooden, two-and-a-half story Georgian-style mansion (named for Adm. Edward Vernon, his former commander in the British navy). George inherited Mount Vernon after Lawrence's death in 1752 and the death of Lawrence's daughter, his immediate heir.

After serving the British in the French and Indian War (as a member of Gen. Braddock's staff he witnessed the am-

## 1775

Voltaire
(1694-1778), age 81
James Oglethorpe
(1696-1785), age 79
Jean-Baptiste Chardin
(1699-1779), age 76
John Wesley
(1703-1791), age 72
Benjamin Franklin
(1706-1790), age 69
Comte de Buffon
(1707-1788), age 68
Carlo Goldoni
(1707-1793), age 68
Linnaeus
(1707-1778), age 68
Charles Wesley
(1707-1788), age 68
William Pitt (the Elder)
(1708-1778), age 67
Samuel Johnson
(1709-1784), age 66
Wilhelm Friedemann Bach
(1710-1784), age 65

**Johann Christoph Friedrich Bach,** age 43; German musician and composer, son of Johann Sebastian Bach. Kapellmeister at Buckeburg and composer of motets, cantatas, oratorios and clavier sonatas, he was named after his father's oldest brother, Johann Christoph Bach (1671–1721), with whom Johann Sebastian lived after the death of his father.

**Pierre Augustin Caron de Beaumarchais,** age 43; French playwright, speculator and secret government agent, born in Paris, the son of a clockmaker. A wealthy widower at 25, he is remembered for two comedies: *Le Barbier de Seville* (1775), which inspired Rossini's opera, and *Le Mariage de Figaro* (1778), which inspired Mozart's. He is also remembered as a procurer of arms for the American colonies during the Revolutionary War.

**Jean Honore Fragonard,** age 43; French rococo painter born in southern France, a favorite at the courts of Louis XV and Louis XVI. Typical of his graceful, frivolous style is the series of panels painted for Mme. Du Barry called *The Progress of Love.* Other famous works are *The Bathers,* in the Louvre, and *The Love Letter,* in the Metropolitan Museum. Deprived of his patrons by the French Revolution, he died forgotten and in poverty.

**Warren Hastings,** age 43; British statesman, first governor general of India (1773–1785), credited with originating British methods of administration. Brought to trial in 1788, with Edmund Burke and Richard Sheridan among the prosecutors, on charges of cruelty and illegal confiscation of property, he was acquitted after a trial that lasted seven years.

bush at the Monongahela River), Washington married and retired to his estate. As a country gentleman, he was occupied with his crops, improvements to his house and property, entertaining his neighbors, dancing at balls, playing cards and billiards, attending the races at Annapolis, foxhunting and attending the meetings of the Virginia House of Burgesses.

But he was not a man who could find complete satisfaction in his own private affairs. When Thomas Fairfax, sixth Baron Fairfax, had come to Virginia in 1747 to settle on his maternal estates, he had taken a liking to young George and sent him along with the party that was to survey and map his six million acres in the Shenandoah Valley. This glimpse of the country beyond the Blue Ridge Mountains had important consequences, arousing in Washington a lifelong passion to see the valley developed into a great agricultural empire linked to the east by a canal from the Potomac to the Ohio River. He was a practical man. So long as the natural development of the colonies could proceed without interference, he would be content to remain a British subject, like Baron Fairfax. But when it became clear that they could not prosper and realize their potential until freed from restrictions imposed by the British, he was ready to join the patriots and theorists and see the matter through to its conclusion.

# 1800

FRANZ JOSEPH HAYDN
Austrian composer
1732-1809

**(Franz) Joseph Haydn,** age 43; Austrian composer, principal founder of the Viennese classical school and first great master of the symphony. As musical director for the Esterhazy family (1766–1790), he composed 80 symphonies, 43 string quartets, 23 operas and numerous sonatas, masses, overtures and oratorios. Among his most admired works are the 12 London Symphonies and two oratorios composed late in life, *The Creation* and *The Seasons*. He was a friend of Mozart's.

Louis XVIII (France)
   (1755-1824), age 45
Gebhard von Scharnhorst
   (1755-1813), age 45
Aaron Burr
   (1756-1836), age 44
William Godwin
   (1756-1836), age 44
Sir Henry Raeburn
   (1756-1823), age 44
William Blake
   (1757-1827), age 43
Antonio Canova
   (1757-1822), age 43
Charles X (France)
   (1757-1836), age 43
Marquis de Lafayette
   (1757-1834), age 43
James Monroe
   (1758-1831), age 42
Horatio Nelson
   (1758-1805), age 42
Noah Webster
   (1758-1843), age 42

# 1775

Thomas Reid
(1710-1796), age 65

Ch'ien Lung
(1711-1799), age 64

David Hume
(1711-1776), age 64

Frederick II of Prussia
(1712-1786), age 63

Francesco Guardi
(1712-1793), age 63

Jean Jacques Rousseau
(1712-1778), age 63

Denis Diderot
(1713-1784), age 62

Karl Philipp Bach
(1714-1788), age 61

Miklos Esterhazy
(1714-1790), age 61

Christoph Gluck
(1714-1787), age 61

Lord Monboddo
(1714-1799), age 61

Etienne de Condillac
(1715-1780), age 60

Jean d'Alembert
(1717-1783), age 58

Jeffrey Amherst
(1717-1797), age 58

David Garrick
(1717-1779), age 58

Horace Walpole
(1717-1797), age 58

Maria Theresa
(1717-1780), age 58

Thomas Gage
(1721-1787), age 54

Peyton Randolph
(1721-1775), age 54

Samuel Adams
(1722-1803), age 53

John Burgoyne
(1722-1792), age 53

Sir William Blackstone
(1723-1780), age 52

Baron Paul d'Holbach
(1723-1789), age 52

Sir Joshua Reynolds
(1723-1792), age 52

Adam Smith
(1723-1790), age 52

Immanuel Kant
(1724-1804), age 51

**Richard Henry Lee,** age 43; American Revolutionary statesman born in Virginia, son of a tobacco planter. It was his distinction, as a member of the Continental Congress, to introduce the motion for independence on June 7, 1776, declaring that "these united colonies are, and of right ought to be, free and independent states." His motion was adopted July 2, 1776.

**Francis Marion,** age c. 43; American planter and Revolutionary soldier born in South Carolina, known as the Swamp Fox. A commander of a militia troop, he used guerrilla-war tactics to great effect, eluding the British in the Caroline swamps after his raids. Joining forces with Light-horse Harry Lee in Nathaniel Greene's victorious campaign, he won more laurels. After the war he served in the South Carolina Senate.

**David Rittenhouse,** age 43; American astronomer and clockmaker born in Pennsylvania. He built an observatory in Norristown, constructed the first telescope in America, and was one of the first to use spider webs in the eyepiece. He helped frame the Pennsylvania constitution and was the first director of the United States Mint in Philadelphia (1792–1795).

GEORGE WASHINGTON
American general and
   first president
1732-1799

**George Washington,** age 43; American general and first president, called the Father of his Country, born in Virginia, the son of a planter. He inherited his brother's estate at 20, living as a gentleman farmer from 27 to 43. After serving as commander-in-chief of the Continental Army (1775–1781), he was unanimously chosen president under the new constitution and inaugurated in New York City in April, 1789. An aristocrat, he distrusted the wisdom of the people, believing them incapable of self-government.

JOSEPH PRIESTLEY
English chemist and
   nonconformist clergyman
1733-1804

**Joseph Priestley,** age 42; English chemist and nonconformist clergyman born in Yorkshire; remembered as the discoverer of "dephlogisticated air" in 1774 (oxygen) and as the author of *Essay on the First Principles of Government* (1768), which suggested to Jeremy Bentham the ideal of "the greatest good of the greatest number." He emigrated to Pennsylvania in 1794 after his open sympathy with the French Revolution had prompted a Birmingham mob to burn his house and chapel.

**Philip John Schuyler,** age 42; American general and statesman born in Albany, N.Y. of one of the wealthiest colonial families. He was an able general, but after the surrender of Fort Ticonderoga in 1777, was replaced as commander of the Saratoga campaign by Horatio Gates. Schuyler resigned from the army in 1779, after being exonerated of charges of negligence, and later served in the United States Senate (1789–1791 and 1797–1798). He was the father-in-law of Alexander Hamilton.

**Daniel Boone,** age 41; American frontiersman born in Pennsylvania, son of English Quakers. From 1767 to 1771 he made exploring forays into the Kentucky region and in 1775, as advance agent for a colonizing expedition, he blazed the famous Wilderness Road. With a party of 30 men, he cleared and marked a 200-mile trail through the Cumberland Gap and into central Kentucky, which from 1790 to 1840 was the principal route of westward migration. Known as a courageous and resourceful woodsman, the hero of many adventures, he was made internationally famous by Lord Byron in *Don Juan*.

**John Adams,** age 40; American statesman and lawyer born in Massachusetts; second president of the United States (1797–1801) and first vice-president. He was an energetic leader in the struggle for independence and a member of the commission that negotiated the peace treaty with Britain. Defeated for reelection in 1800 by Thomas Jefferson, he retired to private life.

**Johann Christian Bach,** age 40; German composer and organist called "the London Bach," youngest son of Johann Sebastian Bach. After two years as church organist in Milan, he became music master to the English royal family and won favor and popularity in London with his symphonies, overtures and chamber music in the rococo style.

**Paul Revere,** age 40; American silversmith and revolutionary patriot born in Boston. An early opponent of British policies, he joined the Sons of Liberty and took part in the Boston Tea Party. As official courier for the Massachusetts Committee of Correspondence, he made his famous midnight ride from Boston to Lexington on April 18, 1775, and achieved immortality for it with the help of Longfellow's poem.

**Patrick Henry,** age 39; American lawyer and Revolutionary statesman born in Virginia. A leader of the radicals and an inflammatory orator, whose rousing phrases "Give me liberty or give me death" and "If this be treason, make the most of it" are familiar to all Americans. He was a member of the Continental Congress from 1774–1776, governor of Virginia from 1776–1779 and 1784–1786 and a vigorous supporter of the Bill of Rights.

**James MacPherson,** age 39; Scottish author, schoolmaster and collector of ancient Gaelic poetry in the Scottish Highlands. In 1762 he published a complete epic poem in six books, called *Fingal,* and in 1763 another, called *Temora,* both ostensibly the work of a third-century poet named Ossian. The poems created a sensation in Europe, but were denounced by Samuel Johnson as forgeries. Goethe expressed his admiration of them, but Macpherson was never able to produce the original manuscripts.

**James Watt,** age 39; Scottish engineer and inventor. As a mechanic at Glasgow University, he was given a Newcomen steam engine to repair, and proceeded to invent the modern condensing steam engine

# 1800

William Pitt (the Younger)
(1759-1806), age 41
Friedrich von Schiller
(1759-1805), age 41
William Wilberforce
(1759-1833), age 41
Luigi Cherubini
(1760-1842), age 40
August von Gneisenau
(1760-1831), age 40
Katsushika Hokusai
(1760-1849), age 40
Comte de Saint-Simon
(1760-1825), age 40
Albert Gallatin
(1761-1849), age 39
August von Kotzebue
(1761-1819), age 39
Johann Fichte
(1762-1814), age 38
John Jacob Astor
(1763-1848), age 37
Charles Bulfinch
(1763-1844), age 37
Josephine
(1763-1814), age 37
Jean Paul Richter
(1763-1825), age 37
Benjamin Latrobe
(1764-1820), age 36
Ann Radcliffe
(1764-1823), age 36
Robert Fulton
(1765-1815), age 35
James Smithson
(1765-1829), age 35
Eli Whitney
(1765-1825), age 35
John Dalton
(1766-1844), age 34
Thomas Malthus
(1766-1834), age 34
Sequoyah
(1766 or 1770-1843),
age 34?
Mme. de Stael
(1766-1817), age 34
Alexander Wilson
(1766-1813), age 34
John Quincy Adams
(1767-1848), age 33

# 1775

Friedrich Klopstock
(1724-1803), age 51
Pierre Laclede
(1724-1778), age 51
Casanova
(1725-1798), age 50
George Mason
(1725-1792), age 50
James Otis
(1725-1783), age 50
Thomas Gainsborough
(1727-1788), age 48
James Cook
(1728-1779), age 47
Horatio Gates
(1727/28-1806), age c.47
Niccolo Piccini
(1728-1800), age 47
Louis de Bougainville
(1729-1811), age 46
Edmund Burke
(1729-1797), age 46
Catherine II of Russia
(1729-1796), age 46
Sir William Howe
(1729-1814), age 46
G. E. Lessing
(1729-1781), age 46
Moses Mendelssohn
(1729-1786), age 46
Thomas Percy
(1729-1811), age 46
Baron von Steuben
(1730-1794), age 45
Josiah Wedgwood
(1730-1795), age 45
Henry Cavendish
(1731-1810), age 44
William Cowper
(1731-1800), age 44

(1765, patented 1769). He manufactured steam engines at Birmingham, in partnership, from 1775 to 1800. The watt, a unit of power, is named for him, and he is said to have originated the term *horsepower*.

EDWARD GIBBON
English historian
1737-1794

**Edward Gibbon,** age 38; English historian, born of a wealthy family; a member of Parliament from 1774–1783 and author of the six-volume *History of the Decline and Fall of the Roman Empire* (1776–1788), a classic renowned for its wealth of detail, its masterful prose style and its controversial section on the Christian religion. He lived in Switzerland the last 11 years of his life.

**John Hancock,** age 38; American merchant and Revolutionary statesman born in Massachusetts. An ardent supporter of the colonial cause, he served in the Massachusetts legislature from 1766–1772 and in the Continental Congress from 1775–1780, again in 1785 and 1786 and as its president from 1775–1777. His signature is the most prominent and elegant on the Declaration of Independence, which he was the first to sign. He was the governor of Massachusetts from 1780–1785 and again from 1787–1793.

**Thomas Paine,** age 38; Anglo-American political writer born in Norfolk, England, son of a corsetmaker. He emigrated to America in 1774, after falling into a state of bankruptcy. He joined the movement for colonial independence with the writing of his pamphlet, *Common Sense* (January 1776). He returned to England in 1787 and published *The Rights of Man* (1791–1792), urging revolution in England, which led to his departure for France, where he was elected to the National Convention. In 1802 he returned to America and retired to a farm in New Rochelle, N.Y.

**Ethan Allen,** age 37; American Revolutionary soldier and land speculator born in Connecticut, remembered for capturing Fort Ticonderoga in 1775 with Benedict Arnold and a small militia company. In a rash attempt to take Montreal, he was captured by the British and held prisoner for three years. As leader of the Green Mountain Boys, he was continuously embroiled in the territorial dispute over the New Hampshire Grants (Vermont), where he owned land.

**John Singleton Copley,** age 37; American portrait painter born in Boston, son of Irish immigrants. Largely self-taught, he was a successful portrait painter at 20. His American portraits are vividly expressive of New England life; many of them, including those of John Hancock, Paul Revere, Samuel Adams and John Quincy Adams, are in the Museum of Fine Arts in Boston. He settled in London in 1775 and painted historical subjects as well as portraits.

**Charles Cornwallis,** age 37; first Marquess Cornwallis, English general and statesman of aristocratic birth, remembered for losing the last battle of the American Revolutionary War. Washington's siege of Yorktown, Va., ended with the surrender of the British on Oct. 19, 1781. Cornwallis was not held responsible and later served with distinction in India, where he was governor general from 1786–1794. In 1805 he was again appointed governor general, but died two months after arriving in India.

**George III,** age 37; elector of Hanover and king of Great Britain and Ireland from 1760–1820, the first of the house of Hanover to be born and educated in England. His reign was a time of industrial progress and a golden age of literature, but largely through his own obstinacy the American colonies were lost. His son, the prince of Wales (later George IV), was regent after 1811, when the growing blindness and mental derangement of the king became evident.

**Benjamin West,** age 37; American painter born in Pennsylvania. After beginning as a portrait painter in Philadelphia at 18, he settled in London in 1763, turned to historical painting and won fame and the patronage of George III. Known as a friend and adviser of young artists, he assisted many American painters in London, including Charles Peale, Gilbert Stuart and John Copley. Two famous paintings are *The Death of General Wolfe* (in the Grosvenor Gallery in London) and *Penn's Treaty With the Indians* (at the Pennsylvania Academy of the Fine Arts in Philadelphia).

**Grigori Aleksandrovich Potemkin,** age 36; Russian statesman, soldier and favorite of Catherine the Great's. He participated in the conspiracy that deposed Peter III and was Catherine's lover for two years. After being succeeded by others, he retained her favor and remained the most powerful man in Russia. He built a harbor at Sevastopol and a fleet on the Black Sea.

**John Rutledge,** age 36; American statesman and jurist born in Charleston, S.C.; second chief justice of the United States Supreme Court (appointed in August 1795) and one of the authors of the Constitution. He studied law in London and returned to become South Carolina's attorney general, governor and chief justice. George Washington appointed him chief justice of the Supreme Court, and he presided at one session, but in December 1795 the Senate refused confirmation.

**James Boswell,** age 35; Scottish lawyer and biographer born in Edinburgh, son of Lord Auchinleck, a jurist. At 23 he met Samuel Johnson, who was 54, cultivated his friendship and recorded for posterity his conversations and mannerisms in his *Life of Samuel Johnson LL. D.* (1791), one of the world's most famous biographies.

**Marquis de Sade** (Donatien Alphonse Francois, comte de Sade), age 35; French writer and soldier born in Paris, notorious for his sexual perversion, called sadism. He fought in the Seven Years' War, married in 1763 and committed himself to a life of pleasure, but for 27 years was confined in prisons and asylums. His novels, *Justine* (1791) and *Juliette* (1797), were translated into English in the 1950s. He died in the Charenton lunatic asylum.

**Haym Salomon,** age 35; American merchant and financier born in Poland of Portuguese-Jewish descent; known as a financial backer of the American Revolution. He emigrated in 1772 and established a mercantile and brokerage business in New York City and later in Philadelphia. He collaborated with Robert Morris in obtaining aid from foreign governments and made large personal loans to the treasury. He also gave financial assistance to Jefferson, Madison and others.

**Benedict Arnold,** age 34; American army officer born in Connecticut, the first known American traitor. An officer of promise but of a jealous

# 1800

Benjamin Constant
(1767-1830), age 33
Maria Edgeworth
(1767-1849), age 33
Andrew Jackson
(1767-1845), age 33
Joachim Murat
(1767-1815), age 33
August von Schlegel
(1767-1845), age 33
Vicomte de Chateaubriand
(1768-1848), age 32
Francis II (Emperor)
(1768-1835), age 32
Ivan Krylov
(1768-1844), age 32
Duncan Phyfe
(1768-1854), age 32
Friedrich Schleiermacher
(1768-1834), age 32
Samuel Slater
(1768-1835), age 32
Tecumseh
(1768?-1813), age 32?
Viscount Castlereagh
(1769-1822), age 31
De Witt Clinton
(1769-1828), age 31
Baron Cuvier
(1769-1832), age 31
Alexander von Humboldt
(1769-1821), age 31
Sir Thomas Lawrence
(1769-1830), age 31
Napoleon I
(1769-1821), age 31
Michel Ney
(1769-1815), age 31
Duke of Wellington
(1769-1852), age 31
Ludwig van Beethoven
(1770-1827), age 30
William Clark
(1770-1838), age 30
G. W. F. Hegel
(1770-1831), age 30
Friedrich Holderlin
(1770-1843), age 30
William Wordsworth
(1770-1850), age 30
E. I. du Pont de Nemours
(1771-1834), age 29

nature and sensitive to slights, he began his treasonable actions after being court-martialed and reprimanded by Washington for arbitrary exercise of his authority. On the night of Sept. 23, 1780, he met with Major Andre of the British army and arranged to surrender his post at West Point. Upon discovery, he went over to the British side. He did not prosper after the war and died in London, near poverty.

**Charles Willson Peale,** age 34; American portrait painter born in Maryland, famous for his portraits of George Washington—seven from life and about 50 from memory. He was sent to London in 1766 by a group of Annapolis citizens to study with Benjamin West. Upon returning in 1769, he became the most popular painter in the colonies and painted about 1,100 portraits of prominent citizens. He married three times and had 17 children.

**Gebhard Leberecht von Blucher,** age 33; Prussian general famous as the conqueror of Napoleon. His victory at Laon in 1814 and occupation of Paris resulted in Napoleon's first exile. After the allied victory at Waterloo, he marched into Paris a second time, in July 1815.

**Nathaniel Greene,** age 33; American Revolutionary general born in Rhode Island. He served with distinction at Trenton, Brandywine and Germantown; was made quartermaster general in 1778; and in 1781 given command of the southern army in Georgia and the Carolinas. In a brilliant campaign he forced the British to retreat to three coastal bases, where they were trapped. He retired to a plantation in Georgia called Mulberry Grove, which was given to him by the state.

**Edmund Cartwright,** age 32; English country clergyman born in Nottinghamshire; inventor of the power loom. After visiting cotton-spinning mills in Derbyshire in 1784, he set to work to apply machinery to weaving and in 1785–1787 patented his loom, which transformed the weaving industry and quickened the industrial revolution. In 1809 Parliament awarded him 10,000 pounds. In 1797 he patented a steam engine that ran on alcohol.

**Count Alessandro Cagliostro** (Giuseppe Balsamo), age 32; Italian adventurer and charlatan born in Palermo of poor parents. He acquired some knowledge of chemistry and traveled in the Orient and throughout Europe, posing as an alchemist and magician and engaging in a variety of fraudulent schemes. In 1789 he returned to Italy, where he was convicted by the Inquisition of heresy and sorcery and confined to a dungeon for the remainder of his life.

**Marquis de Condorcet,** age 32; French writer, mathematician and politician, born in Picardy of a noble family. A moderate in the French Revolution, he was president of the Legislative Assembly in 1792. During the Jacobin reign of terror, he hid for nine months in a friend's house and wrote the famous *Outline of an Historical Picture of the Progress of the Human Mind,* a declaration of faith in human progress. He was arrested while trying to leave Paris and was found dead the next morning.

**Mme. Du Barry** (Jeanne Becu, comtesse Du Barry), age 32; French courtesan, mistress of Louis XV the last five years of his life. An illegitimate child, she was the mistress of Chevalier Jean Du Barry when the king first saw her in 1769. A patron of artists and writers, she was noted for her kindness and lack of ambition. She left the court when the king died in 1774, but 19 years later was arrested by Robespierre and guillotined, on Dec. 7, 1793.

**John Fitch,** age 32; American inventor born in Connecticut. In the Delaware River, on Aug. 22, 1787, he launched the first steamboat built in America. Unable to obtain financial backing for further development, he grew despondent and wrote, "More powerful men than I will win fame and fortune through my discoveries, but no one will remember that poor John Fitch did anything worth speaking of."

**Thomas Jefferson,** age 32; American statesman born in Virginia, son of a planter; third president (1801–1809) and author of the Declaration of Independence. He was a firm believer in democracy, public education, human perfectibility and economy in government. He helped found and design the University of Virginia and doubled the area of the country by purchasing the territory between the Mississippi River and the Rocky Mountains from Napoleon in 1803.

ANTOINE LAVOISIER
French chemist
1743-1794

**Antoine Laurent Lavoisier,** age 32; French chemist born in Paris, one of the founders of modern chemistry and one of the originators of the modern system of chemical nomenclature. He also named the components of water *oxygen* and *hydrogen*. He was guillotined during the French Revolution at the age of 51.

**Jean Paul Marat,** age 32; French physician and Revolutionary leader born in Switzerland, publisher of the paper *Friend of the People,* which urged violence. A member of the radical Jacobin party, he joined Danton and Robespierre in overthrowing the moderate Girondists. He was assassinated in his bathtub in July 1793 by Charlotte Corday.

**William Paley,** age 32; English theologian and philosopher. He lectured at Cambridge, where his *Principles of Moral and Political Philosophy* (1785) became a standard textbook. He also wrote *A View of the Evidences of Christianity* (1794), a refutation of deism; and *Natural Theology* (1802), an argument for the existence of God based on the intricate structure of the universe.

**Meyer Amschel Rothschild,** age 32; German Jewish banker born in Frankfurt-am-Main. From a modest beginning as a moneylender in the Jewish quarter, he rose to eminence as financial agent of the landgrave of Hesse-Kassel and of the British government. His five sons established branch offices in Vienna, London, Naples and Paris, and were made barons by the Austrian emperor.

**Elbridge Gerry,** age 31; American statesman born in Massachusetts; member of the Continental Congress and a signer of the Declaration of Independence. His role as a founding father has been overshadowed by his reputation as a politician. As governor of Massachusetts in 1811, he directed the legislature to redistrict the state in a way to insure Republican control, a technique thereafter known as gerrymandering. He died after two years in office as vice-president under James Madison.

# 1800

Robert Owen
(1771-1858), age 29
Mungo Park
(1771-1806), age 29
Sir Walter Scott
(1771-1832), age 29
Sydney Smith
(1771-1845), age 29
Richard Trevithick
(1771-1833), age 29
Samuel Taylor Coleridge
(1772-1834), age 28
Charles Fourier
(1772-1837), age 28
David Ricardo
(1772-1823), age 28
Friedrich von Schlegel
(1772-1829), age 28
Nathaniel Bowditch
(1773-1838), age 27
William Henry Harrison
(1773-1841), age 27
Louis Philippe (France)
(1773-1850), age 27
Metternich
(1773-1859), age 27
John Randolph
(1773-1833), age 27
Meriwether Lewis
(1774-1809), age 26
Elizabeth Ann Seton
(1774-1821), age 26
Robert Southey
(1774-1843), age 26
Andre Ampere
(1775-1836), age 25
Jane Austen
(1775-1817), age 25
Charles Lamb
(1775-1834), age 25
Walter Savage Landor
(1775-1864), age 25
Friedrich von Schelling
(1775-1854), age 25
J. M. W. Turner
(1775-1851), age 25
John Constable
(1776-1837), age 24
E. T. A. Hoffmann
(1776-1822), age 24
Alexander I (Russia)
(1777-1825), age 23

**Johann Gottfried von Herder,** age 31; German philosopher, critic and clergyman, born in East Prussia, son of a schoolmaster. A prominent literary critic and leading theorist of the romantic movement, he was appointed court pastor at Weimar in 1776 through the influence of Goethe. He compiled an anthology of folk songs from many countries and was one of the first to study comparative religion and mythology.

**Chevalier de Lamarck** (Jean Baptiste Pierre Antoine de Monet, Chevalier de Lamarck), age 31; French naturalist born in Picardy, better known for his errors than his accomplishments. His theory of evolution based on the inheritance of acquired characteristics has been rejected, but he was the first to suggest a division of the animal kingdom into vertebrates and invertebrates and to suggest the zoological classes of Arachnida, Crustacea and Infusoria.

**John Jay,** age 30; American statesman and jurist born in New York City, first chief justice of the United States Supreme Court (1789–1795). He helped negotiate the Treaty of Paris, which ended the Revolution with Great Britain in 1782, and was author, with Hamilton and Madison, of *The Federalist* papers. He also negotiated Jay's Treaty with Great Britain in 1794 and was governor of New York from 1795–1801.

**Mikhail Ilarionovich Kutuzov,** age 30; Russian field marshal. He lost an eye fighting the Turks and lost the Battle of Austerlitz to Napoleon in 1805. As commander-in-chief in 1812, he adopted the strategy of retreating before Napoleon's advance until, 70 miles from Moscow, the Russians and French met in the great Battle of Borodino, Sept. 7, 1812; there were over 100,000 casualties. He continually harried the French army during its disastrous winter retreat from Moscow.

**Henry Mackenzie,** age 30; Scottish novelist, lawyer and public official (comptroller of taxes). He is chiefly remembered for his first novel, *The Man of Feeling* (1771), describing episodes in the life of a good-natured but weak and sentimental hero. He headed the committee which investigated the validity of Macpherson's Ossian.

**Benjamin Rush,** age 30; American physician and statesman born in Pennsylvania. A member of the Continental Congress, a signer of the Declaration of Independence and surgeon general of the Continental army, he was an early advocate of humane treatment for the mentally ill and the author of the first American work on psychiatry, *Medical Inquiries and Observations upon Diseases of the Mind* (1813).

**Count Alessandro Volta,** age 30; Italian physicist and pioneer in electricity, born in Como. He invented the electric battery and was given the title of count by Napoleon in 1801. The volt is named in his honor.

**Anthony Wayne** (Mad Anthony), age 30; American Revolutionary officer born in Pennsylvania. A tanner by trade, he was commissioned a colonel and rose rapidly to brigadier general. One of the most energetic and daring officers of the war, he commanded the center at Brandywine, distinguished himself at Germantown and Monmouth, captured the British garrison at Stony Point and took part in the final Yorktown campaign. In 1794, as commander of the western army, he defeated the Miami Indians near the site of Toledo, Ohio, opening up the Northwest Territory for settlers.

**Goya** (Francisco Jose de Goya y Lucientes), age 29; Spanish painter and etcher born near Saragossa. While he is best known for his powerful etchings depicting the horrors of war and his satirical scenes of urban life, he also painted portraits of the Spanish aristocracy and was court painter to Charles IV. Among his most famous paintings are *Nude Maja* and *Maja Clothed* (in the Prado in Madrid).

**John Paul Jones** (John Paul), age 28; American naval officer born in

Scotland, famous for his victory over the British man-of-war *Serapis* on Sept. 23, 1779. He went to sea at 12 as a cabin boy, rose to captain and was involved in many scrapes. He fled to Virginia after killing a mutinous sailor in Trinidad, adding Jones to his name. After his exploits in the American Revolution, he joined the Russian navy and fought the Turks for two years. He then went to Paris and never returned to America.

JEREMY BENTHAM
English economist and
political theorist
1748-1832

**Jeremy Bentham,** age 27; English economist and political theorist born in London, son of an attorney. An exponent of utilitarianism and an early father of the welfare state, he believed the aim of government should be "the greatest good of the greatest number." He made the phrase famous, although it had been used earlier by the Italian jurist, Beccaria (four years before the publication of Joseph Priestley's *Essay)*, and a century earlier by Francis Hutcheson.

**Jacques Louis David,** age 27; French painter born in Paris, founder of the neoclassical school; court painter to Louis XVI and to Napoleon I, of whom he made several famous portraits. He lived in Brussels after his patron went into exile. His famous paintings include *Death of Marat* (in Brussels) and *Death of Socrates* (in the Metropolitan Museum of Art in New York).

**Conte Vittorio Alfieri,** age 26; Italian dramatist and poet born in Piedmont of a wealthy aristocratic family. Known as the poet of the Italian nationalist movement, he wrote 19 tragic dramas (including *Philip the Second, Antigone, Saul* and *Maria Stuart)* on the theme of liberty versus tyranny. He is also known as the lover of the countess of Albany, daughter of a German prince and wife of Charles Edward Stuart, the Young Pretender (Bonnie Prince Charlie). They are believed to have married after her husband's death in 1788.

JOHANN WOLFGANG
VON GOETHE
German poet, dramatist
and novelist
1749-1832

**Johann Wolfgang von Goethe,** age 26; German poet, dramatist and novelist, born in Frankfurt-am-Main, son of a wealthy lawyer and

Henry Clay
  (1777-1852), age 23
Heinrich von Kleist
  (1777-1811), age 23
Sir Humphrey Davy
  (1778-1829), age 22
William Hazlitt
  (1778-1830), age 22
Stephen Decatur
  (1779-1820), age 21
Francis Scott Key
  (1779-1843), age 21
Lord Melbourne
  (1779-1848), age 21
Clement C. Moore
  (1779-1863), age 21
Thomas Moore
  (1779-1852), age 21
Zebulon Pike
  (1779-1813), age 21
William Ellery Channing
  (1780-1842), age 20
Karl von Clausewitz
  (1780-1831), age 20
Jean Ingres
  (1780-1867), age 20
George Stephenson
  (1781-1848), age 19
John C. Calhoun
  (1782-1850), age 18
Friedrich Froebel
  (1782-1852), age 18
Niccolo Paganini
  (1782-1840), age 18
Martin Van Buren
  (1782-1862), age 18
Daniel Webster
  (1782-1852), age 18
Simon Bolivar
  (1783-1830), age 17
Washington Irving
  (1783-1859), age 17
Augustin de Iturbide
  (1783-1824), age 17
Stendhal
  (1783-1842), age 17
Thomas Sully
  (1783 1872), age 17
Leigh Hunt
  (1784-1859), age 16
Viscount Palmerston
  (1784-1865), age 16

grandson of the *burgomeister*. He is best known for *Faust,* on which he worked most of his life, and *The Sorrows of Young Werther,* written at 25. From 1775 until his death he lived in Weimar and held various administrative posts in the small principality. A conservative in politics, he favored a divided Germany of small states ruled by benevolent monarchs.

**Edward Jenner,** age 26; English physician born in Gloucestershire, originator of the practice of vaccination. Having observed that dairymaids did not get smallpox, he inoculated a small boy with cowpox in 1796 and demonstrated his immunity to smallpox. He published his findings in 1798 but could not explain why it worked.

**Marquis Pierre Simon de Laplace,** age 26; French astronomer and mathematician born in Normandy. He conceived the nebular hypothesis—that the solar system evolved from a nebulous mass of gases and dust—unaware that Immanuel Kant had offered a similar theory some years earlier. He also proved the stability of planetary motions.

**Mirabeau** (Honore Gabriel Victor Riqueti, comte de Mirabeau), age 26; French nobleman and Revolutionary leader and the dominant figure of the first two years; president of the National Assembly (1791). A moderate, he conspired with the king and queen to establish a constitutional monarchy, but did not live to carry out the plan.

**John Stevens,** age 26; American inventor born in New York City, son of a wealthy merchant. Through his efforts the first United States patent laws were enacted in 1790, but he is better known as the builder of the world's first seagoing steamship, the *Phoenix,* which steamed from New York to Philadelphia in 1809.

**Marquis de Jouffroy d'Abbans,** age 24; French engineer and inventor, builder of the first successful steamboat. In 1783 he ran his boat upstream on the Saone River near Lyons for a distance of several miles.

**James Madison,** age 24; American statesman born in Virginia, son of a planter; fourth president of the United States (1809–1817). Called the Father of the Constitution, he took the leading part in the Constitutional Convention of 1787. He was the author, with Hamilton and John Jay, of *The Federalist* and the husband of Dolley Madison.

RICHARD BRINSLEY
SHERIDAN
British dramatist and
politician
1751-1816

**Richard Brinsley Sheridan,** age 24; British dramatist and politician born in Dublin of a prominent Irish family. He is best known as the author of three popular comedies—*The Rivals, The School for Scandal* and *The Critic*—all written in his twenties. He gave up writing for politics, however, before 30, and was a member of Parliament, famous for his oratory, from 1780 to 1812. He took part in the trial of Warren Hastings and was also confidential adviser to the prince of Wales.

**Fanny Burney,** age 23; English novelist born in Norfolk, daughter of the music historian Charles Burney. Her first novel, *Evelina* (1778), was a success and won praise from Samuel Johnson and Edmund Burke, but the next three—*Cecilia, Camilla* and *The Wanderer*—grew increasingly sentimental and moralistic. For five years she was a lady-in-waiting to Queen Charlotte, wife of George III; her *Diary* and *Letters* describe English society during the period 1768–1840.

**George Rogers Clark,** age 23; American Revolutionary frontier officer, born in Virginia, the brother of William Clark. A surveyor by profession, he organized and led an expedition, with the approval of Patrick Henry, the governor of Virginia, to secure the Illinois and Kentucky region for the colonies. He captured the British-held forts of Kaskaskia and Cahokia in Illinois and Vincennes in Indiana. He built Fort Nelson on the site of Louisville, Ky.

**Philip Morin Freneau,** age 23; American poet and journalist born in New York City, called the poet of the American Revolution. He won fame with his long poem *The British Prison-Ship* and his lyrics *The Wild Honeysuckle* and *The Indian Burying Ground.* He strongly opposed Alexander Hamilton and the Federalists.

**Edmund Jennings Randolph,** age 22; American statesman born in Williamsburg, Va., grandson of Sir John Randolph and nephew of Peyton Randolph. Beginning as aide-de-camp to Washington in 1775, he had an active public career as state's attorney general, governor of Virginia, first United States attorney general and secretary of state, succeeding Jefferson in that post.

**George Crabbe,** age 21; English poet born in Suffolk, son of a customs officer. After a year in London, where he was befriended by Edmund Burke, he became a country parson. His best-known poem, *The Village* (1783), is a realistic, unsentimental depiction of rural life, without the trappings of romantic illusion. His poems were admired by Scott, Wordsworth and Byron.

TALLEYRAND
French statesman and
diplomat
1754-1838

**Talleyrand** (Charles Maurice de Talleyrand-Perigord), age 21; French statesman and diplomat known chiefly for his ability to survive under any form of government. Instrumental in Napoleon's rise to power, he was foreign minister from 1799–1807 and, as the French representative at the Congress of Vienna, secured the restoration of the national boundaries of 1789.

# 1800

Zachary Taylor
(1784-1850), age 16
John James Audubon
(1785-1851), age 15
Thomas De Quincey
(1785-1859), age 15
Jacob Grimm
(1785-1863), age 15
Alessandro Manzoni
(1785-1873), age 15
Thomas Love Peacock
(1785-1866), age 15
Davy Crockett
(1786-1836), age 14
Sir John Franklin
(1786-1847), age 14
Wilhelm Grimm
(1786-1859), age 14
Winfield Scott
(1786-1866), age 14
Karl Maria von Weber
(1786-1826), age 14
Francois Guizot
(1787-1874), age 13
Robert Livingston Stevens
(1787-1856), age 13
Emma Willard
(1787-1870), age 13
Lord Byron
(1788-1824), age 12
Sir Robert Peel
(1788-1850), age 12
Arthur Schopenhauer
(1788-1860), age 12
James Fenimore Cooper
(1789-1851), age 11
Jared Sparks
(1789-1866), age 11
Alphonse de Lamartine
(1790-1869), age 10
Leopold I (Belgium)
(1790-1865), age 10
John Ross
(1790-1866), age 10
John Tyler
(1790-1862), age 10
James Buchanan
(1791-1868), age 9
Peter Cooper
(1791-1883), age 9
Michael Faraday
(1791-1867), age 9

**Pierre Charles L'Enfant,** age 21; French architect and engineer born in Paris. A captain of engineers in the Continental Army (1778–1784), he was invited by Washington and Jefferson to draw up plans for the new national capital, but his plans proved too expensive, and he was dismissed in 1792. In the early 20th century, however, his original plans were carried out, and his body was moved to Arlington National Cemetery.

**Louis XVI,** age 21; king of France from 1774–1792, grandson of Louis XV and husband of Marie Antoinette. A victim of circumstances in that he paid for the autocratic excesses of his ancestors, he was deposed by the National Convention after the massacre of the Swiss palace guards by a mob. Tried for treason and condemned to death, he was guillotined on Jan. 21, 1793. He aided America in the Revolutionary War.

**Alexander Hamilton,** age 20; American statesman born in the West Indies, son of a Scottish trader. He went to work at 15 in a counting house following his father's declaration of bankruptcy, and went to the North American colonies at 17 to study at King's College (Columbia). As first Secretary of the Treasury (1789–1795), he established sound fiscal policies and foresaw America's future as a great industrial nation, in contrast to Jefferson's agrarian dreams. He distrusted democracy and favored representation based on wealth and property.

MARIE ANTOINETTE
Queen of France
1755-1793

**Marie Antoinette,** age 20; queen of Louis XVI of France, born in Vienna, daughter of Emperor Francis I and Maria Theresa of Austria. Beautiful, extravagant and pleasure-loving, she was involved in several scandals. After the king's execution she was tried, convicted of treason and guillotined on Oct. 16, 1793. Although cruelly treated during her imprisonment and trial, she behaved bravely.

**John Marshall,** age 20; American jurist born in Virginia, son of a surveyor. As chief justice of the Supreme Court from 1801–1835, appointed by John Adams, he established in his decisions the prestige and power of the court and its indisputable right to rule on the constitutionality of the acts of Congress.

**Sarah Kemble Siddons,** age 20; English actress born in Wales, daughter of Roger Kemble. She traveled from childhood with her father's company of actors and played in London at Drury Lane in 1782. She was acclaimed the greatest tragic actress of her time, unrivaled as Lady Macbeth. Both Gainsborough and Reynolds painted her portrait.

**Gilbert Charles Stuart,** age 20; American painter born in Rhode Island, known chiefly for his three portraits of George Washington. A highly successful portrait artist, he also painted John Adams, Jefferson, Madison, George III, Sarah Siddons and his friend Sir Joshua Reynolds.

**Henry Lee** (Light-horse Harry), age 19; American Revolutionary soldier and statesman born in Virginia; second cousin of Richard Henry Lee and father of Robert E. Lee. In a surprise raid with his light-cavalry troop, he captured Paulus Hook (Jersey City) on Aug. 19, 1779; in the southern campaigns his skillful guerrilla tactics effectively covered the strategic retreat of Nathaniel Greene in the Carolinas (1780–1781). Author of the famous words, "First in war, first in peace, and first in the hearts of his countrymen," he delivered the funeral oration on Washington before both houses of Congress in 1799. He was a member of the Continental Congress from 1786–1788, governor of Virginia from 1792–1795, in the House of Representatives from 1799–1801 and in debtor's prison in 1808–1809. He was also the author of *Memoirs of the War in the Southern Department* (1812).

WOLFGANG AMADEUS
MOZART
Austrian composer
1756-1791

**Wolfgang Amadeus Mozart,** age 19; Austrian composer born in Salzburg of a family of musicians of German descent. A child prodigy on the harpischord, violin and organ, he toured the courts of Europe at six with his father and sister and composed his first opera at 12. Never financially successful, he lived near poverty as a music teacher in Vienna. He is equally famous for his symphonies, chamber music and operas—*The Marriage of Figaro, Don Giovanni, Cosi fan Tutte* and *The Magic Flute.* He died of typhoid fever at 35.

**George Vancouver,** age 18; English navigator and explorer. He accompanied Captain Cook on his second and third voyages and in 1791 commanded an expedition to explore and survey the northwestern coast of America. Sailing by way of the Cape of Good Hope, he took three years for his survey; circumnavigated Vancouver Island; and explored Puget Sound, naming it for his lieutenant Peter Puget. An account of the voyage was published in 1798 in three volumes.

Franz Grillparzer
(1791-1872), age 9
Giacomo Meyerbeer
(1791-1864), age 9
Samuel F. B. Morse
(1791-1872), age 9
Augustin Eugene Scribe
(1791-1861), age 9
Victor Cousin
(1792-1867), age 8
Pius IX (Pope)
(1792-1878), age 8
Gioacchino Rossini
(1792-1868), age 8
Percy Bysshe Shelley
(1792-1822), age 8
Thaddeus Stevens
(1792-1868), age 8
Stephen Austin
(1793-1836), age 7
Sam Houston
(1793-1863), age 7
Henry Schoolcraft
(1793-1864), age 7
William Cullen Bryant
(1794-1878), age 6
Matthew Perry
(1794-1858), age 6
Cornelius Vanderbilt
(1794-1877), age 6
James Gordon Bennett
(1795-1872), age 5
Thomas Carlyle
(1795-1881), age 5
John Keats
(1795-1821), age 5
James Knox Polk
(1795-1849), age 5
Leopold von Ranke
(1795-1886), age 5
Antonio de Santa Anna
(1794/95-1876),
age c.5
Dred Scott
(1795?-1858), age 5?
Augustin Thierry
(1795-1856), age 5
James Bowie
(1796 or 1799-1836),
age 4?
Thomas Bulfinch
(1796-1867), age 4

MAXIMILIEN DE
ROBESPIERRE
French revolutionary and
lawyer
1758-1794

**Maximilien Francois Marie Isidore de Robespierre,** age 17; French revolutionary and lawyer born in Arras. As leader of the radical Jacobin party, he was the most powerful man in the government in 1793–1794 and sent his friends Danton and Desmoulins to the guillotine. In May 1794 he proclaimed the cult of the Supreme Being as the official religion of France. In July 1794 he was arrested by the Revolutionary Tribunal and guillotined, with Saint-Just and 100 of his party, and the so-called Reign of Terror ended.

GEORGES JACQUES
DANTON
French lawyer and
revolutionary
1759-1794

**Georges Jacques Danton,** age 16; French lawyer and revolutionary leader, member of the Jacobins. He incited the riots that culminated in the storming of the royal palace in August 1792. As president of the Committee of Public Safety, he directed foreign policy and military defense. He was arrested and guillotined in April 1794.

ROBERT BURNS
Scottish poet
1759-1796

**Robert Burns,** age 16; Scottish poet born in Ayshire, son of a tenant farmer. From the age of 25 to 27 he wrote most of his familiar poems, which were published as *Poems, Chiefly in the Scottish Dialect,* in 1786. They made him famous in Edinburgh society and won him an appointment in the excise service. In such poems as *The Cotter's Saturday Night; The Jolly Beggars; Tam o' Shanter; Auld Lang Syne; The Banks o' Doon;* and *John Anderson, my Jo,* he immortalized the Scottish countryside and humble peasant life. He died at 37 of rheumatic heart disease.

**Camille Desmoulins,** age 15; French journalist and revolutionary leader. His inflammatory speeches on July 12, 1789, were followed two days later by the storming of the Bastille, which started the Revolution. He opposed the moderate Girondists in 1792, but in 1793 he called for moderation from the ultra-radicals. He was arrested and executed with Danton in April 1794. His young wife was guillotined two weeks later.

**Louis Antoine Leon de Saint-Just,** age 8; French revolutionary leader, a fanatical radical idealist and admirer of Rousseau's political philosophy. He was a trusted ally of Robespierre, a member of the Committee of Public Safety and a leading spirit of the Reign of Terror. He was guillotined with Robespierre in July 1794.

# 1800

George Catlin
(1796-1872), age 4
Jean Baptiste Corot
(1796-1875), age 4
Horace Mann
(1796-1859), age 4
W. H. Prescott
(1796-1859), age 4
Gaetano Donizetti
(1797-1848), age 3
Henrich Heine
(1797-1856), age 3
Ando Hiroshige
(1797-1858), age 3
Sir Charles Lyell
(1797-1875), age 3
Franz Schubert
(1797-1828), age 3
Mary Wollstonecraft Shelley
(1797-1851), age 3
Louis Adolphe Thiers
(1797-1877), age 3
Alfred de Vigny
(1797-1863), age 3
William I (Germany)
(1797-1888), age 3
Auguste Comte
(1798-1857), age 2
Eugene Delacroix
(1798-1863), age 2
Giacomo Leopardi
(1798-1837), age 2
Adam Mickiewicz
(1798-1855), age 2
Jules Michelet
(1798-1874), age 2
Bronson Alcott
(1799-1888), age 1
Honore de Balzac
(1799-1850), age 1
Jacques Halevy
(1799-1862), age 1
Thomas Hood
(1799-1845), age 1
Alexander Pushkin
(1799-1837), age 1

# 1800–1825

The 19th century was the age of European supremacy. Historians generally regard two significant dates, 1815 and 1914, as its beginning and end. It began not with Napoleon's victories, but with his defeat. The significant event of 1815 was the convening of diplomats in Vienna to restore peace after a quarter century of revolution and war. The French Revolution and the Napoleonic wars had shattered the framework of the old regime, and the diplomats met at the Congress of Vienna to structure another. For all of Napoleon's fame and glory, he had a less-lasting influence upon history than two much less famous gentlemen, Prince Klemens von Metternich of Austria and Lord Castlereagh of Great Britain, who in Vienna laid the foundations for a century of peace and progress in Europe. The Congress had begun its deliberations in 1814, but was interrupted in February 1815 by news of Napoleon's escape from Elba and his triumphal march to Paris. After defeating him a second time, they packed him off to St. Helena and returned to finish their business. They were reactionary politicans, but,

## 1800

Samuel Adams
(1722-1803), age 78
Immanuel Kant
(1724-1804), age 76
Friedrich Klopstock
(1724-1803), age 76
Horatio Gates
(1727/28-1806),
age c.72
Niccolo Piccini
(1728-1800), age 72
Louis de Bougainville
(1729-1811), age 71
Sir William Howe
(1729-1814), age 71
Thomas Percy
(1729-1811), age 71
Henry Cavendish
(1731-1810), age 69
William Cowper
(1731-1800), age 69
Jean Honore Fragonard
(1732-1806),
age 68
Warren Hastings
(1732-1818), age 68

**Louis XVIII,** age 45; king of France in 1814–1815 and again from 1815–1824, born in Versailles, grandson of Louis XV and brother of Louis XVI and Charles X. He escaped to Belgium during the Revolution and lived in Germany, Russia and England for 20 years. After Napoleon's downfall he was recalled and crowned king at 59. He ruled with moderation, as a constitutional monarch, and was succeeded by Charles X.

AARON BURR
American political leader
1756-1836

**Aaron Burr,** age 44; American political leader born in New Jersey, third vice-president (1801–1805). Challenging Alexander Hamilton to

for all their love of the old regime, they could not put it back exactly as it had been. They deprived France of all Napoleon's conquests; Austria lost the Netherlands, but gained elsewhere; and other minor boundary adjustments were agreed upon.

Their work was well done. For a century there were no very long wars to impede the remarkable social and industrial progress that changed the face of Europe and indeed the face of the world. The steady progress since 1500 of European science, technology and commerce reached its culmination in the 19th century. With the energies of the Continent harnessed in constructive pursuits, each generation saw an increase in wealth, technology and productivity and improvements in health and sanitation, education and literacy. Most remarkable was the growth of population. It is estimated that in 1815 there were about 200 million people in Europe, or one-fifth of the world's total. In 1914 there were 460 million, or one-fourth of the world's total, not taking into account the 40 million who emigrated overseas and whose descendants in 1914 had multiplied to 200 million. Part of the credit must go to the statesmen who gathered in Vienna to patch up the old regime, and in so doing laid the foundations for a new world.

# 1825

a duel for alleged aspersions on his character, Burr fatally wounded him on July 1804, and was forced to retire from public life. Charged with conspiracy and treason in 1807, he was tried and acquitted by John Marshall, although the nature of the affair is still unclear.

**Gerhard Johann David von Scharnhorst,** age 45; Prussian general and author of books on military science, born in Hanover. After the Prussian defeat by Napoleon (1806–1807), he headed a commission which reorganized the army as a citizens' army and prepared the way for universal military training, which was adopted in 1814.

**William Godwin,** age 44; English writer and political philosopher known for his radical idealism. He maintained that men are rational creatures and can live together in harmony without laws and institutions. The author of several novels, including *The Adventures of Caleb Williams* (1794), he is remembered chiefly as the father-in-law of the romantic poet Shelley.

**Sir Henry Raeburn,** age 44; Scottish portrait painter born near Edinburgh. Apprenticed to a goldsmith at 15, he went to London at 28 and met Sir Joshua Reynolds. After two years in Italy he returned to Scotland in 1787 to become a fashionable painter praised for his technical perfection. He painted over 700 portraits, including those of Sir Walter Scott, Hume, Boswell and James Mackenzie. He was knighted in 1822.

George Stephenson
(1781-1848), age 44
John C. Calhoun
(1782-1850), age 43
Friedrich Froebel
(1782-1852), age 43
Niccolo Paganini
(1782-1840), age 43
Martin Van Buren
(1782-1862), age 43
Daniel Webster
(1782-1852), age 43
Simon Bolivar
(1783-1830), age 42
Washington Irving
(1783-1859), age 42
Stendhal
(1783-1842), age 42
Thomas Sully
(1783-1872), age 42
Leigh Hunt
(1784-1859), age 41
Viscount Palmerston
(1784-1865), age 41
Zachary Taylor
(1784-1850), age 41

Joseph Haydn
(1732-1809), age 68

Joseph Priestley
(1733-1804), age 67

Philip John Schuyler
(1733-1804), age 67

Daniel Boone
(1734-1820), age 66

John Adams
(1735-1826), age 65

Paul Revere
(1735-1818), age 65

James Watt
(1736-1819), age 64

Thomas Paine
(1737-1809), age 63

John Singleton Copley
(1738-1815), age 62

Charles Cornwallis
(1738-1805), age 62

George III (Great Britain)
(1738-1820), age 62

Benajamin West
(1738-1820), age 62

John Rutledge
(1739-1800), age 61

Marquis de Sade
(1740-1814), age 60

Benedict Arnold
(1741-1801), age 59

Charles Willson Peale
(1741-1827), age 59

Gebhard von Blucher
(1742-1819), age 58

Edmund Cartwright
(1743-1823), age 57

Thomas Jefferson
(1743-1926), age 57

William Paley
(1743-1805), age 57

Meyer Rothschild
(1743-1812), age 57

Elbridge Gerry
(1744-1814), age 56

Johann von Herder
(1744-1803), age 56

Chevalier de Lamarck
(1744-1829), age 56

John Jay
(1745-1829), age 55

Mikhail Kutuzov
(1745-1813), age 55

**WILLIAM BLAKE**
English poet and artist
1757-1827

**William Blake,** age 43; English poet and artist born in London, son of a small merchant. An untutored visionary, he disdained the rationalism of his age and developed a private Christianity based on his visions of Jesus Christ and the angels. He supported himself as an illustrator of books; his genius as a lyric poet *(Songs of Innocence* and *Songs of Experience)* went unrecognized until 30 years after his death. These famous lines are his: "And did those feet in ancient time/ Walk upon England's mountains green?/ And was the holy Lamb of God/ On England's pleasant pastures seen?"

**Antonio Canova,** age 43; Italian sculptor born in Venice, apprenticed to a sculptor at 11. His revival of classical simplicity signalled the decline of the baroque. Among his well-known works are monuments to popes Clement XIII and XIV; busts and statues of Napoleon and his family; and *Theseus Vanquishing the Minotaur* and *Cupid and Psyche,* both in the Louvre.

**Charles X,** age 43; king of France from 1824–1830, grandson of Louis XV and brother of Louis XVI and Louis XVIII, whom he succeeded at the age of 67. As the leader of the reactionary party of ultraroyalists, he attempted to restore absolute monarchy and abolish the freedom of the press. He was overthrown by the revolution of July 1830. He abdicated and lived abroad until age 79.

**MARQUIS DE LAFAYETTE**
French statesman and soldier
1757-1834

**Marquis de Lafayette,** age 43; French statesman and soldier remembered for his service to America in the Revolutionary War. As a moderate in the French National Assembly in 1789, he favored a constitutional monarchy and escaped to Flanders after being denounced as a traitor. He became a member of the Chamber of Deputies after 1815.

JAMES MONROE
American statesman and
president
1758-1831

**James Monroe,** age 42; American statesman born in Virginia, son of a planter; fifth president, from 1817–1825. He left college at 18 to fight in the American Revolution, served in the Continental Congress from 1783–1786, and served in the Senate from 1790–1794 as an ally of Jefferson and the anti-Federalists. During his administration, known as the Era of Good Feeling, Florida was acquired (1819) and the Monroe Doctrine, the policy of opposing the extension of European influence into the western hemisphere, was promulgated (1823).

**Horatio Nelson** (Lord Nelson), age 42; British admiral and naval hero born in Norfolk. He grew up in the navy, having entered at 12, and lost his right eye and right arm in battles in 1794 and 1797. He destroyed Napoleon's fleet in the Battle of the Nile in 1798 (and was made Viscount Nelson); in 1805, the British fleet under his command destroyed the combined French and Spanish fleets off Trafalgar, Spain. Nelson lost his life in this battle. The victory—commemorated by Nelson's Column, erected in 1849 in Trafalgar Square in London— ended Napoleon's dreams of invading England.

NOAH WEBSTER
American lexicographer
1758-1843

**Noah Webster,** age 42; American lexicographer born in Connecticut,

John James Audubon
(1785-1851), age 40
Thomas De Quincey
(1785-1859), age 40
Jacob Grimm
(1785-1863), age 40
Alessandro Manzoni
(1785-1873), age 40
Thomas Love Peacock
(1785-1866), age 40
Davy Crockett
(1786-1836), age 39
Sir John Franklin
(1786-1847), age 39
Wilhelm Grimm
(1786-1859), age 39
Winfield Scott
(1786-1866), age 39
Karl Maria von Weber
(1786-1826), age 39
Francois Guizot
(1787-1874), age 38
Robert Livingston Stevens
(1787-1856), age 38
Emma Willard
(1787-1870), age 38
Sir Robert Peel
(1788-1850), age 37
Arthur Schopenhauer
(1788-1860), age 37
James Fenimore Cooper
(1789-1851), age 36
Jared Sparks
(1789-1866), age 36
Alphonse de Lamartine
(1790-1869), age 35
Leopold I (Belgium)
(1790-1865), age 35
John Ross
(1790-1866), age 35
John Tyler
(1790-1862), age 35
James Buchanan
(1791-1868), age 34
Peter Cooper
(1791-1883), age 34
Michael Faraday
(1791-1867), age 34
Franz Grillparzer
(1791-1872), age 34
Giacomo Meyerbeer
(1791-1864), age 34

Henry Mackenzie
(1745-1831), age 55
Benjamin Rush
(1745-1813), age 55
Alessandro Volta
(1745-1827), age 55
Francisco de Goya
(1746-1828), age 54
Jeremy Bentham
(1748-1832), age 52
Jacques Louis David
(1748-1825), age 52
Vittorio Alfieri
(1749-1803), age 51
Johann Wolfgang von Goethe
(1749-1832), age 51
Edward Jenner
(1749-1823), age 51
Pierre de Laplace
(1749-1827), age 51
John Stevens
(1749-1838), age 51
Jouffroy d'Abbans
(1751-1832), age 49
James Madison
(1751-1836), age 49
Richard Sheridan
(1751-1816), age 49
Fanny Burney
(1752-1840), age 48
George Rogers Clark
(1752-1818), age 48
Philip Freneau
(1752-1832), age 48
Edmund Jennings Randolph
(1753-1813), age 47
George Crabbe
(1754-1832), age 46
Pierre L'Enfant
(1754-1825), age 46
Talleyrand
(1754-1838), age 46
Alexander Hamilton
(1755-1804), age 45
John Marshall
(1755-1835), age 45
Sarah Siddons
(1755-1831), age 45
Gilbert Stuart
(1755-1828), age 45
Henry Lee
(1756-1818), age 44

author of the famous *Blue-Backed Speller,* used for many years in American schools. He published his first small dictionary in 1806, *Compendious Dictionary of the English Language;* in 1828 he published, in two volumes, the largest dictionary to that date in America, *An American Dictionary of the English Language.*

**William Pitt** (the Younger), age 41; British statesman born in Kent, second son of William Pitt the Elder. As prime minister from 1784–1801 and from 1804–1806, he formed coalitions in Europe to oppose the French revolutionary and Napoleonic armies, but did not live to see Napoleon's downfall. He was instrumental in the formation of the United Kingdom of Great Britain and Ireland in 1801.

FRIEDRICH VON SCHILLER
German poet and dramatist
1759-1805

**Friedrich von Schiller,** age 41; German poet and dramatist, second only to Goethe in German literature; born in Wurttemberg, son of the overseer of the duke's estate. His nine plays, including *The Robbers,* written at 22, *Mary Stuart* and *The Maid of Orleans,* established him as the leading German dramatist. A romantic idealist and friend of Goethe's, he lived his last five years at Weimar and died of tuberculosis.

**William Wilberforce,** age 41; English politician and humanitarian, founder of the Antislavery Society in 1823 and lifelong crusader in the House of Commons for the abolition of slavery. In 1807 an act of Parliament ended the slave trade, and in 1833, one month after his death, slavery was abolished throughout the British Empire.

(Maria) **Luigi** (Carlos Zenobio Salvatore) **Cherubini,** age 40; Italian composer born in Florence, son of a musician. After settling in Paris in 1788, he gave up Italian-style operas and wrote the French operas that made him famous: *Medee* (1797) and *Les Deux Journees (The Water Carrier,* 1800). He also wrote masses and requiems, including the much admired three-part *Mass in F major.* He was director of the Paris Conservatory from 1821–1841.

**August, Graf Neithardt von Gneisenau,** age 40; German field marshal. He fought the Americans in the Revolutionary War, fought Napoleon at Jena, assisted Scharnhorst in reorganizing the Prussian army (1807–1809) and as Blucher's chief of staff was the principal strategist in the final defeat of Napoleon (1813–1815).

**Katsushika Hokusai,** age 40; Japanese painter and wood engraver, especially famous as a master of printmaking. He produced hundreds of prints of popular subjects, as well as silkscreens and landscape paintings. One famous work is *The Hundred Views of Mount Fuji.*

**Saint-Simon** (Claude Henri Rouvroy, comte de Saint-Simon), age 40; French nobleman (descendant of Charlemagne), staff officer in the American Revolutionary War and social philosopher, born in Paris. One of the founders of modern socialism, he favored the abolition of inheritance rights and the gradual emancipation of women. His major work is *The New Christianity* (1825).

**Albert Gallatin,** age 39; Swiss-American financier and statesman born in Geneva. He came to America in 1780 at 19 and was elected to the House of Representatives in 1795, where he became the leader of the Jeffersonian party. He is chiefly remembered as the longtime Secretary of the Treasury (1801–1814) appointed by Jefferson and kept in the office by Madison. He spoke the famous words: "I know but one way that a nation has of paying her debt and that is 'Spend less than you receive'."

**August Friedrich Ferdinand von Kotzebue,** age 39; German writer and dramatist born in Weimar; the most successful and popular dramatist and librettist of his time, best known for his comedies and melodramas. He was the dramatist for the court theater at Vienna from 1788–1800. His reputation has suffered as a result of his reactionary politics, his attacks on romanticism and his quarrels with Goethe. He published a reactionary political journal in Mannheim until he was stabbed to death by a liberal student.

**Johann Gottlieb Fichte,** age 38; German philosopher, the first outstanding absolute idealist, whose famous *Address to the German Nation* (1808) awakened the spirit of nationalism and encouraged belief in a special German destiny. A disciple of Kant's (whom Kant finally repudiated) and the first rector of the University of Berlin, from 1810–1812, he saw the universe as a moral order, working out a grand design.

**John Jacob Astor,** age 37; German-American fur trader and financier born near Heidelberg. He emigrated in 1784 and entered the fur trade in 1786, dealing directly with Indians. He established trading posts around the Great Lakes, along the Missouri and Columbia rivers, and founded Astoria, Ore. in 1811. By 1817 he had monopolized the Mississippi Valley fur trade. Investing heavily in Manhattan Island real estate, he died the richest man in America.

**Charles Bulfinch,** age 37; American architect born in Boston, son of a physician; famous as a designer of state houses (in Connecticut, Maine and Massachusetts) and for his work on the federal Capitol Building (1818–1830). He also designed Harvard's University Hall, churches and private houses, and laid out Boston Common. He was the father of Thomas Bulfinch (author of *The Age of Fable*).

**Josephine** (Marie Josephine Rose Tascher de la Pagerie), age 37; empress of France from 1804–1809, born in Martinique. The widow of a French army officer, vicomte de Beauharnais (guillotined in 1794), she became the first wife of Napoleon I (married 1796; divorced 1809). She was the grandmother of Napoleon III.

**Jean Paul Richter,** age 37; German writer born in Bavaria. After early poverty, he won success and popularity with his romantic and sentimental novels, remarkable for their warmth and humor. The best known are *Hesperus* (1795); *Life of Quintus Fixlein* (1796, translated by Thomas Carlyle in 1827); and *Titan* (1800–1802), containing a portrayal of Charlotte von Kalb, with whom both he and Schiller were in love. His books were admired by Carlyle and Thomas De Quincey.

**Benjamin Henry Latrobe,** age 36; Anglo-American architect and engineer born in Yorkshire, son of a clergyman. He emigrated in 1796 and assisted Thomas Jefferson in designing the Virginia State Capitol. He also designed the Bank of Pennsylvania in Philadelphia, in the

Samuel F. B. Morse
(1791-1872), age 34
Augustin Eugene Scribe
(1791-1861), age 34
Victor Cousin
(1792-1867), age 33
Pius IX (Pope)
(1792-1878), age 33
Gioacchino Rossini
(1792-1868), age 33
Thaddeus Stevens
(1792-1868), age 33
Stephen Austin
(1793-1836), age 32
Sam Houston
(1793-1863), age 32
Henry Schoolcraft
(1793-1864), age 32
William Cullen Bryant
(1794-1878), age 31
Matthew Perry
(1794-1858), age 31
Cornelius Vanderbilt
(1794-1877), age 31
James Gordon Bennett
(1795-1872), age 30
Thomas Carlyle
(1795-1881), age 30
James Knox Polk
(1795-1849), age 30
Leopold von Ranke
(1795-1886), age 30
Antonio de Santa Anna
(1794/95-1876),
age c.30
Dred Scott
(1795?-1858), age 30?
Augustin Thierry
(1795-1856), age 30
James Bowie
(1796 or 1799-1836),
age 29?
Thomas Bulfinch
(1796-1867), age 29
George Catlin
(1796-1872), age 29
Jean Baptiste Corot
(1796-1875), age 29
Horace Mann
(1796-1859), age 29
W. H. Prescott
(1796-1859), age 29

Greek classic style, and the Roman Catholic cathedral in Baltimore, and rebuilt the national Capitol Building (1815–1817) after it was burned by the British. He died of yellow fever in New Orleans while building the water works.

**Ann Radcliffe** (Ann Ward), age 36; English novelist born in London, author of popular romantic novels of mystery and horror known as Gothic novels; the wife of William Radcliffe, a newspaper editor. Her most famous novel, *The Mysteries of Udolpho* (1794), was satirized by Jane Austen in *Northanger Abbey*.

ROBERT FULTON
American engineer and
   inventor
1765-1815

**Robert Fulton,** age 35; American engineer and inventor born in Pennsylvania. Until the age of 28 he was a professional portrait and landscape painter, but turned to engineering in 1793 and patented various machines. In Paris from 1797–1806, he experimented with steamboats, and upon returning to New York he obtained financial backing and built and launched the first commercially successful steamboat, the *Clermont,* in the Hudson River in August 1807.

**James Smithson,** age 35; English mineralogist, chemist and member of the Royal Society of London, whose estate of over 100,000 pounds eventually was to establish the Smithsonian Institution in Washington, D.C. He was the illegitimate son of Sir Hugh Smithson, who after marrying into the Percy family adopted the name Hugh Percy and was made duke of Northumberland. James Smithson's estate went first to his nephew and then, when his nephew died without heirs, to the United States government.

**John Dalton,** age 34; English chemist and physicist born in Cumberland, remembered as the author of the first modern formulation of the atomic theory in his *New System of Chemical Philosophy* (volume one, 1808). He also studied the aurora borealis and color blindness (Daltonism), with which he was afflicted.

**Thomas Robert Malthus,** age 34; English economist and clergyman born in Surrey. His *Essay on the Principle of Population* (1798) warned of the dangers of overpopulation and predicted that famine, disease, poverty and crime would result. He took a pessimistic view of the future and has proved an accurate prophet.

**Sequoyah,** age 34?; American Indian of the Cherokee Nation, born in Tennessee. Originally a silversmith in Georgia known as George Guess after the white trader believed to be his father, he invented a script of 85 characters representing Cherokee sounds. With it he taught thousands of Cherokees to read and write their own language. The giant sequoia was named for him.

ELI WHITNEY
American inventor
1765-1825

**Eli Whitney,** age 35; American inventor born in Massachusetts and graduated from Yale University in 1792. While visiting a Georgia plantation, he invented a machine for removing the seeds from the fibers of the cotton plant, a cotton engine or "gin" (1793). By eliminating the tedious hand process, Whitney's gin made cotton a profitable crop and the foundation of the American South's economy.

**Mme. de Stael** (Anne Louise Germaine, baronne de Stael-Holstein), age 34; French writer, famous for her literary salon and love affairs, born in Paris, daughter of Jacques Necker, the finance minister whose dismissal in 1789 preceded the storming of the Bastille. At 20 she married Baron Stael-Holstein, a Swiss diplomat. The author of romantic novels and of *De l'Allemagne* (1810), which introduced German romanticism to France, she was banished by Napoleon for her liberal views and lived many years on her Swiss estate with her lover, Benjamin Constant.

**Alexander Wilson,** age 34; Scottish-American ornithologist and poet born in Paisley, Scotland. An apprentice weaver and itinerant peddler of muslins, he emigrated to America in 1794, became a rural schoolteacher and took up the study of birds. His illustrated work *American Ornithology,* in seven volumes (1808–1813), is recognized as a classic and was the first such work in America, preceding Audubon's by 20 years.

JOHN QUINCY ADAMS
American statesman and
president
1767-1848

**John Quincy Adams,** age 33; American statesman and lawyer born in

Gaetano Donizetti
(1797-1848), age 28
Heinrich Heine
(1797-1856), age 28
Ando Hiroshige
(1797-1858), age 28
Sir Charles Lyell
(1797-1875), age 28
Franz Schubert
(1797-1828), age 28
Mary Wollstonecraft
Shelley
(1797-1851), age 28
Louis Adolphe Thiers
(1797-1877), age 28
Alfred de Vigny
(1797-1863), age 28
William I (Germany)
(1797-1888), age 28
Auguste Comte
(1798-1857), age 27
Eugene Delacroix
(1798-1863), age 27
Giacomo Leopardi
(1798-1837), age 27
Adam Mickiewicz
(1798-1855), age 27
Jules Michelet
(1798-1874), age 27
Bronson Alcott
(1799-1888), age 26
Honore de Balzac
(1799-1850), age 26
Jacques Halevy
(1799-1862), age 26
Thomas Hood
(1799-1845), age 26
Alexander Pushkin
(1799-1837), age 26
George Bancroft
(1800-1891), age 25
John Brown
(1800-1859), age 25
Millard Fillmore
(1800-1874), age 25
Thomas B. Macaulay
(1800-1859), age 25
William McGuffy
(1800-1873), age 25
Helmuth von Moltke
(1800-1891), age 25

Massachusetts, sixth president of the United States, from 1825–1829. Defeated for reelection by Andrew Jackson, he ran for Congress and served in the House of Representatives from 1831–1848. The son of John Adams and grandfather of the writer Henry Adams, he was a man of integrity and extraordinary intelligence.

**Benjamin Constant,** age 33; Swiss-French writer and politician born in Lausanne. A member of the Tribunate from 1799–1802, he was banished by Napoleon, only to return many years later to serve in the Chamber of Deputies from 1819–1822 and from 1824–1834 as an advocate of constitutional monarchy. He is remembered as the lover of Mme. de Stael and the author of a semi-autobiographical novel, *Adolphe* (1816).

**Maria Edgeworth,** age 33; English novelist born in Oxfordshire, daughter of a well-to-do inventor and educational theorist. She spent most of her life on her father's estate in Ireland, where she wrote realistic novels of Irish life: *Castle Rackrent* (1800), *Belinda* (1801), *The Absentee* (1812), *Ormund* (1817) and others. She also wrote stories for children.

ANDREW JACKSON
American soldier, statesman
and president
1767-1845

**Andrew Jackson,** age 33; American statesman born in South Carolina, seventh president, from 1829–1837; champion of the frontier farmer, backwoodsman and laborer. As commander of the Tennessee militia, he put down a rebellion of the Creek Indians (1814) and won national fame for his victory over the British in the Battle of New Orleans (1815). During his administration the nation's political parties adopted the convention system and the national debt was paid in full.

**Joachim Murat,** age 33; French cavalry commander and king of Naples (1808–1815) as Joachim I Napoleon. He aided Napoleon in his 1799 coup d'etat, married Napoleon's sister Maria and succeeded Joseph Bonaparte as king of Naples. Defeated by the Austrians in 1815, he was subsequently arrested and executed.

**August Wilhelm von Schlegel,** age 33; German writer and scholar born in Hanover, son of a Lutheran clergyman; professor at Bonn from 1818–1845. With his brother Friedrich, in 1798 he founded the journal *Athenaeum,* the principal organ of German romanticism. He is noted for his translations of Shakespeare and, as a pioneer Sanskrit scholar, of the *Bhagavad-Gita* and the *Ramayana*.

**Francois Rene, vicomte de Chateaubriand,** age 32; French writer and diplomat born in Brittany of a noble family. After living in America for one year (1791–1792), he wrote two stories of Indian life and the American wilderness, *Atala* (1801) and *Rene* (1802), which launched the romantic movement in French literature. Emotional and thoroughly unrealistic, they endowed the savages with the thoughts and feelings of an 18th-century man of sensibility.

**Francis II,** age 32; the last Holy Roman emperor (1792–1806) and the first emperor of Austria (1804–1835), as Francis I; grandson of Maria Theresa. He joined the coalitions against Napoleon (although his daughter, Maria Louisa, married him) and presided over the Congress of Vienna after Napoleon's downfall.

**Ivan Andreyevich Krylov,** age 32; Russian writer of fables born in Moscow. His collection of more than 200 fables, some of which were adapted from Aesop and La Fontaine, won popularity throughout Europe for their satirization of social and political life.

**Duncan Phyfe,** age 32; Scottish-American cabinetmaker born in Scotland. About 1783 he emigrated to America with his parents and was apprenticed to a cabinetmaker near Albany, N.Y. In 1792 he opened a shop in New York City and acquired a reputation for careful workmanship and for the beauty of his chairs, tables and sideboards—virtually all of which were crafted of solid mahogany. His early work is still admired for its graceful design and simple ornamentation.

**Friedrich Ernst Daniel Schleiermacher,** age 32; German Protestant clergyman, theologian and philosopher, born in Breslau; professor of theology at Berlin from 1810–1834. Influenced by Friedrich Schlegel and the romantics, he held that the emotions rather than the reasoning faculties are the seat of human nature and that dogmas rejected by critical rationalism as myths may still be valid as symbols of certain aspects of inner experience. His major work is *The Christian Faith* (1821–1822). He is also known for his translations of Plato (1804–1828).

**Samuel Slater,** age 32; Anglo-American pioneer in the textile industry, born in Derbyshire, England; credited with bringing the Industrial Revolution to America. As a mill worker from the age of 14, he became familiar with the new machines and in 1789, at 21, he slipped away to America in defiance of the law forbidding the emigration of textile workers. In partnership with the firm of Alby & Brown in Providence, R.I., he reproduced from memory the new cotton machinery and in 1790 opened the first mechanized spinning mill in America.

**Tecumseh,** age 32?; American Indian chief of the Shawnee tribe born in Ohio. A renowned warrior and able leader, he maintained that the land was the common possession of all Indians and that no part of it could be sold by a single tribe. After the defeat of his brother, the Shawnee Prophet, at Tippecanoe in 1811, Indian resistance collapsed. He joined the British in the War of 1812 as a brigadier general and was killed in the Battle of the Thames in 1813.

**Viscount Castlereagh** (Robert Stewart, second marquis of Londonderry), age 31; British statesman born in Ireland, son of a landed proprietor. As secretary of war from 1805–1806 and from 1807–1809 and foreign secretary from 1812–1822, he organized the coalitions that defeated Napoleon, appointed the duke of Wellington commander, represented Britain at the Congress of Vienna, sent Napoleon to St. Helena, favored the restoration of the Bourbon monarchy and advocated a moderate peace, restraining the allies from reprisals on France. Overwhelmed by responsibilities, his mind gave way and he slashed his throat at 53. He was buried in Westminster Abbey.

**De Witt Clinton,** age 31; American public official born in New York, son of a Revolutionary War general and nephew of the first governor of New York state. A progressive and efficient administrator, he was mayor of New York City for 10 annual terms between 1803 and 1815 and governor of New York from 1817–1823 and from 1825–1828. He

James Clark Ross
(1800-1862), age 25
David Farragut
(1801-1870), age 24
John Henry Newman
(1801-1896), age 24
Brigham Young
(1801-1877), age 24
Paul Emile Botta
(1802-1870), age 23
Alexandre Dumas (pere)
(1802-1870), age 23
Victor Hugo
(1802-1885), age 23
Louis Kossuth
(1802-1894), age 23
Edwin Landseer
(1802-1873), age 23
Harriet Martineau
(1802-1876), age 23
Hector Berlioz
(1803-1869), age 22
George Borrow
(1803-1881), age 22
Edward Bulwer-Lytton
(1803-1873), age 22
Ralph Waldo Emerson
(1803-1882), age 22
Albert Sidney Johnston
(1803-1862), age 22
Baron von Liebig
(1803-1873), age 22
Prosper Merimee
(1803-1870), age 22
Benjamin Disraeli
(1804-1881), age 21
Ludwig Feuerbach
(1804-1872), age 21
Mikhail Glinka
(1804-1857), age 21
Nathaniel Hawthorne
(1804-1864), age 21
Franklin Pierce
(1804-1869), age 21
Charles Sainte-Beuve
(1804-1869), age 21
George Sand
(1804-1876), age 21
Johann Strauss
(1804-1849), age 21
Eugene Sue
(1804-1857), age 21

was defeated in the presidential race of 1812 by James Madison.

**Baron Cuvier** (Georges Leopold Chretien Frederic Dagobert), age 31; French zoologist; founder of comparative anatomy and councillor of state to Napoleon I. He devised a systematic method of classifying animals in four distinct branches or phyla, but his conviction of the immutability of species, coupled with his reputation, delayed the acceptance of evolutionary theory in France.

**Baron Alexander von Humboldt,** age 31; German naturalist and explorer born in Berlin. He accompanied a French scientific expedition to South America (1799–1804), which explored the Orinoco River, the Amazon and its tributaries and ascended the Andes Mountains. He wrote a lucid, detailed description of his observations. He was the brother of Baron Wilhelm von Humboldt, a philologist and diplomat.

**Sir Thomas Lawrence,** age 31; English portrait painter born in Bristol, son of an innkeeper. He won popularity and royal patronage in his twenties and, after the death of Sir Joshua Reynolds, became the most fashionable painter of his time. He painted Sarah Siddons, Benjamin West and George IV; he is famous for his portraits of children: *The Calmady Children* (in the Metropolitan Museum of Art, New York) and the famous *Pinkie* (in the Huntington Gallery, San Marino, Calif.) He was knighted in 1815.

NAPOLEON BONAPARTE
French soldier and emperor
of France
1769-1821

**Napoleon I** (Napoleon Bonaparte), age 31; French soldier born in Corsica, emperor of France from 1804–1815. Though one of history's supreme military geniuses, brilliantly victorious at Ulm, Austerlitz and Jena, he is better remembered for his failures. The disastrous retreat from Moscow and the debacle at Waterloo have linked his name permanently with the years 1812 and 1815. On the island of St. Helena he dictated his memoirs and died of cancer at 52, six years after Waterloo.

**Michel Ney,** age 31; French general, marshal of France and Prince de la Moskova; commander of the rear guard in the retreat from Moscow. He supported Louis XVIII after the first abdication, but rejoined Napoleon for the Hundred Days and commanded the Old Guard at Waterloo. He was tried for treason and shot Dec. 7, 1815. Napoleon called him "the bravest of the brave."

**DUKE OF WELLINGTON**
(Arthur Wellesley)
British soldier and statesman
1769-1852

**Duke of Wellington** (Arthur Wellesley, the Iron Duke), age 31; British soldier and statesman born in Ireland, fourth son of a titled musician and composer (the earl of Mornington) and relative of John and Charles Wesley. Remembered for his celebrated victory at Waterloo, he was a popular idol of the British public and prime minister from 1828–1830.

**LUDWIG VAN BEETHOVEN**
German composer
1770-1827

**Ludwig van Beethoven,** age 30; German composer born in Bonn of a family of musicians of Flemish origin. He settled in Vienna in 1792 and won recognition and popularity among the aristocracy. He composed nine symphonies, numerous sonatas and string quartets and one opera, *Fidelio*. Totally deaf at 49, he is acknowledged as one of the greatest composers, whose *Ninth Symphony, Moonlight Sonata*, and *Minuet in G* are universally known. His funeral was a public event.

**William Clark,** age 30; American explorer born in Virginia, younger brother of George Rogers Clark. An army lieutenant, he was chosen to accompany Capt. Meriwether Lewis on the famous expedition to open up the Louisiana Purchase to fur traders. They journeyed from St. Louis to the Pacific coast and back (1804–1806), mapping and describing the region, its wildlife and Indian tribes.

Hans Christian Andersen
(1805-1875), age 20
William Lloyd Garrison
(1805-1879), age 20
Ferdinand de Lesseps
(1805-1894), age 20
Giuseppe Mazzini
(1805-1872), age 20
Joseph Smith
(1805-1844), age 20
Alexis de Tocqueville
(1805-1859), age 20
Samuel Wilberforce
(1805-1873), age 20
Elizabeth Barrett Browning
(1806-1861), age 19
Benito Juarez
(1806-1872), age 19
John Stuart Mill
(1806-1873), age 19
Louis Agassiz
(1807-1873), age 18
Giuseppe Garibaldi
(1807-1882), age 18
Joseph Eggleston Johnston
(1807-1891), age 18
Robert E. Lee
(1807-1870), age 18
Henry Wadsworth Longfellow
(1807-1882), age 18
John Greenleaf Whittier
(1807-1892), age 18
Honore Daumier
(1808-1879), age 17
Jefferson Davis
(1808-1889), age 17
Andrew Johnson
(1808-1875), age 17
Napoleon III
(1808-1873), age 17
David Strauss
(1808-1874), age 17
Kit Carson
(1809-1868), age 16
Charles Darwin
(1809-1882), age 16
Edward FitzGerald
(1809-1883), age 16
William E. Gladstone
(1809-1898), age 16
Nikolai Gogol
(1809-1852), age 16

GEORG WILHELM
FRIEDRICH HEGEL
German philosopher
1770-1831

**Georg Wilhelm Friedrich Hegel,** age 30; German philosopher born in Stuttgart. His complex system of metaphysical idealism is unfashionable today, but in the early 19th century large audiences flocked to his lectures. As the philosopher of the national state, he is called the forerunner of totalitarianism and of certain parallel trends in modern sociology, psychology and economics.

**(Johann Christian) Friedrich Holderlin,** age 30; German lyric poet, son of a Protestant clergyman. A brilliant poet, writing Pindaric odes and elegies, he is little known outside Germany and was little appreciated there until the 20th century, when his importance was recognized by Rainer Maria Rilke and Stefan George. He also wrote *Hyperion* (1797–1799), a novel in the form of letters; and an unfinished drama, *The Death of Empedocles*. He suffered an attack of schizophrenia at 32 and was insane after 36.

WILLIAM WORDSWORTH
English poet
1770-1850

**William Wordsworth,** age 30; English poet born in Cumberland, son of the business agent of the earl of Lonsdale. Orphaned at 13, he grew up under the guardianship of two uncles. One of the earliest Romantics, and probably the greatest poet since Milton, he lived an uneventful life in rural England with his wife, daughter and sister, subsisting on inherited income. He was a friend of Southey, Coleridge and Walter Scott. One famous line is, "Plain living and high thinking are no more."

**Eleuthere Irene du Pont de Nemours,** age 29; Franco-American industrialist born in Paris, son of Pierre Samuel du Pont de Nemours, economist and leading physiocrat. He learned how to manufacture gunpowder at the royal powder mills and, after emigrating with his father in 1799, established a gunpowder mill near Wilmington, Del. in 1802, which in the course of time became world famous for the production of nylon for stockings.

**Robert Owen,** age 29; British social reformer and early socialist born in Wales, son of a saddler. A mill worker at 10 and an independent cotton manufacturer at 23, he devoted his life to efforts to improve the conditions of factory labor. His schemes for cooperative living—as at New Harmony, Ind.—ended in failure, but his influence helped to ameliorate the brutal factory conditions of the 19th century. He was the author of *A New View of Society* (1813–1814) and an autobiography (1857 to 1858).

**Mungo Park,** age 29; British explorer born in Falkirk, Scotland, one of the first to penetrate the interior of Africa. Sponsored by a trade association, he explored the Niger and Gambia rivers (1795–1796) and returned to England to write *Travels in the Interior Districts of Africa* (1799). On a second expedition, sponsored by the British government, in 1805, he drowned when his party was attacked by natives.

SIR WALTER SCOTT
Scottish novelist, poet
and historian
1771-1832

**Sir Walter Scott,** age 29; Scottish novelist, poet and historian born in Edinburgh, son of a lawyer. His narrative poems—*The Lay of the Last Minstrel* (1805), *Marmion* and *The Lady of the Lake*—brought fame, but his great popularity and success rested on 2 series of over 20 historical novels, including *Waverley* (1814), *Guy Mannering, Old Mortality* and *Ivanhoe*. At his baronial mansion in Abbotsford, built in 1812, he lived in the style of a country gentleman, but continued to write industriously until his death at 61.

**Sydney Smith,** age 29; English clergyman and wit born in Essex, son of a wealthy landowner. A cofounder of the *Edinburgh Review* in 1802 and a well-known preacher, lecturer and frequenter of literary circles, he is remembered chiefly through anecdotes in other people's memoirs. He was a village parson in Yorkshire from 1809–1828 and canon at St. Paul's in London from 1831–1845.

**Richard Trevithick,** age 29; English engineer born in Cornwall, inventor of the first horseless vehicle to carry passengers. He installed a high-pressure steam engine in a road carriage and on Christmas Eve, 1801, conveyed a few friends through the streets of Cambourne (near

Oliver Wendell Holmes
(1809-1894), age 16

Fanny Kemble
(1809-1893), age 16

Abraham Lincoln
(1809-1865), age 16

Cyrus Hall McCormick
(1809-1884), age 16

Felix Mendelssohn
(1809-1847), age 16

Edgar Allan Poe
(1809-1849), age 16

Pierre Proudhon
(1809-1865), age 16

Alfred Tennyson
(1809-1892), age 16

William Barret Travis
(1809-1836), age 16

P. T. Barnum
(1810-1891), age 15

Camillo di Cavour
(1810-1861), age 15

Frederic Chopin
(1810-1849), age 15

Margaret Fuller
(1810-1850), age 15

Elizabeth Gaskell
(1810-1865), age 15

Asa Gray
(1810-1888), age 15

Leo XIII (Pope)
(1810-1903), age 15

Alfred de Musset
(1810-1857), age 15

Theodore Parker
(1810-1860), age 15

Henry Rawlinson
(1810-1895), age 15

Robert Schumann
(1810-1856), age 15

George Caleb Bingham
(1811-1879), age 14

Theophile Gautier
(1811-1872), age 14

Horace Greeley
(1811-1872), age 14

Franz Liszt
(1811-1886), age 14

Harriet Beecher Stowe
(1811-1896), age 14

Land's End). He also built the first steam locomotive to run on tracks, and in February 1804 pulled five wagons carrying 70 men and ten tons of iron a distance of nine and a half miles in less than two hours.

**Samuel Taylor Coleridge,** age 28; English poet and critic born in Devonshire, youngest son of a clergyman–schoolmaster. He is best known for a few poems of high quality—*The Rime of the Ancient Mariner, Christabel* and *Kubla Khan*—and the prose work *Biographia Literaria.* He is also remembered as an untiring conversationalist and for his unfortunate addiction to opium, taken to relieve the pain of neuralgia.

(Francois Marie) **Charles Fourier,** age 28; French utopian socialist. He believed that social harmony would follow naturally if the artificial restraints of civilization were removed. He proposed the establishment of cooperative communities of 1,620 people each, who would live in a community building (phalanstery) and divide the work among them. Several such communities were established—Brook Farm in Massachusetts was one—but none survived long.

**David Ricardo,** age 28; English economist born in London, of Dutch-Jewish parentage. Entering business as a stock broker at 20, he amassed a fortune in five years, and in 1799 began his lifelong study of economics. In his major work, *The Principles of Political Economy and Taxation* (1817), he expounded the "iron law of wages," which supposedly kept wages at subsistence level. He is known as the founder of the classical school of economics.

(Karl Wilhelm) **Friedrich von Schlegel,** age 28; German critic and exponent of romanticism born in Hanover, younger brother of August von Schlegel. As well as engaging in diplomatic work and lecturing on philosophy in various cities, he wrote extensively: lyric poems; a novel, *Lucinde* (1799); a drama, *Alarcos* (1802); and one of the earliest works in comparative philology, *On the Language and Wisdom of India* (1808). He became a Roman Catholic at 31 and married the daughter of Moses Mendelssohn at 32. He believed unlimited self-realization should be the goal of life.

**Nathaniel Bowditch,** age 27; American mathematician born in Salem, Mass. With no formal education after 10, he taught himself algebra and Latin, went to sea in his twenties, learned navigation and returned to write the *New American Practical Navigator,* which became a standard textbook and is still published by the United States Hydrographic Office. He also translated Laplace's *Celestial Mechanics.*

**William Henry Harrison,** age 27; American general, legislator and ninth president (for one month in 1841); born in Virginia, son of Benjamin Harrison, the revolutionary leader and governor of Virginia. He was governor of Indiana Territory at Vincennes from 1801 to 1813 and general in the war with the Shawnee chief Tecumseh, winning national fame for his victory in the battle of Tippecanoe (in northwest Indiana) in November 1811. He is also famous for his "Log Cabin and Hard Cider" presidential campaign of 1840, which won the election by portraying him as a rough backwoodsman. He took office March 4, 1841 and died April 4 of pneumonia, at 68.

**Louis Philippe,** age 27; king of France from 1830–1848, called the Citizen King. The eldest son of the duke of Orleans, he survived the revolution by joining the Jacobin Club and serving in the revolutionary army. He lived abroad from 1796–1814, including four years in Philadelphia (1796–1800). Proclaimed king in 1830, after the July revolution, he began as a moderate ruler but grew increasingly despotic, lost favor, and was overthrown in February 1848, at 75. He died in exile in England.

**Metternich** (Prince Klemens Wenzel Nepomuk Lothar von Metternich), age 27; Austrian statesman; foreign minister from 1809–1848. As the dominant figure at the Congress of Vienna in 1815, he succeeded in restoring political stability to Europe. He suppressed liberal ideas and movements until the Revolution of 1848 forced him into exile in England. He lived in retirement in Vienna from 1851–1857.

**John Randolph** (John Randolph of Roanoke), age 27; American legislator born in Virginia, cousin of Edmund Jennings Randolph and descendant of Pocahontas. He served in the House of Representatives almost continuously from 1799 to 1829, a noted orator and vigorous champion of individual liberty and states' rights. At his death he freed his 400 slaves and provided for their support.

**Meriwether Lewis,** age 26; American explorer born in Virginia; private secretary to Pres. Jefferson from 1801–1803. As leader of the Lewis and Clark Expedition, he left St. Louis on May 14, 1804, ascended the Missouri River, crossed the Rockies and descended the Columbia River to the Pacific Ocean. He returned to St. Louis on Sept. 23, 1806, having completed the journey on a government grant of $2,500.

**Elizabeth Ann Seton** (Mother Seton), age 26; first native-born American saint, born in New York City, daughter of a physician. She joined the Roman Catholic Church after the death of her husband, William Seton. In 1809 she founded the Sisters of Charity in Emmitsburg, Md., and established a school which marked the beginning of parochial education in the United States. She was beatified by Pope John XXIII in 1963 and canonized in 1974.

ROBERT SOUTHEY
English poet and biographer
1774-1843

**Robert Southey,** age 26; English poet and biographer born in Bristol, author of the children's classic *The Three Bears.* He is also known for his short poems, *The Inscape Rock* and *The Battle of Blenheim,* and for his biography of Lord Nelson. He was a friend of Wordsworth and Coleridge and poet laureate from 1813–1843.

**Andre Marie Ampere,** age 25; French physicist and mathematician born near Lyons. He is known for his contributions to the study of electrodynamics and for his studies of the relationship between electricity and magnetism. The ampere, the basic unit of electrical current, is named for him.

William Makepeace Thackeray
    (1811-1863), age 14
Robert Browning
    (1812-1889), age 13
Charles Dickens
    (1812-1870), age 13
Friedrich von Flotow
    (1812-1883), age 13
Ivan Goncharov
    (1812-1891), age 13
Aleksandr Herzen
    (1812-1870), age 13
Alfred Krupp
    (1812-1887), age 13
Edward Lear
    (1812-1888), age 13
Stephen A. Douglas
    (1813-1861), age 12
John C. Fremont
    (1813-1890), age 12
Friedrich Hebbel
    (1813-1863), age 12
Soren Kierkegaard
    (1813-1855), age 12
David Livingstone
    (1813-1873), age 12
Giuseppe Verdi
    (1813-1901), age 12
Jones Very
    (1813-1880), age 12
Richard Wagner
    (1813-1883), age 12
Mikhail Bakunin
    (1814-1876), age 11
Joseph Hooker
    (1814-1879), age 11
Mikhail Lermontov
    (1814-1841), age 11
Jean Millet
    (1814-1875), age 11
John Lothrop Motley
    (1814-1877), age 11
Charles Reade
    (1814-1884), age 11
Edwin Stanton
    (1814-1869), age 11
Otto von Bismarck
    (1815-1898), age 10
Cochise
    (1815-1874), age 10
George Meade
    (1815-1872), age 10

JANE AUSTEN
English novelist
1775-1817

**Jane Austen,** age 25; English novelist born in Hampshire, youngest of seven children of a clergyman. She wrote three novels in her early twenties: *Pride and Prejudice, Sense and Sensibility* and *Northanger Abbey*. Unable to find a publisher, she wrote no more until finally, many years later, *Sense and Sensibility* was published. She then wrote *Mansfield Park, Emma* and *Persuasion*. These six masterpieces on English country life established her as a major English novelist.

**Charles Lamb,** age 25; English essayist born in London, master of the informal, gently humorous essay: *Essays of Elia* and *Last Essays of Elia*. He also wrote, with his sister, *Tales from Shakespeare*. A book-keeper–clerk for the East India Company for 33 years, he devoted his life to the care of his sister, who in a fit of insanity stabbed their invalid mother to death.

**Walter Savage Landor,** age 25; English poet and prose writer born in Warwick, son of a wealthy doctor. A classicist in a romantic age and a violent-tempered, argumentative man, he is remembered for some short poems and for *Imaginary Conversations* (five volumes) in prose. These famous haughty lines are his: "I strove with none, for none was worth my strife./ Nature I loved and, next to nature, art."

**Friedrich Wilhelm Joseph von Schelling,** age 25; German idealist philosopher; professor at Jena, Wurzburg and Berlin. Closely associated with the Schlegels and Fichte, he attempted a philosophical expression of romanticism. Taking a long, cheery view, he saw the creative impulse working through nature and reason toward ultimate harmony.

**Joseph Mallord William Turner,** age 25; English landscape painter and watercolorist born in London. He achieved early success with romantic landscapes, but in his later pictures, highly praised by John Ruskin, only indistinct objects are visible in a haze of glowing color, as in *Burning of the Houses of Parliament* (at the Philadelphia Museum of Art) and *Interior at Petworth* (at the Tate Gallery in London).

**John Constable,** age 24; English painter born in Suffolk, son of a miller; famous for his scenes of rural England in warm colors, such as *The Hay Wain* in the National Gallery in London. The full-scale study, which many critics prefer, is in the Victoria and Albert Museum, with *A Country Road, Brighton Beach* and *Valley of the Stour*.

**E.T.A. Hoffmann** (Ernst Theodor Amadeus Hoffmann), age 24; German writer and composer born in Koenigsberg, known for his stories of the supernatural, fantastic and grotesque and for his eccentric personality. One of his stories, *The Nutcracker and the Mouse-King*, inspired Tchaikovsky's ballet; three other stories were combined by Offenbach in his opera *Tales of Hoffmann*.

ALEXANDER I
Emperor of Russia
1777-1825

**Alexander I** (Aleksandr Pavlovich), age 23; emperor of Russia from 1801–1825, grandson of Catherine the Great. On a raft in the Memel (Niemen) River at Tilsit in 1807, he signed a treaty of friendship with Napoleon, but rejoined the European coalition after the French invasion and assisted in Napoleon's downfall. His early optimistic liberalism was succeeded by disillusionment, reaction and repression.

HENRY CLAY
American statesman
1777-1852

**Henry Clay,** age 23; American statesman born in Virginia. He moved to Kentucky and became a dominant figure in Congress (spending 12 years in the House and 20 in the Senate) through the force of his oratory. Secretary of state from 1825–1829 and Whig candidate for president in 1832 and 1844, he is famous for saying, "I would rather be right than president."

**Heinrich Wilhelm von Kleist,** age 23; German dramatist and novelist born in Frankfurt-an-der-Oder of a Prussian military family. He fought in the Prussian army from 1792–1799, and, as a passionate nationalist during Napoleon's occupation of Berlin, he was constantly in trouble. Unrecognized in his time, he led an unhappy life and committed sui-

Elizabeth Cady Stanton
(1815-1902), age 10
Anthony Trollope
(1815-1882), age 10
Charlotte Bronte
(1816-1855), age 9
Comte de Gobineau
(1816-1882), age 9
Paul von Reuter
(1816-1899), age 9
Charles Francois Daubigny
(1817-1878), age 8
Frederick Douglass
(c.1817-1895), age c.8
Benjamin Jowett
(1817-1893), age 8
Sir Austen Layard
(1817-1894), age 8
Theodor Mommsen
(1817-1903), age 8
Henry David Thoreau
(1817-1862), age 8
Alexander II (Russia)
(1818-1881), age 7
Pierre Gustave de
Beauregard
(1818-1893), age 7
Emily Jane Bronte
(1818-1848), age 7
Jacob Burckhardt
(1818-1897), age 7
James Anthony Froude
(1818-1894), age 7
Charles Francois Gounod
(1818-1893), age 7
Charles Leconte de Lisle
(1818-1894), age 7
Karl Marx
(1818-1883), age 7
Lewis Henry Morgan
(1818-1881), age 7
Ivan Turgenev
(1818-1883), age 7
Prince Albert
(1819-1861), age 6
Gustave Courbet
(1819-1877), age 6
Edwin Laurentine Drake
(1819-1880), age 6
George Eliot
(1819-1880), age 6

cide with his friend Henrietta Vogel. Today he is compared with Goethe and Schiller. His best-known works are the comedies *The Broken Jug* (1806) and *Amphitryon* (1807); the tragedy *Prince Friedrich von Homburg;* and the novel *Michael Kohlhaas* (1811).

SIR HUMPHREY DAVY
English chemist
1778-1829

**Sir Humphrey Davy,** age 22; English chemist born in Penzance, Cornwall. He isolated several elements, discovered the anesthetic effect of laughing gas (nitrous oxide), proved the diamond to be carbon and invented the miners' safety lamp. Michael Faraday was his assistant. He was knighted in 1812.

**William Hazlitt,** age 22; English essayist, critic and lecturer, born in Kent, son of a Unitarian minister. The family emigrated to America in 1783 and settled in Boston, where the elder Hazlitt founded the first Unitarian church, but he returned to England four years later. Hazlitt is known as a first-rate critic and a lucid prose stylist. *The Spirit of the Age,* a collection of essays, contains discerning appraisals of his contemporaries.

**Stephen Decatur,** age 21; American naval officer born in Maryland, remembered for his daring exploits in the war with Tripoli (1801–1805) and in the War of 1812, when he captured the British ship *Macedonian.* He was fatally wounded in 1820 in a duel with James Barron, a naval officer whom he had refused to reinstate after a court-martial. He is also remembered for the saying, "Our country, right or wrong!"

**Francis Scott Key,** age 21; American lawyer and part-time poet born in Maryland, author of *The Star-Spangled Banner.* After watching the bombardment of Fort McHenry, near Baltimore, by the British fleet on the night of Sept. 13–14, 1814, he was inspired by the sight of the flag, still flying at dawn, to write his poem. The tune was taken from the popular English song *To Anacreon in Heaven.*

**Lord Melbourne** (William Lamb, Second Viscount Melbourne), age 21; British statesman; Whig prime minister in 1834 and from 1835–1841, known principally for his role as political adviser and instructor of the young Queen Victoria, His wife, Lady Caroline Lamb, an author of minor novels, is remembered for her love affair with Lord Byron.

**Clement Clarke Moore,** age 21; American educator and poet born in New York City, son of a Protestant Episcopal clergyman. A biblical scholar and author of a Hebrew lexicon, he is remembered for the poem beginning, "'Twas the night before Christmas, and all through the house," first published in the Troy (N.Y.) *Sentinel* in 1823.

**Thomas Moore,** age 21; Irish poet and lawyer born in Dublin, son of a grocer. He won fame with *Irish Melodies* (1807–1834), which included such famous lyrics as "Believe Me If All Those Endearing Young Charms" and "Oft in the Stilly Night." He also wrote the popular Oriental romance in verse, *Lalla Rookh* (1817). He was a friend of Byron, whose biography he wrote and whose memoirs he destroyed.

**Zebulon Montgomery Pike,** age 21; American army officer and explorer born in New Jersey; discoverer of Pike's Peak in Colorado. He led an exploring party to the headwaters of the Mississippi River (1805–1806) and to the headwaters of the Arkansas River (1806–1807), and discovered the peak named for him. He was killed while attacking York (Toronto) in the War of 1812.

**William Ellery Channing,** age 20; American clergyman and writer born in Newport, R.I.; pastor of the Federal Street Congregational Church in Boston from the age of 23 until his death at 62. One of the organizers of Unitarianism in America, he spoke for humanitarianism and tolerance, in contrast to the dogmatism of the Calvinists. His liberal views influenced Emerson and Oliver Wendell Holmes, among others.

**Karl von Clausewitz,** age 20; Prussian general and writer on military science. He served in the Prussian army in his youth, in the Russian army from 1812–1814 and in the Prussian army again from 1814–1818; fought at Waterloo; and was made director of the war college in 1818. He is famous for his three-volume work on military strategy, *Vom Kriege* (1833).

**Jean Auguste Dominique Ingres,** age 20; French painter born in southern France, near Toulouse, the son of a sculptor. A pupil of David and a leader of the classical school, he is known for the ceiling painting in the Louvre, *Apotheosis of Homer,* and for his many portraits, *(Madame Moitessier)* and nudes *(Nude from the Back)*. He painted the famous *Turkish Women at the Bath* (in the Louvre) at 82.

**Augustin de Iturbide,** age 17; Mexican army officer and emperor as Augustin I, 1822–1823. Commissioned by the Spanish viceroy to suppress revolutionaries, he joined them instead, forced the viceroy to surrender and established Mexican independence in 1821. his provisional government turned into a dictatorship and was soon overthrown in a new revolution, led by Santa Anna. He was captured and shot in 1824.

LORD BYRON
English poet
1788-1824

**Lord Byron** (George Gordon, sixth Baron Byron), age 12; English

Charles Kingsley
(1819-1875), age 6
James Russell Lowell
(1819-1891), age 6
Herman Melville
(1819-1891), age 6
Jacques Offenbach
(1819-1880), age 6
John Ruskin
(1819-1900), age 6
Joseph Seligman
(1819-1880), age 6
Victoria (Great Britain)
(1819-1901), age 6
Walt Whitman
(1819-1892), age 6
Susan B. Anthony
(1820-1906), age 5
James B. Eads
(1820-1887), age 5
Friedrich Engels
(1820-1895), age 5
Jenny Lind
(1820-1887), age 5
Florence Nightingale
(1820-1910), age 5
William Tecumseh
Sherman
(1820-1891), age 5
Herbert Spencer
(1820-1903), age 5
Victor Emmanuel II (Italy)
(1820-1878), age 5
Clara Barton
(1821-1912), age 4
Charles Baudelaire
(1821-1867), age 4
Henry Thomas Buckle
(1821-1862), age 4
Richard Burton
(1821-1890), age 4
Feodor Dostoevsky
(1821-1881), age 4
Mary Baker Eddy
(1821-1910), age 4
Gustave Flaubert
(1821-1880), age 4
Hermann von Helmholtz
(1821-1894), age 4
Matthew Arnold
(1822-1888), age 3

poet born in London; son of Capt. John Byron, the notorious womanizer; grandson of Adm. John Byron (Foul-weather Jack); and grand-nephew of William, fifth Baron Byron, whose title and estates he inherited in 1798. Handsome and talented, he was unfortunately born with a club foot, which did not prevent him from being loved by many women. He created the Byronic hero in *Childe Harold's Pilgrimage:* aloof, moody and antisocial. After 1816 he lived in Venice, Pisa and Greece and died of malaria at 36. These are famous lines: "She walks in beauty like the night/ Of cloudless climes and starry skies."

**Louis XVII** (1785–1795), nominal king of France from 1793–1795, second son of Louis XVI and Marie Antoinette. Imprisoned with the royal family in 1792, he was recognized as king by the royalists after the execution of his father in 1793, although he remained in prison and died there at the age of 10.

PERCY BYSSHE SHELLEY
English poet
1792-1822

**Percy Bysshe Shelley,** age 8; English poet born in Sussex of a land-

# 1825–1850

Of the 40 million people who left Europe in the 19th century, a large majority went to the United States. Between 1820 and 1860 over five million immigrants arrived on its shores, mostly from Great Britain, Ireland and western Germany. Some remained on the Eastern seaboard, but others went West. The West was then Ohio, Indiana, Illinois and

owning family. An atheist, idealist and rebel, he wrote poetry to prop-
agate the political theories of his father-in-law, William Godwin. Shelley
also wrote revolutionary political pamphlets, but is remembered for his
romantic lyrics: "Music, when soft voices die"; "One word is too
often profaned"; et al. A friend of Byron and Leigh Hunt, he drowned
in a storm off the coast of Italy in 1822.

JOHN KEATS
English poet
1795-1821

**John Keats,** age 5; English poet born in London, son of a livery-stable
owner. Orphaned at 15, he was apprenticed to a surgeon–apothecary
and was licensed in 1816, but never practiced. In the next five years he
wrote some of the finest poems in the English language. He contracted
tuberculosis while nursing his brother, and in September 1820, sailed
for Rome, accompanied by Joseph Severn, the painter. He was dead
five months later, at the age of 25. The end came unexpectedly, one
hour before midnight, on the Spanish Steps.

Cesar Franck
   (1822-1890), age 3
Edmond de Goncourt
   (1822-1896), age 3
Ulysses S. Grant
   (1822-1885), age 3
Rutherford B. Hayes
   (1822-1893), age 3
Sir Henry Maine
   (1822-1888), age 3
Gregor Mendel
   (1822-1884), age 3
Frederick Law Olmstead
   (1822-1903), age 3
Louis Pasteur
   (1822-1895), age 3
Heinrich Schliemann
   (1822-1890), age 3
Max Muller
   (1823-1900), age 2
Francis Parkman
   (1823-1893), age 2
Ernest Renan
   (1823-1892), age 2
William Marcy Tweed
   (1823-1878), age 2
Alfred Russell Wallace
   (1823-1913), age 2
Anton Bruckner
   (1824-1896), age 1
Wilkie Collins
   (1824-1889), age 1
Alexandre Dumas (fils)
   (1824-1895), age 1
Stonewall Jackson
   (1824-1863), age 1
Bedrich Smetana
   (1824-1884), age 1

western Kentucky and Tennessee. They floated down the
Ohio River on flatboats or came through the Cumberland
Gap and followed the Wilderness Road. The frontier had
moved beyond the Mississippi; east of the river the worst
perils and hardships of pioneering were past. There were
settled communities everywhere and fairly large towns along
the rivers. By 1820 Kentucky, Tennessee, Ohio, Indiana,
Illinois, Mississippi, Alabama and Louisiana had become
states; in the next quarter century they were transformed
from the rough territories of the primitive frontier into settled,
peaceful and prosperous farmlands.

1850

# 1825

John Adams
(1735-1826), age 90
Charles Willson Peale
(1741-1827), age 84
Thomas Jefferson
(1743-1826), age 82
Chevalier de Lamarck
(1744-1829), age 81
John Jay
(1745-1829), age 80
Henry Mackenzie
(1745-1831), age 80
Alessandro Volta
(1745-1827), age 80
Francisco de Goya
(1746-1828), age 79
Jeremy Bentham
(1748-1832), age 77
Jacques Louis David
(1748-1825), age 77
Johann Wolfgang von Goethe
(1749-1832), age 76
Pierre de Laplace
(1749-1827), age 76
John Stevens
(1749-1838), age 76
Jouffroy d'Abbans
(1751-1832), age 74
James Madison
(1751-1836), age 74
Fanny Burney
(1752-1840), age 73
Philip Freneau
(1752-1832), age 73
George Crabbe
(1754-1832), age 71

It had happened with incredible speed. At the time of the first census in 1790, when the population was still clustered along the Atlantic coastal plain, the total count was 3,929,000 in an area of 869,000 square miles. The frontier then ran through western New York and Pennsylvania (in 1792 Pittsburgh had 130 families), down through eastern Kentucky and Tennessee and into the uplands of Georgia. By 1800, only 10 years later, the Ohio and Mississippi valleys had become the frontier, as thousands of new settlers came down the rivers. They cleared the land, built cabins and barns, planted crops and kept a sharp eye out for marauding Indians.

By 1820 the population, swelled by new immigrants, had reached 9,638,000, and the country's area was 1,749,000

**George Stephenson,** age 44; English inventor and railway builder born near Newcastle. From 1814 to 1822 he built locomotive for hauling coal from mines, and in 1825 he built the first passenger-carrying railway, the Stockton & Darlington line, opened to the public on Sept. 27, 1825. In 1829 he built his faster "Rocket" engine and supervised construction of the Liverpool & Birmingham Railway, opened in 1830. His son Robert supervised construction of the first railway into London, opened in 1838.

**John Caldwell Calhoun,** age 43; American statesman and orator born in South Carolina, foremost champion of the agrarian South and defender of the right of states to nullify federal laws. He served six years in the House of Representatives and 17 in the Senate, was secretary of war and of state and vice-president from 1825–1832. He is also remembered for his historic debates with Daniel Webster in 1833.

MARTIN VAN BUREN
American statesman and president
1782-1862

**Martin Van Buren,** age 43; American statesman born in Kinderhook, N.Y., son of a prosperous Dutch farmer; the eighth president, 1837–1841. He served in the state legislature, as attorney general and as governor and gained control of New York state politics. United States senator from 1821–1826, secretary of state from 1829–1831 and vice-president from 1833–1837, he was elected to succeed Jackson in

square miles. In 1860 the population was 31,443,000 in an area of 2,969,000 square miles, and in the region east of the Mississippi the last traces of raw frontier had vanished; dotted here and there among the rich farmlands were towns where the amenities of civilization were making an appearance. Gradually the settlers improved their farms and replaced their log houses with white weatherboarded houses, complete with green shutters and wide front porches, summer kitchens and smokehouses. Fat cattle grazed in the pastures, fruit ripened in the orchards and growing children romped in the yard. Others, more restless and adventurous, like Huck Finn, "lit out for the wilderness," for the Far West, to rediscover the frontier.

# 1850

1836, but was defeated for reelection in 1840 by William Henry Harrison. The principal event of his term was the Panic of 1837.

**Friedrich Wilhelm August Froebel,** age 43; German educator and founder of the kindergarten system. He made a study of preschool children, devised educational games and activities and, in 1837, in Blankenburg, Thuringia, established the first kindergarten. He encountered opposition, but the system spread and has been universally adopted.

**Niccolo Paganini,** age 43; Italian violinist and composer born in Genoa. A child prodigy, he made his debut at nine and in 1805 became musical director at the court of Napoleon's sister, Maria Anna Elisa, in Tuscany. From 1813 to 1834 he made several tours of Italy and the European capitals, displaying his virtuosity and capitalizing on his Mephistophelian appearance and reputation.

DANIEL WEBSTER
American statesman
1782-1852

**Daniel Webster,** age 43; American statesman born in New Hampshire, famous for his oratory. He served eight years in the House of Representatives and 20 in the Senate and was secretary of state from 1841–1843 and from 1850–1852. Leader of the new Whig party and spokesman for the preservation of the Union, he was one of the three men (with Clay and Calhoun) who dominated American politics in the 1830s and 1840s, overshadowing the presidents.

Ferdinand de Lesseps
(1805-1894), age 45
Benito Juarez
(1806-1872), age 44
John Stuart Mill
(1806-1873), age 44
Louis Agassiz
(1807-1873), age 43
Giuseppe Garibaldi
(1807-1882), age 43
Joseph Eggleston Johnston
(1807-1891), age 43
Robert E. Lee
(1807-1870), age 43
Henry Wadsworth
Longfellow
(1807-1882), age 43
John Greenleaf Whittier
(1807-1892), age 43
Honore Daumier
(1808-1879), age 42
Jefferson Davis
(1808-1889), age 42
Andrew Johnson
(1808-1875), age 42
Napoleon III
(1808-1873), age 42
David Strauss
(1808-1874), age 42
Kit Carson
(1809-1868), age 41
Charles Darwin
(1809-1882), age 41
Edward FitzGerald
(1809-1883), age 41
William E. Gladstone
(1809-1898), age 41

Pierre L'Enfant
(1754-1825), age 71
Talleyrand
(1754-1838), age 71
John Marshall
(1755-1835), age 70
Sarah Siddons
(1755-1831), age 70
Gilbert Stuart
(1755-1828), age 70
Aaron Burr
(1756-1836), age 69
William Godwin
(1756-1836), age 69
William Blake
(1757-1827), age 68
Charles X (France)
(1757-1836), age 68
Marquis de Lafayette
(1757-1834), age 68
James Monroe
(1758-1831), age 67
Noah Webster
(1758-1843), age 67
William Wilberforce
(1759-1833), age 66
Luigi Cherubini
(1760-1842), age 65
August von Gneisenau
(1760-1831), age 65
Katsushika Hokusai
(1760-1849), age 65
Comte de Saint-Simon
(1760-1825), age 65
Albert Gallatin
(1761-1849), age 64
John Jacob Astor
(1763-1848), age 62
Charles Bulfinch
(1763-1844), age 62
Jean Paul Richter
(1763-1825), age 62
James Smithson
(1765-1829), age 60
Eli Whitney
(1765-1825), age 60
John Dalton
(1766-1844), age 59
Thomas Malthus
(1766-1834), age 59

SIMON BOLIVAR
South American
revolutionary
1783-1830

**Simon Bolivar,** age 42; South American revolutionary leader born in Caracas, Venezuela, of a wealthy family and educated by private tutors. He liberated many countries from Spanish rule (1812–1824); but, disillusioned by his failure to establish republican forms of government, he declared he had spent his life "ploughing the seas."

WASHINGTON IRVING
American writer
1783-1859

**Washington Irving,** age 42; American writer born in New York City, son of a wealthy merchant. He represented the family business in England and held various diplomatic posts until 1846, when he retired to a country estate near Tarrytown, N.Y. The first American writer to win international fame, he is known for *The Sketch Book* (1820), containing "Rip Van Winkle" and "The Legend of Sleepy Hollow"; *Alhambra* (1832); and his *Life of Washington* (five volumes, 1855–1859).

**Stendhal** (Marie Henri Beyle), age 42; French novelist, army officer and consular agent, born in Grenoble. His reputation rests on two novels, *The Red and the Black* (1831) and *The Charterhouse of Parma* (1839), which are ranked among the world's greatest. He served in the Moscow campaign, held a minor diplomatic post in Italy (1831–1842) and died before his genius was recognized.

**Thomas Sully,** age 42; Anglo-American painter born in Lincolnshire,

England. He came to America as a boy in 1792, studied painting with his brother and became a leading portrait painter in Philadelphia. On his two trips to England he met Benjamin West and Sir Thomas Lawrence and painted young Queen Victoria. He also painted historical subjects, including the famous *Washington Crossing the Delaware* in the Museum of Fine Arts in Boston.

**Palmerston** (Henry John Temple, third Viscount Palmerston), age 41; British statesman born in Hampshire. As foreign secretary from 1830–1841 and from 1846–1851, he was deeply involved in European politics, enhancing British prestige at home and abroad. He was instrumental in the annexations of Hong Kong. As prime minister from 1855–1858 and from 1859–1865, he vigorously prosecuted the Crimean War and maintained British neutrality in the American Civil War.

ZACHARY TAYLOR
American general and
president
1784-1850

**Zachary Taylor** (Old Rough and Ready), age 41; American general born in Virginia; 12th president, 1849–1850. Entering the army at 24, he served many years on the frontier and, as commander in the Mexican War, defeated Santa Anna in the battle of Buena Vista in 1847. Elected president in 1848, he died of cholera after one year and four months in office.

JOHN JAMES AUDUBON
American naturalist and
artist
1785-1851

**John James Audubon,** age 40; American naturalist and artist born in Haiti, the illegitimate son of a French naval officer. After studying

Nikolai Gogol
(1809-1852), age 41
Oliver Wendell Holmes
(1809-1894), age 41
Fanny Kemble
(1809-1893), age 41
Abraham Lincoln
(1809-1865), age 41
Cyrus Hall McCormick
(1809-1884), age 41
Pierre Proudhon
(1809-1865), age 41
Alfred Tennyson
(1809-1892), age 41
P. T. Barnum
(1810-1891), age 40
Camillo di Cavour
(1810-1861), age 40
Margaret Fuller
(1810-1850), age 40
Elizabeth Gaskell
(1810-1865), age 40
Asa Gray
(1810-1888), age 40
Leo XIII (Pope)
(1810-1903), age 40
Alfred de Musset
(1810-1857), age 40
Theodore Parker
(1810-1860), age 40
Henry Rawlinson
(1810-1895), age 40
Robert Schumann
(1810-1856), age 40
George Caleb Bingham
(1811-1879), age 39
Theophile Gautier
(1811-1872), age 39
Horace Greeley
(1811-1872), age 39
Franz Liszt
(1811-1886), age 39
Harriet Beecher Stowe
(1811-1896), age 39
William Makepeace
Thackeray
(1811-1863), age 39
Robert Browning
(1812-1889), age 38
Charles Dickens
(1812-1870), age 38

# 1825

Sequoyah
(1766 or 1770-1843),
age 59
John Quincy Adams
(1767-1848), age 58
Benjamin Constant
(1767-1830), age 58
Maria Edgeworth
(1767-1849), age 58
Andrew Jackson
(1767-1845), age 58
August von Schlegel
(1767-1845), age 58
Vicomte de Chateaubriand
(1768-1848), age 57
Francis II (Emperor)
(1768-1835), age 57
Ivan Krylov
(1768-1844), age 57
Duncan Phyfe
(1768-1854), age 57
Friedrich Schleiermacher
(1768-1834), age 57
Samuel Slater
(1768-1835), age 57
De Witt Clinton
(1769-1828), age 56
Baron Cuvier
(1769-1832), age 56
Alexander von Humboldt
(1769-1859), age 56
Sir Thomas Lawrence
(1769-1830), age 56
Duke of Wellington
(1769-1852), age 56
Ludwig van Beethoven
(1770-1827), age 55
William Clark
(1770-1838), age 55
G. W. F. Hegel
(1770-1831), age 55
Friedrich Holderlin
(1770-1843), age 55
William Wordsworth
(1770-1850), age 55
E. I. du Pont de
Nemours
(1771-1834), age 54
Robert Owen
(1771-1858), age 54
Sir Walter Scott
(1771-1832), age 54

drawing with Jacques Louis David in France, he returned to America and began observing and painting birds in the Ohio and Mississippi River valleys. His 1,065 life-size drawings in full color were published in England as *Birds of America* (1827–1838) and made him famous. He retired to an estate in New York, which is now Audubon Park.

**Leigh Hunt,** age 41; English poet and essayist born in Middlesex, son of a clergyman. Known chiefly in his time as a rebel, reformer and editor of political journals, he was a friend of Byron and Shelley and author of the well-known *Abou Ben Adhem* ("may his tribe increase").

**Thomas De Quincey,** age 40; English writer born in Manchester, son of a merchant. He ran away from school several times and started to use opium at an early age. His best-known works, written in intricate, ornate prose, are *The Confessions of an English Opium-Eater* (1821) and an essay, *On Murder Considered as One of the Fine Arts* (1827).

**Jacob Grimm,** age 40; German philologist and collector of folklore. He made important contributions to comparative philology, but is better known as the compiler, with his brother Wilhelm, of the world-famous *Grimm's Fairy Tales,* published in German in two volumes (1812 and 1815). He was also a pioneer in comparative mythology.

**Alessandro Manzoni,** age 40; Italian novelist and poet born in Milan of an aristocratic family; author of the popular and highly praised historical novel *I Promessi Sposi (The Betrothed)* (1825–1826). He also wrote religious poetry after his conversion to Roman Catholicism. Verdi composed the *Requiem* in his honor.

**Thomas Love Peacock,** age 40; English novelist and poet born in Dorsetshire, son of a merchant. Employed most of his life by the East India Company, he is known for his comic novels (*Headlong Hall, Nightmare Abbey, Crochet Castle,* etc.) which satirized intellectual fashions of the day and caricatured the romantic poets. He was a close friend of Shelley and the father-in-law of George Meredith.

**Davy Crockett,** age 39; American frontiersman and Indian fighter born in Tennessee, famous for his marksmanship. After the war with the Creek Indians (1813–1814), he was elected twice to the Tennessee legislature and three times to the House of Representatives (1827–1831 and 1833–1835); where his backwoods humor made him popular in Washington society. Defeated for reelection in 1835, he went to Texas and died in the Battle of the Alamo in 1836.

**Sir John Franklin,** age 39; English naval officer and Arctic explorer, born in Lincolnshire. He entered the Royal Navy at 16 and fought at Trafalgar in 1805; he is remembered for his four expeditions to northern Canada, on the last of which he and his crew of 129 officers and men disappeared. His two icebound ships were found east of Victoria Island, with indications that the men had set off on foot.

**Wilhelm Grimm,** age 39; German philologist, brother of Jacob Grimm and collaborator on the famous collection of German folk tales. He also collaborated on a German dictionary.

**Winfield Scott,** age 39; American army officer born in Virginia. He fought in the War of 1812, the Creek and Seminole wars and the Mexican War. Landing at Veracruz, Mexico, he marched inland and occupied Mexico City in September 1847. He is also remembered for organizing the 600-mile forced march of the Cherokees to Oklahoma (1838–1839). As the Whig candidate for president in 1852, he was defeated by Franklin Pierce.

**Karl Maria von Weber,** age 39; German composer and opera conductor born near Lubeck, the son of Baron Anton von Weber. Called the founder of German romantic opera, he conducted operas in Breslau, Prague and Dresden (1804–1826) and wrote 10 extremely popular operas which combined German nationalism with folkloric themes. Of his instrumental music, *Invitation to the Dance,* for piano, is the best known.

**Francois Guizot,** age 38; French historian and statesman born in Nimes. A moderate royalist, he was professor of history at the University of Paris, a cabinet minister and premier in 1847–1848. He also wrote the lengthy *History of the Revolution in England* (six volumes, 1826–1856) and *History of Civilization in Europe* (six volumes, 1829–1832), which emphasized the role of the middle class in the growth of civil liberty.

**Robert Livingston Stevens,** age 38; American engineer and inventor born in Hoboken, N.J., son of the inventor John Stevens. He imported a locomotive from England, the *John Bull* (now in the Smithsonian Institution), and in 1831 began the first steam railway service in New Jersey. His invention of the T-rail and the rail spike opened the way for rapid railway expansion.

EMMA WILLARD
(Emma Hart)
American educator
1787-1870

**Emma Willard** (Emma Hart), age 38; American educator and pioneer in women's education, born in Connecticut. In 1821 she opened the Troy (N.Y.) Female Seminary, a controversial institution which offered collegiate subjects to women, for whom higher education had until then been considered unnecessary and undesirable, because likely to induce a false sense of superiority. She is the author of a volume of poems which includes "Rocked in the Cradle of the Deep."

ARTHUR SCHOPENHAUER
German philosopher
1788-1860

**Arthur Schopenhauer,** age 37; German philosopher born in Danzig

Friedrich von Flotow
(1812-1883), age 38
Ivan Goncharov
(1812-1891), age 38
Aleksandr Herzen
(1812-1870), age 38
Alfred Krupp
(1812-1887), age 38
Edward Lear
(1812-1888), age 38
Stephen A. Douglas
(1813-1861), age 37
John C. Fremont
(1813-1890), age 37
Friedrich Hebbel
(1813-1863), age 37
Soren Kierkegaard
(1813-1855), age 37
David Livingstone
(1813-1873), age 37
Giuseppe Verdi
(1813-1901), age 37
Jones Very
(1813-1880), age 37
Richard Wagner
(1813-1883), age 37
Mikhail Bakunin
(1814-1876), age 36
Joseph Hooker
(1814-1879), age 36
Jean Millet
(1814-1875), age 36
John Lothrop Motley
(1814-1877), age 36
Charles Reade
(1814-1884), age 36
Edwin Stanton
(1814-1869), age 36
Otto von Bismarck
(1815-1898), age 35
Cochise
(1815-1874), age 35
George Meade
(1815-1872), age 35
Elizabeth Cady Stanton
(1815-1902), age 35
Anthony Trollope
(1815-1882), age 35
Charlotte Bronte
(1816-1855), age 34
Comte de Gobineau
(1816-1882), age 34

Sydney Smith
(1771-1845), age 54
Richard Trevithick
(1771-1833), age 54
Samuel Taylor Coleridge
(1772-1834), age 53
Charles Fourier
(1772-1837), age 53
Friedrich von Schlegel
(1772-1829), age 53
Nathaniel Bowditch
(1773-1838), age 52
William Henry Harrison
(1773-1841), age 52
Louis Philippe (France)
(1773-1850), age 52
Metternich
(1773-1859), age 52
John Randolph
(1773-1833), age 52
Robert Southey
(1774-1843), age 51
Andre Ampere
(1775-1836), age 50
Charles Lamb
(1775-1834), age 50
Walter Savage Landor
(1775-1864), age 50
Friedrich von Schelling
(1775-1854), age 50
J. M. W. Turner
(1775-1851), age 50
John Constable
(1776-1837), age 49
Alexander I (Russia)
(1777-1825), age 48
Henry Clay
(1777-1852), age 48
Sir Humphrey Davy
(1778-1829), age 47
William Hazlitt
(1778-1830), age 47
Francis Scott Key
(1779-1843), age 46
Lord Melbourne
(1779-1848), age 46
Clement C. Moore
(1779-1863), age 46
Thomas Moore
(1779-1852), age 46
William Ellery Channing
(1780-1842), age 45

of a family of Dutch origin. His father, a wealthy merchant, drowned in a canal in Hamburg (possibly a suicide). His mother left for Weimar to establish a literary salon, leaving him free to study and travel on an income from the family business. In Dresden from 1814–1818, he wrote his major work, *The World as Will and Idea,* in which he identified the unknowable reality of Kant as a blind will to live, animating all nature. A misogynist and recluse, he lived in a boarding house in Frankfurt after 1833 with a dog as companion. Fame came slowly, but at 70 he was known throughout Europe and, shortly after his death, became the most widely read philosopher of the time.

**Sir Robert Peel,** age 37; British statesman born in Lancashire, son of a textile manufacturer. As home secretary (1822–1830) he reformed the criminal code and, in 1823, abolished the death penalty for many trivial crimes. In 1829 he reorganized the London police force, thereafter called "bobbies." As prime inister (1841–1846) he introduced an income tax and reduced the national debt. He died at 62 after a fall from his horse.

JAMES FENIMORE COOPER
American novelist
1789-1851

**James Fenimore Cooper,** age 36; American novelist born in New Jersey, son of a landowner who founded Cooperstown, N.Y. Expelled from Yale, he spent five years at sea, then married, settled on a country estate and began writing novels at 30. His stories of frontier life and the sea were immediately popular and included *The Spy, The Pathfinder, The Deerslayer* and *The Last of the Mohicans* (1826).

**Jared Sparks,** age 36; American historian born in Connecticut, known for his important collections of historical papers. He gave up the ministry at 34 and published *The Diplomatic Correspondence of the American Revolution* (12 volumes, 1829–1830), *The Writings of George Washington* (12 volumes, 1834–1837), *The Writings of Benjamin Franklin* (10 volumes, 1836–1840) and *The Library of American Biography* (25 volumes, 1834–1848). He was first a professor (1839–1849), then president of Harvard (1849–1853).

**Alphonse Marie Louis de Lamartine,** age 35; French romantic poet and statesman, of the minor nobility. He spent many years in the diplomatic service of Louis XVIII, Charles X and Louis Philippe and was briefly head of the provisional government after the 1848 revolution. Defeated in the presidential election by Louis Napoleon, he retired to private life. He is remembered for his highly successful *Poetic Meditations* (1820) and *New Poetic Meditations* (1823).

**Leopold I,** age 35; first king of Belgium (1831–1865) after its sepration from the Netherlands. A progressive monarch, he was the son of Francis Frederick; duke of Saxe-Coburg-Saalfield; son-in-law of Louis Philippe; and father of the unfortunate Carlotta, empress of Mexico. He is remembered for arranging the marriage of his niece Victoria to his nephew Albert.

**John Ross** (Kooweskoowe), age 35; American Indian chief of the Cherokees, born near Lookout Mountain, Tenn., son of a Scottish father and an Indian mother. As leader of the unsuccessful Cherokee resistance to dispossession of their lands, he accompanied 14,000 Indians on the 600-mile forced march ("the trail of tears") from Georgia to Oklahoma (1838–1839), during which thousands perished of hardship and starvation. From 1839 to 1866 he was chief of the United Cherokee Nation.

**John Tyler,** age 35; American statesman born in Virginia, son of a jurist; tenth president, 1841–1845. Elected vice-president in 1840, he succeeded to the presidency after the death of William Henry Harrison, serving all but the first month of the four-year term. He was never elected president. A states' rights champion, he sided with the South in 1861 and was elected to the Confederate Congress.

**James Buchanan,** age 34; American statesman and learned constitutional lawyer born in Pennsylvania; 15th president, 1857–1861. During his administration the country drifted toward war, and as a moderate he was attacked by both sides. In the last months of his term, after the election of Lincoln, the southern states seceded, but he held that he had been granted no constitutional power to use force against them.

**Peter Cooper,** age 34; American industrialist and philanthropist born in New York City; he built the first steam locomotive in America, the *Tom Thumb,* and financed the laying of the Atlantic cable in 1866. He founded Cooper's Union in New York City (1857–1859) to provide free higher education in science and art for working men.

**Michael Faraday,** age 34; English physicist and chemist born near London, son of a blacksmith. Beginning as laboratory assistant to Sir Humphrey Davy, he experimented with electricity and magnetism and discovered the principle of the electric motor and of mechanical refrigeration, though without realizing their practical value.

**Franz Grillparzer,** age 34; Austrian dramatist born in Vienna, considered by some his country's greatest playwright. His plays, which influenced Hauptmann and Maeterlinck and combined both classic and romantic elements, were until recently little known to the English speaking world. Among his best are three which together comprise a trilogy: *The Golden Fleece* (1822), *King Ottocar* (1825) and *A Dream Is Life* (1834). He was employed by the Austrian civil service from 1815–1856.

**Giacomo Meyerbeer** (Jakob Liebmann Beer), age 34; German operatic composer born in Berlin, son of a banker. He composed German operas and Italian operas, but achieved his greatest success with French grand opera. *Robert le Diable* (1831) and *Les Huguenots* (1836), with librettos by Scribe and spectacular staging, were highly successful and much imitated.

**Samual Finley Breese Morse,** age 34; American artist and inventor born in Massachusetts, son of a clergyman. He began telegraphic experiments at 40 after a successful career as a portrait painter in Boston, Charleston and New York. He devised the Morse code and built an experimental telegraph line from Washington to Baltimore on a government grant of $30,000; he sent the first message on May 24, 1844.

**Augustin Eugene Scribe,** age 34; French dramatist and librettist born in Paris, son of a silk merchant. Prolific and popular, he wrote or

# 1850

Paul von Reuter
(1816-1899), age 34
Charles Francois Daubigny
(1817-1878), age 33
Frederick Douglass
(c.1817-1895),
age c.33
Benjamin Jowett
(1817-1893), age 33
Sir Austen Layard
(1817-1894), age 33
Theodor Mommsen
(1817-1903), age 33
Henry David Thoreau
(1817-1862), age 33
Alexander II (Russia)
(1818-1881), age 32
Pierre Gustave de
Beauregard
(1818-1893), age 32
Jacob Burckhardt
(1818-1897), age 32
James Anthony Froude
(1818-1894), age 32
Charles Francois Gounod
(1818-1893), age 32
Charles Leconte de Lisle
(1818-1894), age 32
Karl Marx
(1818-1883), age 32
Lewis Henry Morgan
(1818-1881), age 32
Ivan Turgenev
(1818-1883), age 32
Prince Albert
(1819-1861), age 31
Gustave Courbet
(1819-1877), age 31
Edwin Laurentine Drake
(1819-1880), age 31
George Eliot
(1819-1880), age 31
Charles Kingsley
(1819-1875), age 31
James Russell Lowell
(1819-1891), age 31
Herman Melville
(1819-1891), age 31
Jacques Offenbach
(1819-1880), age 31
John Ruskin
(1819-1900), age 31

# 1825

Karl von Clausewitz
(1780-1831), age 45
Jean Ingres
(1780-1867), age 45

collaborated on more than 300 plays and 60 librettos. His light, well-constructed comedies and melodramas of middle-class life were flavored with fashionable liberal ideas. Some well-known examples are *A Glass of Water* (1840), *A Chain* (1842) and *Adrienne Lecouvreur* (1849).

**Victor Cousin,** age 33; French educator and philosopher born in Paris. He lectured at the Sorbonne and, as French minister of education, reorganized the primary school system, establishing the policy of philosophical freedom in the universities and introducing the study of the history of philosophy. An eclectic, he believed there is a little bit of truth in every school. He is the author of several histories of philosophy.

**Pius IX** (Pio Nono, Giovanni Maria Mastai-Ferretti), age 33; Italian ecclesiastic; pope from 1846–1878, the first "prisoner of the Vatican" (after the loss of the Papal States). In the longest pontificate of church history, he issued a denunciation *(Syllabus errorum)* of modern errors, including democracy and free speech; affirmed the dogma of the Immaculate Conception; and convened a Vatican Council in 1869 to support the claim of papal infallibility.

GIOACCHINO ANTONIO ROSSINI
Italian operatic composer
1792-1868

**Gioacchino Antonio Rossini,** age 33; Italian operatic composer born in Pesaro in the Papal States of a family of musicians. Between the ages of 18 and 37 he composed nearly 40 highly successful operas, including *The Barber of Seville*. During his long retirement of 39 years enjoyed the honors and rewards of his success. He was the acknowledged master of the *bel canto* style.

**Thaddeus Stevens,** age 33; American lawyer and legislator born in Vermont. A powerful member of the House of Representatives from Pennsylvania (1849–1853 and 1859–1868), he is remembered for his vindictiveness toward the South, his opposition to Lincoln's moderate plan of reconstruction and his insistence that the southern states be treated as conquered provinces and placed under military rule.

**Stephen Fuller Austin,** age 32; first American colonizer in Texas, born in Virginia; called the father of Texas. Carrying out the plan of his father, Moses Austin, to settle 300 Anglo-Saxon families in Texas with the consent of the Mexican governor, he established the first settlement in 1822. The capital was named for him, but he was defeated by Sam Houston in the election for president of Texas.

**Henry Rowe Schoolcraft,** age 32; American ethnologist and pioneer in Indian studies, born in New York, son of a manufacturer. As geologist on an expedition to the Great Lakes in 1820, he made topographical surveys of the region and in 1822 was appointed Indian agent at Sault Ste. Marie, where, with the assistance of his half-Ojibway wife, he began his studies of Indian life and culture. His *Historical and Statistical Information Respecting the Indians of the United States,* in six volumes, was published 1851–1857.

SAM HOUSTON
American soldier and
politician
1793-1863

**Sam Houston,** age 32; American soldier and politician born in Virginia. Before going to Texas in 1833 at the age of 40, he had served in the army, Congress and as governor of Tennessee. After his victory over Santa Anna in the Battle of San Jacinto in April 1836, he was elected first president of the Republic of Texas (1836–1838 and 1841–1844) and first United States senator from Texas (1846–1859).

WILLIAM CULLEN BRYANT
American poet and editor
1794-1878

**William Cullen Bryant,** age 31; American poet and editor born in Massachusetts. He won his reputation as a poet with a single volume of verse published in 1821, and was called the American Wordsworth for his poems of nature *(Thanatopsis* and *To a Waterfowl).* He was also editor and part owner of the New York *Evening Post,* 1829–1878. One famous phrase is, "The melancholy days are come."

**Matthew Calbraith Perry,** age 31; American naval officer born in Rhode Island, called the father of the steam navy for his advocacy of

Joseph Seligman
(1819-1880), age 31
Victoria (Great Britain)
(1819-1901), age 31
Walt Whitman
(1819-1892), age 31
Susan B. Anthony
(1820-1906), age 30
James B. Eads
(1820-1887), age 30
Friedrich Engels
(1820-1895), age 30
Jenny Lind
(1820-1887), age 30
Florence Nightingale
(1820-1910), age 30
William Tecumseh
Sherman
(1820-1891), age 30
Herbert Spencer
(1820-1903), age 30
Victor Emmanuel II (Italy)
(1820-1878), age 30
Clara Barton
(1821-1912), age 29
Charles Baudelaire
(1821-1867), age 29
Henry Thomas Buckle
(1821-1862), age 29
Richard Burton
(1821-1890), age 29
Feodor Dostoevsky
(1821-1881), age 29
Mary Baker Eddy
(1821-1910), age 29
Gustave Flaubert
(1821-1880), age 29
Hermann von Helmholtz
(1821-1894), age 29
Matthew Arnold
(1822-1888), age 28
Cesar Franck
(1822-1890), age 28
Edmond de Goncourt
(1822-1896), age 28
Ulysses S. Grant
(1822-1885), age 28
Rutherford B. Hayes
(1822-1893), age 28
Sir Henry Maine
(1822-1888), age 28

naval steamships. He commanded a squadron in the Mexican War and assisted General Winfield Scott in taking Veracruz in 1847, but is more famous for his expedition to Japan (1853–1854), which resulted in a commercial treaty and the beginning of Japanese contacts with the West.

CORNELIUS VANDERBILT
American steamship and
railroad magnate
1794-1877

**Cornelius Vanderbilt** (Commodore Vanderbilt), age 31; American steamship and railroad magnate, born on Staten Island, New York. In 1810 at the age of 16, he started a freight and passenger ferry between Staten Island and Manhattan. Steamships on the Hudson River and from New York to Boston, Providence, California and Le Havre followed. He sold his steamships in 1862 and invested in railroad stocks; by 1867 he controlled the New York Central Railway. His fortune was estimated at $100 million.

**James Gordon Bennett,** age 30; American newspaper editor and publisher born in Scotland. He emigrated to Nova Scotia in 1819 and worked on New York newspapers from 1826–1832. In May 1835 he started the New York *Herald,* a four-page daily paper, on capital of $500, remaining as editor until 1867. He introduced many features of modern journalism: illustrated news stories, brief editorials criticizing all parties, financial news and sensational news.

THOMAS CARLYLE
British essayist and historian
1795-1881

**Thomas Carlyle,** age 30; British essayist and historian born in Scotland, son of a stone cutter. He won fame as a historian *(The French Revolution,* 1837) and as a popular lecturer *(Heroes and Hero-Worship* and *Past and Present)* and labored 15 years on his biography of Frederick the Great. An enemy of 19th-century materialism and mass industrial democracy, he was the Sage of Chelsea, admired by Emerson, John Stuart Mill, Ruskin and Dickens, who dedicated *Hard Times* to him.

JAMES KNOX POLK
American statesman and
president
1795-1849

**James Knox Polk,** age 30; American statesman born in North Carolina of a prominent family; 11th president, 1845–1849. A longtime Jacksonian congressman and speaker of the House, he emerged as a dark horse in the Democratic convention of 1844 and narrowly defeated Henry Clay in the presidential election. The Mexican War was fought during his administration, and Texas and California were acquired. A hard-working president, he died a few months after leaving office.

**Leopold von Ranke,** age 30; German historian born in Thuringia, professor of history at the University of Berlin from 1825–1871. Called the founder of the modern objective school of history, he influenced generations of historians by insisting on the importance of original source material. His works fill 54 volumes.

ANTONIO LOPEZ
DE SANTA ANNA
Mexican general and
politician
1794/95-1876

**Antonio Lopez de Santa Anna,** age c. 30; Mexican general and

Gregor Mendel
(1822-1884), age 28
Frederick Law Olmstead
(1822-1903), age 28
Louis Pasteur
(1822-1895), age 28
Heinrich Schliemann
(1822-1890), age 28
Max Muller
(1823-1900), age 27
Francis Parkman
(1823-1893), age 27
Ernest Renan
(1823-1892), age 27
William Marcy Tweed
(1823-1878), age 27
Alfred Russell Wallace
(1823-1913), age 27
Anton Bruckner
(1824-1896), age 26
Wilkie Collins
(1824-1889), age 26
Alexandre Dumas (fils)
(1824-1895), age 26
Stonewall Jackson
(1824-1863), age 26
Bedrich Smetana
(1824-1884), age 26
Thomas Henry Huxley
(1825-1895), age 25
Stephanus Paulus Kruger
(1825-1904), age 25
Ferdinand Lassalle
(1825-1864), age 25
Johann Strauss Jr.
(1825-1899), age 25
Walter Bagehot
(1826-1877), age 24
Stephen Foster
(1826-1864), age 24
George B. McClellan
(1826-1885), age 24
Joseph Lister
(1827-1912), age 23
Lew Wallace
(1827-1905), age 23
Meyer Guggenheim
(1828-1905), age 22
Henrik Ibsen
(1828-1906), age 22
George Meredith
(1828-1909), age 22

politician born in Jalapa; commander in the siege of the Alamo. An opportunist who changed sides frequently, he helped Iturbide gain independence for Mexico in 1821, was president many times and dictator from 1853–1855. Forced into exile after the capture of Mexico City in 1847 and again in 1855, he lived in Cuba, Venezuela and the United States; he returned to Mexico in 1874, in his old age, and died in poverty.

**Dred Scott,** age 30?; American Negro born in Virginia, central figure in the Dred Scott case (1856–1857). The servant of an army surgeon, he was taken to Illinois, a free state, and to Wisconsin Territory, remaining four years before returning to a slave state. His suit, arguing that his residence in a state where slavery was illegal had made him free, was denied by the United States Supreme Court.

**Augustin Thierry,** age 30; French historian whose vivid style and narrative skill made history popular in the early 19th century. His fame rests on two books, *History of the Conquest of England by the Normans* (three volumes, 1825) and *Narratives of the Merovingian Era* (two volumes, 1840). He regarded the subjugation of the Gallo-Romans by the invading Franks as the primary fact of French history.

**James Bowie,** age 29?; American pioneer and soldier born in Kentucky or Georgia; the inventor of the Bowie knife. He went to Texas in 1828, became a naturalized Mexican citizen and was a leader in the Texas revolt. As a colonel in the Texas army, he died heroically in the siege of the Alamo, with Crockett, Travis and others, in 1836.

**Thomas Bulfinch,** age 29; American writer born in Massachusetts; son of Charles Bulfinch, the architect. He graduated from Harvard and worked 30 years as a bank clerk in Boston. He is the author of *The Age of Chivalry* (1858); *Legends of Charlemagne* (1863); and *The Age of Fable* (1855), which is still popular and has attained almost the status of a classic.

HORACE MANN
American educator
1796-1859

**Horace Mann,** age 29; American educator born in Massachusetts. As the first secretary of the Massachusetts Board of Education (1837–1848), he introduced ideas and practices which inaugurated the modern era of American public education. The first training school for teachers was established in 1839 through his efforts.

**George Catlin,** age 29; American artist and writer born in Pennsylvania, known for his Indian paintings. He left St. Louis in 1832 and traveled over 5,000 miles by canoe and horseback to make a record for posterity of Indians and their way of life. He exhibited 500 paintings in New York in 1837. Many of his paintings and sketches are in the Catlin Gallery of the National Museum in Washington and in New York's American Museum of Natural History. He is the author of *My Life among the Indians*.

**Jean Baptiste Camille Corot,** age 29; French painter born in Paris, son of a cloth merchant of humble origin; grandson, through his mother, of a rich wine merchant. His early classic style gave way to poeticized, romantic landscapes, which brought enduring success. Famous works include *The Dance of the Nymphs, Recollection of Mortefontaine* and *The Woman in Blue,* all in the Louvre.

**William Hickling Prescott,** age 29; American historian born in Massachusetts, grandson of a revolutionary war officer. Nearly blind after an accident in college, he nevertheless spent his life in historical research. *The History of the Conquest of Mexico* (three volumes, 1843) and *The History of the Conquest of Peru* (two volumes, 1847) are his masterpieces. He also wrote historics of Ferdinand and Isabella and Philip II.

**Gaetano Donizetti,** age 28; Italian operatic composer in the *bel canto* style of Rossini. Of his more than 60 operas and operettas, the best known are *Lucia di Lammermoor* (based on Scott's novel) and the comic opera *Don Pasquale.* He also composed *Anna Bolena,* based on the life story of Henry VIII's second wife.

HEINRICH HEINE
German poet
1797-1856

**Heinrich Heine,** age 28; German lyric poet and prose writer of Jewish parentage born in Duesseldorf. A champion of political liberalism, he lived in Paris after 1831 and is remembered for his bittersweet love songs and ballads, published in 1827 as *Buch de Lieder;* many of them were set to music by Schubert, Schumann, Mendelssohn and Brahms. After 1848 he was confined to bed by an incurable spinal disease, but continued to write, cared for by his wife.

**Ando Hiroshige,** age 28; Japanese landscape painter and printmaker born in Yedo (Tokyo). A popular painter known for the atmospheric effects (rain, mist, moonlight) in his landscapes, he influenced the French impressionists and the American painter James McNeill Whistler. His work is displayed in the Netropolitan Museum of Art in New York and the Museum of Fine Arts in Boston.

**Sir Charles Lyell,** age 28; British geologist born in Scotland. One of the founders of modern geology, he was the first to apply the terms *Eocene, Miocene* and *Pliocene* to the epochs of the Tertiary period. He

Dante Gabriel Rossetti
(1828-1882), age 22
Hippolyte A. Taine
(1828-1893), age 22
Leo Tolstoy
(1828-1910), age 22
Jules Verne
(1828-1905), age 22
Geronimo
(1829-1909), age 21
Anton Rubinstein
(1829-1894), age 21
Chester Alan Arthur
(1830-1886), age 20
Porfirio Diaz
(1830-1915), age 20
Emily Dickinson
(1830-1886), age 20
Francis Joseph I (Austria)
(1830-1916), age 20
Jules de Goncourt
(1830-1870), age 20
Camille Pissarro
(1830-1903), age 20
Christina Rossetti
(1830-1894), age 20
James A. Garfield
(1831-1881), age 19
James Clerk Maxwell
(1831-1879), age 19
Victorien Sardou
(1831-1908), age 19
Philip Sheridan
(1831-1888), age 19
Louisa May Alcott
(1832-1888), age 18
Bjornstjerne Bjornson
(1832-1910), age 18
Lewis Carroll
(1832-1898), age 18
Gustave Dore
(1832/33-1883),
age c.18
Edouard Manet
(1832-1883), age 18
Maximilian (Mexico)
(1832-1867), age 18
Nikolaus Otto
(1832-1891), age 18
Leslie Stephen
(1832-1904), age 18

wrote *The Antiquity of Man Proved by Geology* (1863) and was a friend of Charles Darwin's. He was knighted in 1848.

FRANZ SCHUBERT
Austrian composer
1797-1828

**Franz Schubert,** age 28; Austrian composer born in Vienna, son of a schoolmaster. At the age of 18 he had written an opera, three symphonies and nearly 200 songs. Altogether he wrote 600 songs and set to music the romantic lyrics of Goethe, Schiller and Heine. He is also popularly known for the *Unfinished Symphony* (in B minor). He died of typhoid fever at 31.

**Mary Wollstonecraft Shelley,** age 28; English novelist, daughter of William Godwin and second wife of Shelley (after the suicide of his first wife). She is best known for the famous novel *Frankenstein* (1818), but also wrote *The Last Man* (1826), about an epidemic that destroys the human race, and the semi-autobiographical *Lodore* (1835). She outlived Shelley by 29 years.

**Louis Adolphe Thiers,** age 28; French statesman and historian born in the south of France. In 1821 he joined the liberal opposition to Charles X, held cabinet posts under Louis Philippe, was premier in 1836 and 1840 and, after the war with Prussia, was elected the first president of the Third Republic (1871–1873). He is the author of two monumental works: *History of the French Revolution* (10 volumes, 1823–1827) and *History of the Consulate and the Empire* (20 volumes, 1845–1862).

**Alfred Victor, comte de Vigny,** age 28; French poet, dramatist and novelist; of an aristocratic family. An army officer until the age of 30, he became one of the leaders of the romantic movement and the friend of Victor Hugo. The recurring theme of his *Poems Ancient and Modern* (1826) and the novel *Cinq-Mars* is the plight of the individual in a hostile world.

**William I** (Wilhelm Friedrich Ludwig), age 28; king of Prussia from 1861–1888 and emperor of Germany from 1871–1888. He appointed Otto von Bismarck minister of foreign affairs in 1862, took personal command of the troops in the Franco-Prussian War and was crowned emperor in the palace of Versailles in 1871. He declared he ruled by the favor of God.

**Auguste Comte,** age 27; French philosopher and sociologist, secretary and disciple of Saint-Simon. Called the founder of positivism, which he identified as the third stage of human thought, following the theological and metaphysical stages, he attempted to construct a religion of humanity as the basis of a scientific reorganization of society. He was insane when he died of cancer at 59.

**Eugene Delacroix,** age 27; French painter born near Paris, a leader of the romantic revolt against the classicism of David. He is known for his brilliant coloring and exotic, melodramatic scenes of history and legend. Two paintings are the *Death of Sardanapalus* and the famous *Liberty on the Barricades,* in the Louvre.

**Count Giacomo Leopardi,** age 27; Italian poet and scholar of noble birth. A classicist in a romantic age, he wrote of despair and disillusionment, but his clarity and perfection of form made him the leading modern Italian lyric poet. Chronically ill from childhood and disappointed in love, he died of cholera at 39.

**Adam Mickiewicz,** age 27; Polish poet and dramatist of the romantic school; Poland's greatest poet, and an ardent champion of Polish independence. His works include the drama *The Forefathers* (1825) and *Pan Tadeusz* (1834), his masterpiece, an epic poem on the life of the Polish gentry. He died of cholera in Constantinople.

**Jules Michelet,** age 27; French historian born in Paris of poor parents. He was professor of history at the College de France (1838–1851) and author of the 17-volume *History of France* (1833–1867) and the *History of the French Revolution* (1847–1853), considered masterpieces of French literature in spite of their emotionalism and strong bias against the nobility and clergy.

**Amos Bronson Alcott,** age 26; American teacher and writer born in Connecticut. A transcendentalist and friend of Emerson and Thoreau, with ideas too advanced and liberal for the age, he contributed to the *Dial* and undertook many well-intentioned enterprises, but lived most of his life in poverty. He was the father of Louisa May Alcott.

**Jacques Francois Fromental Elie Halevy,** age 26; French operatic composer born in Paris. He studied under Cherubini and became professor at the Paris Conservatory, where Gounod and Bizet were among his pupils. He wrote over 30 popular operas, but his reputation as a major composer rests on one, *Juive (The Jewess,* 1835). He was the father-in-law of Bizet.

**Thomas Hood,** age 26; English poet and humorist born in London, son of a Scottish bookseller. He edited various popular magazines and wrote humorous verse, but is remembered for his serious poetry: *The Song of the Shirt, The Bridge of Sighs, The Plea of the Midsummer Fairies,* etc. He was a friend of William Hazlitt and Charles Lamb. These familiar lines are his: "I remember, I remember/ The house where I was born."

HONORE DE BALZAC
French novelist
1799-1850

**Honore de Balzac,** age 26; French novelist born in Tours of a middle-

Edward Tylor
(1832-1917), age 18
Edwin Booth
(1833-1893), age 17
Aleksandr Borodin
(1833/34-1887), age c.17
Johannes Brahms
(1833-1897), age 17
Charles Gordon
(1833-1885), age 17
Benjamin Harrison
(1833-1901), age 17
Alfred Nobel
(1833-1896), age 17
Jeb Stuart
(1833-1864), age 17
Lord Acton
(1834-1902), age 16
Gottlieb Daimler
(1834-1900), age 16
Edgar Degas
(1834-1917), age 16
Ernst Haeckel
(1834-1919), age 16
William Morris
(1834-1896), age 16
Sitting Bull
(1831 or 1834-1890),
age 16?
James Thomson
(1834-1882), age 16
James McNeill Whistler
(1834-1903), age 16
Samuel Butler
(1835-1902), age 15
Giosue Carducci
(1835-1907), age 15
Andrew Carnegie
(1835-1919), age 15
Leopold II ( Belgium)
(1835-1909), age 15
Camille Saint-Saens
(1835-1921), age 15
Mark Twain
(1835-1910), age 15
Tz'u Hsi
(1834/35-1908),
age c.15
Joseph Chamberlain
(1836-1914), age 14
W. S. Gilbert
(1836-1911), age 14

class family. After eight or nine years in a Parisian attic, producing melodramatic novels and plays under various pseudonyms, he wrote his first serious novel at 30 and followed it with 100 or more novels and stories collectively titled *The Human Comedy*. His boundless energy and realistic portrayal of French society won him a place among the world's great novelists. In debt all his life, he remained unmarried until five months before his death of apoplexy at 50. He also wrote *Droll Stories,* in a Rabelaisian vein.

ALEXANDER PUSHKIN
Russian poet
1799-1837

**Alexander Pushkin,** age 26; Russian poet born in Moscow, one of whose ancestors was reputedly a black Abyssinian prince. He is chiefly known for his unique novel in verse, *Eugene Onegin,* and for the *Queen of Spades* and other short stories. Called Russia's greatest poet, he was mortally wounded at 37 in a duel supposedly caused by the alleged infidelity of his beautiful wife.

**George Bancroft,** age 25; American historian and public official born in Massachusetts. As secretary of the navy for James K. Polk (1845–1846), he established the United States Naval Academy at Annapolis. His *History of the United States* (10 volumes, 1834–1874) won the qualified praise of Leopold von Ranke, who called it the best history ever written from the democratic point of view. He also wrote *History of the Formation of the Constitution of the United States* (two volumes, 1882).

**John Brown,** age 25; American businessman (with a record of several business failures) who achieved national prominence as a fervid abolitionist. He planned to establish a stronghold in the mountains of Virginia as a refuge for slaves; to this end, in October 1859 he seized the town of Harper's Ferry, Va. (now in West Virginia) and the government arsenal, expecting this to trigger a general insurrection. It did not. After being convicted of treason and hanged, he was made a martyr by Northern abolitionists.

**Millard Fillmore,** age 25; American statesman born in New York; 13th president, 1850–1853, succeeding to the presidency on the death of Zachary Taylor. He favored compromise on the slavery issue and was defeated by Franklin Pierce in the election of 1852. In 1856 he ran unsuccessfully as the candidate of the National American (Know Nothing) Party.

**William Holmes McGuffy,** age 25; American educator born in Pennsylvania; professor of moral philosophy at the University of Virginia

(1845–1873) and author of the famous *McGuffy Eclectic Readers,* used in American schools for two generations. Published from 1837 to 1857 with total sales estimated at 122 million, they were as much concerned with teaching morality as reading and are believed to have played an important part in the formation of American character.

THOMAS BABINGTON
MACAULAY
English historian and
essayist
1800-1859

**Thomas Babington Macaulay,** age 25; first Baron Macaulay, English historian and essayist; member of Parliament and of the Supreme Council of India, where he undertook to reform the criminal code and the educational system. He is known for his essays, his five-volume history of the reigns of James II and William III and his popular ballads *Lays of Ancient Rome.* He was created a baron in 1857 by Queen Victoria.

**Helmuth Karl Bernhard, Graf von Moltke,** age 25; Prussian field marshal and military genius. As Prussian chief of staff (1858–1888) he planned the strategy in the wars with Denmark (1864), Austria (1866) and France (1870–1871). He was the uncle of General von Moltke of World War I.

**James Clark Ross,** age 25; British polar explorer born in London. He entered the navy at 12 and at 18 accompanied his uncle, Capt. John Ross, on an expedition to the Arctic. On his own expedition to the Antarctic (1839–1843) he discovered Victoria Land, the Ross Sea and Ross Island. He is the author of *Voyages of Discovery* (1847).

**David Glasgow Farragut,** age 24; American naval officer born in Tennessee and adopted at seven by a naval commander who entered him in the navy at nine as a midshipman. As a commander in the Union navy in the Civil War, he was assigned blockade duty in the Gulf of Mexico; he captured New Orleans in 1862, gained control of the Mississippi River to Vicksburg and captured Mobile in 1864. He is famous for his fighting words, "Damn the torpedoes."

**Brigham Young,** age 24; American religious leader born in Vermont. A house-and-barn painter by trade, he became head of the Mormon Church after Joseph Smith was shot by a mob in 1844; he led the migration to Utah in 1846–1847. He was indicted for polygamy in 1871, but was not convicted.

**Paul Emile Botta,** age 23; French archaeologist born in Turin, Italy, the son of an Italian physician who became a French citizen. As French consular agent in Mosul, he directed excavations at the village of Khorsabad, discovering the remains of Dar Sharrukin, the ancient Assyrian capital of Sargon II, and recovering statues of Sargon, winged

# 1850

T. H. Green
(1836-1882), age 14
Bret Harte
(1836-1902), age 14
Winslow Homer
(1836-1910), age 14
John Burroughs
(1837-1921), age 13
Grover Cleveland
(1837-1908), age 13
George Dewey
(1837-1917), age 13
John Richard Green
(1837-1883), age 13
James Hickok
(1837-1876), age 13
Hitotsubashi
(1837-1902), age 13
William Dean Howells
(1837-1920), age 13
John Pierpont Morgan
(1837-1913), age 13
Algernon Swinburne
(1837-1909), age 13
Henry Adams
(1838-1918), age 12
Georges Bizet
(1838-1875), age 12
James Bryce
(1838-1922), age 12
Sir Henry Irving
(1838-1905), age 12
William Lecky
(1838-1903), age 12
Ernst Mach
(1838-1916), age 12
John Muir
(1838-1914), age 12
George Otto Trevelyan
(1838-1928), age 12
Paul Cezanne
(1839-1906), age 11
George Custer
(1839-1876), age 11
Willard Gibbs
(1839-1903), age 11
Machado de Assis
(1839-1908), age 11
Modest Mussorgsky
(1839-1881), age 11
Walter Pater
(1839-1894), age 11

bulls and the first cuneiform inscriptions seen by Europeans.

JOHN HENRY NEWMAN
English theologian
1801-1890

**John Henry Newman,** age 24; English theologian born in London, son of a banker. He attained eminence in the Church of England and at the age of 45 was converted to Roman Catholicism. Relegated to obscurity until the death of Pius IX, at the age of 78 he was made a cardinal by Pope Leo XIII. In reply to Charles Kingsley's attacks on Catholicism, he wrote *Apologia pro vita sua,* which was immediately recognized as a classic piece of English prose. He also wrote hymns, including *Lead, Kindly Light.*

**Alexandre Dumas** (Dumas *pere),* age 23; French novelist, son of a mulatto general in Napoleon's army. His grandparents were a French count and a black native (Maria Dumas) of Saint Domingue (Haiti). Author of the celebrated adventure novels *The Three Musketeers* and *The Count of Monte Cristo,* he employed many assistants, produced over 1,000 volumes of fiction and lived in splendor on his estate of Monte Cristo near Paris.

**Victor Marie Hugo,** age 23; French poet, dramatist and novelist, son of a Napoleonic general. His most famous novels are *The Hunchback of Notre Dame* (1831), *Les Miserables* (1862) and *Toilers of the Sea* (1866); two of his plays, *Hernani* and *The King Amuses Himself,* are better known as operas by Verdi: *Ernani* and *Rigoletto.* He lived in voluntary exile on the island of Guernsey during the reign of Napoleon III.

**Louis Kossuth,** age 23; Hungarian revolutionary and leader in the cause of national independence. Through his oratory and his political journal, he won popular support and emerged as a leader in the revolution of 1848 and president of the Hungarian republic, 1848–1849. Forced into exile by the reactionary movement, he lived abroad—in Turkey, the United States (1851–1852), England and Italy.

**Sir Edwin Landseer,** age 23; English painter born in London, son of an engraver. He won wide popularity as a painter of animals, especially thoroughbred dogs, and was commissioned to construct the four huge lions at the foot of Nelson's Column in Trafalgar Square. He was also a fashionable portrait painter, whose subjects included Queen Victoria, Prince Albert and Sir Walter Scott. He was knighted in 1850.

**Harriet Martineau,** age 23; English writer born in Norwich; sister of James Martineau, the Unitarian minister. Deaf from childhood, she won a reputation as an economist with *Illustrations of Political Economy* (1832) and *Poor Laws and Paupers* (1833) and as a social critic with her unflattering *Society in America,* written in 1837 after a visit to the United States. She was a friend of George Eliot and Thomas Carlyle.

**(Louis) Hector Berlioz,** age 22; French composer born near Lyons, son of a country doctor. He gave up his medical studies for music and, after some early disappointments, became a leader of the French romantic movement. He is noted for his dramatic compositions—*Damnation of Faust, Roman Carnival* and the symphony *Romeo and Juliet*—and for the *Requiem Mass.* He toured Europe as a conductor and wrote music criticism.

**George Henry Borrow,** age 22; English writer and linguist, remembered for his books on the gypsies. At 16 he had mastered seven languages, and in the course of his wandering life he learned more than 30 languages and dialects, including Romany. His most popular books were *The Zincali, or the Gypsies in Spain* (1841), *The Bible in Spain* (1843), *Lavengro* (1851) and *Romany Rye* (1857).

**Edward George Earle Lytton Bulwer-Lytton,** age 22; first Baron Lytton, English novelist and politician, of an aristocratic family, son of a general. He wrote a number of novels and successful plays and was a member of Parliament, but is remembered for two novels, the popular and carefully researched historical novel *The Last Days of Pompeii* (1834) and *Reinzi* (1835), on which Wagner based his opera.

**Ralph Waldo Emerson,** age 22; American poet, essayist and lecturer, born in Boston, son of a Unitarian clergyman. He gave up the ministry after three years and embarked on a career as public lecturer, traveling throughout New England, the Atlantic states and the Middle West. In his lectures, which were rewritten and published as essays, he expounded his philosophy of transcendental idealism and individual freedom. The most famous essays are on *Nature, Friendship* and *Self-Reliance.*

**Albert Sidney Johnston,** age 22; American army officer born in Kentucky. He graduated from West Point in 1826 and fought in the Black Hawk War, the Texas war for independence and the Mexican War and was secretary of war for Texas. He joined the Confederate army in 1861 as general in charge of western operations and defeated Gen. Grant in a surprise attack at Shiloh on April 1862, but was killed in action. He was considered one of the South's best generals.

**Justus, Baron von Liebig,** age 22; German chemist born in Darmstadt, who, as professor of chemistry at Giessen (1824–1852) and the University of Munich (1852–1873), trained many of the century's leading scientists. He originated the categorization of foods into fats, carbohydrates and proteins and proved that body heat is the result of the combustion of fats and carbohydrates and that the transformation of inorganic into organic matter occurs only in plants. He is called the father of agricultural chemistry.

**Prosper Merimee,** age 22; French novelist and historian born in Paris. As inspector general of historical monuments and a close friend of Napoleon III and the empress Eugenie, he was an influential figure of his time. He is remembered for his short romantic novels: *The Venus of Ille, Colomba* and *Carmen*—the source of Bizet's opera.

**Ludwig Andreas Feuerbach,** age 21; German philosopher, son of a prominent jurist. Beginning as a Hegelian idealist, he turned to naturalistic materialism and in his most famous book, *The Essence of Christianity* (1841), adopted a psychological approach to religion. Identifying religious feeling with psychological needs, he saw the essence of Christianity as a glorification of man.

**Mikhail Ivanovich Glinka,** age 21; Russian composer born in Smolensk; the first of the nationalist composers, taking his themes from Russian

# 1850

Charles Sanders Peirce
(1839-1914), age 11

John D. Rockefeller
(1839-1937), age 11

Alfred Sisley
(1839-1899), age 11

Carlotta
(1840-1927), age 10

Alphonse Daudet
(1840-1897), age 10

Thomas Hardy
(1840-1928), age 10

Claude Monet
(1840-1926), age 10

Thomas Nast
(1840-1902), age 10

Auguste Rodin
(1840-1917), age 10

William Graham Sumner
(1840-1910), age 10

John Addington Symonds
(1840-1893), age 10

Peter Ilich Tchaikovsky
(1840-1893), age 10

Giovanni Verga
(1840-1922), age 10

Emile Zola
(1840-1902), age 10

James Gordon Bennett
(1841-1918), age 9

Georges Clemenceau
(1841-1929), age 9

Anton Dvorak
(1841-1904), age 9

Edward VII (Great Britain)
(1841-1910), age 9

Oliver Wendell Holmes
(1841-1935), age 9

Hirobumi Ito
(1841-1909), age 9

Pierre Auguste Renoir
(1841-1919), age 9

Henry Stanley
(1841-1904), age 9

Ambrose Bierce
(1842-1914?), age 8

Georg Brandes
(1842-1927), age 8

William James
(1842-1910), age 8

Peter Kropotkin
(1842-1921), age 8

folk tales and songs. Two famous operas are *A Life for the Czar* and *Russlan and Ludmilla*. He also wrote chamber music, songs and a Spanish overture, *Night in Madrid*.

**BENJAMIN DISRAELI**
British statesman and
novelist
1804-1881

**Benjamin Disraeli,** age 21; first earl of Beaconsfield, British statesman and novelist born in London, son of a writer of Spanish-Jewish descent. A member of Parliament from 1837–1880 and conservative prime minister in 1868 and from 1874–1880, he pursued an aggressive imperialist policy. He annexed the Fiji Islands and the Transvaal, waged war with the Afghans and Zulus and had Queen Victoria crowned empress of India in 1876. He is the author of *Conigsby* (1844), *Sybil* (1845) and many other novels.

**NATHANIEL HAWTHORNE**
American novelist and
story writer
1804-1864

**Nathaniel Hawthorne,** age 21; American novelist and story writer born in Salem, Mass. He published his first successful novel, *The Scarlet Letter,* at 46. His earlier stories were collected in *Twice-Told Tales* and *Mosses from an Old Manse.* His major works were weighted with allegory and symbolism and concerned with sin, guilt and pride. *Tanglewood Tales for Girls and Boys,* a retelling of classical legends, was his most popular book.

**Franklin Pierce,** age 21; American statesman born in New Hampshire, son of the governor; 14th president, from 1853–1857. A congressman, senator and brigadier general in the Mexican War, he was put forward as a compromise candidate in the Democratic Convention of 1852 and defeated Gen. Winfield Scott, his commanding officer. He tried to cool the heated slavery issue without much success, and had few friends left at the end of his term.

**Charles Augustin Sainte-Beuve,** age 21; French literary critic, a sympathetic spokesman for the romantic movement and a precursor of modern criticism with his detailed, scholarly analyses. He won fame with his weekly newspaper essays, *Monday Chats,* a featured column for 20 years. He is also famous for his love affair with Victor Hugo's wife.

**George Sand** (Amandine Aurore Lucie Dupin Dudevant), age 21; French novelist born in Paris, daughter of an army officer descended from Polish royalty. An early feminist, socialist, humanitarian and apostle of free love, she was more famous for her lovers (including Chopin) and friends (Liszt, Bizet, Delacroix) than for her novels.

**Johann Strauss,** age 21; Austrian composer and conductor born in Vienna. He toured Europe with his orchestra (1825–1837), popularizing the waltz. He composed 150 waltzes, 14 polkas, 35 quadrilles and 19 marches. His best-known waltzes are *Lorelei* and *Sounds of the Rhine.*

**Eugene Sue,** age 21; French novelist born in Paris. A surgeon in the French navy for six years, he inherited a fortune at 25 and embarked on a writing career. After a false start with upper-class novels, he switched to melodramatic stories of Parisian slum life and won immediate popularity. His best-known novels are *The Mysteries of Paris* (1842–1843) and *The Wandering Jew* (1844–1845); the latter was translated into many languages and made into an opera by Jacques Halevy.

**Hans Christian Andersen,** age 20; Danish author born in Odense, son of a shoemaker. He ran away to Copenhagen at 14 (three years after his father's death) and joined the Royal Theater as an apprentice actor and singer. He wrote plays, novels and travel books from an early age, but won worldwide fame with his fairy tales, published in several volumes from 1835 to 1877. Of his more than 150 stories, the most widely known are *The Ugly Duckling, The Red Shoes* and *The Emperor's New Clothes.*

**William Lloyd Garrison,** age 20; American social reformer born in Massachusetts; editor and publisher (1831–1865) of the *Liberator,* the foremost American antislavery journal. He is remembered principally for his uncompromising campaign against slavery, but he was also opposed to prostitution and injustice to the Indians and supported women's suffrage and prohibition.

**Giuseppe Mazzini,** age 20; Italian revolutionary, organizer of the secret society *Young Italy,* whose aim was the unification of Italy under a republican government. Forced into exile, he continued propagandizing from London and Switzerland and refused a seat in parliament under the unified monarchy of Victor Emmanuel II. He is the author of books on philosophy and literature.

**Alexis de Tocqueville,** age 20; French political writer and statesman of aristocratic birth. Having traveled to the United States in 1831 to study penitentiaries, he also observed the manners, customs, and political system; later, he produced the classic upon which his fame rests, *Democracy in America* (1835–1840). He deplored the loss of many fine qualities and values, but felt that resistance to egalitarianism was futile and that it should be accepted and guided.

**Samuel Wilberforce,** age 20; English churchman, son of William

# 1850

Sidney Lanier
  (1842-1881), age 8
Stephane Mallarme
  (1842-1898), age 8
Jules Massenet
  (1842-1912), age 8
Arthur Sullivan
  (1842-1900), age 8
C. M. Doughty
  (1843-1926), age 7
Edvard Grieg
  (1843-1907), age 7
Henry James
  (1843-1916), age 7
Robert Koch
  (1843-1910), age 7
William McKinley
  (1843-1901), age 7
Karl Benz
  (1844-1929), age 6
Sarah Bernhardt
  (1844-1923), age 6
Robert Bridges
  (1844-1930), age 6
George Washington
Cable
  (1844-1925), age 6
Thomas Eakins
  (1844-1916), age 6
Anatole France
  (1844-1924), age 6
Gerard Manley Hopkins
  (1844-1889), age 6
Andrew Lang
  (1844-1912), age 6
Modjeska
  (1840 or 1844-1909),
  age 6?
Friedrich Nietzsche
  (1844-1900), age 6
Nikolai Rimski-Korsakov
  (1844-1908), age 6
Henri Rousseau
  (1844-1910), age 6
Paul Verlaine
  (1844-1896), age 6
Elie Metchnikoff
  (1845-1916), age 5
Wilhelm Roentgen
  (1845-1923), age 5
George Saintsbury
  (1845-1933), age 5

Wilberforce. As bishop of Oxford from 1845–1869 he was known as a powerful orator, an efficient administrator and a ready controversialist. He is remembered for his heated debates with Thomas Henry Huxley over Darwin's theories and was bishop of Winchester from 1869–1873.

JOSEPH SMITH
American religious leader
1805-1844

**Joseph Smith,** age 20; American religious leader born in Vermont, founder of the Mormon Church. He organized the Church of Jesus Christ of the Latter Day Saints in Fayette, N.Y. in 1830. He later moved to Ohio, Missouri and Illinois, where a group of citizens, outraged by the practice of polygamy, took him from jail and shot him in 1844.

**Elizabeth Barrett Browning,** age 19; English poet, daughter of a wealthy landowner. A semi-invalid from a childhood injury, she eloped at 40 with 34-year-old Robert Browning, settled in Florence, Italy, and eventually recovered her health. She is known for her love lyrics *Sonnets from the Portuguese* and the long, sentimental didactic poem in blank verse *Aurora Leigh*.

FELIX MENDELSSOHN
German composer, pianist
and conductor
1809-1847

**Felix Mendelssohn,** age 16; German composer, pianist and conductor, born in Hamburg, son of a German-Jewish banker and grandson of

Moses Mendelssohn. From an early age he toured Europe as a pianist and conductor and composed such famous works as the *Italian Symphony*, the *Reformation Symphony* and *Overture to a Midsummer Night's Dream*. He also wrote special music for Jenny Lind. Overwork contributed to his early death.

EDGAR ALLEN POE
American poet and
story writer
1809-1849

**Edgar Allan Poe,** age 16; American poet and story writer born in Boston of touring theatrical parents. Left destitute two years later by his mother's death in Richmond, he was reared by John Allan, a Richmond merchant. He married his 14-year-old cousin in 1836 and lived an irregular, often impoverished life in New York and Philadelphia as a journalist and editor. His poems—*The Raven, Ulalume, Annabel Lee*—and his tales of mystery and terror attained worldwide fame. His fictional detective, C. August Dupin, was the literary ancestor of Sherlock Holmes. Mysterious circumstances surrounded his death in Baltimore at 40.

**William Barret Travis,** age 16; American lawyer and soldier born in South Carolina; commander of the defenders of the Alamo. He went to Texas at the age of 22, became a colonel in the Texas army in the revolt against Mexico, and was only 27 when his force of 188 men defended the fort for two weeks against the army of Santa Anna. He was killed when the Alamo fell in March 1836.

**Frederic Chopin,** age 15; Polish composer and pianist born near Warsaw, son of a French language teacher and a Polish mother. He studied piano from the age of four and became a favorite composer of the nobility. His etudes, scherzos, nocturnes and polonaises, with their refinements of melody and harmony, were more suitable for private salons than for concert halls. He died of tuberculosis at 39.

**Mikhail Yurievich Lermontov,** age 11; Russian poet and novelist born in Moscow. An officer of the guards, he was banished twice to the Caucasus for dueling and for anti-czarist sentiments. Admired in his time as a romantic poet second only to Pushkin, he is better known today for his novel *A Hero of Our Times*. He was killed at 26 in a duel.

**Emily Jane Bronte,** age 7; English novelist born in Yorkshire, daughter of an eccentric Anglican clergyman and sister of Charlotte and Anne Bronte. Her single novel, *Wuthering Heights* (1848)—a dark, passionate story set in the Yorkshire moors—brought lasting fame, although she died of tuberculosis in the year of its publication.

# 1850

F. H. Bradley
  (1846-1924), age 4
W. F. Cody
  (1846-1917), age 4
Rudolf Eucken
  (1846-1926), age 4
Carry Nation
  (1846-1911), age 4
Charles Parnell
  (1846-1891), age 4
Henryk Sienkiewicz
  (1846-1916), age 4
William Robertson Smith
  (1846-1894), age 4
Alexander Graham Bell
  (1847-1922), age 3
Thomas Alva Edison
  (1847-1931), age 3
Paul von Hindenburg
  (1847-1934), age 3
Jesse James
  (1847-1882), age 3
Joseph Pulitzer
  (1847-1911), age 3
Albert Pinkham Ryder
  (1847-1917), age 3
Ellen Terry
  (1847-1928), age 3
Arthur James Balfour
  (1848-1930), age 2
Bernard Bosanquet
  (1848-1923), age 2
Wyatt Earp
  (1848-1929), age 2
Paul Gauguin
  (1848-1903), age 2
J. K. Huysmans
  (1848-1907), age 2
Vilfredo Pareto
  (1848-1923), age 2
Augustus Saint-Gaudens
  (1848-1907), age 2
Luther Burbank
  (1849-1926), age 1
Crazy Horse
  (1849?-1877), age 1?
W. E. Henley
  (1849-1903), age 1
William Osler
  (1849-1919), age 1
Ivan Pavlov
  (1849-1936), age 1
Kimmochi Saionji
  (1849/50-1940), age c.1
August Strindberg
  (1849-1912), age 1

# 1850–1875

By 1850 slavery had developed into an explosive issue in the United States, confronting citizens and legislators alike; 1850 was the year of the great debate. John C. Calhoun and Daniel Webster had often clashed in the Senate, but never over so momentous an issue as the Missouri Compromise. The occasion was somewhat marred by Calhoun's inability to speak. He was a dying man and had almost lost his voice. His speech was read to the crowded Senate chamber by Sen. Mason of Virginia. John Caldwell Calhoun was a gaunt man with rugged features—thick grayish-black hair; sunken, yellowish brown eyes; and hollow cheeks. He looked, it was said, like the brilliant, defiant defender of a lost cause.

The basic issue was the contested right of individual states to declare acts of the federal government null and void. Calhoun maintained that the Declaration of Independence had made each of the 13 colonies a sovereign state, and that whenever the federal government usurped powers not granted by the Constitution, any state had the right to declare such acts null and void. The controversy had arisen in 1832 over protective tariff laws which the South opposed. In 1850 the issue was slavery, but the cause of the dispute was the same: the industrial North threatened to dominate and subject to its own laws the agricultural, aristocratic South. For Calhoun, the salvation of the south lay in secession from the Union, for the continuation of policies favoring

## 1850

Duncan Phyfe
(1768-1854), age 82
Alexander von Humboldt
(1769-1859), age 81
Duke of Wellington
(1769-1852), age 81
William Wordsworth
(1770-1850), age 80
Robert Owen
(1771-1858), age 79
Louis Philippe (France)
(1773-1850), age 77
Metternich
(1773-1859), age 77
Walter Savage Landor
(1775-1864), age 75
Friedrich von Schelling
(1775-1854), age 75
J. M. W. Turner
(1775-1851), age 75
Henry Clay
(1777-1852), age 73

**Ferdinand Marie, vicomte de Lesseps,** age 45; French diplomat and builder of the Suez Canal. In 1854 he obtained a concession from the viceroy of Egypt, Said Pasha, for the construction of a ship channel through the Isthmus of Suez, raised the capital by subscription and successfully completed the project (1859–1869). He began the construction of a canal in Panama, but gave up the effort after seven years (1881–1888) for lack of funds.

**Benito Pablo Juarez,** age 44; Mexican statesman and national hero, of Indian parentage. In 1855 he joined the revolt against Santa Anna; he served as provisional president from 1857–1861, as elected president from 1861–1867 and again from 1867–1872, after he execution of Maximilian. Respected for his courage and honesty, he introduced liberal reforms and gave political power to the Indians and mestizos, persons of mixed European and Indian ancestry.

**Louis Agassiz,** age 43; Swiss-American zoologist and geologist born in Switzerland. He emigrated in 1846 and was professor of natural history at Harvard from 1848–1873. He studied the glaciers of Switzerland and was the first to suggest that there had been a prehistoric Ice Age when glaciers covered Europe and North America.

**Joseph Eggleston Johnston,** age 43; American army officer born in Virginia and graduated from West Point in 1829. He fought in the Seminole War and the Mexican War, and joined the Confederate army in 1861 as brigadier general. He won the first Battle of Bull Run and

the north meant the doom of southern agriculture and southern life.

The debate began in the last week of February, 1850. Henry Clay rose to outline the points of the Missouri Compromise, defending it eloquently and urging that compromise was the only way to resolve differences; warning that Southern secession would mean war, for the North would never permit the mouth of the Mississippi River to be held by a foreign power.

A few days later, March 4, Calhoun's speech was read to the Senate. He had never been an orator but had relied on reasoned argument and plain speech to present his case. His speech brought home the fact that compromise was not possible: the South's future was at issue, and the South could not permit the Union, the Constitution, to be used to oppress it.

For Daniel Webster, the spellbinder from New England, the first priority was the preservation of the Union. At 68 he was still a man of impressive appearance, and a master of florid rhetoric. "I speak today," he began, "for the preservation of the Union." He defended the compromise bill in a memorable speech that held the senators silent under his spell and erased from their minds Calhoun's logical arguments. The bill passed. That same year Calhoun died, and the South lost its best champion. A new champion, Jefferson Davis, took up the Southern cause, but it had already been lost. It turned out as Calhoun had predicted; the South seceded and a long, costly war ensued.

# 1875

stopped the Union offensive in the Peninsula Campaign, but lost Vicksburg to Grant and retreated as Sherman advanced. He surrendered on April 26, 17 days after Lee. He served in Congress from 1879–1881.

JOHN STUART MILL
English philosopher and economist
1806-1873

**John Stuart Mill,** age 44; English philosopher and economist born in London, son of a Scottish philosopher-economist who introduced him

James A. Garfield
  (1831-1881), age 44
James Clerk Maxwell
  (1831-1879), age 44
Victorien Sardou
  (1831-1908), age 44
Louisa May Alcott
  (1832-1888), age 43
Bjornstjerne Bjornson
  (1832-1910), age 43
Lewis Carroll
  (1832-1898), age 43
Gustave Dore
  (1832/33-1883),
  age c.43
Edouard Manet
  (1832-1883), age 43
Nikolaus Otto
  (1832-1891), age 43
Leslie Stephen
  (1832-1904), age 43

# 1850

Clement C. Moore
  (1779-1863), age 71
Thomas Moore
  (1779-1852), age 71
Jean Ingres
  (1780-1867), age 70
John C. Calhoun
  (1782-1850), age 68
Friedrich Froebel
  (1782-1852), age 68
Martin Van Buren
  (1782-1862), age 68
Daniel Webster
  (1782-1852), age 68
Washington Irving
  (1783-1859), age 67
Thomas Sully
  (1783-1872), age 67
Leigh Hunt
  (1784-1859), age 66
Viscount Palmerston
  (1784-1865), age 66
Zachary Taylor
  (1784-1850), age 66
John James Audubon
  (1785-1851), age 65
Thomas De Quincey
  (1785-1859), age 65
Jacob Grimm
  (1785-1863), age 65
Alessandro Manzoni
  (1785-1873), age 65
Thomas Love Peacock
  (1785-1866), age 65
Wilhelm Grimm
  (1786-1859), age 64
Winfield Scott
  (1786-1866), age 64
Francois Guizot
  (1787-1874), age 63
Robert Livingston Stevens
  (1787-1856), age 63
Emma Willard
  (1787-1870), age 63
Sir Robert Peel
  (1788-1850), age 62
Arthur Schopenhauer
  (1788-1860), age 62
James Fenimore Cooper
  (1789-1851), age 61
Jared Sparks
  (1789-1866), age 61

to Greek at three and to Plato at 10. He held important posts in the India House in London and was a member of Parliament from 1865–1868, advocating equality for women, compulsory education and birth control. He systematized the philosophy of Jeremy Bentham in *Utilitarianism* (1863) and also wrote *Essay on Liberty* (1859), a classic of liberal thought.

GIUSEPPE GARIBALDI
Italian patriot and soldier
1807-1882

**Giuseppe Garibaldi,** age 43; Italian patriot and soldier born in Nice. After political exile in Uruguay from 1836–1848 and on Staten Island, N.Y. from 1849–1854, where he worked as a candlemaker, he returned to Italy to join Victor Emmanuel II of Sardinia and lead the Red Shirts in a successful war of liberation against Austria.

ROBERT EDWARD LEE
American army officer
1807-1870

**Robert Edward Lee,** age 43; American army officer born in Virginia, son of Henry (Light-Horse Harry) Lee. As commander of the Confederate Army of Northern Virginia, he advanced into Pennsylvania but was defeated at the Battle of Gettysburg, July 1–4, 1863. He was appointed commander-in-chief of the Confederate armies in February 1865, when the Southern cause was already a lost one. He was idolized as a brilliant military strategist and national hero.

**John Greenleaf Whittier,** age 43; American poet born on a Massachusetts farm, son of Quaker parents. Known as the poet of rural New

England, he was a journalist and editor for William Lloyd Garrison for 20 years and wrote his best-known poems late in life. *Snowbound,* written at 60, *The Barefoot Boy* and *Barbara Frietchie* are among his most popular poems. He also wrote many hymns.

HENRY WADSWORTH
LONGFELLOW
American poet
1807-1882

**Henry Wadsworth Longfellow,** age 43; American poet born in Portland, Maine, son of a lawyer; professor of modern languages at Harvard from 1835–1854. The most popular 19th-century American poet, he wrote *The Wreck of the Hesperus, The Village Blacksmith, Excelsior, The Song of Hiawatha, Paul Revere's Ride* and many other well-known poems. The oft-quoted line, "Into each life some rain must fall," is his.

**Honore Daumier,** age 42; French painter and caricaturist born in Marseilles, known for his satirical cartoons of bourgeois society. He drew for comic magazines and in 1832 was imprisoned six months for a caricature of Louis Philippe. Many of his 400 lithographs are admired today as masterpieces. His painting *The Third-Class Carriage* is in the Metropolitan Museum of Art in New York.

**Jefferson Davis,** age 42; American statesman born in Kentucky and reared in Mississippi, son of a planter of Welsh descent. His career was a checkered one, including army frontier service, marriage to Zachary Taylor's daughter (who died of malaria within three months), and plantation-building in the wilderness for seven years; he was a national hero in the Mexican War, Calhoun's successor as Southern spokesman and president of the Confederate States from 1861–1865. He spent two years in prison on charges of treason (subsequently dropped).

**Andrew Johnson,** age 42; American statesman born in North Carolina; 17th president, from 1865–1869. His reputation has suffered from his impeachment by an irresponsible group in Congress, but he was an able man of strong character. Despite his lack of education (his wife taught him to write), he served many years in Congress, as governor of Tennessee and as senator and was elected vice-president in 1864. He assumed the presidency following the assassination of Abraham Lincoln. His moderate program of reconstruction aroused hostility in Congress among the rabidly anti-Southern faction. Elected senator in 1874, he died soon after taking office.

**Napoleon III** (Louis Napoleon), age 42; president of France from 1848–1852 and emperor from 1852–1870; nephew of Napoleon I. During his oppressive reign, Nice was annexed, Cochin China ac-

Edward Tylor
(1832-1917), age 43
Edwin Booth
(1833-1893), age 42
Aleksandr Borodin
(1833/34-1887),
age c.42
Johannes Brahms
(1833-1897), age 42
Charles Gordon
(1833-1885), age 42
Benjamin Harrison
(1833-1901), age 42
Alfred Nobel
(1833-1896), age 42
Lord Acton
(1834-1902), age 41
Gottlieb Daimler
(1834-1900), age 41
Edgar Degas
(1834-1917), age 41
Ernst Haeckel
(1834-1919), age 41
William Morris
(1834-1896), age 41
Sitting Bull
(1831 or 1834-1890),
age 41?
James Thomson
(1834-1882), age 41
James McNeill Whistler
(1834-1903), age 41
Samuel Butler
(1835-1902), age 40
Giosue Carducci
(1835-1907), age 40
Andrew Carnegie
(1835-1919), age 40
Leopold II (Belgium)
(1835-1909), age 40
Camille Saint-Saens
(1835-1921), age 40
Mark Twain
(1835-1910), age 40
Tz'u Hsi
(1834/35-1908),
age c.40
Joseph Chamberlain
(1836-1914), age 39
W. S. Gilbert
(1836-1911), age 39

# 1850

Alphonse de Lamartine
   (1790-1869), age 60
Leopold I (Belgium)
   (1790-1865), age 60
John Ross
   (1790-1866), age 60
John Tyler
   (1790-1862), age 60
James Buchanan
   (1791-1868), age 59
Peter Cooper
   (1791-1883), age 59
Michael Faraday
   (1791-1867), age 59
Franz Grillparzer
   (1791-1872), age 59
Giacomo Meyerbeer
   (1791-1864), age 59
Samuel F. B. Morse
   (1791-1872), age 59
Augustin Eugene Scribe
   (1791-1861), age 59
Victor Cousin
   (1792-1867), age 58
Pius IX (Pope)
   (1792-1878), age 58
Gioacchino Rossini
   (1792-1868), age 58
Thaddeus Stevens
   (1792-1868), age 58
Sam Houston
   (1793-1863), age 57
Henry Schoolcraft
   (1793-1864), age 57
William Cullen Bryant
   (1794-1878), age 56
Matthew Perry
   (1794-1858), age 56
Cornelius Vanderbilt
   (1794-1877), age 56
James Gordon Bennett
   (1795-1872), age 55
Thomas Carlyle
   (1795-1881), age 55
Leopold von Ranke
   (1795-1886), age 55
Antonio de Santa Anna
   (1794/95-1876), age c.55
Dred Scott
   (1795?-1858), age 55?
Augustin Thierry
   (1795-1856), age 55

quired and the Suez Canal built. Defeated in the Franco-Prussian War and deposed, he retired with his family to England and the Third French Republic was established.

**David Friedrich Strauss,** age 42; German theologian and philosopher born in Wurttemberg. His *Das Leben Jesu (The Life of Jesus;* two volumes, 1835–1836) marked a turning point in the study of the Bible in its critical examination of the Gospel narrative, rejecting all supernatural elements. He was not an unbeliever, but religious in an unorthodox way, leaning toward pantheism. His book was translated in 1846 by George Eliot.

**Kit** (Christopher) **Carson,** age 41; American frontiersman, trapper and scout, born in Kentucky. He grew up on the Missouri frontier, joined an expedition to New Mexico in 1829 and acted as guide for the Fremont expeditions (1842–1845). He also served as a guide for Gen. Kearny in the Mexican War, when he accomplished his celebrated feat of crawling through the enemy lines to summon aid.

**Charles Robert Darwin,** age 41; English naturalist born in Shropshire, son of a physician. As an unpaid naturalist, he accompanied in his youth the scientific expedition of *H.M.S. Beagle* to South America and around the world (1831–1836). Twenty years of patient accumulation of facts, combined with a reading of Malthus's *Essay on Population,* produced the theory that demolished the myth of the immutability of species. His great work, *On the Origin of Species by Means of Natural Selection,* published in 1859, inaugurated a new era in the history of thought and science. He was buried in Westminster Abbey close to Newton.

**Edward FitzGerald,** age 41; English poet and scholar born in Suffolk, famous for his translation of *The Rubaiyat of Omar Khayyam* (1859), which became one of the most popular poems of the English language and which is considered as much his creation as Omar Khayyam's, since he selected his quatrains from hundreds and gave them a unity not possessed by the original. He also translated six plays of Calderon's.

**William Ewart Gladstone,** age 41; British statesman born in Liverpool. A member of Parliament almost continuously from 1832 to 1895, prime minister four times (1868–1874, 1880–1885, 1886, 1892–1894) and a liberal opposed to the imperialism of Disraeli, he dominated political life with his brilliant intellect and oratory. He was also a classical scholar and translated Horace and lectured on Homer. The Gladstone bag was named for him.

**Nikolai Vasilievich Gogol,** age 41; Russian novelist and dramatist born in the Ukraine of landowning Cossack parents. With the humorous novel *Dead Souls,* the comedy *The Inspector General* and the short story *The Overcoat,* he introduced realism into Russian literature, ending the romantic era of Pushkin and Lermontov. After a pilgrimage to the Holy Land in 1848, he adopted an ascetic life and died of malnutrition at 42.

**Oliver Wendell Holmes,** age 41; American writer and physician born in Cambridge, Mass., son of a prominent clergyman; professor of anatomy and physiology at Harvard (1847–1882). He won fame with his series of essays *The Autocrat at the Breakfast Table,* published in the *Atlantic Monthly* (which he named and helped found). He was also famous as a raconteur and a poet, author of *The Deacon's Masterpiece or, The Wonderful "One-Hoss Shay."*

**Fanny (Frances Anne) Kemble,** age 41; English actress of the famous Kemble theatrical family, granddaughter of Roger Kemble and niece of Sarah Siddons. She made her debut as Juliet in 1829 at Covent Garden and had great success performers in both comedies and tragedies. She toured the United States from 1832–1834 and gave dramatic readings after 1849 in Europe and America.

ABRAHAM LINCOLN
American statesman and
president
1809-1865

**Abraham Lincoln,** age 41; American statesman born in Kentucky, son of an itinerant laborer; 16th president of the United States, 1861–1865. He served in the Illinois legislature from 1834–1841 and in the House of Representatives from 1847–1849 and ran for the Senate in 1858 but lost. The Civil War began one month after his inauguration and ended five days before his assassination. A staunch defender of democracy and human rights, he delivered a classic oration, the famous Gettysburg Address, on Nov. 19, 1863.

**Cyrus Hall McCormick,** age 41; American inventor and manufacturer born in Virginia, son of an inventor. In 1831 he built a mechanical reaper (patented in 1834) and produced a small number of them for local farmers. He built a factory in Chicago in 1847, the McCormick Harvesting Machine Co. (later the International Harvester Co.) and thereby revolutionized American farming.

**Pierre Joseph Proudhon,** age 41; French radical social theorist, of a poor family, called the father of anarchism. He believed that ethical progress would eventually make centralized government obsolete, but rejected force as a means of political change.

**Alfred Tennyson,** age 41; first Baron Tennyson, English poet born in Lincolnshire, son of a clergyman and one of 12 children. He began writing poetry in boyhood and at 33 was recognized as the foremost English poet. He was granted a government pension of 200 pounds; was made poet laureate in 1850, succeeding Wordsworth; and was made a baron in 1884. Famous poems include *Tears, Idle Tears; The Lotos-Eaters; A Dream of Fair Women; Idylls of the King;* and *In Memoriam.*

**Phineas Taylor Barnum,** age 40; American showman born in Connecticut. He opened the American Museum of Curios in New York City in 1842 with such attractions as the midget Tom Thumb and the original Siamese twins, Chang and Eng. In 1871 he opened a circus in Brooklyn, "The Greatest Show on Earth," and in 1881 he joined James Anthony Bailey (1847–1906) to form Barnum & Bailey Circus— for many years the most exciting summer event of small-town America.

**Conte Camillo Benso di Cavour,** age 40; Italian statesman born in Piedmont. Premier of Sardinia from 1852–1859 and again in 1860–1861, he was one of the leaders of the Italian nationalist movement and

T. H. Green
(1836-1882), age 39
Bret Harte
(1836-1902), age 39
Winslow Homer
(1836-1910), age 39
John Burroughs
(1837-1921), age 38
Grover Cleveland
(1837-1908), age 38
George Dewey
(1837-1917), age 38
John Richard Green
(1837-1883), age 38
James Hickok
(1837-1876), age 38
Hitotsubashi
(1837-1902), age 38
William Dean Howells
(1837-1920), age 38
John Pierpont Morgan
(1837-1913), age 38
Algernon Swinburne
(1837-1909), age 38
Henry Adams
(1838-1918), age 37
Georges Bizet
(1838-1875), age 37
James Bryce
(1838-1922), age 37
Sir Henry Irving
(1838-1905), age 37
William Lecky
(1838-1903), age 37
Ernst Mach
(1838-1916), age 37
John Muir
(1838-1914), age 37
George Otto Trevelyan
(1838-1928), age 37
Paul Cezanne
(1839-1906), age 36
George Custer
(1839-1876), age 36
Willard Gibbs
(1839-1903), age 36
Machado de Assis
(1839-1908), age 36
Modest Mussorgsky
(1839-1881), age 36
Walter Pater
(1839-1894), age 36

Thomas Bulfinch
(1796-1867), age 54
George Catlin
(1796-1872), age 54
Jean Baptiste Corot
(1796-1875), age 54
Horace Mann
(1796-1859), age 54
W. H. Pescott
(1796-1859), age 54
Heinrich Heine
(1797-1856), age 53
Ando Hiroshige
(1797-1858), age 53
Sir Charles Lyell
(1797-1875), age 53
Mary Wollstonecraft Shelley
(1797-1851), age 53
Louis Adolphe Thiers
(1797-1877), age 53
Alfred de Vigny
(1797-1863), age 53
William I (Germany)
(1797-1888), age 53
Auguste Comte
(1798-1857), age 52
Eugene Delacroix
(1798-1863), age 52
Adam Sienkiewicz
(1798-1855), age 52
Jules Michelet
(1798-1874), age 52
Bronson Alcott
(1799-1888), age 51
Honore de Balzac
(1799-1850), age 51
Jacques Halevy
(1799-1862), age 51
George Bancroft
(1800-1891), age 50
John Brown
(1800-1859), age 50
Millard Fillmore
(1800-1874), age 50
Thomas B. Macaulay
(1800-1859), age 50
William McGuffy
(1800-1873), age 50
Helmuth von Moltke
(1800-1891), age 50
James Clark Ross
(1800-1862), age 50

the principal architect of Italian unification. His diplomacy and secret aid to Garibaldi resulted in the crowning of Victor Emmanuel II as king of a united Italy in 1861.

**Margaret Fuller,** age 40; American writer, teacher and early feminist, born in Massachusetts, daughter of a lawyer. A friend of Emerson and the transcendentalists, she wrote literary criticism and *Women in the Nineteenth Century* (1845). She married a handsome Italian marchese in Rome, and on the return voyage was lost, with her husband and child, in a shipwreck off Fire Island, N.Y. in 1850.

**Elizabeth Cleghorn Stevenson Gaskell** (Mrs. Gaskell), age 40; English novelist born in London, daughter of a Unitarian minister. At 22 she married William Gaskell, a Unitarian minister, lived a quiet, domestic life in Manchester, raised a large family and wrote her novels about life in manufacturing towns, including *Sylvia's Lovers* (1863), *Wives and Daughters* (1866) and *Cranford* (1853), her masterpiece. She was a friend of Charlotte Bronte and Charles Dickens.

**Asa Gray,** age 40; American botanist born in New York, a prolific writer for scientific journals, author of many textbooks and professor of botany at Harvard (1842–1888). He helped revise Linnaeus' system of plant classification and with John Torrey produced *Flora of North America* (two volumes, 1838–1843). His *Manual of Botany* (1848) is still a standard reference book.

**Leo XIII** (Gioacchino Vincenzo Pecci), age 40; Italian ecclesiastic; pope from 1878–1903. An accomplished statesman and scholar, he reversed the regressive policies of Pius IX and brought the church back into the modern world. He defined Catholic social ideals and attitudes and urged French Catholics to support the Third Republic. He declared Thomism the official Catholic philosophy and founded the Institute of Thomistic Philosophy at Louvain. He also wrote Latin poetry.

**Alfred de Musset,** age 40; French lyric poet and playwright born in Paris of an aristocratic family. He wrote a number of successful plays but is better known for his passionate love lyrics inspired by a brief romance with George Sand. He died at 46 after a long period of debauchery.

**Theodore Parker,** age 40; American clergyman and writer born in Massachusetts, grandson of the commander of the Minutemen at the Battle of Lexington. As minister of the 28th Congregational Society of Boston, he attracted great crowds with his liberal views on religion. He was a transcendentalist, a contributor to the *Dial* and an antislavery propagandist.

**Sir Henry Cheswick Rawlinson,** age 40; English Orientalist, soldier and government official, born in Oxfordshire; the older brother of George Rawlinson, the historian. He is known for his achievement, while British consul at Baghdad, in deciphering the cuneiform inscriptions of Darius the Great at Behistun, making the ancient Near East accessible to modern scholars. He was knighted in 1855.

**Robert Schumann,** age 40; German romantic composer and musical journalist born in Saxony, the son of a bookseller. He wrote many songs for the lyrics of Heine and Goethe, but his reputation rests mainly on his brilliant piano pieces, such as *Papillons* and *Carnaval,* made popular by his wife Clara, a piano virtuoso. His orchestral works include the *Spring Symphony* and the *Rhenish Symphony*. He suffered periods of mental illness throughout his life and died at 46 in confinement.

**George Caleb Bingham,** age 39; American genre painter born in Virginia and raised in Missouri. After spending a short period in Washington, D.C. as a portrait painter, he returned to Missouri to paint the scenes of river life for which he is famous: *Fur Traders Descending* *the Missouri* (in the Metropolitan Museum of Art in New York), *Raftsmen Playing Cards* (in the City Art Museum in St. Louis) and many others.

**Theophile Gautier,** age 39; prolific French writer (poet, novelist and critic) born in southern France. An influential figure among the romantics, defending art for art's sake against the "bourgeois philistines," he is said to have written enough to fill 300 volumes. He is remembered today for his novel *Mademoiselle de Maupin* (1835).

**Horace Greeley,** age 39; American journalist and editor born in New Hampshire. In 1841 he founded the New York *Tribune* to support the liberal policies of the new Whig party and give working men a dependable paper free of sensationalism. He employed Karl Marx as a European correspondent from 1852 to 1861.

**Franz Liszt,** age 39; Hungarian composer, piano virtuoso and child prodigy. He toured European capitals from the age of 11 and was acclaimed the greatest pianist of his time. His best-known compositions are the 15 or more *Hungarian Rhapsodies*. He was the father-in-law of Richard Wagner.

HARRIET BEECHER STOWE
American writer
1811-1896

**Harriet Beecher Stowe,** age 39; American writer born in Connecticut, daughter of a clergyman; sister of Henry Ward Beecher, a prominent Booklyn clergyman; and wife of Calvin Stowe, also a clergyman. She wrote several novels, but is remembered for *Uncle Tom's Cabin, or Life among the Lowly*. Published in book form in 1852, it sold half a million copies and was translated into 20 languages.

**William Makepeace Thackeray,** age 39; English novelist and humorist born in Calcutta, son of an East India Company official. After gambling away his inheritance, he joined the staff of *Punch* (1842–1854), won fame with *Vanity Fair,* which was published serially (1847–1848) and won financial success with *Pendennis, Henry Esmond* and *The Newcomes*. He rivaled Dickens in popularity and surpassed him as a prose stylist. His Becky Sharp is one of fiction's immortal characters.

**Robert Browning,** age 38; English poet born near London, son of a senior bank clerk with literary interests. He wrote verse and unsuccessful plays in his youth, eloped with Elizabeth Barrett and lived in Florence, Italy until her death. In 1861 he returned to England and eventually won fame with *The Ring and the Book* (1868–1869), a long narrative poem about a Roman murder trial. Other familiar poems include *My Last Duchess, The Lost Leader* and *The Pied Piper of Hamelin*.

# 1875

Charles Sanders Peirce
(1839-1914), age 36
John D. Rockefeller
(1839-1937), age 36
Alfred Sisley
(1839-1899), age 36
Carlotta
(1840-1927), age 35
Alphonse Daudet
(1840-1897), age 35
Thomas Hardy
(1840-1928), age 35
Claude Monet
(1840-1926), age 35
Thomas Nast
(1840-1902), age 35
Auguste Rodin
(1840-1917), age 35
William Graham Sumner
(1840-1910), age 35
John Addington Symonds
(1840-1893), age 35
Peter Ilich Tchaikovsky
(1840-1893), age 35
Giovanni Verga
(1840-1922), age 35
Emile Zola
(1840-1902), age 35
James Gordon Bennett
(1841-1918), age 34
Georges Clemenceau
(1841-1929), age 34
Anton Dvorak
(1841-1904), age 34
Edward VII (Great Britain)
(1841-1910), age 34
Oliver Wendell Holmes
(1841-1935), age 34
Hirobumi Ito
(1841-1909), age 34
Pierre Auguste Renoir
(1841-1919), age 34
Henry Stanley
(1841-1904), age 34
Ambrose Bierce
(1842-1914?), age 33
Georg Brandes
(1842-1927), age 33
William James
(1842-1910), age 33
Peter Kropotkin
(1842-1921), age 33

# 1850

David Farragut
  (1801-1870), age 49
John Henry Newman
  (1801-1896), age 49
Brigham Young
  (1801-1877), age 49
Paul Emile Botta
  (1802-1870), age 48
Alexandre Dumas (pere)
  (1802-1870), age 48
Victor Hugo
  (1802-1885), age 48
Louis Kossuth
  (1802-1894), age 48
Edwin Landseer
  (1802-1873), age 48
Harriet Martineau
  (1802-1876), age 48
Hector Berlioz
  (1803-1869), age 47
George Borrow
  (1803-1881), age 47
Edward Bulwer-Lytton
  (1803-1873), age 47
Ralph Waldo Emerson
  (1803-1882), age 47
Albert Sidney Johnston
  (1803-1862), age 47
Baron von Liebig
  (1803-1873), age 47
Prosper Merimee
  (1803-1870), age 47
Benjamin Disraeli
  (1804-1881), age 46
Ludwig Feuerbach
  (1804-1872), age 46
Mikhail Glinka
  (1804-1857), age 46
Nathaniel Hawthorne
  (1804-1864), age 46
Franklin Pierce
  (1804-1869), age 46
Charles Sainte-Beuve
  (1804-1869), age 46
George Sand
  (1804-1876), age 46
Eugene Sue
  (1804-1857), age 46
Hans Christian Andersen
  (1805-1875), age 45
William Lloyd Garrison
  (1805-1879), age 45

CHARLES DICKENS
English novelist
1812-1870

**Charles Dickens,** age 38; English novelist born in Portsmouth, son of a naval clerk whose imprisonment for debt in 1824 provided much of the material for the experiences described in *David Copperfield.* He achieved early success with *Sketches by Boz* (1836) and *The Pickwick Papers* (1836–1837). He was popular in his time for his early novels of humor and pathos, but is respected today for the later novels of greater social significance and psychological insight: *Bleak House, Great Expectations* and *Our Mutual Friend. A Tale of Two Cities* and the sentimental story *A Christmas Carol* remain widely popular.

**Baron Friedrich Ferdinand von Flotow,** age 38; German composer of light opera born in Mecklenburg-Schwerin. Although intended for the diplomatic service, he studied music in Paris and wrote and produced 29 popular operas, only one of which is still produced; entitled *Martha* (1847), it is notable for the inclusion of Thomas Moore's beautiful melody, *Last Rose of Summer*.

**Ivan Aleksandrovich Goncharov,** age 38; Russian novelist and government official born in Simbirsk, son of a rich merchant. He held various offices in the civil service (1834–1867), wrote a few novels and a book of travel sketches and is remembered for one novel, *Oblomov* (1858), a Russian classic which gave currency to the term *Oblomovism*, denoting the kind of indolent half-existence common to the Russian nobility.

**Aleksandr Ivanovich Herzen,** age 38; Russian writer, political thinker, and revolutionary; an apostle of western ideas and western individualism. He lived mostly in Paris and London, published an influential Russian weekly newspaper and wrote *My Past and My Thoughts* (four volumes, 1852–1855). His enthusiasm for socialism was tempered by his fears of a regimented society.

**Alfred Krupp,** age 38; German arms manufacturer, son of Friedrich Krupp, founder of the Krupp Iron Works at Essen. He developed a method of casting steel and began the manufacture of guns in 1847. The adoption of the Krupp rifle by the Prussian army in 1861 presaged the birth of an industrial giant.

**Edward Lear,** age 38; English humorist and bird and landscape painter, best known for his illustrated nonsense poems, which first appeared in *A Book of Nonsense* (1846), followed by several other volumes. These famous lines are his: ''The Owl and the Pussy-Cat went to sea/ In a beautiful pea-green boat.''

**Stephen Arnold Douglas,** age 37; American politician born in Vermont, called the Little Giant. Famous for his oratory, he was a senator from 1847–1861 and several times a candidate for president. Douglas is remembered for his series of debates with Abraham Lincoln on the slavery issue, which brought national prominence to Lincoln.

**John Charles Fremont,** age 37; American explorer and army officer born in Georgia. From 1842 to 1845 he led three expeditions west, mapped the Oregon Trail and crossed the Rockies to California. In the Mexican War he helped conquer California and became one of the first two senators from California in 1850. Known as a quarrelsome man, he ran for president in 1856 and lost.

**Christian Friedrich Hebbel,** age 37; German dramatist born of poor parents and the author of tragic historical dramas characterized by psychological realism and incorporating Hegelian theories of history. Some examples are: *Judith* (1840), *Julia* (1851), *Michel Angelo* (1851) and the trilogy *The Nibelungen* (1862).

**Soren Kierkegaard,** age 37; Danish philosopher and religious writer born in Copenhagen, son of a wool merchant. Carrying the Protestant attitude to an extreme, he viewed religion as an experience unique to each individual, unrelated to systematic theology or established churches; he attacked modern, liberal, ethics-centered, social-welfare Protestantism as contrary to the Christianity of the New Testament. His major works are *Either/Or* and *Fear and Trembling*.

**David Livingstone,** age 37; Scottish missionary and explorer, famous for his journeys in central Africa. He studied medicine and theology while working in a cotton mill and at 27 secured an appointment as a medical missionary in South Africa. He married another missionary's daughter and organized exploring parties that included his wife and family into the interior. He discoverd Lake Ngami in 1849, the Zambezi River in 1851, Victoria Falls and Lake Nyasa. He died in a native village in 1873 after an unsuccessful search for the source of the Nile.

**Giuseppe Verdi,** age 37; Italian operatic composer born near Parma. Success and popularity came slowly, but with *Rigoletto* (1851), *Il Trovatore* (1852) and *La Traviata* (1853) he attained international fame. His later operas included *Aida* (1871), *Otello* (1887) and *Falstaff*, a comic opera written when he was nearly 80. He was unrivaled as the leading figure of 19th-century Italian opera.

**Jones Very,** age 37; American poet, essayist and mystic, born in Salem, Mass. He wrote sonnets which he believed came to him as revelations of the Holy Ghost. His book *Essays and Poems* (1839) was edited by Emerson and highly praised by Channing and William Cullen Bryant. Somewhat unstable, he spent a short time in an insane asylum in 1838.

**Richard Wagner,** age 37; German composer born in Leipzig. He is best known for the four-part *Ring of the Nibelungen*, based on the 12th-century epic poem *The Nibelungenlied*. Other famous works include *Tannhauser, Lohengrin, Tristan and Isolde, Parsifal* and the comic opera *Die Meistersinger von Nurnberg*. At 57 he married Cosima, the 33-year-old daughter of Franz Liszt, settled at Bayreuth in Bavaria and established the Bayreuth Festival for the production of his music dramas. He is also famous for his many love affairs with married women, his violent temper and his tremendous ego.

**Mikhail Aleksandrovich Bakunin,** age 36; Russian anarchist of an aristocratic family. An officer in the Imperial Guard, he turned to revolutionary activity in his youth, was exiled to Siberia, escaped and thereafter lived in London and Paris, participating in the controversies of radical politics. An atheist and a believer in absolute freedom and extreme individualism, he urged the violent overthrow of governments and institutions.

Sidney Lanier
(1842-1881), age 33
Stephane Mallarme
(1842-1898), age 33
Jules Massenet
(1842-1912), age 33
Arthur Sullivan
(1842-1900), age 33
C. M. Doughty
(1843-1926), age 32
Edvard Grieg
(1843-1907), age 32
Henry James
(1843-1916), age 32
Robert Koch
(1843-1910), age 32
William McKinley
(1843-1901), age 32
Karl Benz
(1844-1929), age 31
Sarah Bernhardt
(1844-1923), age 31
Robert Bridges
(1844-1930), age 31
George Washington Cable
(1844-1925), age 31
Thomas Eakins
(1844-1916), age 31
Anatole France
(1844-1924), age 31
Gerard Manley Hopkins
(1844-1889), age 31
Andrew Lang
(1844-1912), age 31
Modjeska
(1840 or 1844-1909),
age 31?
Friedrich Nietzsche
(1844-1900), age 31
Nikolai Rimski-Korsakov
(1844-1908), age 31
Henri Rousseau
(1844-1910), age 31
Paul Verlaine
(1844-1896), age 31
Elie Metchnikoff
(1845-1916), age 30
Wilhelm Roentgen
(1845-1923), age 30
George Saintsbury
(1845-1933), age 30

# 1850

Giuseppe Mazzini
(1805-1872), age 45
Alexis de Tocqueville
(1805-1859), age 45
Samuel Wilberforce
(1805-1873), age 45
Elizabeth Barrett Browning
(1806-1861), age 44

**Joseph Hooker** (Fighting Joe), age 36; Union general in the American Civil War, born in Massachusetts. He distinguished himself in battle and was made commander of the Army of the Potomac in January 1862. He failed to stop Lee's advance and in June 1863 was relieved of his command at his own request. Less than a week later, his successor, George Meade, won the Battle of Gettysburg.

**Jean Francois Millet,** age 36; French painter born near Cherbourg, known for his landscapes and scenes of peasant life. *The Gleaners* and *The Angelus,* both in the Louvre, and *The Potato Planters, The Sower* and *The Man with a Hoe,* all in American museums, are his most familiar works.

**John Lothrop Motley,** age 36; American historian born in Massachusetts. He gained fame as a specialist in the history of the Netherlands with *The Rise of the Dutch Republic* (three volumes, 1856) and *History of the United Netherlands* (four volumes, 1860-1868), both of which were popular and also highly valued by scholars. He was minister to Austria from 1861-1867 and to Great Britain in 1869-1870.

**Charles Reade,** age 36; English novelist and dramatist, born in Oxfordshire, son of a squire. His successful play *Masks and Faces* (1852), on life in the theater, was rewritten as a novel, *Peg Woffington* (1853), and was followed by several other successful plays and a series of novels on social problems. The historical romance *The Cloister and the Hearth* (1861), on the adventures of the father of Erasmus, is his masterpiece. He was a lifelong, apparently platonic friend of actress Laura Seymour, who kept house for him from 1854-1879.

**Edwin McMasters Stanton,** age 36; American politican born in Ohio. As secretary of war from 1862-1868, he proved a forceful and honest prosecutor of the war, but he fell under the influence of extremists in Congress who opposed President Johnson's reconstruction policies and barricaded himself in his office when asked to resign. After Johnson was acquitted in his impeachment trial, Stanton resigned and died the following year.

**Prince Otto von Bismarck** (the Iron Chancellor), age 35; German statesman; premier of Prussia after 1862 and first chancellor of Germany from 1871-1890. By provoking a series of wars, he forged the divided German principalities into a united nation. He proclaimed William I emperor of Germany in 1871, but retained complete control of domestic and foreign policy. He was dismissed by William II in 1890.

**Cochise,** age 35; chief of the Chiricahua Apaches, born in Arizona. Known for his valor, military skill and integrity, he waged war with the United States Army from 1861-1872 after the unjustified hanging of several of his warriors. Impregnable in his mountain stronghold, he was finally persuaded to make peace and live on a reservation formed from his tribe's territory. He is the subject of a popular Hollywood movie.

**George Gordon Meade,** age 35; Union general in the American Civil War, born in Spain and graduated from West Point in 1835. As brigadier general, he fought at the second Battle of Bull Run, Antietam, Fredericksburg and Chancellorsville. In June 1863 he was made commander of the Army of the Potomac, succeeding Hooker; he won the important Battle of Gettsyburg. He remained in command of the Army of the Potomac throughout the war, but under the direction of Grant.

**Anthony Trollope,** age 35; English novelist born in London, the son of an unsuccessful lawyer and shopkeeper whose wife supported the family by writing novels and the sensational *Domestic Manners of the Americans* (1832). A postal inspector whose work took him to all parts of the British Empire, he still found time to write 50 or 60 novels, the most famous of which are *Barchester Towers* and *The Eustace Diamonds*.

ELIZABETH CADY
STANTON
American feminist
1815-1902

**Elizabeth Cady Stanton,** age 35; American feminist born in New York; wife of Henry Brewster Stanton, the journalist and abolitionist. She organized the first women's rights convention in Seneca Falls, N.Y. in July 1848 and after 1852 was associated with Susan B. Anthony in leading the women's movement. She was the first president of the National Woman Suffrage Association from 1869–1890.

**Charlotte Bronte,** age 34; English novelist born in Yorkshire, daughter of an Irish Anglican clergyman originally named Brunty. The older sister of Emily Bronte, she is remembered for *Jane Eyre*, the story of an English governess in love with her handsome, mysterious and frightening employer. Her other novels—*Shirley, Villette* and *The Professor*—are little known.

**Joseph Arthur, comte de Gobineau,** age 34; French diplomat and writer, an early exponent of the racial superiority of the longheaded, blond Nordics, as expounded in *The Inequality of Human Races* (1854). He was also an Oriental scholar and the author of short stories.

**Baron Paul Julius von Reuter** (Israel Beer Josaphat), age 34; German bank clerk born in Kessel, founder of the Reuter News Agency of London. A pioneer in the field of gathering and transmitting news by telegraph, he began with a telegraph and carrier pigeon service in Aachen in 1849, moved to London in 1851 and became a naturalized citizen and extended his service worldwide. He was made a baron in 1871 by the duke of Saxe-Coburg-Gotha.

**Charles Francois Daubigny,** age 33; French landscape painter born in Paris, son of a painter. He lived for 30 years on a houseboat in the Seine and Oise rivers and painted the river banks, depicting atmospheric effects with great skill. His works, which influenced the Impressionists, include *Evening Landscape* (in the Metropolitan Museum of Art) and *Moonlight* (in the Louvre).

**Frederick Douglass,** age c. 33; American Negro lecturer and writer born in Maryland; the son of Harriet Bailey—a slave—and a white man. He escaped to Massachusetts at 21 and took an active part in the antislavery cause, lecturing and editing an antislavery journal. He wrote his autobiography and was minister to Haiti from 1889–1891.

# 1875

F. H. Bradley
   (1846-1924), age 29
W. F. Cody
   (1846-1917), age 29
Rudolf Eucken
   (1846-1926), age 29
Carry Nation
   (1846-1911), age 29
Charles Parnell
   (1846-1891), age 29
Henryk Sienkiewicz
   (1846-1916), age 29
William Robertson Smith
   (1846-1894), age 29
Alexander Graham Bell
   (1847-1922), age 28
Thomas Alva Edison
   (1847-1931), age 28
Paul von Hindenburg
   (1847-1934), age 28
Jesse James
   (1847-1882), age 28
Joseph Pulitzer
   (1847-1911), age 28
Albert Pinkham Ryder
   (1847-1917), age 28
Ellen Terry
   (1847-1928), age 28
Arthur James Balfour
   (1848-1930), age 27
Bernard Bosanquet
   (1848-1923), age 27
Wyatt Earp
   (1848-1929), age 27
Paul Gauguin
   (1848-1903), age 27
J. K. Huysmans
   (1848-1907), age 27
Vilfredo Pareto
   (1848-1923), age 27
Augustus Saint-Gaudens
   (1848-1907), age 27
Luther Burbank
   (1849-1926), age 26
Crazy Horse
   (1849?-1877), age 26?
W. E. Henley
   (1849-1903), age 26
William Osler
   (1849-1919), age 26
Ivan Pavlov
   (1849-1936), age 26

**Benjamin Jowett,** age 33; English Greek scholar and clergyman; professor at Oxford from 1855. His translation of Plato's *Dialogues* (1871), universally recognized as a classic of English literature, introduced Socrates and his circle to English-speaking people. He also translated Thucydides' *Peloponnesian War* (1881) and Aristotle's *Politics* (1885). He was vice-chancellor at Oxford from 1882–1886.

**Sir Austen Henry Layard,** age 33; English archaeologist and diplomat. His excavations in Mesopotamia (1842–1851) uncovered the remains of Nineveh and other ancient cities, expanding contemporary knowledge of Near Eastern history. He wrote *Nineveh and Its Remains* (1848–1849) and *Discoveries in the Ruins of Nineveh and Babylon* (1853).

**Theodor Mommsen,** age 33; German historian and classical scholar famous for his monumental *History of Rome* (1854–1856), recognized as both a literary and historical classic. A proponent of liberal political views, he strongly opposed the policies of Bismarck. He also wrote scholarly works on Roman law and was awarded the Nobel Prize for literature in 1902.

HENRY DAVID THOREAU
American writer and
naturalist
1817-1862

**Henry David Thoreau,** age 33; American writer and naturalist born in Concord, Mass., a friend of Emerson, Bronson Alcott and other transcendentalists. A lover of nature, he lived two years in the famous cabin in the woods at Walden Pond. He is known for a few essays and two books, *Walden* (1854) and *A Week on the Concord and Merrimack Rivers* (1849), and is world-famous for his intransigent individualism.

**Alexander II** (Aleksandr Nikolaevich), age 32; emperor of Russia from 1855–1881, the nephew of Alexander I. Recognizing that reforms were long overdue, he emancipated the serfs in 1861, abolished corporal punishment and reorganized the army and the judicial and educational systems. He sold Alaska in 1867, and was killed by a bomb-throwing nihilist in St. Petersburg.

**Pierre Gustave Toutant de Beauregard,** age 32; Confederate general in the Civil War, born in Louisiana. A West Point graduate (1838) and engineer on the staff of Gen. Winfield Scott in the Mexican War, he directed the bombardment of Fort Sumter, which began the war. He later became president of a railroad.

**Jacob Christoph Burckhardt,** age 32; Swiss historian of culture born in Basel, son of a clergyman. He is known principally for one book, which has become a classic—*The Civilization of the Renaissance in Italy* (1860), in which he traced the rise of the modern self-conscious individual in the 14th and 15th centuries. He studied under Ranke at the University of Berlin and taught history and art history at the University of Basel.

**James Anthony Froude,** age 32; English historian born in Devonshire. His histories are known for their graceful prose style, strong Protestant bias and emphasis on the role of great men. His principal work is *The History of England from the Fall of Wolsey to the Defeat of the Spanish Armada* (12 volumes, 1856–1870). A close friend and literary executor of Carlyle, he wrote his biography in two volumes.

**Charles Francois Gounod,** age 32; French composer born in Paris, son of a painter. Known in his time as an organist, choirmaster and composer of religious music, he is best known today for two operas— *Faust* (1859) and *Romeo and Juliet* (1867)—both notable for their lyric rather than dramatic qualities.

**Charles Marie Leconte de Lisle,** age 32; French poet born on the island of Reunion, east of Madagascar; son of a French sugar grower. In Paris in 1845 he became a leader of the Parnassian revolt against the emotional excesses of romantic egoism and published *Poemes antiques* (1852), the first of four volumes of verse, displaying the qualities of impersonal restraint and a love of art for art's sake.

**Karl Marx,** age 32; German socialist and political theorist born in Prussia, son of a prosperous Jewish lawyer and grandson of a rabbi. The originator of the idea of modern communism, which he called scientific socialism, he predicted the establishment of a collective dictatorship of the proletariat as the result of a bitter class struggle. His direct influence has been slight in advanced industrial nations with large middle-class populations. His principal works are *The Communist Manifesto* (1848), written in collaboration with Friedrich Engels, and *Capital (Das Kapital,* 1867–1895).

**Lewis Henry Morgan,** age 32; American anthropologist and lawyer born in New York. His interest in the Indians of his locality led to his adoption as a member of the Seneca tribe and to many books on Indian culture. The best known is *Ancient Society* (1877), which introduced the familiar division of human societies into evolutionary stages of savagery, barbarism and civilization.

**Ivan Sergeyevich Turgenev,** age 32; Russian novelist born in Orel, son of a cavalry officer and a wealthy, tyrannical mother. He inherited a great fortune at 32 and lived abroad most of his life, the friend of Flaubert and Henry James and the lover of a celebrated opera singer. An opponent of Slavic isolationism, he surpassed both Tolstoy and Dostoevsky as a prose stylist. His best-known works are *A Sportsman's Sketches* (1852), a collection of stories of peasant life, and the novel *Fathers and Sons* (1862), a portrait of a young Nihilist.

**Prince Albert** (Albert Francis Charles Augustus Emmanuel), age 31; younger son of the duke of Saxe-Coburg-Gotha (a duchy in central Germany) and prince consort to his cousin Victoria, queen of Great Britain (they were married in 1840). He eventually won the affection of the British public, but died of typhoid fever at 42.

**Gustave Courbet,** age 31; French realist painter born in Ornans, son of a landowner. A political radical and director of fine arts of the short-lived Paris Commune of 1871, he was later accused of dynamiting the Vendome Column, imprisoned and ordered to pay the cost of reconstruction. Two famous works are the *Burial at Ornans* (in the Louvre) and *Bonjour, Monsieur Courbet,* a portrait of himself as a carefree backpacker on a country road (in the Musee Fabre in Montpellier).

**Edwin Laurentine Drake,** age 31; American pioneer in the oil industry. A railroad conductor from New Haven, Conn., he drilled the first well at Titusville, Pa. in August 1859 (some 20 years before the

# 1875

Kimmochi Saionji
 (1849/50-1940),
 age c.26
August Strindberg
 (1849-1912), age 26
Samuel Gompers
 (1850-1924), age 25
Lafcadio Hearn
 (1850-1904), age 25
Horatio Kitchener
 (1850-1916), age 25
Pierre Loti
 (1850-1923), age 25
Thomas G. Masaryk
 (1850-1937), age 25
Guy de Maupassant
 (1850-1893), age 25
Robert Louis Stevenson
 (1850-1894), age 25
Arthur Evans
 (1851-1941), age 24
Ferdinand Foch
 (1851-1929), age 24
Adolph von Harnack
 (1851-1930), age 24
Desire Joseph Mercier
 (1851-1926), age 24
Walter Reed
 (1851-1902), age 24
Mrs. Humphrey Ward
 (1851-1920), age 24
Herbert Asquith
 (1852-1928), age 23
Joseph Joffre
 (1852-1931), age 23
Albert A. Michelson
 (1852-1931), age 23
George Moore
 (1852-1933), age 23
Mutsuhito
 (1852-1912), age 23
Vincent van Gogh
 (1853-1890), age 22
Cecil Rhodes
 (1853-1902), age 22
Paul Ehrlich
 (1854-1915), age 21
James G. Frazer
 (1854-1941), age 21
Arthur Rimbaud
 (1854-1891), age 21
John Philip Sousa
 (1854-1932), age 21

invention of the gasoline engine) and struck oil at 69 feet.

**George Eliot** (Mary Ann Evans), age 31; English novelist born in Warwickshire and reared in a strict Protestant family. A scholarly intellectual and friend of Herbert Spencer, she turned to fiction in her late thirties and joined the ranks of the foremost English novelists with *Adam Bede, The Mill on the Floss, Silas Marner* and *Middlemarch,* all realistic portrayals of rural, middle-class English life.

**Charles Kingsley,** age 31; English clergyman and novelist born in Devonshire, son of a clergyman. Known for his popular historical romances *(Hypatia* and *Westward Ho!)* and children's stories *(The Water-Babies),* he was also a liberal social reformer and a prominent churchman, chaplain to Queen Victoria and a canon at Westminster Abbey. His attack on Roman Catholicism led Cardinal Newman to write his *Apologia.*

**James Russell Lowell,** age 31; American poet, essayist and diplomat, member of a prominent New England family. Professor of modern languages at Harvard from 1855–1861, he was the author of *The Vision of Sir Launfal* and *The Bigelow Papers,* composed of satirical verse in Yankee dialect.

**Herman Melville,** age 31; American novelist born in New York City. A friend of Nathaniel Hawthorne, he achieved early but short-lived success with five popular novels: *Typee, Omoo, Mardi, Redburn* and *White-Jacket* (1846–1850), narrations of his experiences at sea and among South Sea natives. He married and lived on a farm, where he wrote *Moby-Dick* (1851), which was not a success. After 20 years as a customs inspector in New York City he died in obscurity; not until the 1920s was *Moby-Dick* hailed as a classic.

**Jacques Offenbach** (Jacob Eberst), age 31; German-French composer born in Cologne. He managed his own theater in Paris after 1855 and wrote and produced over 90 one-act operettas, including *La Vie Parisienne.* His most famous work is the four-act opera *The Tales of Hoffmann,* containing the popular *Barcarolle.*

**Charles Baudelaire,** age 29; French poet and critic, born in Paris. An original, gifted poet and the translator of Edgar Allan Poe's stories, he was notorious for his drug addiction and for charges of immorality brought against him for the content of *Les Fleurs du Mal,* for which he was fined 300 francs.

**Henry Thomas Buckle,** age 29; English historian born near London of a wealthy family. Rejecting the ordinary conception of history as an affair solely of politics and wars, he attempted a scientific history that embraced all aspects of life in relation to the natural environment. He had finished only two volumes of his famous *History of Civilization in England* (1857–1861) before his death at 41, but it has profoundly influenced modern historians.

**Sir Richard Burton,** age 29; English explorer, adventurer and Orientalist, born in Devonshire. He served seven years in the East India Company army and, at 32, disguised as an Afghan pilgrim, journeyed to the holy city of Mecca, a city forbidden to non-believers. He explored East Africa with John Speke and discovered Lake Tanganyika, wrote 43 volumes of travel accounts and completed the first unexpurgated translation of the *Arabian Nights* (16 volumes, 1885–1888). He was knighted in 1886.

**Fedor Mikhailovich Dostoevsky,** age 29; Russian novelist born in Moscow, son of a physician. His long ordeal in a Siberian penal colony, which transformed him from a youthful utopian socialist into a profoundly religious Slavophile, was reflected in his preoccupation with the problems of evil, guilt, suffering and redemption. In his later years, despite his passion for gambling, he became fairly prosperous. His most famous novels are *Crime and Punishment* (1866) and *The Brothers Karamazov* (1880).

**Gustave Flaubert,** age 29; French novelist born in Rouen, son of a physician. After his father's death in 1846, he lived with his mother at Croisset, a suburb of Rouen; except for travels in the Near East and winters in Paris with his literary friends, his was an uneventful life devoted to writing. A perfectionist and brilliant prose stylist, he spent years on each of his novels. *Madame Bovary* and *Sentimental Education* are considered his masterpieces.

**Hermann Ludwig Ferdinand von Helmholtz,** age 29; German physiologist and physicist born at Potsdam. Famous at 26 for his treatise outlining for the first time the principle of the conservation of energy, he also studied the mechanisms of sight and hearing and invented the ophthalmoscope in 1850. He was a professor at various German universities from 1849–1894.

**Matthew Arnold,** age 28; English poet and critic, son of the headmaster of Rugby. He published five volumes of poetry between 1849 and 1858, and thereafter wrote literary and social criticism *(Essays in Criticism* and *Culture and Anarchy).* Inspector of elementary schools from 1851–1886 and professor of poetry at Oxford from 1857–1867, he was an apostle of culture and a determined foe of the materialism of the age. Two familiar poems are *The Scholar Gipsy* and *Dover Beach* ("Where ignorant armies clash by night.").

MARY BAKER EDDY
American religious innovator
1821-1910

**Mary Baker Eddy,** age 29; American religious innovator born in New Hampshire, founder of the Christian Science Church. A semi-invalid most of her life, she found relief in a combination of Bible study and mental healing, expounded in *Science and Health with Key to the Scriptures* (1875). The church, which is not generally recognized as a Christian denomination, was chartered in 1879.

**Cesar Auguste Franck,** age 28; Belgian-French composer and organist born in Liege and taken to Paris as a boy. He was known in his lifetime as an organist at Ste. Clotilde and a teacher at the Paris Conservatory, but was unacknowledged as a composer. He is popular today for his oratorios, symphonic poems, piano pieces and his symphony in D minor.

**John Ruskin,** age 31; English writer and art critic, born in London, son of a wealthy wine merchant. His aesthetic studies, *Modern Paint-*

# 1875

Oscar Wilde
  (1854-1900), age 21
Eugene V. Debs
  (1855-1926), age 20
Arthur Wing Pinero
  (1855-1934), age 20
Josiah Royce
  (1855-1916), age 20
Sigmund Freud
  (1856-1939), age 19
Robert E. Peary
  (1856-1920), age 19
Henri Petain
  (1856-1951), age 19
John Singer Sargent
  (1856-1925), age 19
George Bernard Shaw
  (1856-1950), age 19
Louis Sullivan
  (1856-1924), age 19
Nikola Tesla
  (1856-1943), age 19
Booker T. Washington
  (1856-1915), age 19
Woodrow Wilson
  (1856-1924), age 19
Wovoka
  (1856/58-1932),
  age c.19
Joseph Conrad
  (1857-1924), age 18
Edward Elgar
  (1857-1934), age 18
Georgi Plekhanov
  (1857-1918), age 18
Hermann Sudermann
  (1857-1928), age 18
William Howard Taft
  (1857-1930), age 18
Thorstein Veblen
  (1857-1929), age 18
Rudolf Diesel
  (1858-1913), age 17
Emile Durkheim
  (1858-1917), age 17
Gustaf V (Sweden)
  (1858-1950), age 17
Selma Lagerlof
  (1858-1940), age 17
Max Planck
  (1858-1947), age 17

ers (five volumes), *The Seven Lamps of Architecture* and *The Stones of Venice* (three volumes) are noted for their splendid prose and discerning criticism. Disturbed by the rapid spread of industrialism, he also wrote studies in morality: *Unto This Last, Sesame and Lilies* and *The Crown of Wild Olive*. He lived on a small income, after giving away his large fortune.

**Joseph Seligman,** age 31; German-Jewish financier born in Bavaria, son of a poor weaver. He emigrated to America in 1837 and grew prosperous from his humble trade as a peddler, then sent for his seven brothers and established a retail business and an international banking house, J.&W. Seligman & Co. Called the American Rothschild, he was a financial adviser to Abraham Lincoln and a financial backer of the Union.

**Victoria** (Alexandrina Victoria), age 31; queen of the United Kingdom of Great Britain and Ireland from 1837–1901 and empress of India from 1876–1901; of the house of Hanover, the daughter of Edward, duke of Kent and granddaughter of George III. She succeeded her uncle, William IV, at 18, married Prince Albert of Saxe-Coburg-Gotha and had nine children. Her 63-year reign, the longest in English history, was a time of growing industrialization, imperialism and prosperity for the middle class. It was characterized publicly by a conservative morality and the growth of humanitarianism.

WALT WHITMAN
American poet
1819-1892

**Walt Whitman,** age 31; American poet born on Long Island, N.Y. He worked at various jobs from the age of 12 and had little formal education. He published *Leaves of Grass,* originally a 94-page volume of free verse containing 12 poems, in 1855; he subsequently revised and enlarged the collection several times. A clerk in the office of the attorney general from 1865–1873, he was stricken with paralysis at 54 and lived his ramaining 19 years as a semi-invalid.

**James Buchanan Eads,** age 30; American inventor and engineer born in Indiana. He invented a diving bell and made a fortune recovering valuables from sunken steamboats (1848–1857). Among his engineering exploits were the construction of the famous Eads Bridge across the Mississippi at St. Louis (1867–1874) and the deepening of the mouth of the Mississippi at New Orleans to facilitate river navigation.

**Friedrich Engels,** age 30; German socialist born in an industrial town of the Rhineland, son of a manufacturer; co-author, with Karl Marx, of the *Communist Manifesto*. Living in England after 1850 as a textile manufacturer, he gave Marx financial aid and edited and published his works. He was the author of several political treatises.

SUSAN BROWNELL
ANTHONY
American reformer
1820-1906

**Susan Brownell Anthony,** age 30; American reformer born in Massachusetts, daughter of a Quaker. An early advocate of equal pay for women teachers, higher education for women and temperance for men, she met Elizabeth Cady Stanton at a temperance meeting in 1851, and they joined forces to lead the women's suffrage movement. Their cause finally triumphed in 1928.

**Jenny Lind** (Johanna Maria Lind), age 30; Swedish singer born in Stockholm, called the Swedish Nightingale. Unrivaled as a coloratura soprano, she made her operatic debut at 18 and was enthusiastically received by audiences throughout Europe. Felix Mendelssohn wrote special music for her, and P. T. Barnum brought her to America for a concert tour (1850–1852). Her last public appearance was in 1870.

FLORENCE NIGHTINGALE
English nurse and
humanitarian
1820-1910

**Florence Nightingale,** age 30; English nurse and humanitarian, born in Florence, Italy of wealthy English parents. She introduced improved nursing practices in the Crimean War, established a school for nurses, wrote the first nursing textbook and made nursing a respected medical profession. She is often referred to as "the Lady with the Lamp."

**William Tecomseh Sherman,** age 30; Union general in the American Civil War, born in Ohio. He fought at the first Battle of Bull Run and

Giacomo Puccini
(1858-1924), age 17
Theodore Roosevelt
(1858-1919), age 17
Henri Bergson
(1859-1941), age 16
John Dewey
(1859-1952), age 16
Arthur Conan Doyle
(1859-1930), age 16
Eleanora Duse
(1859-1924), age 16
Havelock Ellis
(1859-1939), age 16
Lady Gregory
(1859?-1932), age 16?
Knut Hamsun
(1859-1952), age 16
Victor Herbert
(1859-1924), age 16
A. E. Housman
(1859-1936), age 16
Sholom Aleichem
(1859-1916), age 16
Francis Thompson
(1859-1907), age 16
William II (Germany)
(1859-1941), age 16
James Barrie
(1860-1937), age 15
William Jennings Bryan
(1860-1925), age 15
Anton Chekhov
(1860-1904), age 15
Gustav Mahler
(1860-1911), age 15
Ignace Jan Paderewski
(1860-1941), age 15
John J. Pershing
(1860-1948), age 15
Raymond Poincare
(1860-1934), age 15
Edward MacDowell
(1861-1908), age 14
Aristide Maillol
(1861-1944), age 14
Fridtjof Nansen
(1861-1930), age 14
Frederic Remington
(1861-1909), age 14
Rabindranath Tagore
(1861-1941), age 14

at Shiloh, Corinth and Vicksburg. On his famous march through Georgia, he left Chattanooga May 6, 1864; reached Atlanta Sept. 2; burned the city; left Atlanta Nov. 15; marched to the sea, leaving a trail of devastation; and entered Savannah Dec. 21. He then marched north through the Carolinas and received Johnston's surrender April 26, 1865.

**Herbert Spencer,** age 30; English philosopher born in Derby, son of an eccentric schoolteacher. He was famous in his day for his *System of Synthetic Philosophy,* developed in several volumes over many years (1860–1896), in which he attempted to sustain the 19th-century faith in social progress with a world view that related all groups of phenomena, "astronomic, geologic, biologic, psychologic, and sociologic," to the unifying principle of evolution. When faith in progress declined, so did his reputation.

**Victor Emmanuel II,** age 30; king of Sardinia from 1847–1878 and first king of Italy from 1861–1878. Assisted by Cavour and Garibaldi, he succeeded in his struggle to free Italy from Austrian domination and establish an independent, unified nation in 1861.

**Clara Barton,** age 29; American school teacher and founder of the American Red Cross. Born in Massachusetts, she taught school from 1839–1854 and began her humanitarian work during the Civil War, distributing supplies to the soldiers and caring for the wounded. She worked for the International Red Cross behind the German lines in the Franco-Prussian War, and in 1881–1882 organized the American Red Cross, serving as its first president from 1882–1904.

**Edmond Louis Antoine Huot de Goncourt,** age 28; French novelist, art critic and diarist, born in Nancy. Together with his brother Julius he produced naturalistic novels depicting the lives of ordinary people in painstaking detail and art criticism. The brothers were inseparable and lived and worked together. The *Goncourt Journal,* their famous 40-year record of the doings of Parisian society, was published in 22 volumes, 1956–1958.

**Rutherford Birchard Hayes,** age 28; American statesman born in Ohio; 19th president, from 1877–1881. He fought in the Civil War; served in Congress from 1865–1867; was governor of Ohio for three terms; and was elected president in a close, disputed election, defeating the Democrat Samuel J. Tilden by an electoral vote of 185 to 184. His term saw the final withdrawal of federal troops from Southern states.

ULYSSES SIMPSON GRANT
American general and president
1822-1885

**Ulysses Simpson Grant,** age 28; American general and statesman, born in Ohio, son of a leather tanner; 18th president, from 1869–1877. He tried various occupations without success—until July 1863, when he captured Vicksburg and 30,000 Confederate troops. As commander-in-chief of the Union armies, he directed the Wilderness Campaign which ended with Lee's surrender. He proved a failure as president, with scandal and graft rampant during his term. He wrote his *Personal Memoirs* in two volumes.

LOUIS PASTEUR
French chemist and
microbiologist
1822-1895

**Louis Pasteur,** age 28; French chemist and microbiologist; inventor of the process of pasteurization, based on his discovery that fermentation and putrefaction of liquids are caused by microorganisms in the atmosphere. His investigations of anthrax and rabies confirmed the germ theory of disease (the greatest medical discovery of all time) and explained why the technique of vaccination introduced by Edward Jenner was successful. He was a professor of chemistry at the Sorbonne from 1867–1889 and the first director of the Pasteur Institute from 1889 to 1895.

GREGOR JOHANN
MENDEL
Austrian botanist and priest
1822-1884

**Gregor Johann Mendel,** age 28; Austrian botanist and priest. He entered a monastery at Brunn (Brno) at 21, and from the breeding experiments he conducted with garden peas formulated the principles known as Mendel's Law, or the basis of the modern theory of heredity. His work was published in 1865.

Frederick Jackson Turner
(1861-1932), age 14
Alfred North Whitehead
(1861-1947), age 14
Claude Debussy
(1862-1918), age 13
Frederick Delius
(1862-1934), age 13
Gerhart Hauptmann
(1862-1946), age 13
O. Henry
(1862-1910), age 13
Maurice Maeterlinck
(1862-1949), age 13
Arthur Schnitzler
(1862-1931), age 13
Edward Westermarck
(1862-1939), age 13
Edith Wharton
(1862-1937), age 13
Gabriele D'Annunzio
(1863-1938), age 12
Henry Ford
(1863-1947), age 12
William Randolph Hearst
(1863-1951), age 12
David Lloyd George
(1863-1945), age 12
Pietro Mascagni
(1863-1945), age 12
George Santayana
(1863-1952), age 12
George Washington Carver
(1864?-1943), age 11?
Richard Strauss
(1864-1949), age 11
Henri de Toulouse-Lautrec
(1864-1901), age 11
Miguel de Unamuno
(1864-1936), age 11
Max Weber
(1864-1920), age 11
Mrs. Patrick Campbell
(1865-1940), age 10
George V (Great Britain)
(1865-1936), age 10
Warren G. Harding
(1865-1923), age 10
Rudyard Kipling
(1865-1936), age 10
Jean Sibelius
(1865-1957), age 10

**Sir Henry Maine,** age 28; English jurist and historian known for his studies of the history of law and institutions, which he interpreted from an evolutionary and aristocratic point of view. He was a professor of law and jurisprudence at both Cambridge and Oxford and a member of the viceroy's council of India from 1863–1869. His most famous works are *Ancient Law* (1861) and *Early History of Institutions* (1875).

**Frederick Law Olmstead,** age 28; American landscape architect born in Connecticut. With Calvert Vaux, he planned and supervised the laying out of Central Park in New York City. He also designed Prospect Park in Brooklyn, South Park in Chicago, the park system of Boston, the grounds of the National Capitol and Jackson Park in Chicago, originally the grounds of the 1893 World's Exposition. He has earned the title of father of American parks.

**Heinrich Schliemann,** age 28; German businessman and archaeologist, famous for his discovery of ancient Troy. He retired from business in 1863 after making a fortune and spent the rest of his life excavating cities in Asia Minor and Greece, searching for remains of the Homeric age. His excavations of Mycenae, Ithaca, Orchomenos and Tiryns brought to public and scholarly attention the forgotten Mycenaean culture.

**Max Mueller** (Friedrich Maximilian Mueller), age 27; German-British philologist and Orientalist born in Dessau, the son of Wilhelm Mueller, a court librarian and poet. He settled in England, was made a professor at Oxford and was engaged by the East Indian Company to bring out a complete edition of the Sanskrit *Rig-Veda*—which he did, in six volumes, from 1849 to 1873. He spent the last 25 years of his life editing *The Sacred Books of the East* (51 volumes). He also wrote influential books on comparative philology, mythology and religion.

**Francis Parkman,** age 27; American historian born in Boston, the son of a prosperous and prominent clergyman. In spite of a nervous disorder and defective vision, he set out in 1846 to explore the West and gathered material for his famous book *The Oregon Trail* (1849). With his two-volume work, *The Conspiracy of Pontiac* (1851), he won a reputation as a historian of the French and British colonial wars.

**(Joseph) Ernest Renan,** age 27; French scholar and historian whose *Life of Jesus* (1863) was the first biography to treat Jesus as a historical figure. It formed the first volume of the seven-volume *History of the Origins of Christianity* (1863–1881). He also wrote *History of the People of Israel* (five volumes, 1887–1893) and was praised by Mommsen as a true scholar despite the beauty of his style.

**William Marcy Tweed** (Boss Tweed), age 27; American politician born in New York City. Beginning as a Democratic alderman, he rose to be grand sachem of Tammany Hall and head of the Tweed Ring, a handful of politicians who stole millions from the city treasury. Exposed by *Harper's Weekly* (with cartoons by Thomas Nast) and the New York *Times* in 1870, he was convicted and served a year in jail.

**Alfred Russell Wallace,** age 27; English naturalist said to have conceived of the theory of natural selection about the same time as Darwin. Actually, in 1858 he had accomplished only an abstract sketch, a stage reached by Darwin 15 years earlier. He wrote *Contributions to the Theory of Natural Selection* in 1870 and defined the line of zoological differentiation between Asia and Australia known as Wallace's Line.

**Anton Bruckner,** age 26; Austrian composer and organist, son of a school teacher. He toured France and England as a virtuoso organist, but his reputation as a composer grew more slowly. His music, which includes nine symphonies and three well-known masses—the D minor, E minor and F minor masses—bears the influence of Wagner and in turn influenced Gustav Mahler.

**Wilkie Collins,** age 26; English novelist born in London, son of a painter; author of the first full-length detective novels in English and of the popular mysteries *The Woman in White* (1860) and *The Moonstone* (1868). He wrote over 30 novels, some of which first appeared in the *Household Words* of his friend, Charles Dickens. He collaborated with Dickens in writing *No Thoroughfare* (1867).

**Alexandre Dumas** (Dumas *fils),* age 26; French playwright and novelist born in Paris, an illegitimate son of Dumas *pere.* His fame rests on his popular dramatization in 1852 of his first novel, *La Dame aux Camelias (Camille).* Verdi's *La Traviata* added to its renown; Sarah Bernhardt made the play a staple of her repertoire; Greta Garbo starred in the first film version.

**Thomas Jonathan Jackson** (Stonewall Jackson), age 26; American army officer born in Virginia and graduated from West Point in 1846. He served in the Mexican War and from 1851–1861 was an instructor at the Virginia Military Institute. As a general in the Confederate army, he stood immovably—like a stone wall—at the first Battle of Bull Run, and fought also in the Shenandoah campaign; at the second Battle of Bull Run; Antietam; at Fredericksburg; and at Chancellorsville. Called the South's most able general after Lee, he was accidentally shot by his own troops and died at 39.

**Bedrich Smetana,** age 26; Czech nationalist composer and conductor. He established a school of music in Prague and appeared as a conductor until 1874, when he became deaf. He is best known for his comic opera *The Bartered Bride* and the symphonic poem *From the Fields and Groves of Bohemia.*

**Thomas Henry Huxley,** age 25; English biologist, essayist and educator; born in London, son of a schoolmaster. As assistant surgeon on the H.M.S. *Rattlesnake* in Australian waters (1846–1850), he made observations of marine life which led to the formulation of the zoological class *Hydrozoa.* Called "Darwin's Bulldog," he was the foremost defender of Darwin's theories and attracted large crowds to his public lectures and debates with Bishop Wilberforce. He wrote *Evolution and Ethics* (1893).

**Stephanus Johannes Paulus Kruger** (Oom Paul), age 25; South African statesman of Dutch descent, born in Cape Colony. As a boy he accompanied his family on the Great Trek northward to escape the encroachments of the British (1836–1840) and became a political and military leader of the Transvaal Republic, of which he was president from 1883–1902. Too old to fight in the Boer War (1899–1902), he went to Europe in an unsuccessful effort to obtain aid and died in Switzerland.

**Ferdinand Lassalle,** age 25; German social reformer born in Breslau, son of a Jewish merchant; called the founder of the German Social Democratic party. A friend of Karl Marx, he engaged in socialist propaganda on behalf of the working classes and urged the formation of cooperative manufacturing associations. He was killed in a duel at 39 by a Hungarian diplomat defending his wife's honor.

**Johann Strauss, Jr.** (the Waltz King), age 25; Austrian composer and conductor born in Vienna. His popularity surpassed that of his father, whom he succeeded as orchestra leader. He composed 400 waltzes, including *The Blue Danube, Tales from the Vienna Woods* and *Voices of Spring.* Of his 16 operettas, the best known are *Die Fledermaus (The Bat)* and *The Gypsy Baron.*

**Walter Bagehot,** age 24; English economist and writer born inxLondon, son of a banker. Of high standing among economists, he was the author of *The English Constitution* (1864) and *Lombard Street* (1873),

# 1875

Charles Steinmetz
(1865-1923), age 10
William Butler Yeats
(1865-1939), age 10
Benedetto Croce
(1866-1952), age 9
Wassily Kandinsky
(1866-1944), age 9
Ramsay MacDonald
(1866-1937), age 9
Gilbert Murray
(1866-1957), age 9
Romain Rolland
(1866-1944), age 9
Sun Yat-sen
(1866-1925), age 9
August von Wassermann
(1866-1925), age 9
H. G. Wells
(1866-1946), age 9
Arnold Bennett
(1867-1931), age 8
Vicente Blasco-Ibanez
(1867-1928), age 8
Gutzon Borglum
(1867 or 1871-1941),
age 8?
Marie Curie
(1867-1934), age 8
Ernest Dowson
(1867-1900), age 8
John Galsworthy
(1867-1933), age 8
Jozef Pilsudski
(1867-1935), age 8
Luigi Pirandello
(1867-1936), age 8
Arturo Toscanini
(1867-1957), age 8
Wilbur Wright
(1867-1912), age 8
W. E. B. Du Bois
(1868-1963), age 7
Stefan George
(1868-1933), age 7
Maxim Gorki
(1868-1936), age 7
Nicholas II (Russia)
(1868-1918), age 7
Edmond Rostand
(1868-1918), age 7
Neville Chamberlain
(1869-1940), age 6

a study of the English banking system. Editor (1860–1877) of the financial journal *The Economist* (founded by his father-in-law), he also wrote literary criticism.

**Stephen Collins Foster,** age 24; American songwriter born near Pittsburgh. A bookkeeper in Cincinnati (1846–1850) with no formal musical training, he gained success and fame writing songs for Christy's Minstrels. An alcoholic, he died in Bellevue Hospital in New York City at 37. Some of his famous songs are *Jeanie with the Light Brown Hair* (1854), *Camptown Races* (1850) and *My Old Kentucky Home* (1853).

**George Brinton McClellan,** age 24; American army officer born in Philadelphia and graduated from West Point in 1846. From November 1861 to March 1862, he was general in chief of the Union armies, but was removed because of his delay in mounting an offensive. He commanded the Army of the Potomac in the Peninsula and Antietam campaigns, but was again removed for his overcautiousness. He ran for president as the Democratic candidate in 1864 against Lincoln, but lost.

**Joseph Lister,** age 23; first Baron Lister, English surgeon born in Essex; professor of surgery from 1860–1893 at the universities of Glasgow, Edinburgh and London. He introduced antiseptic surgery, proving that the sterilization of instruments, using carbolic acid (phenol) or heat, was effective in preventing infection (1865). He also initiated the use of absorbable ligatures. He was made a baron in 1897.

**Lew Wallace,** age 23; American novelist, army officer and lawyer; born in Indiana, son of the governor. A major general in the Union army, he was president of the court that convicted the Confederate commandant of Andersonville prison: the dreadful conditions of this prisoner-of-war camp had led to the deaths of many captured Union soldiers. He is remembered as the author of *Ben Hur*, one of the best-selling novels of all time. He also wrote *The Fair God, The Prince of India* and others, now consigned to oblivion.

**Meyer Guggenheim,** age 22; Swiss-American industrialist and philanthropist and founder of the Guggenheim fortune; born in Switzerland. He emigrated in 1847 and established a retail and importing business in Philadelphia. Late in life he entered the copper-smelting business, built smelters in Colorado and Mexico and a refinery at Perth Amboy, N.J. With the aid of his seven sons he acquired a near-monopoly of the copper industry.

**Henrik Ibsen,** age 22; Norwegian dramatist born in a small town where he worked six years as a pharmacist's apprentice. At 23 he was stage manager of a theater in Bergen and at 29 a theater director in Christiana (Oslo). From 35 to 63 he lived in Italy and Germany and achieved fame only late in life with *A Doll's House* (1879), *Ghosts* (1881), *An Enemy of the People* (1882) and *Hedda Gabler* (1890). His introduction of recognizable middle-class characters and situations signalled the end of the era of romantic drama.

**George Meredith,** age 22; English novelist and poet born in Portsmouth, son of a tailor. His major novels, *The Egoist* and *Diana of the Crossways,* are famous for their difficult opening chapters, although he is generally considered a distinguished prose stylist. The father of Virginia Woolf, Leslie Stephen, is said to have been the model for a character in *The Egoist*.

**Dante Gabriel Rossetti,** age 22; English poet and painter born in London, the son of an exiled Italian patriot. He formed with Holman Hunt and other artists the pre-Raphaelite group, taking their inspiration from the style of Italian painters before Raphael. His contemporaries called him vain and egotistical. His best-known poem is *The Blessed Damozel.*

**Hippolyte Adolphe Taine,** age 22; French historian and critic, son of a lawyer. A 19th-century materialist in his outlook, he attempted a scientific study of human nature and history. His major works are *History of English Literature* (1863–1864) and *The Origins of Contemporary France* (1876–1894).

COUNT LEO TOLSTOY
Russian novelist and
    moral philosopher
1828-1910

**Count Leo Tolstoy** (Lev Nikolaevich Tolstoi), age 22; Russian novelist and moral philosopher, born in central Russia on the family estate of Yasnaya Polyana. An orphan at nine, he was raised by his aunts and educated by French tutors. He produced his first novel, *Childhood,* at 24, but his two greatest novels, *War and Peace* (1869) and *Anna Karenina* (1875–1877), are the work of later years. At about 50 he experienced a religious conversion and thereafter wrote only religious and ethical works: *The Kingdom of God Is Within You* (1893), *What Is Art?* (1898) and others. Rejecting the church, the state and Western civilization, he preached a religion of nonviolence and attracted many followers throughout the world.

GERONIMO
American Apache Chieftain
1829-1909

**Geronimo,** age 21; American Apache Indian born in southern Arizona. Intermittently from 1876 to 1886, he led raids on white settlers in

# 1875

Mahatma Gandhi
    (1869-1948), age 6
Andre Gide
    (1869-1951), age 6
Edgar Lee Masters
    (1869-1950), age 6
Henri Matisse
    (1869-1954), age 6
Edwin Arlington Robinson
    (1869-1935), age 6
Booth Tarkington
    (1869-1946), age 6
Frank Lloyd Wright
    (1869-1959), age 6
Alfred Adler
    (1870-1937), age 5
Ivan Bunin
    (1870-1953), age 5
Lenin
    (1870-1924), age 5
Frank Norris
    (1870-1902), age 5
Jan Christian Smuts
    (1870-1950), age 5
Teitaro Suzuki
    (1870-1966), age 5
Theodore Dreiser
    (1871-1945), age 4
Marcel Proust
    (1871-1922), age 4
Ernest Rutherford
    (1871-1937), age 4
J. M. Synge
    (1871-1909), age 4
Paul Valery
    (1871-1945), age 4
Orville Wright
    (1871-1948), age 4
Roald Amundsen
    (1872-1928), age 3
Calvin Coolidge
    (1872-1933), age 3
Sergei Diaghilev
    (1872-1929), age 3
Haakon VII (Norway)
    (1872-1957), age 3
Piet Mondrian
    (1872-1944), age 3
Bertrand Russell
    (1872-1970), age 3
Ralph Vaughan Williams
    (1872-1958), age 3

the Southwest, was captured and escaped several times. At 57 he settled on a farm at Fort Sill, Okla., and joined the Dutch Reformed Church; he dictated his memoirs and appeared as a popular attraction at the St. Louis World's Fair in 1904.

**Jules Verne,** age 22; French author born in Nantes. He studied law in Paris and wrote plays and opera librettos until he was about 35, when he turned to scientific adventure stories and won immediate success and popularity with *20,000 Leagues Under the Sea, Around the World in 80 Days, Michael Strogoff* and about 50 others. He is often called the forerunner of modern science fiction.

**Anton Rubinstein,** age 21; Russian-Jewish pianist and composer born in the Ukraine. He made his concert debut at nine and became famous throughout Europe as a virtuoso pianist and a rival of Liszt. He composed operas *(The Maccabees),* oratorios *(Paradise Lost),* symphonies *(The Ocean Symphony),* piano concertos and other works. He toured the United States in 1872–1873.

**Chester Alan Arthur,** age 20; American statesman born in Vermont; 21st president, 1881–1885. Appointed collector of the port of New York by Pres. Grant, he was elected vice-president in 1880, and in September 1881 succeeded to the presidency after the assassination of James Garfield. In spite of his record as a machine politician, he proved honest and efficient. Illness prevented him from seeking a second term.

**Porfirio Diaz,** age 20; Mexican general and dictator, a mestizo born in Oaxaca. He supported Juarez in the war with the French, and in 1876 he overthrew the government of Juarez's successor and established himself as president, ruling as a dictator from 1876–1880 and again from 1884–1911, with little regard for the welfare of the people. Overthrown in 1911, he died in exile in Paris at 85.

**Emily Elizabeth Dickinson,** age 20; American poet born in Amherst, Mass., daughter of a lawyer and granddaughter of a founder of Amherst College. She lived all her life in her parents' house; she was shy, eccentric and, in her later years, a recluse. The posthumous publication in 1890 and 1891 of the first two volumes of her 1,775 poems placed her among the greatest American poets. Cryptic and unsentimental, her poetry continues to increase in popularity. These famous lines are hers: "Because I could not stop for Death,/ He kindly stopped for me."

**Francis Joseph I** (Franz Josef), age 20; emperor of Austria from 1848–1916 and king of Hungary from 1867–1916, of the house of Hapsburg-Lorraine; the great-great-grandson of Maria Theresa. His

# 1875–1900

The last quarter of the 19th century was the great age of optimism. In 1875 Queen Victoria, the granddaughter of

reign was the last great age of Austrian political and cultural preeminence. Symptoms of decline appeared as the Italian possessions were lost and leadership of the German confederation was surrendered to Bismarck. Franz Josef died at 86 and was succeeded by his grandnephew, Charles I. Two years later the empire disintegrated into independent national states.

**Jules Alfred Huot de Goncourt,** age 20; French novelist, art critic and diarist. Born in Paris, he was the younger brother of Edmond Goncourt and collaborator in all his writings, including the famous *Goncourt Journal*. He died at 40; his brother outlived him by 26 years.

**Camille Pissarro,** age 20; French landscape painter of the impressionist school; born in the Virgin Islands, the son of a hardware merchant. The oldest of the impressionists, though not their leader, he went to Paris at 25 and helped Monet organize their first exhibition in 1874. He is known for his street scenes of Paris and Rouen, views of the Normandy countryside and sunlit village road scenes. He was the friend and teacher of many younger painters.

**Christina Georgina Rossetti,** age 20; English poet born in London, sister of Dante Gabriel Rossetti. Her reputation rests on *Goblin Market and Other Poems* (1862) and her later short lyrics of a religious, often melancholy nature. She surpassed her brother as a lyricist. She never married.

**Philip Henry Sheridan,** age 19; Union general in the American Civil War, born in Albany, N.Y. He commanded the cavalry of the Army of the Potomac and is credited with forcing Lee's surrender in 1865 by blocking his retreat from Appomattox. He succeeded Sherman as commander of the army in 1884.

**Maximilian** (Ferdinand Maximilian Josepf), age 18; archduke of Austria and emperor of Mexico from 1864–1867; brother of Emperor Francis Joseph I. He accepted the offer of a group of wealthy Mexicans who conspired with Napoleon III to establish an imperial government in Mexico. Juarez was driven across the American border by French troops, and Maximilian was crowned emperor. An ultimatum from the United States in February 1866 caused Napoleon to withdraw his troops, leaving Maximilian defenseless. He was arrested and shot in June 1867.

**James Ewell Brown Stuart** (Jeb Stuart), age 17; Confederate cavalry commander in the American Civil War, famous for his raids that disrupted federal communications. He succeeded Stonewall Jackson as corps commander at Chancellorsville and commanded the cavalry at Gettysburg in July 1863. He was mortally wounded in action in May 1864.

George III, was at age 56 in the 38th year of her reign and possessed of a calm, reassuring presence which convinced her subjects that all was right with the world. There were some minor problems to be solved regarding the conditions of laboring people and the distant parts of the empire, but these would eventually be attended to. It was in the meantime a comfortable, enlightened and humane world.

Carl L. Becker (1873-1945), age 2

Enrico Caruso (1873-1921), age 2

Willa Cather (1873 or 1876-1947), age 2?

Feodor Chaliapin (1873-1938), age 2

Colette (1873-1954), age 2

Lee De Forest (1873-1961), age 2

Ford Madox Ford (1873-1939), age 2

George Edward Moore (1873-1958), age 2

Emily Post (1873-1960), age 2

Sergei Rachmaninoff (1873-1943), age 2

G. K. Chesterton (1874-1936), age 1

Sir Winston Churchill (1874-1965), age 1

Robert Frost (1874-1963), age 1

Ellen Glasgow (1874-1945), age 1

Herbert Hoover (1874-1964), age 1

Amy Lowell (1874-1925), age 1

Guglielmo Marconi (1874-1937), age 1

W. Somerset Maugham (1874-1965), age 1

Arnold Schoenberg (1874-1951), age 1

Gertrude Stein (1874-1946), age 1

Chaim Weizmann (1874-1952), age 1

# 1875

Peter Cooper
(1791-1883), age 84
Pius IX (Pope)
(1792-1878), age 83
William Cullen Bryant
(1794-1878), age 81
Cornelius Vanderbilt
(1794-1877), age 81
Thomas Carlyle
(1795-1881), age 80
Leopold von Ranke
(1795-1886), age 80
Antonio de Santa Anna
(1794/95-1876), age c.80
Jean Baptiste Corot
(1796-1875), age 79
Sir Charles Lyell
(1797-1875), age 78
Louis Adolphe Thiers
(1797-1877), age 78
William I (Germany)
(1797-1888), age 78
Bronson Alcott
(1799-1888), age 76
George Bancroft
(1800-1891), age 75
Helmuth von Moltke
(1800-1891), age 75
John Henry Newman
(1801-1896), age 74
Brigham Young
(1801-1877), age 74
Victor Hugo
(1802-1885), age 73
Louis Kossuth
(1802-1894), age 73

They believed above all in progress. The publication in 1859 of Darwin's book had at first been disturbing, but when Herbert Spencer demonstrated that evolution and social progress were grounded in cosmic laws, many minds were put at ease. In 1860 Spencer had announced his intention of publishing a comprehensive work in several volumes, to be called *A System of Synthetic Philosophy,* which would explain and clarify the principle of evolution. Volumes dropped from the presses at frequent intervals: *First Principles* in 1862; *Principles of Biology,* 1864 and 1867; *The Principles of Sociology,* in three volumes, 1876, 1882 and 1896; *Data of Ethics,* 1879; and *Principles of Ethics,* 1892 and 1893. It was proven conclusively in these volumes that progress was inevitable and that optimism should be the disposition

**James Abram Garfield,** age 44; American statesman and legislator, born in Ohio, the son of a frontier farmer; 20th president, March–September 1881. A farmer and canal boatman in his youth, and a teacher in a small college, he rose to the rank of major general in the Union army and served in Congress from 1863–1880, the last four years as Republican leader with a reputation for his powerful oratory. He was nominated as the Republican candidate for president on the 36th ballot in 1880 and served only six months before being assassinated by a disappointed office seeker. He was the second American president to be assassinated.

**James Clerk Maxwell,** age 44; British physicist born in Edinburgh; first professor of experimental physics at Cambridge. Observing similarities between light waves and electromagnetic waves, he concluded that light is an electromagnetic phenomenon. He is ranked with the greatest scientists for the fundamental nature of his discoveries.

**Victorien Sardou,** age 44; French playwright born in Paris, the son of a school teacher. His more than 70 comedies and semihistorical melodramas were highly popular and were produced with such eminent players as Henry Irving and Sarah Bernhardt. The most successful were *Madame Devil-May-Care* (1893), *Fedora* (1882) and *La Tosca* (1887), the source of Puccini's opera.

**Louisa May Alcott,** age 43; American author born in Pennsylvania, daughter of Bronson Alcott. She took up writing to relieve the family's poverty and won popularity with her children's classics, *Little Women* (1868–1869) and *Little Men* (1871). She was a friend of Emerson and Thoreau.

**Bjornstjerne Bjornson,** age 43; Norwegian poet, dramatist and novelist; son of a clergyman. A leader in the cause of Norwegian independence and author of the national anthem, he is best known for his novels of peasant life, *Arne* and *The Fisher Maiden,* but he also wrote plays that were second only to Ibsen's.

**Lewis Carroll** (Charles Lutwidge Dodgson), age 43; English humorist and author of children's books, born in Cheshire, son of a clergyman. *Alice's Adventures in Wonderland* (1865), *Through the Looking-Glass* (1871) and *The Hunting of the Snark* have attained immortality, along with some of the characters therein—the Mad Hatter, the March Hare and the Cheshire Cat. He also taught mathematics at Oxford from 1855–1881. These famous lines of Jabberwocky are his: "'Twas brillig,

of every reasonable person.

This was the theme of Victoria's diamond jubilee of 1897, celebrating her 60th year of her reign, an occasion of great public rejoicing. She was 78, and her popularity was at its height, for her subjects were enjoying a period of unprecedented prosperity. Her personal honesty and devotion to family life made her a symbol of solid middle-class virtues. Queen Victoria and Herbert Spencer were the gods of the age of progress, representing stabiliy, decency, morality, humanitarianism and eternal progress. Their lives were almost exactly contemporary. When Victoria died in 1901 and Spencer in 1903, the future for England and the Continent looked exceptionally bright; the monarchs were firmly seated on their thrones, and there was not a cloud on the horizon.

# 1900

and the slithy toves/ Did gyre and gimble in the wabe."

**Gustave Dore,** age c. 43; French book illustrator and painter born in Strasbourg. He is said to have illustrated over 120 books—including such classics as the works of Rabelais, Cervantes, Dante, Milton, Balzac and La Fontaine—in a highly individual, theatrical style which is still admired.

**Edouard Manet,** age 43; French painter born in Paris, son of a government official. Not one of the impressionists, although some of his work, such as *The Balcony,* shows their influence, he is famous for two paintings that scandalized the critics: *Olympia* and *Luncheon on the Grass,* in the Louvre. He also painted *The Bar at the Folies Bergere* and a wide variety of scenes of modern life, and attained, only after his death, the recognition he desired.

**Nikolaus August Otto,** age 43; German inventor born in Cologne, the son of an innkeeper; inventor of the first practical small engine. His four-stroke, internal-combustion engine (patented in 1877) was similar to the modern engine but ran on coal gas instead of petroleum distillate. He established a factory at Deutz, with Gottlieb Daimler as manager.

**Sir Leslie Stephen,** age 43; English man of letters born in London of a prominent family. He was the first editor (1882–1891) of the huge *Dictionary of National Biography* and author of *History of English Thought in the Eighteenth Century* (1876). Said to be the original of the modest Vernon Whitford in Meredith's *The Egoist,* he was the son-in-law of Thackeray and father (by his second wife) of Virginia Woolf.

**Sir Edward Burnett Tylor,** age 43; English anthropologist born in London, son of a Quaker owner of a brass foundry. Called the founder of modern anthropology, he won a reputation with *Researches into the Early History of Mankind* (1865), but his principal work is *Primitive Culture* (1871), in which he developed the theory of animism. He was the first professor of anthropology at Oxford, from 1896–1909.

**Edwin Thomas Booth,** age 42; American actor born in Maryland; son of the English actor Junius Brutus Booth. One of the greatest American actors, he appeared on the New York stage from 1862–1865 and from 1866–1873 (he retired temporarily for one year after his brother shot Lincoln) and in England from 1880–1882, alternating in repertory with Sir Henry Irving. He toured California and the West from 1852–

Sigmund Freud
  (1856-1939), age 44
Robert E. Peary
  (1856-1920), age 44
Henri Petain
  (1856-1951), age 44
John Singer Sargent
  (1856-1925), age 44
George Bernard Shaw
  (1856-1950), age 44
Louis Sullivan
  (1856-1924), age 44
Nikola Tesla
  (1856-1943), age 44
Booker T. Washington
  (1856-1915), age 44
Woodrow Wilson
  (1856-1924), age 44
Joseph Conrad
  (1857-1924), age 43
Edward Elgar
  (1857-1934), age 43
Georgi Plekhanov
  (1857-1918), age 43
Hermann Sudermann
  (1857-1928), age 43
William Howard Taft
  (1857-1930), age 43
Thorstein Veblen
  (1857-1929), age 43
Rudolf Diesel
  (1858-1913), age 42
Emile Durkheim
  (1858-1917), age 42
Gustaf V (Sweden)
  (1858-1950), age 42

337

# 1875

Harriet Martineau
  (1802-1876), age 73
George Borrow
  (1803-1881), age 72
Ralph Waldo Emerson
  (1803-1882), age 72
Benjamin Disraeli
  (1804-1881), age 71
George Sand
  (1804-1876), age 71
Hans Christian Andersen
  (1805-1875), age 70
William Lloyd Garrison
  (1805-1879), age 70
Ferdinand de Lesseps
  (1805-1894), age 70
Giuseppe Garibaldi
  (1807-1882), age 68
Joseph E. Johnston
  (1807-1891), age 68
Henry Wadsworth Longfellow
  (1807-1882), age 68
John Greenleaf Whittier
  (1807-1892), age 68
Honore Daumier
  (1808-1879), age 67
Jefferson Davis
  (1808-1889), age 67
Andrew Johnson
  (1808-1875), age 67
Charles Darwin
  (1809-1882), age 66
Edward FitzGerald
  (1809-1883), age 66
William E. Gladstone
  (1809-1898), age 66
Oliver Wendell Holmes
  (1809-1894), age 66
Fanny Kemble
  (1809-1893), age 66
Cyrus Hall McCormick
  (1809-1884), age 66
Alfred Tennyson
  (1809-1892), age 66
P. T. Barnum
  (1810-1891), age 65
Asa Gray
  (1810-1888), age 65
Leo XIII (Pope)
  (1810-1903), age 65
Sir Henry Raeburn
  (1810-1895), age 65

1856 and from 1873–1879. He was noted for his performances as Hamlet, King Lear, Romeo and Othello. He retired in 1891.

**Aleksandr Porfirevich Borodin,** age c. 42; Russian composer born in St. Petersburg, the illegitimate son of a nobleman. A physician and professor of chemistry by vocation, he took up musical composition as a recreation. His familiar works include the unfinished opera *Prince Igor* and *In the Steppes of Central Asia.*

**Johannes Brahms,** age 42; German composer and pianist born in Hamburg, son of a musician. A successful composer in Vienna after 1863, he combined romanticism and classicism to produce such famous works as the symphonies in C minor, D major, E major and E minor; the *Academic Festival Overture;* and the *Tragic Overture.* He was a close friend of Robert and Clara Schumann and a lifelong bachelor.

**Charles George Gordon** (Chinese Gordon), age 42; British soldier born in Woolwich. He fought in the Crimean War and in many parts of the British Empire, suppressed the Taiping Rebellion in China and defended Khartoum for 10 months against the Muslim leader called the Mahdi. He was killed when Khartoum fell in 1885.

**Benjamin Harrison,** age 42; American statesman born in Ohio, grandson of William Henry Harrison; 23rd president, 1889–1893. An Indianapolis lawyer and senator (1881–1887), he is remembered for winning the 1888 election in the Electoral College, despite the fact that Grover Cleveland had received a larger popular vote. A staunch Republican, he followed the party line throughout his administration.

**Alfred Bernhard Nobel,** age 42; Swedish chemist, engineer and manufacturer; born in Stockholm, the son of a manufacturer. He studied engineering in the United States from 1850–1854, invented dynamite in 1866 and established factories throughout the world for the production of explosives. He left $9.2 million to be used for the annual presentation of awards of merit; the first Nobel Prize was awarded in 1901.

**Lord Acton** (John Emerich Edward Dalberg-Acton, first Baron Acton), age 41; English historian of an aristocratic Roman Catholic family. A liberal member of Parliament and a friend of Gladstone, professor of modern history at Cambridge from 1895–1902 and first editor of the *Cambridge Modern History,* he was an influential historian, although he never wrote a book. His lectures were collected and published posthumously.

**Gottlieb Daimler,** age 41; German engineer, inventor and pioneer automobile manufacturer; born in Wurttemberg. He developed the Otto gas engine into a lightweight, high-speed gasoline engine and drove a four-wheeled horseless carriage from Cannstatt to Esslingen in 1884 at a speed of 11 miles per hour. He formed the Daimler Motor Company in 1890 and produced the first modern motor car in 1900, which he called Mercedes after his daughter.

**Edgar Degas,** age 41; French painter and sculptor born in Paris, son of a banker. Although he is sometimes called an impressionist, he did not count himself among them. He is known for his cafe and racetrack scenes and for numberous pastels of young ballerinas. He turned to sculpting in later years when his sight failed, and was almost totally blind at death. One famous work is *L'absinthe,* in the Louvre.

**Ernst Heinrich Haeckel,** age 41; German biologist and philosopher born in Potsdam. Professor of zoology at Jena from 1865–1908, he was the first German advocate and popularizer of Darwinism. He originated the theory that each growing organism passes through stages corresponding to stages in the development of the species. He applied evolutionary theory to philosophy in *The Riddle of the Universe* (1899).

**William Morris,** age 41; English poet, prose writer and craftsman; born in Essex, son of a prosperous businessman. An admirer of medieval craftsmanship, he designed and manufactured furniture, tapestries and textiles and printed fine books. A prolific writer, he is known for his poems *The Story of Sigurd the Volsung* and *The Earthly Paradise* and the prose romance *News from Nowhere* (1891). He actively promoted socialism, in the belief that it would bring the restoration of craftsmanship.

SITTING BULL
American Indian chief and
medicine man
1831 or 1834-1890

**Sitting Bull,** age 41?; American Indian chief and medicine man born in South Dakota, head of the Sioux war council. He is famous for the Battle of the Little Big Horn, on June 25, 1876, during which George Armstrong Custer made his fatal last stand. He was later settled on Standing Rock Reservation and in 1885 appeared in Buffalo Bill's Wild West Show. He was shot by Indian police in 1890 during a disturbance.

JAMES McNEILL WHISTLER
American painter and etcher
1834-1903

**James Abbott McNeill Whistler,** age 41; American painter and etcher born in Massachusetts, son of an army surgeon. In Paris at 21 he became a dandy and met Courbet, Manet and Degas. After moving to London he achieved success as a portrait painter, with Thomas Carlyle

Selma Lagerlof
(1858-1940), age 42
Max Planck
(1858-1947), age 42
Giacomo Puccini
(1858-1924), age 42
Theodore Roosevelt
(1858-1919), age 42
Henri Bergson
(1859-1941), age 41
John Dewey
(1859-1952), age 41
Arthur Conan Doyle
(1859-1930), age 41
Eleanora Duse
(1859-1924), age 41
Havelock Ellis
(1859-1939), age 41
Lady Gregory
(1859?-1932), age 41?
Knut Hamsun
(1859-1952), age 41
Victor Herbert
(1859-1924), age 41
A. E. Housman
(1859-1936), age 41
Sholom Aleichem
(1859-1916), age 41
Francis Thompson
(1859-1907), age 41
William II (Germany)
(1859-1941), age 41
James Barrie
(1860-1937), age 40
William Jennings Bryan
(1860-1925), age 40
Anton Chekhov
(1860-1904), age 40
Gustav Mahler
(1860-1911), age 40
Ignace Jan Paderewski
(1860-1941), age 40
John J. Pershing
(1860-1948), age 40
Raymond Poincare
(1860-1934), age 40
Edward MacDowell
(1861-1908), age 39
Aristide Maillol
(1861-1944), age 39
Fridtjof Nansen
(1861-1930), age 39

# 1875

George Caleb Bingham
  (1811-1879), age 64
Franz Liszt
  (1811-1886), age 64
Harriet Beecher Stowe
  (1811-1896), age 64
Robert Browning
  (1812-1889), age 63
Friedrich von Flotow
  (1812-1883), age 63
Ivan Goncharov
  (1812-1891), age 63
Alfred Krupp
  (1812-1887), age 63
Edward Lear
  (1812-1888), age 63
John C. Fremont
  (1813-1890), age 62
Giuseppe Verdi
  (1813-1901), age 62
Jones Very
  (1813-1880), age 62
Richard Wagner
  (1813-1883), age 62
Mikhail Bakunin
  (1814-1876), age 61
Joseph Hooker
  (1814-1879), age 61
Jean Millet
  (1814-1875), age 61
John Lothrop Motley
  (1814-1877), age 61
Charles Reade
  (1814-1884), age 61
Otto von Bismarck
  (1815-1898), age 60
Elizabeth Cady Stanton
  (1815-1902), age 60
Anthony Trollope
  (1815-1882), age 60
Comte de Gobineau
  (1816-1882), age 59
Paul von Reuter
  (1816-1899), age 59
Charles Francois Daubigny
  (1817-1878), age 58
Frederick Douglass
  (1817-1895), age 58
Benjamin Jowett
  (1817-1893), age 58
Sir Austen Layard
  (1817-1894), age 58

among his subjects. His most famous work is *Arrangement in Black and Gray No. 1: The Artist's Mother,* in the Louvre.

**James Thomson,** age 41; British poet and essayist, born in Scotland, son of a seaman. He grew up in poverty and became an army schoolmaster, a lawyer's clerk and a contributor to popular magazines. His addiction to narcotics intensifed the mood of despair expressed in the famous poem *The City of Dreadful Night* (1874).

**Samuel Butler,** age 40; English novelist born in Nottinghamshire, son of a clergyman. Driven to New Zealand by family quarrels, he raised sheep for five years. He achieved his first success at 37 with *Erewhon,* a utopian novel, but is better known for *The Way of All Flesh,* a satirical attack on Victorian society and morals published a year after his death. He was also noted for his anti-Christian bias.

**Giosue Carducci,** age 40; Italian poet and critic born in Tuscany, the son of a physician with republican sympathies. Considered the national poet of modern Italy, he was a classicist in reaction to the romanticism of his time and author of many volumes of verse and literary criticism. He was a professor at Bologna from 1860–1904 and the winner of the 1906 Nobel Prize for Literature.

ANDREW CARNEGIE
American industrialist
1835-1919

**Andrew Carnegie,** age 40; American industrialist born in Scotland and brought to America at 13 by his family. Hard work, frugality and shrewd investments (in the Pullman Company and oil leases) enabled him to gain control of one-quarter of American steel production in 1899. He retired in 1901 and gave $350 million to cultural and educational institutions; he endowed 1,700 libraries and built Carnegie Hall in New York City in 1891.

**Leopold II,** age 40; king of Belgium from 1865–1909, a cousin of both Queen Victoria and Prince Albert. An energetic monarch, he promoted industrial expansion, encouraged exploration and settlement of the Congo River basin and laid the foundations of the Belgian colonial empire. He was also notorious for his dissolute life and his ruthless methods of colonial exploitation.

**Camille Saint-Saens,** age 40; French composer, pianist and organist, born in Paris. He composed his first symphony at 18, was for 19 years organist at the Church of the Madelaine and made several successful world tours, performing and conducting his own music. He is best known for the opera *Samson et Delila;* the symphonic poem *Danse Macabre;* symphonies in A minor and C minor; and the *Third Symphony,* in E flat minor.

MARK TWAIN (Samuel
Langhorne Clemens)
American humorist and novelist
1835-1910

**Mark Twain** (Samuel Langhorne Clemens), age 40; American humorist and novelist, born in Missouri. Apprenticed to a printer at 12 after his father's death, he was at various times a journeyman printer, river pilot, miner, journalist and lecturer. He found his true vocation at 40, portraying Midwestern rural life with simple realism and humor in *Tom Sawyer* (1876), *Huckleberry Finn* (1884) and *Life on the Mississippi*. As a world celebrity he lectured for many years, but grew disillusioned and cynical toward the end of his life.

**Tz'u Hsi,** age c. 40; Chinese dowager empress, originally named Yehomala, concubine of Emperor Hsien Feng (1831–1861). She was regent for her son, T'ung Chih, from 1862–1873, and for her nephew, Kuang Hsu, from 1875–1889 and from 1898–1908, but in reality was the ruling power from 1861 to 1908. She resisted foreign encroachments and modernization and encouraged anti-foreign secret societies collectively known as *I Ho Ch'uan* (righteous harmonious fists), derisively called Boxers by the British. Before she died in 1908 she named Hsuan T'ung (Henry Pu-Yi), the nephew of her nephew, as successor.

**Joseph Chamberlain,** age 39; British statesman born in London, son of a manufacturer. After retiring from business at 37, he became mayor of Birmingham, a member of Parliament (1876), a member of Gladstone's cabinet and an active champion of social reform at home and colonial expansion abroad. He was the colonial secretary during the Boer War (1899–1902) and the father of Austen and Neville Chamberlain.

**Sir William Schenck Gilbert,** age 39; English playwright and humorist born in London, son of a surgeon. He studied law but turned to writing comic verses, burlesques and melodramas, and became famous for his long collaboration (1871–1896) with composer Arthur Sullivan in producing comic operas: *H.M.S. Pinafore, The Pirates of Penzance, The Mikado* and many more. He was knighted in 1907.

**Thomas Hill Green,** age 39; English idealist philosopher, born in Yorkshire and educated at Oxford, where he taught from 1860 to 1882. He is known for his strong attack on empiricism in his *Introduction to Hume's Treatise on Human Nature* (1874) and *Prolegomena to Ethics* (1883). A political liberal, he believed in popular education and maintained that society is obligated to further the well-being of all its members. He is said to have been the original of Mr. Gray in *Robert Elsmere* by Mrs. Humphrey Ward.

**Bret Harte** (Francis Brett Harte), age 39; American writer born in

Frederic Remington
(1861-1909), age 39
Rabindranath Tagore
(1861-1941), age 39
Frederick Jackson Turner
(1861-1932), age 39
Alfred North Whitehead
(1861-1947), age 39
Claude Debussy
(1862-1918), age 38
Frederick Delius
(1862-1934), age 38
Gerhart Hauptmann
(1862-1946), age 38
O. Henry
(1862-1910), age 38
Maurice Maeterlinck
(1862-1949), age 38
Arthur Schnitzler
(1862-1931), age 38
Edward Westermarck
(1862-1939), age 38
Edith Wharton
(1862-1937), age 38
Gabriele D'Annunzio
(1863-1938), age 37
Henry Ford
(1863-1947), age 37
William Randolph Hearst
(1863-1951), age 37
David Lloyd George
(1863-1945), age 37
Pietro Mascagni
(1863-1945), age 37
George Santayana
(1863-1952), age 37
George Washington Carver
(1864?-1943), age 36?
Richard Strauss
(1864-1949), age 36
Henri de Toulouse-Lautrec
(1864-1901), age 36
Miguel de Unamuno
(1864-1936), age 36
Max Weber
(1864-1920), age 36
Mrs. Patrick Campbell
(1865-1940), age 35
George V (Great Britain)
(1865-1936), age 35
Warren G. Harding
(1865-1923), age 35

# 1875

Theodor Mommsen
(1817-1903), age 58
Alexander II (Russia)
(1818-1881), age 57
Pierre Gustave de
Beauregard
(1818-1893), age 57
Jacob Burckhardt
(1818-1897), age 57
James Anthony Froude
(1818-1894), age 57
Charles Francois Gounod
(1818-1893), age 57
Charles Leconte de Lisle
(1818-1894), age 57
Karl Marx
(1818-1883), age 57
Lewis Henry Morgan
(1818-1881), age 57
Ivan Turgenev
(1818-1883), age 57
Gustave Courbet
(1819-1877), age 56
Edwin Laurentine Drake
(1819-1880), age 56
George Eliot
(1819-1880), age 56
Charles Kingsley
(1819-1875), age 56
James Russell Lowell
(1819-1891), age 56
Herman Melville
(1819-1891), age 56
Jacques Offenbach
(1819-1880), age 56
John Ruskin
(1819-1900), age 56
Joseph Seligman
(1819-1880), age 56
Victoria (Great Britain)
(1819-1901), age 56
Walt Whitman
(1819-1892), age 56
Susan B. Anthony
(1820-1906), age 55
James B. Eads
(1820-1887), age 55
Friedrich Engels
(1820-1895), age 55
Jenny Lind
(1820-1887), age 55
Florence Nightingale
(1820-1910), age 55

Albany, N.Y., son of a school teacher. He went to California at 18 and in his early thirties achieved success with his humorous stories of gold mining camps: *The Luck of Roaring Camp, The Outcasts of Poker Flat* and others. After seven years in the American diplomatic service, he spent his last years in London.

**Winslow Homer,** age 39; American painter born in Boston. After several years as an illustrator for *Harper's Weekly,* he won recognition for his genre paintings of Southern life and Civil War scenes. He also painted, both in oils and watercolors, many forest and mountain scenes. After 1884, when he settled on the coast of Maine, he painted mostly seascapes. A famous watercolor is *Hurricane, Bahamas.*

**John Burroughs,** age 38; American naturalist born in New York. After working as a clerk in Washington, D.C., he settled on a farm at 37 and spent his time observing nature and writing about it. Among his well-known books are *Locusts and Wild Honey* (1879), *Signs and Seasons* (1886) and *Ways of Nature* (1905). He was a friend of Walt Whitman, John Muir and Theodore Roosevelt.

GROVER CLEVELAND
American statesman and
president
1837-1908

**Grover Cleveland,** age 38; American statesman born in New Jersey, son of a clergyman; 22nd (1885–1889) and 24th (1893–1897) president. He gained a national reputation as a reform mayor of Buffalo and as an honest governor of New York (1882–1885), and was elected president in 1884 as the Democratic "clean government" candidate, in opposition to the "Rum, Romanism, and Rebellion" campaign of James G. Blaine. He lost the close election of 1888 to Benjamin Harrison, but was elected for a second term in 1892.

**George Dewey,** age 38; American naval officer born in Vermont. He served under Farragut in the Civil War, and, as commander of the Asiatic squadron at the outbreak of the Spanish-American War, sailed to Manila, entered the harbor stealthily after midnight and at first light destroyed eight Spanish warships. When troop reinforcements arrived in August 1898, he assisted in the capture of Manila and became a national hero.

**John Richard Green,** age 38; English historian and Anglican clergyman born in Oxford. He is famous for his *Short History of the English People* (1874), which was immediately popular and is still read for its literary quality and emphasis on social trends rather than political events. He later expanded it into a four-volume work (1877–1880). His wife was an Irish historian.

**James Butler Hickok** (Wild Bill Hickok), age 38; American scout and frontier marshal born in Illinois, reputedly unsurpassed as a marksman. He was a stage driver; Union scout in the Civil War; deputy marshal at Fort Riley, Kansas (1866); marshal of Hays, Kansas (1869); and marshal of Abilene (1871). He appeared with Buffalo Bill's Show in 1872–1873 as a legendary gunfighter. He was killed at Deadwood, Dakota Territory, in 1876, shot in the back while playing cards.

**Hitotsubashi** (Yoshinobu), age 38; last of the Japanese shoguns. As leader of the isolationist party, he was chosen shogun to succeed Iyenochi in 1867, but resigned a few months later when Mutsuhito became emperor and the Meiji restoration began. The Tokugawa shogunate, founded by Iyeyasu in 1603, came to an end with his resignation.

**William Dean Howells,** age 38; American novelist, critic and editor, born in Ohio. He was appointed American consul in Venice at 24 after writing Lincoln's campaign biography. He wrote several volumes of criticism and over 30 novels, noted for their realism in depicting American life and manners. His best-known titles are *The Rise of Silas Lapham* (1885) and *Indian Summer* (1886). He was the editor of the *Atlantic Monthly* from 1871 to 1881.

**John Pierpont Morgan,** age 38; American financier and industrial organizer, born in Connecticut, the son of an international banker. He founded J. P. Morgan & Company in 1895 and organized the first billion-dollar corporation, United States Steel, in 1901, after buying Carnegie's interests. He also consolidated International Harvester.

**Algernon Charles Swinburne,** age 38; English poet and critic born in London of an old, distinguished family. He defied Victorian moral standards with his first volume of verse, *Poems and Ballads* (1866), celebrating unrestrained sexuality and the life of the senses. Compelled to abandon the sensual life at 42, after dissipation had ruined his health, he lived a quiet though productive life thereafter.

**Henry Brooks Adams,** age 37; American historian, biographer and novelist; born in Boston, the grandson of John Quincy Adams. His fame rests on two books, privately printed in small editions: *Mont-Saint-Michel and Chartres* (1904), an idealization of medieval unity; and *The Education of Henry Adams* (1906), a reflective autobiography in forceful prose. He also wrote a history of the early 19th century in the United States.

**Georges Bizet,** age 37; French composer born near Paris, son of a musician. A youthful prodigy, he met with disappointment and had only small successes. Even *Carmen* (1875), on which he had pinned his hopes, was given an indifferent reception. Today everyone knows Bizet's *Carmen,* but he died at 37 still untouched by fame.

**James Bryce** (Viscount Bryce), age 37; British historian, statesman and diplomat; born in Belfast, Ireland of a Scottish family; professor of civil law at Oxford from 1870–1893. He was ambassador to the United States from 1907–1913, and is remembered for his classic work on American government, *The American Commonwealth* (1888). He also wrote *Modern Democracies* (1922).

**Sir Henry Irving** (John Henry Brodribb), age 37; English actor born in Somersetshire. He appeared in Edinburgh and Manchester theaters from the age of 18 and settled in London in 1866 for a long, successful career that included 24 years (1878–1902) playing opposite Ellen Terry. He made eight American tours between 1883 and 1904 and was the first actor to be knighted, in 1895.

**William Edward Hartpoole Lecky,** age 37; British historian born in Ireland. A liberal member of Parliament, he is famous for three works: *History of the Rise and Influence of the Spirit of Rationalism in Europe* (1865); *History of European Morals from Augustus to Charlemagne*

# 1900

Rudyard Kipling
(1865-1936), age 35
Jean Sibelius
(1865-1957), age 35
Charles Steinmetz
(1865-1923), age 35
William Butler Yeats
(1865-1939), age 35
Benedetto Croce
(1866-1952), age 34
Wassily Kandinsky
(1866-1944), age 34
Ramsay MacDonald
(1866-1937), age 34
Gilbert Murray
(1866-1957), age 34
Romain Rolland
(1866-1944), age 34
Sun Yat-sen
(1866-1925), age 34
August von Wassermann
(1866-1925), age 34
H. G. Wells
(1866-1946), age 34
Arnold Bennett
(1867-1931), age 33
Vicente Blasco-Ibanez
(1867-1928), age 33
Gutzon Borglum
(1867 or 1871-1941),
age 33?
Marie Curie
(1867-1934), age 33
Ernest Dowson
(1867-1900), age 33
John Galsworthy
. (1867-1933), age 33
Jozef Pilsudski
(1867-1935), age 33
Luigi Pirandello
(1867-1936), age 33
Arturo Toscanini
(1867-1957), age 33
Wilbur Wright
(1867-1912), age 33
W. E. B. Du Bois
(1868-1963), age 32
Stefan George
(1868-1933), age 32
Maxim Gorki
(1868-1936), age 32
Nicholas II (Russia)
(1868-1918), age 32

# 1875

William Tecumseh Sherman
   (1820-1891), age 55
Herbert Spencer
   (1820-1903), age 55
Victor Emmanuel II (Italy)
   (1820-1878), age 55
Clara Barton
   (1821-1912), age 54
Richard Burton
   (1821-1890), age 54
Feodor Dostoevsky
   (1821-1881), age 54
Mary Baker Eddy
   (1821-1910), age 54
Gustave Flaubert
   (1821-1880), age 54
Hermann von Helmholtz
   (1821-1894), age 54
Matthew Arnold
   (1822-1888), age 53
Cesar Franck
   (1822-1890), age 53
Edmond de Goncourt
   (1822-1896), age 53
Ulysses S. Grant
   (1822-1885), age 53
Rutherford B. Hayes
   (1822-1893) age 53
Sir Henry Maine
   (1822-1888), age 53
Gregor Mendel
   (1822-1884), age 53
Frederick Law Olmstead
   (1822-1903), age 53
Louis Pasteur
   (1822-1895), age 53
Heinrich Schliemann
   (1822-1890), age 53
Max Muller
   (1823-1900), age 52
Francis Parkman
   (1823-1893), age 52
Ernest Renan
   (1823-1892), age 52
William Marcy Tweed
   (1823-1878), age 52
Alfred Russell Wallace
   (1823-1913), age 52
Anton Bruckner
   (1824-1896), age 51
Wilkie Collins
   (1824-1889), age 51

(1869); and the great work on which he spent 19 years, *History of England in the Eighteenth Century* (eight volumes, 1878–1890).

**Ernst Mach,** age 37; Austrian physicist and philosopher born in Moravia, after whom the Mach number, indicating the ratio of the speed of an object to the speed of sound, is named. His research in the field of ballistics was but a small part of his work, for he is better known as a philosopher of science; a forerunner of logical positivism, he maintained that science should be restricted to the investigation of what can be perceived by the senses.

**John Muir,** age 37; Scottish-American naturalist born in Dunbar, Scotland and brought to America at 11. An ardent conservationist, he was instrumental in the establishment of Yosemite National Park and played a part in persuading Theodore Roosevelt, with whom he went on camping trips, to set aside 148 million acres of forest. He wrote *Our National Parks* (1901) and *The Yosemite* (1912).

**Sir George Otto Trevelyan,** age 37; English historian of a distinguished family—son of a British civil servant in India and nephew of Lord Macaulay. He served as private secretary to his father in India, as a member of Parliament from 1865–1897 and as cabinet minster and wrote *The Life and Letters of Lord Macaulay* (1876) and *The American Revolution* (six volumes, 1899–1914), which was highly praised in America.

PAUL CEZANNE
French painter
1839-1906

**Paul Cezanne,** age 36; French painter born in Provence, son of a banker. He studied with Pissarro and exhibited with the impressionists, but developed a postimpressionist style notable for its accentuation of geometric forms and slight distortions that emphasize the solidity of objects. He painted mostly still lifes *(The Blue Vase)* and landscapes *(Mont Sainte-Victoire,* in the Metropolitan Museum of Art).

**George Armstrong Custer,** age 36; American army officer born in Ohio and graduated from West Point in 1861. The youngest general in the Union army, he was present at Lee's surrender, and after the war was lieutenant colonel of the Seventh Cavalry, on frontier duty. In the famous Battle of the Little Big Horn River in the Black Hills of Dakota, he and his 200 men were killed by a large force of Indians led by Sitting Bull and Crazy Horse on June 25, 1876.

(Josiah) **Willard Gibbs,** age 36; American mathematical physicist born in Connecticut, son of a philologist. A professor at Yale from 1871–1903, he is considered by many the greatest American scientist for his complex mathematical theorems which formed the basic principles of physical chemistry. His importance was first recognized in Europe.

**Joaquim Maria Machado de Assis,** age 36; Brazilian novelist born in Rio de Janeiro, son of a Negro house painter and a Portuguese mother. Called Brazil's greatest novelist, he also wrote poetry and short stories, but is best known for two novels—*Epitaph of a Small Winner* (1881) and *Dom Casmurro* (1900)—both blithely pessimistic in tone. He was the first president of the Brazilian Academy of Letters.

**Modest Petrovich Mussorgsky,** age 36; Russian composer born near Pskov, son of a landowner. A nationalist composer, of the group that included Borodin and Rimski-Korsakov, he is known for the opera *Boris Gudunov,* based on Pushkin's play, and the piano suite *Pictures at an Exhibition.* He died of tuberculosis.

**Walter Horatio Pater,** age 36; English essayist and critic, born in London and educated at Oxford, where he remained—a studious, life-long bachelor. He is known for two popular and influential works: *Studies in the History of the Renaissance* (1873), and the reflective historical novel of the time of Marcus Aurelius, *Marcus the Epicurean* (1885). He was a painstaking prose stylist and a defender of the pursuit of beauty as the most worthwhile activity of life.

**Charles Sanders Peirce,** age 36; American philosopher born in Massachusetts, son of a Harvard professor. Called the founder of pragmatism, he first used the term in an article in *Popular Science* magazine in 1878. His attempt to find in the consequences of ideas their ultimate meaning was developed further by William James, John Dewey and other American pragmatists.

**Alfred Sisley,** age 36; French painter born in Paris of English parents; one of the leading impressionists. His poetic, dreamlike landscapes were little noticed in his lifetime, although three months after his death of throat cancer, his pictures brought high prices. Among his well-known works are *The Flood at Port Marly* and *Snow at Louveciennes,* both in the Louvre.

JOHN D. ROCKEFELLER
American oil magnate
1839-1937

**John Davison Rockefeller,** age 36; American oil magnate born in Richford, N.Y. Starting work as a bookkeeper at 16, he entered the oil-refining business at 23, formed Standard Oil Company at 31, and at 39 controlled 90 percent of the oil-refining industry in the United States. When he retired in 1911, his fortune was estimated at $1 billion.

**Carlotta, or Carlota** (Marie Charlotte Amelie), age 35; empress of

# 1900

Edmond Rostand
(1868-1918), age 32
Neville Chamberlain
(1869-1940), age 31
Mahatma Gandhi
(1869-1948), age 31
Andre Gide
(1869-1951), age 31
Edgar Lee Masters
(1869-1950), age 31
Henri Matisse
(1869-1954), age 31
Edwin Arlington Robinson
(1869-1935), age 31
Booth Tarkington
(1869-1946), age 31
Frank Lloyd Wright
(1869-1959), age 31
Alfred Adler
(1870-1937), age 30
Ivan Bunin
(1870-1953), age 30
Lenin
(1870-1924), age 30
Frank Norris
(1870-1902), age 30
Jan Christian Smuts
(1870-1950), age 30
Teitaro Suzuki
(1870-1966), age 30
Theodore Dreiser
(1871-1945), age 29
Marcel Proust
(1871-1922), age 29
Ernest Rutherford
(1871-1937), age 29
J. M. Synge
(1871-1909), age 29
Paul Valery
(1871-1945), age 29
Orville Wright
(1871-1948), age 29
Roald Amundsen
(1872-1928), age 28
Calvin Coolidge
(1872-1933), age 28
Sergei Diaghilev
(1872-1929), age 28
Haakon VII (Norway)
(1872-1957), age 28
Piet Mondrian
(1872-1944), age 28

# 1875

Alexandre Dumas (fils)
(1824-1895), age 51
Bedrich Smetana
(1824-1884), age 51
Thomas Henry Huxley
(1825-1895), age 50
Stephanus Paulus Kruger
(1825-1904), age 50
Johann Strauss
(1825-1899), age 50
Walter Bagehot
(1826-1877), age 49
George B. McClellan
(1826-1885), age 49
Joseph Lister
(1827-1912), age 48
Lew Wallace
(1827-1905), age 48
Meyer Guggenheim
(1828-1905), age 47
Henrik Ibsen
(1828-1906), age 47
George Meredith
(1828-1909), age 47
Dante Gabriel Rossetti
(1828-1882), age 47
Hippolyte Adolphe Taine
(1828-1893), age 47
Leo Tolstoy
(1828-1910), age 47
Jules Verne
(1828-1905), age 47
Geronimo
(1829-1909), age 46
Anton Rubinstein
(1829-1894), age 46
Chester Alan Arthur
(1830-1886), age 45
Porfirio Diaz
(1830-1915), age 45
Emily Dickinson
(1830-1886), age 45
Francis Joseph I (Austria)
(1830-1916), age 45
Camille Pissarro
(1830-1903), age 45
Christina Rossetti
(1830-1894), age 45
Philip Henry Sheridan
(1831-1888), age 44

Mexico from 1864–1867, born near Brussels, the daughter of Leopold I of Belgium. She married Maximilian, the archduke of Austria, in 1857, and accompanied him to Mexico. When his position as emperor became desperate, she went to Europe in a vain attempt to obtain aid. After his execution her mind gave way, and she was confined in a chateau in Belgium until her death at 87.

**Alphonse Daudet,** age 35; French novelist born in the south of France, son of a silk manufacturer. He is famous for *Letters from My Windmill* (1869), a collection of realistic, humorous stories of Provencal life and the novels *Tartarin of Tarascon* and *Tartarin on the Alps,* also popular for their warmth and good humor. His son, Leon, was a prominent royalist.

THOMAS HARDY
English novelist and poet
1840-1928

**Thomas Hardy,** age 35; English novelist and poet born in Dorsetshire. His somber novels of rural English life—*The Return of the Native, Tess of the D'Urbervilles* and *Jude the Obscure*—are highly praised by critics, but were not popular. Disappointed with their reception, he turned to poetry at 55. Many critics consider his poetry superior to his fiction.

**Claude Monet,** age 35; French landscape painter and leader of the impressionists, son of a shopkeeper of Le Havre. It was one of his paintings, entitled *Impression: Sunrise,* that gave the group its name. Noted for his passion to record exactly what the eye sees, he often painted the same scene at different hours of the day to show the changing effects of light and atmosphere. *Morning on the Seine* was a favorite subject.

**Thomas Nast,** age 35; cartoonist born in Landau, Germany and brought to America at six. As an artist for several New York papers, he became famous for his biting political cartoons, which helped undo the corrupt Tweed Ring in New York City. He originated the elephant and donkey as symbols of the Republican and Democratic parties, and was the United States consul in Ecuador in 1902.

**Francois Auguste Rene Rodin,** age 35; French sculptor born in Paris. He is world famous for such sculptures as *The Kiss, The Thinker* (in the Rodin Museum in Paris), *John the Baptist* and *The Burghers of Calais.* He also made portrait busts of Clemenceau, Proust and Shaw and statues of Hugo and Balzac.

**William Graham Sumner,** age 35; American economist and sociologist, born in New Jersey. A Protestant Episcopal clergyman and professor of political and social science at Yale from 1872–1910, he is remembered chiefly for a work of his later years, *Folkways* (1907), a discursive study of the force and influence of long established human customs and traditions. He was a *laissez-faire* economist.

**John Addington Symonds,** age 35; English poet and literary historian, born in Bristol, son of an eminent physician. He is remembered for his classic, authoritative *Renaissance in Italy* (seven volumes, 1875–1886). He also wrote biographies of Shelley, Whitman and other poets, as well as several volumes of verse, and made the standard English translation of the autobiography of Benvenuto Cellini.

PETR ILICH TCHAIKOVSKY
Russian composer
1840-1893

**Petr Ilich Tchaikovsky,** age 35; Russian composer born in the Ural Mountain region, the son of a mine inspector. He taught harmony at the Moscow Conservatory from 1866–1878 and thereafter lived on an annual subsidy from a wealthy widow he never met. His immensely popular works include the fourth, fifth and sixth symphonies, the *1812 Overture, March Slav,* and the operas *Eugene Onegin* and *The Queen of Spades.* His ballet scores—*Swan Lake, Sleeping Beauty* and *The Nutcracker*—are unsurpassed.

**Giovanni Verga,** age 35; Italian novelist and story writer, born in Catania, Sicily, of a landowning family. A realist, faithfully depicting middle-class Sicilian life, with a sympathetic eye for the unfortunate peasants, he has been compared by his admirers to Zola. *The House by the Medlar Tree* and *Little Novels of Sicily* were translated by D. H. Lawrence. His story *Cavalleria Rusticana* was the source of Mascagni's opera.

**Emile Zola,** age 35; French novelist born in Paris, son of a Greek-Italian civil engineer and a French mother. An uncompromising naturalist, he portrayed his characters as the helpless victims of heredity and environment. His novels include the well-known *L'Assommoir,* on alcoholism; *Nana,* on prostitution in high society; and *Germinal,* on class conflict in a mining town. His famous letter *J'accuse* caused a revival of popular interest in the celebrated Dreyfus affair, resulting in Dreyfus' exoneration and release from prison.

**James Gordon Bennett,** age 24; American newspaper publisher born in New York City, son of the elder James Gordon Bennett (1795–1872), whom he succeeded in 1867 as manager of the New York *Herald.* He is famous for having financed Henry Stanley's expedition to Africa to find David Livingstone (1869–1871), along with other spectacular undertakings.

**Georges Clemenceau,** age 34; French statesman, born near Nantes, son of a working-class radical. In America from 1865–1869 as a

Bertrand Russell
(1872-1970), age 28
Ralph Vaughan Williams
(1872-1958), age 28
Carl L. Becker
(1873-1945), age 27
Enrico Caruso
(1873-1921), age 27
Willa Cather
(1873 or 1876-1947),
age 27?
Feodor Chaliapin
(1873-1938), age 27
Colette
(1873-1954), age 27
Lee De Forest
(1873-1961), age 27
Ford Madox Ford
(1873-1939), age 27
George Edward Moore
(1873-1958), age 27
Emily Post
(1873-1960), age 27
Sergei Rachmaninoff
(1873-1943), age 27
G. K. Chesterton
(1874-1936), age 26
Sir Winston Churchill
(1874-1965), age 26
Robert Frost
(1874-1963), age 26
Ellen Glasgow
(1874-1945), age 26
Herbert Hoover
(1874-1964), age 26
Amy Lowell
(1874-1925), age 26
Guglielmo Marconi
(1874-1937), age 26
W. Somerset Maugham
(1874-1965), age 26
Arnold Schoenberg
(1874-1951), age 26
Gertrude Stein
(1874-1946), age 26
Chaim Weizmann
(1874-1952), age 26
Albert I (Belgium)
(1875-1934), age 25
D. W. Griffith
(1875-1948), age 25
Carl Gustav Jung
(1875-1961), age 25

journalist and teacher, he returned to France to become leader of the radicals in the Chamber of Deputies from 1876–1893. As premier from 1906–1909, he opposed French colonialism; as forceful wartime premier, from 1917–1920, he opposed leniency toward Germany at the Versailles Conference following the victory of the Allies.

**Anton Dvorak,** age 34; Czech composer born in Bohemia, son of an innkeeper; the first Bohemian composer to win world recognition. He wrote his famous symphony in E minor, *From the New World,* while in New York City as director of the National Conservatory of Music, from 1892–1895. He is also known for his *Slavonic Dances,* chamber music and many piano pieces, including *Humoresque*.

**Edward VII** (Albert Edward), age 34; king of the United Kingdom of Great Britain and Ireland and emperor of India from 1901–1910, of the house of Saxe-Coburg-Gotha; son of Queen Victoria, whom he succeeded at the age of 60. He married Alexandra, the daughter of the king of Denmark, and had three daughters and two sons. He was a popular monarch, known as the Peacemaker for his frequent visits to European capitals to promote international harmony. He was succeeded by his son George V.

OLIVER WENDELL
HOLMES
American jurist
1841-1935

**Oliver Wendell Holmes,** age 34; American jurist born in Boston, son of Oliver Wendell Holmes, the writer. Justice of the Massachusetts Supreme Court for 20 years (1882–1902) and of the United States Supreme Court for 30 years (1902–1932), to which he was appointed by Theodore Roosevelt, he was a forceful liberal, known as the Great Dissenter for his frequent disagreement with the conservative majority.

**Hirobumi Ito,** age 34; Japanese statesman, an important figure in the emergence of Japan as a modern nation. A supporter of Western ideas, he studied in Europe and visited the United States in 1871. Premier four times from 1886 to 1901, he waged war with China in 1894–1895, and with Saionji drew up a new constitution in 1888–1889. He was assassinated by a Korean at Harbin.

**Pierre Auguste Renoir,** age 34; French painter born in Limoges, son of a tailor. He grew up in poverty and painted chinaware in a factory at 13. The subjects of his paintings—buxom nudes, flowers, social scenes, beautiful women and children in pretty clothes—present an optimistic, pleasing view of life. Two famous paintings are *Mme. Charpentier and Her Children* (Metropolitan Museum) and *Le Moulin de la Galette* (Louvre). He was a friend of Monet and Sisley and father of Jean Renoir, the filmmaker.

**Sir Henry Morton Stanley** (John Rowlands), age 34; journalist and explorer born in Wales and brought up in a workhouse. He shipped as a cabin boy from Liverpool to New Orleans and was adopted by a New Orleans merchant named Henry Stanley (1859). His finding of Livingstone in Africa was but one episode in an adventurous life, which included fighting on both sides of the American Civil War and helping Leopold II of Belgium open up the Congo for exploitation. He is the author of *In Darkest Africa* (two volumes, 1890).

**Ambrose Gwinnett Bierce,** age 33; American journalist and short-story writer born in Ohio, known for his sardonic and cynical stories, collected in *Tales of Soldiers and Civilians* (1891), and for the *Devil's Dictionary* (1906). He went to Mexico in 1913 and was never seen again.

**Georg Morris Brandes** (original surname, Cohen), age 33; Danish literary critic of Jewish parentage, born in Copenhagen. Acknowledged the foremost critic of his age, he was a follower of Taine and Spencer and a defender of realism against romanticism. A professor in Copenhagen and Berlin, he wrote *Main Currents in Nineteenth-Century Literature* (six volumes, 1872–1890), and studies of Shakespeare, Goethe, Voltaire and others.

**William James,** age 33; American philosopher and psychologist born in New York City, son of a wealthy amateur philosopher. Professor of psychology and philosophy at Harvard, 1880–1901, he was one of the founders of pragmatism, a philosophy that would judge the truth of any notion only by its practical consequences. He wrote *The Will to Believe and Other Essays in Popular Philosophy* (1897) and *The Varieties of Religious Experience* (1902).

**Petr Alekseevich Kropotkin,** age 33; Russian anarchist born in Moscow of a wealthy family. From the age of 30 he engaged in anarchist propaganda, was imprisoned several times and lived in England after 1886. A benevolent rather than a violent anarchist, he urged brotherhood and cooperation as a natural and reasonable way of life. He is the author of *The Conquest of Bread* (1888) and *Mutual Aid* (1902).

**Sidney Lanier,** age 33; American poet born in Georgia of an aristocratic Southern family. He spent some time in a Union prison in the Civil War, and after a period of ill health and poverty settled in Baltimore (1873), played in the symphony orchestra and lectured on English literature at Johns Hopkins University. His poetry, though melodic, is considered somewhat ornate. He died of tuberculosis at 39.

**Stephane Mallarme,** age 33; French poet born in Paris, leader of the symbolists (a school that eschewed direct statement, preferring suggestion and ambiguity). His difficult and obscure verse influenced Eliot, Proust and Joyce. His best-known poem is *Afternoon of a Faun*, which inspired Debussy's *Prelude*. Manet painted his portrait.

**Jules Emile Frederic Massenet,** age 33; French composer born in the Loire Valley of a prosperous family. A professor at Paris Conservatory, 1878–1894, he wrote oratorios, cantatas and orchestral suites, but is best known for his operas: *Manon, Le Cid, Thais* and *Don Quichotte.*

**Sir Arthur Sullivan,** age 33; English composer born in London, son of a bandmaster. He is world famous for his long collaboration with W. S. Gilbert in producing 14 comic operas that are still much admired and frequently performed. He also wrote *Onward, Christian Soldiers; The Lost Chord;* and one grand opera, *Ivanhoe.* He was knighted in 1883.

**Charles Montagu Doughty,** age 32; English linguist, writer and traveler; born in Suffolk, son of a clergyman. His single well-known book, *Travels in Arabia Deserta* (1888), is recognized today as a master-

# 1900

Antonio Machado
(1875-1939), age 25
Thomas Mann
(1875-1955), age 25
Maurice Ravel
(1875-1937), age 25
Rainer Maria Rilke
(1875-1926), age 25
Albert Schweitzer
(1875-1965), age 25
Sherwood Anderson
(1876-1941), age 24
Mohammed Ali Jinnah
(1876-1948), age 24
C. F. Kettering
(1876-1958), age 24
Jack London
(1876-1916), age 24
George Macaulay Trevelyan
(1876-1962), age 24
Mary Garden
(1877-1967), age 23
Hermann Hesse
(1877-1962), age 23
Riza Shah Pahlavi
(1877-1944), age 23
Pancho Villa
(1877-1923), age 23
Martin Buber
(1878-1965), age 22
George M. Cohan
(1878-1942), age 22
John Masefield
(1878-1967), age 22
Ferenc Molnar
(1878-1952), age 22
Carl Sandburg
(1878-1967), age 22
Upton Sinclair
(1878-1968), age 22
Albert Einstein
(1879-1958), age 21
E. M. Forster
(1879-1970), age 21
Paul Klee
(1879-1940), age 21
Vachel Lindsay
(1879-1931), age 21
Will Rogers
(1879-1935), age 21
Joseph Stalin
(1879-1953), age 21

piece. He traveled through Arabia disguised as an Arab, gathering facts on desert life and customs which he described in vivid, highly individual prose.

**Edvard Hagerup Grieg,** age 32; Norwegian composer born in Bergen, son of a musical mother who taught him the piano. Aided by a government subsidy at 31, he drew on folk themes and wrote over 100 songs and two *Peer Gynt* suites, for which he is world famous. His *Piano Concerto in A Minor* is also well known.

**Henry James,** age 32; American novelist born in New York City, the younger brother of William James. He settled in England in 1876 and wrote several successful short novels, including *Daisy Miller* (1879) and *Washington Square* (1881). His later novels, such as *The Ambassadors* and *The Wings of the Dove,* explored subtleties of thought and feeling in an idealized European aristocracy. As his style grew more intricate and his sentences more complex, his popularity declined. Among his best-known stories is *The Turn of the Screw.* In 1915, just before his death, he became a British subject.

**Robert Koch,** age 32; German physician and bacteriologist born in Hanover, whose discoveries led to the control of several diseases. He isolated the bacteria that cause anthrax (1876), tuberculosis (1882), and Asiatic cholera (1883). In 1896 he developed an effective vaccine for rinderpest, the African cattle plague.

**William McKinley,** age 32; American statesman born in Ohio, son of a manufacturer; 25th president, 1897–1901, and the third president to be assassinated. In alliance with Mark Hanna, the political boss, he was elected congressman, governor of Ohio, and president, defeating William Jennings Bryan in 1896. His administration saw the acquisition of the Philippine Islands and Hawaii and the emergence of the United States as a world power after the Spanish-American War (1898). He was reelected in 1900 but was shot by an anarchist less than a year later.

**Karl Benz,** age 31; German mechanical engineer and pioneer automobile manufacturer born in Karlsruhe, Baden. In 1885 he built a three-wheeled vehicle driven by an internal-combustion gas engine (patented January 1886, five months after Daimler's patent) and began manufacturing motor cars in Mannheim. He also invented the differential drive. The firms of Daimler and Benz merged in 1926.

SARAH BERNHARDT (Rosine Bernard)
French actress
1844-1923

**Sarah Bernhardt** (Rosine Bernard), age 31; French actress born in Paris. She appeared in dramas by Hugo, Racine, Shakespeare and

Sardou (who wrote several plays especially for her) and was known the world over as "the divine Sarah." Her greatest successes were in *Camille* by Dumas *fils*, and Rostand's *L'Aiglon*. She appeared in the United States 1886–1889 and made two silent films in 1912.

**Robert Seymour Bridges,** age 31; English poet born in Kent of a wealthy family. He studied medicine and practiced (1875–1882) before turning to poetry. An experimenter in new verse forms, he wrote *The Testament of Beauty* (1929), considered his masterpiece, and compiled an anthology, *The Spirit of Man* (1916). He was poet laureate from 1913 to 1930.

**George Washington Cable,** age 31; American writer born in New Orleans, famous in his time in Europe and America for his novels and stories of old New Orleans. A link between the romantic Southern writers and modern realists, he is best known for the collection of stories *Old Creole Days* (1879), and the novel *The Grandissimes* (1889), both warm but unsentimental portrayals of the French in New Orleans.

**Thomas Eakins,** age 31; American painter born in Philadelphia; instructor at the Pennsylvania Academy of the Fine Arts, 1873–1886. Sometimes called the greatest American painter, he was a realist known for his sporting scenes, depictions of surgical operations in progress and portraits, including one of Walt Whitman. One famous painting is *Max Schmitt in a Single Scull* (Metropolitan Museum).

**Anatole France** (Jacques Anatole Francois Thibault), age 31; French novelist and critic born in Paris, the son of a bookseller. A gentle skeptic, he is known for his fine prose style in such novels as *The Crime of Sylvestre Bonnard* (1881), *Thais* (1890) and the political satire, *Penguin Island* (1908).

**Gerard Manley Hopkins,** age 31; English poet born near London of a Protestant family. Converted to Roman Catholicism, he entered the Jesuit order at 24 and became a priest at 33 and a professor of Greek at Dublin University at 40. Unknown as poet except to his friends, he introduced techniques—most notably, a system of prosody called "sprung rhythm—that influenced T. S. Eliot and other modern poets and is greatly admired today. He died of typhoid fever at 44. These lines are his: "Margaret, are you grieving/ Over Goldengrove unleaving?"

**Andrew Lang,** age 31; Scottish scholar, folklorist and translator of Homer (in the standard prose translations of Butcher and Lang and of Lang, Leaf and Myers). His studies in folklore and mythology include *Custom and Myth* (1884), *Myth, Literature, and Religion* (1887) and *The Making of Religion* (1898). Among children he is better known for the popular Fairy Books: Orange, Green, Pink, Lilac, Brown, Crimson, Blue and so on.

**Modjeska** (Helena Opid Modjeska), age 31?; actress born in Cracow, Poland. A leading actress in Warsaw before she emigrated to America in 1876, she was famous for her portrayals of Shakespeare's tragic heroines and Dumas's Camille. She introduced Ibsen to America when she played Nora in *A Doll's House* in 1883 in Louisville.

**Friedrich Wilhelm Nietzsche,** age 31; German philosopher born in Saxony, son of a Lutheran clergyman. An implacable foe of Christianity, he is more admired for the original style and sweeping force of his writing than for the truth and wisdom of his philosophy. In *Thus Spake Zarathustra, Antichrist,* and *The Genealogy of Morals,* he extolled the "will to power" as the essence of life. A misogynist, he lived a solitary, unsettled life in Switzerland and Italy, until the onset of insanity at 45 ended his career. He was cared for thereafter by his mother and sister.

**Nikolai Andreevich Rimski-Korsakov,** age 31; Russian composer,

## 1900

Wallace Stevens
  (1879-1955), age 21
Leon Trotsky
  (1879-1940), age 21
Yoshihito
  (1879-1926), age 21
Emiliano Zapata
  (1877/79-1919),
  age c.21
Jacob Epstein
  (1880-1959), age 20
Michel Fokine
  (1880-1942), age 20
Ibn Saud
  (c.1880-1953),
  age c.20
Helen Keller
  (1880-1968), age 20
John L. Lewis
  (1880-1969), age 20
Douglas MacArthur
  (1880-1964), age 20
H. L. Mencken
  (1880-1956), age 20
Robert Musil
  (1880-1942), age 20
Sean O'Casey
  (1880-1964), age 20
Oswald Spengler
  (1880-1936), age 20
Wilhelmina (Netherlands)
  (1880-1962), age 20
Leonard Woolley
  (1880-1960), age 20
Bela Bartok
  (1881-1945), age 19
Ernest Bevin
  (1881-1951), age 19
Alexander Fleming
  (1881-1955), age 19
John XXIII (Pope)
  (1881-1963), age 19
Kemal Ataturk
  (1881-1938), age 19
Aleksandr Kerenski
  (1881-1970), age 19
Pablo Picasso
  (1881-1973), age 19
Teilhard de Chardin
  (1881-1955), age 19
Stefan Zweig
  (1881-1942), age 19

born near Novgorod of an aristocratic family. A professor at St. Petersburg Conservatory from 1871–1908, he is especially known for the brilliance of his instrumentation as manifested in the symphonic works *Capriccio Espagnol* and *Scheherazade*. He wrote 16 operas, including *The Snow Maiden* and *The Golden Cockerel*. He was the teacher of Stravinsky.

**Henri Rousseau,** age 31; French painter born in the department of Mayenne (NW France). Called a primitive or naive artist, he took up painting at 40—befriended by established artists, among them Picasso—after many years in the customs service, and without technical training produced a number of fantasy pictures that possess a dreamlike quality in spite of (or perhaps because of) their inexpert drawing. Two famous examples are *The Sleeping Gypsy* and *The Dream* (Metropolitan Museum).

**Paul Verlaine,** age 31; French symbolist poet notorious for his violent, disorderly life. He is famous for his musical verse, highly praised by readers of French and losing much in translation due to its use of cadences peculiar to that language. After serving a term in prison for the attempted murder of Rimbaud, he divided his time between periods of intoxication and periods of repentance.

**Elie Metchnikoff,** age 30; Russian bacteriologist born in Kharkov. Professor of zoology at Odessa 1870–1882, in 1895 he succeeded Pasteur as director of the Pasteur Institute in Paris and is credited with the discovery of the function of white blood cells as destroyers of harmful bacteria in the bloodsteam.

**Wilhelm Conrad Roentgen,** age 30; German physicist born in Prussia, professor at various German universities. He announced to a scientific body at Würzburg in 1895 his discovery of short-wave radiations which he called X rays; a discovery which revolutionized the practice of medicine. He was awarded the first Nobel Prize in physics in 1901.

**George Edward Saintsbury,** age 30; English critic, journalist and historian, born in Southampton. After 20 years as a London journalist, he became a professor of English literature at Edinburgh University (1895–1915) and acquired a reputation as a leading critic. He wrote *Nineteenth-Century Literature* (1896) and *A History of Criticism* (three volumes, 1900–1904).

**Francis Herbert Bradley,** age 29; English philosopher; brother of A. C. Bradley, the critic. An absolute idealist, he attacked 19th-century hedonism in *Ethical Studies* (1876) and wrote *Appearance and Reality* (1893) to expound his own metaphysical system, maintaining that the contradictions inherent in all experience are proof of its unreality, while only the Absolute Whole is truly real.

**William Frederick Cody** (Buffalo Bill), age 29; American scout, buffalo hunter and showman, born in Iowa. He supplied buffalo meat for train construction crews (1867–1868), was an Indian scout for the United States Cavalry from 1868–1872 and an actor from 1872–1883. In 1883 he organized and managed Buffalo Bill's Wild West Show, which toured the United States and Europe with great success for 18 years. He retired to Wyoming, where the town of Cody was named for him.

**Rudolf Christoph Eucken,** age 29; German philosopher of the idealist school, professor at Jena (1874–1926) and winner of the 1908 Nobel Prize for literature. Ethical activism was the keynote of his philosophy, which enjoyed a great vogue in his time. He is the author of *The Truth of Religion* (1901), *The Life of the Spirit* (1909) and other volumes.

**Carry Amelia Moore Nation,** age 29; American reformer born in Kentucky. She divorced her first husband, an alcoholic, and married

David Nation, a minister and lawyer. In 1900 in Kansas she began a violent campaign against the sale and consumption of alcohol, destroying liquor supplies and saloon property with a hatchet. A heavy woman standing six feet tall, she was often imprisoned, shot at and otherwise attacked, but lived to be 65.

**Charles Stewart Parnell,** lage 29; Irish statesman and nationalist leader. He promoted the cause of Irish independence by uniting the various Irish factions and introducing in the British Parliament in 1886 the first Home Rule bill. His political downfall occurred three years later, after he was named in another man's divorce action.

**Henryk Sienkiewicz,** age 29; Polish novelist and journalist educated in Warsaw. He won popularity with his novels on Polish history and was a newspaper correspondent in the United States 1876–1878. He became world famous with his novel *Quo Vadis?*, which has often been dramatized and produced in films.

**William Robertson Smith,** age 29; Scottish biblical scholar and Orientalist. He became a center of controversy when articles he had written for the ninth edition of the *Encyclopedia Brittanica* resulted in his dismissal from his professorship, although the final result of the affair was the liberalization of Protestant theology. He was co-editor of the *Brittanica* in 1880 and editor-in-chief 1887–1888. *The Religion of the Semites* (1889) is considered his most important book.

**Alexander Graham Bell,** age 28; inventor born in Edinburgh, son of an educator. He emigrated in 1871 and became an American citizen in 1882. At 18 he began the experiments that resulted in the first transmission of speech by wire on March 10, 1876. The telephone was introduced at the Philadelphia Centennial Exposition of 1876 and the Bell Telephone Company organized in 1877. He died at his summer home in Nova Scotia at 75.

THOMAS ALVA EDISON
American inventor
1847-1931

**Thomas Alva Edison,** age 28; American inventor born in Ohio. A newsboy at 12 on the Grand Trunk Railway and a successful inventor at 22 with a workshop in Newark, New Jersey, he invented the phonograph (1877, using a tinfoil cylinder as recorder); the incandescent lamp (1879); and the kinetoscope (1888). He also produced the first talking motion pictures in 1913. His more than 1,000 inventions transformed daily life in America and established him as the world's greatest inventor.

**Paul von Hindenburg,** age 28; German general and chief of staff from 1916–1918 during the First World War. The Hindenburg Line, a

## 1900

Eamon De Valera
(1882-1975), age 18
Arthur Eddington
(1882-1944), age 18
Jean Giraudoux
(1882-1944), age 18
William F. Halsey
(1882-1959), age 18
James Joyce
(1882-1941), age 18
Jacques Maritain
(1882-1973), age 18
Anna Pavlova
(1882-1931), age 18
Franklin D. Roosevelt
(1882-1945), age 18
Igor Stravinsky
(1882-1971), age 18
Sigrid Undset
(1882-1949), age 18
Virginia Woolf
(1882-1941), age 18
Clement Attlee
(1883-1967), age 17
Walter Gropius
(1883-1969), age 17
Franz Kafka
(1883-1924), age 17
John Maynard Keynes
(1883-1946), age 17
Benito Mussolini
(1883-1945), age 17
Jose Ortega y Gasset
(1883-1955), age 17
Maurice Utrillo
(1883-1955), age 17
Anton von Webern
(1883-1945), age 17
William Carlos Williams
(1883-1963), age 17
Grigori Zinoviev
(1883-1936), age 17
Amedeo Modigliani
(1884-1920), age 16
Hideki Tojo
(1884/85-1948),
age c.16
Harry S. Truman
(1884-1972), age 16
Alban Berg
(1885-1935), age 15
Niels Bohr
(1885-1962), age 15

system of trenches constructed across northern France, resisted Allied attacks from March 1917 to October 1918. He was elected president of the German republic in 1925 and reelected in 1932, defeating Adolph Hitler. Yielding to pressure, he appointed Hitler chancellor in January 1933, and died the following year.

**Jesse Woodson James,** age 28; American outlaw born in Missouri. At 19 he and his brother Frank became leaders of a band of desperadoes who captured the public fancy with their spectacular holdups of banks and trains. Their downfall came when the governor of Missouri offered $10,000 for Jesse, dead or alive. He was killed in 1882, at 35, in St. Joseph, Mo., by Robert Ford, a member of another gang. Frank James was tried and acquitted and lived out his life peacefully.

**Joseph Pulitzer,** age 28; journalist and publisher born in Hungary. Immigrating to the United States at 17 and a citizen at 20, he founded a newspaper empire based on sensationalism and prolabor policies, established the Pulitzer Prizes, first awarded in 1917, and endowed the Columbia University School of Journalism. Nearly blind and afflicted with a severe nervous disorder at 40, he spent his later years in a soundproof house at Bar Harbor, Maine, or on his 300-foot yacht, the *Liberty,* but retained control of his papers.

**Albert Pinkham Ryder,** age 28; American painter born in Massachusetts, known for his somber landscapes and marines. Ranked among the greatest American painters, he lived a reclusive life dedicated to art. Two familiar works are *Toilers of the Sea* and *The Curfew Hour* (Metropolitan Museum).

**Ellen Terry,** age 28; English actress born in Coventry of a theatrical family. She made her stage debut at nine in boys' roles and at 31 became Sir Henry Irving's leading lady. Her greatest successes were in *The Merchant of Venice* and *Much Ado About Nothing.* She also appeared in Shaw's plays and retired in 1925 after being made Dame of the British Empire.

**Arthur James Balfour,** age 27; first earl of Balfour, British statesman; prime minister from 1902–1905 and author of the Balfour Declaration of 1917, expressing British approval of the establishment of a Jewish state in Palestine. He was also a philosopher, the author of *A Defence of Philosophic Doubt* (1879), *Theism and Humanism* (1915) and other books.

**Bernard Bosanquet,** age 27; English idealist philosopher and disciple of T. H. Green. As a lecturer at Oxford from 1871–1881 and professor of moral philosophy at St. Andrews from 1903–1908, he was part of the late 19th-century reaction against empiricism. Among his important works are *The Philosophical Theory of the State* (1899) and *The Value and Destiny of the Individual* (1913).

**Wyatt Berry Earp,** age 27; American marshal and gunfighter, born in Illinois. As deputy marshal in Dodge City, Kansas, 1876–1877, he pacified the lawless town and moved on to Tombstone, Arizona, to become deputy U.S. marshal of the Arizona Territory. He survived the famous gunfight at the O.K. Corral on Oct. 26, 1881, and died at 81 in Los Angeles.

**Paul Gauguin,** age 27; French postimpressionist painter born in Paris, son of a French journalist and a Peruvian mother of French and Spanish descent. He gave up his office job at 40, abandoned his wife and family and embarked for Tahiti, where he lived from 1891–1893 and 1895–1901, much of the time in poverty and ill health. He died of syphillis at 54 in the Marquesas. His work is noted for its massive, simplified forms, impassive figures and exotic backgrounds, as in *Women of Tahiti* (Louvre) and *Tahitian Landscape* (Metropolitan Museum). His life inspired Somerset Maugham's novel, *The Moon and Sixpence* (1919).

**Joris Karl Huysmans,** age 27; French novelist of Dutch descent born in Paris. A government employee for 30 years, he wrote several novels, only one of which, *Against the Grain* (1884), is well known. It is an account of an aesthete seeking sensual experience of all kinds, an ancestor of the decadents of the 1890s.

**Vilfredo Pareto,** age 27; Italian economist and antidemocratic sociologist born in Paris, son of an Italian nobleman and a French mother. An engineer for many years, at 45 he became a professor of political economy at the University of Lausanne. His contention that sociology should be an experimental science, employing the methods of physics, may be partly responsible for its preoccupation with detail. In *The Mind and Society* (1916) he developed his theory of the cyclical rise and fall of governing elites.

**Augustus Saint-Gaudens,** age 27; American sculptor of French descent born in Dublin and brought to New York in infancy, son of a shoemaker. The leading American sculptor of the late 19th century, he is best known for the seated figure of Lincoln in Lincoln Park, Chicago; the Adams Memorial in Rock Creek Cemetery, Washington, D.C.; and the equestrian statue of General Sherman in Central Park, New York City.

**Luther Burbank,** age 26; American horticulturist born in Massachusetts; famous for developing new varieties of vegetables, fruits and flowers. After his first success with the Burbank potato, he moved to Santa Rosa, California (1875), and produced improved varieties of plums, raspberries, blackberries, apples, peaches, tomatoes, asparagus, lilies, roses and poppies. He is the author of *How Plants Are Trained to Work for Men* (eight volumes, 1921).

**Crazy Horse,** age 26?; American Indian chief of the Oglala Sioux tribe born in the Black Hills of the Dakotas; renowned as a courageous war chief. Resisting efforts of the United States Army to remove his people to a reservation, he defeated the army in two battles in 1876. In June he joined Sitting Bull to annihilate General Custer's force. Subsequently forced to surrender, he was stabbed to death at 28 while attempting to escape.

**William Ernest Henley,** age 26; English poet and editor born in Gloucestor, son of a bookseller. Though crippled by tuberculosis, he led an active life as editor of various London magazines for nearly 20 years, and first published such writers as Kipling, Yeats and H. G. Wells. He was a friend of Robert Louis Stevenson, with whom he collaborated on four plays. His most famous poem is *Invictus*, with the familiar lines: "I thank whatever gods may be/ For my unconquerable soul."

**Sir William Osler,** age 26; Canadian physician born in Ontario. As professor of medicine at Johns Hopkins University, 1889–1904, and at Oxford, 1905–1919, he played an important part in the development of modern medical practice. He is the author of *The Principles and Practice of Medicine* (1892) and *A Concise History of Medicine* (1919). He was made a baronet in 1911.

**Ivan Petrovich Pavlov,** age 26; Russian physiologist, professor at St. Petersburg and director of experimental medicine at various institutions. He is famous for his demonstration of conditioned reflexes in dogs—for which he received the 1904 Nobel Prize in physiology and medicine—and from which developed the school of psychology known as behaviorism. He survived the revolution and continued his work under the Soviets.

**Kimmochi Saionji,** age c. 26; Japanese liberal statesman born in

Jerome Kern
(1885-1945), age 15
D. H. Lawrence
(1885-1930), age 15
Sinclair Lewis
(1885-1951), age 15
Francois Mauriac
(1885-1970), age 15
Chester Nimitz
(1885-1966), age 15
George Patton
(1885-1945), age 15
Ezra Pound
(1885-1972), age 15
Karl Barth
(1886-1968), age 14
David Ben-Gurion
(1886-1973), age 14
Diego Rivera
(1886-1957), age 14
Ludwig Mies van der Rohe
(1886-1969), age 14
Paul Tillich
(1886-1965), age 14
Chiang Kai-shek
(1887-1975), age 13
Le Corbusier
(1887-1965), age 13
Bernard Montgomery
(1887-1976), age 13
Sigmund Romberg
(1887-1951), age 13
Heitor Villa-Lobos
(1887-1959), age 13
Irving Berlin
(1888-        ), age 12
Richard E. Byrd
(1888-1957), age 12
T. S. Eliot
(1888-1965), age 12
Katherine Mansfield
(1888-1923), age 12
Eugene O'Neill
(1888-1953), age 12
Marc Chagall
(1887/89-        ),
age c.11
Charles Chaplin
(1889-1977), age 11
Amelita Galli-Curci
(1889-1963), age 11
Martin Heidegger
(1889-1976), age 11

Kyoto. He lived 10 years in France, observing Western ways, held various cabinet posts under Ito, and as premier 1906–1908 and 1911–1912 promoted the modernization effort. He headed the Japanese delegation to the Paris Peace Conference in 1919 and remained an influential elder statesman until his death at 91.

**August Strindberg,** age 26; Swedish dramatist and novelist born in Stockholm, legitimate son of an impoverished nobleman and a servant girl. He was successful at 30 with his satirical novel, *The Red Room,* but is better known for his dramas centering on the battle of the sexes: *The Father, Miss Julie* (which became a film, an opera and a ballet), and *Dance of Death.* He wrote over 70 plays, which are considered equally as important as those of Ibsen and Chekhov for their influence on modern drama.

**Samuel Gompers,** age 25; American labor leader born in London and brought to America by his parents at 13. A cigarmaker by trade, he became president (1874–1881) of his local labor union and helped found the Federation of Organized Trades and Labor Unions in 1881. When it was reorganized in 1886 as the American Federation of Labor, he became its first president (1886–1924). By focusing on the goals of higher wages and shorter hours and rejecting radical and socialistic programs, he set the American labor union movement on its current course.

**Lafcadio Hearn,** age 25; Greek-Irish-Japanese writer born on a Greek island, son of an Irish army surgeon and a Greek mother. He came to America in 1867 and worked on Cincinnati and New Orleans papers for 20 years, before abandoning the West to become a Japanese citizen. He married a Japanese girl, took a Japanese name, and wrote stories and novels in English *(Some Chinese Ghosts)* revealing his love of the exotic and macabre.

**Horatio Herbert Kitchener,** age 25; first Earl Kitchener of Khartoum, British soldier born in Ireland. He campaigned in South Africa and India and became a great popular hero for his reconquest of the Sudan from the Khalifa, successor of the Mahdi. As secretary of state for war in 1914, at the outbreak of World War I, he undertook a vast expansion of the British army and was alone in predicting it would be a long war. He was drowned in 1918, when his ship struck a German mine and sank off the Orkney Islands.

**Pierre Loti** (Louis Marie Julien Viand), age 25; French novelist and naval officer born in Rochefort. He spent most of his life in the navy, retiring at 60, but from the age of 30 wrote a series of novels with exotic backgrounds. *An Iceland Fisherman* (1886), a story of Breton fishermen, and *Ramuntcho* (1897), on Basque peasant life, are his best novels, and somewhat more somber than the rest.

**Thomas G. Masaryk,** age 25; Czech statesman born in Moravia, first president of Czechoslovakia, 1918–1935. A professor at the University of Prague and a member of the Austrian parliament before World War I, he organized the Czech independence movement from London and is called the father of modern Czechoslovakia. He is the author of *The Making of a State.*

**Guy de Maupassant,** age 25; French short-story writer of noble birth, born in Normandy. He learned the art of fiction from Flaubert, a family friend, and won immediate popularity with his finely crafted, sardonic stories: *The Piece of String, Miss Harriet, Mademoiselle Fifi, The Necklace,* and 300 others. Committed to an asylum at 42, suffering from syphillis, paralysis and insanity, he died the following year.

**Robert Louis Stevenson,** age 25; Scottish novelist, essayist, and poet, born in Edinburgh, the son of a civil engineer and grandson of a designer and builder of lighthouses. What was intended as a boys' adventure novel, *Treasure Island* (1883), won unexpected success among a new adult reading public that wanted simple, uncomplicated prose. *Kidnapped* (1886) and *The Strange Case of Dr. Jekyll and Mr. Hyde* (1886) increased his popularity. Chronically ill, he settled in Samoa with his wife in 1889 and died five years later at 44, leaving his last novel, *Weir of Hermiston,* unfinished; it is often described as potentially his best. He also wrote the popular *Child's Garden of Verses* (1885).

**Sir Arthur Evans,** age 24; English archaeologist famous for his discovery of the ancient Minoan civilization of Crete. From 1898 to 1935 he excavated the site of the city of Knossos and reported his findings in *The Palace of Minos* (four volumes, 1921–1935). The Minoan script known as Linear B was not deciphered until later—by Michael Ventris, and English architectural student, in 1952–1956.

**Ferdinand Foch,** age 24; French soldier. A professor of strategy and director of the war college at the outbreak of World War I, he commanded the 10th army corps and played a decisive role in stopping the German advance at the Marne (1914). He directed the action in the Battle of the Somme (1916) and, as supreme commander of the Allied forces in 1918, directed the final victorious offensive.

**Adolph von Harnack,** age 24; German Protestant theologian and church historian born in what is now Estonia (USSR), the son of a Protestant theologian. A professor at various German universities, he is noted for his great work, *The History of Dogma* (four volumes, 1886–1890), which profoundly influenced modern theology. He also wrote *Monasticism* (1895) and *What Is Christianity?* (1900).

**Desire Joseph Mercier,** age 24; Belgian churchman and philosopher; professor of philosophy at Louvain and leader in the 20th-century revival of Thomism in Europe. As primate of Belgium (1906) and cardinal (1907), he was the spiritual leader and spokesman for Belgium during the German occupation (1914–1918), while King Albert was with the army. He issued a series of pastoral letters which resulted in his house arrest, and wrote *Cardinal Mercier's Own Story* (1920).

WALTER REED
American army surgeon
1851-1902

**Walter Reed,** age 24; American army surgeon born in Virginia. A professor of bacteriology at the Army Medical College in Washington, D.C. (after 15 years of frontier service), he was commissioned in 1900 to investigate the cause of yellow fever. He identified the mosquito, *Aedes aegypti,* as the carrier and recommended its extermination. Walter Reed Hospital in Washington, D.C., is named in his honor.

**Mrs. Humphrey Ward** (Mary Augusta Arnold Ward), age 24; English novelist born in Tasmania and reared in England, the niece of

# 1900

Adolph Hitler
(1889-1945), age 11
Edwin Hubble
(1889-1953), age 11
Jawaharlal Nehru
(1889-1964), age 11
Arnold Toynbee
(1889-1975), age 11
Ludwig Wittgenstein
(1889-1951), age 11
Charles de Gaulle
(1890-1970), age 10
Dwight Eisenhower
(1890-1969), age 10
Ho Chi Minh
(1890-1969), age 10
Waslaw Nijinsky
(1890-1950), age 10
Boris Pasternak
(1890-1960), age 10
Harold Alexander
(1891-1969), age 9
Rudolf Carnap
(1891-1970), age 9
Par Lagerkvist
(1891-1974), age 9
Sergei Prokofiev
(1891-1953), age 9
Erwin Rommel
(1891-1944), age 9
Arthur Compton
(1892-1962), age 8
Francisco Franco
(1892-1975), age 8
Darius Milhaud
(1892-1974), age 8
Edna St. Vincent Millay
(1892-1950), age 8
Tito
(1892-1980), age 8
Robert Watson-Watt
(1892-1973), age 8
Jomo Kenyatta
(1893?-1978), age 7?
Mao Tse-tung
(1893-1976), age 7
Vladimir Mayakovsky
(1893-1930), age 7
Cole Porter
(1893-1964), age 7
E. E. Cummings
(1894-1962), age 6

Matthew Arnold and the wife of Thomas Humphrey Ward, an editor. She was one of the most popular novelists of her time, and her most successful novel, *Robert Elsmere* (1888), could be found on every English drawing-room table. Its thematic subject—Christianity as a social gospel rather than a mystical, dogmatic religion—was of great topical interest.

**Herbert Henry Asquith,** age 23; first earl of Oxford and Asquith, English statesman of a middle-class family. A liberal member of Parliament (1886–1924) and prime minister (1908–1916), he is notable for inaugurating a broad program of social welfare, including old-age pensions (1908) and unemployment insurance (1911). He also secured passage in 1911 of an act abolishing the veto power of the House of Lords. He took Great Britain into World War I, but his coalition cabinet proved unworkable, and he was succeeded by Lloyd George.

**Joseph Jacques Cesare Joffre,** age 23; French soldier. As commander-in-chief of the French army, he is credited with directing the orderly French retreat before the German advance in 1914. After the horrible Battle of Verdun (1916), he was replaced as commander and given an advisory role.

**Albert Abraham Michelson,** age 23; American physicist born in Germany and brought to the United States at the age of two. He became head of the physics department at the University of Chicago (1892–1929) and won world renown for two feats: the measurement of the speed of light (186,000 miles per second) and the Michelson-Morley experiment, which demonstrated that the motion of the earth through space is not measurable. He received the Nobel Prize for physics in 1907.

**George Moore,** age 23; Irish novelist born in County Mayo, son of a member of Parliament. A self-dramatizing dandy who frequented Parisian cafes and knew all the great figures of art and literature, he was nevertheless a prolific writer. *Esther Waters* (1894) is his best novel, but he is better known for the semifictional autobiographical works, *Confessions of a Young Man* (1888) and *Hail and Farewell* (three volumes, 1911–1914).

**Mutsuhito** (Meiji), age 23; emperor of Japan 1867–1912. His reign, known as the Meiji restoration, marked the termination of the Tokugawa shogunate, the end of feudalism and the birth of modern Japan. Western ideas, laws and methods were introduced; the Gregorian calendar was adopted, and the Russo-Japanese War was won (1904–1905). The capital was moved to Tokyo (1869).

**Vincent van Gogh,** age 22; Dutch painter and etcher, son of a Protestant clergyman. A maladjusted religious zealot in youth, he took up painting at 27 and produced works that achieved phenomenal popularity 50 years after his tragic suicide at 37. In brilliant colors, with swirling brush strokes, he painted the fields, flowers and trees of Provence. One of many familiar works is the *Cornfield with Cypress Trees* (National Gallery, London).

**Cecil John Rhodes,** age 22; British diamond magnate and imperialist born near London, the son of a clergyman. Sent to South Africa at 17 for his health to work on his brother's cotton farm, he joined the diamond prospectors at Kimberley and in one year made a large fortune. At 35 he controlled diamond production in Kimberley and formed the British South African Company, which developed and controlled the area to the north (Rhodesia and Zambia). He died at 49 of a heart ailment, leaving six million pounds to establish the Rhodes scholarships.

**Paul Ehrlich,** age 21; German bacteriologist and chemotherapist born in Silesia. In 1909 he discovered Salvarsan, a chemical effective in the cure of syphillis and the first synthetic chemical agent used in the treatment of disease.

**Sir James George Frazer,** age 21; Scottish anthropologist and classical scholar born in Edinburgh, the son of the owner of a chemical firm. He is famous for his lengthy study of magic and religion, *The Golden Bough* (two volumes, 1890; expanded to 12 volumes, 1911–1915). He also wrote *Folk-Lore in the Old Testament* (three volumes, 1918) and translated Pausanias' *Hellados Periegesis* (six volumes, 1898). He was knighted in 1914.

**Arthur Rimbaud,** age 21; French symbolist poet and vagabond famous for his difficult, obscure verse, written before the age of 20. He gave up poetry for the life of a trader in Abyssinia, dealing in coffee, slaves and guns. He died in a Marseilles hospital at 37. His best-known poem is *A Season in Hell*.

**John Philip Sousa,** age 21; American bandmaster and composer born in Washington, D.C., of Portuguese and German descent, the son of a trombone player. After leading the U.S. Marine Corps Band 1880–1892, he organized his own band and toured the United States and Europe with great success for many years. He wrote over 100 marches, including the *Washington Post March* and *The Stars and Stripes Forever*.

**Oscar Wilde,** age 21; Irish poet and dramatist born in Dublin, the son of a surgeon. He is remembered for his witty drawing-room comedies; *Lady Windemere's Fan, A Woman of No Importance, An Ideal Husband* and *The Importance of Being Earnest*. He also wrote a popular novel, *The Picture of Dorian Gray;* a familiar poem, *The Ballad of Reading Gaol;* and a serious drama in French, *Salome,* produced in Paris with Sarah Bernhardt, and made into an opera by Richard Strauss. After his imprisonment (1895–1897) for sodomy, he lived in obscurity and poverty in Paris and died at 46.

**Eugene Victor Debs,** age 20; American socialist born in Indiana. A locomotive fireman in youth, he was active in the labor-union movement until 1897, when he organized the Social Democratic Party of America (renamed the Socialist Party in 1901). He ran for president in 1900, 1904, 1908, 1912 and again in 1920, when he received one million votes while in prison for opposing the war.

**Sir Arthur Wing Pinero,** age 20; English dramatist born in London. He wrote his first play, *200 Pounds a Year,* at 22 and followed it with dozens of popular farces and sentimental comedies. He turned to problem plays with *The Profligate* (1889) and enjoyed a long, successful career as a semiserious dramatist. *The Second Mrs. Tanqueray* (1893), about a woman with a questionable past, is his best-known play.

**Josiah Royce,** age 20; American philosopher born in northern California; foremost modern American idealist and professor at Harvard 1892–1916. Among his many books are *The Spirit of Modern Philosophy* (1892) and *The World and the Individual* (1900). Even in an age that has turned away from traditional idealism, his books are still read.

**Wovoka** (Jack Wilson), age c. 19; American Paiute Indian born in Nevada, the originator of the Ghost Dance and regarded by his followers as a messiah. His visions, combined with Indian traditions and influences from the Shaker religion, moved him to predict the end of the earth and the disappearance of all whites, followed by the earth's rejuvenation and rebirth of Indians living and dead, who would thenceforth live in peace and plenty. The religion spread rapidly among western Indians, who believed that performing the Ghost Dance would hasten the day.

## 1900

Edward VIII (Great Britain)
(1894-1972), age 6
Aldous Huxley
(1894-1963), age 6
Nikita Khrushchev
(1894-1971), age 6
Norbert Wiener
(1894-1964), age 6
George VI (Great Britain)
(1895-1952), age 5
Oscar Hammerstein II
(1895-1960), age 5
Paul Hindemith
(1895-1963), age 5
Juan Peron
(1895-1974), age 5
Edmund Wilson
(1895-1972), age 5
F. Scott Fitzgerald
(1896-1940), age 4
Bernard De Voto
(1897-1955), age 3
William Faulkner
(1897-1962), age 3
Thornton Wilder
(1897-1975), age 3
Bertolt Brecht
(1898-1956), age 2
Alexander Calder
(1898-1976), age 2
Chou En-lai
(1898-1976), age 2
George Gershwin
(1898-1937), age 2
Henry Moore
(1898-     ), age 2
Leo Szilard
(1898-1964), age 2
Jorge Luis Borges
(1899-     ), age 1
Federico Garcia Lorca
(1899-1936), age 1
Ernest Hemingway
(1899-1961), age 1
Vladimir Nabokov
(1899-1977), age 1

# 1900-1925

The first quarter of the 20th century belonged to America, and more particularly to the United States. The country came into prominence as a world power during World War I and after the war, when President Wilson went to Versailles to write the peace treaty. The year 1914 is regarded as a watershed by most historians, dividing two eras and signaling the end of 19th-century European civilization, for royalty everywhere were losing their thrones as American-style democracies were established. But while it was the end of an era in Europe, it was the beginning of a better and brighter age in America.

The conditions of everyday life underwent more change in this quarter century than in the previous hundred years, or in the 500 years before that. Women took to wearing short skirts for the first time in centuries; they cut their hair short, painted their faces and wore high heels and silk stockings. It was the age of the flapper and the bootlegger, but also of the Model T Ford, electric trolley cars and electric street lighting (replacing gas lights which were lit each evening

## 1900

Leo XIII (Pope)
   (1810-1903), age 90
Giuseppe Verdi
   (1813-1901), age 87
Elizabeth Cady Stanton
   (1815-1902), age 85
Theodor Mommsen
   (1817-1903), age 83
John Ruskin
   (1819-1900), age 81
Victoria (Great Britain)
   (1819-1901), age 81
Susan B. Anthony
   (1820-1906), age 80
Florence Nightingale
   (1820-1910), age 80
Herbert Spencer
   (1820-1903), age 80
Clara Barton
   (1821-1912), age 79
Mary Baker Eddy
   (1821-1910), age 79
Frederick Law Olmstead
   (1822-1903), age 78
Max Muller
   (1823-1900), age 77

SIGMUND FREUD
Austrian neurologist and
   psychoanalyst
1856-1939

**Sigmund Freud,** age 44; Austrian neurologist and founder of psychoanalysis, born in Moravia of middle-class Jewish parents who moved to Vienna when he was three. His unprecedented search for psychological rather than physiological explanations of mental and emotional disorders led to the theory and practice of *psychoanalysis*, a term he originated in 1896. He was the first to develop systematically the concept of the subconscious mind, laying the foundation for modern psychology. Although not widely acknowledged in his lifetime, his ideas have become part of the fabric of contemporary thought, exercis-

by a boy going around on a bicycle); of paved streets and sidewalks, hot-and-cold running water and central heating (with a coal furnace in the basement); of vacuum sweepers, sewing machines, refrigerators and electric fans; of the phonograph, the movies, the radio; of dance bands and the foxtrot, the Ziegfeld Follies and spectator sports. It was the age of Jack Dempsey, Babe Ruth, Douglas Fairbanks, Charlie Chaplin and Rudolph Valentino. In 1900 automobiles were the sport of the rich; there were 8,000 registered in the country. In 1925 there were 17 million registered automobiles.

It was a brand-new age. It appeared as if the old, stodgy world of the 19th century, when women braided their long hair in coils and wore heavy floor-length skirts and men wore stiff bowler hats, high-button shoes, celluloid collars and heavy, unpressed woolen suits—it appeared as if that world had been swept under the rug and a new, shining world created in its place. While in Europe the tragic costs of the World War had brought dismay and disillusionment, the United States changed from an untried, undeveloped land into a world power flushed with victory, with unshakable faith in its own destiny, knowing that it was the best in the world and getting better.

# 1925

ing a particularly profound influence upon subsequent developments in literature.

**Robert Edwin Peary,** age 44; American Arctic explorer born in Pennsylvania; first man to reach the North Pole. As a U.S. Navy civil engineer, he began explorations in Greenland in 1886 and proved it to be an island. After several unsuccessful attempts, he reached the Pole on April 6, 1909, accompanied by Matthew Henson and four Eskimos.

**Henri Philippe Petain,** age 44; French army officer; hero of the Battle of Verdun (1916) in World War I and commander-in-chief of the French armies in 1917, under Marshall Foch. As premier in June, 1940, he surrendered to Adolph Hitler and became head of the Vichy collaborationist government. In 1945 he was brought to trial and convicted of treason, but his sentence of death was commuted to life imprisonment by De Gaulle. Sent to an island off the coast of Brittany, he died there at 95.

**John Singer Sargent,** age 44; American painter born in Florence, Italy, of wealthy American parents. He established himself in Europe as a fashionable portrait painter, with Ellen Terry and Robert Louis Stevenson among his subjects, and on frequent trips to America painted Theodore Roosevelt, Woodrow Wilson, Edwin Booth and John D. Rockefeller. The famous *Madame X* is in the Metropolitan Museum of Art in New York.

**George Bernard Shaw,** age 44; British playwright and critic born in Dublin, of English parents—his father an unsuccessful businessman, his mother a music teacher. His first successful play, *Arms and the Man* (1894), was made into an operetta, *The Chocolate Soldier,* in 1908 and was followed by a series of satirical dramas on social and religious problems of the time: *Major Barbara, Heartbreak House,*

Bela Bartok
(1881-1945), age 44
Ernest Bevin
(1881-1951), age 44
Alexander Fleming
(1881-1955), age 44
John XXIII (Pope)
(1881-1963), age 44
Kemal Ataturk
(1881-1938), age 44
Aleksandr Kerenski
(1881-1970), age 44
Pablo Picasso
(1881-1973), age 44
Teilhard de Chardin
(1881-1955), age 44
Stefan Zweig
(1881-1942), age 44
Eamon De Valera
(1882-1975), age 43
Arthur Eddington
(1882-1944), age 43
Jean Giraudoux
(1882-1944), age 43
William F. Halsey
(1882-1959), age 43

# 1900

Alfred Russell Wallace
  (1823-1913), age 77
Stephanus Paulus Kruger
  (1825-1904), age 75
Joseph Lister
  (1827-1912), age 73
Lew Wallace
  (1827-1905), age 73
Meyer Guggenheim
  (1828-1905), age 72
Henrik Ibsen
  (1828-1906), age 72
George Meredith
  (1828-1909), age 72
Leo Tolstoy
  (1828-1910), age 72
Jules Verne
  (1828-1905), age 72
Geronimo
  (1829-1909), age 71
Porfirio Diaz
  (1830-1915), age 70
Francis Joseph I (Austria)
  (1830-1916), age 70
Camille Pissarro
  (1830-1903), age 70
Victorien Sardou
  (1831-1908), age 69
Bjornstjerne Bjornson
  (1832-1910), age 68
Sir Leslie Stephen
  (1832-1904), age 68
Edward Tylor
  (1832-1917), age 68
Benjamin Harrison
  (1833-1901), age 67
Lord Acton
  (1834-1902), age 66
Gottlieb Daimler
  (1834-1900), age 66
Edgar Degas
  (1834-1917), age 66
Ernst Haeckel
  (1834-1919), age 66
James McNeill Whistler
  (1834-1903), age 66
Samuel Butler
  (1835-1902), age 65
Giosue Carducci
  (1835-1907), age 65
Andrew Carnegie
  (1835-1919), age 65

etc. *Pygmalion* (1912) is better known in its adaptation as the musical comedy *My Fair Lady*.

**Louis Henri Sullivan,**. age 44; American architect born in Boston, a pioneer in modern functional architecture. He abandoned Victorian Gothic ornamentation for simple, uncluttered lines. Among his many notable buildings in the Midwest are the Wainwright Building in St. Louis (1890) and the Carson Pirie, Scott store in Chicago (1904).

**Nikola Tesla,** age 44; Croation-American inventor and pioneer in electric power, born in Austria-Hungary. He came to America at 28 and in 1888 patented a small alternating-current motor. In 1889 in association with Westinghouse Company, he put on the market the first electric appliance, a three-blade fan. He also designed the power system at Niagara Falls, the world's first large-scale generating plant (1891–1896).

**Booker Taliaferro Washington,** age 44; American Negro educator born in Virginia, son of a mulatto slave and a white man. He worked his way through Hampton Institute, became an instructor, and in 1881 was appointed to establish, at Tuskegee, Alabama, a trade and professional school for blacks, which he eventually developed into a large, successful institution. He was an eloquent public speaker and the author of *Up From Slavery* (1901).

**(Thomas) Woodrow Wilson,** age 44; American statesman and educator born in Virginia; 28th president, 1913–1921. Formerly president of Princeton University (1902–1910), he was a forceful public speaker whose addresses were models of political oratory. His administration was notable for the passage of women's suffrage and child labor laws, and the establishment of the Federal Reserve System. He maintained neutrality in World War I until German submarines attacked American ships. A paralytic stroke in October 1919, left him an invalid, and he died in 1924.

**Joseph Conrad** (Teodor Jozef Konrad Korzeniowski), age 43; English novelist born in Poland. Entering the British merchant service as a youth, he became a ship's captain and a British subject at 29 and at 37 retired from the sea to write. His novels and stories are psychological character studies, mostly with an Eastern or tropical-sea setting, and include *Almayer's Folly, Lord Jim, Chance, Victory, Nostromo* and *Heart of Darkness*. Despite his flawless English prose, he never lost his strong Polish accent in speaking.

**Sir Edward Elgar,** age 43; English composer born near Worcestor, son of the organist of St. George's Roman Catholic Church. He is best known for his oratorios: *The Dream of Gerontius, The Apostles* and *The Kingdom;* and for his five *Pomp and Circumstance* marches, but he also wrote symphonic works in the romantic style. He was knighted in 1904 and made a baronet in 1931.

**Georgi Valentinovich Plekhanov,** age 43; Russian political philosopher, called the founder of Russian philosophic Marxism. He spent much of his life in exile in Geneva, and was associated for a time with Lenin, but disagreed with Bolshevik policy, rejected terrorism, and after the revolution retired from public life. He is the author of *Essays on the History of Materialism* (1896) and other works which influenced Russian Marxist theory.

**Hermann Sudermann,** age 43; German naturalistic dramatist and novelist born in East Prussia. Among his best-known novels are *Dame Care* (1887), on the defeat of youthful aspiration by hardship and poverty, and *The Song of Songs* (1908). His most successful plays were *Magda* (1893), in which appeared Sarah Bernhardt, Mrs. Patrick Campbell and Eleanora Duse; and *The Joy of Living* (1902).

**William Howard Taft,** age 43; American statesman and jurist born in Cincinnati, the son of a cabinet officer and diplomat; 27th president, 1909–1913; chief justice of the Supreme Court, 1921–1930, appointed by Warren Harding. He was also the first civilian governor of the Philippine Islands, 1901–1904. After defeating William Jennings Bryan in the election of 1908, he maintained the policies of his friend and predecessor, Theodore Roosevelt, but with less vigor.

**Thorstein Bunde Veblen,** age 43; American economist and sociologist born in Wisconsin, the son of Norwegian immigrants. A critic of established institutions, he stressed the conflicting interests of social classes and deprecated culture and classical learning as disserviceable anachronisms in an industrial age. Author of *The Theory of the Leisure Class* (1899), he was the first to use the phrase "conspicuous consumption."

**Rudolf Christian Karl Diesel,** age 42; German mechanical engineer born in Paris. He invented and built (1893–1897) an internal-combustion engine to run on crude oil, which was universally adopted for driving locomotives and trucks. He drowned in 1913 while crossing the English Channel.

**Emile Durkheim,** age 42; French sociologist born in Lorraine, one of the founders of modern sociology. He traced the origin of religious and moral values to a collective consciousness, or social mind, and opposed attempts to offer psychological explanations of social facts. His most important works are *The Division of Labor in Society* (1893), *Suicide* (1897) and *The Elementary Forms of the Religious Life* (1912).

**Gustaf V** (Gustavus), age 42; king of Sweden, 1907–1950, of the house of Bernadotte (descended from a Napoleonic general). During his reign Sweden emerged as a progressive, democratic state with a high standard of living. A popular monarch, he walked the streets of Stockholm unguarded and died at 92.

**Selma Lagerlof,** age 42; Swedish novelist born in Varmland. A teacher in a girls' school, she published a successful novel, *Gosta Berlings,* in 1891, and followed it with dozens of novels and stories of peasant life, with themes taken from Swedish folklore. She also wrote *The Miracles of the Antichrist* (1897), a story of Sicily, and *The Ring of the Lowenskolds* (1925–1928). She was the winner of the 1909 Nobel Prize for literature.

**Max Karl Ernst Ludwig Planck,** age 42; German physicist born in Kiel, the son of a jurist. A pioneer of modern physics, in 1900–1901 he developed the quantum theory (a quantum is a unit of energy and the theory relates to the way energy is emitted), an important contribution to the understanding of atomic structure. He is called a forerunner of the atomic age.

**Giacomo Puccini,** age 42; Italian operatic composer born near Pisa, the son of a musician. After becoming famous at 35 with *Manon Lescaut,* he wrote many other popular operas with exotic settings: *La Boheme, Tosca, Madame Butterfly* and *Girl of the Golden West.* He died of throat cancer leaving *Turandot* unfinished.

**Theodore Roosevelt,** age 42; American statesman born in New York City of a wealthy, prominent family; 26th president, 1901–1909. He commanded a volunteer cavalry regiment, the Rough Riders, in the Spanish-American War and returned a hero, to be elected governor of New York (1899) and vice-president (1901), succeeding to the presidency upon the assassination of William McKinley in September. He vigorously enforced the Sherman Anti-Trust Act and began construction of the Panama Canal. A conservationist and big-game hunter, he wrote *The Winning of the West, The Strenuous Life* and *African Game Trails.*

# 1925

James Joyce
(1882-1941), age 43
Jacques Maritain
(1882-1973), age 43
Anna Pavlova
(1882-1931), age 43
Franklin D. Roosevelt
(1882-1945), age 43
Igor Stravinsky
(1882-1971), age 43
Sigrid Undset
(1882-1949), age 43
Virginia Woolf
(1882-1941), age 43
Clement Attlee
(1883-1967), age 42
Walter Gropius
(1883-1969), age 42
John Maynard Keynes
(1883-1946), age 42
Benito Mussolini
(1883-1945), age 42
Jose Ortega y Gasset
(1883-1955), age 42
Maurice Utrillo
(1883-1955), age 42
Anton von Webern
(1883-1945), age 42
William Carlos Williams
(1883-1963), age 42
Grigori Zinoviev
(1883-1936), age 42
Hideki Tojo
(1884/85-1948),
age c.41
Harry S. Truman
(1884-1972), age 41
Alban Berg
(1885-1935), age 40
Niels Bohr
(1885-1962), age 40
Jerome Kern
(1885-1945), age 40
D. H. Lawrence
(1885-1930), age 40
Sinclair Lewis
(1885-1951), age 40
Francois Mauriac
(1885-1970), age 40
Chester Nimitz
(1885-1966), age 40

# 1900

Leopold II (Belgium)
(1835-1909), age 65
Camille Saint-Saens
(1835-1921), age 65
Mark Twain
(1835-1910), age 65
Tz'u Hsi
(1834/35-1908), age c.65
Joseph Chamberlain
(1836-1914), age 64
W. S. Gilbert
(1836-1911), age 64
Bret Harte
(1836-1902), age 64
Winslow Homer
(1836-1910), age 64
John Burroughs
(1837-1921), age 63
Grover Cleveland
(1837-1908), age 63
George Dewey
(1837-1917), age 63
Hitotsubashi
(1837-1902), age 63
William Dean Howells
(1837-1920), age 63
John Pierpont Morgan
(1837-1913), age 63
Algernon Swinburne
(1837-1909), age 63
Henry Adams
(1838-1918), age 62
James Bryce
(1838-1922), age 62
Sir Henry Irving
(1838-1905), age 62
William Lecky
(1838-1903), age 62
Ernst Mach
(1838-1916), age 62
John Muir
(1838-1914), age 62
George Trevelyan
(1838-1928), age 62
Paul Cezanne
(1839-1906), age 61
Willard Gibbs
(1839-1903), age 61
Joachim Machado de Assis
(1839-1908), age 61
Charles Sanders Peirce
(1839-1914), age 61

**Henri Louis Bergson,** age 41; French philosopher born in Paris of Polish-Jewish and Irish descent. He postulated a dynamic elan vital (life force), incomprehensible to the intellect, as the driving force of the evolutionary process. His ability to write and lecture on philosophy in clear, understandable language made him world famous. His major work is *Creative Evolution* (1907).

**John Dewey,** age 41; American philosopher and educator born in Vermont, the son of a grocer. His philosophy of instrumentalism, drived from William James' pragmatism, denied the absolute and eternal nature of truth and the value of mental activity as an end in itself. He believed the mind to be essentially an instrument for solving practical problems of existence and was a pioneer in progressive education.

**Sir Arthur Conan Doyle,** age 41; British physician and writer born in Edinburgh. He practiced medicine for eight years and wrote the first Sherlock Holmes story, *A Study in Scarlet,* in 1887. This was followed by about 60 more with the same two principal characters, immortalizing them and making their creator world famous. He also wrote historical novels *(The White Company)* and histories of the Boer War and World War I. He was knighted in 1902.

**Eleanora Duse,** age 41; Italian actress born in Milan. A member of her father's traveling company from the age of 13, she formed her own company at 27 and toured Europe with great success. She appeared on the New York stage in *Camille* in 1893. After retiring at 50, she returned to the stage 12 years later and died in 1924, in Pittsburgh, while on tour.

**Havelock Ellis,** age 41; English psychologist and sociologist born in Surrey. His pioneer work, *Studies in the Psychology of Sex* (seven volumes, 1897–1928), opened the way for rational discussion of problems of sex. The first volume was banned as obscene; the last was accepted without a ripple of protest. He also wrote *The Dance of Life* (1923), *Little Essays on Love and Virtue* (1922), and predicted the eventual acceptance of eugenic practices.

**Lady Augusta Persse Gregory,** age 41?; Irish playwright and patron of the theater born in County Galway. She married Sir William Gregory, a retired civil servant, and after his death in 1892 she dedicated herself to the theater. One of the founders and first director of the Abbey Theatre in Dublin, she wrote many of the plays produced there, including *Spreading the News* (1904) and *The Rising of the Moon* (1907).

**Knut Hamsun** (Knut Pedersen), age 41; Norwegian novelist, winner of the 1920 Nobel Prize for literature. Before his first successful novel, *Hunger* (1890), he lived a wandering life, working as a laborer and street-car conductor in Chicago (1886–1888). His novels, among them *Pan* (1894) and *The Growth of the Soil* (1917), reflect his own alienation and hostility to industrial society and democracy. His popularity declined after his collaboration with the Nazis in World War II. He lived to be 92.

**Victor Herbert,** age 41; Irish-American composer and conductor born in Dublin. He emigrated at 27 and became a cellist at the Metropolitan Opera House in New York (1886–1898) and the conductor of the Pittsburgh Symphony Orchestra (1898–1904). His more than 40 popular operettas, including *The Fortune Teller* (1989), *Babes in Toyland* (1903), *The Red Mill* (1906), *Naughty Marietta* (1910) and *Princess Pat* (1915), brought him fame and fortune. He also wrote musical scores for the Ziegfeld Follies.

**Alfred Edward Housman,** age 41; English poet and classical scholar born in Worcestershire, near the Shropshire hills. A professor of Latin, he published only two small volumes of verse, *A Shropshire Lad*

(1896) and *Last Poems* (1922), but is one of the best-loved poets of the 20th century. The transiency of love, beauty and life were the favorite themes of his poignant lyrics.

**Sholom Aleichem,** age 41; pen name (meaning "Peace be with you") of Solomon Rabinowitz, a Yiddish short-story writer born near Kiev in the Ukraine. Living in America after 1906, he became known as the sympathetic chronicler of Eastern European Jewish life of the late 19th century. *Fiddler on the Roof* is based on his stories.

**Francis Thompson,** age 41; English religious poet born in Lancashire, the son of a physician. He studied medicine but failed to pass the examinations and lived in poverty and ill health, addicted to drugs for most of his life. His fame rests on one poem, *The Hound of Heaven*. He also wrote a life of St. Ignatius of Loyola.

**William II** (Friedrich Wilhelm Viktor Albert), age 41; emperor of Germany and king of Prussia 1888–1918; grandson of Queen Victoria and cousin of George V of England. His aggressive colonial policy and expansion of the German navy contributed to the outbreak of World War I. After Germany's defeat, he fled to Holland, where he lived in comfortable exile until his death in 1941.

**Sir James Matthew Barrie,** age 40; Scottish playwright and novelist born near Dundee, the son of a weaver. Success came with his romantic novels *The Little Minister* (1891) and *Sentimental Tommy* (1895), lasting fame and worldwide recognition with the fantasy play *Peter Pan* (1904). His other successful plays were *Quality Street* (1901), *The Admirable Crichton* (1902)—perhaps his best—*What Every Woman Knows* (1908) and *Dear Brutus* (1917). He was made a baronet in 1913.

**William Jennings Bryan,** age 40; American politician and orator born in Illinois. As the "boy orator from the River Platte," he was the popular idol of the Populist movement of the 1890s; he served as a congressman from Nebraska from 1891–1895 and was the Democratic candidate for president in 1896, 1900 and 1908. As assistant prosecutor in the famous Scopes trial, he won the case but died five days later. He is the author of *The Bible and Its Enemies* (1921).

ANTON CHEKHOV
Russian dramatist and
short-story writer
1860-1904

**Anton Pavlovich Chekhov,** age 40; Russian dramatist and short-story writer born in Taganrog on the Sea of Azov. A descendant of serfs, he was a master of the modern short story and a dramatist whose four great plays revolutionized the theater. He portrayed with realism the stagnant pre-revolution Russian society of the late 19th and early 20th centuries. He married an actress from the Moscow Art Theater and lived in the Crimea after 1897 because of poor health. He died of tuberculosis at 44.

# 1925

George Patton
  (1885-1945), age 40
Ezra Pound
  (1885-1972), age 40
Karl Barth
  (1886-1968), age 39
David Ben-Gurion
  (1886-1973), age 39
Diego Rivera
  (1886-1957), age 39
Ludwig Mies van der
  Rohe
  (1886-1969), age 39
Paul Tillich
  (1886-1965), age 39
Chiang Kai-shek
  (1887-1975), age 38
Le Corbusier
  (1887-1965), age 38
Bernard Montgomery
  (1887-1976), age 38
Sigmund Romberg
  (1887-1951), age 38
Heitor Villa-Lobos
  (1887-1959), age 38
Irving Berlin
  (1888-    ), age 37
Richard E. Byrd
  (1888-1957), age 37
T. S. Eliot
  (1888-1965), age 37
Eugene O'Neill
  (1888-1953), age 37
Marc Chagall
  (1887/89-    ),
  age c.36
Charles Chaplin
  (1889-1977), age 36
Amelita Galli-Curci
  (1889-1963), age 36
Martin Heidegger
  (1889-1976), age 36
Adolph Hitler
  (1889-1945), age 36
Edwin Hubble
  (1889-1953), age 36
Jawaharlal Nehru
  (1889-1964), age 36
Arnold Toynbee
  (1889-1975), age 36
Ludwig Wittgenstein
  (1889-1951), age 36

# 1900

John D. Rockefeller
(1839-1937), age 61

Carlotta
(1840-1927), age 60

Thomas Hardy
(1840-1928), age 60

Claude Monet
(1840-1926), age 60

Thomas Nast
(1840-1902), age 60

Auguste Rodin
(1840-1917), age 60

William Graham Sumner
(1840-1910), age 60

Giovanni Verga
(1840-1922), age 60

Emile Zola
(1840-1902), age 60

James Gordon Bennett
(1841-1918), age 59

Georges Clemenceau
(1841-1929), age 59

Anton Dvorak
(1841-1904), age 59

Edward VII (Great Britain)
(1841-1910), age 59

Oliver Wendell Holmes
(1841-1935), age 59

Hirobumi Ito
(1841-1909), age 59

Pierre Auguste Renoir
(1841-1919), age 59

Henry Stanley
(1841-1904), age 59

Ambrose Bierce
(1842-1914?), age 58

Georg Brandes
(1842-1927), age 58

William James
(1842-1910), age 58

Peter Kropotkin
(1842-1921), age 58

Jules Massenet
(1842-1912), age 58

Sir Arthur Sullivan
(1842-1900), age 58

C. M. Doughty
(1843-1926), age 57

Edvard Grieg
(1843-1907), age 57

Henry James
(1843-1916), age 57

**Gustav Mahler,** age 40; Austrian composer and conductor born in Bohemia, son of a shopkeeper. He directed the Imperial Opera in Vienna from 1897–1907 and was conductor of the Metropolitan Opera in New York from 1908–1910 and of the New York Philharmonic Orchestra from 1909–1911. He composed nine operas as well as many songs and song cycles. Mahler died at 50.

**Ignace Jan Paderewski,** age 40; Polish virtuoso pianist, composer and statesman. The most popular pianist of his time, whose name became a household word, he made his debut in Vienna in 1887 and thereafter established himself as the foremost interpreter of Chopin. He was active in the cause of Polish independence and premier in 1919. His most famous composition is the *Minuet in G.*

**John Joseph Pershing,** age 40; American army officer born in Missouri and graduated from West Point in 1886. He fought the Indians in the West, the Spanish in Cuba, the Moros in the Phillippines and commanded the American Expeditionary Force in Europe (1917–1919). Because of his stubborn resistance, the American troops were not incorporated into French and British armies but operated as a separate force. He wrote *My Experiences in the World War* (1931), which won the Pulitzer Prize for history.

**Raymond Poincare,** age 40; French statesman; cousin of Jules Poincare, the mathematician. As wartime president from 1913–1920 he sustained morale and discouraged defeatism with his eloquent oratory. He was premier in 1912–1913, from 1922–1924 and from 1926–1929, and inflexible in his demand for full payment of German reparations.

**Edward Alexander MacDowell,** age 39; American composer born in New York City. His well-known works include the symphonic poems *Hamlet and Ophelia* and *Lancelot and Elaine;* two piano concertos; the *Indian Suite;* and shorter pieces such as *Woodland Sketches,* all showing the influence of Grieg, Dvorak and other Europeans. His summer home in Peterborough, N.H., is now the MacDowell Colony for artists and writers.

**Aristide Maillol,** age 39; French neoclassical sculptor born in a small town near Perpignan. A painter, woodcarver and tapestry weaver before turning to sculpture in his late thirties, he is known for his massive yet graceful female nudes and for the Cezanne monument in Paris.

**Fridtjof Nansen,** age 39; Norwegian Arctic explorer, scientist and statesman. In 1888 he led the first expedition across the ice fields of Greenland, and on his polar expedition of 1893–1896 he reached 86 degrees 14 minutes north before being forced to turn back. He was a professor of zoology and oceanography, the first Norwegian minister to Great Britain, 1906–08, and winner of the Nobel Peace Prize in 1922 for refugee work. He also wrote *Eskimo Life* (1891).

**Frederic Remington,** age 39; American genre painter and sculptor born in New York City, known for his colorful paintings of cowboys and Indians on the Western plains. One of the best known of his more than 3700 paintings, drawings and illustrations is *Cavalry Charge on the Southern Plains* in the Metropolitan Museum, New York City. The bronze sculpture *Bronco Buster* is also there.

**Sir Rabindranath Tagore,** age 39; Hindu poet born in Calcutta of a wealthy family; winner of the 1913 Nobel Prize for literature. A prodigious writer of verse, plays, novels and stories which conveyed the message of peace and brotherhood, he traveled and lectured throughout the world and was knighted in 1915 by George V. Among his works, written in Bengali and translated into English by himself, are the poems *Gitanjali* (1912), *The Gardener* (1913), *The Crescent Moon* (1913) and *Songs of Kabir* (1915), and the play *The Post Office* (1914).

**Frederick Jackson Turner,** age 39; American historian born in Wisconsin; professor of history at Harvard from 1910–1924. He is known as the originator of the frontier theory, emphasizing the significance of the receding frontier in the development of American social and economic life. Author of *The Rise of the New West* (1906), *The Frontier in American History* (1920) and *The Significance of Sections in American History* (1932), he was the winner of the 1933 Pulitzer Prize for history.

**Alfred North Whitehead,** age 39; English mathematician and philosopher; collaborator with his pupil, Bertrand Russell, on *Principia mathematica* (three volumes, 1910–1913), an important work in theoretical mathematics. He taught mathematics at Cambridge from 1885–1911 and at the University of London from 1911–1924, and was professor of philosophy at Harvard from 1924–1936. He also wrote popular books on philosophy.

**Claude Debussy,** age 38; French composer born in a suburb of Paris of a poor family. Called a forerunner of modern music, he is much admired for his piano compositions, such as *The Isle of Mirth* and *Suite Bergamasque* (containing *Clair de Lune)*. His orchestral works include *La Mer* and *L'Apres-Midi d'un Faune* and are noted for their dreamlike quality and harmonic innovations.

**Frederick Delius,** age 38; English composer born in Yorkshire, the son of a German wool merchant. His compositions, influenced by European romantics, include the opera *A Village Romeo and Juliet* (1907); the orchestral piece *North Country Sketches* (1914); and the choral works, *Sea Drift* (1903) and *Song of the High Hills* (1912). Although blind and paralyzed in his last years, he continued to work and in 1929 attended a festival of his works organized by Sir Thomas Beecham.

**Gerhart Hauptmann,** age 38; German dramatist born in Silesia, the son of an innkeeper; winner of the 1912 Nobel Prize for literature and foremost modern German playwright. *Before the Dawn* (1889) introduced naturalism to the German stage and was followed by other dramas of social realism, including *The Weavers* (1892), considered to be his best. He also wrote novels, an epic poem and fantasy plays *(The Sunken Bell,* 1897), but is remembered for his early naturalistic dramas.

**O. Henry** (William Sydney Porter), age 38; American writer born in North Carolina of a middle-class family. He spent three years as a bank teller in Austin, Texas, and three years in prison for embezzling the bank's funds. Settling in New York City in 1902, he grew rich and famous writing hundreds of stories about ordinary people for popular magazines, usually with surprise endings. One famous example is *The Gift of the Magi.* He died of tuberculosis at 47.

**Maurice Maeterlinck,** age 38; Belgian writer born in Ghent, an exponent of symbolism in drama. His best-known plays are *Pelleas et Melisande* (1892), the source of Debussy's opera, and *The Blue Bird* (1909), now a children's classic. He also wrote *The Life of the Bee,* an attempt to poeticize natural science.

**Arthur Schnitzler,** age 38; Austrian playwright, novelist and physician; born in Vienna, the son of a prominent physician. His light-hearted comedies of love—including *Merry-Go-Round* (1903), which became the film *La Ronde* in 1955—brought success and fame, but he adopted a more serious tone in his later dramas, *The Vast Domain* (1911) and *Professor Bernhardi* (1912). These and the autobiographical novel *The Road to the Open* (1908) are imbued with a resigned, worldly skepticism.

**Edward Alexander Westermarck,** age 38; Finnish social philosopher and anthropologist born in Helsinki. He wrote in English and was a

# 1925

Charles de Gaulle
(1890-1970), age 35
Dwight Eisenhower
(1890-1969), age 35
Ho Chi Minh
(1890-1969), age 35
Waslaw Nijinsky
(1890-1950), age 35
Boris Pasternak
(1890-1960), age 35
Harold Alexander
(1891-1969), age 34
Rudolf Carnap
(1891-1970), age 34
Par Lagerkvist
(1891-1974), age 34
Sergei Prokofiev
(1891-1953), age 34
Erwin Rommel
(1891-1944), age 34
Arthur Compton
(1892-1962), age 33
Francisco Franco
(1892-1975), age 33
Darius Milhaud
(1892-1974), age 33
Edna St. Vincent Millay
(1892-1950), age 33
Tito
(1892-1980), age 33
Robert Watson-Watt
(1892-1973), age 33
Jomo Kenyatta
(1893?-1978), age 32?
Mao Tse-tung
(1893-1976), age 32
Vladimir Mayakovsky
(1893-1930), age 32
Cole Porter
(1893-1964), age 32
E. E. Cummings
(1894-1962), age 31
Edward VIII (Great Britain)
(1894-1972), age 31
Aldous Huxley
(1894-1963), age 31
Nikita Khrushchev
(1894-1971), age 31
Norbert Wiener
(1894-1964), age 31
George VI (Great Britain)
(1895-1952), age 30

# 1900

Robert Koch
  (1843-1910), age 57
William McKinley
  (1843-1901), age 57
Karl Benz
  (1844-1929), age 56
Sarah Bernhardt
  (1844-1923), age 56
Robert Bridges
  (1844-1930), age 56
George Washington Cable
  (1844-1925), age 56
Thomas Eakins
  (1844-1916), age 56
Anatole France
  (1844-1924), age 56
Andrew Lang
  (1844-1912), age 56
Modjeska
  (1844-1909), age 56
Friedrich Nietzsche
  (1844-1900), age 56
Nicolai Rimski-Korsakov
  (1844-1908), age 56
Henri Rousseau
  (1844-1910), age 56
Elie Metchnikoff
  (1845-1916), age 55
Wilhelm Roentgen
  (1845-1923), age 55
George Saintsbury
  (1845-1933), age 55
F. H. Bradley
  (1846-1924), age 54
William Frederick Cody
  (1846-1917), age 54
Rudolf Eucken
  (1846-1926), age 54
Carry Nation
  (1846-1911), age 54
Henryk Sienkiewicz
  (1846-1916), age 54
Alexander Graham Bell
  (1847-1922), age 53
Thomas Alva Edison
  (1847-1931), age 53
Paul von Hindenburg
  (1847-1934), age 53
Joseph Pulitzer
  (1847-1911), age 53
Albert Pinkham Ryder
  (1847-1917), age 53

professor of sociology at the University of London 1907–1936. A defender of conservative morality in *The History of Human Marriage* (1891), he traced the origin of marriage to the apes. He also wrote *The Future of Marriage in Western Civilization* (1936).

**Edith Wharton** (Edith Newbold Jones), age 38; American writer born in New York City of a wealthy family of high social standing; the wife of Edward Wharton, a banker. Her novels depict the social world and conventions of the very wealthy. Famous titles include *The Age of Innocence* (1920) and *Old New York* (1924), a collection of four short novels. *Ethan Frome* (1911), a novel of New England, is her masterpiece.

**Gabriele D'Annunzio,** age 37; Italian poet, novelist and soldier; born in Abruzzi, the son of a landowner. One of his best-known novels, *The Flame* (1900), relates the story of his love affair with Eleanora Duse, for whom he wrote most of his plays. He was known as a melodramatic *poseur* and was an outspoken supporter of Mussolini.

HENRY FORD
American automobile
manufacturer
1863-1947

**Henry Ford,** age 37; American automobile manufacturer born on a farm near Dearborn, Michigan, the son of Irish immigrants. Starting out as a machinist, he organized the Ford Motor Company in 1903 and produced the first inexpensive automobile, the Model T, in 1909. He revolutionized factory production methods by introducing the assembly line in 1913.

**William Randolph Hearst,** age 37; American publisher born in San Francisco, whose father was a mining magnate and a senator. He founded a newspaper chain (18 big-city dailies and nine popular magazines) and gained a reputation for his conservative politics and the "yellow" journalism of his publications, calculated to appeal to the least-educated classes. He grew enormously wealthy and lived ostentatiously in the manner of a medieval baron, but soon after his death in 1951 the publishing empire declined, with changing times and changing tastes.

**David Lloyd George,** age 37; British statesman of Welsh descent born in Manchester. A sharp-tongued liberal member of Parliament for 54 years, he helped secure the passage of unemployment- and sickness-insurance legislation. As prime minister 1916–1922, he saw the Allies victorious in the world war and played a principal role in the formulation of the Versailles Treaty. He died one month before the end of World War II.

**Pietro Mascagni,** age 37; Italian composer born in Leghorn. He is famous for a single work, the popular opera *Cavalleria Rusticana* (1890), in the violently emotional Italian style known as *verismo*. A conductor and music teacher all his life, he wrote 16 other operas which are seldom produced today.

**George Santayana** (Jorge Augustin de Santayana), age 37; Spanish-American philosopher born in Madrid, the son of an official of the Spanish colonial civil service. Although born in Spain of Spanish parents, he was educated in Boston and wrote in English. After teaching at Harvard for 23 years, he retired at 49 and returned to Europe. He saw the universe as neither moral nor rational, but rather as purely mechanical in its operation. Besides his philosophical and critical works, he wrote the novel *The Last Puritan* (1935), and a three-volume auto-biography entitled *Persons and Places* (1944).

GEORGE WASHINGTON
CARVER
American botanist and
agricultural chemist
1864?-1943

**George Washington Carver,** age 36?; American Negro botanist and agricultural chemist born in Virginia of slave parents. He worked his way through Iowa State College and became a teacher and agricultural-research director at Tuskegee Institute. In his efforts to improve the economy of the South and the lot of the Negro, he discovered hundreds of industrial uses for the peanut, the sweet potato and the soybean, making these crops profitable. His birthplace was made a national monument in 1953.

**Richard Strauss,** age 36; German composer and conductor born in Munich. One of the last German romantics, he is known for the operas *Salome* (1905) and *Der Rosenkavalier* (1911) and for the symphonic poems *Don Juan, Death and Transfiguration* and *Thus Spake Zarathustra.* He was honorary head of the music department of the Third Reich. Strauss was unrelated to the Austrian Johann Strauss.

**Henri de Toulouse-Lautrec,** age 36; French painter and poster designer of noble lineage, born in southern France. He is as famous for his physical deformity, alcoholism, and sordid associations as for his postimpressionist paintings. His familiar works include portraits of the music-hall entertainer, Yvette Guilbert and the model, Suzanne Valadon (Utrillo's mother) as well as scenes of cabarets, circuses and race-tracks. He died at 36 after a paralytic stroke.

**Miguel de Unamuno y Jugo,** age 36; Spanish philosopher, essayist and novelist; born in Bilbao of Basque origin. A professor of Greek and rector (1901–1914) at the University of Salamanca, he was exiled by Primo de Rivera and lived in Paris from 1924–1930, returning to Spain upon the establishment of the republic. His novels, *Mist* (1914)

Oscar Hammerstein II
(1895-1960), age 30
Paul Hindemith
(1895-1963), age 30
Juan Peron
(1895-1974), age 30
Edmund Wilson
(1895-1972), age 30
F. Scott Fitzgerald
(1896-1940), age 29
Bernard De Voto
(1897-1955), age 28
William Faulkner
(1897-1962), age 28
Thornton Wilder
(1897-1975), age 28
Bertolt Brecht
(1898-1956), age 27
Alexander Calder
(1898-1976), age 27
Chou En-lai
(1898-1976), age 27
George Gershwin
(1898-1937), age 27
Henry Moore
(1898-      ), age 27
Leo Szilard
(1898-1964), age 27
Jorge Luis Borges
(1899-      ), age 26
Federico Garcia Lorca
(1899-1936), age 26
Ernest Hemingway
(1899-1961), age 26
Vladimir Nabokov
(1899-1977), age 26
Aaron Copland
(1900-      ), age 25
Ignazio Silone
(1900-      ), age 25
Kurt Weill
(1900-1950), age 25
Thomas Wolfe
(1900-1938), age 25
Walt Disney
(1901-1966), age 24
Enrico Fermi
(1901-1954), age 24
Hirohito
(1901-      ), age 24
Andre Malraux
(1901-1976), age 24

# 1900

Ellen Terry
   (1847-1928), age 53
Arthur James Balfour
   (1848-1930), age 52
Bernard Bosanquet
   (1848-1923), age 52
Wyatt Earp
   (1848-1929), age 52
Paul Gauguin
   (1848-1903), age 52
J. K. Huysmans
   (1848-1907), age 52
Vilfredo Pareto
   (1848-1923), age 52
Augustus Saint-Gaudens
   (1848-1907), age 52
Luther Burbank
   (1849-1926), age 51
William Ernest Henley
   (1849-1903), age 51
William Osler
   (1849-1919), age 51
Ivan Pavlov
   (1849-1936), age 51
Kimmochi Saionji
   (1849/50-1940), age c.51
August Strindberg
   (1849-1912), age 51
Samuel Gompers
   (1850-1924), age 50
Lafcadio Hearn
   (1850-1904), age 50
Horatio Kitchener
   (1850-1916), age 50
Pierre Loti
   (1850-1923), age 50
Thomas G. Masaryk
   (1850-1937), age 50
Sir Arthur Evans
   (1851-1941), age 49
Ferdinand Foch
   (1851-1929), age 49
Adolph von Harnack
   (1851-1930), age 49
Desire Joseph Mercier
   (1851-1926), age 49
Walter Reed
   (1851-1902), age 49
Mrs. Humphrey Ward
   (1851-1920), age 49
Herbert Asquith
   (1852-1928), age 48

and *Abel Sanchez* (1917), are well known but his major work is *The Tragic Sense of Life in Men and Nations* (1913), an affirmation of faith in the importance of the individual.

**Max Weber,** age 36; German sociologist and economist born in Erfurt. An influential figure in modern sociology because of his concern with developing a methodology, he rejected Marx's economic determinism and searched instead for religious roots of modern institutions—a point of view demonstrated in the well-known *Protestant Ethic and the Spirit of Capitalism* (1904–1905) and *Collected Essays on the Sociology of Religion* (1920).

**Mrs. Patrick Campbell** (Beatrice Stella Tanner), age 35; English actress born in London, the daughter of an English father and an Italian mother. She married in 1884 and continued to use her husband's name after he was killed in the Boer War in 1900. A dark-haired beauty noted for her rudeness and wit, she appeared in plays by Pinero, Shakespeare, Ibsen and Shaw (who wrote the role of Eliza Dolittle in *Pygmalion* especially for her). In her later years she played a few small roles in films.

**George V** (George Frederick Ernest Albert), age 35; king of the United Kingdom of Great Britain and Northern Ireland and emperor of India from 1910–1936, of the house of Saxe-Coburg-Gotha (called the house of Windsor after 1917); second son of Edward VII and grandson of Victoria. The momentous developments of his reign include World War I, the Irish insurrection, the first Labour Party government, worldwide economic depression and the rise of totalitarianism.

**Warren Gamaliel Harding,** age 35; American newspaper editor and statesman born in Ohio, the son of a farmer; 29th president, 1921–1923. A conservative Republican, he opposed the League of Nations and favored a high protective tariff. After the Teapot Dome scandal rocked his administration, he went on a speaking tour and died of a heart attack in the San Francisco Palace Hotel in August 1923. He was succeeded by Calvin Coolidge.

**Rudyard Kipling,** age 35; English writer born in Bombay, India, of English parents. He was a journalist at 17 and at 22 published his first book of stories, *Plain Tales from the Hills.* He married an American woman and lived for four years in Vermont, where he wrote *The Jungle Books* (1894 and 1895) and *Captains Courageous* (1897). Settling permanently in Sussex in 1902, he became the most popular writer of his time, known as the interpreter of India and the empire. He also wrote *Kim* (1901), *Barrack-Room Ballads* (1892) and *The Recessional,* for Queen Victoria's diamond jubilee in 1897.

**Jean Sibelius,** age 35; Finnish composer, the most renowned of his country, and a late representative of 19th-century romanticism. He drew his themes from nature and folklore and is best known for his seven symphonies (1899–1924), the symphonic poems, *Finlandia* and *The Oceanides,* and the popular *Valse Triste* (1903). He lived to be 91.

**Charles Proteus Steinmetz,** age 35; electrical engineer born in Breslau, Germany. He emigrated to America in 1889 and became a consulting engineer for electric companies. His researches into the nature of alternating current and his more than 100 inventions helped domesticate electricity and turn it into an obedient household servant. He invented the lightning arresters for high-power transmission lines.

**William Butler Yeats,** age 35; Irish poet and dramatist born near Dublin, the son of a Protestant portrait painter. A romantic in his youth, writing of love and Irish folklore, he established himself with his later collections of verse *The Wild Swans of Coole* (1917), *The Winding Stair* (1933), etc., as a major poet of the 20th century, despite the peculiarity of his metaphysical and historical views and his preoccupation with theosophy and the occult. He also wrote plays for the Abbey Theatre in Dublin, which he helped found.

**Benedetto Croce,** age 34; foremost Italian philosopher of the early 20th century, born in Aquila, the son of a landed proprietor, and orphaned at 17 by an earthquake. His four-volume *Philosophy of the Spirit* (1902–1917), reacting to late 19th-century materialism, endeavored to show the way back to a belief in the spirit. He held that the sciences construct mental fictions, that the uniformity they discover is not within nature but within human mental processes. A political liberal, he retired from public life when Mussolini came to power.

**Wassily Kandinsky,** age 34; Russian painter born in Moscow, generally regarded as one of the originators of modern abstract art. He gave up a law career at 30 to study painting in Munich and in 1910 produced the first nonrepresentational picture in Europe. Influenced by theosophy, he wrote *Concerning the Spiritual in Art* (1912), explaining the theory of his painting.

**James Ramsay MacDonald,** age 34; British statesman and Labour Party leader born in Scotland; prime minister (January–October 1924) of the first Labour government in British history. He was also prime minister in the second Labour cabinet, 1929–1931, and head of a coalition government dominated by Conservatives, 1931–1935, for which he was repudiated by his own party and deprived of the party chairmanship.

**Gilbert Murray,** age 34; British classical scholar born in Sydney, Australia; professor of Greek at Glasgow 1889–1899 and at Oxford 1908–1936. He is known for his translations of Greek drama and his many books on Greek literature and religion, including the well-known *Four Stages of Greek Religion* (1912), which he enlarged to *Five Stages* in 1925. He originated the phrase "failure of nerve" in speaking of the late classical period.

**Romain Rolland,** age 34; French novelist, playwright and biographer; best known for his giant novel *Jean-Christophe* (1904–1912), the life story of a musical genius in the modern world. Rolland received the 1915 Nobel Prize for literature. A pacifist and liberal humanitarian, he lived in Switzerland during World War I.

**Sun Yat-sen,** age 34; Chinese statesman born near Macao; principal founder of the Chinese republic (1911). In exile from 1895 to 1911, living in Hawaii, the United States, England and Japan, he returned after the Manchu dynasty had been overthrown by a revolution, and was made provisional president of the new republic. In 1912 he resigned in favor of Yuan Shih-k'ai, named by the abdicating emperor to form a republican government, but he retained great influence. After his death of cancer in 1925, rival warlords dominated the country.

**August von Wassermann,** age 34; German bacteriologist, the pupil of Robert Koch. He is noted for his discovery in 1906 of a method of detecting the presence of syphilis in the blood, known as the Wassermann reaction, which is widely used for early diagnosis. He also developed vaccines for cholera, tetanus and typhoid fever.

**Herbert George Wells,** age 34; English novelist and popularizer of history and science; born in Kent, the son of a shopkeeper who began life as a domestic servant. A pioneer in science fiction, he wrote *The Time Machine* (1895), *The Invisible Man* (1897) and *The War of the Worlds* (1898). He also wrote novels of contemporary life and the popular *Outline of History* (1920), and devised numerous utopian schemes for the improvement of the world.

**Arnold Bennett,** age 33; English novelist born in Staffordshire, the

Sukarno
(1901–1970), age 24
Marian Anderson
(1902–    ), age 23
Charles Lindbergh
(1902–1974), age 23
Richard Rodgers
(1902–1980), age 23
John Steinbeck
(1902–1968), age 23
Erskine Caldwell
(1903–    ), age 22
Louis Leakey
(1903–1972), age 22
George Orwell
(1903–1950), age 22
Alan Paton
(1903–    ), age 22
Evelyn Waugh
(1903–1966), age 22
Graham Greene
(1904–    ), age 21
Christopher Isherwood
(1904–    ), age 21
Isaac Bashevis Singer
(1904–    ), age 21
John O'Hara
(1905–1970), age 20
Anthony Powell
(1905–    ), age 20
Jean-Paul Sartre
(1905–1980), age 20
Hannah Arendt
(1906–1975), age 19
Samuel Beckett
(1906–    ), age 19
Hsuan T'ung
(1906–1967), age 19
Dmitri Shostakovich
(1906–1975), age 19
W. H. Auden
(1907–1973), age 18
Rachel Carson
(1907–1964, age 18
Louis MacNeice
(1907–1963), age 18
James Michener
(1907–    ), age 18
Simone de Beauvoir
(1908–    ), age 17
Lyndon Johnson
(1908–1973), age 17

# 1900

Joseph Joffre
   (1852-1931), age 48
Albert A. Michelson
   (1852-1931), age 48
George Moore
   (1852-1933), age 48
Mutsuhito
   (1852-1912), age 48
Cecil Rhodes
   (1853-1902), age 47
Paul Ehrlich
   (1854-1915), age 46
James G. Frazer
   (1854-1941), age 46
John Philip Sousa
   (1854-1932), age 46
Oscar Wilde
   (1854-1900), age 46
Eugene V. Debs
   (1855-1926), age 45
Arthur Wing Pinero
   (1855-1934), age 45
Josiah Royce
   (1855-1916), age 45
Wovoka
   (1856/58-1932), age c.44

son of a solicitor. He wrote highly successful novels depicting lower middle-class life in English industrial towns. *The Old Wives' Tale* (1908), *Clayhanger* (1910) and *Hilda Lessways* (1911) are generally considered to be his best.

**Vicente Blasco Ibanez,** age 33; Spanish novelist born near Valencia. A supporter of the republican cause, he lived in exile on the Riviera during the dictatorship of Primo de Rivera (1923–1930). His most popular novels were *The Naked Maja* (1906) and *The Four Horsemen of the Apocalypse* (1916), the latter a story of World War I which was translated into many languages and made into a popular silent film.

**Gutzon Borglum,** age 33?; American sculptor born in Idaho, the son of Danish immigrants. On the face of a granite mountain in South Dakota, at an elevation of 500 feet, he carved the heads, 50 to 70 feet in height of four American presidents. Known as the Mount Rushmore Memorial, it was accomplished in the years 1927–1941. He also executed the equestrian statue of General Sheridan in Washington and the large marble head of Lincoln in the Capitol Rotunda.

MARIE CURIE (Marja
   Sklodowska)
Polish-French physicist
1867-1934

**Marie Curie** (Marja Sklodowska), age 33; Polish-French physicist born in Warsaw. She married Pierre Curie, the French physicist, in 1895, and together they investigated the radioactivity of uranium and discovered two new elements, polonium (1898) and radium (1902), for which they received the 1903 Nobel Prize for physics. She succeeced her husband as professor at the University of Paris in 1906 and was awarded the 1911 Nobel Prize in chemistry.

**Ernest Christopher Dowson,** age 33; English lyric poet born in Kent of a prosperous family. After the death of his father and the suicide of his mother, he was plagued with debts, illness and alcoholism, and died of tuberlosis at 32. Identified with the fin de siecle decadents, he wrote both erotic and religious verse. One famous line is, "They are not long, the days of wine and roses."

**John Galsworthy,** age 33; English novelist and playwright born in Surrey of an upper-middle-class family. In *The Forsyte Saga,* a series of novels published 1906–1921, he portrayed convincingly the lives and attitudes of the wealthy industrial class of England. He also wrote plays on contemporary problems, but these were less successful and less popular than his novels.

**Jozef Pilsudski,** age 33; Polish statesman, general and dictator. A socialist agitator for independence before World War I, he cooperated in the formation of a Polish republic after the war, but in 1926 he overthrew the government in a military coup d'etat and exercised supreme power as the minister of war and commander-in-chief of the army until his death in 1935.

**Luigi Pirandello,** age 33; Italian dramatist, novelist and short-story writer, born in Sicily. A teacher of literature at a girls' school in Rome for 30 years and the author of many volumes of short stories, he is famous for his pessimistic, well-constructed plays: *Six Characters in Search of an Author* (1921), *Henry IV* (1922), and *As You Desire Me* (1930). For several summers, he toured Europe with his own company.

**Arturo Toscanini,** age 33; Italian conductor born in Parma; conductor at La Scala, in Milan, of the Metropolitan Opera in New York City, the New York Philharmonic Orchestra and the NBC Symphony Orchestra, retiring in 1954. Considered by many the greatest conductor of modern times and unrivaled as an interpreter of Beethoven and Brahms, he is also credited with restoring the proper style to Italian opera. He was a friend of Verdi.

**Wilbur Wright,** age 33; American aviation pioneer born in Indiana; the builder, with his younger brother Orville, of the first practical airplane. On Dec. 17, 1903, at Kitty Hawk, North Carolina, their 750-pound machine powered with a 12-horsepower motor stayed in the air 59 seconds and traveled 852 feet. On Oct. 5, 1905, at Dayton, Ohio, their plane flew 24¼ miles in 38 minutes. Wilbur died of typhoid fever at 45.

**William Edward Burghardt Du Bois,** age 32; American Negro educator and writer born in Massachusetts. He graduated from Harvard and for many years (1897–1910 and 1932–1944) taught at Atlanta University. As editor (1910–1932) of *Crisis,* the organ of the National Association for the Advancement of Colored People, he was a prominent figure in early movements for racial equality. He is the author of *The Souls of Black Folks* (1903) and an *Autobiography* (1968).

**Stefan George,** age 32; German poet born in a town on the Rhine of a wealthy family. His esoteric poetry, influenced by the French Parnassians and symbolists, was written for an intellectual elite. A disciple of Nietzsche, he was an enemy of realism in literature, and of humanism, democracy and progress. The Nazis claimed him as their national poet, but he disdained the honors and went into exile in Switzerland, where he died.

**Maxim Gorki** (pen name, meaning "the bitter one," of Aleksei Maksimovich Peshkov), age 32; Russian novelist, playwright and short-story writer. Orphaned at nine, he lived as a vagabond for 15 years, joined the Bolshevik party, and after the revolution helped establish "socialist realism" as the approved style of writing. He is best known for his play *The Lower Depths* (1902), which portrays the life of the poor.

**Nicholas II** (Nikolai Aleksandrovich), age 32; czar of Russia 1894–1917. His continuation of the repressive policies of his father, Alexander III, and his military defeat by Japan led to the short-lived revolution of 1905. Inadequate preparation for World War I, military losses, the disorganization of the economy and the threat of famine resulted in the revolution of 1917 and his abdication. He was executed with his entire family by the Bolsheviks in July of 1918, and was the last of the czars.

**Edmond Rostand,** age 32; French dramatist and poet born in Marseilles, the son of a journalist. After his first volume of verse (1890) he turned to the theater and wrote successful romantic dramas. His two greatest successes were the famous *Cyrano de Bergerac* (1897) and *L'Aiglon* (1900), written for Sarah Bernhardt. *Chantecler* (1910) was also an outstanding success in Paris and New York City.

**Neville Chamberlain,** age 31; British statesman, the son of Joseph

Claude Levi-Strauss
(1908-      ), age 17
Richard Wright
(1908-1960), age 17
Malcolm Lowry
(1909-1957), age 16
Kwame Nkrumah
(1909-1972), age 16
Eudora Welty
(1909-      ), age 16
Eero Saarinen
(1910-1961), age 15
Gian-Carlo Menotti
(1911-      ), age 14
Ronald Reagan
(1911-      ), age 14
Wernher von Braun
(1912-1977), age 13
John Cheever
(1912-1982), age 13
Lawrence Durrell
(1912-      ), age 13
Eugene Ionesco
(1912-      ), age 13
Jackson Pollock
(1912-1956), age 13
Minoru Yamasaki
(1912-      ), age 13
Benjamin Britten
(1913-1976), age 12
Albert Camus
(1913-1960), age 12
Gerald Ford
(1913-      ), age 12
Richard Nixon
(1913-      ), age 12
Norman Borlaug
(1914-      ), age 11
Ralph Ellison
(1914-      ), age 11
Jonas Salk
(1914-      ), age 11
Dylan Thomas
(1914-1953), age 11
Tennessee Williams
(1914-      ), age 11
Saul Bellow
(1915-      ), age 10
Arthur Miller
(1915-      ), age 10
Harold Wilson
(1916-      ), age 9

Chamberlain. After retiring from the hardware-manufacturing business in Brimingham, he became lord mayor in 1915, a member of Parliament in 1918 and conservative prime minister in 1937. By his notorious appeasement of Hitler at Munich in September 1938, he believed he was gaining time for British rearmament. He declared war on Germany in September 1939, and was succeeded by Winston Churchill in May 1940, after a vote of no confidence. He died in November of the same year.

MOHANDAS KARAMCHAND
GANDHI (Mahatma Gandhi)
Hindu nationalist and
spiritual leader
1869-1948

**Mohandas Karamchand Gandhi** (Mahatma Gandhi), age 31; Hindu nationalist and spiritual leader. After practicing law in South Africa (1893–1914), he returned to India and rose to leadership in the Indian National Congress. His fasts and civil disobedience campaigns played an important part in the struggle for Indian independence. Revered by the Hindus for his ascetic life, he was an enemy of progress. He was fatally shot in New Delhi in 1948 by a Hindu zealot.

**Andre Gide,** age 31; French novelist and critic born in Paris, the son of a professor of law; nephew of the economist, Charles Gide. He inhertied a large fortune at 26 and became a prominent figure of the French literary world. A hesitant hedonist with religious and moral scruples, he wrote *The Immoralist, Straight Is the Gate* and *The Counterfeiters*. He also wrote *Corydon* (1924) in defense of homosexuality.

**Edgar Lee Masters,** age 31; American poet and writer born in Kansas, the son of a lawyer and a lawyer himself, practicing in Chicago 1892–1920. His *Spoon River Anthology* (1915) was inspired by the region in central Illinois where he grew up, near the Spoon River. He also wrote biographies of Walt Whitman, Vachel Lindsay and Mark Twain.

**Henri Matisse,** age 31; French painter born in Picardy, the son of a grain dealer. His surface decorative effects and elimination of the illusion of a third dimension identify him as a pioneer of modern art. As an appreciation for modern art grew in the twenties, his vivid female nudes, still lifes and interiors made him rich and famous. Famous examples of his work include the *Decorative Figure on an Ornamental Background, Large Interior in Red* and *Meditation*.

**Edwin Arlington Robinson,** age 31; American poet born in Maine. Except for ten years in the New York Custom House (a position obtained for him by Theodore Roosevelt), he managed to give his full time to poetry, living on the patronage of friends, and won the Pulitzer Prize for poetry three times. Two famous poems are *The Man against the Sky* and *Tristram*.

**Booth Tarkington,** age 31; American novelist and playwright born in Indianapolis, the son of a lawyer. He achieved success with his first novel, *The Gentleman from Indiana* (1899), and won wide popularity with his novels of boyhood, *Penrod* (1914) and *Seventeen* (1916). In *The Magnificent Ambersons* (1918) and *Alice Adams* (1921), he portrayed midwestern urban life with humor and sentiment.

**Frank Lloyd Wright,** age 31; American architect born in Wisconsin. He began his career as an employee of Louis Sullivan's architectural firm in Chicago and continued in the new style of functional simplicity with his houses free of the elaborate "gingerbread" decoration of the 19th century. His houses of this period (1893–1908) marked a new era of residential design. He also contributed to the development of the skyscraper, 1912–1936, and the use of glass-and-metal walls. Famous buildings include the Imperial Hotel in Tokyo (1916–1922); the Price Tower in Bartlesville, Oklahoma (1955); and the Solomon R. Guggenheim Museum in New York City (1959); his last commission.

**Alfred Adler,** age 30; Austrian psychiatrist born in Vienna. He was an early associate of Sigmund Freud but later rejected his emphasis on the sexual roots of behavior and formed his own school. He attributed personality disorders to a feeling of personal inferiority and originated the phrase "inferiority complex." He wrote *The Theory and Practice of Individual Psychology* (1918).

**Ivan Alekseevish Bunin,** age 30; Russian novelist and story writer of an aristocratic but impoverished family; winner of the 1933 Nobel Prize for literature. His novels, describing a Russian society in decline, include *The Village* (1910) and *The Well of Days* (1930). *The Gentleman from San Francisco* is his best-known story. He also translated Longfellow's *Hiawatha* into Russian.

**Lenin** (Vladimir Ilich Ulyanov), age 30; Russian revolutionary leader and founder of Soviet Russia, born in Simbirsk (Ulyanovsk) on the Volga River. An agitator for reform early in life, he was exiled several times. He returned to Russia after the revolution in February, overthrew the moderate provisional government of Kerenski, and seized power for the Bolsheviks in November of 1917. After a paralytic stroke in 1923, he lost the power of speech and died in January 1924, setting off a power struggle that ended with Joseph Stalin as dictator.

**Frank Norris** (Benjamin Franklin Norris), age 30; American novelist born in Chicago of a wealthy family. In his short life of 32 years, he was a war correspondennt in South Africa and Cuba and produced several outstanding novels in the realistic manner of Zola: *McTeague* (1899), about San Francisco slum life; *The Octopus* (1901), about wheat farmers; and *The Pit* (1903), about grain speculators. The latter two were parts of an unfinished trilogy, *The Epic of Wheat*. He was the brother-in-law of Kathleen Norris, the popular novelist.

**Jan Christian Smuts,** age 30; South African soldier and statesman born in Cape Colony. Although a Boer of Dutch descent, he cooperated with the British and was a member of the government after the formation of the Union of South Africa as a British dominion in 1910. As commander-in-chief of the British forces in Africa during World War I, he terminated the German colonial empire with his victories in German Southwest Africa and German East Africa. He was prime minister of the Union of South Africa 1919–1924 and 1939–1948.

**Teitaro Suzuki,** age 30; Japanese scholar and authority on Buddhism, credited with introducing Zen Buddhism to the West. He studied in the United States 1897–1909, lectured at Tokyo University and at various European schools, and wrote many books, including *Essays in Zen Buddhism* (three volumes, 1927–1933) and *An Introduction to Zen Buddhism* (1949).

# 1925

Indira Gandhi
(1917-      ), age 8
John F. Kennedy
(1917-1963), age 8
Robert Lowell
(1917-1977), age 8
Andrew Wyeth
(1917-      ), age 8
Gamal Nasser
(1918-1970), age 7
Anwar Sadat
(1918-1981), age 7
Aleksandr Solzhenitsyn
(1918-      ), age 7
Edmund Hillary
(1919-      ), age 6
Mohammed Riza Pahlavi
(1919-1980), age 6
J. D. Salinger
(1919-      ), age 6
John Paul II (Pope)
(1920-      ), age 5
Julius Nyerere
(1921-      ), age 4
Christian Barnard
(1923-      ), age 2
Norman Mailer
(1923-      ), age 2
Jimmy Carter
(1924-      ), age 1

**Theodore Dreiser,** age 29; American novelist born in Indiana, the younger brother of Paul Dresser (composer of *My Gal Sal* and *On the Banks of the Wabash*). His first novel, *Sister Carrie* (1901), aroused protests over its frank treatment of sex and was withdrawn from publication. He was a clumsy stylist but a forceful writer, concerned with social problems, and a member of the Communist Party. His most successful book was *An American Tragedy* (1925).

**Marcel Proust,** age 29; French novelist born in Paris, the son of a Jewish mother and a wealthy Roman Catholic physician on the faculty of the University of Paris. At 34 he withdrew from the fashionable salons he had frequented, secluded himself in a cork-lined room and spent 17 years writing his seven-part novel, *Remembrance of Things Past* (published 1913–1927), which is an anatomy of upper-class French society; an exhaustive exploration of the narrator's sensations, experiences and memories. It is so difficult and lengthly a book that few persons have read every word.

**Ernest Rutherford,** age 29; first Baron Rutherford of Nelson, British physicist born in New Zealand; a pioneer in nuclear physics. As professor of experimental physics at Cambridge 1919–1937, he investigated the nature of radioactivity and formulated the modern theory of atomic structure: that the atom consists of a hard nucleus surrounded by orbiting electrons. He was knighted in 1914 and made a baron in 1931.

**John Millington Synge,** age 29; Irish dramatist born near Dublin of a middle-class Protestant family. In 1898 he took the advice of W. B. Yeats and made the first of five annual visits to the primitive Aran Islands in Galway Bay. The result was his completion of five plays of peasant life, all produced by the Abbey Theatre, three of which are classics: *Riders to the Sea, Playboy of the Western World* and *Deidre of the Sorrows*. He died one month before his 38th birthday.

**Paul Valery,** age 29; French poet and essayist born in a Mediterranean seaport, the son of a Corsican customs officer and an Italian mother. His poetry, written in his youth, is difficult and virtually untranslatable, but his essays on a variety of intellectual topics, published in a series of volumes entitled *Variety* (1924–1944), are admired for their acuteness of perception and distinction of style.

**Orville Wright,** age 29; American pioneer in aviation born in Dayton, Ohio; younger brother of Wilbur Wright, with whom he collaborated in building and flying the first practical airplane. He outlived his brother by 36 years.

**Roald Amundsen,** age 28; Norwegian polar explorer, the leader of a successful Antarctic expedition (1910–1912) in which he became the first man to reach the South Pole (December 14, 1911). On an earlier expedition (1903–1906), he proved there really was a Northwest Passage by sailing through the northern seas from the Atlantic to the Pacific. He disappeared in 1928 on a flight to rescue the Italian explorer, Umberto Nobile. He is the author of *North West Passage* (1908).

**Calvin Coolidge,** age 28; American statesman born in Vermont, the son of a storekeeper; 30th president, 1923–1929. As Republican governor of Massachusetts, 1919–1921, he broke the 1919 Boston police strike with the state militia, declaring they had no right to strike against the public safety. Elected vice-president in 1920, he succeeded to the presidency in 1923 after the death of Harding, and was reelected in 1924. His administration strongly supported big business.

**Sergei Pavlovich Diaghilev,** age 28; Russian ballet producer born in Novgorod of an upper-class family. He organized the Ballets Russes company in Paris in 1909 (known as the Ballet Russe de Monte Carlo after 1923) to introduce Russian ballet to the West, with Michel Fokine as choreographer and Nijinsky and Pavlova as principal dancers. Known as a tyrannical perfectionist, he produced ballets in Europe for 20 years and toured the United States in 1916. He died in 1929.

**Haakon VII,** age 28; king of Norway 1905–1957, second son of Frederick VIII, king of Denmark. A constitutional monarch, he was the first king of an independent Norway, after its separation from Sweden. During his reign Norway became a modern, progressive nation—a pioneer in unemployment insurance, old-age pensions and women's suffrage. He married the daughter of Edward VII of Great Britain.

**Piet Mondrian,** age 28; Dutch abstract painter. He studied and taught in Amsterdam and in 1910 went to Paris. There, under the influence of cubism, he developed a geometric style he called neoplasticism. He lived in New York City from 1940 to 1944 and died there.

**Bertrand Arthur William Russell,** age 28; third Earl Russell, English mathematician and philosopher; the grandson of a prime minister and a descendant of the dukes of Bedford. He collaborated with A. N. Whitehead on *Principia mathematica* (1910–1913), wrote popular books on philosophy and social reform and actively participated in left-wing progressive movements and demonstrations. He was the best educated man of his time, said George Santayana, but a many-sided fanatic.

**Ralph Vaughan Williams,** age 28; English composer born in Gloucestershire, considered the foremost English composer of his time. Of his nine symphonies, the best known are the *London* (1914) and the *Pastoral* (1922). Among his other compositions are orchestral work, *Fantasia on Greensleeves* (1935); the song cycle, *On Wenlock Edge* (1909); and several operas, including *Riders to the Sea* (1937).

**Carl Lotus Becker,** age 27; American historian born in Iowa, known for his studies of the American Revolutionary War period, written in exceptionally lucid prose. He taught history at the University of Kansas 1902–1916 and at Cornell University 1917–1941. He is the author of *The Declaration of Independence* (1922), *The Heavenly City of the Eighteenth-Century Philosophers* (1932) and *Our Great Experiment in Democracy* (1924).

**Enrico Caruso,** age 27; Italian operatic tenor born in Naples. A mechanic in his youth, he made his debut at 21 and was soon a leading tenor at La Scala. He appeared in New York in 1903 in *Rigoletto* and remained for many years the chief attraction of the Metropolitan Opera, unrivaled for the beauty and power of his voice. He died at 48.

**Willa Cather,** age 27?; American novelist born in Virginia and reared in Nebraska. She extolled the heroic virtues of pioneer American families in *O Pioneers!* (1913) and *My Antonia* (1918) and depicted the conflict between urban and rural values in *One of Ours* (1922). She is known as a superb stylist, especially in her later novels, *Death Comes to the Archbishop* (1927) and *Shadows on the Rock* (1933).

**Feodor Ivanovich Chaliapin,** age 27; Russian bass singer born in Kazan (near the Volga River). Singing in grand opera in St. Petersburg from the age of 21, he became a French citizen after the Russian revolution, and appeared in New York City in 1907 and from 1921 to 1929, achieving his greatest success in *Boris Gudunov*. As a concert singer, he popularized *The Song of the Volga Boatman*.

**Colette** (Sidonie Gabrielle Claudine Colette), age 27; French novelist of the demimonde born in Normandy, the daughter of an army officer. After a series of minor novels, she gained attention with *Cheri* (1920) and *The Last of Cheri* (1926), portraying the intimate relationship of a young man and an older woman. *Gigi* (1945), about the training of a young girl for the profession of love, was made into a musical film. She was married three times and after her first divorce was a music-hall entertainer for eight years.

**Lee De Forest,** age 27; American inventor born in Iowa, called the father of radio. In 1906 he invented the audion vacuum tube, the key component of radio and television until the invention of the transistor in 1947. In 1910 he broadcast an opera performance, and in the world's first news broadcast reported the election results of 1916.

**Ford Madox Ford** (Ford Madox Hueffer), age 27; English novelist and critic born in Surrey, the son of a German music critic. *The Good Soldier* (1915) and *No More Parades* (1925) are among his best novels; *The Inheritors* (1901) and *Romance* (1903) were written in collaboration with Joseph Conrad. He also wrote a biography of Conrad (1924).

**George Edward Moore,** age 27; English philosopher educated at Cambridge University, where he remained as lecturer 1911–1925 and professor of philosophy 1925–1939. He is known for *Principia ethica* (1903), a closely reasoned investigation of the nature of the good. He provided no answers or systematic doctrines, but gave a brilliant demonstration of the way philosophical investigations should be conducted. He lectured in the United States 1940–1944.

**Emily Price Post,** age 27; American authority on etiquette born in Baltimore of a wealthy family of high social standing. Educated in private schools, she wrote a few novels and in 1922 published *Etiquette,* which sold a million copies and established her as the highest authority on matters of good taste and good manners.

**Sergei Vassilievich Rachmaninoff,** age 27; Russian composer, pianist and conductor; born near Novgorod on his family's estate. A celebrated piano virtuoso and the last of the romantic composers, he is known particularly for the *Second Piano Concerto* and the preludes in C sharp minor and G minor. He lived in New York City after 1918 and died in Beverly Hills.

**Gilbert Keith Chesterton,** age 26; English essayist, novelist and poet, born in London. He wrote a popular novel, *The Man Who Was Thursday* (1908), and a series of Father Brown detective stories (1911–1935), but is remembered for his collections of essays—*Heretics* (1905), *Tremendous Trifles* (1909), etc.—wittily defending his conservative, Roman Catholic views with the clever use of paradox. He was also famous for his corpulence.

SIR WINSTON CHURCHILL
British statesman and author
1874-1965

**Sir Winston Leonard Spencer Churchill,** age 26; British statesman and author descended from the duke of Marlborough. He served in the British army in his youth—in India, South Africa, and the Sudan—and as a cabinet minister for many years, but attained his greatest fame when, as wartime prime minister 1940–1945, he became a symbol of Britain's dogged resistance to the Nazis. As conservative prime minister 1951–1955, he refused to accede to the dismemberment of the empire. He is the author of *A History of the English-speaking Peoples* (four vols., 1956–1958).

**Robert Lee Frost,** age 26; American poet born in San Francisco, called the poet of rural New England. He arrived in Massachusetts at 11 and engaged in various occupations—including teaching and farming—until the publication of his first volume of verse *A Boy's Will* at 39. In his fifties he was a professor of English at Amherst, Harvard and other schools. He was awarded the Pulitzer Prize for poetry four times.

**Ellen Glasgow,** age 26; American novelist born in Virginia of an aristocratic Southern family. She lived a quiet, unmarried life in Richmond and wrote realistic novels on the social history of the South, reflecting the transition from its domination by aristocratic society to the rise of commercialism and a new middle class. Some well-known titles are *The Battle-ground* (1902), *Barren Ground* (1925) and *In This Our Life* (1941).

**Herbert Clark Hoover,** age 26; American statesman born in Iowa; 31st president, 1929–1933. A mining engineer with offices in New York and London, he came to public notice for his work on various relief commissions during and after World War I. He was secretary of commerce 1921–1929 and was elected president in 1928. After the stock-market crash in October 1929, his political support ebbed away, as he adopted an ineffective policy of waiting for prosperity to reappear.

**Amy Lowell,** age 26; American poet and critic born in Massachusetts, a member of the famous Lowell family which included James Russell Lowell. Influenced by Ezra Pound and the imagists, she published an anthology, *Some Imagist Poets* (1915–1917), and became their leader and principal spokesman. She also published several volumes of verse and criticism, and a two-volume biography of John Keats.

**Marchese Guglielmo Marconi,** age 26; Italian inventor born in Bologna, the son of an Italian nobleman and an Irish mother. He built the first practical system of wireless (radio) telegraphy in 1895. In 1899 he sent signals across the English Channel and in 1901 across the Atlantic. Transatlantic wireless service became available to the public in 1907.

**William Somerset Maugham,** age 26; English novelist born in Paris, where his father was on the British embassy staff. An expert narrative technique, combined with realism, skepticism and the use of exotic Eastern backgrounds, established him as one of the most successful writers of his time. His most familiar novels are: *Of Human Bondage* (1915), *The Moon and Sixpence* (1919), and *The Razor's Edge* (1944). The short-story collection, *The Trembling of a Leaf* (1921), contains the famous "Miss Thompson," dramatized as *Rain* by John Colton.

**Arnold Schoenberg,** age 26; Austrian-American composer born in Vienna; leader of the ultra-modern school. His early works were in the romantic tradition, but in 1908 he began composing atonal music and by 1923 had developed his 12-tone technique, which was adopted by Alban Berg and Anton von Webern. He emigrated to America in 1933, became a citizen in 1941, and taught at the University of California 1936–1944.

**Gertrude Stein,** age 26; American writer born in Pennsylvania. She settled in Paris in 1903 and became famous for her unconventional, free-style writing and her literary salon, where Hemingway, Picasso and others met. Her best-known works are *The Autobiography of Alice*

# 1900

B. *Toklas* and the opera, *Four Saints in Three Acts*.

**Chaim Weizmann,** age 26; Jewish chemist and Zionist leader born in Russia; first president of Israel. Active in the Zionist movement from youth, he became a British subject in 1910, taught chemistry in Manchester, and in 1920 was elected president of the World Zionist Organization (1920–1931 and 1935–1946). When the Republic of Israel was established in 1948, he became provisional president 1948–1949, and was the first elected president, serving 1949–1952.

**Albert I** (Albert Leopold Clement Marie Meinrad), age 25; king of Belgium 1909–1934 and hero of World War I; nephew of Leopold II. A popular monarch, he traveled widely and introduced reforms in the administration of the Congo. At the outbreak of the war he took personal command of the army in the face of the German invasion, remained with the troops at Ypres throughout the war, and led the final offensive in 1918. He was killed by a fall while mountain climbing.

**David Wark Griffith,** age 25; American motion picture producer and director born in Kentucky. An actor in stock companies and early films, he became an independent producer in 1913 and introduced techniques and practices that transformed the movies into an art form. His films include *Birth of a Nation* (1915), *Intolerance* (1916), *Broken Blossoms* (1919) and *Orphans of the Storm* (1921).

**Carl Gustav Jung,** age 25; Swiss psychiatrist born in Basel. He came under the influence of Sigmund Freud in 1907 but by 1912 had begun to develop his own school of analytic psychology, which would attempt to understand neuroses by analyzing the patient's present maladjustment instead of analyzing his childhood experiences. He originated the classification of personalities as either extroverted or introverted and wrote *Psychology of the Unconscious* (1912).

**Antonio Machado,** age 25; Spanish poet and playwright born in Seville; known for his austere, philosophical lyrics. A loyalist in the Civil War, he left Spain when Franco triumphed, crossed the Pyrenees on foot, and died a month later. His complete poems, many of which have been translated into English, appeared in 1936.

**Thomas Mann,** age 25; German novelist and essayist born in Lubeck, the son of a prosperous merchant and grandson of a Brazilian woman of Portuguese origin; younger brother of Heinrich Mann. At 26 he achieved international fame with his first long novel, *Buddenbrooks*, its theme the conflict between an artistic temperament and middle-class society. His other important novels are *The Magic Mountain* (1924), the four-part *Joseph and His Brothers* (1934–1944) and *Doctor Faustus* (1947). He left Germany in 1933, living in America 1938–1953, and in Zurich 1953–1955.

**Maurice Joseph Ravel,** age 25; French composer born near Biarritz; younger professional rival of Debussy, with whom he has often been compared for the similar impressionism of his piano pieces and chamber music. His most popular works were the two ballets, *Daphnis et Chloe* (1912) and *Bolero* (1928). Afflicted with a nervous disorder, he was unable to work during the last five years of his life and died at 62.

**Ranier Maria Rilke,** age 25; German poet born in Prague, the son of a Jewish mother and a Catholic father of aristocratic birth. A major poet of the 20th century, he lived a solitary, wandering life, visiting Tolstoy in Russia and acting as secretary to Rodin 1905–1906. He is best known for the *Duino Elegies* (1925), begun in 1910–1912, when he was the guest of Princess Maria von Thurn und Taxis-Hohenlohe at Duino Castle, near Trieste. He died of blood poisoning at 51.

**Albert Schweitzer,** age 25; Alsatian philosopher, musicologist and mission doctor, world famous for his humanitarian work in French Equatorial Africa. Somtimes identified as French, he was born in

Upper Alsace when it was German. He was the son of a Lutheran clergyman, wrote his books in German, and was interned by the French as an enemy alien in World War I. In *The Quest for the Historical Jesus* (1906) and other theological works, he maintained that Jesus was not an ethical teacher but a herald announcing the end of the world, that his ethics were "interim ethics"—for a day, a week or a month.

**Sherwood Anderson,** age 24; American novelist and short-story writer born in Ohio. At 40 he left his job as the manager of a paint factory to join in the literary renaissance of Chicago and wrote *Windy McPherson's Son* (1916), *Poor White* (1920) and *Dark Laughter* (1925). His collection of stories of small-town life—*Winesburg, Ohio* (1919)—is perhaps his best-known work.

**Mohammed Ali Jinnah,** age 24; Indian statesman and Muslim leader born in Karachi; principal founder of Pakistan. As president of the All-Indian Muslim League, he worked for Hindu–Muslim unity until 1940, when he proposed the creation of separate Muslim areas and the formation of an independent state. In 1947 the British approved of the partition of India, and he was appointed the first governor general of the dominion of Pakistan. He died the following year.

**Charles Franklin Kettering,** age 24; American engineer, inventor and manufacturer, born in Ohio. His invention of the automobile self-starter in 1917, which replaced the hand crank, struck the first blow for equality of the sexes; the motor car, formerly reserved for strong-armed men, passed into the hands of women and teenagers. He was the manager of General Motors Research Corporation 1917–1947.

**Jack London** (John Griffith London), age 24; American writer born in San Francisco. His adventurous early life as a sailor, gold prospector and vagrant, was climaxed by world fame at 27 with the publication of his novel, *The Call of the Wild*. His 40 or 50 other adventure stories, including *White Fang* and *The Sea-Wolf,* made him rich as well as famous. A socialist and International Workers of the World sympathizer, he also wrote the semiautobiographical *Martin Eden* (1909). He died at 40 of an overdose of morphine.

**George Macaulay Trevelyan,** age 24; English historian born in Stratford-on-Avon, third son of the historian Sir George Otto Trevelyan. A professor of modern history at Cambridge 1927–1940 and master of Trinity College 1940–1951, he wrote many important and popular books—*British History in the Nineteenth Century* (1922), *History of England* (1926), *England Under Queen Anne* (three volumes, 1930–1934), etc.—all of them lucidly and imaginatively written.

**Mary Garden,** age 23; operatic soprano born in Aberdeen, Scotland and was brought to America as a child. She made her Paris debut in 1900 and in 1902 was chosen by Debussy for the premiere performance of *Pelleas et Melisande.* She appeared in New York in 1907 and sang with the Chicago Opera Company 1910–1931. She was also noted for her dramatic ability, so noticeable in Salome's "dance of the seven veils" that it caused a scandal in Chicago.

**Hermann Hesse,** age 23; German novelist and poet born in Swabia, the son of a Protestant missionary. He is chiefly remembered for his later novels, which were influenced by psychoanalytic theory and Oriental mysticism. Some of his well-known titles are *Demian* (1919), *Siddhartha* (1922) and *Steppenwolf* (1927). He was the winnner of the 1946 Nobel Prize for literature.

**Riza Shah Pahlavi,** age 23; Persian army officer and founder of modern Iran. As the commander of a Cossack force in 1921, he expelled the Russians and made himself minister of war and commander-in-chief of the army. As premier in 1923 and shah in 1925, he encouraged Westernization and industrialization and in 1935 changed the name of the country from Persia to Iran. Forced to abdicate in 1941 in favor of his son, Mohammed Riza Pahlavi, he died in exile in South Africa.

**Pancho Villa** (Francisco Villa), age 23; Mexican bandit and revolutionist. He changed sides frequently in the revolutions of 1910–1915, and after being driven into northern Mexico, crossed the border and raided a town in New Mexico in March 1916. With orders from President Wilson to capture him dead or alive, General Pershing pursued him into Mexico but failed to catch him. He was assassinated in 1923.

**Martin Buber,** age 22; Austrian-Jewish philosopher and Hasidic scholar born in Vienna. He taught at the University of Frankfurt-am-Main, Germany, 1924–1938, and was a professor at the Hebrew University in Jerusalem 1938–1951. His philosophy of religious existentialism is set forth in his famous book, *I and Thou* (1922). He also wrote many books on the Eastern Jewish sect of Hasidism.

**George Michael Cohan,** age 22; American composer and actor born in Rhode Island, into a family of vaudeville actors of Irish descent. He wrote, produced and acted in scores of successful, fast-paced musical shows, which were the first to depart from the traditional Viennese-style operettas of Victor Herbert. He wrote such familiar tunes as "You're a Grand Old Flag," "Give My Regards to Broadway," and "Over There."

**John Masefield,** age 22; English poet born in Ledbury. He went to sea as a boy and wrote *Salt-Water Ballads* (1902). He wrote plays, fiction and an autobiography *(In the Mill,* 1941), but is best known for his long narrative poems, treating realistic themes in plain, vigorous verse: *The Everlasting Mercy* (1911), *The Widow in The Bye Street* (1912) and *The Daffodil Fields* (1913). He was poet laureate 1930–1967.

**Ferenc Molnar,** age 22; Hungarian playwright and novelist born in Budapest, the son of a wealthy merchant. A successful playwright at 30, he is known for his light comedies such as *Liliom* (1909), which became the Broadway and film musical *Carousel; The Guardsman* (1910) and *The Play's the Thing* (1925). He came to America in 1940, wrote film scripts, and died in New York City.

**Carl Sandburg,** age 22; American poet and biographer born in Illinois, the son of Swedish immigrants. His volumes of free verse in the American idiom include *Chicago Poems* (1916), *Smoke and Steel* (1920) and *The People, Yes* (1936). He is also known as a collector and singer of folk songs and the author of a six-volume biography of Abraham Lincoln.

**Upton Beall Sinclair,** age 22; American novelist and social reformer born in Baltimore. After the success of *The Jungle* (1906), a novel exposing the dreadful conditions in the Chicago stockyards, he wrote other "muckraking" novels: *The Money Changers* (1908), *King Coal* (1917) and *Oil!* (1921). He wrote over 80 books, including 11 "Lanny Budd" novels on world events in his later years, and is considered an earnest reformer rather than a creative writer of the first rank.

**Albert Einstein,** age 21; German-Jewish-American theoretical physicist born in Ulm, the son of an electrical engineer. Despite his international reputation as one of the greatest scientific intellects of all time, his German citizenship was revoked in 1933 and his prperty confiscated; fortunately he was on a lecture tour in Belgium. In his later years, after becoming an American citizen, he worked on the unified-field theory, searching for one set of laws governing electrons within the atom and stars in the heavens, but with only partial success. His most famous postulate is $E=mc^2$, or energy equals mass times the speed of light squared.

**Edward Morgan Forster,** age 21; English novelist and essayist born in London. Although not widely popular, his five novels, including *A Room with a View* (1908) and *A Passage to India* (1924), established him as an important modern writer, concerned with the conflict between human feelings and restrictive social conventions. He also wrote two books of essays: *Abinger Harvest* (1936) and *Two Cheers for Democracy* (1951).

**Paul Klee,** age 21; Swiss painter born in Bern, the son of a musician. A friend of Kandinsky in Munich in 1911, he was present at the birth of abstract art. He produced thousands of works and became one of the most successful abstract painters, noted for the fantastic shapes and exotic colors of his paintings.

**Vachel Lindsay,** age 21; American poet born in Illinois. He studied painting 1900–1905, but gave it up for poetry and had a precarious livelihood until the publication of *General William Booth Enters Heaven and Other Poems* in 1913. Other volumes followed, including *The Congo* (1914) and *The Chinese Nightingale* (1917). He lectured and recited his poems throughout the United States and at Oxford University in England. His later years were clouded by poverty and illness.

**Will Rogers,** age 21; American humorist born in Indian Territory (Oklahoma). A real cowboy in his youth, he entered vaudeville at 26 with a lasso act, added a humorous monologue in 1912 and in 1915 appeared in the Ziegfeld Follies. From his books *(The Cowboy Philosopher on Prohibition,* 1919) and, after 1926, his daily newspaper column, he gained a national reputation as a folk humorist and political satirist. He also appeared in motion pictures and died in a plane crash in Alaska in 1935.

**Joseph Stalin** (Josif Vissarionovich Djugashvili), age 21; Russian revolutionist and dictator born near Tiflis, Georgia, the son of a shoemaker. After Lenin's death in 1924, he exiled or executed many of the old Bolsheviks, abandoned the aim of world revolution, established a police state, and attempted to establish socialism in one country by force and terror. He was hated and feared and is remembered by most with horror.

**Wallace Stevens,** age 21; American poet and insurance executive born in Pennsylvania. His poetry, published in many volumes from 1923–1954, is difficult, philosophical and written with great precision of language; he is one of the leading modern poets. He was vice-president, 1934–1955, of a Hartford, Connecticut, insurance company.

LEON TROTSKY
Russian revolutionist
1879-1940

**Leon Trotsky** (Lev Davidovich Bronstein), age 21; Russian revolutionist born in the Ukraine, the son of wealthy Jewish parents. An anticzarist agitator from the age of 17, he joined Lenin in organizing the Bolshevik seizure of power in 1917, but lost control of the party to Stalin after Lenin's death and was exiled in 1929. A brilliant theoretician, he wrote many books, including *The Revolution Betrayed* (1937), and was assassinated in 1940 in Mexico by a young Spaniard believed to be a Stalinist agent.

**Yoshihito** (Taisha), age 21; emperor of Japan 1912–1926, the son of Mutsuhito. During his reign Japan attained the status of a world power and joined the Allies against Germany in World War I. He was succeeded by his son Hirohito.

**Emiliano Zapata,** age c.21; Mexican revolutionist and agrarian reformer born in the state of Morelos in southern Mexico. An Indian tenant farmer, he recruited an army of Indians and called for a redistribution of the land. Idolized by his followers, he gained considerable power in the south from 1911 to 1916, but achieved no permanent results. He was killed by a government agent in 1918.

**Jacob Epstein,** age 20; British sculptor born in New York City of Russian-Polish-Jewish parents. He settled in London in 1905 and became a British subject in 1910. Among his famous works are Oscar Wilde's tomb in Paris and the statue of Rima (of W. H. Hudson's *Green Mansions)* in Hyde Park, London. He is also famous for bronze busts of Conrad, Einstein and Shaw, executed in his peculiar rough-hewn style. He was knighted in 1954.

**Michel Fokine,** age 20; Russian ballet dancer and choreographer born in St. Petersburg and trained in the imperial ballet school. He breathed new life into the stylized Russian ballet with his choreography for *Les Sylphides* (1903) and *Cygne* (1905, for Pavlova). As choreographer of Diaghilev's Ballets Russes in Paris in 1909–1914, he is credited with creating modern ballet. He became an American citizen in 1932.

**Ibn Saud** (Abdul Aziz ibn Saud), age c.20; king of Saudi Arabia 1932–1953, born in Riyadh, son of the sultan of Nejd. Called the founder of Saudi Arabia, in 1901 he recovered the throne of Nejd from which his father had been exiled, replaced the patriarchal system with a modern administration, invaded and conquered the Hejaz (1924–1925) and renamed the two kingdoms the kingdom of Saudi Arabia (1932). The discovery of oil there in 1938 made him one of the richest men in the world.

**Helen Adams Keller,** age 20; American author and lecturer born in Alabama. Blind and deaf from the age of 19 months, she learned to read Braille, write on a typewriter, read lips with her fingers and to speak at the age of 10. She graduated from Radcliffe College in 1904, lectured, appeared in vaudeville and wrote several books, among others *The Story of My Life* (1903) and *The World I Live In* (1908).

**Henry Louis Mencken,** age 20; American writer and editor born in Baltimore, the son of a prosperous cigar manufacturer. On the staff of the Baltimore newspapers from 1899 until his retirement, and co-editor of *Smart Set* magazine 1914–1923, he was famous in his time for the wit and asperity with which he attacked middle-class smugness and puritanical morals. He is the author of *The American Language* (1918) and three volumes of autobiography—*Happy Days, Newspaper Days,* and *Heathen Days,* 1940–1943.

**Robert Musil,** age 20; Austrian novelist born in the province of Carinthia, the son of an engineer. He wrote short stories and two plays but is known for his complex three-volume novel, *The Man without Qualities* (1930–1943), which examines Viennese society before the First World War with wit and subtlety. He left Vienna in 1938 and died in Switzerland.

**Sean O'Casey,** age 20; Irish playwright born in Dublin of Protestant parents. He grew up in the slums and depicted them with realism, bitterness and humor in *Juno and the Paycock* (1924) and *The Plough and the Stars* (1926), both produced by the Abbey Theatre. He was active in the Irish national movement.

JOHN LLEWELLYN LEWIS
American labor leader
1880-1969

**John Llewellyn Lewis,** age 20; American labor leader born in Iowa of Welsh descent. A coal miner like his father, he joined the United Mine Workers' union and in 1920 became its president. Through his aggressive organizing of industrial unions 1935–1940 as founder and head of the Congress of Industrial Organizations (CIO), he made possible the immense gains of the labor force achieved before and after World War II. He resigned as president of the United Mine Workers in 1960.

**Douglas MacArthur,** age 20; American army officer born in Arkansas, the son of a Spanish-American War general. He graduated from West Point in 1903 and was its superintendent 1919–1922. As supreme Allied commander in the Southwest Pacific in World War II, he was a hero to some and a self-dramatizing egotist to others. He commanded the occupation forces in Japan 1945–1951 and the U.S. forces in Korea 1950–1951, until relieved of his command in April 1951, by President Truman. MacArthur Park in Los Angeles is named for him.

**Oswald Spengler,** age 20; German philosopher, world famous for his two-volume *Decline of the West,* published 1918–1922, but written before the war. Drawing upon the 19th-century philosophy of history written by the Russian, Nikolai Danilevsky, he compared the rise and fall of civilizations to the growth and decay of living organisms. He believed Western civilization had entered its final stage.

**Wilhelmina** (Wilhelmina Helena Pauline Maria), age 20; queen of the Netherlands 1890–1948. A constitutional monarch popular with her subjects, she became a symbol of Dutch resistance in World War II and established a government-in-exile in England. She abdicated in 1948 in favor of her daughter Juliana and lived in retirement for 14 years.

**Sir Charles Leonard Woolley,** age 20; English archaeologist known for his discovery of the Royal Graves of Ur of the ancient land of Sumer. Directing the joint British Museum/University of Pennsylvania expedition (1922–1934), he unearthed the earliest remains of Sumerian civilization which had then been discovered. He wrote *Ur of the Chaldees* (two volumes, 1934) and *The Beginning of Civilization* (1963).

**Franz Kafka,** age 17; German writer born in Prague of well-to-do parents. Although sometimes called an Austrian or a Czech writer, he belonged to the German-Jewish community of Prague and wrote in German. In precise, lucid prose, he presented an incomprehensible world, half real and half fantasy, in which his characters experienced frustration, guilt and anxiety. His three short unfinished novels, *The Trial, The Castle* and *Amerika,* were all published posthumously. In *The Metamorphosis,* his most famous story, the hero turns into a cockroach. In poor health all his life, he died of tuberculosis at 41.

**Amedeo Modigliani,** age 16; Italian painter and sculptor born in Leghorn. Living in Paris after 1906, he was influenced in his painting by Picasso and Matisse and in his sculptures by primitive and African art; the effect of the African influence may be seen in his elongated heads.

# 1925–1950

In 1925 there were 17 million automobiles in the United States. Horse-drawn buggies and carriages had disappeared from city streets, although horses were still to be seen drawing delivery vans and pulling wagons full of ice, milk and fruits and vegetables. Those families who did not own motor cars rode the trolley cars to work and to the market. In the country, however, and the smaller towns, large numbers of horses were still used for transport. Some of the more prosperous farmers drove to town in Model T Fords, but the buggies standing along Main Street on a Saturday afternoon outnumbered the cars. Horses were still used in farm work everywhere, for only a very few tractors had appeared. Statistically, there were 16½ million horses and six million mules in the United States in 1925, together somewhat more than the number of automobiles, though less than the 21 million horses and five million mules of ten years earlier.

George Otto Trevelyan
    (1838-1928), age 87
John D. Rockefeller
    (1839-1937), age 86
Carlotta
    (1840-1927), age 85
Thomas Hardy
    (1840-1928), age 85
Claude Monet
    (1840-1926), age 85
Georges Clemenceau
    (1841-1929), age 84
Oliver Wendell Holmes
    (1841-1935), age 84

**Bela Bartok,** age 44; Hungarian composer, piano virtuoso and collector of folk music. He taught piano for many years at the Academy of Music in Budapest and went to America in 1940 as a war refugee. He had only moderate success and died penniless in 1945 in a New York City hospital, but is recognized today as an original modern composer. His works include the opera, *Bluebeard's Castle,* and *Music for Strings, Percussion and Celesta* (1936).

**Ernest Bevin,** age 44; British labor leader and statesman born in Somersetshire, one of the founders of the British Labour Party. A union organizer from his early manhood on, in 1922 he consolidated 32 unions to form the powerful Transport and General Workers' Union. He was a labor minister in Churchill's cabinet 1940–1945 and a foreign minister in the Labour government of Clement Attlee, 1945–1950.

**Sir Alexander Fleming,** age 44; British bacteriologist born in Scotland; professor at the University of London 1928–1948. He discov-

He died of tuberculosis after a short life marked by poverty, alcoholism and disease.

**Katherine Mansfield** (Kathleen Mansfield Beauchamp Murry), age 12; British short-story writer born in New Zealand. She went to school in London 1903–1906 and returned in 1908. She led an unhappy life, contracted tuberculosis early and died at 34, but is called one of the originators of the modern short story. Her sensitive, finely crafted stories were published in several volumes, including *In a German Pension* (1911), *The Garden Party* (1922) and *The Dove's Nest* (1923). She married John Middleton Murry, the critic and friend of D. H. Lawrence.

Despite the reduction in their number, horses were still the mainstay of the family farm.

The second quarter of the 20th century will be forever infamous as the time when man ungratefully abandoned his faithful friend and servant. The horse played no small part in the ascendancy of man. For centuries he pulled plows, doubling and tripling productivity; he pulled stagecoaches and carriages, reducing travel times by more than half; he carried men into battle, took families to church on Sunday and gently carried on his back the four-year-old learning to ride. Man mastered the world only after he had transformed himself into a superhuman creature, half-man and half-horse, a centaur; and then in cold ingratitude, he turned his back on this industrious companion, allowing his numbers to dwindle to the point of near extinction.

In 1950 the number of horses had shrunk to five million, and most of these were thoroughbred racing horses, saddle horses and show horses. The farm horse, old Dobbin or Reuben, the patient horse of all work who thought he was one of the family, has virtually disappeared. He will soon be only a memory, like the family farm which was his home.

ered penicillin in 1928, after observing that secretions from the mold, *Penicillium notatum*, destroyed bacteria on his culture plates. Not until 1940 was its effectiveness and safety fully established. He was knighted in 1944.

**John XXIII** (Angelo Giuseppe Roncalli), age 44; Italian ecclesiastic; pope 1958–1963. In 1962 he convened a church council (Vatican II) to effect reforms within the church and promote the unity of all Christians, and in 1963 he issued the famous encyclical, "Peace on Earth." A large, corpulent man with none of the qualities of a pinched ascetic, he won the affecton of non-Catholics as well as Catholics throughout the world.

**Kemal Ataturk,** age 44; Turkish general and statesman born in Salonika; first president of the Turkish republic, 1923–1938, and the founder of modern Turkey. After Muhammad VI, the last sultan of the Ottoman Empire, was deposed in 1922, Ataturk abolished polygamy, monas-

Hannah Arendt
(1906-1975), age 44
Samuel Beckett
(1906-    ), age 44
Dmitri Shostakovich
(1906-1975), age 44
W. H. Auden
(1907-1973), age 43
Rachel Carson
(1907-1964), age 43
Louis MacNeice
(1907-1963), age 43
James Michener
(1907-    ), age 43

# 1925

Georg Brandes
   (1842-1927), age 83
C. M. Doughty
   (1843-1926), age 82
Karl Benz
   (1844-1929), age 81
Robert Bridges
   (1844-1930), age 81
George Washington Cable
   (1844-1925), age 81
George Saintsbury
   (1845-1933), age 80
Rudolf Eucken
   (1846-1926), age 79
Thomas Alva Edison
   (1847-1931), age 78
Paul von Hindenburg
   (1847-1934), age 78
Ellen Terry
   (1847-1928), age 78
Arthur James Balfour
   (1848-1930), age 77
Wyatt Earp
   (1848-1929), age 77
Luther Burbank
   (1849-1926), age 76
Ivan Pavlov
   (1849-1936), age 76
Kimmochi Saionji
   (1849/50-1940), age c.76
Thomas G. Masaryk
   (1850-1937), age 75
Arthur Evans
   (1851-1941), age 74
Ferdinand Foch
   (1851-1929), age 74
Adolph von Harnack
   (1851-1930), age 74
Desire Joseph Mercier
   (1851-1926), age 74
Herbert Asquith
   (1852-1928), age 73
Joseph Joffre
   (1852-1931), age 73
Albert A. Michelson
   (1852-1931), age 73
George Moore
   (1852-1933), age 73
James G. Frazer
   (1854-1941), age 71
John Philip Sousa
   (1854-1932), age 71

teries and Eastern dress, adopted the Gregorian calendar and the Roman alphabet, and laid plans for the industrialization of the coutry.

**Aleksandr Feodorovich Kerenski,** age 44; Russian revolutionary leader; premier July-November 1917, as head of the provisional republican government. His indecisiveness and failure to win the army's support enabled the Bolsheviks to seize power. He fled to Paris and eventually to America and died in 1970.

**Pablo Picasso,** age 44; Spanish painter and sculptor born in Malaga, recognized as the foremost modern painter. He worked in many styles, passing successively through different stages now dubbed his blue, rose, angular plane, cubist, and neoclassic periods. His most famous work is the 12-by-26 foot black-and-white mural, *Guernica*, painted in 1937 in denunciation of the destruction by German aircraft of this Basque town. He also designed scenery for the Ballet Russe 1917–1928.

**Pierre Teilhard De Chardin,** age 44; French paleontologist and philosopher. Ordained a Jesuit priest in 1911, he became known for his attempts to reconcile evolution with Catholic doctrine. His conclusions, which were coolly received in both religious and scientific circles, were published in *The Phenomenon of Man* (1955). As advisor to the Geologic Survey of China, he was in China when the skull of Peking man was discovered (1929).

**Stefan Zweig,** age 44: Austrian-Jewish novelist, biographer and poet; born in Vienna, of a wealthy family. A writer imbued with the ideals of prewar European culture, he is known for his biographies of Marie Antoinette, Erasmus and Balzac, and for the novel *Amok* (1923). In *The World of Yesterday* (1943), he recalled with affection a vanished era. He went to England in 1934, to New York in 1940 and to Brazil in 1941, where he and his wife committed suicide (1942).

**Eamon De Valera,** age 43; Irish statesman born in New York City, the son of a Spanish artist and an Irish mother. As an infant, he was taken to his mother's family in County Limerick and grew up in a laborer's cottage. The leader of the Irish independence movement from 1916, he was president of the Irish Free State 1932–1957, premier of Eire 1937–1948, premier of the Republic of Ireland 1951–1954 and 1957–1959 and president 1959–1973, retiring at 91.

**Sir Arthur Stanley Eddington,** age 43; Englisn astronomer and physicist; professor of astronomy at Cambridge and director of the Royal Observatory at Greenwich. One of the first to clarify and explain the theory of relativity in words rather than equations, he is also known for his work on the motion and constitution of the stars. He wrote *The Internal Constitution of the Stars* (1926) and *The Nature of the Physical World* (1928).

**Jean Giraudoux,** age 43; French playwright, novelist and career diplomat; recognized as the leading French dramatist between the wars for such plays as *Amphitryon 38* (1929), *Tiger at the Gate* (1935) and *The Madwoman of Chaillot* (1943). His plays are witty, stylish, and sometimes frothy, but with an undercurrent of pessimism. He was the wartime director of propaganda 1940–1944, for the Vichy government.

**William Frederick Halsey,** age 43; American naval officer born in New Jersey and graduated from Annapolis in 1904. As commander of the Allied naval forces in the South Pacific in World War II, he directed the three-day battle (November 13–15, 1942) off Guadalcanal in which 23 Japanese ships were sunk. He commanded the U.S. Third Fleet in the Pacific from June 1944 to November 1945, and directed the aerial bombardment of Japan.

**James Joyce,** age 43; Irish novelist born in a Dublin suburb and educated in Jesuit schools. He left Ireland as a young man and lived in Trieste, Zurich and Paris as a language teacher. His novel, *Ulysses* (1922), in a brilliant display of verbal virtuosity, describes a day in the life of Leopold Bloom, a Jewish newspaper advertising salesman in Dublin, through the sequence of his own thoughts. *Finnegan's Wake* (1939), another very long novel, relates the dreams of H. C. Earwicker, a Dublin saloonkeeper, and those of his wife and two sons, all of whom remain asleep throughout the narrative.

**Jacques Maritain,** age 43; French philosopher born in Paris of a Protestant family. He studied under Henri Bergson and was converted to Roman Catholicism in 1906. A liberal interpreter of Thomism, he believed the church should not remain aloof from secular affairs. He was a professor of philosophy at the Catholic Institute in Paris 1913–1940, at Columbia University 1940–1944, and Princeton University 1948–1957, and the author of *Man and the State* (51), *Christianity and Democracy* (1942) and other works.

**Anna Pavlova,** age 43; Russian ballerina born in St. Petersburg and trained at the imperial ballet school. The most accomplished and celebrated dancer of her time, she joined Diaghilev's Ballets Russes in Paris in 1909, where Michel Fokine created many dances especially for her. She made her New York debut in 1910 and returned in 1925.

FRANKLIN DELANO
ROOSEVELT
American president
1882-1945

**Franklin Delano Roosevelt,** age 43; 32nd American president 1933–1945; born in Hyde Park, New York, of a wealthy family; a distant cousin of Theodore Roosevelt. The most popular president of modern times and a persuasive radio orator, he introduced a number of reforms collectively known as the New Deal, including old-age security and unemployment insurance. His cordial collaboration with Winston Churchill on strategy brought victory to the Allies in World War II. From 1921 a semi-invalid from polio, he died of a cerebral hemmorhage shortly before the end of the war.

**Sigrid Undset,** age 43; Norwegian novelist born in Denmark, the daughter of a Norwegian archaeologist; winner of the 1928 Nobel Prize for literature. After her early successful novels of medieval Norway, she turned to the portrayal of contemporary life with *The Wild Orchid* (1929), *The Burning Bush* (1930) and *The Faithful Wife* (1936). She also wrote short stories, poems and essays on her Roman Catholic faith.

**Virginia Woolf,** age 43; English novelist and essayist born in London;

Simone de Beauvoir
(1908-      ), age 42
Lyndon Johnson
(1908-1973), age 42
Claude Levi-Strauss
(1908-      ), age 42
Richard Wright
(1908-1960), age 42
Malcolm Lowry
(1909-1957), age 41
Kwame Nkrumah
(1909-1972), age 41
Eudora Welty
(1909-      ), age 41
Eero Saarinen
(1910-1961), age 40
Gian-Carlo Menotti
(1911-      ), age 39
Ronald Reagan
(1911-      ), age 39
Wernher von Braun
(1912-1977), age 38
John Cheever
(1912-1982), age 38
Lawrence Durrell
(1912-      ), age 38
Eugene Ionesco
(1912-      ), age 38
Jackson Pollock
(1912-1956), age 38
Minoru Yamasaki
(1912-      ), age 38
Benjamin Britten
(1913-1976), age 37
Albert Camus
(1913-1960), age 37
Gerald Ford
(1913-      ), age 37
Richard Nixon
1913-      ), age 37
Norman Borlaug
(1914-      ), age 36
Ralph Ellison
(1914-      ), age 36
Jonas Salk
(1914-      ), age 36
Dylan Thomas
(1914-1953), age 36
Tennessee Williams
(1914-      ), age 36
Saul Bellow
(1915-      ), age 35

# 1925

Eugene V. Debs
   (1855-1926), age 70
Arthur Wing Pinero
   (1855-1934), age 70
Sigmund Freud
   (1856-1939), age 69
Henri Petain
   (1856-1951), age 69
John Singer Sargent
   (1856-1925), age 69
George Bernard Shaw
   (1856-1950), age 69
Nikola Tesla
   (1856-1943), age 69
Wovoka
   (1856/58-1932), age c.69
Edward Elgar
   (1857-1934), age 68
Hermann Sudermann
   (1857-1928), age 68
William Howard Taft
   (1857-1930), age 68
Thorstein Veblen
   (1857-1929), age 68
Gustaf V (Sweden)
   (1858-1950), age 67
Selma Lagerlof
   (1858-1940), age 67
Max Planck
   (1858-1947), age 67
Henri Bergson
   (1859-1941), age 66
John Dewey
   (1859-1952), age 66
Arthur Conan Doyle
   (1859-1930), age 66
Havelock Ellis
   (1859-1939), age 66
Lady Gregory
   (1859?-1932), age 66?
Knut Hamsun
   (1859-1952), age 66
A. E. Housman
   (1859-1936), age 66
William II (Germany)
   (1859-1941), age 66
James Barrie
   (1860-1937), age 65
William Jennings Bryan
   (1860-1925), age 65
Ignace Jan Paderewski
   (1860-1941), age 65

the daughter of Sir Leslie Stephen, an eminent man of letters; and wife of the critic Leonard Woolf. A member of the Bloomsbury group of London intellectuals, she is known for her impressionistic and poetic stream-of-consciousness novels: *Mrs. Dalloway* (1925), *To the Lighthouse* (1927) and *The Waves* (1931). Fearing insanity, she drowned herself at 59.

IGOR FEDOROVICH
STRAVINSKY
Russian-American composer
1882-1971

**Igor Fedorovich Stravinsky,** age 43; Russian-American composer born near St. Petersburg. His most popular early works, while he lived in Paris, were the ballets, *The Firebird* (1910), *Petrouchka* (1911), and *The Rite of Spring* (1913). His later works include the ballet, *Orpheus* (1947) and the opera, *The Rake's Progress* (1951). A leader in the ultramodern school, he lived in California after 1939, continuing to compose to an advanced age. He died at 89.

**Clement Richard Attlee,** age 42; first Earl Attlee, British statesman born in London; prime minister 1945–1951. A social service worker early in life, he became the Labour Party prime minister and nationalized important industries, introduced national health insurance, and began dismantling the British Empire. He was made an earl in 1955, and wrote *Twilight of Empire* (1963).

**Walter Gropius,** age 42; German-Architect born in Berlin, where he practiced 1910–1914 and 1928–1934 and became a leader in the new functional architecture, designing many spectacular glass-and-metal buildings. After practicing in London 1934–1937, he went to America and became the head of Harvard University's School of Architecture. The United States Embassy in Athens is one of his most famous buildings.

**John Maynard Keynes,** age 42; first baron of Tilton; English economist born in Cambridge, the son of a university lecturer. He made his fortune speculating in international currencies, but won his reputation with *The General Theory of Employment, Interest, and Money* (1936), a defense of large-scale government spending to increase employment. His theories particularly relating to unbalanced budgets, have profoundly influenced the economic policies of many countries.

**Jose Ortega y Gasset,** age 42; Spanish philosopher born in Madrid, the son of a prominent journalist. A professor of philosophy at the University of Madrid and the intellectual leader of the antimonarchists, he lived in exile after the outbreak of the Spanish Civil War, in Paris, Buenos Aires, Lima and Lisbon. *The Revolt of the Masses* (1930) made him internationally famous for its acute analysis of Western society. He also wrote *The Dehumanization of Art* and other essays.

BENITO MUSSOLINI
Italian dictator
1883-1945

**Benito Mussolini** (Il Duce), age 42; Italian dictator 1922–1943 and founder of the Fascist Party. After gaining power through his aggressive tactics as head of the four-million member nationalist party, he suppressed all opposition and suspended parliamentary government and free speech. Deposed in 1943 after the Allied invasions, he was briefly restored by the Germans, but was recaptured, tried and executed in April 1945.

**Maurice Utrillo,** age 42; French painter born in Paris, an illegitimate son of Suzanne Valadon, the painter's model immortalized by Toulouse-Lautrec. He was legally adopted at seven by Miguel Utrillo, a Spanish writer. An alcoholic at 18, he took up painting as therapy and became famous for his somber street scenes and cathedrals in various shades of white. One famous example is the *Notre Dame de Clignancourt*. He spent his last years in a luxurious villa near Paris.

**Anton von Webern,** age 42; Austrian composer and conductor born in Vienna, a pupil and disciple of Arnold Schoenberg. His extremely short compositions, employing the 12-tone technique, have not been popular, although they influenced other composers, including Stravinsky. His music was banned by the Nazis in 1938 and in 1945 he was accidentally killed by an American soldier of the occupation forces.

**William Carlos Williams,** age 42; American poet, novelist and physician; born in New Jersey. He was a general practitioner in Rutherford, New Jersey, most of his life, meanwhile establishing a reputation as a leading 20th-century American poet. In his poetry, the best known of which is the long poem *Paterson* (1946–1958), he recorded, in everyday speech, his observations of American life. He also wrote four novels, including *White Mule* (1937).

**Grigori Evseevich Zinoviev** (Hirsch Apfelbaum), age 42; Russian communist leader born in southern Russia; one of the old Bolsheviks eliminated by Stalin. An associate of Lenin as early as 1903, he returned with him from Switzerland in 1917, became a member of the Politburo and the president of the Third International Party. He was accused of conspiring with Trotsky in 1927 and expelled from the party. Accused again in 1936, he confessed in the famous Moscow trials and was executed in August 1936.

**Hideki Tojo,** age c.41; Japanese general and statesman born in Tokyo; minister of war in 1940 and prime minister in 1941, two months before

# 1950

Arthur Miller
(1915-      ), age 35
Harold Wilson
(1916-      ), age 34
Indira Gandhi
(1917-      ), age 33
John F. Kennedy
(1917-1963), age 33
Robert Lowell
(1917-1977), age 33
Andrew Wyeth
(1917-      ), age 33
Gamal Nasser
(1918-1970), age 32
Anwar Sadat
(1918-1981), age 32
Aleksandr Solzhenitsyn
(1918-      ), age 32
Edmund Hillary
(1919-      ), age 31
Mohammed Riza Pahlavi
(1919-1980), age 31
J. D. Salinger
(1919-      ), age 31
John Paul II (Pope)
(1920-      ), age 30
Julius Nyerere
(1921-      ), age 29
Christian Barnard
(1923-      ), age 27
Norman Mailer
(1923-      ), age 27
Jimmy Carter
(1924-      ), age 26
Robert F. Kennedy
(1925-1968), age 25
Yukio Mishima
(1925-1970), age 25
Elizabeth II (Great Britain)
(1926-      ), age 24
Fidel Castro
(1927-      ), age 23
Gunter Grass
(1927-      ), age 23
Edward Albee
(1928-      ), age 22
Gabriel Garcia Marquez
(1928-      ), age 22
Martin Luther King Jr
(1929-1968), age 21
Edwin Aldrin
(1930-      ), age 20

John J. Pershing
(1860-1948), age 65

Raymond Poincare
(1860-1934), age 65

Aristide Maillol
(1861-1944), age 64

Fridtjof Nansen
(1861-1930), age 64

Rabindranath Tagore
(1861-1941), age 64

Frederick Jackson Turner
(1861-1932), age 64

Alfred North Whitehead
(1861-1947), age 64

Frederick Delius
(1862-1934), age 63

Gerhart Hauptmann
(1862-1946), age 63

Maurice Maeterlinck
(1862-1949), age 63

Arthur Schnitzler
(1862-1931), age 63

Edward Westermarck
(1862-1939), age 63

Edith Wharton
(1862-1937), age 63

Gabriele D'Annunzio
(1863-1938), age 62

Henry Ford
(1863-1947), age 62

William Randolph Hearst
(1863-1951), age 62

David Lloyd George
(1863-1945), age 62

Pietro Mascagni
(1863-1945), age 62

George Santayana
(1863-1952), age 62

George Washington Carver
(1864?-1943), age 61?

Richard Strauss
(1864-1949), age 61

Miguel de Unamuno
(1864-1936), age 61

Mrs. Patrick Campbell
(1865-1940), age 60

George V (Great Britain)
(1865-1936), age 60

Rudyard Kipling
(1865-1936), age 60

Jean Sibelius
(1865-1957), age 60

the attack on Pearl Harbor. As leader of the military party and the most powerful man in the government, he directed Japanese military operations throughout World War II. He attempted suicide in September 1945, but was arrested as a war criminal, tried and executed in December 1948.

HARRY S. TRUMAN
American statesman and
    president
1884-1972

**Harry S. Truman,** age 41; American statesman born in Missouri, the son of a farmer; 33rd president, 1945–1953. A county judge before being elected to the U.S. Senate in 1934, he became vice-president in January 1945, and president three months later. He authorized deployment of the atomic bomb and assisted European recovery through the Marshall Plan. A popular figure during his long retirement, he is remembered for his vigor and integrity.

**Alban Berg,** age 40; Austrian composer born in Vienna, pupil and friend of Arnold Schoenberg. He is best known for the opera *Wozzeck* (1917–1921), in which Schoenberg's atonality is blended with elements of the Viennese tradition. The opera *Lulu,* a purer expression of the 12-tone technique, was left unfinished.

**Niels Bohr,** age 40; Danish physicist born in Copenhagen. A pupil of Ernest Rutherford at Cambridge University, he made important contributions to the development of the atom bomb and worked on the secret wartime project at Los Alamos, New Mexico, 1943–1945.

**Jerome David Kern,** age 40; American composer born in New York City and reared in Newark, New Jersey, where his father owned a general merchandising store. An important figure in the transition from Viennese-type operettas to modern musical comedies, he is known for such shows as *Very Good Eddie* (1915), *Sunny* (1925), *Show Boat* (1927) and *Roberta* (1933). His familiar and enduring songs include "They Didn't Believe Me" (1914), "Ol' Man River" (1927) and "Smoke Gets in Your Eyes" (1933).

**David Herbert Lawrence,** age 40; English novelist born in Nottinghamshire, the son of a coal miner. Afflicted with tuberculosis, he lived many years abroad in Italy and New Mexico, after eloping at 27 with a professor's wife whom he later married. His incorporation of psychoanalytic theory into his novels impressed the critics, but his frank treatment of sex caused many of his books to be suppressed. The most famous are *Sons and Lovers* (1913) and *Lady Chatterley's Lover* (1928). He also wrote travel books and literary criticism.

**Sinclair Lewis,** age 40; American novelist born in Minnesota, the son of a physician. He wrote six unsuccessful novels before the outstanding success of *Main Street* in 1920, which convincingly described the dullness of small-town middle-class life in the Midwest of the twenties. *Babbitt, Arrowsmith, Elmer Gantry* and *Dodsworth* were also successful, but were followed by a series of minor novels. He was the first American writer to receive the Nobel Prize for literature (1930).

**Francois Mauriac,** age 40; French novelist born in Bordeaux of a middle-class Roman Catholic family. With more literary skill than Sinclair Lewis and with a religious orientation, he portrayed the dark side of French provincial life. *The Desert of Love* (1925) and *Viper's Tangle* (1932) rank high among 20th-century works of fiction. He received the 1952 Nobel Prize for literature.

**Chester William Nimitz,** age 40; American naval officer born in Texas and graduated from Annapolis in 1905. As commander of the Pacific Fleet from December 1941 to November 1945 he planned the strategy that Admiral Halsey and others executed to defeat the Japanese in the South Pacific in World War II.

**George Smith Patton,** age 40; American army officer born in California and graduated from West Point in 1909. He commanded a tank brigade in the First World War, and in 1944 in World War II, he commanded the Third Army, which led the American push through France after the Normandy landing. A bold and capable leader, though not universally admired, he was fatally injured in an auto accident in Germany.

**Ezra Pound,** age 40; American poet and critic born in Idaho. He lived in London, Paris and Italy, 1908–1945, and won fame with his long poem *The Cantos* (1925–1948), but his reputation declined after the airing of his propaganda broadcasts for the Fascists in World War II. Committed to a mental hospital in Washington in 1945, he returned to Italy after his release in 1958.

**Karl Barth,** age 39; Swiss Protestant theologian born in Basel. He taught in Bonn, Germany, until expelled by the Nazis in 1935. Called an important modern theologian, he turned away from liberal theology to restore belief in the fundamental dogmas of Christianity, stressing the necessity of faith, obedience, and a feeling of awe. His principal works are *Church Dogmatics,* in several volumes, and *The Word of God and the Word of Man* (1924).

DAVID BEN-GURION
Israeli statesman and
president
1886-1973

**David Ben-Gurion** (David Grun), age 39; Israeli statesman born in Poland. He emigrated to Palestine in 1906 and was expelled by the Turks during World War I; after Palestine became a British mandate in

Neil Armstrong
    (1930-        ), age 20
Harold Pinter
    (1930-        ), age 20
John Updike
    (1932-        ), age 18

# 1925

William Butler Yeats
  (1865-1939), age 60
Benedetto Croce
  (1866-1952), age 59
Wassily Kandinsky
  (1866-1944), age 59
Ramsay MacDonald
  (1866-1937), age 59
Gilbert Murray
  (1866-1957), age 59
Romain Rolland
  (1866-1944), age 59
Sun Yat-sen
  (1866-1925), age 59
August von Wassermann
  (1866-1925), age 59
H. G. Wells
  (1866-1946), age 59
Arnold Bennett
  (1867-1931), age 58
Vicente Blasco-Ibanez
  (1867-1928), age 58
Gutzon Borglum
  (1867 or 1871-1941),
  age 58?
Marie Curie
  (1867-1934), age 58
John Galsworthy
  (1867-1933), age 58
Jozef Pilsudski
  (1867-1935), age 58
Luigi Pirandello
  (1867-1936), age 58
Arturo Toscanini
  (1867-1957), age 58
W. E. B. Du Bois
  (1868-1963), age 57
Stefan George
  (1868-1933), age 57
Maxim Gorki
  (1868-1936), age 57
Neville Chamberlain
  (1869-1940), age 56
Mahatma Gandhi
  (1869-1948), age 56
Andre Gide
  (1869-1951), age 56
Edgar Lee Masters
  (1869-1950), age 56
Henri Matisse
  (1869-1954), age 56
Edwin Arlington Robinson
  (1869-1935), age 56

1922, he played a leading part, as head of the Jewish Labor Party, in the formation of the independent state of Israel. He was the first prime minister, 1948–1953, and again 1955–1963 and wrote *Israel: a Personal History* (1971).

**Diego Rivera,** age 39; Mexican mural painter known for the massive, simplified figures of peasants and workers in his giant murals. Living in Europe 1907–1909 on a government scholarship and again 1912–1921, he became acquainted with Cezanne and Picasso and was converted to Communism. He painted murals for many public buildings in Mexico City and in the United States.

**Ludwig Mies Van Der Rohe,** age 39; German-American architect born in Aachen as Ludwig Mies, the son of a master mason. Called one of the founders of modern architecture, he became famous for his glass-and-metal skyscrapers in Berlin, emigrated to America in 1937, and taught at the Armour Institute in Chicago 1940–1958. Among his notable works are the Seagram Building in New Yrk designed with Philip Johnson and the Chicago Federal Center.

**Paul Johannes Tillich,** age 39; Protestant theologian born in Prussia, the son of a Lutheran clergyman. He left Germany in 1933 and taught at the Union Theological Seminary in New York City (1933–1954), at Harvard (1954–1962), and at the University of Chicago (1962–1965). He constructed a system that would accommodate both modern scientific concepts and the ideas of existential philosophy as elucidations of Christian doctrine, expounding it in his principal work, *Systematic Theology* (three volumes, 1951–1963).

**Chiang Kai-shek,** age 38; Chinese general, statesman and nationalist leader. He joined the party of Sun Yat-sen in his youth; after Sun's death, as generalissimo of the southern army, he occupied Peking (1928) and assumed leadership of the nationalist government. Years of warfare with the Japanese and the Communists ended with his expulsion from the mainland in 1949. On the island of Taiwan he established and maintained a strong regime, which claimed to be the legitimate government of China.

**Le Corbusier** (Charles Edouard Jenneret), age 38; Swiss architect born near Geneva. A pioneer of modern functional architecture, he is known for the simplicity of his designs and for his use of sheet glass and synthetic materials. He designed buildings throughout the world—from Rio de Janeiro to·Chandigarh, India—including the Carpenter Center for Visual Arts at Harvard University.

**Bernard Law Montgomery,** age 38; first Viscount Montgomery of Alamein; British army officer born in Ireland. He is famous for his whirlwind campaign as commander of the British Eighth Army in Africa, which routed the Germans under Erwin Rommel and secured northern Africa for the Allies. He also participated in the Normandy campaign, as field commander of ground forces, and after the war he was deputy supreme commander of the NATO forces (1951–1958).

**Sigmund Romberg,** age 38; Hungarian-American composer born in Nagy Kaniza, Hungary, of middle-class parents who wanted him to be an engineer. He visited New York at 22 and remained, becoming a rival of Victor Herbert. In his 40-year career he wrote the music for 56 shows, adapting Viennese romanticism to American taste in such famous operettas as *Maytime* (1917), *The Student Prince* (1924), *The Desert Song* (1926) and *The New Moon* (1928).

**Heitor Villa-lobos,** age 38; Brazilian composer born in Rio de Janeiro, the son of a writer. Living in Paris in the '20s, he came under the influence of Ravel, although his principal source of inspiration remained Brazilian folk music. Of his nearly 3,000 works, the most representative are the *Fifth Symphony* (1920), the opera *Malazarte*

(1921), and a series of suites called *Bachianas Brasileiras* (1930–1944). He also composed ballets, oratorios, string quartets and piano music commissioned by Artur Rubenstein.

**Irving Berlin** (Israel Baline), age 37; American composer of popular music born in a small Russian town, the son of a Jewish cantor. He wrote music lyrics of songs that have been a part of American life for half a century, including "Alexander's Ragtime Band" (1911), "White Christmas" and "There's No Business Like Show Business." His songs ran the gamut from "God Bless America" to "You Can't Shake Your Shimmy on Tea" (1919).

**Richard Evelyn Byrd,** age 37; American aviator and polar explorer born in Virginia; a descendant of William Byrd, the colonial tobacco planter and founder of Richmond. He flew over both poles and led five Antarctic expeditions (1928–1956), surveying, mapping and making meteorological studies. On his fourth expedition (1946–1947), he discovered a large ice-free region in the interior.

THOMAS STEARNS ELIOT
American-English poet
    and critic
1888-1965

**Thomas Stearns Eliot,** age 37; poet and critic born in St. Louis, Missouri; the grandson of a Unitarian clergyman who helped found Washington University. He went to London in 1914 and became a British subject in 1927. His long poem *The Waste Land* (1922), expressing a postwar mood of disillusionment, established his reputation and profoundly influenced modern poetry. An Anglo-Catholic in his later years, he wrote poems and plays *(Murder in the Cathedral,* 1935; and *The Cocktail Party,* 1949) on religious themes. He was awarded the 1948 Nobel Prize for literature.

EUGENE GLADSTONE
    O'NEILL
American playwright
1888-1953

**Eugene Gladstone O'Neill,** age 37; American playwright born in New York City, the son of an actor. Influenced by Ibsen and Strindberg,

# 1925

Booth Tarkington
  (1869-1946), age 56
Frank Lloyd Wright
  (1869-1959), age 56
Alfred Adler
  (1870-1937), age 55
Ivan Bunin
  (1870-1953), age 55
Jan Christian Smuts
  (1870-1950), age 55
Teitaro Suzuki
  (1870-1966), age 55
Theodore Dreiser
  (1871-1945), age 54
Ernest Rutherford
  (1871-1937), age 54
Paul Valery
  (1871-1945), age 54
Orville Wright
  (1871-1948), age 54
Roald Amundsen
  (1872-1928), age 53
Calvin Coolidge
  (1872-1933), age 53
Sergei Diaghilev
  (1872-1929), age 53
Haakon VII (Norway)
  (1872-1957), age 53
Piet Mondrian
  (1872-1944), age 53
Bertrand Russell
  (1872-1970), age 53
Ralph Vaughan Williams
  (1872-1958), age 53
Carl L. Becker
  (1873-1945), age 52
Willa Cather
  (1873 or 1876-1947),
  age 52?
Feodor Chaliapin
  (1873-1938), age 52
Colette
  (1873-1954), age 52
Lee De Forest
  (1873-1961), age 52
Ford Madox Ford
  (1873-1939), age 52
George Edward Moore
  (1873-1958), age 52
Emily Post
  (1873-1960), age 52
Sergei Rachmaninoff
  (1873-1943), age 52

he introduced serious psychological themes into American drama. His well-known plays include *Desire under the Elms* (1924), *Strange Interlude* (1927), and *Mourning Becomes Electra* (1931), the latter a trilogy transmuting the themes and plots of Aeschylus' Orestcia from a treatment of the Trojan War to one of the civil war as experienced in New England. Among his later plays are *The Iceman Cometh* (1946) and *A Touch of the Poet* (1957). He was the winner of the 1936 Nobel Prize for literature.

MARC CHAGALL
Russian painter
1887/89-

**Marc Chagall,** age c.36; Russian painter born in Vitebsk; a significant modern painter in whose scenes of Russian village life, and scenes from his own life, the influence of cubism is apparent. He painted several spectacular murals, two of which, measuring 30 by 36 feet, are in the lobby of the Metropolitan Opera House in New York. He lived in France after 1922, except for a period spent in the United States, 1941–1949.

**Charles Spencer Chaplin,** age 36; English motion-picture comedian, director and producer; born in London, the son of a music-hall entertainer. A comic genius, he rose from poverty, with the aid of his brother Sydney, to become the world's favorite comedian. He made his first film in Los Angeles in 1914 and followed it with such masterpieces as *The Kid, The Floorwalker, City Lights* and *Modern Times.* Married to Eugene O'Neill's daughter and living in Switzerland after 1952, he published his autobiography in 1964 and was knighted in 1975.

**Amelita Galli-Curci,** age 36; Italian operatic soprano born in Milan. She appeared in *Rigoletto* in Rome in 1909, in Chicago in 1916, and New York in 1918. A younger contemporary of Mary Garden and one of the world's greatest singers, she was a popular attraction of the Metropolitan Opera Company 1921–1930. She died at 74 in La Jolla, Calif.

**Martin Heidegger,** age 36; German philosopher; professor at the universities of Marburg and Freiburg. Ignoring the traditional problems of epistemology and metaphysics, he focused on the human obligation to find meaning and significance in finite existence without the consoling psychological effects of religious faith. His principal work, *Being and Time* (1927), influenced the French existentialists.

**Adolph Hitler,** age 36; German dictator born in Austria. Named chancellor by President von Hindenburg in 1933, he assumed full power at Hindenburg's death the following year. In the Second World War, which began with his invasion of Poland in September 1919, he conquered Denmark, Norway, the Netherlands, Belgium, France and Greece, and invaded Russia. In 1945, after the tide had turned in favor of the United States, Britain and Russia, he committed suicide. Considered half mad, he shook the foundations of civilized society.

**Edwin Powell Hubble,** age 36; American astronomer born in the Missouri Ozarks; research director at Mount Wilson Observatory in California and director of the 200-inch telescope at Mount Palomar Observatory. In 1925 he proved that some of the nebulae observed in the Milky Way are actually vast, incredibly distant star systems (galaxies) that are apparently receding from our galaxy.

JAWAHARLAL NEHRU
Indian statesman and
nationalist leader
1889-1964

**Jawaharlal Nehru,** age 36; Indian statesman and nationalist leader born in Allahabad, the son of an attorney of the Brahman caste. A brilliant and highly educated man, he rose to prominence in the independence movement as principal aide to Gandhi, and was India's first prime minister, from 1947 until his death. He is the author of many books, including *Toward Democracy* (1941), and the father of Indira Gandhi.

**Arnold Joseph Toynbee,** age 36; English historian born in London, the son-in-law of Gilbert Murray. A professor at the University of London 1919–1955, he is famous for *A Study of History* (12 volumes, 1934–1961), a detailed examination and comparison of the origins, development and decline of 20 historical civilizations, coming to the familiar conclusion that decline is attributable to moral failure rather than material and environmental circumstances.

**Ludwig Wittgenstein,** age 36; Austrian-British philosopher born in Vienna. After studying with Bertrand Russell, he served in the Austrian army in World War I and worked as a schoolteacher and architect before returning to England at 40. There he became a professor at Cambridge University and a British subject at 49. His fame rests on the *Tractatus logico-philosophicus* (1922), which purported to prove that all metaphysical propositions, including his own, are nonsense.

**Ho Chi Minh,** age 35; Vietnamese Communist leader; president of North Vietnam 1954–1969. From 1940 to 1945 he organized a guerilla force, expelled the Japanese, established the Democratic Republic of Vietnam with himself as president and successfully resisted French attempts to regain control. After the division of the country into North and South in 1954 by an international conference at Geneva, its reunification under Communist rule became his aim and was achieved after his death.

**Waslaw Nijinsky,** age 35; Russian ballet dancer of Polish descent

# 1925

G. K. Chesterton
   (1874-1936), age 51
Sir Winston Churchill
   (1874-1965), age 51
Robert Frost
   (1874-1963), age 51
Ellen Glasgow
   (1874-1945), age 51
Herbert Hoover
   (1874-1964), age 51
Amy Lowell
   (1874-1925), age 51
Guglielmo Marconi
   (1874-1937), age 51
W. Somerset Maugham
   (1874-1965), age 51
Arnold Schoenberg
   (1874-1951), age 51
Gertrude Stein
   (1874-1946), age 51
Chaim Weizmann
   (1874-1952), age 51
Albert I (Belgium)
   (1875-1934), age 50
D. W. Griffith
   (1875-1948), age 50
Carl Gustav Jung
   (1875-1961), age 50
Antonio Machado
   (1875-1939), age 50
Thomas Mann
   (1875-1955), age 50
Maurice Ravel
   (1875-1937), age 50
Rainer Maria Rilke
   (1875-1926), age 50
Albert Schweitzer
   (1875-1965), age 50
Sherwood Anderson
   (1876-1941), age 49
Mohammed Ali Jinnah
   (1876-1948), age 49
Charles Kettering
   (1876-1958), age 49
George Macaulay Trevelyan
   (1876-1962), age 49
Mary Garden
   (1877-1967), age 48
Hermann Hesse
   (1877-1962), age 48
Riza Shah Pahlavi
   (1877-1944), age 48

born in Kiev and trained at the imperial ballet school in St. Petersburg. He made his debut at 17 and joined Diaghilev's Ballets Russes in Paris in 1909 for a short, spectacular career that ended in 1919 with insanity and confinement in an asylum. One of the world's greatest dancers, he held audiences spellbound in such ballets as *The Specter of the Rose* and *The Rite of Spring*.

CHARLES DE GAULLE
French general and
   president
1890-1970

**Charles Andre Joseph Marie de Gaulle,** age 35; French soldier and statesman born in Lille. A general in the French army in 1940, he fled to England when French defenses collapsed, organized the Free French forces, and assumed leadership after the war: he was president 1945–1946, premier in 1958, and first president of the Fifth Republic, 1959–1969. A forceful, domineering personality, he attempted to restore the power and prestige France had enjoyed before its capitulation. He retired in 1969 to write his memoirs.

DWIGHT DAVID
EISENHOWER
American general and
   president
1890-1969

**Dwight David Eisenhower,** age 35; American general and statesman born in Texas, the son of a railway mechanic who became a Kansas farmer; 34th president, 1953–1961. He graduated from West Point in 1915, was commanding officer at a training camp in the First World War, commander-in-chief of the U.S. forces in Europe from July 1942, and commander-in-chief of the Allied forces in Europe from

December 1943, directing the crucial landings in Sicily, Italy and Normandy. As president, he was popular and inspired confidence, but his accomplishments are hard to define.

**Boris Leonidovich Pasternak,** age 35; Russian poet, translator and novelist; born in Moscow, the son of a painter. He won recognition in Russia for his several volumes of verse, but his international reputation stems from *Doctor Zhivago*, a novel written in his later years, which is a story set in Russia in the years 1905 to the Second World War. It was banned in Russia, because of the author's interest in individual freedom, and he was not permitted to accept the Nobel Prize for literature.

**Harold Rupert Alexander,** age 34; first Earl Alexander of Tunis; British field marshall. He fought in France 1914–1918, on the northwest frontier of India 1934–1938, and was acclaimed for his orderly evacuation under fire of British troops from Dunkirk in 1940. He directed the landings of Allied troops in Sicily and Italy in 1943 and after the war was made governor of Canada, 1946–1952.

**Rudolf Carnap,** age 34; German–American philosopher born in Wuppertal (near Dusseldorf). A founder of logical positivism and a member of the Vienna Circle, he taught philosophy in Vienna 1926–1931. Rejecting metaphysical and ethical speculation as meaningless, he held that the aim of philosophy should be not to construct propositions, but to analyze and clarify the propositions of empirical science. He was a professor at the University of Chicago 1936–1952 and at UCLA 1954–1962.

**Par Fabian Lagerkvist,** age 34; Swedish poet, dramatist and novelist; winner of the 1951 Nobel Prize for literature. An important modern writer whose plays include *The Man Without a Soul* (1936) and *Victory in the Dark* (1939), he was an enemy of totalitarianism and concerned with the moral/philosophical problem of good and evil. Among his well-known novels are *The Dwarf* (1944), *Barabbas* (1950) and *The Sibyl* (1956).

**Sergei Sergeevich Prokofiev,** age 34; Russian composer and pianist born in the Ukraine. From 1918 to 1921 he toured Japan and the United States as a concert pianist and lived in Paris 1922–1933, where Diaghilev produced his ballet *The Buffoon*. Among his best-known works are the opera *The Love for Three Oranges* (1921), and the fairy tale for narrator and orchestra, *Peter and the Wolf* (1936). His lively music was popular in Russia, where he lived after 1933.

**Erwin Rommel,** age 34; German general called the "Desert Fox" for his brilliant North African campaign. Formerly a member of Hitler's bodyguard, he commanded an armored division in the invasion of France and commanded German forces in Africa, 1941–1943, where he outmaneouvered the British and forced them back to El Alamein in Egypt. After the British offensive under Montgomery had driven the Germans from Africa, he was accused of plotting against Hitler and forced to take poison (1944).

**Arthur Holly Compton,** age 33; American physicist born in Ohio. As a professor of physics at the University of Chicago (1923–1945), he contributed to the development of the atomic bomb, but is better known for his work on X rays and cosmic rays, and for the discovery of the Compton effect (a change in the wavelength of X rays and gamma rays under certain conditions), which verified the quantum theory. He was awarded the 1927 Nobel Prize for physics, jointly with C. T. R. Wilson.

**Francisco Franco,** age 33; Spanish soldier and dictator, the son of a naval officer. As a young officer, he defeated the Riff chieftain, Abd el-Krim, in Morocco in 1926; and as commander of the insurgent

Martin Buber
  (1878-1965), age 47
George M. Cohan
  (1878-1942), age 47
John Masefield
  (1878-1967), age 47
Ferenc Molnar
  (1878-1952), age 47
Carl Sandburg
  (1878-1967), age 47
Upton Sinclair
  (1878-1968), age 47
Albert Einstein
  (1879-1955), age 46
E. M. Forster
  (1879-1970), age 46
Paul Klee
  (1879-1940), age 46
Vachel Lindsay
  (1879-1931), age 46
Will Rogers
  (1879-1935), age 46
Joseph Stalin
  (1879-1953), age 46
Wallace Stevens
  (1879-1955), age 46
Leon Trotsky
  (1879-1940), age 46
Yoshihito
  (1879-1926), age 46
Jacob Epstein
  (1880-1959), age 45
Michel Fokine
  (1880-1942), age 45
Ibn Saud
  (c.1880-1953),
  age c.45
Helen Keller
  (1880-1968), age 45
John L. Lewis
  (1880-1969), age 45
Douglas MacArthur
  (1880-1964), age 45
H. L. Mencken
  (1880-1956), age 45
Robert Musil
  (1880-1942), age 45
Sean O'Casey
  (1880-1964), age 45
Oswald Spengler
  (1880-1936), age 45

forces in the civil war (1936–1939), he crushed the republican opposition with aid from Germany and Italy. Assuming the powers of a dictator, he headed an oppressive regime until his death in 1975.

**Darius Milhaud,** age 33; French composer born in southern France. From 1940–1947 he was a professor of composition at Mills College in Oakland, California, and returned to France in 1947. He composed mostly for the theater: operas, ballets and motion-picture scores. *The Nothing Doing Bar* (1920) is one of his best-known ballets.

**Edna St. Vincent Millay,** age 33; American poet born in Maine. She graduated from Vassar, lived in Greenwich Village in the '20s, and first attracted notice with *The Harp Weaver and Other Poems,* a collection which won the 1923 Pulitzer Prize for poetry. She married a coffee importer, moved to an upstate farm, and published many volumes of verse, including *Wine from These Grapes* (1934) and *Conversations at Midnight* (1937). One of the most popular poets of her time, her verse was admired for its lyric quality.

**Tito** (Josip Broz), age 33; Yugoslav Communist leader born in a Croatian village, the son of a blacksmith; president of Yugoslavia 1953–1980. A metal worker and labor leader, he organized guerilla forces in World War II and harried the Nazi invaders. After the war his party established a Communist state and resisted Russian intervention. He died at 88, the last survivor of contemporary World War II leaders.

**Sir Robert Alexander Watson-Watt,** age 33; British physicist born in Scotland. In 1935 he built a radio-detecting device (radar—*r*adio *d*etecting *a*nd *r*anging) capable of locating aircraft 100 miles away. After its development into a practical, efficient system, it proved to be an invaluable tool in the defense of Britain in World War II. He was knighted in 1942.

**Jomo Kenyatta,** age 32?; African nationalist leader born near Nairobi; the first president of Kenya. A member of the Kikuyu tribe, he was educated at a mission school and studied two years at Moscow University. In 1948 he helped organize the Mau Mau terrorists, for which he was imprisoned 1953–1959. In 1963 the country was granted independence, and in 1964 he was elected president of the Republic of Kenya.

**Mao Tse-tung,** age 32; Chinese Communist leader of peasant origin; founder of the People's Republic of China. In 1928 he organized, with Chu Teh, the Fourth Chinese Red Army and waged civil war with the Nationalists under Chiang Kai-shek. In 1934 to 1936 they made the 6,000-mile Long March to a stronghold in northwest China; and after the Japanese had been expelled, civil war resumed. In October of 1949, Mao established the People's Republic, which he controlled until his death. In 1939 he married an actress, Chiang Ching, 20 years younger than himself.

**Vladimir Mayakovsky,** age 32; Russian poet and playwright born in Georgia in southern Russia. A member of the Bolshevik party at 14, he was made the official poet of the Soviet government in 1917 and thereafter wrote only propagandist verse. Called the greatest Soviet poet, he is known for two satirical plays, *The Bedbug* (1928) and *The Bathhouse* (1929). He committed suicide at 37.

**Edward Estlin Cummings,** age 31; American poet and painter knwon as e e cummings; born in Massachusetts, the son of a Harvard lecturer and clergyman. The eccentricities of his punctuation and capitalization often drew attention away from his conventional themes. He was also a successful painter and the author of *The Enormous Room* (1922), a novel about World War I.

COLE PORTER
American composer and
lyricist
1893-1964

**Cole Porter,** age 32; American composer and lyricist born on a 750-acre farm in Indiana of a wealthy family, and educated at Yale and Harvard universities. His witty lyrics and melodious tunes made his two dozen musical comedies outstanding successes and brought a new level of sophistication to the American musical stage. Such songs as "Night and Day" (1932), "Begin the Beguine" (1935), "Let's Do It" (1928), "In the Still of the Night" and "What Is This Thing Called Love?" (1929) have become unforgettable classics.

**Edward VIII** (Edward Albert Christian George Andrew Patrick David), age 31; king of Great Britain and Northern Ireland and emperor of India from January to December, 1936; the first bachelor king of England since George III. After his abdication to make legally possible his marriage to an American divorcee, he was made governor of the Bahama Islands, 1940–1945, and thereafter lived as a private citizen, mostly in France and the United States. He is the author of *A King's Story* (1951) and *Windsor Revisited* (1960).

**Aldous Leonard Huxley,** age 31; English novelist and critic born in Surrey, the grandson of Thomas Henry Huxley. His early novels, which gained him a reputation as a witty and cynical satirist, include *Crome Yellow* (1921), *Antic Hay* (1923), *Point Counter Point* (1928) and *Brave New World* (1932). After settling in California in 1937, he turned to Eastern philosophy and abandoned the writing of satire.

**Nikita Sergeevich Khrushchev,** age 31; Russian Communist leader, the son of a miner; secretary of the Communist Party 1953–1964 and premier of the USSR 1958–1964. A shrewd politician with a jovial manner, he rose through the ranks to the highest office of Russian government, and favored peaceful coexistence with the West. In 1964 a sudden coup by Brezhnev and Kosygin quietly deposed him and sent him into retirement.

**Norbert Wiener,** age 31; American mathematician born in Missouri. A child prodigy who attended college at 11, he was a professor at the Massachusetts Institute of Technology 1932–1960. He made important contributions to the science of automation, which he called *cybernetics,* expanding it to include the study of communication and control systems in living organisms as well as in the mechanical and electrical systems designed to replace them.

**George VI** (Albert Frederick Arthur George), age 30; king of Great Britain and Northern Ireland 1936–1952 and emperor of India 1936–

# 1925

Wilhelmina (Netherlands)
(1880-1962), age 45
Leonard Woolley
(1880-1960), age 45

1948. A steady, confidence-inspiring monarch, the second son of George V, he succeeded to the throne after the abdication of his brother, Edward VIII. The momentous developments of his reign included the Second World War, the decline of empire, the establishment of a welfare state, and the devaluation of the British pound. He was succeeded by his daughter Elizabeth II.

**Oscar Hammerstein II,** age 30; American lyricist and librettist born in New York City, the grandson of the operatic impresario, Oscar Hammerstein I. He wrote the lyrics of dozens of the most familiar songs in a career that extended from his early collaboration with Vincent Youmans, Rudolf Friml and Jerome Kern (from which came "Rose Marie" in 1924, and "Ol' Man River" in 1927) to his collaboration with Richard Rodgers on *Okalhoma!, South Pacific, The Sound of Music* (1959) and others.

**Paul Hindemith,** age 30; German composer and violinist born in Hanau, a leading composer of the early 20th century, of both atonal and tonal music. After his music was banned by the Nazis, he went to Turkey to reorganize musical studies in the schools, was a professor at Yale University 1941–1953, and at the University of Zurich 1953–1963. His best-known works include the opera *Mathis the Painter* (1938), on the life of Matthias Grunewald, and the symphony drawn from the opera.

**Juan Domingo Peron,** age 30; Argentine army office and political leader; president 1946–1955 and 1973–1974. The strongest of the fascist colonels who overthrew the government in 1943, he had the support of organized labor during his presidency, but worsening economic conditions led to his expulsion in another coup in 1955. After 18 years in exile, he returned to the presidency in 1973 but died the following year.

**Edmund Wilson,** age 30; American critic born in New Jersey, the son of the state attorney general. His industriousness as editor and author of a continuous stream of books of criticism established him as the leading American man of letters of his time. Known for his acute analyses and the clarity of his style, he was the author of *Axel's Castle, The Triple Thinkers, The Wound and the Bow, Upstate* and many others.

**Francis Scott Key Fitzgerald,** age 29; American novelist born in Minnesota, a descendant of Francis Scott Key and the son of a commercial traveler. *This Side of Paradise* (1920), *The Beautiful and the Damned* (1921) and two collections of short stories, *Flappers and Philosophers* (1920) and *Tales from the Jazz Age* (1922), made him famous as the chronicler of the twenties. His later years were clouded by alcoholism and debt, and he died in Hollywood at 44. *The Great Gatsby* (1925) is called his masterpiece.

**Bernard Augustine De Voto,** age 28; American writer and editor born in Utah, known for his scholarly books on the American West. He taught English at Northwestern University and Harvard, wrote several books on Mark Twain and was the official editor of the Mark Twain manuscripts at Harvard. His best-known works are *Across the Wide Missouri* (1947) and *The Course of Empire* (1952).

**Thornton Niven Wilder,** age 28; American novelist and playwright born in Wisconsin, the son of a consular officer. He taught English at the University of Chicago 1930–1936, but had already achieved success with the novel *The Bridge of San Luis Rey* (1927); a minor classic which won the Pulitzer Prize for fiction; and *The Woman of Andros* (1930). His most successful plays were *Our Town* (1938) and *The Skin of Our Teeth* (1942), both Pulitzr prize winners, and *The Matchmaker* (1954), which became the musical comedy *Hello, Dolly.*

WILLIAM FAULKNER
American novelist
1897-1962

**William Faulkner,** age 28; American novelist born in Mississippi, the son of a livery-stable owner who became the business manager of the University of Mississippi. In the mythical county of Yoknapatawpha, with its decaying aristocracy and new commercialism, he potrayed the dark, violent side of modern life. His reputation as a major novelist rests on *The Sound and the Fury* (1929), *As I Lay Dying* (1930), *Light in August* (1932) and *Absalom, Absalom* (1936). He was the winner of the 1949 Nobel Prize for literature.

**Bertolt Brecht,** age 27; German playwright and poet born in Augsberg of a middle-class family. He is best known for his collaboration with Kurt Weill on *The Threepenny Opera* (1928)—a musical drama of the German underworld of the twenties based on John Gay's *Beggar's Opera* (1728)—and for the play *Mother Courage* (1941). A Communist from his youth, he directed the East German state theater after World War II.

**Alexander Calder,** age 27; American sculptor born in Philadelphia of a family of sculptors. His father sculpted the figures of Audubon and William Penn in the American Hall of Fame and his grandfather made an equestrian statue of General Mead for Fairmount Park. He is known for his abstract sculptures, made of pieces of metal and bent wire, called *mobiles* and *stabiles*.

**Chou En-lai,** age 27; Chinese Communist leader born in Szechwan of a prominent Mandarin family. He helped Mao Tse-tung found the Chinese Communist Party and participated in the Long March (1934–1935) of the Red Army. After the establishment of the People's Republic, he became its premier and foreign minister and was still the premier at his death, universally recognized as a shrewd and able statesman.

**George Gershwin,** age 27; American composer born in Brooklyn, the son of Russian-Jewish immigrants. In collaboration with his older brother, Ira, who wrote the lyrics, he produced many successful musical comedies and is remembered for such popular tunes as "Fascinating Rhythm" (1924), "Bidin' My Time" (1930), "Embraceable You" (1930) and "Summertime." He also composed symphonic pieces such as *Rhapsody in Blue* (1923) and *An American in Paris* (1926).

**Henry Moore,** age 27; English sculptor born in Yorkshire. His highly original modern sculptures are instantly recognizable for their smooth, rounded shapes and hollows, and their rather bulky reclining figures. A well-known example is the bronze group at the Lincoln Center for the Performing Arts in New York City.

# 1925

**Leo Szilard,** age 27; Hungarian-American physicist born in Budapest. He taught at the University of Berlin 1923–1933, emigrated to England in 1933, and to the United States in 1938. With Enrico Fermi he achieved the first nuclear chain reaction, in 1942 at the University of Chicago. He opposed the bombing of Japanese cities and after the war gave up nuclear studies to teach biophysics.

**Jorge Luis Borges,** age 26; Argentine short-story writer, poet and essayist; born in Buenos Aires of a well-to-do family, and educated in Geneva and at Cambridge University. His writing is often philosophical and obscure and not widely popular, but is highly regarded by critics for its sophisticated and fantastic humor. His work includes the collection of short stories, *Ficciones* (1944) and the collection of essays, *Otras Inquisiciones* (1960, *Other Inquisitions).*

**Federico Garcia Lorca,** age 26; Spanish poet and dramatist born near Granada of a wealthy landowning family. His *First Book of Gypsy Ballads* (1928) made him famous throughout the Spanish-speaking world. His most popular plays are the three tragedies on peasant and gypsy life of Andalusia: *Blood Wedding* (1933), *Yerma* (1934) and *The House of Bernarda Alba* (1935). He was arrested and murdered by Fascist soldiers in 1936.

ERNEST HEMINGWAY
American novelist and
   story writer
1899-1961

**Ernest Hemingway,** age 26; American novelist and story writer born in Illinois, the son of a prosperous physician. He achieved his first major success with the novel *The Sun Also Rises* (1926), about disillusioned American expatriates in Europe. He is more often praised for his terse, straightforward style than for the substance of his books, which concentrate on the physical life and neglect the life of the spirit. *For Whom the Bell Tolls* (1940) and the short novel, *The Old Man and the Sea* (1952), are among his best works. He was the winner of the 1954 Nobel Prize for literature.

**Vladimir Nabokov,** age 26; Russian-American novelist, poet and critic; born in St. Petersburg of an aristocratic family. A cosmopolitan, he lived in Western Europe (1917–1940) and began writing in English after he emigrated to America in 1940. He is widely known for one book, *Lolita* (1955), which was followed by less sensational and often obscure novels; an autobiography, *Speak, Memory,* was published in 1966.

**Ignazio Silone,** age 25; Italian novelist and socialist born in central Italy. A bitter enemy of Fascism, he wrote realistic novels of Italian peasant life, exposing the injustice of a brutal regime and eloquently defending Christian and human values. *Fontamara* (1933), *Bread and Wine* (1937) and *The Seed Beneath the Snow* (1940) are perhaps his best novels.

AARON COPLAND
American composer
1900-

**Aaron Copland,** age 25; American composer born in Brooklyn, the son of Russian-Jewish immigrants. His works, many of them embodying folk themes, include *Lincoln Portrait* (1942); the ballets *Billy the Kid* (1938) and *Appalachian Spring* (1944); a song cycle, *Twelve Poems of Emily Dickinson* (1950); and scores for the films *Of Mice and Men* (1939) and *Our Town* (1940). Called the representative American composer of his time, he has also taught, lectured and written books on music.

**Kurt Weill,** age 25; German-American composer born in Dessau. His early success, *The Threepenny Opera* (1928), with Bertolt Brecht's libretto, was followed after his emigration to America in 1935 by successful musical plays: *Knickerbocker Holiday* (1938), *Lady in the Dark* (1941) and *Lost in the Stars* (1949), based on Alan Paton's novel. Two of his famous songs are "Mack the Knife" and "September Song."

**Thomas Clayton Wolfe,** age 25; American novelist born in North Carolina. An English instructor at New York University 1924–1930, he achieved immediate success with his first novel, *Look Homeward, Angel* (1929) and followed it with three more long novels: *Of Time and the River* (1935), *The Web and the Rock* (1939) and *You Can't Go Home Again* (1940). All are about an idealistic young man's search for values, written in a highly charged, emotional style. He died of tuberculosis at 38.

**Walt Disney** (Walter Elias Disney), age 24; American cartoonist and pioneer in animated cartoon films, born in Chicago. He began making cartoon films in Los Angeles in 1923 and after much experimentation hit upon the popular characters of Mickey Mouse (1928) and Donald Duck. His Disneyland amusement park opened in Orange County, California in 1955, and became a popular tourist attraction, drawing visitors from all over the world.

**Andre Malraux,** age 24; French writer, revolutionary, and public official; born in Paris. From his active participation in the Communist revolution in China and in the Spanish Civil War, he gathered material for his novels, *Man's Fate* (1933) and *Man's Hope* (1936). He later became an enthusiastic follower of General de Gaulle and served as the minister of cultural affairs 1959–1969. He also wrote a three-volume work on aesthetics, *The Voices of Silence* (1947–1949).

ENRICO FERMI
Italian-American physicist
1901-1954

**Enrico Fermi,** age 24; Italian-American physicist born in Rome. He taught physics at the universities of Florence and Rome and was a professor at Columbia University in New York City 1939–1945. He conducted research on the quantum theory and atomic structure, and in 1940 supervised construction of the first nuclear reactor. In 1942 at the University of Chicago, he created the first chain reaction and thereafter worked on the atomic bomb at Los Alamos, New Mexico. He is called the father of the bomb.

HIROHITO
Emperor of Japan
1901-

**Hirohito,** age 24; emperor of Japan; son of Yoshihito, whom he succeeded in 1926, and grandson of Mutsuhito (Meiji). For the first two decades of his reign, the militarists were in control and waged war in Manchuria and China and with the Allies. After Japan's crushing defeat in 1945, a democratic government was established with the cooperation of the emperor, and Japan developed into one of the world's most progressive industrial countries.

**Sukarno,** age 24; Indonesian nationalist leader and first president of the republic of Indonesia, born on the island of Java. He aided the Japanese against the Dutch in World War II, and after the defeat of Japan he declared Indonesia independent, in August of 1945. As president from 1945 to 1967, he headed an authoritarian government with strong ties to Communist China. In 1966 an anticommunist group headed by Suharto seized power and kept Sukarno under house arrest from 1967 until his death.

**Marian Anderson,** age 23; American Negro contralto born in Philadelphia. She made her concert debut in 1924 and in 1933 made a triumphal tour of Europe which established her reputation worldwide. She was the first Negro soloist to sing with the Metropolitan Opera Company in New York, appearing in 1955 in Verdi's *The Masked Ball*. Her rich contralto voice had no equal in her time.

CHARLES AUGUSTUS
LINDBERGH
American aviator
1902-1974

**Charles Augustus Lindbergh,** age 23; American aviator born in Detroit, the son of a congressman of Swedish descent. His nonstop flight from New York to Paris—May 20–21, 1927—made aviation history and achieved for him the status of a national hero. He later became an object of criticism for leaving America to live in England after the kidnapping and death of his infant son. His isolationism early in World War II also aroused criticism. He is the author of *We* (1936).

**Richard Charles Rodgers,** age 23; American composer born on Long Island, the son of a New York physician. For many years one of the most successful popular composers, he is famous for such outstanding musical comedies as *The Girl Friend* (1926) and *Pal Joey* (1940) with Lorenz Hart; and *Oklahoma!* (1943), *South Pacific* (1949) and *The King and I* (1951) with Oscar Hammerstein II.

**John Steinbeck,** age 23; American novelist and story writer born in California. The lives of migrant farm workers formed the subject of many of his books: *Tortilla Flat* (1935), *In Dubious Battle* (1936), and *Of Mice and Men* (1937). His greatest novel, *The Grapes of Wrath* (1939), which was made into a film in 1940, described the plight of dispossessed farmers of the Oklahoma dust bowl. *East of Eden* (1952) and *Winter of Our Discontent* (1961) are later novels.

**Erskine Caldwell,** age 22; American novelist and story writer born in Georgia. Among his realistic novels about the life of poor sharecroppers in the South, the best known are *Tobacco Road* (1932), dramatized in 1933 for a successful run on Broadway, and *God's Little Acre* (1933); both are extremely popular for their humor and plain speech.

**Louis Seymour Bazett Leakey,** age 22; British archaeologist and anthropologist born in Kenya, the son of missionary parents. He grew up among the natives of Kenya but was educated at Cambridge University. His fossil discoveries (1959–1962) in Olduvai Gorge in Tanzania, made hime world famous. They seemed to indicate that man is much older than had formerly been believed and that hominids existed 1,750,000 years ago.

**George Orwell** (Eric Arthur Blair), age 22; English novelist and essayist born in India, the son of a British civil servant. *Burmese Days* (1934), *Down and Out in Paris and London* (1933) and *Homage to Catalona* (1938) relate the experiences of his early life. His best novels are *Animal Farm* (1945) and *1984* (1948), a prophetic look at a regimented and dehumanized society of the future. He also published several volumes of essays, distinguished by their originality of thought and style.

**Alan Stewart Paton,** age 22; South African novelist born in Natal. His successful novel, *Cry, the Beloved Country* (1948), about the racial problem in South Africa, was translated into many languages and made into a musical play, *Lost in the Stars* (1949). His second novel, *Too Late the Phalarope* (1953) and his short stories also depict the African racial conflict with compassion and understanding. He helped found the Federal Party in 1953 to oppose apartheid.

**Evelyn Arthur St. John Waugh,** age 22; English novelist born in London, the son of an editor and the younger brother of Alec Waugh. His novels of British upper-class life—*Decline and Fall* (1928), *Vile Bodies* (1930), *A Handful fo Dust* (1934) and others—place him among the foremost satirists of English literature. *Brideshead Revisited* (1945) is a serious novel on the fortunes of an aristocratic family and *The Loved One* (1948) a broad satire on American funeral customs.

**Graham Greene,** age 21; English novelist born in Hertfordshire. He began writing novels while working as a journalist and had his first success with the spy story *Stamboul Train,* or *Orient Express* (1932), which was followed by the somewhat more serious *A Gun for Sale,* or *This Gun for Hire* (1936). His more ambitious novels are *Brighton Rock* (1938), *The Heart of the Matter* (1948), and *The End of the Affair* (1951), which combine exciting plots with soul-searching inner dramas.

**Christopher William Bradshaw Isherwood,** age 21; English writer born in Cheshire. His stories of Berlin between the wars, *The Last of Mr. Norris* (1935) and *Goodbye to Berlin* (1939), established his reputation as a leading writer. The stories were the source of a play, *I Am a Camera* (1951), and a musical, *Cabaret* (1966). After his arrival in the United States in 1939 and residence in California, he turned to Indian philosophy and made new translations of some of the Upanishads.

**Isaac Bashevis Singer,** age 21; Polish-American-Jewish writer born in

# 1950–1975

In 1910 one hour and four minutes of human labor were required to produce a bushel of wheat; in 1965 six minutes were required. In 1910 two hours and 46 minutes were required to produce a bale of cotton; in 1965, 18 minutes were required. This phenomenal increase in the rate of production reflects the speed of technological change which in the 20th century transformed the appearance of America and its way of life almost beyond recognition. Technology continued its rapid advance through the third quarter of the century, making possible such marvels as giant earth-moving machines, ditch-diggers, oversize drills, ever larger

Poland, the younger brother of Israel Joshua Singer. He emigrated to New York in 1935 and wrote first in Yiddish for the *Jewish Daily Forward,* but his reputation spread beyond the Jewish community as he translated some of his novels and stories into English. Jewish life and folklore are his subjects in the novel *The Family Moskat* (1950), and the autobiographical *In My Father's Court* (1966).

**John Henry O'Hara,** age 20; American novelist and short-story writer born in Pennsylvania. Beginning as a journalist in New York City, he was successful at 29 with his first novel, *Appointment in Samarra* (1934), which was followed by many others—including *Butterfield 8* (1935), *Pal Joey* (1940) and *Ten North Frederick* (1955)—all of them realistic, detailed portrayals of modern urban life.

**Anthony Dymoke Powell,** age 20; English novelist born in London and reared wherever his father, an officer in the British army, was stationed. His principal work is a series of 12 novels under the general title of *A Dance to the Music of Time* (after the painting by Poussin), which chronicles the fortunes of the English upper class after the First World War. From the first volume in 1951, *A Question of Upbringing,* to the last in 1976, *Hearing Secret Harmonies,* the series portrays sympathetically England's Silver Age.

**Jean-Paul Sartre,** age 20; French playwright, novelist and philosopher, born in Paris. As the postwar prophet of existentialism he gained worldwide attention, but lost much of his audience when he turned to Marxism. His principal works are the exposition his philosophy, *Being and Nothingness* (1943); the novels *Nausea* (1938) and *The Age of Reason* (1945); and the plays *No Exit* (1944) and *The Respectful Prostitute* (1946). A brilliant but difficult writer, he gave up writing in 1975 because of near blindness.

**Hsuan T'ung** (Henry Pu-Yi), age 19; last emperor of the Manchu dynasty of China, 1908–1912; grandnephew of the dowager empress, Tz'u Hsi. Elected emperor at the age of two, with his father, Prince Ch'un, as regent, he abdicated at six when the republic was established. He lived in retirement until crowned emperor of Manchukuo (Manchuria) by the Japanese in 1934. Captured by the Russians in 1945, he was charged as a war criminal and imprisoned until 1959, when he was released by Mao Tse-tung. When he died at 61, he was a gardener and librarian in Peking.

and more complicated agricultural machines and all manner of hoists and lifts that replaced human muscle. As automation and computers appeared in factories and offices, and an increasingly specialized technology enabled scientists to send men to the moon, the amenities of domestic life were also tremendously improved, with the advent of refrigeration, television and air conditioning.

But as the 20th century advanced, technological innovations ceased to capture the imagination of a people grown accustomed to miracles. Much more startling were the cumulative effects of this progress upon the social, economic and political life of the era. These effects had been slow in appearing, manifesting themselves at first only superficially in changing styles of dress, etiquette and entertainment; their full force was revealed in the third quarter of the centu-

# 1950

ry, when a multitude of concomitant new attitudes, new standards and values and new philosophies of life challenged and threatened established traditions. The unrest of youth, the civil rights and feminist movements and the migrations to and from urban centers were only the most conspicuous of many developments triggered by the inexorable march of technology.

The rise in the living standards of the poorest and least educated in the industrial countries, those who in earlier centuries had been denied the benefits of prosperity, was

Henri Petain
(1856-1951), age 94
George Bernard Shaw
(1856-1950), age 94
Gustaf V (Sweden)
(1858-1950), age 92
John Dewey
(1859-1952), age 91
Knut Hamsun
(1859-1952), age 91
William Randolph Hearst
(1863-1951), age 87
George Santayana
(1863-1952), age 87
Jean Sibelius
(1865-1957), age 85
Benedetto Croce
(1866-1952), age 84
Gilbert Murray
(1866-1957), age 84
Arturo Toscanini
(1867-1957), age 83
W. E. B. Du Bois
(1868-1963), age 82
Andre Gide.
(1869-1951), age 81
Edgar Lee Masters
(1869-1950), age 81
Henri Matisse
(1869-1954), age 81
Frank Lloyd Wright
(1869-1959), age 81
Ivan Bunin
(1870-1953), age 80
Jan Christian Smuts
(1870-1950), age 80
Teitaro Suzuki
(1870-1966), age 80
Haakon VII (Norway)
(1872-1957), age 78

**Hannah Arendt,** age 44; German-American political writer born in Hanover. She emigrated to America in 1941, became a citizen in 1950, and was a professor at the University of Chicago and the New School for Social Research in New York City. Her three most important books are *Origins of Totalitarianism* (1951), *The Human Condition* (1958) and *Eichmann in Jerusalem* (1963), on Nazi war crimes.

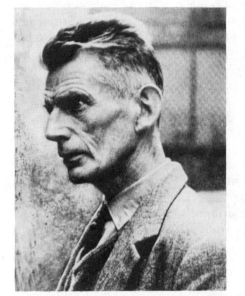

SAMUEL BECKETT
Irish-French playwright
1906-

**Samuel Beckett,** age 44; Irish-French playwright and novelist born in Dublin. He settled in Paris in 1937 and wrote mostly in French. His famous play, *Waiting for Godot,* whose theme is nothing less than the futility of existence, was published in Paris in 1953.

**Wystan Hugh Auden,** age 43; Anglo-American poet born in York and educated at Oxford. A youthful radical whose early poems established him as a poet of social protest; recognized as one of the most influential poets of his generation for his constant experimentation with verse forms and techniques. His many volumes of verse include *The Age of Anxiety,* which won the 1948 Pulitzer Prize for poetry. He became an American citizen in 1946.

**Rachel Louise Carson,** age 43; American marine biologist and writer born in Pennsylvania. A teacher of zoology at the University of Maryland until 1936 and a biologist with the U.S. Fish and Wildlife Service until 1952, she wrote *Under the Sea Wind* (1941), but her greatest success was *The Sea Around Us* (1951), notable for its writing as well as its scientific accuracy. *Silent Spring* (1962) was the first book to draw attention to the dangers of insecticides.

reflected to some degree in improved conditions elsewhere; in Russia, China, Africa and southern Asia, native peoples declared their independence, threw off colonial rule and entered the modern world, making their first acquaintance with its comforts and amenities. Consequently, more people were living well than ever before in history. The rise of the underprivileged classes to a better way of life, their increased public prominence, and their consequent influence upon the color and tone of everyday life was indeed the outstanding characteristic of this quarter century.

DMITRI SHOSTAKOVICH
Russian composer
1906-1975

**Dmitri Shostakovich,** age 44; Russian composer born in St. Petersburg. His first two operas, *The Nose* (1929) and *Lady Macbeth of Mzensk* (1934), were acclaimed by public and critics alike, but were attacked by the Communist Party—the one as decadent, the other as counter-revolutionary. He amended his musical style and in 1966 was made a Hero of Socialist Labor. His best-known symphonies are the *Fifth* (1937), celebrating the 20th anniversary of the revolution, the *Seventh* or *Leningrad Symphony* (1942) and the *Ninth* (1945).

**Louis MacNeice,** age 43; British poet and classical scholar born in Belfast and educated at Oxford. He lectured in Birmington and London and after 1941 was a producer for the BBC. His early theme of social protest is not apparent in the later collections *(Ten Burnt Offerings,* 1952; and *Visitations,* 1958), which are witty and restrained commentaries on modern life. He is also known for his verse translations of Aeschylus' *Agamemnon* and Goethe's *Faust.*

**James Albert Michener,** age 43; American writer born in New York City. His teaching career was terminated by service in the South Pacific in World War II, where he gathered material for his collection of stories, *Tales of the South Pacific* (1947), which won the Pulitzer Prize for fiction and was made into a musical comedy *(South Pacific)* by Rodgers and Hammerstein. A series of highly successful novels followed, among them *Return to Paradise* (1951), *Sayonara* (1954), *Hawaii* (1959) and *Centennial* (1974).

**Simone de Beauvoir,** age 42; French writer and disciple of Jean-Paul

# 1950

Bertrand Russell
(1872-1970), age 78
Ralph Vaughan Williams
(1872-1958), age 78
Colette
(1873-1954), age 77
Lee De Forest
(1873-1961), age 77
G. E. Moore
(1873-1958), age 77
Emily Post
(1873-1960), age 77
Sir Winston Churchill
(1874-1965), age 76
Robert Frost
(1874-1963), age 76
Herbert Hoover
(1874-1964), age 76
W. Somerset Maugham
(1874-1965), age 76
Arnold Schoenberg
(1874-1951), age 76
Chaim Weizmann
(1874-1952), age 76
Carl Gustav Jung
(1875-1961), age 75
Thomas Mann
(1875-1955), age 75
Albert Schweitzer
(1875-1965), age 75
Charles Kettering
(1876-1958), age 74
George Macaulay Trevelyan
(1876-1962), age 74
Mary Garden
(1877-1967), age 73
Hermann Hesse
(1877-1962), age 73
Martin Buber
(1878-1965), age 72
John Masefield
(1878-1967), age 72
Ferenc Molnar
(1878-1952), age 72
Carl Sandburg
(1878-1967), age 72
Upton Sinclair
(1878-1968), age 72
Albert Einstein
(1879-1955), age 71
E. M. Forster
(1879-1970), age 71

Sartre. A teacher of philosophy before the war, she became famous with her brilliant postwar novels, *All Men Are Mortal* (1946) and *The Mandarins* (1955), written in the existential vein. Among her nonfiction books, *The Second Sex* (1949–1950), which initiated the contemporary feminist movement, is a study in the status of women; *The Coming of Age* (1970) is a study of the aged of many cultures.

LYNDON BAINES
JOHNSON
American statesman and
president
1908-1973

**Lyndon Baines Johnson,** age 42; American legislator and statesman born in Texas; 36th president, 1963–1969. Succeeding to the presidency in 1963 after the assassination of John F. Kennedy and reelected by an overwhelming majority in 1964, he profited from his 24 years in Congress to secure the passage of a large amount of social legislation. His ever deepening involvement of the U.S. in the war in Vietnam, however, disenchanted many of his followers.

**Claude Levi-Strauss,** age 42; Belgian-French anthropologist born in Brussels. After four years in Brazil, 1935–1939, studying tropical-forest Indians, he taught at a number of schools and became a professor of anthropology at the College de France (1959) and a leading figure in French intellectual circles as the founder of structural anthropology. He is the author of *From Honey to Ashes* (1967), *The Raw and the Cooked* (1969) and other volumes.

RICHARD WRIGHT
American writer
1908-1960

**Richard Wright,** age 42; American Negro writer born on a plantation in Mississippi. Struggling up from poverty, he achieved success with *Native Son* (1940), a bitter novel about a black man in Chicago in the '30s, which was made into both a play (1941) and a film (1950). His autobiography, *Black Boy* (1945), was equally successful and equally bitter about racial prejudice. He lived in Paris after the war.

**Malcolm Lowry,** age 41; English novelist born in Cheshire, the son of a cotton broker. He is known chiefly for one novel, *Under the Volcano* (1947); written in an exaggerated, rhetorical style, it is nonetheless highly praised for its penetrating analysis of the erosion of the character of an alcoholic Englishman in Mexico. An alcoholic himself, he lived an unsettled life in the Far East, Spain, Paris, Hollywood, Cuernavaca (Mexico) and Toronto. He died in England at 47.

**Kwame Nkrumah,** age 41; African political leader born in the Gold Coast, the son of a goldsmith, and educated at mission schools and in London. As a leader in the nationalist movement he became prime minister in 1957 when the Gold Coast achieved independence, and first president (1960–1966) of the new Republic of Ghana. When he was visiting Peking in 1966, his dictatorial government was overthrown. He took refuge in Guinea and lived there until his death.

**Eudora Welty,** age 41; American novelist and story writer born in Mississippi. Her collections of short stories, portraying the lives of Mississippians with humor, compassion and realism, include *A Curtain of Green* (1941) and *The Bride of Innisfallen* (1955). Her best-known novels are *Delta Wedding* (1946), *The Ponder Heart* (1954) and *The Optimist's Daughter* (1972), a short, tersely written novel of social and moral significance which won the Pulitzer Prize for fiction.

EERO SAARINEN
Finnish-American architect
1910-1961

**Eero Saarinen,** age 40; Finnish-American architect, the son of a prominent architect who emigrated to America in 1923. Among the original designs which made him world famous are the auditorium and chapel at the Massachusetts Institute of Technology in Cambridge (1955), the American embassies in Oslo (1959) and London (1960), Dulles International Airport (1962), and the Trans World Airlines Terminal at Kennedy International Airport in New York (1962).

**Gian-Carlo Menotti,** age 39; Italian-American composer born in central Italy. His celebrated operas in English for which he wrote the librettos, include *The Medium* (1946); *The Consul* (1950), a Pulitzer Prize winner; *The Saint of Bleecker Street* (1954), another Pulitzer prize winner; and *Amahl and the Night Visitors* (1951), which is shown annually at Christmas time on television. He taught composition in

# 1950

Joseph Stalin
   (1879-1953), age 71
Wallace Stevens
   (1879-1955), age 71
Jacob Epstein
   (1880-1959), age 70
Ibn Saud
   (c.1880-1953), age 70
Helen Keller
   (1880-1968), age 70
John L. Lewis
   (1880-1969), age 70
Douglas MacArthur
   (1880-1964), age 70
H. L. Mencken
   (1880-1956), age 70
Sean O'Casey
   (1880-1964), age 70
Wilhelmina (Netherlands)
   (1880-1962), age 70
Leonard Woolley
   (1880-1960), age 70
Ernest Bevin
   (1881-1951), age 69
Alexander Fleming
   (1881-1955), age 69
John XXIII (Pope)
   (1881-1963), age 69
Aleksandr Kerenski
   (1881-1970), age 69
Pablo Picasso
   (1881-1973), age 69
Teilhard de Chardin
   (1881-1955), age 69
Eamon De Valera
   (1882-1975), age 68
William F. Halsey
   (1882-1959), age 68
Jacques Maritain
   (1882-1973), age 68
Igor Stravinsky
   (1882-1971), age 68
Clement Attlee
   (1883-1967), age 67
Walter Gropius
   (1883-1969), age 67
Jose Ortega y Gasset
   (1883-1955), age 67
Maurice Utrillo
   (1883-1955), age 67
William Carlos Williams
   (1883-1963), age 67

Philadelphia 1941–1955 and in 1958 founded the Spoleto art festival in Italy.

**Ronald Wilson Reagan,** age 39; American political leader and motion-picture actor born in Illinois; 40th president, elected in 1980. A moderately successful actor for many years, he learned something of the rough and tumble of politics as president of the Screen Actors Guild for six terms. As the governor of California, 1967–1975, he pursued conservative Republican policies. In a time of severe inflation and rising unemployment, he defeated the single-term incumbent, Jimmy Carter, in the presidential election.

**Wernher Von Braun,** age 38; German-American engineer and rocket expert. From 1937 to 1945 he directed German rocket research and developed the V-2 liquid-fuel rocket of World War II. After becoming an American citizen, he headed the Redstone guided-missle program and developed rockets for the Apollo moon flights. He wrote *First Men to the Moon* (1960).

**John Cheever,** age 38; American novelist and short-story writer born in Massachusetts. His books are detailed depictions of the way of life in affluent Northeastern suburbs, with a touch of satire and intimations of worse times ahead. His principal works are the novels *The Wapshot Chronicle* (1957), *The Wapshot Scandal* (1964) and *Bullet Park* (1969), and several volumes of short stories.

**Lawrence Durrell,** age 38; British novelist born in India of Irish parents. His novels convey the exoticism of foreign places, particularly of the Middle East, where he was in the diplomatic service. Love and intrigue in Alexandria, Egypt, are the themes of the four elaborately written novels of the *Alexandria Quartet: Justine* (1957), *Balthazar* (1958), *Mountolive* (1958) and *Clea* (1960).

**Eugene Ionesco,** age 38; Rumanian-French playwright born near Bucharest. He spent his childhood in Paris and returned there in 1938 to write, in French, highly successful plays enlivened with humor, which include *The New Tenant* (1956) and *Rhinoceros* (1959), which was made into a film starring Zero Mostel. His themes were the senselessness of existence and the absurdity of bourgeois values.

**Jackson Pollock,** age 38; American painter born in Cody, Wyoming, the son of a farmer. Beginning as a Works Progress Administration art project painter (1938–1942), he developed an original abstract style and unconventional techniques, which included dripping paint on a canvas stretched on the floor. He died in an automobile accident at 44 at the height of his career as the leading American abstract painter.

MINORU YAMASAKI
American architect
1912-

**Minoru Yamasaki,** age 38; American architect born in Seattle of Japanese descent. One of the leading modern architects, he has created many spectacular designs including the Lambert–St. Louis Municipal Air Terminal, the Reynolds Metal Company building in Detroit, and the Century Plaza Hotel in West Los Angeles.

BENJAMIN BRITTEN
English composer
1913-1976

**Benjamin Britten,** age 37; English composer born in East Suffolk in the seaside resort of Lowestoft (the easternmost point in England). Sometimes called the foremost English composer since Henry Purcell, he is best known for his modern operas; *Peter Grimes* (1945), *Billy Budd* (1951), *Gloriana* (1953)—written for the coronation of Elizabeth II—*The Turn of the Screw* (1954), and others. He also composed a great choral work, *War Requiem* (1962), and many song cycles.

**Albert Camus,** French-Algerian writer born in Algeria, son of a farm laborer. A journalist in Paris after 1940, he was active in the Resistance and published his first novel, *The Stranger,* in 1946. *The Plague* (1947) and *The Fall* (1956) followed, in vigorous, lucid prose which won him the 1957 Nobel Prize for literature. He ranks high among modern French writers and has been called an existentialist, although he rejected the designation. He died in an automobile accident in France at 46.

GERALD RUDOLPH FORD
American statesman and
   president
1913-

**Gerald Rudolph Ford,** age 37; American legislator and statesman

# 1950

Harry S. Truman
  (1884-1972), age 66
Niels Bohr
  (1885-1962), age 65
Sinclair Lewis
  (1885-1951), age 65
Francois Mauriac
  (1885-1970), age 65
Chester Nimitz
  (1885-1966), age 65
Ezra Pound
  (1885-1972), age 65
Karl Barth
  (1886-1968), age 64
David Ben-Gurion
  (1886-1973), age 64
Diego Rivera
  (1886-1957), age 64
Ludwig Mies van der Rohe
  (1886-1969), age 64
Paul Tillich
  (1886-1965), age 64
Chiang Kai-shek
  (1887-1975), age 63
Le Corbusier
  (1887-1965), age 63
Bernard Montgomery
  (1887-1976), age 63
Sigmund Romberg
  (1887-1951), age 63
Heitor Villa-Lobos
  (1887-1959), age 63
Irving Berlin
  (1888-      ), age 62
Richard E. Byrd
  (1888-1957), age 62
T. S. Eliot
  (1888-1965), age 62
Eugene O'Neill
  (1888-1953), age 62
Marc Chagall
  (1887/89-      ), age c.61
Charles Chaplin
  (1889-1977), age 61
Amelita Galli-Curci
  (1889-1963), age 61
Martin Heidegger
  (1889-1976), age 61
Edwin Hubble
  (1889-1953), age 61
Jawaharlal Nehru
  (1889-1964), age 61

born in Nebraska; 38th president, 1974-1977. A longtime congressman from Michigan (1949-1973) and Republican minority leade 1965-1973, he was appointed vice-president by President Nixon in December 1973, to succeed Spiro Agnew. When Richard Nixon resigned in August 1974, Ford became the first president to hold office without being elected. He resisted efforts of the Congress to overspend and succeeded in controlling inflation, but lost the election of 1976 by a narrow margin.

RICHARD MILHOUS NIXON
American statesman and
president
1914-

**Richard Milhous Nixon,** age 37; American legislator and statesman born in California, the son of a storekeeper; 37th president, 1969-1974. He gained a reputation in Congress as a fervid anti-Communist and was elected vice-president in 1952 and 1956 as the running mate of Dwight Eisenhower; and president 1968 and 1972, winning the support of many former enemies by his performance. The Watergate affair proved his undoing, and he was forced to resign and retire to private life less than two years after being reelected.

**Norman Ernest Borlaug,** age 36; American agronomist born in Iowa, the principal leader of the Green Revolution. He headed a team of international scientists in Mexico in the 1940s, working to improve the yield of wheat and rice plants and to develop disease-resistant strains. The results were miraculous, as the new varieties doubled and tripled yields in many Middle East and Latin American countries. He was awarded the 1970 Nobel Peace Prize for his efforts to eradicate hunger.

**Ralph Waldo Ellison,** age 36; American Negro writer born in Oklahoma. His novel, *The Invisible Man* (1952), heralded the launching of the civil-rights movement of the sixties. Highly praised for its literary quality, it describes the feelings of a black man in a world that ignores him. In 1970 he was appointed a professor at New York University.

**Jonas Edward Salk,** age 36; American physician and microbiologist born in New York City; famous for developing a vaccine for infantile paralysis (poliomyelitis). Engaged for many years in virus research at the universities of Michigan and Pittsburgh, he succeeded in producing an effective vaccine, which was first distributed nationwide in 1955, and for which he received a Congressional Gold Medal.

**Dylan Thomas,** age 36; Welsh poet and short-story writer born in South Wales, the son of a schoolteacher. He worked as a newspaper reporter in Wales, went to London in 1934, and won almost instant recognition as a major poet. *The Map of Love* (1939) and *Portrait of the Artist as a Young Dog* (1940), biographical sketches, made him famous in America. After the war he made poetry-reading tours and died of alcoholism in New York City at 39. His most famous poem is *Do Not Go Gentle into That Good Night* (1952).

TENNESSEE WILLIAMS
American dramatist
1914-

**Tennessee Williams** (Thomas Lanier Williams), age 36; American dramatist born in Mississippi. His first success came in 1945 with *The Glass Menagerie*, after which he quickly became one of the most popular American playwrights. *A Streetcar Named Desire* won the 1948 Pulitzer Prize for drama and *Cat on a Hot Tin Roof* won the 1955 Pulitzer Prize for drama. Many of his plays are psychological studies of frustrated or lonely people, and many have been filmed.

SAUL BELLOW
Canadian-American novelist
1915-

**Saul Bellow,** age 35; Canadian-American novelist born in Quebec of Russian-Jewish parentage. After a boyhood in the slums of Montreal, he was taken to Chicago, where he graduated from Northwestern University and became a teacher. One of the most successful of serious contemporary novelists, he is known for *The Adventures of Augie March* (1953), *Herzog* (1964), *Mr. Sammler's Planet* (1976), and the short masterpiece *Seize the Day* (1956).

**Indira Gandhi,** age 33; Indian political leader born in Allahabad and educated in India and at Oxford; the daughter of Jawaharlal Nehru and wife of Feroze Gandhi, a lawyer who died in 1960. She worked with

# 1950

Arnold Toynbee
(1889-1975), age 61
Ludwig Wittgenstein
(1889-1951), age 61
Charles de Gaulle
(1890-1970), age 60
Dwight Eisenhower
(1890-1969), age 60
Ho Chi Minh
(1890-1969), age 60
Waslaw Nijinsky
(1890-1950), age 60
Boris Pasternak
(1890-1960), age 60
Harold Alexander
(1891-1969), age 59
Rudolf Carnap
(1891-1970), age 59
Par Lagerkvist
(1891-1974), age 59
Sergei Prokofiev
(1891-1953), age 59
Arthur Compton
(1892-1962), age 58
Francisco Franco
(1892-1975), age 58
Darius Milhaud
(1892-1974), age 58
Edna St. Vincent Millay
(1892-1950), age 58
Tito
(1892-1980), age 58
Robert Watson-Watt
(1892-1973), age 58
Jomo Kenyatta
(1893?-1978), age 57?
Mao Tse-tung
(1893-1976), age 57
Cole Porter
(1893-1964), age 57
E. E. Cummings
(1894-1962), age 56
Edward VIII (Great Britain)
(1894-1972), age 56
Aldous Huxley
(1894-1963), age 56
Nikita Khrushchev
(1894-1971), age 56
Norbert Wiener
(1894-1964), age 56
George VI (Great Britain)
(1895-1952), age 55

her father in the independence movement and was his aide after he became prime minister. As prime minister 1966–1977, she followed a policy of neutrality which was more neutral toward the West than to the Eastern bloc. Ousted in 1977 by opponents of her sterilization program, she was returned to office in the election of 1979.

ARTHUR MILLER
American playwright
1915-

**Arthur Miller,** age 35; American playwright born in New York City, the son of a small manufacturer. He achieved outstanding success in 1947 with *All My Sons* and with *Death of a Salesman* in 1949, which won the Pulitzer prize. Many first-rate plays followed, including *After the Fall* (1963), inspired by his marriage with Marilyn Monroe. His plays express a serious concern with moral problems confronting the individual and society.

HAROLD WILSON
British statesman
1916-

**Harold Wilson,** age 34; British statesman born in Yorkshire and educated at Oxford University where he lectured on economics 1937–1940. He entered Parliament in 1945 and became a leader of the left wing of the Labour Party. As prime minister, 1964–1970, he proposed closing British military bases east of Suez, imposed wage-and-price controls, and devalued the pound. A highly intelligent, able statesman in a difficult time, he was again prime minister 1974–1976.

**John Fitzgerald Kennedy,** age 33; American legislator and statesman born in Massachusetts; the son of Joseph Kennedy, a financier; 35th president, 1961–1963. A congressman 1947–1953 and senator 1953–1960, he was elected president in 1960 and served less than two years before his assassination in Dallas, Texas, in November of 1963. A popular president, with an engaging personality and youthful appearance, he intensified the American involvement in Vietnam but became a national hero after his death.

**Robert Lowell,** age 33; American poet born in Boston, the cousin of Amy Lowell and grandnephew of James Russell Lowell. A leading modern poet of great technical ability, he was a convert to Roman Catholicism, active in social and political reform movements, and was married to two writers, Jean Stafford and Elizabeth Hardwick, successively. *Lord Weary's Castle* (1946) won the Pulitzer Prize for poetry.

ANDREW NEWELL WYETH
American painter
1917-

**Andrew Newell Wyeth,** age 33; American genre painter born in Pennsylvania, the son of a painter and illustrator. His subjects are the people and places of the Northeastern states; many are painted in watercolor. *Christina's World* in the Museum of Modern Art, New York City, is one of his best-known paintings.

GAMAL ABDEL NASSER
President of Egypt
1918-1970

**Gamal Abdel Nasser,** age 32; Egyptian army officer and statesman; first president of the Republic of Egypt, 1956–1970. In 1952, as a

# 1950

Oscar Hammerstein II
(1895-1960), age 55
Paul Hindemith
(1895-1963), age 55
Juan Peron
(1895-1974), age 55
Edmund Wilson
(1895-1972), age 55
Bernard De Voto
(1897-1955), age 53
William Faulkner
(1897-1962), age 53
Thornton Wilder
(1897-1975), age 53
Bertolt Brecht
(1898-1956), age 52
Alexander Calder
(1898-1976), age 52
Chou En-lai
(1898-1976), age 52
Henry Moore
(1898-     ), age 52
Leo Szilard
(1898-1964), age 52
Jorge Luis Borges
(1899-     ), age 51
Ernest Hemingway
(1899-1961), age 51
Vladimir Nabokov
(1899-1977), age 51
Aaron Copland
(1900-     ), age 50
Ignazio Silone
(1900-     ), age 50
Kurt Weill
(1900-1950), age 50
Walt Disney
(1901-1966), age 49
Enrico Fermi
(1901-1954), age 49
Hirohito
(1901-     ), age 49
Andre Malraux
(1901-1976), age 49
Sukarno
(1901-1970), age 49
Marian Anderson
(1902-     ), age 48
Charles Lindbergh
(1902-1974), age 48
Richard Rodgers
(1902-1980), age 48
John Steinbeck
(1902-1968), age 48

lieutenent colonel, he led the coup that deposed King Farouk; in 1954 he was made premier, and in 1956 elected president. He nationalized the Suez Canal in 1956, lost a disastrous war to Israel in 1967 and completed the Aswan Dam in 1970.

**Anwar al-Sadat,** age 32; Egyptian statesman, successor to Nasser as president in 1970. Continuing to implement Nasser's policies, he proved an able and enlightened statesman. In 1972 he expelled Soviet military advisers and technicians and initiated more cordial relations with the West, which culminated in a series of conferences to negotiate a settlement of the Arab–Israeli dipute. He was assassinated in 1981.

**Aleksandr Isaevich Solzhenitsyn,** age 32; Soviet Russian writer of Cossack descent; reared by his mother, a teacher, after his father died in an accident. His first novel, *One Day in tne Life of Ivan Denisovich,* relates his experiences after being sentenced to eight years in prison for anti-Stalinist remarks. Subsequent novels published in English translation are *The First Circle* (1968), *Cancer Ward* (1969) and *The Gulag Archipelago* (1974), which documented the brutal conditions in Soviet labor camps and resulted in his deportation.

**Sir Edmund Percival Hillary,** age 31; New Zealand explorer and mountain climber born in Auckland; first man to reach the summit of Mount Everest. A climber of many years' experience, he joined the British Mount Everest expedition of 1953 and on May 29 reached the top with the Nepalese guide, Tenzing Norkay. He was knighted the same year by Queen Elizabeth. In 1958 he led an overland expedition to the South Pole. He is the author of *High Adventure* (1955).

MOHAMMED REZA
PAHLAVI
Shah of Iran
1919-1980

**Mohammed Riza Pahlavi,** age 31; shah of Iran 1941–1979; born in Teheran, the son of Riza Shah Pahlavi, who was deposed by British and Russian troops in World War II for collaborating with the Germans. He encouraged the increase of literacy and the emancipation of women, distributed land to peasant farmers and built a strong army. After the Islamic revolution forced him into exile, he lived in Mexico, Panama and Egypt, undergoing treatment for cancer.

**John Paul II** (Karol Jozef Wojtyla), age 30; Polish ecclesiastic and first Slavic pope; elected October 1978, following the 34-day pontificate of John Paul I. The son of a retired army surgeon, he was ordained at 26, made archbishop of Krakow at 44 and cardinal at 47. Called the Pilgrim Pope, he travels frequently overseas, addressing immense, enthusiastic crowds, as an apostle of human rights and peace. Fluency in many languages enhances his considerable personal charm. An unsuccessful attempt was made upon his life in Vatican City in May 1981.

JEROME DAVID SALINGER
American novelist and
  story writer
1919-

**Jerome David Salinger,** age 31; American novelist and story writer born in New York City, the son of an Irish mother and a prosperous Jewish importer. Holden Caulfield, the hero of *The Catcher in the Rye* (1951), was the prototype of the rebellious adolescents of the '50s and '60s, who took him to their hearts. The collection of short stories, *Franny and Zooey* (1961), was also extremely popular. Living in seclusion in rural New Hampshire, he virtually stopped writing in 1965.

**Julius Kambarage Nyerere,** age 29; African political leader, the son of a tribal chief; first president of Tanzania. He attended the University of Edinburgh and taught in mission schools. When Tanganyika was granted independence by Britain in 1961, he became the first prime minister, and after Tanganyika and Zanzibar were joined in the United Republic of Tanzania, he became the first president (1964) and began nationalizing its major industries.

**Christian Neethling Barnard,** age 27; South African surgeon, the son of a Dutch Reformed clergyman, educated at the University of Cape Town and the University of Minnesota. He taught surgery at the University of Cape Town and in December 1967, made medical history by performing the first human-heart-transplant operation. The patient survived with the new heart for 18 days. In his second operation, performed in January 1968, the patient survived 563 days. He is the author of *One Life* (1970).

**Norman Mailer,** age 27; American writer born in New Jersey, reared in Brooklyn, and trained as an engineer at Harvard University. *The Naked and the Dead* (1948), called one of the best World War II novels, made him famous at 25. *Barbary Shore* (1951) and *The Deer Park* (1955) were less successful. A participant in liberal and radical causes, he writes in an informal, witty, and sometimes exhibitionist style and has generally been more successful as a journalist than a novelist.

**James Earl Carter** (Jimmy Carter), age 26; American naval officer and statesman born in Georgia, the son of a peanut warehouser and state legislator; the governor of Georgia 1971–1975 and 39th president, 1977–1981. He graduated from Annapolis in 1946 and after seven years in the navy resigned his commission to manage the family business. Although an intelligent and efficient administrator, he projected an image of indecisiveness. In a period of severe inflation, rising unemployment and seeming national decline, he was defeated for reelection in 1980.

**Robert Francis Kennedy,** age 25; American politician and public

# 1950

Erskine Caldwell
(1903-    ), age 47
Louis Leakey
(1903-1972), age 47
George Orwell
(1903-1950), age 47
Alan Paton
(1903-    ), age 47
Evelyn Waugh
(1903-1966), age 47
Graham Greene
(1904-    ), age 46
Christopher Isherwood
(1904-    ), age 46
Isaac Bashevis Singer
(1904-    ), age 46
John O'Hara
(1905-1970), age 45
Anthony Powell
(1905-    ), age 45
Jean-Paul Sartre
(1905-1980), age 45
Hsuan T'ung
(1906-1967), age 44

official born in Massachusetts, the younger brother of John F. Kennedy. As attorney general, 1961–1964, he strictly enforced civil-rights laws; and as senator, 1965–1968, he was a tireless defender of the poor and under privileged; he had become a strong contender for the Democratic presidential nomination at the time of his assassination in Los Angeles at 43.

**Yukio Mishima,** age 25; Japanese novelist, essayist, playwright and actor; born in Tokyo of a Samurai family. In the postwar period of rapid Westernization, he cultivated the arts of karate and swordsmanship and wrote novels glorifying the heroic ideals of feudal Japan. *The Temple of the Golden Pavilion* (1956) and the four-volume *The Sea of Fertility* (1969–1972) are considered his best novels. A violent, extraordinarily talented man—and an enemy of modernity—he committed ritual suicide at 45.

ELIZABETH II
Queen of England
1926-

**Elizabeth II** (Elizabeth Alexandra Mary), age 24; queen of Great Britain and Northern Ireland, of the house of Windsor; the daughter of George VI, whom she succeeded in 1952. She married Philip Mountbatten, the duke of Edinburgh in 1947 and had four children. Troubled economic conditions and a diminishing political and military role in the world marked her reign, although the majority of people enjoyed a higher standard of living than ever before. Her proper and decorous conduct made her popular with her subjects.

**Fidel Castro,** age 23; Cuban revolutionary leader and premier. As a young lawyer in 1952, he led the underground opposition to the dictator, Fulgencio Batista; establishing a base in the mountains of Oriente province, he waged guerilla warfare, forcing Batista out in 1959. He enjoyed popular support in Cuba and at first in the United States, but gradually embraced Communism and cultivated the friendship of the Soviet Union, under whose strong influence he has fallen.

**Gunter Wilhelm Grass,** age 23; German novelist, playwright, poet and *Luftwafe* veteran, born in Danzig (Odansk, Poland). He has written poetry and plays, but is better knwon for his novels: *The Tin Drum* (1959), which made him famous; *Cat and Mouse* (1961); *Dog Years* (1963); and *Local Anesthetic* (1969). With fantastic humor, symbolism and ambiguity, his novels attack contemporary social and political problems.

**Gabriel Garcia Marquez,** age 22; Columbian writer, born in poverty, called a major Latin-American novelist. He worked as a journalist in Bogota, wrote short stories, and in 1967 published the long novel, *One Hundred Years of Solitude,* which was translated into English in 1972 and established his reputation beyond the Spanish-speaking world. Filled with humor, satire, fantasy and gross exaggeration, it tells the story of the mythical city of Macondo and its founders; on other levels may be taken as a history of Colombia and of human experience.

EDWARD FRANKLIN ALBEE
American playwright
1928-

**Edward Franklin Albee,** age 22; American playwright born in Washington, D.C.; the adopted son of Reed A. Albee, of the Keith–Albee theaters. He left his adoptive parents and worked at a variety of jobs before his first successful play. His best-known plays are both brilliant and bitter: *Who's Afraid of Virginia Woolf?* (1962), his masterpiece, and *A Delicate Balance* (1966), the Pulitzer prize winner made into a film with Katherine Hepburn.

**Martin Luther King Jr.** (Michael Luther King), age 21; American Baptist minister and civil-rights leader born in Georgia. One of the leaders of the 1955 boycott of the Montgomery, Alabama, bus system, he helped found in 1957 the Southern Christian Leadership Conference, which played an important part in altering the social and economic status of Negroes in America. Because of his many achievements and his insistence on nonviolent methods, he was awarded the Nobel Peace Prize in 1964. He was assassinated in 1968.

**Edwin Eugene Aldrin,** age 20; American astronaut born in New Jersey and graduated from West Point in 1951; second man to walk on the moon. A combat jet pilot in the Korean War, he entered the astronaut-training program in 1964 and made several space flights, and a 5½-hour space walk, before undertaking the Apollo XI flight which landed him and Neil Armstrong on the moon.

**Neil Alden Armstrong,** age 20; American astronaut born in Ohio; first man to walk on the moon, in July of 1969. A navy combat pilot in the Korean War and a civilian test pilot after the war at Edwards Air Force Base in California, he was the first civilian to enter the astronaut-training program (1962). He commanded the Apollo XI lunar flight with Air Force Colonel Edwin Aldrin and Lieutenant Colonel Michael Collins as crew members.

**Harold Pinter,** age 20; English dramatist born in London's East End, the son of a Jewish tailor; foremost British dramatist of his time. He was a repertory actor with various road companies for 10 years and wrote his first play in 1957. Among his successes are *The Birthday Party* (1958), *The Caretaker* (1960), *The Homecoming* (1964)—made into a film—and *Old Times* (1970). His highly unconventional plays, with little overt violence, have a pervasive air of mystery and terror; audiences generally find them puzzling but also engrossing.

**John Updike,** age 18; American novelist and story writer born in Pennsylvania and educated at Harvard and Oxford, the son of a high school teacher. In careful, precise prose, he portrays individuals coping with the complex problems of modern society. His well-known novels include *Rabbit, Run* (1960); *The Centaur* (1962, *Couples* (1968), and *Rabbit Redux* (1971)—in which a middle-aged man confronts the problems of the disorderly 1960s.

# INDEX

Montgomery, Bernard 394
Moore, Clement C. 282
Moore, George 358
Moore, George Edward 378
Moore, Henry 403
Moore, Thomas 282
More, Thomas 173
Morgan, John Pierpont 343
Morgan, Lewis Henry 323
Morris, William 339
Morse, Samuel B. 293
Motley, John Lothrop 320
Mozart, Wolfgang Amadeus 261
Muawiya 94
Mueller, Lucas (see Cranach, Lucas, the Elder)
Mueller, Max (Friedrich Maximilian) 330
Muhammad (see Mohammed)
Muhammad I 153
Muhammad II (the Great) 161
Muhammad III 196
Muhammad IV 215
Muir, John 344
Mu'izz, al- (see Moizz)
Murad I 146
Murad II 156
Murad III 190
Murad IV 206
Murasaki Shikibu 119
Murat, Joachim 272
Murillo, Bartolome Esteban 209
Murray, Gilbert 371
Murry, Kathleen Mansfield (see Mansfield, Katherine)
Musil, Robert 384
Musset, Alfred de 316
Mussolini, Benito 391
Mussorgsky, Modest 345
Mutsuhito 358

Nabokov, Vladimir 404
Nabonidus 4
Nadir Shah 228
Nansen, Fridtjof 366
Napier, John 191
Napoleon I 274
Napoleon III 313
Nashe, Thomas 196
Nasser, Gamal 419
Nast, Thomas 346
Nation, Carry 352
Nebuchadnezzar II 2
Nehemiah 16
Nehru, Jawaharlal 397
Nelson, Horatio (Lord) 267
Nero 56
Nerva, Marcus Cocceius 56
Nestorius 80
Newcomen, Thomas 221
Newman, John Henry 304
Newton, Isaac 216
Ney, Michel 274

Nicholas II 373
Nicholas of Cusa 156
Nicias 16
Nietzsche, Friedrich 351
Nightingale, Florence 327
Nijinsky, Waslaw 397
Nimitz, Chester 393
Nixon, Richard 416
Nkrumah, Kwame 413
Nobel, Alfred 338
Nobunaga 188
Norris, Frank 375
Nyerere, Julius 421

O'Casey, Sean 384
Occam (Ockham), William of 144
Odoacer 84
Offenbach, Jacques 324
Ogadai 136
Oglethorpe, James Edward 230
O'Hara, John 409
Olaf I 118
Olmstead, Frederick Law 330
Omar 92
Omar Khayyam 125
O'Neill, Eugene 395
Origen 67
Orkhan 143
Ortega y Gasset, Jose 390
Orwell, George 407
Osler, William 355
Osman 142
Othman (Muslim caliph) 93
Othman (Ottomon emperor) (see Osman)
Otis, James 243
Otto, Nikolaus 337
Otto I (the Great) 114
Ousmequin (see Massasoit)
Ovid 48
Owen, Robert 277

Paderewski, Ignace Jan 366
Paganini, Niccolo 287
Paine, Thomas 252
Palestrina, Giovanni 185
Paley, William 255
Palladio, Andrea 182
Palmerston, Viscount 289
Papin, Denis 217
Papinian 64
Paracelsus, Philippus Aureolus 178
Pareto, Vilfredo 335
Park, Mungo 277
Parker, Theodore 316
Parkman, Francis 330
Parmenides 12
Parmigiano, Il 181
Parnell, Charles 353
Pascal, Blaise 210
Pasternak, Boris 399
Pasteur, Louis 329
Paston, John 159
Pater, Walter 345

Paton, Alan 408
Patrick, Saint 80
Patton, George 393
Paul, Oom (see Kruger, Stephanus Paulus)
Paul, Saint 54
Paul III 179
Paulus, Julius 66
Pausanius (Sparta) 10
Pausanius (Greece) 64
Pavlov, Ivan 355
Pavlova, Anna 389
Peacock, Thomas Love 290
Peale, Charles Willson 254
Peary, Robert E. 361
Pederson, Knut (see Hamsun, Knut)
Peel, Robert 292
Peele, George 193
Peirce, Charles Sanders 345
Peisistratus 5
Pelagius 78
Penn, William 216
Pepin the Short 101
Pepo, Cenni di (see Cimabue, Giovanni)
Pepys, Samuel 215
Percy, Thomas 247
Pericles 13
Peron, Juan 402
Perry, Matthew 295
Pershing, John J. 366
Pertinax, Publius Helvius 63
Perugino, Il 165
Peshkov, Alexsei (see Gorki, Maxim)
Petain, Henri 361
Peter, Saint 53
Peter I (the Great) 223
Petrarca, Francesco (see Petrarch)
Petrarch 145
Petronius, Gaius 56
Phidias 13
Philip, King (American Indian) 215
Philip II (France) 135
Philip II (Macedonia) 24
Philip II (Spain) 185
Philip IV (Spain) 206
Philip IV (the Fair) (France) 143
Philip V (Spain) 226
Philo Judaeus 50
Phyfe, Duncan 273
Picasso, Pablo 388
Piccini, Niccolo 245
Pico della Mirandola 169
Pierce, Franklin 306
Piero della Francesca 159
Piero di Cosimo
Pietro, Guido di (see Angelico, Fra)
Pike, Zebulon 283
Pilate, Pontius 52
Pilsudski, Jozef 372
Pindar 11
Pinero, Arthur Wing 359
Pinter, Harold 423

Pirandello, Luigi  373
Pisarro, Camille  335
Pitt, William, the Elder  235
Pitt, William, the Younger  268
Pius IX  294
Pizarro, Francisco  172
Planck, Max  363
Plantagenet, Henry  (see Henry II)
Plassey, Baron of  (see Clive, Robert)
Plato  21
Plautus, Titus Maccius  34
Plekhanov, Georgi  362
Plessis, Armand Jean du  (see
    Richelieu, Duc de)
Pliny the Elder  55
Pliny the Younger  60
Plotinus  66
Plutarch  58
Pocahontas  199
Po Chu-i  104
Poe, Edgar Allen  309
Poincare, Raymond  366
Poisson, Jeanne Antoinette  (see
    Pompadour, Mme. de)
Polk, James Knox  297
Pollock, Jackson  414
Polo, Marco  141
Polybius  38
Pompadour, Mme. de  241
Pompey the Great  44
Ponce de Leon, Juan  170
Pope, Alexander  228
Poquelin, Jean Baptiste  210
Porphyry  70
Porter, Cole  401
Porter, William Sydney  (see Henry, O.)
Porus  25
Posidonius  42
Post, Emily  378
Potemkin, Grigoir  253
Pound, Ezra  393
Poussin, Nicolas  203
Powell, Anthony  409
Praxiteles  24
Prescott, W.H.  299
Prevost, Abbe  230
Priestley, Joseph  250
Prior, Matthew  221
Prokofiev, Sergei  399
Propertius, Sextus  49
Protagoras  16
Proudhon, Pierre  315
Proust, Marcel  376
Ptolemy (astronomer)  60
Ptolemy I Soter  26
Ptolemy II  30
Ptolemy II Euergetes  32
Publicola  (see Valerius, Publius)
Puccini, Giacomo  363
Pulitzer, Joseph  354
Purcell, Henry  219
Pushkin, Alexander  302
Pu-Yi, Henry  (see Hsuan T'ung)

Pyrrhus  29
Pythagoras  6

Rabelais, Francois  178
Rachmaninoff, Sergei  378
Racine, Jean Baptiste  216
Radcliffe, Ann  270
Raeburn, Henry  265
Raleigh, Walter  192
Rameau, Jean Philippe  226
Randolph, Edmund Jennings  259
Randolph, John  229
Randolph, John, of Roanoke  279
Randolph, Peyton  241
Randolph, William  218
Ranke, Leopold von  297
Raphael  175
Ravel, Maurice  380
Rawlinson, Henry  316
Reade, Charles  320
Reagan, Ronald  414
Reed, Walter  357
Reid, Thomas  237
Rembrandt  207
Remington, Frederic  366
Renan, (Joseph) Ernest  330
Renoir, Pierre Auguste  348
Reuter, Paul von  321
Revere, Paul  251
Reynolds, Joshua  243
Rhodes, Cecil  358
Ricardo, David  278
Richard I (the Lionhearted)  133
Richard II  151
Richard III  167
Richardson, Samuel  229
Richelieu, duc de  202
Richter, Jean Paul  269
Ricimer  83
Rijn, Rembrandt van  (see Rembrandt)
Rilke, Rainer Maria  380
Rimbaud, Arthur  359
Rimini, Francesca da  (see Francesca
    da Rimini)
Rimski-Korsakov, Nikolai  351
Riqueti, Honore  (see Mirabeau,
    Comte de)
Rittenhouse, David  250
Rivera, Diego  394
Riza Shah Pahlavi  381
Robbia, Luca della  155
Robert I  143
Robert of Lincoln  (see Grosseteste,
    Robert)
Robespierre, Maximilien de  262
Robinson, Edwin Arlington  374
Robusti, Jacobo  183
Rockefeller, John D.  345
Rodgers, Richard  407
Rodin, Auguste  346
Roentgen, Wilhelm  352
Rogers, Will  383
Roland  103

Rolf the Ganger  (see Rollo)
Rolland, Romain  371
Rollo  110
Romberg, Sigmund  394
Rommel, Erwin  399
Romulus Augustulus  85
Roncalli, Angelo Giuseppe
    (see John XXIII)
Ronsard, Pierre de  184
Roosevelt, Franklin D.  389
Roosevelt, Theodore  363
Ross, James Clark  303
Ross, John  293
Rossetti, Christina  335
Rossetti, Dante Gabriel  332
Rossini, Gioacchino  294
Rostand, Edmond  373
Rothschild, Meyer Amschel  255
Rousseau, Henri  352
Rousseau, Jean Jacques  238
Rouvroy, Claude Henri  (see
    Saint-Simon, Comte de)
Rovere, Francesco della  (see Sixtus IV)
Rovere, Giuliano della  (see Julius IV)
Rowlands, John  (see Stanley, Henry)
Roxana  27
Royce, Josiah  359
Rubens, Peter Paul  198
Rubinstein, Anton  334
Rudolf I of Hapsburg  139
Ruisdael, Jacob van  211
Rumi, Jalal ud-Din  138
Rurik  110
Rush, Benjamin  256
Ruskin, John  325
Russell, Bertrand  377
Rutherford, Ernest  376
Rutledge, John  253
Ryder, Albert Pinkham  354

Saadi  (see Sadi)
Saadia ben Joseph  112
Saarinen, Eero  413
Sachs, Hans  178
Sadat, Anwar  420
Sade, Marquis de  253
Sadi  136
Sainte-Beuve, Charles  307
Saint-Gaudens, Augustus  355
St. John, Henry  224
Saint-Just, Louis Antoine de  263
Saint-Saens, Camille  340
Saintsbury, George  352
Saint-Simon, Comte de  269
Saionji, Kimmochi  355
Saladin (Salah-al-Din)  132
Salinger, J.D.  421
Salk, Jonas  416
Sallust  46
Salome  55
Salomon, Haym  253
Sama, Anjin  (see Adams, Will)
Samudragupta  73